NEGOTIATION
Readings, Exercises, and Cases

NEGOTIATION
Readings, Exercises, and Cases

Third Edition

Roy J. Lewicki
The Ohio State University

David M. Saunders
McGill University

John W. Minton
Pfeiffer University

Boston   Burr Ridge, IL   Dubuque, IA   Madison, WI
New York   San Francisco   St. Louis
Bangkok   Bogotá   Caracas   Lisbon   London   Madrid   Mexico City
Milan   New Delhi   Seoul   Singapore   Sydney   Taipei   Toronto

Irwin/McGraw-Hill

A Division of The **McGraw·Hill** Companies

NEGOTIATION: READINGS, EXERCISES, AND CASES

This book is printed on acid-free paper.

3 4 5 6 7 8 9 0 DOC/DOC 9 3 2 1 0 9

ISBN 0–256–21591–X

Vice president and editorial director: *Michael W. Junior*
Publisher: *Craig S. Beytien*
Senior sponsoring editor: *John E. Biernat*
Editorial assistant: *Erin Riley*
Marketing manager: *Ellen Cleary*
Editing associate: *Christine Vaughan*
Senior production supervisor: *Madelyn S. Underwood*
Compositor: *Shepherd, Inc.*
Typeface: *10/12 Times Roman*
Printer: *R.R. Donnelley & Sons Company*

Library of Congress Cataloging-in-Publication Data

Negotiation: readings, exercises, and cases.--3rd ed./ [edited by]
 Roy J. Lewicki, David M. Saunders, John W. Minton.
   p.   cm.
  Includes index.
  ISBN 0-256-21591-X
  1. Negotiation in business.   2. Negotiation.   3. Negotiation--Case
studies.   I. Lewicki, Roy J.   II. Saunders, David M.   III. Minton,
John W., 1946-
HD58.6.N45   1999
658.4′052--dc21   97-44924

http://www.mhhe.com

We dedicate this book to all negotiation and meditation professionals who try to make the world a better place.

About the Authors

Roy J. Lewicki is professor of management and human resources at the Max M. Fisher College of Business, The Ohio State University. He has authored or edited 19 books, as well as numerous research articles. Professor Lewicki received the first David Bradford Outstanding Educator award from the Organizational Behavior Teaching Society for his contributions to the field of teaching in negotiation and dispute resolution; he has won several teaching awards at The Ohio State University.

David M. Saunders is associate dean—masters programs and director of the MBA Program at McGill University in Montreal, Canada, where he is also an associate professor—organization behavior and human resource management. Dr. Saunders has coauthored three brooks on negotiation and has published articles in many professional journals. He also codeveloped the McGill Negotiation Simulator, a computer-based interactive video simulation of negotiation.

John W. Minton is the Jefferson–Pilot Professor of Management at Pfeiffer University in Misenheimer and Charlotte, North Carolina. He has been a visiting assistant professor at Duke University and an assistant and associate professor at Appalachian State University. Professor Minton trains and consults in a variety of managerial and operational areas; he is also involved in volunteer dispute resolution at the state and local levels.

Preface

Managers negotiate every day. During an average day, a manager may negotiate with

The boss, over a budget request.

Subordinates, over a work deadline.

A supplier, about a quality problem in the raw materials.

A banker, over the interest rate of a business loan.

A government official, regarding compliance with environmental regulations.

A real estate agent, over the lease on a new warehouse.

Her/his spouse, over who will walk the dog.

His/her child, over who will walk the dog (still an issue after losing the previous negotiation).

In short, negotiation is a common, everyday activity that most people use to influence others and to achieve personal objectives. In fact, negotiation is not only a common activity but an essential activity to living an effective and satisfying life. We all need things—resources, information, cooperation, and support from others. And others have these needs as well. Negotiation is a process by which we attempt to influence others to help us achieve our needs, while at the same time taking their needs into account. It is a fundamental skill, not only for successful management but for successful living.

In 1985, Roy Lewicki and Joseph Litterer published the first edition of this book. As they were preparing that volume, it was clear that the basic processes of negotiation had received only selective attention in both the academic and practitioner literature. Scholars of negotiation had generally restricted examination of these processes to basic theory development and laboratory research in social psychology, to a few books written for managers, and to an examination of negotiation in complex settings such as diplomacy and labor–management relations. Efforts to draw from the broader study of techniques for influence and persuasion, to integrate this work into a broader understanding of negotiation, or to apply this work to a broad spectrum of conflict and negotiation settings were only beginning to occur.

In the past several years this world has changed significantly. There are several new professional associations (the Conflict Management Division of the Academy of Management and the International Association of Conflict Management) that have devoted themselves exclusively to facilitating research and teaching in the fields of negotiation and conflict management. There are several new journals (*Negotiation Journal, International Journal of Conflict Management, International Negotiation*) that focus exclusively on research in these fields. There are new funding agencies, such as the National Institute for Dispute Resolution, whose mission has been to enhance the development of new research and training materials. Finally, through the generosity of the Hewlett Foundations, there are a number of new university centers that have de-voted themselves to enhancing the quality of teaching, research, and service in the negotiation and conflict management fields. Many schools now have several courses in negotiation and conflict management—in schools of business, public policy, psy-chology, social work, education, and natural resources. And development has occurred on the practitioner side as well. Books, seminars, and training courses on negotiation and conflict management abound. And, finally, mediation has become an extremely popular process as an alternative to litigation for handling divorce, community dis-putes, and land-use conflicts. In pragmatic terms, all of this development means that as we assembled this third edition, we have had a much richer and more diverse pool of resources from which to sample. The net result for the student and instructor is a highly improved book of readings and exercises that contains many new articles, cases, and exercises, which represent the very best and most recent work on negotia-tion and the related topics of power, influence, and conflict management.

A brief overview of this book is in order. The Readings portion of the book is or-dered into 13 sections: (1) the Nature of Negotiation, (2) Prenegotiation Planning, (3) Strategy and Tactics of Distributive Bargaining, (4) Strategy and Tactics of Inte-grative Negotiating, (5) Communication and Cognitive Biases, (6) Finding Negotia-tion Leverage, (7) Ethics in Negotiation, (8) Social Context, (9) Teams and Group Ne-gotiations, (10) Individual Differences, (11) Global Negotiations, (12) Managing Difficult Negotiation Situations: Individual Approaches, and (13) Managing Difficult Negotiation Situations: Third-Party Approaches.

The next portion of the book presents a collection of role-play exercises, cases, and self-assessment questionnaires that can be used to teach about negotiation processes and subprocesses. **Complete information about the use or adaptation of these materials for several classroom formats is provided in our accompanying In-structor's Manual, which faculty members may obtain from their local McGraw Hill–Irwin representative, or by calling (800) 634–3963 or visiting the McGraw-Hill Web site at www.mhhe.com.**

For those readers familiar with the earlier editions of this book, the most visible changes in this edition are to the book's content and organization, as follows:

1. The content of this edition is substantially new. Almost half of the readings are new to this edition, and almost all of the exercises and cases are either new to this edi-tion or have been revised and updated.

2. We have reorganized the book slightly. We have organized the Readings portion of the book into the sections described above. We have combined discussion of interde-pendence with the introduction to negotiation, have included cognitive biases in the communication section, have combined power and persuasion under the heading leverage, and have better highlighted approaches to take when negotiations go wrong.

3. The structure of this book parallels that of a completely revised textbook, *Negotiation* by Lewicki, Minton, and Saunders, also published by McGraw Hill–Irwin. These books can be used together, and we encourage instructors to contact their local Mc-Graw Hill–Irwin representative for an examination copy (call 800–634–3963, or visit the Web site at www.mhhe.com).

This book could not have been completed without the assistance of numerous people. We especially thank

- The many authors and publishers who granted us permission to use or adapt their work for this book and whom we have recognized in conjunction with specific exercises, cases, or articles.

- The many negotiation instructors and trainers who inspired several of the exercises in this book and who have given us excellent feedback on the previous editions of this book.

- The staff of McGraw Hill–Irwin, especially our current editor, John Biernat, and our previous editors, Kurt Strand and Karen Johnson.

- Our families, who continue to provide us with the time and support required to finish this project.

In conclusion, we are very saddened by the recent untimely death of two very good friends and colleagues. Both played important roles in the field of negotiation and in creating the earlier versions of this text. Professor Joseph Litterer, Professor Emeritus of the University of Massachusetts, worked with Roy to develop the first version of this book in 1985. Joe was a wonderful coauthor and inspiration, and we are indebted to him for the creativity and vision that provided the intellectual foundation for this volume. Professor Jeffrey Rubin, of Tufts University and the Harvard Negotiation Program, was a major leader and pioneer in negotiation research and teaching. The field of negotiation has been shaped tremendously by Jeff's boundless energy, commitment, creativity, and skills, and his intellectual legacy will pervade this discipline for years to come. Thanks, Joe and Jeff, for the intellectual and personal gifts that you have made to us as authors, and to the field of negotiation.

Roy J. Lewicki
David M. Saunders
John W. Minton

Contents

Section Twelve: Managing Difficult Negotiation Situations: Individual Approaches   397

Section Thirteen: Managing Difficult Negotiation Situations: Third-Party Approaches   419

Exercises   471

NEGOTIATION
Readings, Exercises, and Cases

The Nature of Negotiation

When most people hear the word *negotiation* they usually think of large, complex, formal deliberations: contract talks between labor and management, discussion of a trade agreement or a treaty between the diplomats of two different nations, or a meeting of several businesspersons and attorneys to complete a corporate merger or acquisition. Yet these are only a few of the many situations we can call negotiation. In fact, all of us negotiate every day, for example, in one or more of the following situations:

- We arrive at an intersection simultaneously with three other cars; somehow, we need to decide who is going to go through the intersection in what order.
- We need to decide how to share a scarce resource—a computer terminal or a library book.
- We must work out an arrangement with other people to share the tasks and chores of daily living—for example, cleaning the apartment, walking the dog, going to the grocery store, or doing the laundry.
- We need to influence someone to change his or her mind—for example, to agree to accept our paper three days after the due date, to waive the fine on our overdue library book, or to give us a pay raise.

The list is endless. Regrettably, however, many of these situations are not often recognized as negotiations. As a result, we may not handle them as effectively as we might. One purpose of this book is to learn how to manage these situations more effectively, by recognizing that they *are* negotiations, and by applying negotiation principles to them.

WHEN IS NEGOTIATION NEEDED?

A negotiation situation is one in which

1. Two or more parties must make a decision about their interdependent goals and objectives.
2. The parties are committed to peaceful means for resolving their dispute.
3. There is no clear or established method or procedure for making the decision.

Like most definitions, this one means the most to those who already understand the nature of what we are trying to define. Let's take an example. Two people who work in the same office want to take their vacation during the first two weeks in July;

however, both cannot be away at the same time. In some organizations there are established procedures for making such decisions: the person with the most seniority gets preference. This procedure may be formalized—that is, it may be part of the company rules or the union contract—or it may simply be an informal tradition in the organization. In any event, there is a rule that can be referred to and used. An alternative way is to refer the decision to a senior manager. But when no senior manager is available or when there are no rules, what are the parties to do? They could flip a coin, but some would feel this decision is too important to be left to chance. They could fight over it, but this hardly seems to be the kind of problem one goes to battle over. At this point, the most reasonable and viable alternative is for the parties to negotiate—that is, to discuss their preferences for taking the vacation, attempt to understand each other's preferences, and find a way to settle the problem amicably.

FEAR OF NEGOTIATING

Even after many parties recognize the importance of negotiation as a mechanism for making decisions, solving problems, and managing conflicts—and the prevalence of negotiation in our daily lives—they still back off. They find the prospect of negotiating uncomfortable, even distasteful. They say, "Negotiating isn't for me. I don't negotiate. I don't need to learn anything about negotiation!"

The fact is that we *all* negotiate! In fact, it is impossible *not* to negotiate! Every day we are in situations where we must coordinate our preferences with those of others, influence other people to our way of thinking, or resolve potential conflicts. However, there are several reasons why people find negotiation unpleasant or believe they can avoid it.

First, the basis of most negotiations is some form of conflict—a conflict of preferences, priorities, or perspectives. Many people are afraid of conflict. Conflict makes them uncomfortable or insecure, and they would prefer to minimize or avoid conflict. Other people want to avoid conflict with the person with whom they must negotiate— a boss, a spouse, a close friend—because they are afraid that they won't perform well, or will endanger their relationship with that person. While these concerns are understandable and very realistic, it is important to understand several things:

- Given all of the situations in which we are interdependent with others— sharing a scarce resource, coordinating our actions, engaging in give and take— conflict is unavoidable. Daily we come into contact with people who have preferences and priorities different from our own, and we must learn to live and work together with them and to resolve these differences.
- If we truly fear conflict, we will probably either avoid taking any position—and not get what we want—or we will take an arbitrary and (probably) unrealistic position, and still not get what we want.
- Negotiation does not have to be a hostile, bloody, or psychologically intimidating process to be successful. In fact, if it is any of these, it is likely to be highly unsuccessful.

A second reason people fear negotiation is that many of us have the idea that to be successful at negotiation we need to be verbally glib—very articulate, very persuasive, a fast and smooth talker, even a con artist. We do not see ourselves as having any of these skills, and wouldn't want them even if we could have them. Thus, if we don't have them, we must not be good negotiators; moreover, we probably could never stand up effectively against those people who, by this definition, are good negotiators!

People's fear of negotiation does have some basis, for conflict is threatening to some people, and some negotiators are skilled con artists! But our experience is that these fears—like many other fears—are greatly exaggerated and are compounded by the normal fear one has of learning any new skill. Learning a new skill is a little scary and intimidating—particularly when we have to practice it in public, in front of people we think are better at it than we are. But, like so many other things, developing a new skill is far less difficult than we think it is! One purpose of this book—and the related practice activities (role plays and simulations)—is to help the student overcome the fear of negotiating. This fear can be overcome through mastery of the concepts presented here and practice of the related skills.

More important, it is also the purpose of this book to present a comprehensive perspective on effective negotiation. As the reader will discover, effective negotiation is not likely to require quick wit, fast talking, and deviousness or deception! In fact, in most of our daily negotiations, these qualities are more likely to get us into trouble than to help us get what we want. Instead, we will show that there are many other, far more important, skills and qualities to effective negotiation—ones we can feel more comfortable with and master very quickly.

Negotiation is a complex human activity. It involves a dynamic interpersonal process. It requires the intellectual ability to understand the key factors that tend to shape and characterize different negotiation situations. It requires skills, both behavioral and analytical, to diagnose negotiation problems and select the correct strategies and approaches. It also requires an understanding of one's own personality and one's system of personal ethics and values, because these will affect how we perceive situations and how we determine the appropriate strategy and tactics. Finally, negotiation is a learnable process. We do not have to be born with the skill. Most of us can improve with a few lessons, a bit of coaching, and some tips on how to do it better. This book provides the tools and resources to learn to negotiate better and to gain greater confidence in one's negotiating ability and potential.

SCOPE OF THIS BOOK

This book represents a compilation of articles on negotiation and related topics: conflict, conflict resolution, power, influence, and persuasion. Most of the articles were selected from newspapers, magazines, and management journals. We chose them because they made very good points, were very readable, and were not unnecessarily theoretical or technical.

The organization of the readings parallels an accompanying textbook (*Negotiation,* third ed., by Roy J. Lewicki, John W. Minton, and David M. Saunders) and is divided into four parts. The first part, Fundamental Processes of Negotiation, examines some critical aspects common to all negotiations and has four sections: (1) The Nature of Negotiation, (2) Prenegotiation Planning, (3) Strategy and Tactics of Distributive Bargaining, and (4) Strategy and Tactics of Integrative Negotiating. The second part,

Fundamental Subprocesses of Negotiation, examines three critical subprocesses of negotiation: (1) Communication and Cognitive Biases, (2) Finding Negotiation Leverage, and (3) Ethics in Negotiation. The third part, Individual, Group, and Cultural Contexts of Negotiation, examines the broader contexts of negotiations in four sections: (1) Social Context, (2) Teams and Group Negotiations, (3), Individual Differences, and (4) Global Negotiations. Finally, the fourth part of the readings portion of the book, Managing Difficult Negotiation Situations, is divided into two sections: (1) Individual Approaches and (2) Third-Party Approaches.

This comprehensive reading section is followed by a collection of 27 exercises, including role-play scenarios and simulations, questionnaires, and eight cases. More will be said about these resources when each is introduced.

INTRODUCTION TO SECTION ONE:
THE NATURE OF NEGOTIATION

The purpose of the articles in Section One is to provide a broad introduction to the nature of negotiation as well as to the basic dynamics of conflict and its management. Leonard Greenhalgh explores these basic dynamics in the first article, "Managing Conflict." Greenhalgh begins his article as we did—by pointing out that conflict is inherent in the life of organizations. Conflict occurs whenever there are scarce resources, when people have different interests at stake, or when parties try to limit each other's power to control a situation. Conflict is not necessarily bad or good, but it is inevitable. And since it is both inevitable and a central part of organizational life, managers must understand how to deal with it effectively. Greenhalgh uses the article to develop a "diagnostic model" of conflict, suitable to be used both by parties to a conflict and by third parties who are evaluating ways to resolve a dispute. He offers seven specific perceptual dimensions of disputes, which provide the foundations of this diagnostic model; the ends of each dimension represent the degree to which a conflict is more or less easy to resolve. The perceptual dimensions include the nature of the issues in question, the magnitude of the stakes, the type of interdependence between the parties, the continuity of the parties' interaction (short term versus long term), the structure of the parties, the involvement of third parties, and the perceived progress of the conflict (the "balance of power" between the parties). Greenhalgh ends the article by addressing some of the skills necessary to manage conflict effectively in today's organizations.

In the second article in this section, "Strategic Choice," Dean Pruitt and Jeffrey Rubin suggest that there are five basic strategies for managing conflict: contending, problem solving, yielding, withdrawing, and inaction. Negotiator preferences for conflict resolution strategies are determined by the strength of two concerns: concern about one's own outcomes and concern about the other person's outcomes. These two concerns are not opposite ends of the same dimension; rather, the concerns are uncorrelated because their intensity varies independently (knowing the extent to which a negotiator is concerned about his or her own needs tells us nothing about how concerned the person is about the other person's needs, and vice versa). This article clarifies the determinants of preferences for the five strategies for resolving conflict and enables the reader to make these choices with more conscious control.

In the final article in this section, "Consider Both Relationships and Substance When Negotiating Strategically," Grant Savage, John Blair, and Ritch Sorenson suggest that both relationships and substance need to be considered when using negotiation to resolve conflict. Similar to the dual-concern model presented in the previous article, the substantive outcomes and relationship outcomes are independent. Savage, Blair, and Sorenson suggest that negotiators should consider the other person's evaluation of the relationship and the negotiation outcome before choosing a conflict resolution strategy. Managers are advised to answer four questions (Is the substantive outcome very important to me? Is the relationship outcome very important to me? Is the substantive outcome very important to the other party? Is the relationship outcome very important to the other party?) before selecting a conflict resolution strategy. The article contains suggested strategies for the 16 possible combinations of answers to the four questions, and a good description of tactics for use during different stages of conflict resolution.

Managing Conflict

Leonard Greenhalgh

Managers or change agents spend a substantial proportion of their time and energy dealing with conflict situations. Such efforts are necessary because any type of change in an organization tends to generate conflict. More specifically, conflict arises because change disrupts the existing balance of resources and power, thereby straining relations between the people involved. Since adversarial relations may impede the process of making adaptive changes in the organization, higher-level managers may have to intervene in order to implement important strategies. Their effectiveness in managing the conflict depends on how well they understand the underlying dynamics of the conflict—which may be very different from its expression—and whether they can identify the crucial tactical points for intervention.

CONFLICT MANAGEMENT

Conflict is managed when it does not substantially interfere with the ongoing functional (as opposed to personal) relationships between the parties involved. For instance, two executives may agree to disagree on a number of issues and yet be jointly committed to the course of action they have settled on. There may even be some residual hard feelings—perhaps it is too much to expect to manage feelings in addition to relationships—but as long as any resentment is at a fairly low level and does not substantially interfere with other aspects of their professional relationship, the conflict could be considered to have been managed successfully.

Conflict is not an objective, tangible phenomenon; rather, it exists in the minds of the people who are party to it. Only its manifestations, such as brooding, arguing, or fighting, are objectively real. To manage conflict, therefore, one needs to empathize, that is, to understand the situation as it is seen by the key actors involved. An important element of conflict management is persuasion, which may well involve getting participants to rethink their current views so their perspective on the situation will facilitate reconciliation rather than divisiveness.

Influencing key actors' conceptions of the conflict situation can be a powerful lever in making conflicts manageable. This approach can be used by a third party intervening in the conflict or, even more usefully, by the participants themselves. But using this perceptual lever alone will not always be sufficient. The context in which the conflict occurs, the history of the relationship between the parties, and the time available will have to be taken into account if such an approach is to be tailored to the situation. Furthermore, the conflict may prove to be simply unmanageable: one or both parties may wish to prolong the conflict or they may have reached emotional states that make constructive interaction impossible; or, perhaps the conflict is "the tip of the iceberg" and resolving it would have no significant impact on a deeply rooted antagonistic relationship.

Table 1 presents seven perceptual dimensions that form a useful diagnostic model that shows what to look for in a conflict situation and pinpoints the dimensions needing high-priority attention. The model can thus be used to illuminate a way to make the conflict more manageable. The point here is that conflict becomes more negotiable between parties when a minimum number of dimensions are perceived to be at the "difficult-to-resolve" pole and a maximum number to be at the "easy-to-resolve" pole. The objective is to shift a viewpoint from the difficult-to-resolve pole to the easy-to-resolve one. At times, antagonists will deliberately resist "being more reasonable" because they see tactical advantages in taking a hard line. Nevertheless, there are strong benefits for trying to shift perspectives; these benefits should become apparent as we consider each of the dimensions in the model.

Issues in Question

People view issues on a continuum from being a matter of principle to a question of division. For example, one organization needed to change its channel of distribution. The company had sold door-to-door since its founding, but the labor market was drying up and the sales force was becoming increasingly understaffed. Two factions of executives sprung up: the supporters were open to the needed change; the resisters

TABLE 1   Conflict Diagnostic Model

	Viewpoint Continuum	
Dimension	Difficult to Resolve	Easy to Resolve
Issue in question	Matter of principle	Divisible issue
Size of stakes	Large	Small
Interdependence of the parties	Zero-sum	Positive-sum
Continuity of interaction	Single transaction	Long-term relationship
Structure of the parties	Amorphous or fractionalized, with weak leadership	Cohesive, with strong leadership
Involvement of third parties	No neutral third party available	Trusted, powerful, prestigious, and neutral
Perceived progress of the conflict	Unbalanced: one party feeling the more harmed	Parties having done equal harm to each other

argued that management made a commitment to the remaining sales force and, as a matter of principle, could not violate the current sales representatives' right to be the exclusive channel of distribution.

Raising principles makes conflict difficult to resolve because by definition one cannot come to a reasonable compromise; one either upholds a principle or sacrifices one's integrity. For some issues, particularly those involving ethical imperatives, such a dichotomous view may be justified. Often, however, matters of principle are raised for the purpose of solidifying a bargaining stance. Yet, this tactic may work *against* the party using it since it tends to invite an impasse. Once matters of principle are raised, the parties try to argue convincingly that the other's point of view is wrong. At best, this approach wastes time and saps the energy of the parties involved. A useful intervention at this point may be to have the parties acknowledge that they *understand* each other's view but still believe in their own, equally legitimate point of view. This acknowledgment alone often makes the parties more ready to move ahead from arguing to problem solving.

At the other extreme are divisible issues where neither side has to give in completely; the outcome may more or less favor both parties. In the door-to-door selling example, a more constructive discussion would have ensued had the parties been able to focus on the *economic* commitment the company had to its sales force, rather than on the *moral* commitment. As it was, the factions remained deadlocked until the company had suffered irrevocable losses in market share, which served no one's interests. Divisible issues in this case might have involved how much of the product line would be sold through alternative channels of distribution, the extent of exclusive territory, or how much income protection the company was willing to offer its sales force.

Size of Stakes

The greater the perceived value of what may be lost, the harder it is to manage a conflict. This point is illustrated when managers fight against acquisition attempts. If managers think their jobs are in jeopardy, they subjectively perceive the stakes as being high and are likely to fight tooth and nail against the acquisition. Contracts providing for continued economic security, so-called golden parachutes, reduce the size of the stakes for those potentially affected. Putting aside the question of whether such contracts are justifiable when viewed from other perspectives, they do tend to make acquisition conflicts more manageable.

In many cases the perceived size of the stakes can be reduced by persuasion rather than by taking concrete action. People tend to become emotionally involved in conflicts and as a result magnify the importance of what is really at stake. Their "egos" get caught up in the winning/losing aspect of the conflict, and subjective values become inflated.

A good antidote is to postpone the settlement until the parties become less emotional. During this cooling-off period they can reevaluate the issues at stake, thereby restoring some objectivity to their assessments. If time does not permit a cooling off, an attempt to reassess the demands and reduce the other party's expectations may be possible: "There's no way we can give you 100 percent of what you want, so let's be realistic about what you can live with." This approach is really an attempt to induce an attitude change. In effect, the person is being persuaded to entertain the thought "If I can get by with less than 100 percent of what I was asking for, then what is at stake must not be of paramount importance to me."

A special case of the high-stakes/low-stakes question is the issue of precedents. If a particular settlement sets a precedent, the stakes are seen as being higher because future conflicts will tend to be settled in terms of the current settlement. In other words, giving ground in the immediate situation is seen as giving ground for all time. This problem surfaces in settling grievances. Thus, an effective way to manage such a conflict is to emphasize the uniqueness of the situation to downplay possible precedents that could be set. Similarly, the perceived consequences of organizational changes for individuals can often be softened by explicitly downplaying the future consequences: employees are sometimes assured that the change is being made "on an experimental basis" and will later be reevaluated. The effect is to reduce the perceived risk in accepting the proposed change.

Interdependence of the Parties

The parties to a conflict can view themselves on a continuum from having "zero-sum" to "positive-sum" interdependence. Zero-sum interdependence is the perception that if one party gains in an interaction, it is at the expense of the other party. In the positive-sum case, both parties come out ahead by means of a settlement. A zero-sum relationship makes conflict difficult to resolve because it focuses attention narrowly on personal gain rather than on mutual gain through collaboration or problem solving.

Consider the example of conflict over the allocation of limited budget funds among sales and production when a new product line is introduced. The sales group fights for a large allocation to promote the product in order to build market share. The production group fights for a large allocation to provide the plant and equipment necessary to turn out high volume at high-quality levels. The funds available have a fixed ceiling, so that a gain for sales appears to be a loss for production and vice versa. From a zero-sum perspective, it makes sense to fight for the marginal dollar rather than agree on a compromise.

A positive-sum view of the same situation removes some of the urgency to win a larger share of the spoils at the outset. Attention is more usefully focused on how one party's allocation in fact helps the other. Early promotion allocations to achieve high sales volume, if successful, lead to high production volume. This, in turn, generates revenue that can be invested in the desired improvements to plant and equipment. Similarly, initial allocations to improve plant and equipment can make a high-quality product readily available to the sales group, and the demand for a high-quality product will foster sales.

The potential for mutual benefit is often overlooked in the scramble for scarce resources. However, if both parties can be persuaded to consider how they can both benefit from a situation, they are more likely to approach the conflict over scarce resources with more cooperative predispositions. The focus shifts from whether one party is getting a fair share of the available resources to what is the optimum initial allocation that will jointly serve the mutual long-run interests of both sales and production.

Continuity of Interaction

The continuity-of-interaction dimension concerns the time horizon over which the parties see themselves dealing with each other. If they visualize a long-term interaction—a *continuous* relationship—the present transaction takes on minor significance, and the conflict within that transaction tends to be easy to resolve. If, on the other hand, the transaction is viewed as a one-shot deal—an *episodic* relationship—the parties will have little incentive to accommodate each other, and the conflict will be difficult to resolve.

This difference in perspective is seen by contrasting how lawyers and managers approach a contract dispute. Lawyers are trained to perceive the situation as a single episode: the parties go to court, and the lawyers make the best possible case for their party in an attempt to achieve the best possible outcome. This is a "no-holds-barred" interaction in which the past and future interaction between the parties tends to be viewed as irrelevant. Thus, the conflict between the parties is not really resolved; rather, an outcome is imposed by the judge.

In contrast, managers are likely to be more accommodating when the discussion of a contract is viewed as one interaction within a longer-term relationship that has both a history and a future. In such a situation, a manager is unlikely to resort to no-holds-barred tactics because he or she will have to face the other party again regarding future deals. Furthermore, a continuous relationship permits the bankrolling of favors: "We helped you out on that last problem; it's your turn to work with us on this one."

Here, it is easy, and even cordial, to remind the other party that a continuous relationship exists. This tactic works well because episodic situations are rare in real-world business transactions. For instance, people with substantial business experience know that a transaction is usually not completed when a contract is signed. No contract can be comprehensive enough to provide unambiguously for all possible contingencies. Thus trust and goodwill remain important long after the contract is signed. The street-fighting tactics that may seem advantageous in the context of an episodic orientation are likely to be very costly to the person who must later seek accommodation with the bruised and resentful other party.

Structure of the Parties

Conflict is easier to resolve when a party has a strong leader who can unify his or her constituency to accept and implement the agreement. If the leadership is weak, rebellious subgroups who may not feel obliged to go along with the overall agreement that has been reached are likely to rise up, thereby making conflict difficult to resolve.

For example, people who deal with unions know that a strong leadership tends to be better than a weak one, especially when organizational change needs to be accomplished. A strongly led union may drive a hard bargain, but once an agreement is reached the deal is honored by union members. If a weakly led union is involved, the agreement may be undermined by factions within the union who may not like some of the details. The result may well be chronic resistance to change or even wildcat strikes. To bring peace among such factions, management may have to make further concessions that may be costly. To avoid this, managers may find themselves in a paradoxical position of needing to boost the power of union leaders.

Similar actions may be warranted when there is no union. Groups of employees often band together as informal coalitions to protect their interests in times of change. Instead of fighting or alienating a group, managers who wish to bring about change may benefit from considering ways to formalize the coalition, such as by appointing its opinion leader to a task force or steering committee. This tactic may be equivalent to cooptation, yet there is likely to be a net benefit to both the coalition and management. The coalition benefits because it is given a formal channel in which the opinion leader's viewpoint is expressed; management benefits because the spokesperson presents the conflict in a manageable form, which is much better than passive resistance or subtle sabotage.

Involvement of Third Parties

People tend to become emotionally involved in conflicts. Such involvement can have several effects: perceptions may become distorted, nonrational thought processes and arguments may arise, and unreasonable stances, impaired communication, and personal attacks may result. These effects make the conflict difficult to resolve.

The presence of a third party, even if the third party is not actively involved in the dialogue, can constrain such effects. People usually feel obliged to appear reasonable and responsible because they care more about how the neutral party is evaluating them than by how the opponent is. The more prestigious, powerful, trusted, and neutral the third party, the greater is the desire to exercise emotional restraint.

While managers often have to mediate conflicts among lower-level employees, they are rarely seen as being neutral. Therefore, consultants and change agents often end up serving a mediator role, either by design or default. This role can take several forms, ranging from an umpire supervising communication to a messenger between parties for whom face-to-face communication has become too strained. Mediation essentially involves keeping the parties interacting in a reasonable and constructive manner. Typically, however, most managers are reluctant to enlist an outsider who is a professional mediator or arbitrator, for it is very hard for them to admit openly that they are entangled in a serious conflict, much less one they cannot handle themselves.

When managers remain involved in settling disputes, they usually take a stronger role than mediators: they become arbitrators rather than mediators. As arbitrators, they arrive at a conflict-resolving judgment after hearing each party's case. In most business conflicts, mediation is preferable because the parties are helped to come to an agreement in which they have some psychological investment. Arbitration tends to be more of a judicial process in which the parties make the best possible case to support their position: this tends to further polarize rather than reconcile differences.

Managers can benefit from a third-party presence, however, without involving dispute-resolution professionals per se. For example, they can introduce a consultant into the situation, with an *explicit* mission that is not conflict intervention. The mere presence of this neutral witness will likely constrain the disputants' use of destructive tactics.

Alternatively, if the managers find that they themselves are party to a conflict, they can make the conflict more public and produce the same constraining effect that a third party would. They also can arrange for the presence of relatively uninvolved individuals during interactions; even having a secretary keep minutes of such interactions encourages rational behavior. If the content of the discussion cannot be disclosed to lower-level employees, a higher-level manager can be invited to sit in on the discussion, thereby discouraging dysfunctional personal attacks and unreasonable stances. To the extent that managers can be trusted to be evenhanded, a third-party approach can facilitate conflict management. Encouraging accommodation usually is preferable to imposing a solution that may only produce resentment of one of the parties.

Perceived Progress of the Conflict

It is difficult to manage conflict when the parties are not ready to achieve a reconciliation. Thus, it is important to know whether the parties believe that the conflict is escalating. The following example illustrates this point.

During a product strategy meeting, a marketing vice president carelessly implied that the R&D group tended to overdesign products. The remark was intended to be a humorous stereotyping of the R&D function, but it was interpreted by the R&D vice president as an attempt to pass on to his group the blame for an uncompetitive product. Later in the meeting, the R&D vice president took advantage of an opportunity to point out that the marketing vice president lacked the technical expertise to understand a design limitation. The marketing vice president perceived this rejoinder as ridicule and therefore as an act of hostility. The R&D vice president, who believed he had evened the score, was quite surprised to be denounced subsequently by the marketing vice president, who in turn thought he was evening the score for the uncalled-for barb. These events soon led to a memo war, backbiting, and then to pressure on various employees to take sides.

The important point here is that from the first rejoinder neither party wished to escalate the conflict; each wished merely to even the score. Nonetheless, conflict resolution would have been very difficult to accomplish during this escalation phase because people do not like to disengage when they think they still "owe one" to the other party. Since an even score is subjectively defined, however, the parties need to be convinced that the overall score is approximately equal and that everyone has already suffered enough.

DEVELOPING CONFLICT MANAGEMENT SKILLS

Strategic decision making usually is portrayed as a unilateral process. Decision makers have some vision of where the organization needs to be headed, and they decide on the nature and timing of specific actions to achieve tangible goals. This portrayal, however, does not take into account the conflict inherent in the decision-making process; most strategic decisions are negotiated solutions to conflicts among people whose interests are affected by such decisions. Even in the uncommon case of a unilateral decision, the decision maker has to deal with the conflict that arises when he or she moves to *implement* the decision.

In the presence of conflict at the decision-making or decision-implementing stage, managers must focus on generating an *agreement* rather than a decision. A decision without agreement makes the strategic direction difficult to implement. By contrast, an agreement on a strategic direction doesn't require an explicit decision. In this context, conflict management is the process of removing cognitive barriers to agreement. Note that agreement does not imply that the conflict has "gone away." The people involved still have interests that are somewhat incompatible. Agreement implies that these people have become committed to a course of action that serves some of their interests.

People make agreements that are less than ideal from the standpoint of serving their interests when they lack the *power* to force others to fully comply with their wishes. On the other hand, if a manager has total power over those whose interests are affected by the outcome of a strategic decision, the manager may not care whether or not others agree, because total power implies total compliance. There are few situations in real life in which managers have influence that even approaches total power, however, and power solutions are at best unstable since most people react negatively to powerlessness per se. Thus it makes more sense to seek agreements than to seek power. Furthermore, because conflict management involves weakening or removing barriers to agreements, managers must be able to diagnose successfully such barriers. The model summarized in Table 1 identifies the primary cognitive barriers to agreement.

Competence in understanding the barriers to an agreement can be easily honed by making a pastime of conflict diagnosis. The model helps to focus attention on specific aspects of the situation that may pose obstacles to successful conflict management. This pastime transforms accounts of conflicts—from sources ranging from a spouse's response to "How was your day?" to the evening news—into a challenge in which the objective is to try to pinpoint the obstacles to agreement and to predict the success of proposed interventions.

Focusing on the underlying dynamics of the conflict makes it more likely that conflict management will tend toward resolution rather than the more familiar response of suppression. Although the conflict itself—that is, the source—will remain alive, at best, its expression will be postponed until some later occasion; at worst, it will take a less obvious and usually less manageable form.

Knowledge of and practice in using the model is only a starting point for managers and change agents. Their development as professionals requires that conflict management become an integral part of their use of power. Power is a most basic facet of organizational life, yet inevitably it generates conflict because it constricts the autonomy of those who respond to it. Anticipating precisely how the use of power will create a conflict relationship provides an enormous advantage in the ability to achieve the desired levels of control with minimal dysfunctional side effects.

Strategic Choice

Dean Pruitt

Jeffrey Z. Rubin

Peter Colger has to make a decision. For months he has been looking forward to taking his two weeks of vacation at a quiet mountain lodge where he can hunt, fish, and hike to lofty scenic overlooks. Now his wife Mary has rudely challenged this dream. She has told him that she finds the mountains boring and wants to go to Ocean City, Maryland, a busy seaside resort that Peter dislikes intensely. Peter must decide what strategy to employ in this controversy.

. . . Five general strategies are available to Peter. He can engage in *contentious behavior* and try to prevail—for example, by arguing for the merits of a mountain vacation, indicating that he had already made up his mind, threatening to take a separate vacation if Mary does not agree, or even making a large deposit on a room in a mountain hotel. He can take a *problem-solving* approach and try to find a way to go to both places or to a vacation spot that satisfies both sets of interests. He can *yield* to Mary's demands and agree to go to the seashore. He can be *inactive* (do nothing) in the hope that the issue will simply go away. Or he can *withdraw* from the controversy—for example, by deciding not to take a vacation.

The aim of this chapter is to examine the conditions that determine how Peter (and, more generally, anyone facing a conflict) decides among these basic strategies. We will focus mainly on the first three strategies (contending, problem solving, and yielding), which we call the "coping strategies" because . . . they involve active efforts to resolve the controversy.

NATURE OF THE STRATEGIES

Contending refers to any effort to resolve a conflict on one's own terms without regard to the other party's interests. Parties who employ this strategy maintain their own aspirations and try to persuade the other party to yield. Various tactics are available to parties who choose this strategy. They include making threats, imposing penalties with the understanding that they will be withdrawn if the other concedes, and taking preemptive actions designed to resolve the conflict without the other's consent (such as making a deposit at a mountain hotel in our example). If the parties are trying

Reprinted from Dean Pruitt and Jeffrey Z. Rubin, *Social Conflict* (New York: McGraw-Hill, Inc., 1986). Used with permission of McGraw-Hill, Inc.

to reach a negotiated settlement of the controversy, contending may also involve presenting persuasive arguments, making demands that far exceed what is actually acceptable, committing oneself to an "unalterable" position, or imposing a deadline.

By contrast, *problem solving* entails an effort to identify the issues dividing the parties and to develop and move toward a solution that appeals to both sides. Parties who employ this strategy maintain their own aspirations and try to find a way of reconciling them with the other party's aspirations.

The agreement developed in problem solving can take the form of a compromise (an obvious alternative that stands partway between the two parties' preferred positions), or it can take the form of an integrative solution (a creative reconciliation of the two parties' basic interests). The difference between a compromise and an integrative solution is illustrated by two options that were discussed during the Camp David negotiations . . . A compromise proposal, in which Egypt and Israel would each get half the Sinai, was unacceptable to both sides. The key to settlement was an integrative solution, in which Egypt got the Sinai and Israel got diplomatic recognition and military guarantees.

Various tactics are available to implement the strategy of problem solving. These include risky moves such as conceding with the expectation of receiving a return concession, mentioning possible compromises as talking points, and revealing one's underlying interests. They also include cautious moves such as hinting at possible compromises, sending disavowable intermediaries to discuss the issues, communicating through back channels, and communicating through a mediator.

Although problem solving has been described so far as an individual activity, it can also be a joint enterprise involving both parties. For example, two people can exchange accurate information about their underlying interests, collectively identify new issues in light of this information, brainstorm to seek alternative ways of dealing with the issues, and sometimes even work together to evaluate these alternatives. Joint problem solving is an excellent way to locate mutually acceptable solutions, but it is sometimes impractical because one party is not ready for it or the parties do not trust each other. Hence, individual problem solving must at times be substituted.

Yielding, which involves lowering one's aspirations, need not imply the total capitulation that we saw in the vacation example. It can also imply a partial concession. For example, Peter Colger might decide to forsake his secondary goal of hiking to mountain overlooks in order to make it easier to find a mutually acceptable agreement. He could then engage in problem solving, seeking a quiet resort that permits fishing and hiking where his wife can also accomplish her major goals.

Withdrawing and *inaction* are similar to each other in that they involve termination of efforts to resolve the controversy. They differ in that withdrawing is a permanent termination, whereas inaction is a temporary move that leaves open the possibility of resuming efforts to cope with the controversy. Withdrawing is usually a distinct strategy, but it may at times be hard to distinguish from contending or yielding. For example, if I withdraw from a controversy with my son over the use of my car, I automatically win and thus gain a contentious advantage. If my son withdraws, he is essentially yielding to my viewpoint.

CHOOSING A STRATEGY

There are trade-offs among the five basic strategies, in the sense that choosing one of them makes selecting the others less likely. Inaction and withdrawing are totally incompatible with each other and with the three coping strategies. Though sometimes found in combination with each other, the coping strategies are also somewhat incompatible. There are three reasons for this latter incompatibility. First, the coping strategies are alternative means of moving toward the same end, agreement with the other party. If it is not possible to use one of them, a person is more likely to employ the others. Second, these strategies require different psychological orientations; for example, it does not seem quite right to try to push another party around while yielding to or working with that party. Third, these strategies tend to send out contradictory signals to the other party. Yielding often implies weakness, which is incompatible with putting effective pressure on the other. Contending can undermine the other party's trust, which is an important element of effective problem solving.

Because of these trade-offs, there are indirect as well as direct antecedents of all five strategies. Direct antecedents, as we would expect, directly affect the likelihood of adopting a strategy. Indirect antecedents affect this likelihood by encouraging or discouraging one of the other strategies.

Most of the rest of this chapter is devoted to two theoretical notions about the determinants of choice among the basic strategies. The first, which is summarized in a *dual concern model,* traces strategic choice to the relative strength of concern about own and other's outcomes. The second, which we call the *perceived feasibility perspective,* attributes this choice to the perceived likelihood of success and the cost of enacting the various strategies. These two theoretical notions are complementary in the sense that each deals with issues ignored by the other.

A good deal of evidence will be cited in support of these theoretical notions, most of it derived from laboratory experiments on simulated negotiation. *Negotiation,* a form of conflict behavior, occurs when two parties try to resolve a divergence of interest by means of conversation. Laboratory experiments on this phenomenon place subjects (usually undergraduates) in a simulated negotiation setting and manipulate theoretically relevant variables. Careful measurements of reactions to these variables are taken. A more detailed discussion of this kind of research can be found in Pruitt (1981) and Rubin and Brown (1975).

The chapter ends with a discussion of the forces that determine the vigor with which the three coping strategies are enacted.

THE DUAL CONCERN MODEL

The dual concern model appears in Figure 1. It postulates two types of concerns: *concern about own outcomes,* which is shown on the abscissa, and *concern about the other party's outcomes,* which is shown on the ordinate. These concerns are portrayed as ranging from indifference (at the zero point of the coordinate) to very great concern.

The two concerns in this model are defined as follows: Concern about own outcomes means placing importance on one's own interests—one's needs and values—in the realm under dispute. People with a strong concern about their own outcomes are

FIGURE 1   The Dual Concern Model

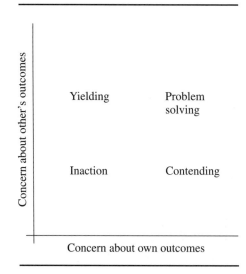

highly resistant to yielding; in other words, their aspirations tend to be rigid and high.[1] Concern about the other's outcomes implies placing importance on the other's interests—feeling responsible for the quality of the other's outcomes. This concern is sometimes *genuine,* involving an intrinsic interest in the other's welfare. However, it is more often *instrumental,* being aimed at helping the other in order to advance one's own interests. Thus, for example, dependence on another person often encourages efforts to build a working relationship with that person by trying to satisfy his or her needs.

Although this is not shown in Figure 1, it is theoretically possible for people to have negative concerns about the other party's outcomes and even about their own outcomes. In other words, we might have extended the coordinates in the figure downward and to the left. A few points about negative concerns will be made in this chapter but not enough to warrant introducing further complexity into the formal statement of the model.

The dual concern model makes the following predictions about the antecedents of strategic choice: Problem solving is encouraged when there is a strong concern about both own and other's outcomes. Yielding is encouraged by a strong concern about only the other's outcomes. Contending is encouraged by a strong concern about only one's own outcomes. Inaction is encouraged when concern about both parties' outcomes is weak. The model makes no predictions about the antecedents of withdrawing.

The dual concern model has its origins in Blake and Mouton's (1964) managerial grid and has been adapted to the analysis of conflict by various authors (Blake and Mouton, 1979; Filley, 1975; Gladwin and Walter, 1980; Rahim, 1983; Ruble and

---

1. See Kelley, Beckman, and Fischer (1967) for a sophisticated discussion of the concept of resistance to yielding.

Thomas, 1976; Thomas 1976). Other labels are sometimes given to the dimensions in this model. For example, concern about own outcomes is sometimes called assertiveness, and concern about other's outcomes is sometimes called cooperativeness.

Other versions of the dual concern model (Filley, 1975; Thomas, 1976) postulate a fifth strategy called compromising, which is ordinarily shown in the middle of the figure because it is viewed as due to a moderate concern about both self and other. We do not take this approach, because we see no need to postulate a separate strategy in order to explain the development of compromises. We see compromises as arising from one of two sources—either lazy problem solving involving a half-hearted attempt to satisfy the two parties' interests, or simple yielding by both parties.

Thomas (1976) notes that the two concerns in the dual concern model are often erroneously reduced to a single dimension, with selfishness (concern about own outcomes) on one end and cooperativeness (concern about other's outcomes) on the other. This is an improper simplification, because it is clear that both concerns can be strong at the same time. People can be both selfish and cooperative (leading them to engage in problem solving in an effort to reconcile both parties' interests). By postulating dual concerns, we are forced to distinguish between two ways of cooperating with the other party, yielding and problem solving. These were not sufficiently separated in a prior theory of strategic choice (Deutsch, 1973), which proposed only a single motivational dimension ranging from competition to cooperation. Postulating dual concerns also forces us to distinguish between two ways of advancing one's own interests, contending and problem solving.

Determinants of Concern about Own Outcomes

The strength of concern about own outcomes differs from situation to situation and from person to person. For example, person A may be relatively indifferent about the location and quality of his or her vacation, whereas this may be a matter of great concern for person B. Person A, on the other hand, may have a much deeper concern about the quality of his or her work on the job.

Concern about own outcomes can be traced to a number of determinants. One is the importance of the values affected by these outcomes. Person B may have an extremely taxing job, which produces a great need for rest and relaxation during his or her vacation, whereas person A may not have such strong needs. When a spouse challenges these vacation preferences, person A is likely to yield or be inactive, whereas person B will make an effort to salvage these preferences via contentious or problem-solving activities.

Another determinant of concern about own outcomes in any one realm is the importance of outcomes in other realms. People do not have an infinite amount of time or energy, so they cannot pursue all of their interests with equal intensity. A strong concern about one issue often leads to a weak concern about others. For example, person A may be relatively indifferent to the issue of quality of vacation because of being wrapped up in his or her job, the campaign for a nuclear freeze, or some other absorbing activity.

Concern about own outcomes also tends to be low when people are afraid of conflict. This is because resistance to yielding, which is produced by a high concern about own outcomes, tends to engender conflict. Fear of conflict is a personality predisposition for some people. It is also produced by certain situations, such as being attracted to—or dependent on—another person but distrustful of the other's opinion of the self (Hancock and Sorrentino, 1980). Situations such as this, which are said to involve "false cohesiveness" (Longley and Pruitt, 1980), are especially common at the beginning of a relationship when people are feeling each other out. Research on newly formed romantic couples suggests that such sentiments can block all forms of assertiveness, including both contentious and problem-solving behavior (Fry, Firestone, and Williams, 1983).

Concern about Own Group's Outcomes.   The forces mentioned so far affect individuals acting on their own behalf. But the parties to conflict are often groups. Hence we must inquire into the antecedents of the concern that is frequently felt by group members about the outcomes achieved by their group.

Especially strong concerns about the fate of the group tend to develop in cohesive groups whose members share a similar life situation and discuss their common fate with one another. This is particularly likely when the members of such groups regard themselves as part of a broader social movement, making common cause with similar groups in other locations (Kriesberg, 1982).

When the parties are groups or organizations, actual conflict behavior is usually carried out by representatives. Research on negotiation (Benton and Druckman, 1973) suggests that representatives are usually more reluctant to yield than are individuals bargaining on their own behalf. This is because they are trying to please their constituents and typically view their constituents as nonconciliatory. The effect disappears in those infrequent cases where the constituent is revealed to have a conciliatory bias (Benton and Druckman, 1974).

Other studies suggest that representatives are especially reluctant to yield under conditions that make them anxious to please their constituents, such as when they have low status in their groups (Kogan, Lamm, and Trommsdorff, 1972), are distrusted by their constituents (Wall, 1975), wish to continue associating with their constituents (Klimoski, 1972), or have female as opposed to male constituents (Forcey, Van Slyck, Carnevale, and Pruitt, 1983). All of these conditions can be viewed as enhancing concern about own side's outcomes.

Accountability to constituents has much the same effect. A representative is accountable to the extent that he or she must report the outcome of the negotiation to powerful constituents. Accountable representatives are especially reluctant to concede in negotiation (Bartunek, Benton, and Keys, 1975), suggesting that they are particularly concerned about group outcomes. As a result, they are more likely to adopt a contentious or problem-solving approach than to yield (Ben-Yoav and Pruitt, 1984b).

Quite often, constituents instruct their representatives to achieve high outcomes and are dissatisfied when they come home with less. This also serves to bolster the concern felt by representatives for their side's outcomes.

Determinants of Concern about the Other Party's Outcomes

As mentioned earlier, concern about the other party's outcomes takes two basic forms: *genuine* concern, based on an intrinsic interest in the other's welfare, and *instrumental* concern, aimed at advancing one's own interests. There is an important difference between these two forms of concern. Because instrumental concern is aimed at impressing the other, it is stronger when the other is more concerned about his or her own outcomes. By contrast, genuine concern aims at serving the other regardless of the other's degree of self-interest.

Genuine concern about the other party's outcomes is fostered by various kinds of interpersonal *bonds,* including attraction (Clark and Mills, 1979), perceived similarity (Hornstein, 1976), and kinship or common group identity (Hatton, 1967). Genuine concern is also fostered by a positive mood (Isen and Levin, 1972) and by taking helpful actions toward someone (not necessarily the party with whom one is now in conflict) in the recent past, especially if there were no clear external incentives for this action (Freedman and Fraser, 1966; Uranowitz, 1975).

Instrumental concern about the other party's outcomes is common whenever one sees oneself as dependent on the other—when the other is seen as able to provide rewards and penalties. An example is the expectation of further negotiation in the future. Dependence leads to the conclusion that it is desirable to build a relationship with the other now. Hence one tries to impress the other with one's concern about his or her welfare.

Dependence is by no means a one-way street. Mutual dependence is quite common and can encourage either mutual yielding or mutual problem solving. The impact on mutual problem solving is illustrated by a case study of mediation between two managers in the same company (Walton, 1969). It was not until both men discovered that they could be hurt by one another that they began trying to solve the problems they were having with each other.

For people to be aware of their dependence on another party, it is often necessary for them to project themselves into the future. This point is important for understanding conflict, because people embroiled in escalating conflicts often lose awareness of the future. They concentrate so hard on winning in the present that they lose track of the importance of maintaining good relations with the other party. In such situations, future perspective can be regained in a number of ways. One is to take time out from the controversy—to become disengaged for a while. Research suggests that such a "cooling-off period" enhances cooperativeness in settings where parties are basically interdependent (Pilisuk, Kiritz, and Clampitt, 1971).

Although bonds and dependencies usually foster concern about the other party's outcomes, under certain conditions they can produce exactly the opposite reaction—antagonism toward the other and adoption of contentious tactics. This reaction occurs when people to whom we are bonded—friends, relatives, people we admire—fail to fulfill their minimum obligations or severely frustrate us. Our bonds to these people can actually encourage more anger and aggression than we would otherwise feel, because we believe they owe us preferential treatment. A similar reaction occurs when people on whom we are dependent are unresponsive to our needs (Gruder, 1971). The ordinary reaction to dependence is concern about the other party's needs. But if the other is perceived as taking advantage of this concern, it often seems necessary to reverse gears and retaliate in order to motivate the other to be more responsive. (These reactions are outside the scope of the dual concern model, which deals only with positive concern about the other's outcomes.)

Predictions from the Model

The dual concern model has received support in three recent studies. These studies made use of a laboratory simulation of negotiation in which two participants play the roles of buyer and seller in a wholesale market. Their task is to reach agreement on the prices of three appliances: typewriters, vacuum cleaners, and sewing machines. Each participant has a benefit schedule showing the profit that his or her firm will make at each price level. The participants are allowed to talk about their benefit schedules but not to show them to each other. The benefit schedules are constructed so that there are hidden solutions that provide much greater benefit to both parties than those that are obvious at first, but these solutions can be achieved only if one or both parties engage in problem solving. In all three studies, the two concerns specified in the dual concern model were manipulated independently of each other in a 2×2 design. Both subjects in a dyad always received the same combination of concerns.

In the first two studies, concern about own outcomes was manipulated by means of instructions about the lower limit of profit the subjects could achieve. High concern was produced by telling both subjects privately that their firms required them to achieve no less than a particular profit level ($4,600); low concern was produced by telling them nothing about a lower limit on profit. The researchers reasoned that the former condition would encourage more resistance to yielding than the latter.

The first study (Pruitt, Carnevale, Ben-Yoav, Nochajski, and Van Slyck, 1983) involved a manipulation of genuine concern about the other's outcomes. High concern was produced by putting the participants in a good mood, which has been shown to induce a desire to be helpful (Isen and Levin, 1972). Just before the beginning of negotiation, both subjects received gifts from a confederate of the experimenter. There were no gifts in the low-concern condition. The second study (Ben-Yoav and Pruitt, 1984a) involved a manipulation of strategic concern. High concern was produced by giving the subjects an expectation of cooperative future interaction. They were told that they would have to work together toward a common goal on a task following the negotiation. The aim of this instruction was to make them feel dependent on each other and hence desirous of developing a working relationship. In the low-concern condition, they were told that they would be working alone on a subsequent task.

The average joint benefit (sum of the two parties' profits) achieved in the first two studies is shown in Figure 2. In both studies, a combination of high concern about own outcomes and high concern about the other's outcomes (shown in the upper-right-hand cell) produced especially high joint benefit. This result is evidence of active problem-solving behavior, as predicted by the dual concern model. Other evidence of problem solving in this condition is the fact that the negotiators were especially likely to give each other information about the entries in their profit schedules. A combination of high concern about own outcomes and low concern about the other's outcomes (lower-right-hand cell) produced moderately low joint benefit. Contentious statements such as persuasive arguments and threats were especially common in this condition, again supporting the dual concern model. A combination of low concern about own outcomes and high concern about the other's outcomes (upper-left-hand cell) produced the lowest joint benefit of all, suggesting the yielding (aspiration collapse) predicted by the dual concern model.

FIGURE 2   Joint Benefit Achieved in Studies 1 and 2

	No limit	Limit			No limit	Limit
Positive mood	8540	9890		Expectation of cooperative future interaction	8175	9425
No mood	8900	8960		No expectation of cooperative future interaction	8675	8650
	Study 1				Study 2	

The results of these two studies show that, as predicted by the dual concern model, concern about the other party's outcomes is a two-edged sword. In conjunction with concern about own outcomes, it leads to problem solving and (when both parties share the same concerns) especially high joint benefit. But when concern about own outcomes is weak, concern about the other party's outcomes produces yielding and especially low joint benefit.

In the third study (Ben-Yoav and Pruitt, 1984b), concern about the other party's outcomes was again manipulated by the presence versus absence of an expectation of cooperative future interaction. Concern about own outcomes was manipulated by means of high versus low accountability to constituents. Under high accountability, the constituents (who were confederates) were able to divide the money earned in the negotiation and write an evaluation of the outcomes achieved by their negotiators. Under low accountability, the negotiators divided the money earned, and no evaluations were written.

The results for joint benefit are shown in Figure 3. As predicted by the dual concern model, high accountability in the absence of an expectation of cooperative future interaction encouraged heavy contentious verbalizations and low joint benefit (as shown in the lower-right-hand cell). But the impact of accountability was completely reversed when there was an expectation of future interaction. In this condition (upper-right-hand cell), accountability encouraged especially high joint benefit, presumably because it fostered heavy joint problem solving.

These results suggest that accountability, and hence concern about own outcomes, is also a two-edged sword. Under normal conditions, it fosters contentious behavior and low joint benefit. But under conditions that encourage a desire for good relations between the opposing parties, it fosters problem solving and high joint benefit.

In summary, the dual concern model postulates that strategic choice is determined by the strength of two concerns: concern for own outcomes and concern for the other party's outcomes. When both concerns are strong, people prefer problem solving; when the former concern is strong, they prefer contending; when the latter

FIGURE 3   Joint Benefit Achieved in Study 3

	Accountability	
	Low	High
Expectation of cooperative future interaction	8600	9770
No expectation of cooperative future interaction	8840	8300

concern is strong, they prefer yielding; and when both concerns are weak, inaction is likely to be found. Concern about own outcomes produces high, rigid aspirations. It tends to be strong when the interests at stake are important, when outcomes in other realms are unimportant, when there is low fear of conflict, when there is high accountability to constituents, and when constituents insist that their representative achieve a high level of benefit. Concern about the other party's outcomes can be either genuine or instrumental (strategic). Genuine concern is fostered by interpersonal bonds of all types and by good mood. Instrumental concern is fostered by a desire to develop a working relationship with a person on whom one is dependent. The predictive value of this model has been demonstrated in three studies.

THE PERCEIVED FEASIBILITY PERSPECTIVE

Choice among the five basic strategies is also a matter of perceived feasibility—the extent to which the strategy seems capable of achieving the concerns that give rise to it and the cost that is anticipated from enacting each strategy. Considerations of feasibility supplement those specified by the dual concern model. The dual concern model indicates the strategies preferred under various combinations of concern about own and other's outcomes. But for a strategy actually to be adopted, it must also be seen as minimally feasible. If not, another strategy will be chosen, even if it is less consistent with the current combination of concerns.

For example, take parties who are concerned about both their own and the other party's outcomes. Problem solving is their preferred strategy. But if this strategy seems infeasible or too risky, they are likely to shift to yielding or contending, their next best alternatives. Which of these is chosen is determined both by the relative strength of the two concerns and by other considerations of feasibility and cost. If the parties are more concerned about the other's outcomes than their own, they adopt a yielding approach, provided that this seems reasonably feasible. If they are more concerned about their own outcomes than the other's, they shift to contentious behavior, also provided that this seems reasonably feasible.

For another example, take parties who are concerned mainly about their own outcomes. Contending is their preferred strategy because it holds the promise of getting something for nothing. But problem solving is a close second if the contentious approach appears infeasible or costly. Indeed, problem solving often seems the most feasible way of pursuing one's own interests.

The next three sections deal with the perceived feasibility of three of the fundamental strategies under consideration in this chapter: problem solving, contending, and inaction.

Perceived Feasibility of Problem Solving

Problem solving seems more feasible the greater the *perceived common ground* (PCG). PCG is a party's assessment of the likelihood of finding an alternative that satisfies both parties' aspirations. The more likely it seems that such an alternative can be found, the more feasible problem solving appears to be. PCG is greater (1) the lower the Party's own aspirations, (2) the lower the Other's aspirations as perceived by Party, and (3) the greater the perceived integrative potential (PIP)—that is, Party's faith that alternatives favorable to both parties exist or can be devised.

This definition implies that PCG is the mirror image of perceived conflict. As PCG goes up, conflict, in the sense of perceived divergence of interest, goes down.

The reader may be surprised to learn that lower aspirations make problem solving seem more feasible. Superficially, this seems inconsistent with the point made earlier that lack of concern about one's own interests (which produces low aspirations) reduces the likelihood of problem solving. However, these two points are not contradictory. We are talking about two countervailing forces that are simultaneously activated when concern about own interests is low. The one makes problem solving seem more feasible, and the other (by permitting the strategy of yielding) makes problem solving seem less necessary.

Perceived integrative potential (PIP), a component of PCG, needs further elaboration. At any given point in negotiation, some alternatives are known and the availability of others is suspected. PIP is high when there are known alternatives that provide high benefit to both parties. It is moderately high when it seems probable that such alternatives can be developed—the more definite the prospects for developing such an alternative, the higher is PIP. It is low when there seems little prospect of finding mutually beneficial alternatives.

Greater clarity about the concepts of PIP and PCG is provided by the graphs in Figure 4. The abscissa in these graphs maps Party's own benefits; the ordinate, Party's perception of Other's benefits. The heavy points in these graphs refer to known alternatives, the medium points to alternatives that seem potentially discoverable, and the light points to long shots. The location of a point in the space shows the perceived value of that alternative to the two parties. The vertical lines in these graphs refer to Party's own aspirations and the horizontal lines to Other's perceived aspirations.

FIGURE 4   Four Levels of Perceived Common Ground

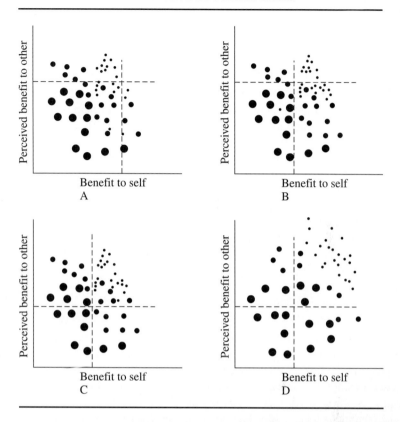

PCG is greater the more points there are to the northeast (above and to the right) of the intersection of the aspiration lines and the darker these points are. PCG is greater in Figure 4B than in Figure 4A because Party's own aspirations are lower. It is greater in Figure 4C than in Figure 4B because Other's perceived aspirations are also lower. It is greater in Figure 4D than in Figure 4C because of greater PIP—that is, greater perceived likelihood that mutually beneficial alternatives can be developed (as shown by the fact that the darker points are farther from the origin in the northeast direction).

Determinants of Perceived Integrative Potential.   A number of conditions contribute to PIP and hence to the likelihood that problem solving will be employed.

1. *Faith in own problem-solving ability.* Some people are good communicators and/or understand well how to devise mutually beneficial alternatives. Hence their experience leads them to see considerable integrative potential in almost any situation. Others, less well endowed, are likely to view conflict as more intractable and to adopt strategies of yielding or contending rather than problem solving.

2. *Momentum.* Momentum refers to prior success at reaching agreement in the current controversy. The more frequent and recent such successes have been, the greater will be Party's faith that these successes can be reproduced in the future and that problem solving is worthwhile. Momentum can sometimes be encouraged by scheduling easier issues earlier in a negotiation agenda, so that a solid foundation of success has been built by the time more difficult issues are encountered.

3. *Availability of a mediator.* Mediators often serve as communication links between the parties, coordinating movement toward compromise or helping to develop integrative solutions. Their availability should make problem solving seem more likely to be successful.

   An example of the latter mechanism can be seen in the British reaction to the Argentine occupation of the Falkland Islands in 1982. Yielding was ruled out on the grounds of cost to the British image. Inaction seemed inadvisable because every day of the occupation enhanced the legitimacy of the Argentine action. In short, the choice was between contending and problem solving. At first it appeared that there might be integrative potential; American Secretary of State Alexander Haig was trying to mediate the crisis. Hence the British adopted a problem-solving strategy, working with Haig while defending their basic interests by moving their fleet slowly toward South America. However, PIP disappeared with the failure of Haig's mission, making problem solving seem quite infeasible. As a result, the British adopted an exclusively contentious approach, an all-out invasion of the islands.

4. *Other's perceived readiness for problem solving.* Problem solving seems more feasible to the extent that Other seems ready to participate in this process. There are two reasons for this. One is increased PIP, because joint problem solving is usually more efficient than unilateral problem solving. The second is that problem solving seems less risky when Other is not taking a contentious approach, because under those conditions there is less danger in allowing oneself to look weak.

   Trust.   The perception that Other is ready for problem solving, and hence that there is integrative potential, is sometimes a function of trust—that is, of Party's perception that Other is concerned about Party's interests. Research (Kimmel, Pruitt, Magenau, and Konar-Goldband, 1980) suggests that trust encourages problem solving when Party is otherwise inclined to adopt this strategy, presumably by making problem solving seem feasible.

   Although trust allows people to adopt a problem-solving strategy, it is no guarantee that this strategy will be adopted. Indeed, trust can sometimes have quite the opposite effect, encouraging high, inflexible aspirations defended by contentious behavior.

   Whether trust encourages problem solving or contending depends at least in part on Other's perceived resistance to yielding—that is, the apparent firmness of Other's aspirations. A trusted Other whose aspirations do not seem firm will be expected to give in to Party's demands. Hence contentious behavior seems especially feasible. But if Other's aspirations seem firm, trust implies instead that Other will cooperate if and only if Party cooperates. This encourages Party to adopt a problem-solving strategy.

   Evidence that problem solving is encouraged by a combination of trust and perceived firmness comes from several bargaining experiments. All of these studies examined bargainer response to helpful actions from the other party, which actions presumably engendered trust. When the other party had been helpful, bargainers were more willing to cooperate if the other also (1) had high threat capacity (Lindskold and Bennett, 1973; Michener, Vaske, Schleifer, Plazewsksi, and Chapman, 1975); (2) had a tough constituent (Wall, 1977); (3) had been unyielding or competitive in the past (Deutsch, 1973; Harford and Solomon, 1967); or (4) had been unwilling to make unilateral concessions in the past (Komorita and Esser, 1975; McGillicuddy, Pruitt, and Syna, 1984). These four conditions presumably enhance Party's perception that Other has firm aspirations.

Trust develops in a number of ways. It is encouraged by a perception that the other party has a positive attitude toward us, is similar to us, or is dependent on us. As an example of the latter point, Solomon (1960) has shown that trust is greater when one sees oneself as having a capacity to punish the other for failing to cooperate.

Trust also tends to develop when one has been helpful toward the other party (Loomis, 1959). This prediction is implied by dissonance (Festinger, 1957) and self-perception (Bem, 1972) theories. It also follows from the assumption that the other will reciprocate one's helpful behavior.

We tend to trust people who have been helpful or cooperative, especially if their help is directed toward us (Cooper and Fazio, 1979) and has occurred recently (Kelley and Stahelski, 1970). Trust is an especially common response when the other's helpful behavior is seen as voluntary and not as a product of environmental forces. Hence we tend to trust others whose helpful behavior is not required by their role (Jones and Davis, 1965) or seems to be costly to them (Komorita, 1973). All of these circumstances encourage problem solving by enhancing perceived integrative potential.

Perceived Feasibility of Contending

Contending seems more feasible the lower the other's apparent resistance to yielding. There is not much point in putting pressure on an opponent who has ultra-strong feelings, has powerful and resolute constituents, or has already yielded to the bare bone of need. Other tactics, such as yielding and problem solving, are more likely to be adopted. But if the other's aspirations (however high they may be) seem relatively easy to dislodge, contentious behavior gets a boost.

The points just made imply that contentious behavior is often self-liquidating, a victim of both failure and success. If it fails, this indicates that Other's resistance is greater than originally thought, so Party will abandon the tactic. If it succeeds and Other yields, Other's resistance to further yielding is likely to grow because Other will come closer and closer to his or her limit. Again, Party must eventually abandon the tactic.

The feasibility of contending is also a function of Party's apparent capacity to employ contentious tactics and of Other's apparent capacity to counter them. Does Party have good arguments? Does Other have counterarguments? Is Party adept at arguing his or her case? How effective is Other as a debater? Can Party reward or punish Other? How good are Other's defenses against such tactics? Does Party have ways to commit himself or herself credibly? Is Other capable of undoing these commitments?

Capacities such as these are sometimes lumped together under the familiar concepts of "power" and "counterpower." These concepts have some merit in that they allow us to make a few broad generalizations. For example, we can generalize that more-powerful people have higher aspirations and make greater use of heavy contentious tactics, regardless of the source of their power. But there is a tendency to overuse these concepts in social science theory, making facile generalizations with little real meaning (see, e.g., Morgenthau, 1967). The problem is that there are many kinds of power, each with a different set of properties (French and Raven, 1959).

In a stable long-term relationship, each party's capacity to employ contentious tactics tends to be matched by the other's level of resistance, so that there is relatively little advantage to either party in employing contentious tactics. Hence, on important issues where the parties cannot easily yield, joint problem solving is most likely to be the strategic choice. This is true even when threat capacity greatly favors one side, as in a relationship between master and slave. Joint problem solving is not uncommon in such relationships, though the outcome is likely to benefit the master far more than the slave. The slave's situation produces aspirations that are so low that his or her resistance to further yielding is strong enough to balance the master's superior threat capacity.

Perceived Cost.   Contentious behavior, particularly in its more severe forms, runs the risk of alienating the other party and starting a conflict spiral. There is also some danger of third-party censure. Such considerations can deter contentious behavior, particularly when one is dependent on the other party or on watchful third parties.

Costs are also associated with constituent *surveillance,* which has a complicated relationship to the use of contentious tactics. Surveillance must be distinguished from accountability to constituents. Representatives are accountable to the extent that they can be rewarded or punished on the basis of the outcomes they generate for their constituents. They are under surveillance when their actual conflict behavior (e.g., how they negotiate) is being observed. Representatives who are being observed by their constituents usually fear getting out of line with these constituents' expectations. If they believe the constituents favor toughness, they will tend to adopt contentious behavior; if they see the constituents as conciliatory, they will avoid contending. These points are supported by a study of the joint effect of surveillance and sex of constituent (Forcey, Van Slyck, Carnevale, and Pruitt, 1983) on strategic choice. Surveillance by male constituents was found to enhance negotiator contentiousness, whereas surveillance by female constituents was found to diminish contentiousness. This makes sense if we assume that the subjects subscribed to the usual stereotype that men favor a tough approach and women a conciliatory approach to interpersonal relations.

Perceived Feasibility of Inaction

Inaction is obviously the greatest time waster of the strategies. Hence *time pressure* should discourage use of this strategy and, if Party remains engaged in the controversy, encourage the three coping strategies.

There are two sources of time pressure: cost per unit time of engaging in the controversy and closeness to a deadline. In negotiation, time pressure can be due to any cost of continued negotiation, including time lost from other pursuits, the expense of maintaining negotiators in the field, or rapid deterioration of the object under dispute (such as fruits and vegetables). Deadlines are points in the future at which significant costs are likely to be experienced if the controversy has not been resolved. At a strike deadline, the union pulls the workers out of the factory; at a hiring deadline, the job offer is withdrawn. The closer one is to a deadline and the larger the penalty for passing that deadline without agreement, the greater the time pressure and hence the less likely one is to enact the strategy of inaction.

An example of the impact of time pressure on strategic choice can be seen in the 1968 student rebellion in Mexico City, which occurred just before the Olympic Games in that city. As the opening of the games approached, the Mexican government became increasingly concerned about the continuing student disorder. In effect, deadline pressures were increasing, and the existing impasse with the students seemed less and less tolerable. All three of the coping strategies were employed in quick succession. First, the government yielded to a few student demands and then entered into problem-solving discussions. Finding the latter unsuccessful, the government then took the contentious (to say the least) approach of shooting hundreds of students at a rally.

All three coping strategies are possible in the face of time pressure, but research (Pruitt and Drews, 1969) suggests that the favorite strategy is yielding. This is presumably because yielding is the fastest way to move toward agreement. It follows that contending and problem solving are adopted in the face of time pressure only when there is heavy resistance to yielding.

In summary, we have argued that perceived feasibility—assessment of effectiveness and cost—affects strategic choice. This consideration supplements the forces specified in the dual concern model. Thus, for example, problem solving is adopted when one is concerned about both own and other's outcomes provided that there is some perceived possibility of success at a reasonable cost. The perceived feasibility of problem solving is a function of perceived common ground (PCG), the perception that an alternative can be found that satisfies both parties' aspirations. PCG, in turn, is a function of own and perceived other's aspirations and of perceived integrative potential (PIP), the apparent likelihood of identifying mutually beneficial alternatives. Perceived feasibility of contending is a positive function of perceived power and an inverse function of Other's apparent resistance to yielding. Perceived feasibility of inaction diminishes with increased time pressure.

ANTECEDENTS OF WITHDRAWING

The dual concern model and the perceived feasibility perspective and not very useful in understanding the conditions under which people withdraw from a conflict. Hence, we must turn to other considerations.

People decide to withdraw when the benefit they expect from a controversy falls below their limit—that is, their minimal aspiration.

The benefit they expect is determined in part by how far they think the other party will concede. Thus I am unlikely to withdraw from negotiation with an auto dealer if he or she proposes a moderate price for an attractive car and seems willing to go lower. It is also determined in part by perceived integrative potential. If a jointly acceptable package of price, car, and accessories looks easy to devise, I am also unlikely to withdraw.

Logically speaking, the limit should be set at the level of benefit that can be achieved by withdrawing (Fisher and Ury, 1981), and this is often the case. For example, in negotiating with a car dealer, I should set my limit at the lowest price I would have to pay another dealer for a comparable car. However, in actual practice, people often get locked into unrealistic limits through a process of premature commitment. For example, before going to buy a car, I may tell my friends that I intend to pay no more than $6,250, and I may even announce this figure to the dealer as a contentious gambit. Unless I am willing to renege on this commitment, $6,250 becomes my effective limit, and I must withdraw if the dealer does not accept it. (It follows that the contentious strategy of positional commitment is risky unless one is fairly certain about what the other will accept.)

THE VIGOR OF STRATEGIC BEHAVIOR

Implementation of the three coping strategies can be more or less *vigorous*. In the case of contentious behavior, vigor refers to the heaviness of the actions taken. Shouts are more vigorous than persuasive communications, blows more vigorous than shouts, shots more vigorous than blows. In the case of problem solving, vigor refers to the creativity of the problem-solving effort. At the low end of vigor is a simple, dull effort to coordinate the making of concessions toward an obvious compromise. At the high end is an active effort to understand the other's interests and a thoughtful search for a way to reconcile these interests with one's own. In the case of yielding, vigor refers simply to how far one drops one's aspirations. Vigor has no meaning with respect to the strategies of inaction or withdrawing.

There are various determinants of how vigorous a strategy will be. One set of determinants is embodied in the dual concern model (Figure 1). The stronger the concerns specified by this model, the more vigorous will be the predicted strategy. Thus, if concern about own outcomes is weak, greater concern about the other party's outcomes will produce more profound yielding. If concern about the other's outcomes is weak, greater concern about own outcomes will encourage more extreme contentious behavior. If neither concern is weak, problem solving will be more vigorous and creative the stronger are the dual concerns.

It is common for parties who have adopted a coping strategy to begin less vigorously and move toward greater vigor if earlier efforts do not achieve agreement. Such gradualism ensures that no greater costs will be incurred than are necessary to achieve their goals. This point is most obvious in the realm of contentious behavior. Like the United States in the Vietnam War, parties usually begin cautiously and escalate only if they are unsuccessful.

Two of the coping strategies have a paradoxical feature: If they are adopted, the vigor with which they are enacted is a function of some of the same conditions that *discourage* their being adopted in the first place.

One of these strategies is contending. As mentioned earlier, the expectation of resistance from the other party discourages contentious behavior. But suppose that other conditions (such as being a highly accountable representative with no dependence on the other) predispose a party to contend. What is the effect of expected resistance then? Our hypothesis is that it promotes the use of heavier contentious tactics. If the other looks like a pushover, it should be easy to get a concession by simple stonewalling or persuasive argumentation. But if the other's position seems engraved in stone, heavier guns will be needed, in the form of threats or other coercive actions.

Problem solving is the other strategy that exhibits this paradoxical feature. Low PCG discourages problem solving. But it also encourages a creative form of problem solving when this strategy is adopted for other reasons. Suppose, for example, that there is a complete stalemate—both parties are totally unwilling to yield and contentious tactics seem useless. If withdrawing is infeasible and inaction also seems unattractive (perhaps because of time pressure), problem solving is the only possible approach. To the extent that PCG is low (whether because of high aspirations, a perception that the other party has high aspirations, or minimal PIP), it will seem necessary to employ a more creative effort in order to reach agreement . . .

CONCLUSIONS

This chapter has presented a preliminary theory about the conditions that affect the choice people make among the five strategies available to them in conflict: contending, problem solving, yielding, inaction, and withdrawing. This theory consists mainly of a dual concern model, supplemented by some ideas about the effect of feasibility considerations. The theory also implies some paradoxical hypotheses about determinants of the vigor with which certain of the strategies are employed. Strangely, the same conditions that make contending and problem solving seem less feasible cause these strategies to be employed with greater vigor if they happen to be adopted.

Consider Both Relationships and Substance When Negotiating Strategically

Grant T. Savage

John D. Blair

Ritch L. Sorenson

When David Peterson, director of services for Dickerson Machinery, arrives at his office, he notes four appointments on his schedule. With his lengthy experience in negotiating important contracts for this large-equipment repair service, he does not take long to identify the agenda for each appointment.[1]

A steering clutch disk salesman from Roadworks will arrive at 8:30 A.M. Peterson has relied for years on disks supplied by Caterpillar and knows those disks can provide the 8,000 hours of service Dickerson guarantees. Price is an issue in Peterson's selection of a supplier, but more important is a guarantee on the life span of the part.

A meeting is scheduled at 9:30 with a mechanic who has swapped a new company battery for a used battery from his own truck. This "trade" is, of course, against company policy, and the employee has been reprimanded and told his next paycheck will be docked. However, the mechanic wants to discuss the matter.

A representative for Tarco, a large road-building contractor, is scheduled for 10:00 A.M. Peterson has been interested in this service contract for a couple of years. He believes that if he can secure a short-term service contract with Tarco, Dickerson's high-quality mechanical service and guarantees will result in a long-term service relationship with the contractor. The night before, Peterson had dinner with Tarco's representative, and this morning he will provide a tour of service facilities and discuss the short-term contract with him.

A meeting with management representatives for union negotiations is scheduled for 1:00 P.M. That meeting will probably last a couple of hours. Peterson is concerned because the company has lost money on the shop undergoing contract talks, and now the union is demanding higher wages and threatening to strike. The company cannot

---

Reprinted from *Academy of Management Executive* 3, no. 1 (February 1989), pp. 37–47. Used with permission.

1. The incidents reported in this vignette and throughout the article are based on actual experiences in a multistate machinery servicing company.

afford a prolonged strike, but it also cannot afford to increase pay at current service production rates. Negotiating a contract will not be easy.

CHOOSING NEGOTIATION STRATEGIES

Peterson's appointments are not unique. Researchers and scholars have examined similar situations. What strategic advice does the negotiation literature offer for handling these four situations?

One of the best developed approaches is *game theory,* which focuses on maximizing substantive outcomes in negotiations.[2] Peterson would probably do well by focusing on only the best possible outcome for Dickerson Machinery in his meetings with the salesman and the employee: He already has a good contract for a steering wheel clutch, but if the salesman can offer a better deal, Peterson will take it; and in the case of the employee, Peterson will hear him out but foresees no need to deviate from company policy.

In contrast, an exclusive focus on maximizing the company's substantive outcomes would probably not work in the other two situations: Tarco may continue being serviced elsewhere unless enticed to try Dickerson; and during the union negotiations, strategies to maximize outcomes for management only could force a strike.

Another well-developed strategic approach is *win-win problem solving.* It is designed to maximize outcomes for both parties and maintain positive relationships.[3] This approach could work in the union negotiation, but the outcome would probably be a compromise, not a true win-win solution.

Win-win negotiation probably is not the best strategy in the other three situations. Either Roadwork's salesman meets the guarantee and beats current prices, or he does not; trying to find a win-win solution would probably be a waste of time. Similarly, because the meeting with the employee will occur after company rules have been applied, a win-win solution is probably not in the company's best interest. Lastly, an attempt to maximize the company's substantive outcomes in a short-term service contract with Tarco could hinder long-term contract prospects.

Any one approach to negotiation clearly will not work in all situations. Executives need a framework for determining what strategies are best in different situations. We believe the best strategy depends on desired outcomes. In this article, we characterize the two major outcomes at issue in the previous examples as *substantive* and *relationship* outcomes. Although both types of outcome have been discussed in the literature, relationship outcomes have received much less attention. Our contention is that a systematic model of strategic choice for negotiation must account for both

---

2. See H. Raiffa, *The Art and Science of Negotiation* (Cambridge, MA: Harvard University Press, 1982), for a discussion of how game theory can help negotiators maximize their substantive outcomes under a diverse set of situations.

3. Both R. Fisher and W. Ury, *Getting to Yes: Negotiating Agreements without Giving In* (Boston: Houghton-Mifflin, 1981) and A. C. Filley, "Some Normative Issues in Conflict Management," *California Management Review,* 21, no. 2 (1978), pp. 61–65, treat win-win problem solving as a principled, collaborative process.

substantive and relationship outcomes. In articulating such a model, we suggest that executives can approach negotiation strategically by assessing the negotiation context; considering unilateral negotiation strategies; transforming unilateral into interactive negotiation strategies; and monitoring tactics and reevaluating negotiation strategies.

ASSESSING THE NEGOTIATION CONTEXT

A crucial context for any negotiation is the manager's current and desired relationship with the other party. Unfortunately, in their rush to secure the best possible substantive outcome, managers often overlook the impact of the negotiation on their relationships. This oversight can hurt a manager's relationship with the other party, thus limiting his or her ability to obtain desired substantive outcomes now or in the future.

Each interaction with another negotiator constitutes an *episode* that draws from current and affects future relationships. Intertwined with pure concerns about relationships are concerns about substantive outcomes. Many times negotiators are motivated to establish or maintain positive relationships and willingly "share the pie" through mutually beneficial collaboration. Other negotiations involve substantive outcomes that can benefit one negotiator only at the expense of the other (a fixed pie). These cases often motivate negotiators to discount the relationship and claim as much of the pie as possible.

Most negotiations, however, are neither clearly win-win nor win-lose situations, but combinations of both (an indeterminate pie). Such mixed-motive situations, in which both collaboration and competition may occur, are particularly difficult for managers to handle strategically.[4] The relationship that exists prior to the negotiation, the relationship that unfolds during negotiations, and the desired relationship often will determine whether either negotiator will be motivated to share the pie, grab it, or give it away.

In any case, managers should keep existing and desired relationships in mind as they bid for substantive outcomes. For example, when negotiators are on the losing end of a win-lose negotiation, they should examine the implications of taking a short-term loss. During his third appointment, Peterson's willingness to make only minimal gains in service contracts for the short term may create a positive relationship that will lead to a lucrative, long-term contract with Tarco. The relative importance of possible substantive and relationship outcomes should help executives decide whether and how to negotiate. To guide their decision process, managers should begin by assessing their relative power and the level of conflict between them and the other party. Both are key determinants of their current relationship with the other party.

Exhibit 1 illustrates the negotiation context, showing those aspects of the situation and negotiation episode that shape relationship and substantive outcomes. Existing levels of power and conflict influence (1) the relationship between the executive

---

4. See S. Bacharach and E. J. Lawler, *Power and Politics in Organizations: The Social Psychology of Conflict, Coalitions, and Bargaining* (San Francisco, CA: Jossey-Bass, 1980) for a recent discussion of mixed-motive negotiation situations.

EXHIBIT 1   Assessing the Negotiation Context

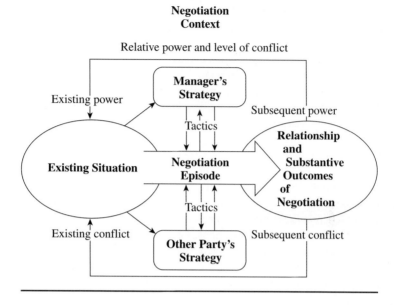

and the other party and (2) the negotiation strategies they choose. These strategies are implemented through appropriate tactics during a negotiation episode—a one-on-one encounter, a telephone call, or a meeting with multiple parties—and result in substantive and relationship outcomes.

The multiple arrows linking strategies, tactics, and the negotiation episode in Exhibit 1 show the monitoring process through which both the manager and the other party refine their strategies and tactics during an episode. A complex and lengthy negotiation, such as a union contract negotiation, may include many episodes; a simple negotiation may be completed within one episode. Each episode, nonetheless, influences future negotiations by changing the manager's and the other party's relative power, the level of conflict between them, and their relationship.

Relative Power

The relative power of the negotiators establishes an important aspect of their relationship: the extent of each party's dependence on the other. Researchers have found that individuals assess their power in a relationship and choose whether to compete, accommodate, collaborate, or withdraw when negotiating with others.[5] Managers can assess their power relative to the other party by comparing their respective abilities to

---

5. See L. Putnam and C. E. Wilson, "Communicative Strategies in Organizational Conflicts: Reliability and Validity of a Measurement Scale," in M. Burgoon, ed., *Communication Yearbook* 6 (Newbury Park, CA: Sage Publications, 1982), pp. 629–52. See also R. A. Cosier and T. L. Ruble, "Research on Conflict Handling Behavior: An Experimental Approach," *Academy of Management Journal* 24 (1981), pp. 816–31.

induce compliance through the control of human and material resources. To what extent do they each control key material resources? To what extent do they each control the deployment, arrangement, and advancement of people within the organization?[6]

These questions will help managers determine whether their relationship with the other party is based on independence, dependence, or interdependence. Additionally, these questions should help executives consider how *and* whether their relationship with the other party should be strengthened or weakened. Often managers will find themselves or their organizations in interdependent relationships that have both beneficial and detrimental aspects. These relationships are called mixed-motive situations in the negotiation literature because they provide incentives for both competitive and cooperative actions.

In his relationship with the Roadwork salesman, Peterson has considerable power. He is satisfied with his current vendor and has other vendors wanting to sell him the same product. The numerous choices available allow him to make demands on the salesman. Similarly, Peterson has more relative power than the mechanic. On the other hand, he has relatively little power with Tarco, since the contractor can choose from a number of equipment-service shops. Moreover, Tarco's representative did not make the initial contact and has not actively sought Dickerson's services.

Level of Conflict

The level of conflict underlying a potential negotiation establishes how the negotiators perceive the affective dimension of their relationship—that is, its degree of supportiveness or hostility. Managers can assess the relationship's level of conflict by identifying the differences between each party's interests. On what issues do both parties agree? On what issues do they disagree? How intense and how ingrained are these differences?[7]

Answers to these questions will reveal whether negotiations will easily resolve differences and whether the relationship is perceived as supportive or hostile. These questions, like the questions about relative power, should also help executives consider how *and* whether the relationship should be strengthened or weakened. Very few negotiations begin with a neutral relationship. Indeed, the affective state of the relationship may be a primary reason for negotiating with a powerful other party, especially if the relationship has deteriorated or been particularly supportive.

In Peterson's case, neutral to positive relationships exist with the Roadwork salesman and the Tarco representative. However, his relationships with the mechanic

---

6. Power as the ability to induce compliance is discussed in J. March and H. Simon, *Organizations* (New York: Wiley, 1958) and in P. Blau, *Exchange and Power in Social Life* (New York: Wiley, 1964). Two recent books discussing power from a material-resource perspective are H. Mintzberg's *Power in and Around Organizations* (Englewood Cliffs, NJ: Prentice Hall, 1983), and J. Pfeffer's *Power in Organizations* (Marshfield, MA: Pitman, 1981). A. Giddens, *The Constitution of Society: Outline of the Theory of Structuration* (Berkeley: University of California Press, 1984), discusses power from a critical-theory perspective within the field of sociology, emphasizing how power involves control over human resources.

7. For discussions of conflict intensity and durability, see I. R. Andrews and D. Tjosvold, "Conflict Management under Different Levels of Conflict Intensity," *Journal of Occupational Behaviour* 4 (1983), pp. 223–28, and C. T. Brown, P. Yelsma, and P. W. Keller, "Communication-Conflict Predisposition: Development of a Theory and an Instrument," *Human Relations* 34 (1981), pp. 1103–17.

and the union are potentially hostile. For example, management and union representatives have already had confrontations. Their conflict may escalate if the relationship is not managed and both sides are not willing to make concessions.[8]

Considering a Unilateral Negotiation Strategy

Before selecting a strategy for negotiation, a manager should consider his or her interests and the interests of the organization. These interests will shape the answers to two basic questions: (1) Is the substantive outcome very important to the manager? and (2) Is the relationship outcome very important to the manager?

Four *unilateral* strategies (see Exhibit 2) emerge from the answers: *trusting collaboration, firm competition, open subordination,* and *active avoidance.*[9] We call these unilateral strategies because in using them, managers consider only their own interests or the interests of their organization, ignoring for the time being the interests of the other party.

The unilateral strategies presented in Exhibit 2 are similar to the conflict management styles suggested by the combined works of Blake and Mouton, Hall, and Kilmann and Thomas.[10] However, while we agree that personalities and conflict-management preferences influence a person's ability to negotiate, our selection of terms reflects our focus on strategies instead of styles. For example, Johnston used the term "subordination" to refer to a strategy similar to the conflict-management style variously termed "accommodation" (Kilmann and Thomas), "smoothing" (Blake and Mouton), or "yield-lose" (Hall).[11] We, however, see using the openly subordinative strategy as more than simply "rolling over and playing dead" or "giving away the store." Rather, this strategy is designed to strengthen long-term relational ties, usually at the expense of short-term substantive outcomes. Our discussion below also goes beyond Johnston's conception, showing how a negotiator can focus the openly subordinative strategy according to his or her substantive goals.

---

8. See M. Deutsch, *The Resolution of Conflict* (New Haven: Yale University Press, 1973), for a discussion of how spiraling conflicts can be both inflamed and controlled.

9. For further discussions on these basic strategies, see C. B. Derr, "Managing Organizational Conflict: Collaboration, Bargaining, and Power Approaches," *California Management Review* 21 (1978), pp. 76–82; Filley, "Some Normative Issues in Conflict Management"; Fisher and Ury, *Getting to Yes*; R. Johnson, "Negotiation Strategies: Different Strokes for Different Folks," in R. Lewicki and J. Litterer, eds., *Negotiation: Readings, Exercises, and Cases* (Homewood, IL: Richard D. Irwin, 1985), pp. 156–64; D. A. Lax and J. K. Sebenius, *The Manager as Negotiator: Bargaining for Cooperation and Competitive Gain* (New York: The Free Press, 1986); and D. G. Pruitt, "Strategic Choice in Negotiation," *American Behavioral Scientist* 27 (1983), pp. 167–94.

10. For an overview of the contributions by these and other conflict-management researchers, see the special issue on "Communication and Conflict Styles in Organizations," L. L. Putnam, ed., *Management Communication Quarterly* 1, no. 3 (1988), pp. 291–45. See also R. Blake and J. Mouton's "The Fifth Achievement," *Journal of Applied Behavioral Science* 6 (1970), pp. 413–26; J. Hall's *Conflict Management Survey: A Survey of One's Characteristic Reaction to and Handling of Conflicts Between Himself and Others* (Conroe, TX: Teleometrics, 1986); and R. H. Kilmann and K. W. Thomas, "Interpersonal Conflict-Handling Behavior as Reflections of Jungian Personality Dimensions," *Psychology Reports* 37 (1975), pp. 971–80, and "Developing a Forced-Choice Measure of Conflict-Handling Behavior: The 'Mode' Instrument," *Educational & Psychological Measurement* 37 (1977), pp. 309–25.

11. See notes 9 and 10 above; especially see Johnston, "Negotiation Strategies."

EXHIBIT 2   Considering a Unilateral Negotiation Strategy

Is the substantive
outcome very important
to the manager?

	Yes	No
Yes Is the relationship outcome very important to the manager? **No**	*Strategy C1* **Trustingly collaborate** When both types of outcomes are very important *Situation 1*	*Strategy S1* **Openly subordinate** When the priority is on relationship outcomes *Situation 2*
	Strategy P1 **Firmly compete** When the priority is on substantive outcomes *Situation 3*	*Strategy A1* **Actively avoid negotiating** When neither type of outcome is very important *Situation 4*

Our view is consistent with research that suggests that individuals adopt different strategies in different relational contexts.[12] We anticipate that managers' success with these unilateral strategies depends on their ability to exhibit a variety of conflict styles. To highlight the role of relationship and substantive priorities, we describe these four unilateral strategies in their most extenuated, ideal form, and articulate their underlying assumptions. In many ways our descriptions are classic depictions of each type of strategy. Two of these strategies—competition and collaboration—are frequently discussed in the conflict and negotiation literature.

1. *Trusting Collaboration (C1).* In general, if both relationship and substantive outcomes are important to the organization, the manager should consider *trusting collaboration.* The hallmark of this strategy is openness on the part of both parties. By encouraging cooperation as positions are asserted, the executive should be able to

---

12. M. L. Knapp, L. L. Putnam, and L. J. Davis, "Measuring Interpersonal Conflict in Organizations: Where Do We Go From Here?" *Management Communication Quarterly* 1 (1988), pp. 414–29; Putnam and Wilson, "Communicative Strategies in Organizational Conflicts"; and J. Sullivan, R. B. Peterson, N. Kameda, and J. Shimada, "The Relationship between Conflict Resolution Approaches and Trust—A Cross Cultural Study," *Academy of Management Journal* 24 (1981), pp. 803–15.

achieve important relationship and substantive outcomes. The executive seeks a win-win outcome both to achieve substantive goals *and* maintain a positive relationship.

Trustingly collaborative strategies generally are easiest to use and most effective when the manager's organization and the other party are interdependent and mutually supportive. These circumstances normally create a trusting relationship in which negotiators reciprocally disclose their goals and needs. In this climate, an effective problem-solving process and a win-win settlement typically result.

2. *Open Subordination (S1).* If managers are more concerned with establishing a positive relationship with another party than obtaining substantive outcomes, they should openly subordinate. We use the term *subordination* instead of *accommodation* to differentiate this strategic choice from a conflict-management style. An openly subordinative strategy is a yield-win strategy that usually provides desired substantive outcomes to the other party but rarely to the manager. A subordinative strategy may be used regardless of whether the manager exercises more, less, or equal power relative to the other party. Our argument is that subordination can be an explicit strategic negotiation behavior—not simply a reflection of power. If the manager has little to lose by yielding to the substantive interests of the other party, open subordination can be a key way for him or her to dampen hostilities, increase support, and foster more interdependent relationships.

3. *Firm Competition (P1).* If substantive interests are important but the relationship is not, the manager should consider *firmly competing.* This situation often occurs when managers have little trust for the other party or the relationship is not good to begin with. In such situations, they may want to exert their power to gain substantive outcomes. To enact this competitive strategy, they may also become highly aggressive, bluffing, threatening the other party, or otherwise misrepresenting their intentions. Such tactics hide the manager's actual goals and needs, preventing the other party from using that knowledge to negotiate its own substantive outcomes. Not surprisingly, the credibility of the executive's aggressive tactics and, thus, the success of the firmly competitive strategy often rests on the organization's power vis-à-vis the other party. When following a firmly competitive strategy, the manager seeks a win-lose substantive outcome and is willing to accept a neutral or even a bad relationship.

4. *Active Avoidance (A1).* Managers should consider *actively avoiding negotiation* if neither the relationship nor the substantive outcomes are important to them or the organization. Simply *refusing* to negotiate is the most direct and active form of avoidance. Executives can simply tell the other party they are not interested in or willing to negotiate. Such an action, however, will usually have a negative impact on the organization's relationship with the other party. Moreover, managers must determine which issues are a waste of time to negotiate. We treat avoidance, like subordination, as an explicit, strategic behavior rather than as an option taken by default when the manager is uncertain about what to do.

However, we recognize that these unilateral strategies are most successful only in a limited set of situations. In the next section we include various *interactive* modifications that make these classic, unilateral strategies applicable to a wider set of negotiation situations.

INTERACTIVE NEGOTIATION STRATEGIES

Before using the unilateral strategies suggested by Exhibit 2, the executive should examine the negotiation from each party's perspective. The choice of a negotiation strategy should be based not only on the interests of the executive or organization, but also on the interests of the other party. The manager should anticipate the other party's substantive and relationship priorities, assessing how the negotiation is likely to progress when the parties interact. This step is crucial because the unilateral strategies described above could lead to grave problems if the other party's priorities differ. For example, when using either trusting collaboration or open subordination, the manager is vulnerable to exploitation if the other party is concerned only about substantive outcomes. When anticipating the other party's substantive and relationship priorities, executives should consider the kinds of actions the other party might take. Are those actions likely to be supportive or hostile? Will they represent short-term reactions or long-term approaches to the substantive issues under negotiation? Are those actions likely to change the party's degree of dependence on, or interdependence with, the organization? The answers will depend on (1) the history of the executive's relations with the other party and (2) the influence of key individuals and groups on the manager and the other party.

In short, executives should take into account both their own and the other party's substantive and relationship priorities in choosing a negotiating strategy. Exhibit 3 is a decision tree designed to help managers decide which strategy to use. The left side represents, in a different form, the analysis in Exhibit 2; thus, Exhibit 3 also shows how the manager's substantive and relationship priorities lead to *unilateral strategies* based solely on the manager's position. The right side illustrates how these unilateral strategies may be continued, modified, or replaced after the manager considers the other party's potential or apparent priorities.[13]

Managers should examine the appropriateness of a unilateral negotiation strategy by accounting for the other party's priorities before they use it. Sometimes such scrutiny will simply justify its use. For example, when both substantive and relationship outcomes are important to an executive, the appropriate unilateral strategy is trusting collaboration. If the manager anticipates that the other party also values both substantive and relationship outcomes (see Exhibit 3, Situation 1), he or she would continue to favor this strategy. At other times, scrutiny of the other party's priorities may suggest some modifications. We discuss next each of the interactive variations of the classic, unilateral strategies.

1. *Principled Collaboration (C2).* The C1 collaborative strategy assumes that the other party will reciprocate whenever the executive discloses information. However, if the manager negotiates openly and the other party is not open or is competitive, the manager could be victimized. Under such circumstances, the manager should use the

---

13. We call these strategies *interactive* because they take into account the interactive effect of the manager's and the other party's anticipated or actual priorities concerning substantive and relationship outcomes. Interactive strategies based on anticipating the other party's priorities, as we later discuss in some length, may be changed to reflect more closely the actual priorities of the other party, as revealed through the interaction during a negotiation episode.

EXHIBIT 3 Selecting an Interactive Strategy

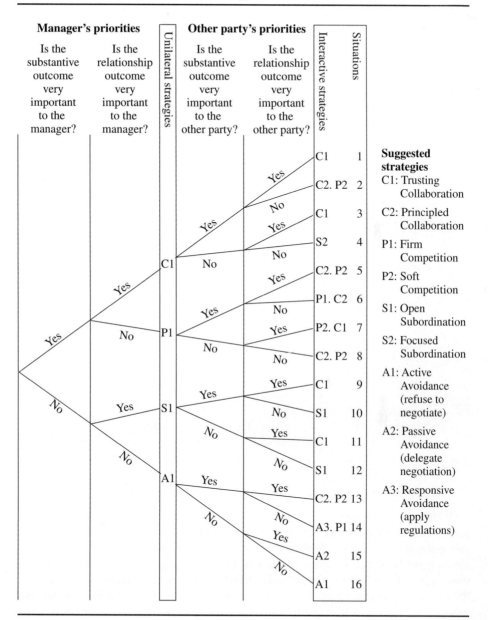

modified collaborative strategy of principled collaboration.[14] Rather than relying on only trust and reciprocity, the manager persuades the other party to conduct negotiations based on a set of mutually agreed upon principles that will benefit each negotiator.

2. *Focused Subordination (S2).* The openly subordinative strategy (S1) assumes that the substantive outcome is of little importance to the organization. Sometimes, however, an organization has both substantive and relationship interests, but the other party has little stake in either interest. By discovering and then acquiescing to those key needs that are of interest only to the other party, the manager can still gain some substantive outcomes for the organization while assuring a relatively positive relationship outcome. Here, managers both create substantive outcomes for the other party and achieve substantive outcomes for themselves or their organization.

3. *Soft Competition (P2).* Under some circumstances the directness of the firmly competitive strategy (P1) may need to be softened. For example, even though the manager may place little importance on the relationship outcome, this relationship may be very important to the other party. If the other party is powerful and potentially threatening, the manager would be wise to use a competitive strategy that maintains the relationship. Here the executive would avoid highly aggressive and other "dirty" tactics.

4. *Passive Avoidance (A2).* If the manager does not consider either the relationship or the substantive outcome important but the other party views the negotiation as important for a relationship outcome, the manager probably should *delegate* the negotiation. By passively avoiding the negotiation, the manager allows someone else within the organization to explore possible outcomes for the organization and keep the relationship from becoming hostile. Delegating ensures that possible opportunities are not ignored while freeing the executive from what appears to be a low-priority negotiation.

5. *Responsive Avoidance (A3).* By contrast, if the manager considers neither the relationship nor the substantive outcome important and the other party considers the substantive outcome important and the relationship unimportant, the manager should *regulate* the issue. Direct interaction with the other party is not necessary; the manager can be responsive but still avoid negotiating by either applying standard operating procedures or developing new policies that address the other party's concern.

Transforming Unilateral Strategies

The model of strategic choice in Exhibit 3 connects unilateral and interactive negotiation strategies. In many instances the interactive strategies are modifications of the unilateral strategies. We base the decision to modify or replace a unilateral strategy almost exclusively on the manager's and other party's differing outcome priorities. Three outcome conditions and three sets of assumptions influence the choice of interactive strategies.

1. *Outcome Condition 1: The manager may value the relationship, but the other party may not.* For example, a manager who assumes that trust and cooperation will result in a fair outcome may be taken advantage of by another party who is concerned with only substantive outcomes.[15] Hence, we suggest either principled collabo-

---

14. See Fisher and Ury, *Getting to Yes.*

15. See, for example, L. L. Cummings, D. L. Harnett, and O. J. Stevens, "Risk, Fate, Conciliation and Trust: An International Study of Attitudinal Differences among Executives," *Academy of Management Journal* 14 (1971), pp. 285–304.

ration or soft competition for such cases to ensure that the other party does not take advantage of the manager (see Exhibit 3, Situation 2). On the other hand, the manager may simply want to create a long-term business relationship with someone who currently is interested in neither substantive nor relationship outcomes. In these cases the manager should choose to subordinate in a focused fashion—rather than to trustingly collaborate—to establish a relationship with the other party (see Exhibit 3, Situation 4).

2. *Outcome Condition 2: The manager may not value the relationship, but the other party may.* Given only their own substantive priorities, managers would firmly compete or actively avoid negotiation under these circumstances. However, if the other party is interested in the relationship, the manager may not have to compete firmly to obtain desired substantive outcomes. The manager may collaborate or softly compete and still gain substantive goals without alienating the other party (see Exhibit 3, Situations 5–8). Such strategies may also foster a long-term relationship with substantive dividends for the manager.

Similarly, in situations where neither substantive nor relationship outcomes are important to the manager but the relationship is important to the other party, the manager may choose an interactive strategy other than avoidance. The other party is in a position to choose a subordinative strategy and may offer substantive incentives to the manager. If the manager chooses principled collaboration or soft competition, he or she may gain some positive substantive outcomes (see Exhibit 3, Situation 13).

3. *Outcome Condition 3: Both parties may value the relationship, but the manager may not value substantive outcomes.* In these cases, whether or not the other party is interested in substantive outcomes, the manager may choose a trustingly collaborative strategy to maintain positive ties with the other party (see Exhibit 3, Situations 9 and 11).

4. *Transformation Assumptions.* Underlying these three outcome conditions are three sets of assumptions. First, we assume that most relationships will involve some mixture of dependence and interdependence as well as some degree of supportiveness and hostility. Second, we assume that most negotiators will view the relationship outcome as important under four separate conditions—high interdependence, high dependence, high supportiveness, or high hostility—or possible combinations of those conditions. Third, from a manager's perspective, each of the basic strategies has a different effect with regard to power and conflict: (1) collaborative strategies strengthen the interdependence of the manager and the other party while also enhancing feelings of supportiveness, (2) subordinative strategies increase the other party's dependence on the manager while also deemphasizing feelings of hostility, and (3) competitive strategies decrease the manager's dependence on the other party but may also escalate feelings of hostility.

Thus many of the interactive negotiation strategies in Exhibit 3 seek to enhance interdependent relationships or favorably shift the balance of dependence within a relationship. These same strategies also attempt to dampen feelings of hostility or heighten feelings of supportiveness.

Illustrations of Negotiation-Strategy Transformations

To demonstrate more concretely how Exhibit 3 works, we will examine how Dickerson's Peterson might act if he were to follow the decision tree to choose his negotiation strategies.

1. From Avoidance to Collaboration or Competition.   In planning to meet with the steering clutch salesman, Peterson first considers whether the substantive outcome is very important to Dickerson Machinery. Because the company already has a satisfactory source for clutch disks, the substantive outcome is not very important. Second, Peterson considers the importance of the relationship outcome. Given that Dickerson Machinery currently has no ties with Roadworks and Peterson foresees no need to establish a long-term relationship, the relationship outcome is not very important either. Based on Peterson's priorities only, unilateral avoidance strategy (A1) seems appropriate.

However, Peterson now considers the salesman's priorities. First, is the substantive outcome important to the salesman? Obviously, it is—Roadworks is a struggling, new company and needs new clients. Second, is the relationship outcome important to Roadworks? Because the salesman works on a commission with residuals, he probably desires a long-term sales contract, so the relationship outcome is important. The salesman's priorities suggest that he would probably collaborate trustingly (C1).

After answering the questions forming the decision tree in Exhibit 3 (see Situation 13), Peterson has two options for an interactive strategy. Since he is in a position of power, he does not need to make concessions. Moreover, the salesman may have products worthy of consideration. Thus, Peterson can engage in principled collaboration (C2) or softly compete (P2). In other words, he can collaborate based on principles, taking a strong stand on what he expects in a sales contract; or he can softly compete by making product demands that do not offend the salesman.

2. From Collaboration to Subordination.   For the situation with the contractor, the relationship outcome is very important to Dickerson Machinery but the immediate, substantive outcome is not. Peterson realizes that Dickerson needs Tarco's business for long-term stability but does not need to make a profit in the short term. Therefore, his unilateral strategy would be to subordinate openly (S1). He decides to change his strategy from the trustingly collaborative (C1) approach he has used in past dealings with Tarco.

As Peterson considers the contractor's priorities, he anticipates that the substantive outcome is important to Tarco but the relationship outcome is not. Tarco's representative has made clear the need for reliable service at the lowest possible price; conversely, Tarco has not responded to Peterson's bids to provide service for more than two years. Peterson recognizes, based on Exhibit 2, that Tarco can compete firmly (P1). After assessing both parties' priorities using the decision tree (see Exhibit 3, Situation 10), he decides he should continue with an interactive strategy of open subordination (S1). Such a strategy is more likely to induce Tarco's representative to offer a contract than the trustingly collaborative strategy he has used previously. For example, he is prepared to subordinate by offering a "winter special" to reduce labor costs by 10 percent, cutting competitive parts costs by 15 percent, and providing a new paint job at 50 percent the normal costs or providing a six-month deferment on payment, all in addition to paying for the trip to the plant.

3. From Competition to Collaboration.   Peterson's analysis of the negotiation with the labor union includes an assessment of the recent history of and level of conflict between the union and the company. Previous episodes in this contract negoti-ation have led both the union and Dickerson Machinery to change their priorities. Dur-ing the first few episodes, both parties focused on only substantive outcomes and ignored relationship outcomes, using firmly competitive strategies. Also, during these earlier episodes, both sides' demands hardened to the point where the union threatened to strike and management threatened to give no increases in wages or benefits.

Now, however, Peterson believes that both substantive and relationship outcomes are important to Dickerson. The company wants to find a way to increase productivity without giving much of an increase in pay and benefits. It also does not want to lose good mechanics or stimulate a strike. Dickerson's unilateral strategy under these new conditions should be trustingly collaborative (C1).

From analyzing the union's position, Peterson realizes that both the substantive and relationship outcomes should be important to the union. His informal discussions with union representatives have assured him that both sides are now concerned about maintaining the relationship. Nonetheless, the union clearly wants an increase in pay and benefits even though it also does not want a strike. In short, the union now is likely to trustingly collaborate but could easily shift its priorities and choose to firmly compete.

As he enters the negotiation strategy session this afternoon, Peterson plans to rec-ommend to the management negotiation team the use of a principled collaborative (C2) strategy (see Exhibit 3, Situation 2). Because of the current instability in the rela-tionship, he does not want to provide the union with any opportunity to exploit a per-ceived weakness that a more trustingly collaborative strategy might create.

Monitoring and Reevaluating Strategies

After implementing their interactive strategy, managers should monitor the other party's tactics. How the other party acts will signal its strategy. Based on the other par-ty's tactics, executives can (1) determine if their assumptions and expectations about the other party's strategy are accurate and (2) modify, if needed, their strategies during this and subsequent negotiation episodes. Exhibit 1 provides an overview of this process. The arrows linking strategies to tactics and the negotiation episode represent how tactics (1) are used to implement a strategy (first arrow), (2) provide information to each party (second, reversed arrow), and (3) may affect the choice of alternative strategies during a negotiation episode (third arrow).

Monitoring Tactics

More specifically, we view tactics in two ways: (1) as clusters of specific actions associated with the implementation of one strategy or another, and (2) as actions that derive their strategic impact from the particular phase of the negotiation in which they are used. In Exhibit 4, we combine these two perspectives to provide executives with descriptions of competitive, collaborative, and subordinative tactics across vari-ous phases of negotiation. We suggest that most negotiations go through four phases: (1) the search for an arena and agenda formulation, (2) the stating of demands and offers, (3) a narrowing of differences, and (4) final bargaining.[16] Not every negotiation will involve all of these phases. Rather, these phases characterize typical negotiations in mixed-motive situations. Hence, a specific phase may be skipped or never attained.[17]

For example, the search for an arena in which to carry out discussions may be unnecessary for some ongoing negotiations; however, most negotiations will initially involve some Phase 1 interaction about the items to be discussed. During the second phase, both the managers and the other party express their preferences and establish their commitments to specific issues and outcomes. The third phase may be skipped, although it usually occurs if the manager and the other party are far apart in their preferences and commitments. Both sides may add or delete bargaining items or shift preferences to avoid an impasse. The fourth phase completes the negotiation: The manager and the other party reduce their alternatives, making joint decisions about each item until a final agreement is reached.

Exhibit 4 should help managers recognize (1) how using certain tactics during various phases of a negotiation is essential to implementing their strategy and (2) how the tactics of the other party reflect a particular strategic intent. An unanticipated strategy implemented by the other party may indicate that the executive inaccurately assessed the negotiation context or under- or overestimated the strength of the other party's priorities. Hence, once the manager recognizes the other party's actual strategy, he or she should reassess the negotiation, repeating the process discussed in previous sections to check the appropriateness of his or her strategies.

Sometimes, however, the other party's use of an unanticipated strategy does not mean the executive's assessment of the negotiation context was inaccurate. In Exhibit 3, some combinations of the manager's and other party's priorities result in the listing of two interactive strategies. Managers should normally use the first (left-hand) strategies in these listings. The secondary (right-hand) strategies are suggested as countermoves the executive should use if the other party uses a strategy different from the one expected, but the executive remains convinced that his or her diagnosis is accurate.

---

16. Different researchers offer varying descriptions of negotiation phases. See L. Putnam, "Bargaining as Organizational Communication," in R. D. McPhee and P. K. Tompkins, eds., *Organizational Communication: Traditional Themes and New Directions* (Beverly Hills, CA: Sage, 1985), for a summary of this research. Ann Douglas proposed the first three-step model in "The Peaceful Settlement of Industrial and Intergroup Disputes," *Journal of Conflict Resolution* 1 (1957), pp. 69–81. However, this model and subsequent three-stage models do not consider the search for the arena as a component phase of a negotiation. P. Gulliver, *Disputes and Negotiations: A Cross-Cultural Perspective* (New York: Academic Press, 1979), proposes an eight-stage model of negotiation, remedying that oversight. Our proposed four-phase model condenses and draws extensively from Gulliver's work.

17. Additionally, we view the phases of negotiation as conceptually separate from our notion of negotiation episodes (see Exhibit 1). All four phases may take place during one episode, particularly if the negotiation involves a single issue of low concern to one or another negotiator. On the other hand, during very complex negotiations stretching over a period of months, numerous episodes may constitute each phase.

EXHIBIT 4 Using Tactics across Negotiation Phases

Negotiation Phases	Negotiation Tactics		
	Competitive	*Collaborative*	*Subordinative*
The search for an arena and agenda formulation	• Seek to conduct negotiations on manager's home ground • Demand discussion of manager's agenda items; curtail discussions of other party's items • Ignore or discount the other party's demands and requests	• Seek to conduct negotiations on neutral ground • Elicit the other party's agenda items and assert manager's items; incorporate both • Consider other party's demands and requests	• Seek to conduct negotiations on the other party's ground • Elicit the other party's agenda items and subvert manager's items • Concede to the other party's demands and requests
The stating of demands and offers	• Insist other party make initial offers or demands on all items • Respond with very low offers or very high demands • Commit to each item; exaggerate manager's position and discredit other party's	• Alternate initial offers and demands on items with other party • Respond with moderate offers or moderate demands • Indicate reasons for manager's commitment to item outcomes; probe the other party's reasons	• Make initial offers or demands on all other party-relevant items • Make high offers or low demands • Accept the other party's commitments to items; explain manager's commitments
A narrowing of differences	• Demand that other party make concession; back up demand with threats • Delete, add, or yield only on low manager-interest items • Magnify degree of manager's concessions; downplay other party's	• Seek equitable exchange of concessions with the other party • Delete, add, or yield items if mutual interests converge • Honestly assess manager's and other party's concessions	• Concede to the other party's demands • Delete, add, or yield to any other party-relevant item • Acknowledge the other party's concessions; downplay manager's concessions
Final bargaining	• Seek large concessions from the other party • Concede only minimally on high manager-interest items • Use concessions on low manager-interest items as bargaining chips	• Seek equitable exchange of concessions from the other party • Seek mutually beneficial outcomes when conceding or accepting concessions on items	• Yield to the other party's relevant preferences by accepting low offers and making low demands

Reevaluating Negotiation Strategies

Take, for example, Peterson's appointment with the mechanic who had swapped a battery from a company truck with his own used battery. Going into the negotiation Peterson decides that his unilateral strategy should be trusting collaboration: The mechanic is highly skilled and would be hard to replace, yet the infraction is a serious matter. He also anticipates that the employee will be interested primarily in retaining a good relationship with Dickerson's management. Hence, Peterson decides to stick with trusting collaboration as his interactive strategy (see Exhibit 3, Situation 3).

However, during the first five minutes of the meeting, Peterson's efforts to discuss returning the battery to the company and removing the infraction from the mechanic's personnel record are repeatedly rebuffed by the employee. Instead, the mechanic threatens to retire early from Dickerson and collect the benefits due him unless Peterson transfers him. Peterson recognizes that the mechanic is employing competitive tactics to set the agenda, which reflects an interest in substantive outcomes but little concern for relationship outcomes.

As the negotiation enters the next phase, Peterson considers the mechanic's apparent priorities and reevaluates his own priorities. Now neither the substantive nor the relationship outcomes are very important to him. He knows that Dickerson has no opening for the mechanic at any other shop; moreover, if the employee wants to leave, the relationship is of little value. Based on this reassessment (see Exhibit 3, Situation 14), Peterson sees that he has two interactive strategic options: He can regulate the matter (A3) by pressing criminal charges or compete firmly (P1) with the employee.

Rather than withdraw from the interaction, Peterson decides to compete firmly and tells the mechanic that unless the battery is returned, he will do everything he can legally do to prevent the mechanic from receiving optimal severance benefits. If the employee refuses to return the battery, Peterson can still request Dickerson's legal department to file criminal charges against him (A3) as a way to publicize and enforce a legitimate regulatory approach designed to help the company avoid this kind of negotiation.

DISCUSSION

Most of the negotiation literature focuses on substantive outcomes without systematically considering the ways negotiations affect relationships. The approach we have taken underscores how negotiation strategies should address both parties' substantive and relationship priorities. Further, we encourage executives proactively to view negotiation as an indeterminate, reiterative, and often confusing process. It requires them to anticipate and monitor the other party's actions. The other party's tactics will inform managers as to whether their assumptions about the other party's priorities and strategy are correct. Based on this assessment, managers can modify their negotiation strategies as needed during current or future episodes.

Managers should need, however, a few caveats about our advice:

1. Underlying the strategic choice model in Exhibit 3 is the assumption that most negotiations are of the mixed-motive sort; that is, the manager and other party usually

negotiate over several substantive items. Some items have potential outcomes that can benefit both negotiators; others have potential outcomes that can benefit only one negotiator. Under these conditions, collaborative, competitive, and subordinative strategies may all come into play as the negotiators seek either win-win, win-lose, or yield-win substantive outcomes. Our emphasis in the model is on win-win substantive outcomes brought about through collaborative strategies (C1 and C2).

2. We assume that most relationships will involve some mixture of dependence and interdependence. Furthermore, we posit that most negotiators will view the relationship outcome as important when it is characterized by either high interdependence or high dependence. Collaborative strategies will strengthen the interdependence of the organization and the other party, subordinative strategies will increase the other party's dependence on the organization, and competitive strategies will decrease the organization's dependence on the other party. Our advice about negotiation strategies is directed particularly toward managers who want to enhance relationships of interdependence or favorably shift the balance of dependence within a relationship.

3. We also recognize that the history and level of conflict between an organization and another party strongly influence each negotiator's attitude toward the existing relationship. Feelings of hostility, we assume, will be escalated by a competitive strategy; in contrast, feelings of hostility will be deemphasized by a subordinative strategy. Following this same logic, feelings of supportiveness will be enhanced by a collaborative strategy. Several of the strategies suggested in Figure 3—trusting collaboration, soft competition, open subordination, and passive and responsive avoidance—attempt to dampen hostilities and increase supportiveness between the manager and the other party.

4. Our advice to executives is simultaneously well supported and speculative. On one hand, the classic (unilateral) strategies suggested in Exhibit 3 are fairly well supported within the negotiation literature; the link between these strategies and both relationship and substantive outcomes is the special focus of our approach. On the other hand, the effectiveness of the interactive strategies suggested in Exhibit 3 remains open to continuing empirical investigations. We have developed this interactive model of strategic choice by linking our concerns about relationship outcomes with what is currently known about the basic strategies of negotiations.

Although the three sets of assumptions we make about relationships are usually warranted in most organization-related negotiations, executives should carefully consider whether their situations fit with these constraints before using our strategic choice model (Exhibit 3). However, regardless of the situation, we believe that managers will generally be more effective negotiators when they carefully assess both (1) the relationship and the substantive aspects of any potential negotiation and (2) what is important to the other party and what is important to them.

Prenegotiation Planning

Successful professional negotiators agree on one thing: the keys to success in negotiation are preparation and planning. Persuasive presentation, skillful communication, nimble shifting of position, and a host of other skills used during actual negotiations are important, but they cannot overcome the disadvantage created by poor planning, nor can they help negotiators who have locked themselves into untenable positions before or during the early stages of negotiation. Further, while using interpersonal skills can help negotiators reap the most from a strategy, a well-laid plan has its own strength, and even modest skills can see it through to an acceptable conclusion. Sections Three and Four discuss two major types of negotiation: distributive and integrative (win-lose and win-win). This section addresses the operational and strategic process of planning and preparing for negotiations of either sort.

There are at least two levels or stages of preparation for negotiation. One involves getting ready for a specific negotiation, when we want to learn more about the other party, the situation we face, and so on. The other involves making ourselves ready to negotiate at any time. Professional runners prepare for the next race, but they have also been preparing themselves all year, in fact for many years, to run races. Given that we are all going to face negotiation situations regularly, we need to know how to prepare properly.

Conflict is a part of life, welcomed by some, regretted by others, but present nonetheless. Nowhere is this more so than in negotiation. Some bargaining is obviously competitive, as when two parties have different and mutually exclusive objectives (such as haggling over the price of something). Even in integrative negotiating, when the parties are working toward joint or convergent goals, there may still be substantial conflict about how much each will contribute or how much each will benefit. Hence conflict, while varying in intensity, is inherent in any negotiation situation and needs to be planned and prepared for.

Using the words *preparation* and *planning* may imply that negotiation is inherently systematic, rational, and predictable. Preparation and planning do pay off, but not in such a deterministic fashion. There is no inherently proper way of determining the best settlement in negotiation; settlements are always arbitrary. In addition, negotiations are rarely completely cool, harmonious, generous, or mutually supportive. There is frequently a troublesome trade-off between individual and joint interests. These conditions may be accentuated and multiplied when one or perhaps both parties perceive the relationship as competitive, as an effort to win at the other party's expense. Doing this, of course, engenders defensiveness, distrust, and counter-offensiveness, usually resulting in a less satisfactory outcome for both parties.

One key message has been that these conditions can be reduced and subordinated by structuring the relationship as a collaborative one in which parties work together on joint or mutually supportive goals, work to trust each other, and find ways to cooperate.

It is overly simplistic to suggest that in integrative negotiating there is cooperation while in distributive bargaining cooperation does not exist. Even in distributive bargaining, there must always be a certain minimal level of cooperation. Suppose that you are selling a used car and drive a hard bargain, getting as much as the buyer can possibly pay while withholding special features such as an extra set of stereo speakers, snow tires, and so on. You may have "won" in the sense of getting as much as possible from the situation; and the other party may have "lost" as much as possible because he or she did not get any concessions from you in what was a heated, highly competitive negotiation. Yet you will have nothing if the other party does not cooperate and go through with the deal. In most states, for a limited amount of time after a deal has been reached, people can walk away from an agreement to purchase a house, a car, or most major appliances. In less legal types of arrangements, such as an adjustment made between two managers about the transfer of materials between their departments, both parties have to continue to perceive an advantage for the agreement to work. These aspects of negotiation may be difficult to understand fully at first. The readings in this section should help to that end.

Robert Kuhn's article "How to Plan the Strategies" (from his 1988 book *Dealmaker*) differentiates between incremental and strategic thinking. While both are appropriate and necessary, the former involves "satisficing," or reacting to contingencies, and the latter involves a more proactive, creative approach to the future. Specifically, strategic thinking must deal with surprise, with the unforeseen and the unanticipated. Kuhn states that a good strategy defines one's approach, linking goals to tactics while searching for competitive advantages and distinct competencies. He cautions, though, against putting too much faith in strategy as an inviolable process, stating that the "mirage of control is the problem of strategy." He also warns against focusing on gimmicks or tricky tactics in lieu of solid strategizing.

Continuing with the preparation theme, Bill Scott's "Preparing for Negotiations" (from his 1981 book *The Skills of Negotiating*) builds on preparation, subject to three assumptions: that the negotiation planners have done their homework regarding the other side, that they know "the rules governing the negotiating territory," and that the negotiation will be a simple one (i.e., that it will be accomplished in just a few meetings). Scott suggests that the conduct of negotiation preliminaries attend to setting the purpose, plan, pace, and place of the negotiation, and to making it a positive experience for the other party.

Finally, Deborah Tannen's "Framing and Reframing" (from her book *That's Not What I Meant!*) emphasizes the important ways in which we use conversation to "frame" or add meaning to what we say or do. As Tannen states, "Framing is a way of showing how we mean what we say or do and figuring out how others mean what they say or do." Research has shown that framing dynamics are present in our perceptions, cognitive dynamics, and use of language in conflict situations. How we talk about a problem or issue, and the language we tend to use, can strongly shape how we perceive and think about that issue or problem. In this context, Tannen emphasizes the indirect, informal ways that conversation frames meaning through our choice of words, tone of voice, and nonverbal signals, as well as the context in which the communication occurs. Both in this specific context and in the broader ways that a frame can shape the way we see, think about, and talk about a negotiation problem, understanding framing dynamics is critical to understanding how to prepare and present a negotiation issue to the other party.

How to Plan the Strategies

Robert Kuhn

STRATEGY IS MORE THINKING THAN DOING

Strategy is an ancient term derived from warfare. It depicts the fighting plans of battlefield commanders. One can envision generals hunched over detailed relief maps, moving armies as if pawns. One can visualize wars being won and lost by subtle shifts of thrust, parry, and feint.

Strategy in deal making is a directed plan. It defines the approach. It links overall goals with operational tactics. It has specific, clear-cut objectives and describes the actions and reactions of decision makers to the shifts and changes of conditions. Strategy for a dealmaker is like a hammer for a carpenter or a bat for a baseball player. It is the tool that gets the job done. The better your strategy, the better your deals.

In this sense, strategy is the search for *competitive advantage,* for areas of relative strength that can coax, coddle, or coerce favorable outcomes. Competitive advantage seeks to capitalize on your *distinctive competencies,* those aspects of the deal-making process where your side excels or can excel compared with the other side.

Assessing mutual strengths and weaknesses is the key to devising the best deal-making strategy. Compare your strengths and weaknesses to those of your opponent in the context of the deal issues. The result of this assessment is a series of alternative strategies. These various options for deal-making direction are then evaluated for probable outcomes, and the best are chosen to put into action.

Creativity promotes strategy formulation.

Consistency directs strategy evaluation.

Structure controls strategy implementation.

There is, however, a dark side to strategy. Its presence can fool dealmakers into thinking they've got a good grip on a situation when they haven't got a handle on anything. The more the strategic sophistication, at times the stronger the strategic illusion. The mirage of control is the problem of strategy.

It has been said that corporate strategy is like a ritual rain dance. It has no effect on the weather that follows, of course, but it makes those who do it feel they are in complete charge. Often when we use strategic planning, we are laboring to improve the dancing, not the weather.

From Robert Kuhn, *Dealmaker* (New York: John Wiley & Sons, Inc., 1988), pp. 64–72. Reprinted by permission of John Wiley & Sons, Inc.

WAYS OF THINKING: INCREMENTAL VERSUS STRATEGIC

Strategic planning is not sorcery; strategic hocus-pocus will not conjure up instant deal closing. Strategic planning is just a way of thinking about a transaction. It can be best understood in contrast to its opposite, incremental planning. The best dealmakers function well in both modes. While the strategic process leads to original thinking in devising alternative options, the incremental mode can be fertile soil for the spontaneous sprouting of "aha" insights.

Incremental Thinking

Operating in the incremental mode, the dealmaker begins *reactively* by recognizing an immediate problem, some unexpected shock, whether opportunity or threat. The dealmaker then searches selectively through a restricted variety of potential solutions, making marginal movements from the status quo, evaluating each tiny step in order. Deviations from current policy are considered sequentially and widened progressively until the first satisfactory solution is found. Such an agreeable answer is accepted immediately and all other alternatives, even if potentially better, are ignored.

Herbert Simon's idea of *bounded rationality* controls here.[1] Dealmakers can't ever know *everything;* so if they want to do *anything,* they must replace *optimizing,* finding the best answer, with *satisficing,* finding an acceptable answer. According to bounded rationality, problems in the real world need only be solved satisfactorily, not perfectly.

Strategic Thinking

Operating in the strategic mode, dealmakers begin *proactively* by defining general goals and setting specific objectives. They scan the deal-making environment seeking opportunities and threats and analyze both sides for relative strengths and weaknesses. The key here is deal-making strengths and weaknesses in the light of the opportunities and threats in a search for competitive advantages.

What emerges from this dynamic, creative process is a set of alternatives. Each is evaluated for probable consequences. Strategic choice is made with the guideline of internal consistency: Which set of strategies best matches goals and strengths? Implementation (including step and time sequencing), feedback, and review complete the process.

It is a common misconception to judge incremental decision making bad, and strategic decision making good. Each is good, but in its own arena. One would not resolve an ugly personality clash in the strategic mode, just as one would not formulate a comprehensive plan in the incremental mode. Learn when to stay incremental and when to jump strategic.

STRATEGY AND SURPRISE

Strategic thinking, to be truly strategic, must deal with surprise. The unanticipated must be anticipated; the unforeseen, seen. If everything is assumed to be known,

---

1. Herbert Simon, *Administrative Behavior* (New York: Free Press, 1976).

if your deal-making future is expected to emulate your deal-making past, then the process is simple extension (trending), and strategy is playing no part. Strategic deal making must be concerned with radical change, discontinuity, sharp breaks with the past, even violent twists from current paths. Dealmakers must plan for the unplanned.

SCOPE OF STRATEGY

Strategic thinking works for individuals as well as for companies. People can apply the thought processes for making personal decisions and planning personal deal making. For example, you can use the strategic method to resolve whether to push for a still higher salary at a prospective job or to negotiate a better position at your current job.

An honest assessment of your strengths and weaknesses in light of the employment opportunities and threats (e.g., the prospective vs. current job) can be a critical part of the process. Careful consideration of diverse alternatives in light of overall lifetime goals is certainly worth the effort. (One would not, of course, need strategic thinking to make the vast majority of daily deals. Lifetime goals are irrelevant for buying a car or settling time-to-bed arguments with kids.)

WHEN PLANNING STRATEGY

What to do first when planning your strategy? When negotiating or structuring a deal, do *not* focus on conjuring up tricky tactics. Gimmicks do not achieve. Plots sicken as they thicken.

Devising the plan must come first. Where do you want to go, and how will each step of the process help get you there? See ends from beginnings. Have a clear vision of the proposed path—even though that path will twist and turn often. Keep ultimate results in current focus. After each step of the deal, try to reconstruct your objectives. Are you proceeding on target? Or have you drifted? If you've strayed off course, can you get back on? Or should you now consider altering your objectives to conform to the new reality? Negotiating deals is a continuous series of course corrections and target shifts.

STRATEGIC ATTITUDES

There are three general kinds of strategic attitudes in deal making. They are (1) simple and direct, (2) press and push, and (3) cool and aloof.

Simple and Direct

Come right to the point. Say what you mean. The straightforward approach may be startlingly effective, disarming the other side and driving to quick resolution. Go simple and direct when

You've worked with the other side before.

The deal is bogging down.

Immediate closure is a goal.

Press and Push

Here's where the shoving starts. Sensitive points are squeezed. To be effective, the pressing and pushing should be subtle. If the other side thinks that you are twisting arms they will become resentful. Pressure is not some evil, alien torture. It is often the mechanism to get a deal closed.[2] Press and push when

Your side is stronger.

The other side needs a quick close.

You want to assess limits.

Cool and Aloof

This approach uses reverse psychology. Play hard to get. Let the other side sell themselves. It can be marvelously effective. If you give points too quickly, if you're too compromise minded, the other side may worry that they've undershot their potential. (I've been there, kicking myself when the positive response came a mite too easily.) Avoid tempting your opponents: awakening latent greed is not smart. The key here is making the other side work when exacting the concession. Be cool and aloof when

The other side is stronger.

Your side is under time pressure.

You have other alternative deals.

TACTICS TO CONSIDER

Attitudes and approaches to negotiating vary. In some situations, the "drip" is preferred, letting out demands little by little so as not to scare off the other side. In different situations, the "drop" is preferred, with the whole load being dumped at once. The following 12 tactics are used commonly in negotiations. . . . If you choose to use them, know how to thrust. If they're used against you, know how to parry. Consistency is vital here: tactics must be matched to strategy.

1. *Patience.* You wait. However anxious, you don't show it. Patience is a devastating weapon when the other side is highly volatile. When you set the pace, you control the deal.

2. *Slow agony.* The deal moves at a crawl. Every issue takes inordinate amounts of time. Delays are frequent. Slow agony never says no; the deal never actually stalls. This is an interesting defense against high pressure.

---

2. On arrival in the United States, my father-in-law had to be pressured and tricked by a real estate agent to make an excellent purchase of a small apartment building. Having been buffeted by the business ways of his old country, my father-in-law was highly skeptical of everyone. There's no doubt that, left unpressured and untricked, he would have never bought anything. His investment of $15,000 grew to over $400,000 in 15 years, not to mention all the years of income, free rent, and meaningful work.

3. *Apathy.* Overt concern is minimal. Whether the deal goes or blows appears immaterial. You request without energy and respond without passion. Apathy defends against high pressure.

4. *Empathy/sympathy.* Concern is shown for the other side. This is a powerful tactic for breaking deadlocks and bridging gaps. Such feelings should be genuine. Do not feign personal concern; compassion as a ruse is off-limits. Use empathy/sympathy when you mean it.

5. *Sudden shifts.* Whim and caprice do not build solid reputation. Consistency is important, but sometimes it equals sluggishness, even obstinacy. When talks are turgid and momentum has dissipated, unexpected changes can dislodge blockage and overcome obstacles. You have nothing to lose by shaking the tree.

6. *Faking.* Dealmakers are like football halfbacks, able to feint one way and run the other. Faking is more trading than lying. Fake when you want to protect a particular point. For example, you might insist on all cash in selling your home (or business) just to be able to maintain your price when you finally "concede" some seller financing—which you planned to concede all along.

7. *Walking.* Closing your briefcase and leaving the room. A dead deal. This tactic is less extreme than it looks. After all, you can always reopen negotiations (though some of your credibility is lost). Walking works when the other side has more basic power and has pushed too hard too long. Quitting is the ultimate leveler.

8. *Fait accompli.* The threat to take unilateral action. The deal, or something about it, would be irrevocably changed. For example, when a financially troubled company negotiates with creditors, each side can threaten to file bankruptcy proceedings—which would put all decisions in the hands of the court. Use fait accompli when you control a critical issue—but use it cautiously.

9. *Salami.* Cut a little here, a little there, and soon the salami is all gone. Some negotiators grind for small gain—but they never stop. The deal's never done. You must stop these people. Strict limits are the antidote for salami tactics.

10. *Limits.* Allow the other side to go so far but no farther. Setting boundaries can be imposing, even riveting. Don't do it often, but always make it count. Set your limits once and stick to them. Use this tactic when the other side keeps pushing.

11. *Deadlines.* Countdowns are contentious. Calendar pressure is troublesome. One must never make a hasty decision under time constraint. Try to force yourself to go even a bit slower than normal. If the deal evaporates, it evaporates. It's far better to pass a dozen good deals than to make one bad one.

12. *Antagonism.* Not a good tactic. More is accomplished by seeking personal harmony even during professional disputes. Nonetheless people are antagonistic, some deliberately as a technique, others because that's just the way they are. Disarm the antagonism by sidesteps, not body blocks, by leveraged angles not frontal assaults. Direct confrontation rarely works. Try gentle correction, tinged with humor. "I see the new day hasn't brought forth a new attitude." "I can't toughen my position because you can't get more upset."

WHAT TO DO?

You are a buyer negotiating to buy a new home. You currently rent an apartment and have no pressure to move quickly. The sellers, however, have serious concerns. They have moved to a new city and have already bought another home. What to do?

Time is a strength to you and a weakness to them. Draw up a series of alternatives related to time. You might give a short deadline for your offer if you feel pressure is the right tactic. Conversely, you might grant extra time to the sellers. Evaluating the different options requires careful analysis of the personalities of the people. The high-pressure strategy might be more effective if the sellers are unable to maintain two mortgages or cannot be bothered with unfinished business in their old city. The sympathetic strategy would be more effective if the sellers show appreciation by making an easier agreement. It is also possible to hedge your bets: try one approach, and if it doesn't work, shift to the other. (Think carefully about the order.)

Preparing for Negotiations

Bill Scott

It is critically important, when one's strategy is toward cooperation to mutual advantage, to build firm foundations at the start of the negotiation meeting. But before we can lay firm foundations, we must have made a good job of preparing the ground.

Time after time, one finds negotiators having two cries. On the one hand, "We just didn't have time to do our preparation properly before the meeting." On the other hand, after the meeting, "Well, that has certainly taught me that I ought to be more careful about the way I prepare."

There is no substitute for adequate preparation.

We shall deal with the subject in this chapter, making three sets of assumptions:

1. That the negotiator will have done his homework on the content issues for negotiation. That is, the buyer will have researched all specifications, quantities, market competition, market prices, and so on. The banker will be aware of the availability of funds, the appropriate rate of interest, the status of the client, and so on.

2. That the negotiator is familiar with the rules governing the negotiating territory. The company rules for purchasing or for selling, the trade and/or international rules that apply, the essential legal matters.

3. We assume that the deal is one which can be settled within one or two meetings . . .

This chapter will give suggestions about

- Conducting the preliminaries.
- A general approach to the planning of negotiations.
- The essence of the negotiating plan.
- Physical preparation.

CONDUCTING THE PRELIMINARIES

Other Party comes to a meeting bringing with him not only knowledge of the basic facts. He brings also his own way of conducting negotiations, his expectations about the way that our Party will behave, and his counterintentions.

Whether he has done his preparations systematically or not at all, he will bring impressions and opinions which will influence his conduct.

Reprinted from Bill Scott, *The Skills of Negotiating* (Brookfield, VT: Gower, 1981), pp. 77–87. Used with permission of Gower Publishing Co., Old Post Road, Brookfield, VT 05036.

To help him to bring the right attitudes and information, we need to have explored beforehand as far as possible the purpose of the meeting and the agenda of items which we will discuss. This may have been done through correspondence or by telephone or even, for major negotiations, through preliminary meetings between representatives.

A great deal of Other Party's basic values are deeply ingrained. We cannot much influence them during the preliminaries, but we can and do influence his opinions of us and his expectations about the way we shall behave, which in turn influence the way he will prepare to behave with us.

In part his expectations will be based on factors outside our control, such as the stories he has heard about us, the sort of relationship he would expect with a different Party in our situation, and the experience he has had with other organizations in our own industry and culture.

He may have more direct evidence about us: evidence from dealings which he or his colleagues have had with our organization, evidence of the manner in which we negotiate and of the effectiveness with which we have implemented previous deals.

There remain, however, the preliminaries through which we can ourselves influence him. The manner in which we communicate beforehand needs to reflect our interest in dealing with him, our integrity, our cooperativeness. To create the most positive expectations we need to apply the basic ground rules for communication between people distant from one another; to be prompt and polite, clear, concise, and correct.

We need also to be sensitive in the volume of our preliminary work. Sometimes we have to deal with businesses which seem virtually to resist paperwork. Such organizations always appreciate some brief statement on paper, covering issues like purpose, time, and estimated duration; but with them, anything more than one sheet of paper is irritating and counterproductive.

For other organizations, where formality rules strongly, there is a need for meticulous detail in preliminary exchanges. Indeed, the preliminaries can escalate, almost to become the most important part of the negotiating process.

To summarize: it is important in the way we conduct the preliminaries to help the Other Party to prepare himself for the negotiations, and to ensure he enters the negotiating room looking forward to a desirable relationship.

GENERAL APPROACH TO PLANNING

In principle, preparations for negotiation should lead to a plan which is simple and specific, yet flexible.

It must be sufficiently simple for the negotiator himself easily to carry the headlines in his own thinking. He must have these headlines, these principles of his plan, very clear in his mind, so clear that he can handle the heavy ongoing content of the negotiation with Other Party (making great demands on his conscious energy) yet at the same time subconsciously be able to relate to his plan.

Such simplicity is hard to achieve.

The plan must be specific: it cannot be simple without being very specific. No room for reservations or elaborations.

Yet it must be flexible. The negotiator must be able to listen effectively to Other Party, to see the relationship of Other Party's thinking to his own plans, and to adjust flexibly.

So the aim of our preparation is to produce a plan which is simple and specific, yet flexible.

That is the ideal, but the reality is usually very different. The negotiator hunts out the information, reads through the correspondence in the files, talks to half a dozen colleagues with interest in the negotiation—each putting a different picture—and is under pressure to be on his way to the motorway or the airport with very little time to form this ragged mass of impulses into any coherent pattern.

His need now is for a discipline, for a general approach which he can use quickly and which he can apply to many different types of negotiation.

The general approach we use is in three stages:

Ideas stage.

Thesis sentence.

Analysis stage.

The aim of the *ideas stage* is to make a quick review of the area for negotiation and at the same time to clear one's own mind. It corresponds to the brainstorming stage in Preparation of Information, but is now in two steps. Step 1 is quickly to jot down all one's jumbled ideas about the negotiation . . . Step 2 is to jot down our thoughts about Other Party on another sheet of paper. What they do, where they are, what they look like, what we know of the individuals, what we know they want from the negotiation, what we guess they want, and what else we would like to know. Again, random thoughts (Figure 1).

This ideas stage has led us to the production of two sheets of paper, one with random ideas on the subject and one with random ideas on the Other Party. Having been filled in, having got our minds cleared, these sheets have already largely served their purpose. They should now be put away (not necessarily thrown away—they just might serve some useful purpose later in our preparations).

Our conscious energy is now free to prepare our plans, uncluttered by the jumble of thoughts that was previously there; and the first step in this *analytical stage* is to prepare a thesis sentence.

This thesis sentence is a statement in general terms of what we hope to achieve from the negotiation process. It is a statement for our own guidance, and may sometimes differ from the general purpose of the negotiation as defined to/agreed with Other Party.

The thesis sentence needs to be simple, so we should try to specify it within a maximum of 15 to 20 words. If it takes more, the negotiator has not sufficiently simplified his thinking about why he is entering the negotiating process.

It is critical that his thinking should be so sharp. If he finds it difficult to state his purpose within 20 words, then he needs to spend more time on clearing his mind, drafting his thoughts about the purpose of the meeting, then pruning and modifying until he gets inside the maximum of 20 words (Figure 2).

Continuing the analysis stage, the second step is to develop a plan for handling the negotiation meeting.

FIGURE 1   Random Thoughts about Other Party

Jensen Electric Supply

30 years relationship
Annual golf match
Good customers
Tough but fair
Enjoy dealing
Probably see Alf
Hope not Doug
Are they in trouble?
Maybe need help
Maybe we need to
     protect
Is whole region in
     trouble
Or just them?

Know our
     processes
Keep it friendly

The need now is to produce an ordered approach to the conduct of the negotiation, together with a statement of one's opening position.

THE ESSENCE OF THE PLAN

The control of any meeting hinges on three of the four Ps . . . : the *purpose* of the meeting, the *plan* for the meeting and the *pace* of the meeting. (The *personalities* element, the introduction of the people and their roles, should be a routine, not a part of the plan specific to any one meeting.) Our preparation must cover those three Ps:

FIGURE 2   Thesis Sentence

Jensen – Generator Contract

Thesis.   To ensure goodwill, check their business strength, and get best compensation.

- The *purpose* spelled out in one sentence which can be offered to Other Party as "our view of the purpose of this meeting." It should be "our declared view" of the purpose, not necessarily the same as the thesis sentence.
- The *plan* or agenda must be kept simple. The human brain has the ability to keep a clear image of only a few agenda topics throughout a negotiation meeting—about four main items. If in the preparation one tries to give equal significance to, say, seven or eight main points, then the brain is overstretched. It cannot later have a sharp recollection of so many main points. It cannot easily, during the negotiation, relate all that is going on to the prepared plan.

  So at the analysis stage we are concerned to prepare our plans for the negotiation meeting under about four main headings.
- The *pace*—in terms of "how long"—should also be estimated.

The practical way to go about this preparation is—after going through the brainstorming stage and preparing the thesis sentence—to plan the agenda. Aim for the ideal of *four* main agenda points, subheading each if need be.

- In negotiations "toward agreement," a sequence I regularly find useful is "Ours — Theirs — Creative possibilities — Practical actions." "Ours" may, in one session, be "what we hope for from the negotiation," with the corresponding "theirs" being what they hope for; then the creative possibilities for the two of us working together; and, finally, what we should do before we meet again.
- In a later session, the same sequence might become "Our offer — Their offer — Overlaps and problems — Action needed to resolve problems."
- And for the next meeting, "Where we'd got to and what we each had to do — Our new position — Their new position — What is agreed and what remains to be done."

Having got the plan worked out, we should "top" it with a statement of purpose (already considered when building our thesis sentence, though not necessarily to be repeated verbatim); and we should "tail" it with an estimate of the time we shall need (Figure 3).

FIGURE 3   Plan for Meeting

Jensen – Generator Contract

Purpose   *Agree settlement*

Plan   *Their reasons/our problems*
Any creative possibilities?
How to settle?
What settlement?

Pace   *11·00 – 12·00*

Finally, the plan needs reducing to key words printed on a postcard.

The purpose of this final stage of planning is to provide a document which the negotiator can have in front of him in the negotiating room. He then needs the key statements prominent and visible at one glance of the eyes. He needs them as prompters for his subconscious, so that he can still control the negotiating process, even when his conscious energy is absorbed in the content of the negotiation (Figure 4).

In addition to this procedural preparation for a negotiation, there is another item to which we have already attached much importance. This is the opening statement to be made at the outset of the negotiating process. It should be systematically prepared. . . .

Following this preliminary work the negotiator goes into the negotiating room properly prepared both to control the process of negotiating, and to present his own position.

What about the room he is going into?

THE PHYSICAL PREPARATION

In this section we shall look briefly at the negotiating room, the layout of the room and the need for services.

The negotiating room itself needs to have the obvious facilities—light, heating, air, noise-proofing.

More contentious are the furnishing and the layout of the room. Negotiators seem to need a table at which to be seated—they seem to feel defenseless without a table between them. But what sort of table? A rectangular table—or the typical businessman's desk—leads to parties being seated opposite to one another. This immediately creates a head-on physical confrontation.

FIGURE 4   Prompter for Control of Negotiation

Generator Contract
To Agree Settlement
    Reasons/Problems
    Creative?
    How Settle?
    How Much?

11·00 – 12·00

Negotiators recognize that they feel differently on the rare occasions when they sit at round tables. In any poll of negotiators there will be a hefty majority who find it more comfortable and more constructive to use a round table than to use either a rectangular or a square one.

Should negotiators, whether at round or rectangular tables, split into their respective teams or should they intermix? It depends on the mood and style of the negotiations.

Where the parties are relaxed and collaborative, then the relaxation and collaboration are heightened by intermixing. At the extreme this would lead to each negotiator in a team being seated between two negotiators from the Other Party; but that would be contrived only by a formal approach to seating positions. Within an agreement-oriented group, the ice-breaking period leads to informality in the choice of seating positions. It is a purely random matter as to whether one walks up to the table with and sits beside a member of Own or of Other Party.

Where the negotiation process is more conflicting, then it is natural that the parties will gather together, probably on opposite sides of the table. This is both for psychological and for practical reasons. Psychologically, the mood is of "all together against them." Practically, either party may want to refer to papers which they want to keep obscured from Others (impracticable if Others are neighbors) or they may want to sit together so that they can pass notes within their team.

Incidentally neither the regular reference to secret papers nor the passing of notes is a symbol of good negotiators. Energy is needed for the exchanges with Other Party and not for private transactions. It is more skillful to take a recess either to check on the private papers or to handle private communication with colleagues.

It is not only the shape of table that is important—it is also size. There is a comfortable distance at which individuals or groups of individuals may sit from one another. If the parties are sitting a little closer, then the atmosphere becomes warmer. If they are sitting a lot closer, then they become uncomfortable and heated. If the distance apart is, on the other hand, too much, then the parties become remote and the discussion becomes academic.

Apart from the question of the room and the furnishing, the host needs to make suitable provisions for sustenance and for the well-being of Other Party. A special courtesy is in providing Other Party with a room which they can use for recesses, together with such other facilities as typing, telex, and telephone.

SUMMARY

1. The preparation for a negotiation meeting needs discipline. It needs time and the regular use of the same approach.
2. We suggest a disciplined approach of:
   a. Brainstorming.
   b. Thesis sentence.
   c. Planning.
3. The preparation needs to cover purpose, plan, and pace of the meeting.
4. The opening statement should be prepared equally carefully.
5. Physical arrangements influence the form of the subsequent negotiations.

Framing and Reframing

Deborah Tannen

Raised voices at the next table let you know that a fight is brewing. You are surprised to hear, seconds later, a burst of laughter. What you took for a fight was actually robust conversation.

You slap your friend on the back, or give him a poke, and somehow he knows you are feeling friendly toward him, not angry. But when Uncle Charlie pinches Little Butch lovingly on the cheek, it hurts, and Butch conceives a determined dislike for Uncle Charlie.

Marie makes a remark about Gordon's poor taste in ties; he looks hurt and protests that several people specifically complimented him on it. Maria laughs, gives him an affectionate push and says, "Can't you take a joke?"

These fleeting understandings and misunderstandings are a matter of *framing*—another term and concept developed by Gregory Bateson. Framing is a way of showing how we mean what we say or do and figuring out how others mean what they say or do. It is another aspect of indirectness in conversation. Signals and devices . . . serve to frame our utterances through metamessages about what we think is going on, what we're doing when we say something, and our attitudes toward what we say and the people we say it to.

This chapter illustrates the process of framing on the various levels of conversation. Subtle signals like pitch, tone of voice, intonation, and facial expression work, along with the words we say, to frame each utterance as serious, joking, teasing, angry, polite, rude, ironic, and so on. These small, passing frames reflect and create the larger frames that identify the activities going on. For example, utterances framed as giving information contribute to the framing of a larger activity, "teaching." Teasing and complimenting can be part of a larger frame, "courting." And giving advice can be part of being protective. Everything about the way we say something contributes to establishing the footing that frames our relationships to each other.

Framing can be done only indirectly, through metamessages. If you try to name a frame, you indirectly invoke a different one. Sometimes we feel put down by others' apparent kindness because their concern entails a subtle and unflattering reframing of our worlds. When stated and perceived frames conflict, we feel hamstrung, caught in what Bateson called a double bind. To deal with reframing that makes us uncomfortable, we can tackle the problem directly, by metacommunicating, or indirectly, by counter-reframing. Many of us instinctively stay in the frames set by others; some of us instinctively resist them. The best approach is to recognize when we feel reframed, and accept or resist it according to the situation.

Let's look more closely at these aspects of framing.

WHAT'S A FRAME?

The following example of different styles of indirectness—which will sound very familiar now—also illustrates framing.

Monica asks Jay, "Where should we go for dinner?" He names a restaurant; they go there; the food is terrible. Monica mumbles, disgruntled, "It was terrible when I had lunch here with Sondra too." Jay feels tricked: "Why didn't you say so?" She is self-righteous: "You didn't ask me." And she goes on to accuse him: "You don't care what I want. We always do what you want anyway."

To Jay, it seems that Monica never says what she wants and then gets angry when she doesn't get it. What is he supposed to be, a mind reader? He can't imagine that she knows what she wants but is reluctant to impose it on him without first getting a sense of what he wants. When she asks where they should go for dinner, she expects him to respond vaguely (for example, "What are you in the mood for?") and turn the question back on her. She might then counter with something slightly less vague: "Nothing too heavy" or "I had a late lunch." Asking where he would like to go is a way to start a negotiation in which they both indicate what they would like and how strongly they feel about it, so they can agree on something that will satisfy both. But instead of a negotiation, she hears a demand from Jay about what he wants.

For her part, Monica can't imagine that when Jay names a restaurant he's just throwing out an idea—his way of starting a negotiation. He intends the restaurant he mentions as a suggestion, not a demand. Since she expects a negotiation to start vague and work its way in, and he expects it to start specific and work its way out, she never gets a chance to say what she wants and blames him for not caring, and he thinks she doesn't know or won't say what she wants and is always forcing him to decide.

When Monica asks, "Where would you like to go for dinner?" she doesn't wave a flag that says QUESTION: STEP ONE IN NEGOTIATION. When Jay throws out the name of a restaurant, he doesn't hold up a banner that says SUGGESTION: STEP ONE IN NEGOTIATION. Yet that is how they mean what they say—how they're framing their talk. Our words don't come with INSTRUCTIONS FOR USE. We don't label our utterances with the name of the frame. If we tried to, we'd have a paragraph of framing for every word of talk—and we'd need to frame the framing as such, in infinite regress.

FRAMES GO NAMELESS

Since framing, by its very nature, is signaled indirectly, naming the frame invokes a different frame. If a parent says to an adolescent son, "I'd like to have a little chat with you," he may respond, "What did I do now?" He expects something far weightier than a "little chat," which can only come about by the way, when it's not labeled. If you have to state "I'm talking to you" or "I'm trying to explain," you are probably no longer just talking or explaining but have advanced to a state of exasperation. When all is well, frames do their work unnoticed and unnamed.

If you try to get others to name their frames by asking them how they meant what they said, or what they think they're doing by saying it, they are likely to hear your question as a challenge or a criticism. They may offer a counterchallenge: "What do you *mean* what do I mean?!" Because we expect communication to proceed on its own steam, calling intentions into question in itself sends a troubling metamessage of lack of rapport.

For the most part, speakers and hearers agree, more or less, on how they're framing their conversation. For example, Shirley and Eric are talking on the phone. Suddenly Eric snaps, "Stop it!" Shirley isn't offended; she realizes that he is addressing not her but his dog, even though she can't see where he's looking. She can hear where his voice is looking in the way he speaks. There isn't time or need for Eric to say, "Wait a minute. I'm going to interrupt my conversation with you to address my dog, who has just begun to make a dinner of the carpet."

Unlike humans, dogs can identify frames only by tone of voice and other nonverbal signals, not by the meaning of words spoken. This led Eric's dog to a confusion in frames. Having correctly surmised that Eric was talking to his dog, Shirley remarked that she was surprised to hear him address the dog with a Southern accent. Eric said he always used that accent when he spoke to the dog, and he demonstrated further: "Like I say to him, 'Go git that ball!' " The dog, however, still in earshot, could not understand the words "I say to him," and therefore missed the framing of this as a quote: "*Illustrating* what I say to the dog when I want to play with him." Instead, the dog took what he heard as an invitation to play and began dashing about the room looking for something to fetch. (He settled on a stuffed frog.)

There are situations in which humans also have trouble identifying frames. One such situation is in writing. In writing, we can't use conversational signals, so we have to label or somehow flag our shifts in frames—with section headings, transition phrases, and introductory words like "In summary" or "To begin." We don't need those frame labels in speaking because we identify frame switches orally by our voice quality. That's why, when reading a transcript of conversation, it is difficult to determine how something was meant. (This has significant implications for legal proceedings which depend on a "verbatim" record of testimony or transcripts of recordings of conversation as evidence.)

If we compose speech in our heads and then write the words we would have spoken, all the elements of voice quality (pitch, timing, intonation) are lost—and so may be the frame that lets others know how we mean what we say. That's why letters are often misinterpreted. The meaning of the words is clear but a reader often misses the attitude of the writer to that meaning and toward the person addressed: Is it quizzical, affectionate, annoyed, teasing?

A professor was grading an assignment written by a particularly good student, one with whom she had a friendly relationship. The professor had made much, in class, of the necessity of limiting assignments to the number of pages allowed. The student had kept to the page limit, but she had squeezed in a lot of words by printing her assignment on a word processor that had tiny print. The professor teased the student in her written comments: "Using the word processor is a kind of cheating." The student lost a night's sleep, feeling she had seriously been accused of cheating. Had the professor made her remark in person, the student would have seen by the professor's smile and friendly manner that the accusation was teasing, not serious.

When something significant is at stake, many people prefer to discuss things on the phone rather than write about it, and would rather talk in person than on the phone. They sense that when it's important to make clear how you mean what you say, you have a better chance of doing so if you can frame your meaning with voice quality, and a still better chance if you also have nonverbal signals such as facial expression, gestures, and posture working to frame meaning as well.

When a radio station tests its emergency warning system, it has to frame the noise very explicitly: "This is a test. This is only a test." The danger of audiences' missing the frame was seen when Orson Welles read H. G. Wells's *The War of the Worlds* on the radio. Many listeners who tuned in late believed they were hearing an announcement of the real end of the world. If they had picked up a book and turned to the middle, they wouldn't have been frightened because the book physically frames its words as fiction. Radio depends on talk alone for framing.

Sometimes readers miss explicit framing even in print. A man who was unused to reading the *New York Times* picked up a copy in a friend's house. He looked up from his reading with a veil of panic across his face and said, "This is an upsetting paper to read." It turned out he had read a prediction of the imminent end of the world—and hadn't noticed that the page was framed by a box and the words PAID ADVERTISEMENT discreetly displayed in the corner.

EXPLOITING FRAMES: ADS AND JOKES

Advertisers regularly make use of our framing habits. Patent-medicine ads on television used to feature men in white coats reporting laudatory information about products. The white coat, serious demeanor, and sober tone of voice framed the man as a doctor and the information he gave as scientifically sound, without the ad's saying either. Modern advertisers have become more sophisticated; it is no longer common to see actors posing as doctors in white coats, but similar framing effects are achieved by authoritative sounding voices, or by actors appearing casual, warm, and friendly, talking in tones that imply they are taking the audience into their confidence.

Many jokes depend for their effect on our framing habits by suggesting one line of interpretation, then suddenly switching frames at the end. For example, the one about the man who appears in town carrying a whip and offers to take travelers to the next town for half the usual fare. A group forms; they pay their fares and follow him, assuming he has left his horse and wagon around the corner. As they round the corner—and the next—they figure he's left his wagon at the outskirts of town. Leaving town, they conclude his wagon must be at the first way station. Well on their way to the next town—on foot—they protest: Where are his horse and wagon? "Who said anything about a wagon?" he asks. "I said I'd take you to the next town, and I'm taking you." He didn't have to say anything about a horse and wagon. The whip did the framing for him. And in hearing the joke, listeners have to switch frames at the end, revising their interpretation of the meaning of "take." Executing such a frame shift is what is thought of as "getting" a joke.

Jokes, advertisements, and con games intentionally make use of our framing habits. But because framing is done indirectly rather than explicitly, our talk can be misinterpreted when we don't intend to mislead. Like other forms of indirectness, framing constitutes both the armor and the soft underbelly of communication.

FRAMES IN PUBLIC: I'M WORKING, I'M OFF DUTY

Differences in conventional ways of framing can cause confusion and misinterpretation in public settings. For example, "mainstream" American conventions require workers to look busy even if they aren't, but some cultural styles require people to look "cool"—that is, not busy—even if they are. A customer walks into a post office and is pleased to see that there are no other customers before her, and the clerk isn't busy. He's singing to himself, dancing in place, and dawdling with some papers, moving slowly and casually, showing no signs of focused attention. So the customer is annoyed when the clerk makes no move to help her or even to acknowledge her approach.

But the clerk really was doing something important. When he finished, he turned to her and cheerfully served her. If he had displayed toward his task an air of great attention and preoccupation, with focused movements, she would have gotten the metamessage "I'm busy" before she approached and wouldn't have expected immediate service. (In fact, he could just as easily have used these signals to give the impression of being busy when he wasn't.)

FOOTING

Anne was expecting an important piece of express mail on the day a severe snowstorm paralyzed the city. The next day she called the post office and asked whether she had any chance of getting her express mail. The man who answered the telephone said, "No, ma'am!" She asked, "Isn't there going to be any delivery of express mail?" He said, peremptorily and with a derisive laugh, "No, ma'am! Whatever is here is going to stay here and whatever isn't isn't. Nothing's coming in or out." His tone was saying that this was obvious. She was getting annoyed. "Well, couldn't I come and get it?" "No!" he snapped, his annoyance reaching a peak. "The post office is closed. The only reason I'm here is because I couldn't get home last night." At that Anne's frustration melted. She said, "Oh, I'm sorry. It's nice of you to answer the phone."

When Anne heard someone answer the phone, her frame was established: "open for business." But for the stranded postal worker the obvious frame was "off duty." Telling her that he couldn't get home the night before not only clued Anne in on his frame but also changed the footing on which he was talking to her—from "uncooperative employee" to "person to person."

Footing is a term used by sociologist Erving Goffman to refer to a kind of frame that identifies the relationship between speakers. The same information can be communicated with different footings—and radically different effects. Imagine a man who insists he cannot let you into the swimming pool without your card, saying, "How do I know you're not trying to sneak in?" Imagine the difference in effect if he says, "I wish I could let you in. I don't think the policy makes sense either, but I can't go against policy." In the latter instance, the footing between the card checker and client is "you and me against the system." In the first, it's "me and the system against you."

Frame changes like this can make things better—or worse. A university professor turned up at the field house of the university where she teaches and discovered that she didn't have her identification card. The student attendant at the entrance insisted she couldn't enter without it. She explained that she was on the faculty, that she swam regularly, and that her colleague, another faculty member who was with her, could identify her. The student maintained that she had better look again for her card because he couldn't let her in without it.

The professor searched in vain through her purse. Finally she pointed out that she had forgotten her card once before, and the attendant had simply entered her number into the computer. The young man said that he was also going to do that, but if he made her search for her card first, she would think twice before forgetting it again. This changed the frame from "doing my job" to "teaching you a lesson." Given the role differences, this frame puts the student on an insolent footing with respect to the professor.

THE POWER AND DANGER OF FRAMES

The professor wrote a letter of complaint to the director of the field house. He replied that he was sure she had misinterpreted the intentions of the student who was just doing his job.

The power of frames is that they do their work off the record. By letting us mean what we say without saying what we mean in so many words, they allow us to renege, perhaps sincerely, by saying, "I didn't mean it that way," or by accusing, "What's wrong with you? You're imagining things." This defensive payoff for us as framers is a liability for us when we're uncomfortable with the frames set by others. It's far harder to challenge the way something was framed than it is to challenge a direct statement.

Most of us feel a strong impulse to sail with the framing winds. Changing course against the prevailing winds takes a great effort and risks scuttling the conversational boat. But there are two main ways to manage conversational frames rather than being blown about by them. Both ways entail changing the frame by stepping outside it. One is metacommunicating, and the other is changing the frame without talking about it.

BREAKING THE FRAME

The best example to illustrate the drive to stay in the frame and the two ways to step outside it is a personal experience, so I'll break the frame of impersonal exposition that I've established . . .—change the footing on which I address the reader—and describe my personal experience here. (I've signaled this shift in footing explicitly because in print I can't signal it by softening my tone of voice, shifting to a more relaxed bodily stance, smiling, and so on.)

I was lecturing to a large audience. Two people sitting in the first row—a couple—were giving me trouble. They kept making derisive comments, launching long questions that challenged my assertions and derailed me from the course of my lecture. The metamessage of their comments and questions was that all I was saying was stupid and wrong.

This had never happened to me before. So I dealt with it by using the tools that had always worked in the past to reframe critical questions as not disruptive: I kept my cool; I thanked the questioners for raising interesting points, and in answering their questions, I talked about issues I wanted to address anyway. But these tools weren't sturdy enough for this reframing job because the couple didn't do their part in supporting my reframing. They didn't stop at one, two, or three questions; they called out instead of raising their hands to be recognized; they responded at length to my answers, so each question led to an extended exchange; and they tenaciously kept talking over my attempts to shorten their long responses.

As I became more unnerved by the long interruptions and challenges to my credibility, I began to make jokes at their expense. Finally, I responded to a particularly destructive challenge—the man's scornful observation that obviously people who would misunderstand each other are not very intelligent—with an impassioned, stunningly articulate, and well-reasoned explication of the error of equating ways of talking with such value-laden and unfounded attributions as intelligence. Only my closest friends would have recognized my enhanced fluency and eloquence as a sign of anger. At the end of the lecture I felt like a victor following a battle: exhausted and emotionally spent, but relieved that I had prevailed.

Although I did prevail in this struggle with the contentious couple, I realized the next morning that I had not handled the situation well at all because I had stayed in the frame they had set: a battle that involved me with them as the center of attention and catapulted them out of a large audience onto center stage. Each time I responded at length to their attacks, I reinforced that frame and encouraged them to fire another round. What I should have done was break the frame, either by metacommunicating—directly talking about what was going on—or by indirectly changing it.

METACOMMUNICATING

Metacommunicating is the term Gregory Bateson used to refer to talking about communication—naming the frame. I could have stated outright that the extended interruptions were preventing me from getting to the points I had prepared or even that I was feeling under attack. I could also have analyzed the immediate interaction in the terms of my lecture. For example, the woman had vigorously objected to my conclusion that people sometimes make impressions different from their intentions. Leaning forward out of her front-row seat, she had protested, "Surely if you're a sensitive person, you see the impression you're making, and if it's different from what you intend, then you change what you're doing!" I could have asked if she was intending right then to disrupt my lecture, appear rude, and upset me. Had she noticed that she was making that impression? Did she consider herself a sensitive person?

But calling attention to the disruptiveness of their behavior would have reinforced the battle frame by naming it and making the confrontation open. Talking about my personal reaction would have aggravated it and presented me in a more vulnerable stance than was congruent with my role as lecturer. In other words, metacommunicating changes the frame, but it also gives substance to the old frame by making it the subject of the new one, metacommunication. Metacommunicating itself caries a metamessage of involvement—like calling someone to tell him you never want to talk to him again.

Another way of stepping outside the frame would have been to say, "There are 75 people in this room. You've already asked a lot of questions; let's give some of the others a chance." This changes the frame without naming it. In this way I could have reestablished control not by flexing my muscles on the specific issue ("I'm running this show and you're bugging me") but by exercising an unrelated control (giving everyone a chance to ask questions). Such a reframing would block further disruptions and dislodge this couple from the center of attention as a by-product rather than as the focus of the reframing.

REFRAMING IN THE FRAME OF APPROVAL

Luck presented me with the perfect continuation of this example. The next day I had my frames changed in a very different way—in the guise of approval and support. I gave a talk to a small group of psychotherapists. Far from attacking my assertions, they enthusiastically embraced them. They took my ideas and reframed them in psychological terms: for example, "I see what you mean; he was hostile." Unfortunately, what was offered as a show of understanding was actually evidence of lack of it. My point was precisely that the behavior mistakenly seen as hostile was really a well-intentioned act in a different style.

An even more powerful type of reframing in that setting went like this. I decided to use my experience of the night before to demonstrate the concept of frames, as I have just done here. As soon as I finished explaining what had happened, and before I proceeded to analyze it, the psychotherapist sitting next to me reached out, touched my shoulder, and said, "Let's role-play that." This gesture reframed the interaction, casting me as a patient and her as my therapist!

Metacommunicating in this case would be to say, "Hey, I'm not your patient!" To resist the reframing without naming the frame would be to say, "Wait, I haven't finished talking about these examples."

It is as frustrating to be praised as to be criticized if we feel the praise is based on a frame that isn't ours—like the complaint in the song "Killing Me Softly": "telling my whole life in his words." We want to tell our own lives in our own words. And it is frustrating to be helped (as I was "helped" to role-play an interaction I had found difficult) if that help establishes a footing with which we don't feel comfortable. It's no fun being embraced if the embrace cuts off your breath.

REFRAMING AS PUT-DOWN

Sometimes you feel put down by what others say, and you're not sure why, especially if they appear to be saying something kind.

Shortly after her divorce, Marjorie took a trip to London over the Christmas holiday. When she said good-bye to her friends Julian and Barb, Barb patted her lovingly on the arm and said with a smile, "You don't have to go all the way to London not to be alone on Christmas. Next year you can spend Christmas with us."

Marjorie said thank you for the kind offer. But she felt rotten. Her exciting trip to London was reframed as a pathetic attempt to avoid being alone on the holiday. Yet because the reframing was done by an apparently generous gesture, she didn't think of objecting. Even if she had thought of it, she wouldn't have said anything because any objection would introduce a contentious tone into the thus-far harmonious interchange.

Such a communication is confusing because it's a double bind: the message and metamessage conflict. The message says "We're your friends; we want you to be happy." The metamessage says "You poor thing," and that makes you *feel* like a poor thing—and feel correspondingly miserable.

Another time Marjorie was expecting a visit from Caroline—a friend who happened to be, like Marjorie, a successful stockbroker. When she mentioned to Sophia that Caroline would be staying at her house, Sophia said, "Oh, good, you'll have a chance to pick her brains." This reframed the friendly visit from a peer as a situation in which Marjorie was the lucky beneficiary of a visit by a superior. In this sense, it's insulting, reducing Marjorie's status. But the insult isn't in the proposition, it's in the assumptions underlying it—in other words, in the framing.

A group of friends is having dinner at a restaurant. They are in the habit of tasting each other's food, especially if it is something interesting. Karen offers Laura a taste of her roast duck, and Laura accepts. Then she offers Karen a taste of her scallops, and Karen declines, saying soothingly, "You don't have so many. You keep them."

Suddenly Laura feels like a pig because she's hogging her own dinner. Karen turned down Laura's offer in a way that framed her refusal as magnanimous, and it was made even more so because she had just given of her duck. Karen seemed to imply that she wanted to taste the scallops but would deny herself so as not to take any away from Laura. (Perhaps Karen was actually expecting Laura to offer again, more insistently.) True magnanimity would have consisted in pretending not to want any, so Laura could eat all her scallops without feeling she was depriving Karen.

Karen's magnanimity, framed by the way she declined the offer, underlies the classic "martyred mother" stance ("Don't mind me—I'll just sit here in the dark.") It's an ironic twist by which you want to be magnanimous but want credit for it too—and taking credit for being magnanimous reframes the other's behavior as depriving you. It is not necessary to see this as intentionally destructive on the part of guilt inspirers. It is sufficient that they want their magnanimity on record. The reframing of the other's behavior is a by-product of that frame.

FRAME SAVERS AND FRAME BREAKERS

A man and a woman are walking down the street. A car approaches the intersection at the same time they do. The driver of the car stops at the corner and signals them to cross in front of him. Such apparent kindness is, in a sense, inappropriately self-aggrandizing. If there is a crosswalk, it is the law, not the driver's magnanimity, that requires him to let the pedestrians cross. By waving them across, the driver takes credit for an externally defined situation, like Karen's converting Laura's own scallops into a gift from her.

How does the couple at the corner respond to this reframing? The woman quickens her pace and hurries across the street. The man backs up and signals the driver of the car to go ahead while he waits.

The woman's instinct is to accept the frame set by the driver: "I'm allowing you to cross." She quickens her pace to return kindness for kindness by avoiding keeping the driver waiting more than necessary. The man's instinct is to resist the driver's frame and substitute his own: "No, *I'm* allowing *you* to go ahead."

Whereas it might seem as though the right to go ahead gives one the upper hand, that is only the message level. On the metamessage level, the one who *decides* who goes ahead has the upper hand, regardless of who gets to go. This is why many women do not feel empowered by such privileges as having doors held open for them. The advantage of going first through the door is less salient to them than the disadvantage of being granted the right to walk through a door by someone who is framed, by his magnanimous gesture, as the arbiter of the right-of-way.

Most of us tend either to resist or to yield to frames. Those who instinctively resist frames set by others tend to balk when they feel pushed. Those who instinctively fit inside the frames set by others tend to yield when they feel pushed. We are more likely to respond according to our habits than to the specifics of the situation.

It would be better to learn to respond one way or the other—to go with the frame or resist—depending on the situation. The first step toward this exercise of control is to recognize when we feel uncomfortable with the frames we're put in and understand the ways of talking that are doing the framing. The second is to practice ways of resisting that framing or of changing frames by talking differently. In some cases, it may even be worthwhile to metacommunicate: to talk about the frame, with or without using the term.

FRAMES ARE DYNAMIC

Frames are not static, like picture frames, but are constantly evolving lines of interpretation, continually negotiated footings. The framing that is going on at any moment is part of what establishes the frame for what goes on next, and is partly created by the framing that went before. The footing we establish at any moment is occasioned by the footing that was established the moment before—and the year before.

At any point, each person is both reacting to and causing a reaction in others. Most of us tend to see ourselves as responding to what others say, without realizing that what they are saying may be a reaction to us. We are keenly aware that we said what we did because of what she said, but it may not occur to us that she said what she did because of what we said—just before, yesterday, or last year. Communication is a continuous stream in which everything is simultaneously a reaction and an instigation, an instigation and a reaction. We keep moving in a complex dance that is always different but made up of familiar steps. The constantly shifting rhythm and sequence is adjusted by subtle metamessages that frame what's going on from moment to moment.

Strategy and Tactics
of Distributive Bargaining

Earlier in this volume, we referred to different types of bargaining situations as different "structures" of bargaining. In this section and the next, we will examine two major structures of bargaining and how they pose different conditions and problems for negotiators.

In distributive bargaining, two parties have different but interdependent goals. When two parties are in a situation where they have incompatible goals, the condition is described as a fixed-sum, variable-share payoff structure, also known as a win-lose situation. In labor negotiations, labor and management are looking at the profits being made by the company (the sum) and negotiating as to what share the workers will get as a salary increase and how much the firm will keep as profit. There is a clear conflict of interest, and each party is motivated to obtain the largest share. This type of bargaining is also referred to as competitive negotiating, hard bargaining, or win-lose negotiating.

The more one party knows about the other's strategy, the better able that party is to plan negotiations and know what can probably be obtained. Hence, much effort before and during negotiation is directed to getting as much information as possible about the other party. Of course, the same process holds true for the other side; hence, it is to each side's advantage to keep its own information as private as possible while trying to learn about the other side. Therefore, in distributive bargaining, we face a situation where both parties are attempting to obtain as much information about the other as possible and, at the same time, to give out as little information as they can.

All negotiation strategies and tactics involve risk. While distributive bargaining tactics appear exciting and can yield large gains, they are not without the potential for large losses. Perhaps the largest potential loss involves the negotiator's reputation. Indiscriminate use of "dirty tricks" will eventually be identified in even the smoothest of hard bargainers who use them. The cost of being discovered? An irritated other party who may seek revenge, withdraw his or her business, or cause an unpleasant confrontation. Recipients of dirty tricks have the following options available: ignore them, respond with their own tricks, or discuss the tactic and offer to change the bargaining process. Finally, *dirty tricks* is a loaded term. People draw different ethical boundaries in their lives and when they negotiate, so don't assume that the ethics of the people with whom you negotiate are the same as yours! We'll have more to say about ethics in Section Seven.

In the first article in this section, "Winning at the Sport of Negotiation," Kathy Aaronson presents 12 of her favorite bargaining tactics from sales negotiations. For Aaronson, negotiation is a sport where making a good deal is like scoring a touchdown. Given that you are the quarterback, you need to learn the essential plays to win each game. Aaronson discusses how to use some of the classic tactics of distributive negotiation: delay, limited authority, nibbling, and so on. The other message in the article is to label the tactics that you use (and that you see others use) so that your playbook (tactics available) can be as complete as possible for the next game (negotiation).

In the article "Negotiation Techniques," Charles Craver discusses negotiation strategies and tactics that are used by some of the best distributive negotiators: lawyers. Craver divides the negotiation process into three stages (information, competitive, cooperative) and offers important insights about strategies and tactics for each stage. While the article is full of examples from the legal profession, the information contained in the competitive negotiation section of the article is applicable to anyone who wants to sharpen his or her hard-bargaining skills.

In the final article in this section, "Secrets of Power Negotiating," Roger Dawson presents 12 "gambits" or strategies that every distributive bargainer should be able to use in "power bargaining" situations. Dawson breaks negotiations into three phases (opening, middle, closing) and suggests gambits that are useful at each stage. He compares negotiating to the game of chess—people play by the rules and respond predictably to the moves that you make. Dawson believes that the best distributive negotiators always make sure that the other negotiator feels that he or she got a good deal, and presents numerous examples in this article showing how to make this happen.

Winning at the Sport of Negotiation

Kathy Aaronson

HOW TO TACKLE (AND EMPLOY) THE MOST COMMON BUSINESS NEGOTIATION TACTICS

In order to negotiate successfully and to buffer yourself from experiencing the negotiation emotionally, you must learn to recognize and develop negotiating tactics. Once you have used a tactic or experienced it being used on you, you can *label* it as such. That tactic then becomes just one in a series of possible plays—part of the negotiating game—rather than an attempt to wound or overpower you personally. The following 12 tactics are major negotiating skills.

Tactic 1: Delay

When you have the power, use it; when you don't, delay.

Say you start a job in which you are promised a salary review and the opportunity to make another $1,000 a month after six months on the job. You go into your manager's office and say, "Well, it's my six-month anniversary. Could we please discuss my salary review?"

He says, "I just don't have time now, but I'll get back to you shortly."

A week goes by, and he says, "Give me 10 days—I'm going out of town." Now you're over the moon with frustration, because you've been delayed.

Presidents of companies often can negotiate a contract with an entire foreign country, but cannot negotiate a simple compensation plan with their secretaries. This supervisor may be delaying because he doesn't know how to negotiate with you. He needs to be taught *how* to give you a raise.

When people delay, they frequently need more information to get them "unstuck"—with all the necessary information before them, it will be more difficult to justify a delay.

My suggestion in the case of the salary raise would be for you to go back into the manager's office and say, "I have a feeling you've been delaying this because you need more information from me. And you'd feel more comfortable if I gave you more information about why you should give me a raise."

Reprinted by permission of The Putnam Publishing Group from *Selling on the Fast Track* by Kathy Aaronson. Copyright © 1989 by Sales Athlete, Inc.

You might prepare a grid illustrating every month you've been working down the far left side, with the amount of money earned per month. Another sheet would show the number of hours worked per day, the number of accounts and dollar volume of the accounts. On the next page would be another grid, showing in blue the income you've brought into the company, and in the green the income you've earned.

Give your supervisor a copy of this material and say, "I know you have to go through channels, so you could just attach a memorandum to this if you like." You have empowered him with information.

Tactic 2: Silence and Bracketing

Coupled with a tactic called bracketing, silence is very, very powerful. Information gathering is best achieved through silence. When we bracket the attention of the information giver or person we're negotiating with, we direct their concentration to a specific area of the negotiation, then listen aggressively—carefully, silently and without jumping to respond—to everything they have to say on that subject.

If I simply say, "Let's discuss for a moment a succulent, juicy hamburger," and then I'm silent, you would fill that silence with your gut-level reaction to the specific issue of juicy hamburgers. Your response might be, "Oh, the *best* hamburger I ever had was at Joe's, and now you've got me craving another one." Or, "I don't eat meat, and the very mention of that turns my stomach." Whether your response is positive or negative is not the point: I have *bracketed* your attention to the subject, then used silence for a period to retrieve information regarding how you feel about the subject.

* * * * *

Tactic 3: Limited Authority

We've all heard this one: "I'll take this upstairs and see what we can do." "I've got to talk to my partner." "My agent makes those decisions." "I've got to send that to my lawyer."

When you've reached a point of closure and are stopped by the limited authority tactic, most likely your prospect *has* the authority, but has discovered some objection to your product, service, or idea that leads him to this point of impasse. Your move is to discover what that objection is by "repackaging" the information for the person of supposedly higher authority.

Example: "You want to review this with your attorney. How does your attorney best like to review information for his approval?"

Your prospect responds: "Well, I send it over, and he reviews it, and sends it back, and we review it together over the phone."

You say: "Well, I'd like to give you the information to present your attorney. What do you suggest I emphasize?" And reposition your presentation so that it removes any mistrust and any misunderstandings that hold potential legal problems. Because you've intuited that what he's said to you is that he doesn't trust your presentation is legally in order.

If you suspect it's the client's accountant who needs to review your proposal, ask "In what format does your accountant prefer to evaluate projects?" Once the person tells you the objections he feels his accountant will have to your presentation, you can reorganize your material as though you were presenting it to the accountant.

You are actually engaging in role-playing. Your prospect takes on the persona of the accountant—or spouse or partner or attorney—and you reorganize your material as though you were presenting it to this invisible third person.

When the invisible objector is "my partner," you ask, "What aspect of the business does your partner oversee?"

"Administration." You would then refocus your presentation as though you were presenting it to an administrator. You may actually even engage in a little outright role-playing: "Let's say you were your partner, and I were presenting this to you. . ."

Tactic 4: The Bottom Line

This is the point below which you will not go. If the bottom line is that you can't discount a product, all of your energy must be put toward selling it for full value. You've likely heard the adage in sales and marketing: "If you have two aspirin in your pocket and don't know how to sell them, you might as well take them for all the good they'll do you." The bottom line is that you don't waste time redesigning aspirin, you direct your energy toward selling aspirin to people who need aspirin.

Whatever your product, service, or idea, at the bottom line there is a price and there are benefits. The strategy is to identify people or organizations that need it, can afford to pay for it, and can abide by the policies and procedures of the organization that employs you.

When you're negotiating, and you hit your bottom line, you cannot charge any less or redesign your offering. When you accept the bottom line, your creative problem-solving strength is directed toward those prospects who need and want what you are selling.

The bottom line is your scorecard—the description of your product, its pricing, corporate policy regarding credit terms, volume, availability, delivery time, guarantee, and quality assurance. The configurations of these components determine the bottom line for sales athletes. The key is that you go into negotiations fully understanding what your bottom line is, and prepared to ascertain the bottom line of your prospect.

Imagine a client says his fiscal year ends December 31. The company wants your product but wants you to come back January 1, and here it is October 1. Their unspoken bottom line is that they won't have any money until January 1. Between October 1 and January 1 your competition could come in and usurp this client's enthusiasm for your product. Therefore, you may want to talk to your manager and see if you can arrange a purchase order with credit terms—buy now, pay 90 days later.

Or a client company says, "I can get your product cheaper elsewhere, and I must buy on the basis of price only." In fact, you know your product withstands heat, cold, and pressure, or has a benefit above all the other products in the field that justifies its higher price . . . Your bottom line is that you won't discount, so you use creative problem-solving skills to justify the pricing of your product and close the sale.

Tactic 5: "No"

The great value of getting a "No" from your prospect is that you can ask "Why?" and everything he tells you in response comprises precisely the circumstances under which he will buy. A "no" thus doesn't signal the end—it is the point at which the prospect trusts you enough to tell you he is not going to buy. "No" can be parlayed to a point where true feelings are disclosed, bottom lines are revealed, and where it becomes clear to you what objections you must meet in order to sell your product, service, or idea.

Tactic 6: Nibbling

Children are experts at this. Nibbling is the ability to withdraw and then return, but keep the pressure on:

"May I go to the movie?"

"First clean your room, and I'll think about it."

Five minutes later: "May I go to the movie, please?"

"Well, did you clean your room?"

"No."

"Clean your room first."

Ten minutes later: "I *almost* finished cleaning it. Now may I go to the movie?"

In sales, you can use nibbling as a positive negotiating tool to continually keep the subject in front of the prospect until the problem is resolved. The "touchdown" strategy requires nibbling. You can nibble as you relate to your territory like a cop on the beat, continually going back to check on client prospects, seeing them and also being seen.

Tactic 7: Expectation and Control

This is where you say, "This part is not negotiable, but that part is." All of your prospect's energy becomes redirected to the area that is negotiable. You let the prospect know what the product does and does not do, so that the prospect is not blind in his belief about your product. This is positive, clear, friendly, and honest.

Tactic 8: Auction

"I can get it cheaper (better, faster) somewhere else . . ." This is the single most powerful tool in the hands of a buyer. If you don't know your competition, or don't know what mood they're in today, you're up against the auctioning tactic.

When confronted with this, ask what the cheaper rate is. Give your prospect more details of your presentation. Explain that the price is not negotiable, but that something else is (a better service contract, the color choices, or the delivery time).

You might say, "This is how we do business—we have trucks that work, that send our product out on time, people that stand on the docks to ensure quality control. Our competitors don't. If you're at all concerned that things might shut down or a problem be created for you should our product not arrive, we're going to ask that you consider paying a little more to make sure it does arrive on time."

Tactic 9: Concessions

Concessions, however slight, should be given very carefully, treated like gold, wrapped in silver, and presented like a gift to a monarch. They can be the key to bonding a relationship in negotiating.

* * * * *

Frequently, a mistake is made in the guise of "inducement closes." A prospect has decided not to buy, and has said something like, "It just doesn't fit." The salesperson then throws in an inducement: "If you buy it by Friday, I'll give you 10 percent off." Meanwhile, the prospect still doesn't think the product or service fits his corporation or his equipment. Salespeople may have a whole list of valuable inducements and just throw them on the prospect's desk in hopes that something will induce a sale.

Use concessions to *build* interest. That way, you can also withdraw them. You say: "If you buy five dozen, you get a display rack." The prospect says: "I'll take three dozen and a display rack." Your response is: "No, I'm sorry, I have to withdraw the rack offer because we have found that if you commit to five dozen you will build repeat business. If you buy only three dozen you won't have the depth of merchandise necessary to generate repeat sales, or to develop a reputation of being a vendor of this item."

You have offered a concession, then taken it away, thereby creating an incentive for buying on your terms and getting the concession back.

Tactic 10: Rationale

If in fact what anyone is looking for in negotiation is satisfaction, recognize that satisfaction doesn't necessarily have to be what the person is asking for.

I divide my time between lecturing and corporations. A very big problem with my work is that when I'm giving a presentation to corporations I can't take phone calls, and when I'm with a corporate client I also can't take phone calls. This means I am not always reachable. Phone calls usually come from people with a problem. At my office, therefore, there must be someone who can handle the callers so that, although they have asked for something (to speak to me) and have not received it, they leave feeling taken care of because they have been given a rationale that satisfies.

If you are to make a mistake in negotiation, it should be that you give too much rationale that satisfies rather than not enough. I once thought someone was absolutely ripping me off. The client said, "Let me break it down for you," and when he gave his rationale, the reality was that I was not being ripped off. I left satisfied even though I did not get what I originally thought I should have gotten.

Frequently people are remiss with creditors because they are embarrassed that they cannot pay their bills. If, however, they pick up the phone and say, "Listen, there's a strike, I cannot pay in full, but let me work something out" they can negotiate to everyone's satisfaction through rationale.

Tactic 11: Message-Sending

During negotiations, messages will come your way verbally, visually, and in writing. Understanding this tactic is crucial to reading your adversary.

If all of a sudden someone stands up and looks jittery, don't talk through it. Recognize that something has just transpired. Read the nervous laughter, the jiggling foot. If all of a sudden someone starts crying—and that has happened in negotiations—the response to the message would be not to concentrate on price or services, but to move the person from an emotional position back to an intellectual position.

People send written messages, usually of a less dramatic nature but needing to be read with the same sensitivity as visual or verbal cues. A client you've been doing business with for years stops returning your calls—that's a message. Or pays his bills more slowly than usual—that's a message.

Tactic 12: Deadlines

. . . Frequently deadlines are artificial. They can remove profitability from an account, and when you test them you learn they are in fact there because of the belief that you won't service on time.

"I need it Friday."

"Why?"

"I'm going on vacation for three weeks." That's a deadline.

" I need it Friday."

"Why?"

"We go into production Tuesday." That's a test. To which the response might be, "Well, to get it to you Friday, we will have to FedEx it, which is an extra cost. You'll either have to pay or it will remove the profit from us. Whereas if we send it our usual way, we guarantee it will get there by 9:00 A.M. Monday, which is 24 hours before your production start."

Those are just the beginnings of a grab bag of tactics you'll see and use in negotiations. Once you begin recognizing and labeling such common moves, you'll see how much fun it is to identify and name your own. Labeling tactics makes them easier to tackle and helps you to buffer yourself from interpreting them emotionally.

* * * * *

Negotiation Techniques

Charles B. Craver

Practicing lawyers negotiate constantly—with their partners, associates, legal assistants, and secretaries; with prospective clients and actual clients; and with opposing parties on behalf of clients. Although practitioners tend to use their negotiation skills more often than their other lawyering talents, few have had formal education about the negotiation process.

The process consists of three formal phases:

- The information phase, where each party endeavors to learn as much about the other side's circumstances and objectives as possible.

- The competitive phase, where negotiators try to obtain beneficial terms for their respective clients.

- The cooperative phase, where if multiple-item transactions are involved, parties may often enhance their joint interests.

THE INFORMATION PHASE

The focus of this phase is always on the knowledge and desires of the opposing party. It is initially helpful to employ general, information-seeking questions instead of those that may be answered with a yes or no. Expansive interrogatories are likely to induce the other party to speak. The more that party talks, the more he is likely to divulge.

Where negotiators have effectively used open-ended questions to induce the other party to disclose its opening position and its general legal and factual assumptions, they should not hesitate to resort to specific inquiries to confirm suspected details. They can do this by asking the other side about each element of its perceived position. What exactly does that party hope to obtain, and why? What are the underlying motivational factors influencing that side's articulated demands?

Negotiators must try to learn as much as possible about the opposing side's range of potential and actual choices, its preferences and their intensity, its planned strategy, and its strengths and weaknesses. Bargainers need to be aware that the opponent's perception of a situation may be more favorable to their own than they anticipated. Even the most proficient negotiators tend to overstate their side's weaknesses and overestimate the opposing party's strengths. Only through patient probing of their adversary's circumstances can they hope to obtain an accurate assessment.

The order in which parties present their initial demands can be informative. Some negotiators begin with their most important topics in an effort to produce an expeditious resolution of those issues. They are anxiety-prone, risk-averse advocates who wish to diminish the tension associated with the uncertainty inherent in the negotiation process. They believe they can significantly decrease their fear of not being able to settle by achieving expeditious progress on their primary topics. Unfortunately they fail to appreciate that this approach may enhance the possibility of a counterproductive impasse. If their principal objectives correspond to those of their adversary, this presentation sequence is likely to cause an immediate clash of wills.

Other negotiators prefer to begin bargaining with their less significant subjects, hoping to make rapid progress on these items. This approach is likely to develop a cooperative atmosphere that will facilitate compromise when the more disputed subjects are explored.

Negotiators must decide ahead of time what information they are willing to disclose and what information they must disclose if the transaction is going to be fruitful. Critical information should not always be directly provided. If negotiators voluntarily apprise the other side of important circumstances, this may appear self-serving and be accorded little weight. If, however, they slowly disclose such information in response to opponent questions, what they divulge will usually be accorded greater credibility.

Where an adversary asks about sensitive matters, blocking techniques may be used to minimize unnecessary disclosure. Such techniques should be planned in advance and should be varied to keep the opposing party off balance. A participant who does not wish to answer a question might ignore it, and the other side might go on to some other area.

Where a compound question is asked, a negotiator may respond to the beneficial part of it. Skilled negotiators may misconstrue a delicate inquiry and then answer the misconstrued formulation; they may respond to a specific question with general information or to a general inquiry with a narrow response. On occasion, negotiators may handle a difficult question with a question of their own. For example, if one party asks whether the other is authorized to offer a certain sum, that side may ask about the first party's willingness to accept such a figure.

Many negotiators make the mistake of focusing entirely on their opponents' stated positions. They assume that such statements accurately reflect the desires of the other side. Making this assumption may preclude the exploration of options that might prove mutually beneficial. It helps to go behind stated positions to try to ascertain the underlying needs and interests generating these positions. If negotiators understand what the other party really wants to achieve, they can often suggest alternatives that can satisfy both sides sufficiently to produce an accord.

THE COMPETITIVE PHASE

Once the information phase ends, the focus usually changes from what the opposing party hopes to achieve to what each negotiator must get for his client. Negotiators no longer ask questions about each other's circumstances; they articulate their own side's demands.

"Principled" Offers and Concessions

Negotiators should develop a rational basis for each item included in their opening positions. This provides the other party with some understanding of the reasons underlying their demands, and it helps to provide the person making those demands with confidence in the positions. Successful negotiators establish high, but rational, objectives and explain their entitlement to these goals.

When negotiators need to change their position, they should use "principled" concessions. They need to provide opponents with a rational explanation for modifications of their position.

For example, a lawyer demanding $100,000 for an injured plaintiff might indicate willingness to accept $90,000 by saying that there is a 10 percent chance that the plaintiff might lose at trial or a good probability that the jury in a comparative-negligence jurisdiction will find that the plaintiff was 10 percent negligent. This lets the other party know why the change is being made, and it helps to keep the person at the $90,000 level until he is ready to use a "principled" concession to further reduce the demand.

Argument

The power-bargaining tactic lawyers use most often involves legal and nonlegal argument. Factual and legal arguments are advanced. Public policy may be invoked in appropriate situations. Emotional appeals may be effective in some circumstances. If an argument is to be persuasive, it must be presented objectively.

Effective arguments should be presented in a comprehensive, rather than a conclusionary, fashion. Factual and legal information should be disclosed with appropriate detail. Influential statements must be insightful and carefully articulated. They must not only be fully comprehended, but they must go beyond what is expected.

Contentions that do not surprise the receiving parties will rarely undermine their confidence in their preconceived position. But assertions that raise issues opponents have not previously considered will likely induce them to recognize the need to reassess their perceptions.

Threats and Promises

Almost all legal negotiations involve use of overt or at least implicit threats. Threats show recalcitrant parties that the cost of disagreeing with offers will transcend the cost of acquiescence. Some negotiators try to avoid use of formal "threats," preferring less-challenging "warnings." These negotiators simply caution opponents about the consequences of their unwillingness to accept a mutual resolution.

If threats are to be effective, they must be believable. A credible threat is one that is reasonably proportionate to the action it is intended to deter—seemingly insignificant threats tend to be ignored, while large ones tend to be dismissed. Negotiators should never issue threats unless they are prepared to carry them out, since their failure to do so will undermine their credibility.

Instead of using negative threats that indicate what consequences will result if the opposing party does not alter its position, negotiators should consider affirmative promises that indicate their willingness to change their position simultaneously with the other party. The classic affirmative promise—the "split-the-difference" approach—has been used by most negotiators to conclude a transaction. One side promises to move halfway if only the other side will do the same.

Affirmative promises are more effective than negative threats at inducing position changes, since the first indicates that the requested position change will be reciprocated. A negative threat merely suggests dire consequences if the other side does not alter its position. They are more of an affront to an opponent than affirmative promises, and, as a result, are more disruptive of the negotiation process.

Silence and Patience

Many negotiators fear silence, since they are afraid that they will lose control of the transaction if they stop talking. The more they talk, the more information they disclose and the more concessions they make. When their opponents remain silent, such negotiators often become even more talkative.

When negotiators have something important to say, they should say it and then keep quiet. A short comment accentuates the importance of what they are saying and provides the other party with the chance to absorb what was said. This rule is crucial when an offer or concession is being made. Once such information has been disclosed, it is time for the other side to respond.

Patience can be used effectively with silence. Where the other negotiator does not readily reply to critical representations, he should be given sufficient time to respond. If it is his turn to speak, the first party should wait silently for him to comment. If the first party feels awkward, he should look at his notes. This behavior shows the silent party that a response will be required before further discussion.

Limited Authority

Many advocates like to indicate during the preliminary stages that they do not have final authority from their client about the matter in dispute. They use this technique to reserve the right to check with their client before any tentative agreement can bind their side.

The advantage of a limited-authority approach—whether actual or fabricated—is that it permits the party using it to obtain a psychological commitment to settlement from opponents authorized to make binding commitments. The unbound bargainers can then seek beneficial modifications of the negotiated terms based on "unexpected" client demands. Since their opponents do not want to let such seemingly insignificant items negate the success achieved during the prior negotiations, they often accept the alterations.

Bargainers who meet opponents who initially say they lack the authority to bind their clients may find it advantageous to say that they also lack final authority. This will permit them to "check" with their own absent principal before making any final commitment.

A few unscrupulous negotiators will agree to a final accord with what appears to be complete authority. They later approach their opponent with apparent embarrassment and explain that they did not really have this authority. They say that their principal will require one or two modifications before accepting the other terms of the agreement. Since the unsuspecting opponent and his client are now committed to a final settlement, they agree to the concessions.

Negotiators who suspect that an adversary might use this technique may wish to select—at the apparent conclusion of their transaction—the one or two items they would most like to have modified in their favor. When their opponent requests changes, they can indicate how relieved they are about this, because their own client is dissatisfied. Then they can offer to exchange their items for those their adversary seeks. It is fascinating to see how quickly the opponent will now insist on honoring the initial accord.

The limited-authority situation must be distinguished from the one where an opponent begins a negotiation with no authority. This adversary hopes to get several concessions as a prerequisite to negotiations with a negotiator with real authority.

Negotiators should avoid dealing with a no-authority person, since he is trying to induce them to bargain with themselves. When they give their opening position, the no-authority negotiator will say that it is unacceptable. If they are careless, they will alter their stance to placate the no-authority participant. Before they realize what they have done, they will have made concessions before the other side has entered the process.

Anger

If negotiators become angry, they are likely to offend their opponent and may disclose information that they did not wish to divulge. Negotiators who encounter an adversary who has really lost his temper should look for inadvertent disclosures which that person's anger precipitates.

Negotiators often use feigned anger to convince an opponent of the seriousness of their position. This tactic should be used carefully, since it can offend adversaries and induce them to end the interaction.

Some negotiators may respond with their own retaliatory diatribe to convince their adversary that they cannot be intimidated by such tactics. A quid-pro-quo approach involves obvious risks, since a vituperative exchange may have a deleterious impact on the bargaining.

Negotiators may try to counter an angry outburst with the impression that they have been personally offended. They should say that they cannot understand how their reasonable approach has precipitated such an intemperate challenge. If they are successful, they may be able to make the attacking party feel guilty and embarrassed, shaming the person into a concession.

Aggressive Behavior

Such conduct is usually intended to have an impact similar to that associated with anger. It is supposed to convince an opponent of the seriousness of one's position. It can also be used to maintain control over the agenda.

Those who try to counter an aggressive bargainer with a quid-pro-quo response are likely to fail, due to their inability to be convincing in that role. Negotiators who encounter a particularly abrasive adversary can diminish the impact of his techniques through the use of short, carefully controlled interactions. Telephone discussions might be used to limit each exchange. Face-to-face meetings could be held to less than an hour. These short interactions may prevent the opponent from achieving aggressive momentum.

A few aggressive negotiators try to undermine their opponent's presentation through use of interruptions. Such behavior should not be tolerated. When negotiators are deliberately interrupted, they should either keep talking if they think this will discourage their opponent or they might say that they do not expect their opponent to speak while they are talking.

Uproar

A few negotiators try to obtain an advantage by threatening dire consequences if their opponent does not give them what they want. For example, a school board in negotiations with a teachers' union might say that it will have to lay off one-third of the teachers due to financial constraints. It will then suggest that it could probably retain everyone if the union would accept a salary freeze.

Negotiators confronted with such predictions should ask themselves two crucial questions: What is the likelihood that the consequences will occur? and What would happen to the other party if the consequences actually occurred? In many cases, it will be obvious that the threatened results will not occur. In others, it will be clear that the consequences would be as bad or worse for the other side as for the threatened party.

Bargainers occasionally may have to call an opponent's bluff. If union negotiators were to indicate that they could accept the layoffs if the school board would only raise salaries of the remaining teachers by 30 percent, the board representatives would probably panic. They know the school system could not realistically function with such layoffs. They were merely hoping that the union would not come to the same realization.

Settlement Brochures and Video Presentations

Some lawyers, particularly in the personal injury field, try to enhance their bargaining posture through settlement brochures or video presentations. A brochure states the factual and legal bases for the claim being asserted and describes the full extent of the plaintiff's injuries. Video presentations depict the way in which the defendant's negligent behavior caused the severe injuries the plaintiff has suffered.

Brochures are often accorded greater respect than verbal recitations, due to the aura of legitimacy generally granted to printed documents. Use of brochures may bolster the confidence of the plaintiff's lawyer and may enable him to seize control of the negotiating agenda at the outset. If the plaintiff's lawyer is fortunate, the opponent will begin by suggesting that the plaintiff is seeking too much for pain and suffering. This opening might implicitly concede liability, as well as responsibility for the property damage, medical expenses, and lost earnings requested.

Those presented with settlement brochures or video reenactments should not accord them more respect than they deserve. Lawyers should treat written factual and legal representations just as they would identical verbal assertions.

If lawyers are provided with settlement brochures before the first negotiating session, they should review them and prepare effective counterarguments, which they can state during settlement discussions.

Lawyers should not allow their adversary to use a settlement brochure to seize control of the agenda. Where appropriate, they may wish to prepare their own brochure or video to graphically depict their view of the situation.

Boulwareism

This technique gets its name from Lemuel Boulware, former vice president for labor relations at General Electric. Boulware was not enamored of traditional "auction" bargaining, which involves using extreme initial positions, making time-consuming concessions, and achieving a final agreement like the one the parties knew from the outset they would reach. He decided to determine ahead of time what GE was willing to commit to wage and benefit increases and then formulate a complete "best-offer-first" package. He presented this to union negotiators on a "take-it-or-leave-it" basis unless the union could show that GE had made some miscalculation or that changed circumstances had intervened.

Boulwareism is now associated with best-offer-first or take-it-or-leave-it bargaining. Insurance company adjusters occasionally try to establish reputations as people who will make one firm, fair offer for each case. If plaintiff does not accept that proposal, they plan to go to trial.

Negotiators should be hesitant to adopt Boulwareism. The offeror effectively tells the other party that he knows what is best for both sides. Few lawyers are willing to accord such respect to the view of opposing counsel.

Boulwareism deprives the opponent of the opportunity to participate meaningfully in the negotiation process. A plaintiff who might have been willing to settle a dispute for $50,000 may not be willing to accept a take-it-or-leave-it first offer of $50,000. The plaintiff wants to explore the case through the information phase and to exhibit his negotiating skill during the competitive phase. When the process has been completed, he wants to feel that his ability influenced the final outcome.

Negotiators presented with take-it-or-leave-it offers should not automatically reject them simply because of the paternalistic way in which they have been extended. They must evaluate the amount being proposed. If it is reasonable, they should accept it. Lawyers should not permit their own negative reaction to an approach to preclude the consummation of a fair arrangement for their clients.

Br'er Rabbit

In *Uncle Remus, His Songs and His Sayings* (1880), Joel Chandler Harris created the unforgettable Br'er Rabbit. When the fox captured Br'er Rabbit, Br'er Rabbit used reverse psychology to escape. He begged the fox to do anything with him so long as he did not throw him in the brier patch. Since the fox wanted to punish the rabbit, he chose the one alternative the rabbit appeared to fear most and flung him in the brier patch. Br'er Rabbit was thus emancipated.

The Br'er Rabbit technique can occasionally be used against win-lose opponents who do not evaluate their results by how well they have done but by an assessment of how poorly their adversary has done. They are only satisfied if they think the other side has been forced to accept a terrible argument.

The Br'er Rabbit approach has risks. Although adroit negotiators may induce a careless, vindictive opponent to provide them with what is really desired, they must recognize that such a device will generally not work against a normal adversary. A typical win-win bargainer would probably accept their disingenuous representations and provide them with the unintended result they have professed to prefer over the alternative that has been renounced.

Mutt and Jeff

In the Mutt and Jeff routine, a seemingly reasonable negotiator professes sympathy toward the "generous" concessions made by the other, while his partner rejects each new offer as insufficient, castigating opponents for their parsimonious concessions. The reasonable partner will then suggest that some additional concessions will have to be made if there is to be any hope of satisfying his associate.

Single negotiators may even use this tactic. They can claim that their absent client suffers from delusions of grandeur, which must be satisfied if any agreement is to be consummated. Such bargainers repeatedly praise their opponent for the concessions being made, but insist that greater movement is necessary to satisfy the excessive aspirations of their "unreasonable" client when their client may actually be receptive to any fair resolution. The opponent has no way of knowing about this and usually accepts such representations at their face value.

Negotiators who encounter these tactics should not directly challenge the scheme. It is possible that their opponents are not really engaged in a disingenuous exercise. One adversary may actually disagree with his partner's assessment. Little is to be gained from raising a Mutt and Jeff challenge. Allegations about the tactics being used by such negotiators will probably create an unproductive bargaining atmosphere—particularly in situations where the opponents have not deliberately adopted such a stratagem.

Those who interact with Mutt and Jeff negotiators tend to make the mistake of directing their arguments and offers to the unreasonable participant to obtain approval when it is often better to seek the acquiescence of the reasonable adversary before trying to satisfy the irrational one. In some instances, the more conciliatory opponent may actually agree to a proposal characterized as unacceptable by his associate. If the unified position of the opponents can be shattered, it may be possible to whipsaw the reasonable partner against the demanding one.

It is always important when dealing with unreasonable opponents to consider what might occur if no mutual accord is achieved. If the overall cost of surrendering to such an adversary's one-sided demands would clearly be greater than the cost associated with not settling, the interaction should not be continued.

Belly-Up

Some negotiators act like wolves in sheepskin. They initially say they lack negotiating ability and legal perspicuity in a disingenuous effort to evoke sympathy and to lure unsuspecting adversaries into a false sense of security. These negotiators "acknowledge" the superior competence of those with whom they interact and say that they will place themselves in the hands of their fair and proficient opponent.

Negotiators who encounter a belly-up bargainer tend to alter their initial position. Instead of opening with the tough "principled" offer they had planned to use, they modify it in favor of their pathetic adversary, who praises them for their reasonableness, but suggests that his client deserves additional assistance. They then endeavor to demonstrate their ability to satisfy those needs. The belly-up participant says the new offer is a substantial improvement, but suggests the need for further accommodation. By the time the transaction is finished, the belly-up bargainer has obtained everything he wants. Not only are his opponents virtually naked, but they feel gratified at having assisted such an inept bargainer.

Belly-up bargainers are the most difficult to deal with, since they effectively refuse to participate in the process. They ask their opponent to permit them to forgo traditional auction bargaining due to their professed inability to negotiate. They want their reasonable adversary to do all the work.

Negotiators who encounter them must force them to participate and never allow them to alter their planned strategy and concede everything in an effort to form a solution acceptable to such pathetic souls. When belly-up negotiators characterize initial offers as unacceptable, opponents should make them respond with definitive offers. True belly-up negotiators often find it very painful to state and defend the positions they espouse.

Passive-Aggressive Behavior

Instead of directly challenging opponents' proposals, passive-aggressive negotiators use oblique, but highly aggressive, forms of passive resistance. They show up late for a scheduled session and forget to bring important documents. When they agree to write up the agreed-upon terms, they fail to do so.

Those who deal with a passive-aggressive opponent must recognize the hostility represented by the behavior and try to seize control. They should get extra copies of important documents just in case their opponent forgets to bring them. They should always prepare a draft of any agreement. Once passive-aggressive negotiators are presented with such a fait accompli, they usually execute the proffered agreement.

THE COOPERATIVE PHASE

Once the competitive phase has been completed, most parties consider the process complete. Although this conclusion might be warranted where neither party could possibly obtain more favorable results without a corresponding loss being imposed on the other party, this conclusion is not correct for multi-issue, nonconstant sum controversies.

During the competitive phase, participants rarely completely disclose underlying interests and objectives. Both sides are likely to use power-bargaining techniques aimed at achieving results favorable to their own circumstances.

Because of the anxiety created by such power-bargaining tactics, Pareto optimal arrangements—where neither party may improve its position without worsening the other side's—are usually not generated. The parties are more likely to achieve merely "acceptable" terms rather than Pareto optimal terms due to their lack of negotiation efficiency. If they were to conclude the process at this point, they might well leave a substantial amount of untapped joint satisfaction at the bargaining table.

Once a tentative accord has been achieved, it is generally advantageous for negotiators to explore alternative trade-offs that might simultaneously enhance the interests of both sides. After the competitive phase, one party should suggest transition into the cooperative phase. The parties can initial or even sign their current agreement, and then seek to improve their joint results.

Each should prepare alternative formulations by transferring certain terms from one side to the other while moving other items in the opposite direction. When these options are shown, each negotiator must candidly indicate whether any of the proposals are preferable to the accord already achieved.

Exploring alternatives need not consume much time. Negotiators may substantially increase their clients' satisfaction through this device, and the negotiators lose little if no mutual gains are achieved.

If the cooperative phase is to work effectively, candor is necessary. Each side must be willing to say whether alternatives are more or less beneficial for it.

On the other hand, this phase continues to be somewhat competitive. If one party offers the other an option much more satisfactory than what was agreed upon, he might merely indicate that the proposal is "a little better." Through this technique, he may be able to obtain more during the cooperative phase than would be objectively warranted.

SATISFYING CLIENTS

Lawyers who understand these common negotiating techniques can plan their strategies more effectively. They can enhance their skill in the information phase, increase the likelihood that they will achieve acceptable agreements during the competitive phase, and endeavor to maximize the gains obtained for their clients in the cooperative phase.

Secrets of Power Negotiating

Roger Dawson

THE MYTH OF "WIN-WIN"

You have probably heard that the objective of negotiation is a win-win solution—a creative way that you and the other person can walk away from the table, both having truly won. Two people have one orange. They assume the best they can do will be to split the orange down the middle—but as they discuss their needs, they find that one wants the orange for juice, and the other wants the rind for a cake. There needn't be a winner and a loser. Both of them can win.

Oh, sure!

That *could* happen in the real world—but not often enough to make the concept meaningful. Let's face it: in a negotiation, chances are that the other side is out for the same thing as you. If they're buying, they want the lowest price, and you want the highest. If they're selling, they want the highest price, and you want the lowest. They want to take money out of your pocket and put it right into theirs.

Power Negotiating takes a different position. It teaches you how to win at the negotiating table but leave the other person *feeling* that he won. And feeling that permanently. He'll be thinking what a great time he had negotiating with you and how he can't wait to see you again.

The ability to make others feel that they won is so important that I would almost give you that as a definition of a Power Negotiator. You come away from the negotiating table knowing that you won and knowing that you have improved your relationship with the other person.

You play Power Negotiating just like the game of chess—by a set of rules. In negotiating, your counterpart doesn't have to know the rules. But in general, he will respond predictably to moves you make.

If you play chess, you know the strategic moves are called Gambits (a word that suggests an element of risk). There are Beginning Gambits to get the game started in your direction. There are Middle Gambits to keep the game moving in your direction. And there are Ending Gambits to use when you get ready to checkmate or, in sales parlance, close the sale. As negotiations progress, you'll find that every advance depends on the atmosphere you created in the early stages.

Excerpted from *Secrets of Power Negotiating* by Roger Dawson. Reprinted with permission of Career Press.

Ask for More Than You Expect to Get

This Gambit embodies one of the cardinal rules of Power Negotiating. Henry Kissinger said: "Effectiveness at the negotiating table depends upon overstating demands."

Asking for more than you expect raises the perceived value of what you are offering. And it prevents deadlocking.

Let me give you a contrary example: Before the Persian Gulf War, President Bush presented Saddam Hussein with a very clear and precise opening position. But it was not a true *negotiating* position, because it was also his bottom line. He left no room for any concession to the Iraqi side, to give them a little victory and make it easier for them to withdraw from Kuwait. The President did not overstate his demands at all—he announced that Iraq had to pull out of Kuwait. Therefore, nothing happened at the conference table, which resulted in a deadlock and a military conflict. This was no accident. Bush's position was meant to create a deadlock—to provide a reason to go in and take care of Iraq militarily, since we didn't want them to pull out voluntarily today, only to reappear later. But in your negotiation, you may *inadvertently* create deadlocks because you don't have the courage to *ask for more than you expect to get.*

Sometimes it may be intimidating for you to ask for that much. You simply don't have the courage to make sufficiently way-out proposals. There are many reasons why you should learn to do so anyway.

First of all, you never know: When you ask for more than you expect, you might just get it. You don't know how the universe is aligned that day. Perhaps your patron saint is looking down at you over a cloud thinking, "Look at that nice person, working so hard . . ." The only way to find out is to ask.

Here's a rule of thumb about asking: The less you know about whomever you're up against, the higher your initial position should be. Why? He may be willing to pay more than you think. If he's selling, he may be willing to take far less than you think. In any case, in a new relationship, you will look more cooperative to the other side if you're in a position to make larger concessions.

So, start with your Maximum Plausible Position (MPP)—which is the most you can ask for and still appear credible. Note: Your MPP is probably much higher than you think. We all fear being ridiculed, so you are probably tempted to ask for less than the maximum that the other side would find plausible. You must be on guard against *yourself.*

So, stake out your MPP—and imply flexibility. If you're a salesman, you might say to the buyer, "We may be able to modify this position once we know your needs more precisely, but based on what we know so far about the quantities you'd be ordering, our best price would be in the region of $2.25 per widget." You want him to think, "That's outrageous, but there does seem to be some flexibility there, so I'll invest some time negotiating."

Power Negotiators know that first offers seem extreme but are only the beginning; they know that they will work their way toward a solution both sides can accept. When football players or airline pilots go on strike, initial demands from both sides are outlandish. By making the other side move, eventually, both sides can tell the press that they won in negotiations, and both can be magnanimous in victory.

An attorney friend of mine in Amarillo, Texas, was representing a buyer of a piece of real estate. Even though he had a good deal, he dreamed up 23 paragraphs of requests to make of the seller. Some of them were absolutely ridiculous. He felt sure half of them would get thrown out right away. To his amazement, the seller took strong objection to only one sentence in one of the paragraphs.

Even then, he didn't give in right away. He held out for a couple of days before he reluctantly agreed to strike the sentence. And although my friend gave away only that one sentence in 23 paragraphs of requests, the seller felt he had won.

How much more should you ask than you expect to get?

Get the other side to state a position first. If there is no pressure on you, be bold enough to say, "You approached me. The way things are satisfies me. If you want to do this, you'll have to make a proposal to me."

The car dealer is asking $15,000 for the car. You want it for $13,000. So put the price you want in a bracket between what he is asking and what you will offer up front: Offer $11,000.

One of your employees wants to spend $400 on a new desk. You think $325 is reasonable. Say that it can't be more than $250.

In other words, your proposal should be as far from what you want in your direction as the other guy's proposal is in the other direction. If you end up in the middle, you make your objective. You won't always end up in the middle, but how often it happens will amaze you.

Never Say Yes to the First Offer

Why not? If you do, it triggers two negative thoughts in your counterpart's mind:

1. "I could have done better."
2. "Something must be wrong."

Suppose you are a buyer for a maker of aircraft engines meeting with a salesman for a manufacturer of engine bearings. Bearings are a vital component for you, and your regular supplier has let you down. If you can't make an agreement with this company, your assembly line will shut down within 30 days. And if you can't supply the engines on time, it will invalidate your contract with the aircraft manufacturer who gives you 85 percent of your business.

In these circumstances, the price of the bearings you need is not a high priority. But the thought occurs to you: "I'll be a good negotiator. Just to see what happens, I think I'll make him a super-low offer."

He quotes you $250 each, which surprises you because you have been paying $275. You respond, "We've been paying only $175." He responds, "OK, we can match that."

In thousands of seminars over the years, I've posed a situation like this to audiences and can't recall getting anything other than the two negative responses listed above. It isn't the price. It's the immediate response to the proposal without a struggle that sends up a warning flag in most people.

I was president of a real estate company in Southern California that had 28 offices. One day, a magazine salesman came in trying to sell me advertising space. I knew it was an excellent opportunity, and he made me a very reasonable offer that required a modest $2,000 investment. Because I love to negotiate, I used Gambits on him and got him down to an incredible price of $800. That made me wonder if I could do even better, and I used the Gambit called Higher Authority and said: "This looks fine. I just have to run it by my board of directors. They're meeting tonight."

A couple of days later, I called him and said: "I felt I wouldn't have any problem selling the board of directors on that $800, but they're so difficult to deal with right now. The budget is giving everyone headaches. They did make a counteroffer, but it is so low, I am frankly embarrassed to tell you what it is."

"How much did they agree to?"

"$500."

"I'll take it."

And I felt cheated. I still felt I could have done better. In other words, if you're too agreeable, it makes the other side uneasy. There are several ways to avoid the mistrust that can develop in your relationship.

1. Flinch.   Always react with shock and surprise at the other side's proposals.

The truth of the matter is that when people make a proposal to you, they are watching for your reaction. A concession often follows a Flinch. If you don't Flinch, it makes the other person a tougher negotiator. He may not have thought for a moment you would go along with his request, but if you don't Flinch at something outrageous, he may decide to see how far he can get you to go.

Flinching is critical because most people believe what they see more than what they hear. It's safe to assume that with at least 70 percent of the people with whom you will negotiate, the visual overrides the auditory. Don't dismiss Flinching as childish or too theatrical until you've tried it.

A woman told me that she Flinched when selecting a bottle of wine in one of Boston's finest restaurants, and the wine steward immediately dropped the price by $5. A man told me a simple Flinch took $2,000 off the price of a Corvette.

If you're not negotiating face-to-face, you can gasp in shock and surprise. Phone Flinches can be very effective.

2. Avoid Confrontation.   What you say in the first few moments often sets the climate of a negotiation. That's one problem I have with the way lawyers negotiate. Your first communication from them is likely to be a threat. In one workshop I taught that included some lawyers, most of them would start a negotiation exercise with a vicious threat and become more abusive from there. I had to stop the exercise and tell them never to be confrontational early on if they wanted to settle a case without expensive litigation. (I doubted their motives on that score.)

If the other side takes a position with which you disagree, don't argue. That only intensifies their desire to be proved right. Get in the habit of agreeing initially and turning it around. Use the Feel, Felt, Found Formula:

> "I understand exactly how you Feel about that. Many other people have Felt exactly the same way. But you know what we have always Found? When we took a closer look, we Found . . ." (that they changed their minds, of course).

At the very least, this approach gives you time to think. By the time you get around to saying what you found on a closer look, you will have found what you need to say.

Play the Reluctant Buyer or Reluctant Seller

One of my Power Negotiators owns real estate worth probably $50 million, owes $35 million in loans, and therefore has a net worth of about $15 million. Many smaller investors bring him purchase offers, eager to acquire one of his better-known properties. I have seen him make thousands of dollars with the Reluctant Seller Gambit.

He reads the offer quietly and slides it thoughtfully back across the table, scratches above one ear, and says: "I don't know. Of all my properties, I have very special feelings for this one. I was thinking of keeping it and giving it to my daughter for her college graduation present. I really don't think I would part with it for anything less than the full asking price. But it was good of you to make me this offer, and so that you won't have wasted your time, what is the very best price you feel you could give me?"

Many times, I have seen him make thousands of dollars in a few seconds.

Now, put yourself on the other side of the desk for a moment and become the Reluctant Buyer. Let's say you're in charge of buying new computer equipment for your company. How can you get the best possible price? My suggestion is to have the supplier come to your offices and go through the whole presentation. Ask all the questions you can possibly think of, then say: "I really appreciate all the time you've taken. You've obviously put a lot of work into this presentation, but unfortunately, it's not the way we want to go; however, I sure wish you the best of luck."

Pause to examine the crestfallen expression on the salesman's face as he slowly puts away his presentation materials. Then, at the very last moment, as his hand reaches for the doorknob on the way out, come out with the following magic expression. It is one of those expressions in negotiating that, used at the right moment, yields amazingly predictable results. Say: "You know, I really do appreciate the time you took here. Just to be fair to you, what is the very lowest price you would take?"

Would you agree that the first price you were quoted was probably not the bottom? It's a good bet. The first price was probably what I call the "wish number." If you'd signed off on that, the salesman would have shoved the contract into his briefcase, burned rubber all the way back to the office, and run in screaming, "You won't believe what just happened to me!"

When you play the Reluctant Buyer, you'll get a second quote, in which the salesman will probably give away half his negotiating range—between the "wish number" and his lowest possible price, which I call the "walk-away" price. He'll typically respond with: "Well, I tell you what. I like your company. It's the end of our quarter, and we're in a sales contest. If you'll place the order today, I'll give it to you for the unbelievably low price of $200,000 . . ."

It's a game. When someone plays Reluctant Buyer to *you,* the correct response is: "I don't think there's any flexibility in our price, but if you'll tell me what it would take to get your business (getting the other side to commit to a number first), I'll take it to my people (using a Higher Authority as a foil) and see what I can do for you with them (setting up to play Good Guy/Bad Guy)."

The Vise Technique

The Vise is this simple little expression: "You'll have to do better than that."

A veteran negotiator will simply come back at you with: "Just how much better do I have to do?" But it's amazing how often an inexperienced one will give away a big chunk of his range, simply because you did that.

Once you've used that phrase, shut up. Don't say another word. One client called me to say that by using this simple phrase, he got a price $14,000 less than he was prepared to pay.

Are you wondering: "Was that a $50,000 proposal that got knocked down by $14,000, or a multimillion-dollar proposal—in which case, $14,000 is no big deal?" It doesn't matter. The point is that he made $14,000 in those two minutes that it took him to scrawl that phrase on a bid. That would be $420,000 per hour. You'll never make money faster than you do when you're negotiating.

The dollars you save or lose in negotiating are bottom-line dollars, not gross income dollars. I've trained executives at retailers and health maintenance organizations (HMOs) whose profit margin is only 2 percent. They do a billion dollars' worth of business a year, but they bring in only 2 percent in bottom-line profits. In a company like that, a $2,000 concession at the negotiating table has the same effect as a $100,000 sale.

You're probably in an industry that does better than that. In this country, the average profit margin is about 5 percent of gross sales. For such a company, a $2,000 concession at the negotiating table is the equivalent of $40,000 in sales. How long would you be willing to work to get a $40,000 sale?

Perhaps when you read these Gambits you're thinking, "Roger, you've never met the guys I deal with in my business. They make Attila the Hun look like Ann Landers. They'll never fall for that kind of thing." Fair enough. But try these techniques. Time and again, students have told me: "I never thought that would work, but it did. It's amazing." The first time you Flinch or use the Vise on the other person and walk out of negotiations with $1,000 in your pocket that you didn't expect to get, you'll become a believer, too. Negotiating is a game that is played by a set of rules. If you learn the rules well, you can play the game well.

Don't Worry about Price

After two decades of sales training, I am convinced that price is a bigger concern to the people selling than it is to those they're selling to. People want to pay more, not less. Customers who may be asking you to cut your price may be secretly wishing they could pay more. Seriously.

I was the merchandise manager at the Montgomery Ward store in Bakersfield, California, which is not a large town. But in a chain of more than 600 stores, ours ranked 13th in volume. Why? The head office left us alone and allowed us to sell to the needs of the local population. We did a huge business in home air conditioners, because in Bakersfield, it's not unusual for it to be 100 degrees Fahrenheit at midnight. A blue-collar home in that city then cost around $30,000. The air conditioners we sold them cost $10,000 to $12,000. The customers were willing to pay that price, but it was very hard to break in new salesmen because they couldn't believe anybody would pay $12,000 to put an air conditioner in a $30,000 house.

But if I could get these same salesmen to succeed to the point where they made big money and installed air conditioners in their own homes, suddenly they didn't find the price outrageous and would dismiss price objections from customers as if they didn't exist.

Beginning stockbrokers are the same. It's very hard for them to ask a client to invest $100,000 when they don't know where their own lunch money is going to come from. But once they become affluent, their sales snowball.

One of my clients tells me that if three products are on a store shelf—let's say three toasters—and the features of each are described on the carton, customers will most frequently select the highest-priced item. But if a salesman working for minimum wage comes along to assist them, he can't justify spending money on the best and talks the customer down to the low-end or the middle-of-the-line toaster.

The key is the description on the carton. You must give customers a *reason* to spend more money, but if you can do that, they want to spend more money, not less. I think that spending money is what Americans do best. We spend $6 trillion a year in this country. And that's when we're spending our own hard-earned, after-tax dollars. What if you're asking someone at a corporation to spend the company's money? One thing better than spending your own money is spending someone else's money. And corporate expenditures are tax deductible, so Uncle Sam is going to pick up 40 percent of the bill.

Let's face it, does what you pay for something really matter? If you're going to buy a new automobile, does it matter if you spend $20,000 or $21,000? Not really. You'll soon forget what you paid, and the slight increase in payments is not going to affect your lifestyle. What matters is the feeling that you got the best possible deal.

If you're trying to get someone to spend money, all you have to do is give him a reason and convince him there is no way to get a better deal.

Even when dealing with the federal government, price is far from the most important thing. I asked a Pentagon procurement officer point-blank if the government has to buy from the lowest bidder.

"Heavens no," he said. "We'd really be in trouble if that were true. The rules say we should buy from the lowest bidder whom we feel is capable of meeting specifications. We're far more concerned with a company's experience and its ability to get a job done on time."

In a company that doesn't have legal requirements to put out requests for bids, price probably counts for even less. AT&T keeps my telephone business even though it's more expensive than Sprint or MCI and has never pretended otherwise. I stay because the service has been trouble-free and simple to use for many years, and I have more important things concerning me than switching long-distance companies to save a few pennies per call. So don't exacerbate the price problem by assuming that price is uppermost in the other person's mind. Assume that it isn't.

As negotiations proceed, don't narrow the negotiation down to just one issue. If everything is resolved and the only issue left is price, then clearly somebody has to win, and clearly somebody does have to lose. But as long as you keep more than one issue on the table, you can work trade-offs so that the other fellow doesn't mind conceding on price because you are able to offer something in return.

Find other ways to make him feel he's winning.

Higher Authority

Once you're in negotiations, it's always good for you to postpone a decision and plead that you have to run the deal by some outside person with Higher Authority. The other side will make more concessions to people they *don't* see or know than they will to you alone.

But by the same token, you will be frustrated over and over if this Gambit is used on you. When I was a real estate broker, I taught our agents that before they put buyers into their cars to show them properties, they must always say: "Just to be sure I understand, if we find exactly the right home for you today, is there any reason you couldn't make a decision today?"

Here's something you can count on when dealing with another person: Any concession you make will lose its value quickly. A material object may appreciate in value over the years, but the value of services declines rapidly after you have performed them. Consequently, when you make a concession, you must ask for a reciprocal concession right away, because two hours later, what you have done will count for little or nothing.

That's one reason why you always have to settle your fee before you perform a service. When a real estate salesman offers to help someone get rid of a property, a 6 percent fee doesn't sound enormous—but the minute the realtor has found the buyer, that 6 percent suddenly starts to sound like a tremendous amount of money.

Don't Split the Difference

When you are negotiating price, don't offer to split the difference that is keeping you and the person on the other side from agreement. Let him suggest that. You can usually get him to do so if you point out how long you have been negotiating and what a comparatively small sum is keeping you apart.

It makes all the difference psychologically to someone if *he* makes a suggestion and gets you to agree to it, as opposed to unwillingly accepting a proposal from you. It may seem a very subtle thing, but it's a significant factor in determining who feels he has won.

If your counterpart splits the difference with you and moves half the distance toward your price, you can invoke a Higher Authority—maybe it's your partners or your board. After a delay of hours or days, you come back and say that your Higher Authority is not being cooperative and has vetoed the new offer; then point out how it seems too bad that a little difference—between what you're asking and what he just offered—should derail everything. If you keep that up long enough, he will probably offer to split the difference again. So you have that much more bottom-line profit. But even if he won't do it a second time, if you wind up splitting the difference as he first proposed, he will feel he won—because he proposed it.

Set It Aside

In negotiations, you will often find that you are in complete disagreement on one issue. It's easy for an inexperienced negotiator to feel that the whole deal is threatened, but you can handle an impasse on one issue by the Set Aside Gambit: "Let's just set that aside for a moment and talk about some of the other issues, may we?" If you resolve minor issues that you can discuss easily, you'll put momentum into the negotiations again. The other side will be much more flexible after you've reached agreement on the smaller issues.

A stalemate is something different. That's when both sides are still talking but seem unable to make any progress. At this point, you must change the dynamics of the meeting to reestablish momentum.

Change the people in the negotiating team. Remove any member who may have irritated the other side. Change the venue by proposing to continue over lunch or dinner. Ease the tension—tell a funny story, talk about their hobbies or a piece of gossip that's in the news. Explore the possibility of extended credit, a reduced deposit, restructured payments, or a change in specifications, packaging, or delivery method. Remember that the other side may be reluctant to raise these issues for fear of appearing to be in poor financial condition.

Discuss methods of sharing the risk with the other side.

The Art of Concession

In negotiations over price, be sure you don't set up a pattern in the way you make concessions. Don't make equal-size concessions. That will certainly make the other side expect that another concession of just the same size is practically his right. And never make the final concession a big one. It never looks final if it's big. To refuse a further, smaller concession after you have just made a big one makes you seem difficult and only creates needless hostility.

Make Time Your Ally

The longer you can keep the other party involved in negotiations, the more likely he is to move around to your point of view. Think of the tugboats in the Hudson River off Manhattan. A tiny tugboat can move a huge ocean liner if it does it a little bit at a time. If the tugboat captain were to back off, rev up the engines, and try to force the ocean liner around, it wouldn't do any good. If you have enough patience, you can change anybody's mind a little bit at a time.

Unfortunately, this works both ways. The longer you spend in a negotiation, the more likely you are to make concessions.

An 80/20 split surfaces repeatedly in apparently unrelated fields. In the 19th century, the economist Vilfredo Pareto, who studied the distribution of wealth in Italy, pointed out that 80 percent of the wealth was concentrated in the hands of 20 percent of the people. Sales managers tell me that 80 percent of the business is done by 20 percent of the salespeople. Schoolteachers tell me that 20 percent of the children cause 80 percent of the trouble.

It also seems true that on account of the incredible pressure that time can put on a negotiation, 80 percent of the concessions in a negotiation will occur in the last 20 percent of the time available. If demands are presented early on, neither side may be willing to yield, and the entire transaction can fall apart. But if additional demands or problems surface in the final 20 percent of the time available for the negotiation, both sides will be more flexible.

Think back to the last time you bought a piece of real estate. Probably it took about 10 weeks from signing the initial contract until you actually became the owner of the property. Now think of the concessions that were made in the last 2 weeks. Weren't both sides more yielding at that point?

One rule that obviously follows from this: If you have a deadline pushing you in a negotiation, never reveal that fact to the other side. He'll be sure to squeeze you for concessions at the last minute.

If you have flown to Dallas to resolve a negotiation with a hotel developer, and you have a return flight at six o'clock, of course you want to make that flight—but don't let the other people know. If they do know, be sure they know that you have a backup flight at nine o'clock—and that if you need to, you can stay over until you work out a mutually satisfactory arrangement.

The power that comes from knowing the other side's time limit was shown when President Lyndon Johnson wanted to negotiate with the Vietnamese in time to do his party some good in the election of November 1968. He sent our negotiator, Averell Harriman, to Paris with very clear instructions: Get something done, fast, right now, Texas style.

Harriman rented a suite at the Ritz Hotel in Paris on a week-to-week basis. Vietnamese negotiator Xuan Thuy rented a villa in the countryside for two and a half years. Then the Vietnamese proceeded to spend week after week after week talking to us about the shape of the table.

Did they really care about the shape of the table? Of course not. They were projecting, successfully, that they were not under any time pressure. They were trying to exploit Johnson's November deadline. On November 1, only five days before the election, Johnson called a halt to the bombing of Vietnam.

The Most Dangerous Moment

You are at your most vulnerable at the point when you think the negotiations are over, just after the other party has agreed to go ahead. Making a huge sale has excited you. You're feeling good. At such times, you tend to give away things you otherwise wouldn't. Watch your emotions.

If the other side chooses this moment to Nibble at the deal for some concession now, you're likely to think: "Oh no, I thought we had resolved everything. I don't want to take a chance on going back to the beginning and renegotiating the whole thing. If I do that, I might lose the whole sale. I'm better off just giving in on this little point."

Don't lay yourself open to last-minute Nibbles—some of which could negate the benefit of the deal for you. Your protection is to say *you don't have the authority* to make any concessions now. If the other side persists and wants extra training, installation, extended warranties, or anything else, show them the hard price in writing. Don't let the euphoria of finishing a negotiation cost you the store.

Your Most Powerful Weapon

If there's one thing that I can impress upon you that will make you 10 times more powerful as a negotiator, it's this: Learn to develop walk-away power. Often, there's a point you pass in the heat of negotiation when you will no longer walk away. You start thinking:

I'm going to buy this car. I'm going to get the best price I can, but I'm not leaving until I get it."

"I'm going to hire this person. For the lowest salary and benefits that I can—but I won't let him get away."

"I have to take this job. I'm going to fight for the best pay and benefits, but I have to take this job."

"I have to make this sale. I can't walk out of here without a commitment."

The minute you're no longer willing to say, "I'm prepared to walk away from this," I guarantee you will lose in the negotiations.

So don't pass that point. There's no such thing as a sale you have to make at any price, or the only car or home for you, or a job or employee you can't do without. The minute you think there is, you've lost.

When people tell me they made a mistake in negotiations, this is always a part of the problem. They passed the point where they were willing to walk away.

Many years ago, my daughter bought her first car. She fell in love with the car, and the dealer knew it. Then she came back from the place and wanted me to go down with her to negotiate a better price. I sat her down and said, "Julia, are you prepared to come home without the car?"

She said, "No, I'm not, I want it, I want it." She was in trouble.

"Julia, you might as well get your checkbook out and give them what they're asking, because you've set yourself up to lose. We've got to be prepared to walk away."

We walked out of the showroom twice in the two hours we spent negotiating over the car and bought it for $2,000 less than she would have paid for it. How much money was she making while she was negotiating? She was making $1,000 an hour. We'd all go to work for $1,000 an hour, wouldn't we? You never make money faster than when you're negotiating.

Strategy and Tactics
of Integrative Negotiating

Integrative (or collaborative) negotiating occurs when both parties work together toward common or compatible goals. For integrative negotiating to occur, the parties first must agree on the overall goal. This discovery usually depends on the accurate exchange of information, just the opposite of what is typically sought in distributive (or competitive) bargaining. This need to share rather than to conceal information is different from what many people expect to occur during a negotiation. People often find it difficult to accept and do what is necessary to achieve success in integrative negotiating.

The need to share information requires negotiators to collaborate. Barbara Gray, in the article "Collaboration: The Constructive Management of Differences" (from her 1989 book, *Collaborating*) identifies collaboration as a necessary skill, given the failure of more "traditional" individual and collective problem-solving strategies in these turbulent times. Gray sees collaboration as an approach critical to understanding and addressing negotiations marked by multiple, often competing, interests. Collaboration, here, is defined as "a process through which parties who see different aspects of a problem can constructively explore their differences and search for solutions that go beyond their own limited vision of what is possible." Gray's collaboration is a reasonable alternative to confrontation, as well as the foundation for effective integrative negotiating. Her description of collaboration includes a number of characteristics typically attributed to integrative negotiation:

- Resolution of conflict.
- Advancement of a shared vision.
- Implication of interdependencies.
- Emergence of solutions by dealing constructively with differences.
- Joint ownership of resolution decisions.

Terry Anderson, in the article "Step into My Parlor: A Survey of Strategies and Techniques for Effective Negotiation," develops an integrative negotiation model from a practitioner's perspective, highlighting the integrative (or "symbiotic") process by contrasting with the competitive (or "predatory") process. Anderson notes that the pursuit of a positive relationship with the other party tends to moderate the drive for material or substantive victory typical of competitive negotiation. By contrasting symbiosis ("creating value") with predation ("claiming value"), he suggests that, in addition to traditional win-win outcomes, integrative processes may offer attractive alternatives. For instance, allowing the other party to achieve relative substantive success in a current negotiation may be balanced out by the establishment of a stronger relationship that might pay off and "balance the account" in subsequent encounters.

The final reading in this section, "Some Wise and Mistaken Assumptions about Conflict and Negotiation," is an excerpt from an address given by Jeffrey Rubin at the Society for the Psychological Study of Social Issues. Rubin discusses the subtle differences between *resolutions* and *settlements,* suggesting that settlements involve changed *behaviors,* while resolutions involve changed *attitudes.* Recognizing that attitudes are more deeply held and more difficult to change than behaviors (i.e., actions), negotiation is offered as a vehicle to enable behavioral change, which might—or might not—lead to attitudinal change. Regardless, settlement achieves conflict cessation. The article goes on to note that collaborative efforts are often not based on altruistic motives, but on the existence of a negotiator's "enlightened self interest"—the realization that the negotiator tends to do well only to the extent that the other party does well too. The relational aspect of negotiation is also indicated in Rubin's assertion "Rarely does one negotiate in the absence of future consequences."

Collaboration: The Constructive Management of Differences

Barbara Gray

The world must be kept safe for differences.

Clyde Kuckholn

THE NEED TO MANAGE DIFFERENCES

Our society is at a critical juncture. Constructive approaches for confronting difficult societal problems are essential to managing our global future. The pace at which new problems are generated is rapid, and individual organizations are hard pressed to make effective or timely responses. As a result, problems are piling up; new problems are cropping up daily, while yesterday's problems often go unsolved. Problems range in scope from local (such as allocating water rights for local development) to global (such as preventing deterioration of the ozone layer, which shields our planet from ultraviolet radiation).

This pileup of problems and the inability of organizations to contend with them reflects the turbulence of our environment. Under turbulent conditions organizations become highly interdependent with others in indirect but consequential ways (Emery and Trist, 1965, 1972; Trist, 1977). Under these circumstances it is difficult for individual organizations to act unilaterally to solve problems without creating unwanted consequences for other parties and without encountering constraints imposed by others. Because of this interdependence, the range of interests associated with any particular problem is wide and usually controversial.

Consider the situation in Franklin Township, a rural community adjacent to a growing midwestern university town.

In 1970 Franklin Township was a thriving farming community comprising many large family farms. Over the next 15 years Franklin Township's population increased from 759 to 975 residents as a few scattered tracts of farmland were sold for development. By the mid-1980s, developers began eyeing the township as a potential bedroom community. When an 80-acre tract of farmland was sold to a local farmer whose family had lived in the area since 1830, township residents breathed a sigh of relief. Development had been coming too fast, creating traffic and excessive demands on the local water system operated by the township's water company.

Reprinted from B. Gray, *Collaborating: Finding Common Ground for Multiparty Problems*, 1989, pp. 1–25. © Jossey-Bass. Used with permission.

Local residents were shocked a few months later when the farmer submitted plans to the township supervisors for a development of 80 one-acre lots. The community mobilized quickly, and 57 people showed up at the supervisors' meeting to protest the development. Many residents expressed concerns about overtaxing an already inadequate water supply. They carried a petition demanding the supervisors oppose the development and threatened to sue the water company and the township if they did not. The previous summer these residents had gone without water on several occasions during dry spells, and they feared the situation would worsen when 80 additional faucets were turned on.

A second group of residents, dubbed the "horse people," complained that the development would block their access to the riding trails in the state game lands that abutted the proposed development. These residents requested an easement for public access to the game lands. Objections also came from the residents whose private road was to become the gateway to the new homes and from the fruit farmer whose irrigation system depended on private wells close to the proposed development.

Franklin Township is a simple illustration of a situation in which the interests of multiple parties have become intertwined. The parties in the Franklin Township scenario include a neighbor-turned-developer, part-time township supervisors, local interest groups such as the "horse people," water company authorities, a local commercial farmer, and ordinary citizens concerned about taxes, traffic, and so forth. From many of their perspectives, the solution to the problem seems black-and-white—either support or oppose the development. Yet, for the township supervisors, the problem is more complex. They are faced with several questions: How should the township supervisors handle the developer's request for permits? How should they respond to the opposition from homeowners? What is the developer's responsibility to the community? Are the residents' concerns legitimate? Is it prudent to expect the water system to accommodate the new level of demand? What if other farmers followed suit and similar developments were proposed?

The township supervisors have several options. One is the "ostrich approach." They can postpone making a decision for as long as possible and hope the problem will go away. That outcome is, of course, unlikely since township ordinances usually mandate a specific response period. A second option is to take sides with one or more of the parties. There are several possible consequences of this choice, including escalation of the conflict, as township supervisors in North Salem, New York, recently discovered (Foderaro, 1988). In North Salem a developer sued the supervisors, charging that a new zoning ordinance was exclusionary. Dissension among the supervisors over development also caused one to resign and another to lose a bid for reelection.

Other options are available to the supervisors in Franklin Township. They can adopt a "hands off, let the experts decide" approach in which they rely on legal or engineering advisers to make the decisions for them. A fourth option, the traditional approach, involves holding public hearings in which interested parties can vent their concerns. These, however, frequently churn up issues and raise community expectations, often well beyond what responsible public officials can reasonably deliver. Though well intended, both of these options also often lead to less than satisfactory solutions.

One reason the solutions are unsatisfactory is that they are often not accepted by the public. For highly controversial issues, it is likely at least some of the public will not accept the decision of public officials, even when these officials decide only after conscientiously gathering and weighing information from all interested parties. Often, these officials must spend countless future hours justifying their decision after the fact. This problem occurs because parties who gave input do not know if or how their interests were considered during decision making (Delbecq, 1974; Wondolleck, 1985). Because parties are not privy to the process by which their interests and those of others are evaluated, those who gave input initially often feel betrayed when the final solution does not satisfy their requests (Carpenter and Kennedy, 1988). The problem of acceptance increases if the decision threatens basic values or creates a situation of high perceived risks for some stakeholders (Klein, 1976).

Seasoned public officials often become thick skinned, shrugging off the conflict with the adage "You can't please everyone." Unfortunately, heated issues do not die easily and often reemerge in an escalated form.

Additionally, there is growing evidence that for complex problems of this type, individual and collective efforts to solve them are often suboptimal because even well-intentioned decision makers do not really understand the interests they are trying to reconcile (Fisher and Ury, 1981; Wondolleck, 1985; Lax and Sebenius, 1986). Research has shown, for example, that it is often possible to improve on an agreement through a procedure called postsettlement settlement (Raiffa, 1985). In this procedure, parties reach a preliminary agreement and then invite a third party to review it and recommend improvements that benefit all of the parties. Often these opportunities for joint gains lie in trade-offs that the parties were unable to recognize for themselves (Lax and Sebenius, 1986). Procedures that encourage parties to search for these joint gains have the potential to produce better agreements and to prevent escalation.

In light of this, consider a fifth option available to the Franklin Township supervisors. They can assemble a representative sample of the stakeholders (those with a stake in the problem) and let them work out an agreement among themselves. The stakeholders in this case include the developer, the commercial fruit farmer, the township supervisors, the "horse people," the water company board, the homeowners concerned about water, and the homeowners concerned about traffic. This option has the advantage of dealing with interrelated issues in the same forum, since the township supervisors do not have jurisdiction over the water company but do have authority to approve or disapprove the rest of the development plan. Getting all the stakeholders together to explore their concerns in a constructive way allows them to search for a solution they can all accept and averts the potential for escalation of the conflict. Additionally, the supervisors do not abdicate their responsibility, because they must agree to any decision that is reached. This approach is called collaboration.

COLLABORATION AS AN ALTERNATIVE

Collaboration is a process through which parties who see different aspects of a problem can constructively explore their differences and search for solutions that go beyond their own limited vision of what is possible. Collaboration is based on the simple adages that "two heads are better than one" and that one by itself is simply not good enough! Those parties with an interest in the problem are termed stakeholders. Stakeholders include all individuals, groups, or organizations that are directly influenced by actions others take to solve the problem. Each stakeholder has a unique appreciation of the problem. The objective of collaboration is to create a richer, more comprehensive appreciation of the problem among the stakeholders than any one of them could construct alone. The term *problem domain* will be used here to refer to the way a problem is conceptualized by the stakeholders (Trist, 1983).

A kaleidoscope is a useful image to envision what joint appreciation of a domain is all about. As the kaleidoscope is rotated, different configurations of the same collection of colored shapes appear. Collaboration involves building a common understanding of how these images appear from their respective points of view. This understanding forms the basis for choosing a collective course of action.

Collaboration is not really a new concept. It is not unlike the town meeting concept, which is a cornerstone of the democratic process. Town meetings turn on the principles of local participation and ownership of decisions. Collaboration reflects a resurgence of interest in those fundamental principles. Any one of the stakeholders in Franklin Township could suggest that they try collaboration. Because of their responsibility for rendering a permit decision, however, the township supervisors are in the best position to initiate a collaborative dialogue. Their role in such a process would be to help the parties articulate their interests and to facilitate a reconciliation.

Questions like those facing the supervisors and residents of Franklin Township are being asked in communities around the world. In some, like Franklin Township, the issues are controversial. In other cases, such as those concerning the cleanup of toxic dumps or the destruction of the ozone layer, the issues are scientifically and politically complex, involve many interested parties, and are often hotly contested.

Not all occasions for collaboration are conflict induced. In some cases, parties may have a shared interest in solving a problem that none of them alone can address. The opportunity for collaborating arises because stakeholders recognize the potential advantages of working together. They may need each other to execute a vision that they all share. Managing a joint business venture is a good example. Addressing the problem of illiteracy in a community is another. Parties come together because each needs the others to advance their individual interests. Opportunities for collaborating are arising in countless arenas in which business, government, labor, and communities are finding their actions interconnected with those of other stakeholders. In the next section, several public- and private-sector opportunities for constructive collaboration are considered.

OPPORTUNITIES FOR COLLABORATING

Situations that provide opportunities for collaborating are many and varied. They include joint ventures among selected businesses, settlement of local neighborhood or environmental disputes, revitalization of economically depressed cities, and resolution of major international problems. These opportunities can be classified into two general categories: resolving conflicts and advancing shared visions.

Resolving Conflict

Collaboration can be used effectively to settle disputes between the parties in multiparty conflict. Collaboration transforms adversarial interaction into a mutual search for information and for solutions that allow all those participating to insure that their interests are represented. Often, parties in conflict are motivated to try collaboration only as a last-ditch effort when other approaches have reached impasse or have produced less than acceptable outcomes. Parties will try collaboration only if they belief they have something to gain from it. In protracted stalemates, for example, the cost to all parties of inaction may be a sufficient incentive to induce collaboration.

Collaboration has been used to settle hundreds of site-specific environmental disputes (Bingham, 1986), important product liability cases, intergovernmental disputes, and many other community controversies involving transportation, housing, and mortgage lending. Within the environmental area, Bingham (1986) has identified six broad categories within which collaborative solutions to disputes have been sought: land use, natural resource management and public land use, water resources, energy, air quality, and toxics.

The potential for collaboration in international affairs also appears promising. Within the last year a number of major political conflicts have moved from stalemate to early dialogue, signaling a growing potential to search for alternatives to violence. In addition, the list of major global issues in which the interests of several nation-states, nongovernmental organizations (NGOs), and multinational corporations intersect continues to grow. Salient issues include a variety of property rights issues related to the use of the seas and exploration in Antarctica, global environmental issues such as the future of rain forests and control of acid rain, and transnational technology issues such as the management of international telecommunications. For problems of this scope, international collaboration is essential for finding solutions.

The chlorofluorocarbons treaty reached in Montreal in March 1987 provides one model of successful international collaboration. The treaty is historical because it is the first international agreement designed to avert a global disaster (Benedick, 1988). The treaty restricts the production of chemicals (chlorofluorocarbons and others) that erode the stratospheric ozone layer, which protects the earth from the sun's damaging ultraviolet rays. Stakeholders included chlorofluorocarbon producers in several countries, NGOs such as environmental groups and the United Nations Environment Program, members of the scientific community, and governments from the North and the South. Forty-eight countries have signed the treaty, and it is awaiting formal ratification by the countries involved. In addition to the freeze on production, the treaty paves the way for discussions of longer-term strategies to preserve the ozone layer.

Advancing Shared Visions

Collaborations induced by shared visions are intended to advance the collective good of the stakeholders involved. Some are designed to address socioeconomic issues such as illiteracy, youth unemployment, housing, or homelessness, which cut across public- and private-sector interests. Collaborating is also becoming increasingly crucial to successful business management, as companies see advantages in sharing research and development costs (Dimancescu and Botkin, 1986) and exploring new markets through joint ventures (Perlmutter and Heenan, 1986). The proliferation of joint ventures in the auto industry alone has surprised analysts, who a decade ago were predicting a major shakeout in that industry would force many automakers to go out of business (Holusha, 1988).

Public-private partnerships that have sprung up to address deteriorating conditions in U.S. cities are illustrative of collaborative efforts across sectors to advance shared visions. In these partnerships, public and private interests pool their resources and undertake joint planning to tackle economic redevelopment, education, housing, and other protracted problems that have plagued their communities. In the area of education, for example, representatives of industry, labor, and schools have teamed up to deal with youth unemployment and juvenile crime (Elsman and The National Institute for Work and Learning, 1981). These and other partnerships such as the Boston Compact, the Greater Baltimore Committee, the Newark Collaboration, and the Whittier Alliance in Minneapolis began with stakeholders articulating a desirable future they collectively wanted to pursue.

Successfully advancing a shared vision, whether in the public or the private sector, requires identification and coordination of a diverse set of stakeholders, each of whom holds some but not all of the necessary resources. To be successful, coordination must be accomplished laterally without the hierarchical authority to which most managers are accustomed. These circumstances require a radically different approach to organizing and managing, especially for international joint ventures.

> The challenge of managing these coalitions is staggering, given the complexity of the stakeholder network that often involves at least two foreign governments. As a result, interorganizational relations must be carefully worked through in order to gain the advantages of such a union [Heenan and Perlmutter, 1979, p. 82].

Even when parties agree initially on a shared vision, collaboration among them is not necessarily free of conflict. Conflicts inevitably ensue over plans for how the vision should be carried out. And further problems typically arise when stakeholders try to implement their agreements. Overcoming the barriers created by different institutional cultures is frequently a formidable task. Getting the business community and a major urban school district to work together on problems of youth employment, for example, requires considerable adaptation on the part of each. Similar obstacles must be overcome by Japanese and American managers who are trying to implement a management system for a new joint venture (Holusha, 1988).

Nature of Collaborative Problems

It should be clear by now that there is no shortage of problems for which collaboration offers a decided advantage over other methods of decision making. The characteristics of these problems can be described generally as follows:

- The problems are ill defined, or there is disagreement about how they should be defined.
- Several stakeholders have a vested interest in the problems and are interdependent.
- These stakeholders are not necessarily identified a priori or organized in any systematic way.
- There may be a disparity of power and/or resources for dealing with the problems among the stakeholders.
- Stakeholders may have different levels of expertise and different access to information about the problems.

- The problems are often characterized by technical complexity and scientific uncertainty.
- Differing perspectives on the problems often lead to adversarial relationships among the stakeholders.
- Incremental or unilateral efforts to deal with the problems typically produce less than satisfactory solutions.
- Existing processes for addressing the problems have proved insufficient and may even exacerbate them.

Problems with these characteristics have been dubbed "messes" (Ackoff, 1974) or metaproblems (Chevalier, 1966). What is needed to deal constructively with problems of this type is an alternative model of how to organize to solve them. This book proposes a model of organizing based on collaboration among the parties rather than on competition, hierarchy, or incremental planning (Trist, 1977). This book offers a comprehensive treatment of collaborative dynamics in the hope that potential parties will appreciate how they can use collaboration to successfully address multiparty problems. Let us turn now to an in-depth look at what collaborating entails.

DYNAMICS OF COLLABORATION

Collaboration involves a process of joint decision making among key stakeholders of a problem domain about the future of that domain. Five features are critical to the process: (1) the stakeholders are interdependent, (2) solutions emerge by dealing constructively with differences, (3) joint ownership of decisions is involved, (4) stakeholders assume collective responsibility for the future direction of the domain, and (5) collaboration is an emergent process.

Collaboration Implies Interdependence

Collaboration establishes a give and take among the stakeholders that is designed to produce solutions that none of them working independently could achieve. Therefore, an important ingredient of collaboration is interdependence among the stakeholders. Initially, the extent of interdependence may not be fully appreciated by all the parties. Therefore, the initial phase of any collaboration usually involves calling attention to the ways in which the stakeholders' concerns are intertwined and the reasons why they need each other to solve the problem. Parties in conflict especially lose sight of their underlying interdependence. Heightening parties' awareness of their interdependence often kindles renewed willingness to search for trade-offs that could produce a mutually beneficial solution. In the collaborations investigated in this book, external events often propel reexamination of taken-for-granted interdependencies.

Solutions Emerge by Dealing Constructively with Differences

Respect for differences is an easy virtue to champion verbally and a much more difficult one to put into practice in our day-to-day affairs. Yet differences are often the source of immense creative potential. Learning to harness that potential is what collaboration is all about.

Consider the parable of the elephant and the blind men. Several blind men walking through the jungle come upon an elephant. Each approaches the elephant from a different angle and comes into contact with a different part of the elephant's anatomy. The blind man who contacts the elephant's leg declares, "Oh, an elephant is like a tree trunk." Another, who apprehends the elephant's tail, objects to the first's description, exclaiming, "Oh, no, the elephant is like a rope." A third, grasping the elephant's large, floppy ear, insists, "You are both wrong; the elephant is like a fan." Clearly, each man, from his vantage point, has apprehended something important and genuine about the elephant. Each one's perception of elephant is accurate, albeit limited. None of the blind men, through his own inquiries, has a comprehensive understanding of the phenomenon called "elephant." Together, however, they have a much richer and more complete perspective.

Like the blind men, most of us routinely make a number of assumptions that limit our ability to capitalize on this creative potential. One assumption that we frequently make is that our way of viewing a problem is the best. Best to us may mean the most rational, the fairest, the most intelligent, or even the only way. No matter what the basis, we arrive at the conclusion that our way is superior to any other. Thus we lose sight of the possibility that multiple approaches to the elephant yield multiple perceptions about what is possible and what is desirable.

Even if we grant that multiple perceptions are possible, we can easily fall prey to another common assumption; that is, we conclude that different interpretations are, by definition, opposing interpretations. But here we need to distinguish between interpretations that differ from each other and those that are truly opposed. As Fisher and Ury have aptly pointed out, "Agreement is possible precisely because interests differ" (1981, p. 44). Without differing interests, the range of possible exchanges between parties would be nonexistent. Because parties' interests do vary, as do the resources and skills they have to solve a problem, they are able to arrange trade-offs and to forge mutually beneficial alliances.

It is also frequently the case that as we strive to articulate our differences, we discover that our underlying concerns are fundamentally the same. These shared concerns may have been masked by the different ways we described or framed the problem or may have been obscured by strong emotions that deafened us to the messages coming from the other parties. Parties in conflict are known to engage in selective listening and to pay more attention to information that confirms their preconceived stereotypes of their opponents. Stereotypes cause us to discount the legitimacy of the other's point of view and cause both sides to ignore data that disconfirm their stereotypes (Sherif, 1958). Stereotypes also restrict the flow of information between the parties. Without this exchange of information, the parties cannot discover clues about their shared or differing interests that may contain the seeds of an agreement.

Stereotyping figures prominently in the type of complex multiparty disputes addressed in this book. Frequently the parties have had a long history of interaction, fighting out their differences in legislative and judicial arenas. Working on opposite sides in these arenas allows the parties to continually reconfirm their stereotypic impressions with hard evidence (about the other side's motives, values, and willingness to reach accommodation). Collaboration operates on the premise that the assumptions that disputants have about the other side and about the nature of the issues themselves are worth testing. The premise is that testing these assumptions and allowing a constructive confrontation of differences may unlock heretofore disguised creative potential. Through such exploration stakeholders may discover new options that permit constructive mergers of interests previously unimagined or judged infeasible.

Collaboration Involves Joint Ownership of Decisions

Joint ownership means that the participants in a collaboration are directly responsible for reaching agreement on a solution. Unlike litigation or regulation, in which intermediaries (courts, regulatory agencies, legislators) devise solutions that are imposed on the stakeholders, in collaborative agreements the parties impose decisions on themselves. They set the agenda; they decide what issues will be addressed; they decide what the terms will be. Any agreements that are reached may be free-standing contracts, or they may serve as input to a legal or a public policy process that ratifies, codifies, or in some other way incorporates the agreements. Clearly where matters of public policy are under consideration, collaboration cannot serve as a substitute for constitutional decision-making processes. However, it can "provide a sense of direction, smooth social conflict, and speed formal processes" (Dunlop, 1986, p. 24).

When collaboration occurs, the various stakeholders bring their idiosyncratic perceptions of the problem to the negotiations. Each holds assumptions, beliefs, and viewpoints that are consistent with their independent efforts to confront the problem. Through collaboration these multiple perspectives are aired and debated, and gradually a more complete appreciation of the complexity of the problem is constructed. This more complete appreciation forms the basis for envisioning new alternatives that take into account the stakeholders' multiple interests. Thus, the outcome of collaboration is a weaving together of multiple and diverse viewpoints into a mosaic replete with new insights and directions for action agreed on by all the stakeholders. Three key steps in reaching a joint decision include (1) the joint search for information about the problem, (2) the invention of a mutually agreed upon solution about the pattern of future exchanges between stakeholders, and (3) ratification of the agreement and plans for implementing it.

Stakeholders Assume Collective Responsibility
for Future Direction of the Domain

One outcome of collaboration is a set of agreements governing future interactions among the stakeholders. Trist (1983) refers to this as self-regulation of the domain. During collaboration a new set of relationships among the stakeholders is negotiated as they address the problem at hand. The process of collaborating essentially restructures the socially accepted rules for dealing with problems of this type. The negotiations may also restructure the rules governing how stakeholders will interact with respect to the problem in the future. That is, formal or informal contracts about the nature of subsequent exchanges among the stakeholders are forged during collaboration. Collaboration may lead to increased coordination among the stakeholders, although that is not a necessary outcome of the process.

Collaboration Is an Emergent Process

Collaboration is essentially an emergent process rather than a prescribed state of organization. By viewing collaboration as a process, it becomes possible to describe its origins and development as well as how its organization changes over time. Hence, collaboration can be thought of as a temporary and evolving forum for addressing a problem. Typically, collaborations progress from "underorganized systems" in which individual stakeholders act independently, if at all, with respect to the problem (Brown, 1980) to more tightly organized relationships characterized by concerted decision making among the stakeholders.

Collaboration as it is defined here should be distinguished from the terms *cooperation* and *coordination* as used by Mulford and Rogers (1982). They use these terms to classify static patterns of interorganizational relations. Coordination refers to formal institutionalized relationships among existing networks of organizations, while cooperation is "characterized by informal trade-offs and by attempts to establish reciprocity in the absence of rules" (Mulford and Rogers, 1982, p. 13). While these distinctions may be useful for distinguishing formal and informal relationships, they do not capture the dynamic evolutionary character of the phenomenon described in this book. To presume that the parties in a collaborative effort are already part of an organized relationship underrepresents the developmental character of the process and ignores the delicate prenegotiations that are often necessary to bring stakeholders together initially.

Both cooperation and coordination often occur as part of the process of collaborating. The process by which reciprocity is established informally in the absence of rules is as important to collaboration as the formal coordination agreements that eventually emerge. Skillful management of early interactions is often crucial to continued collaboration, since these informal interactions lay the groundwork for subsequent formal interactions.

Once initiated, collaboration creates a temporary forum within which consensus about the problem can be sought, mutually agreeable solutions can be invented, and collective actions to implement the solutions can be taken. Understanding how this process unfolds is critical to successfully managing the kinds of multiparty and multiorganizational relations described earlier in the chapter.

Envisioning interorganizational relations as processes rather than as outcomes in which stakeholders assume decision-making responsibility for their collective future permits investigation of how innovation and change in currently unsatisfactory exchange relationships can occur. If collaboration is successful, new solutions emerge that no single party could have envisioned or enacted. A successful example can best illustrate the dynamics of collaboration.

SUCCESSFUL COLLABORATION

Pernicious stereotypes and misinformation precipitated a major conflict between government agencies and citizens in the community surrounding Three Mile Island Nuclear Reactor. The conflict surfaced over plans for cleanup of the reactor, which was badly damaged during a catastrophic accident in 1979. Through an unprecedented intervention, called the Citizens' Radiation Monitoring Program, local residents and the federal and state governments collaboratively generated credible information to assuage residents' fears about radiation exposure during the initial phase of the cleanup (see Gricar and Baratta [1983] for a more detailed description).

Citizens' Radiation Monitoring Program

The accident at Three Mile Island (TMI) in March 1979 released small but significant levels of radioactivity into the atmosphere, exposing residents of the area surrounding TMI to a maximum radiation dosage twice that of average yearly background levels. Despite reports of no immediate or long-term health effects from the accident, many residents were concerned about the risks associated with radiation exposure. These concerns were heightened when Metropolitan Edison (the operator of Three Mile Island) proposed releasing low levels of radioactive krypton gas into the atmosphere as the first step in the proposed cleanup of the reactor. The full extent of damage to the reactor could not be determined until the gas it contained was removed. The staff of the Nuclear Regulatory Commission (NRC) had determined that the purge would not endanger the health and safety of the public (TMI Support Staff, 1980).

At the time public trust in Met Ed and the NRC was seriously eroded because of the widespread belief that these agencies had deliberately misled the public about radiation levels during the accident. The NRC's own special inquiry into the accident attributed what it called "public misconceptions about risks" to "a failure to convey credible information regarding the actual risks in an understandable fashion to the public" (Rogovin, 1980). This mistrust prompted several communities to appeal to the governor and to the president for independent sources of information about radiation levels. Concern about the risks grew to extreme proportions in March 1980 during public meetings on the environmental impact of the purge. Public opposition to the proposed purge was so fierce that it drowned out the NRC's announcement that a community monitoring program was under way.

In February, the U.S. Department of Energy (DOE) assembled a team of representatives (called the Technical Working Group) from the Environmental Protection Agency, the Pennsylvania Department of Environmental Resources (DER), the Pennsylvania State University, and EG&G Idaho (a technical consultant to Met Ed) to design and implement the Citizens' Radiation Monitoring Program. The program's purpose was to ensure that citizens in the vicinity of TMI received accurate and credible information about radiation levels during the purge. The program was based on the premise that citizens were more likely to believe information generated by themselves or by their neighbors than by government officials, whose credibility they considered questionable. Through the program, local citizens conducted routine monitoring of radiation levels using equipment provided by the Department of Energy.

The Technical Working Group (TWG) sought input on the design of the program from officials of three counties and 12 municipalities that fell within a five-mile radius of TMI. Each community nominated four citizens to serve as monitors. The monitors included teachers, secretaries, engineers, housewives, police officers, and retirees. They ranged in age from early twenties to senior citizens. Their political persuasions about nuclear power ran the gamut from pro- to antinuclear. The monitors were given an intensive "crash course" on radiation and its effects and detection methods, and were given hands-on training so that they could operate the monitoring equipment and interpret the measurements for their fellow citizens.

Each participating community drew up its own monitoring schedule and selected the locations for its monitoring equipment. The citizen monitors posted daily results of the monitoring in the townships, and the TWG disseminated the results to the local media and to the participating agencies.

The Citizen's Radiation Monitoring Program represents a dramatic departure from typical government efforts to communicate with the public. In this case, traditional efforts by government agencies to disseminate public information were grossly ineffective and only increased public mistrust of the agencies. Following months of technical review of Met Ed's proposal for the purge, the NRC tried at public meetings to present a rational argument in support of the purge. Both the meetings and the environmental assessment itself focused exclusively on the technical aspects of reactor decontamination. Rational arguments, however, meant little to citizens whose calculation of the risks involved was much more personal. The accident clearly had left social and psychological scars on the community (Scranton, 1980; Kemeny, 1979; Brunn, Johnson, and Ziegler, 1979) and had created widespread uncertainty about safety. Because of general unfamiliarity with radiation and its effects, the lack of credible information, and the imperceptible nature of radiation itself, the public had little basis for judging either the level of danger or its seriousness. With no precedents to consider, it is not surprising that public fears about potential risks were running high.

Perceptions by public officials that those who resisted were troublemakers or fanatics only fueled the controversy. By underestimating the degree to which emotional concerns for safety shaped public attitudes, these officials reduced their own credibility and further escalated public mistrust.

Collaboration in this case occurred among the Department of Energy, the other agencies involved in the Technical Working Group, and the local municipalities and counties.

Let us examine this case with respect to the five features of collaboration described above. First, how were the stakeholders interdependent? The stakeholders in this case were interdependent because neither Met Ed nor the community could afford not to begin cleanup of the reactor. Leaving the krypton gas inside the reactor posed an unknown risk to the public and prevented Met Ed from determining the extent of damage from the accident. Thus safe but timely decontamination of the reactor was critical.

Second, how were differences handled? Initially in this case there were very different perceptions about safety and about the credibility of those agencies disseminating safety information. Prior to the monitoring program, Met Ed and the government agencies had relied on a rational, technocratic approach to educate the public and had dismissed the citizens' concerns as irrational. The monitoring program was an acknowledgment that these differing perceptions of risk needed to be addressed, not ignored. Enlisting local citizens as monitors was a novel and unprecedented step by these agencies, which typically relied on narrow, technically oriented solutions.

Third, were the stakeholders jointly involved in decision making? The initial proposal for citizen monitoring came from the mayor of one of the affected communities. Exploratory meetings involved several, but not all, stakeholder groups. Once the DOE made the decision to go ahead, decision making was shared among several agencies in the TWG, and, to a lesser extent, the local communities and their citizen monitors participated in making decisions about the execution of the program. Met Ed, a key stakeholder, was purposely excluded from the group because its participation would likely have damaged the credibility of the entire effort. Thus, this process did not provide for full participation by all the stakeholders, but it did incorporate widespread representation in the overall planning.

Fourth, who assumed responsibility for the future direction of the domain? This case graphically illustrates how responsibility for ensuring that credible information about radiation levels was available to the communities surrounding TMI was shared among the stakeholders. The DOE supplied the financial resources; EG&G Idaho, the EPA, and the DER contributed technical expertise and staff; the university designed the equipment and provided training and organizational expertise; and the citizens donated their time and talent to carry out the monitoring.

Finally, to what extent was the collaboration emergent? The process of collaborating grew out of a major public controversy. At the outset, mechanisms for managing the differing interests and coordinating a viable plan of action were underdeveloped. The Citizens' Radiation Monitoring Program emerged through a series of steps. It began with the citizens' opposition to the venting and their plea for credible information. This was followed by the formation of the TWG, involvement of the communities, creation of the training program, and, finally, the monitoring itself. Because of the urgency of the situation, the entire collaborative process lasted only five months.

The consequences of this collaborative effort are summarized below:

- Met Ed was allowed to execute a critical first step in the reactor cleanup process.

- Residents in the community received information they could trust to judge their own levels of radiation exposure. A survey conducted before and after the training indicated a significant increase in the monitors' belief that they could get accurate information about radiation levels and that they had sufficient information to make a judgment about their own safety (Gricar and Baratta, 1983).

- Residents who participated as monitors gained a deeper appreciation for the technical issues associated with nuclear power and engaged in rational dialogue and debate with each other on contested topics during the training program.

In addition to the above outcomes, the Citizens' Radiation Monitoring Program demonstrated that government, communities, and the private sector often hold very different perceptions about a problem. Without a frank and open dialogue characterized by reason and respect, these perceptions cannot be examined. Had the NRC proceeded with the purge without community guarantees about credible information, the conflict would only have escalated, probably to the level of violence.

BENEFITS OF COLLABORATING

When collaboration is used to address multiparty problems, several benefits are possible (see Table 1).

First, collaboration increases the quality of solutions considered by the parties because solutions are based on a broad, comprehensive analysis of the problem. The collective capacity to respond to the problem is also increased as stakeholders apply a variety of complementary resources to solving it. Collaboration also offers a way to reopen negotiations when impasse imperils more traditional processes. More important, use of collaboration early in a multiparty conflict can minimize the possibility that impasse will occur.

TABLE 1   The Benefits of Collaboration

- Broad comprehensive analysis of the problem domain improves the quality of solutions.
- Response capability is more diversified.
- It is useful for reopening deadlocked negotiations.
- The risk of impasse is minimized.
- The process ensures that each stakeholder's interests are considered in any agreement.
- Parties retain ownership of the solution.
- Parties most familiar with the problem, not their agents, invent the solutions.
- Participation enhances acceptance of solution and willingness to implement it.
- The potential to discover novel, innovative solutions is enhanced.
- Relations between the stakeholders improve.
- Costs associated with other methods are avoided.
- Mechanisms for coordinating future actions among the stakeholders can be established.

The process of collaborating builds in certain guarantees that each party's interests will be protected. It does so by continually remanding ownership of the process and any decisions reached to the parties themselves. Parties often assume that by collaborating they will lose any individual leverage they have over the problem. This concern about loss of control is deceptive, however. It is rare in any multiparty conflict that any party satisfies 100 percent of their interests and incurs no costs while the other parties gain nothing. Collaborative processes protect each party's interests by guaranteeing that they are heard and understood. In addition, the processes are structured to ensure that ownership of the solution remains with the participants since ratification hinges on their reaching agreement among themselves.

> Instead of trying to restrict participation, a common tactic, the professional manager gains more control over the situation by ensuring that all the necessary parties are there at the table, recognizing that parties in a dispute often engage in adversarial behavior because no other approach is available to protect their interests [Carpenter and Kennedy, 1988, p. 26].

Parties retain control during collaboration precisely because *they* must be the ones to adopt or reject the final agreement.

Ownership of the process and of the outcomes generates two additional benefits. The parties themselves, who are most familiar with the problem, not their agents, fashion the solution. Additionally, commitment to the solution is generally high as a result of collaboration. Investment in a process of building a comprehensive appreciation of the problem and designing a solution jointly enhances the parties' acceptance of the solution and their commitment to carry it out (Delbecq, 1974).

By focusing on interests and encouraging the exploration of differences, the potential to discover novel, innovative solutions like the Citizens' Radiation Monitoring Program is enhanced. Even when parties are unable to reach closure through collaboration, some benefits from collaborating are still possible. Collaborating usually leaves parties with a clearer understanding of their differences and an improved working relationship. These outcomes permit the parties to amicably "agree to disagree" or to accept a decision imposed by a traditional dispute resolution forum in lieu of reaching a collaborative agreement. Sometimes parties reach agreement on all but one or two areas and turn to a judicial or administrative agency to resolve the remaining disagreements.

Collaboration also has the potential to reduce the costs parties incur from acting alone or the costs associated with protracted conflict among the stakeholders. Although it is difficult to make reliable comparisons (of the cost of collaborating versus not doing so), it is reasonable to assume that collaboration can reduce the cost of hiring intermediaries (such as attorneys in legal disputes), the cost of research and development (R&D) expenditures for partners in R&D consortia, and a myriad of social costs stemming from protracted inaction on critical social and international problems.

Finally, through collaboration stakeholders can develop mechanisms to coordinate their future interactions. Through this coordination, stakeholders take concerted rather than disconnected actions to manage the problem domain, and interdependencies become more predictable.

REALITIES OF COLLABORATING

Just as it is important to articulate the benefits of collaborating, it is equally important to dispel the notion that collaboration is a cure for all evils. There are many circumstances in which stakeholders are unable or unwilling to engage each other in this way. Collaboration is not always an appropriate alternative. For example, when one party has unchallenged power to influence a domain, collaboration does not make sense . . .

Nor is collaboration an idealistic panacea. Realistically, collaboration involves difficult issues that have often eluded simple solutions in the past. Many multiparty problems are political in nature because they involve "distributional" issues. In distributional disputes the stakeholders are concerned about the allocation of funds, the setting of standards, or the siting of facilities. Groups in distributional disputes are contesting "a specific allocation of gains and losses" (Susskind and Cruikshank, 1987, p. 19). Allocating gains and losses, however, involves the allocation of risks that, as the Three Mile Island case illustrated, are perceived very differently by different stakeholders. Moreover, perceptions of risk often have deep psychological and emotional roots. Dealing with these emotional attachments is a tricky business. Success depends as much on the process of legitimizing parties' interests as on the substantive outcomes. The design of meetings between stakeholders is crucial to success. Many well-intended efforts to involve the public in government decisions, for example, are exercises in frustration and often exacerbate rather than improve the situation because careful attention to the process of managing differences is neglected (Wondolleck, 1985; Carpenter and Kennedy, 1988).

Thus, solving complex multiparty problems requires more than sound economic policies and technological breakthroughs. It also demands careful attention to the process of making decisions. Successful collaborations are not achieved without considerable effort on the part of the participating stakeholders and usually not without the skill and forbearance of a convening organization and/or a skilled third party. Often parties perceive real risks to collaborating, if only because the process is unfamiliar and the outcomes are uncertain. Unless issues like these and more serious ones such as concerns about cooptation or lack of fairness are dispelled up front, attempts at collaboration will not succeed. It is often the convener or third party who initially proposes the possibility of collaborating and who then shepherds the parties through a collaborative process. Hence, for collaboration to occur, someone must introduce a mind set, a vision, a belief in the creative potential of managing differences, and must couple this mind set with a constructive process for designing creative solutions to complex multiparty problems.

. . . Negotiation is not used here to denote specific tactics of positional bargaining, which are often associated with collective bargaining or buyer-seller transactions. Instead, negotiation is used in the broader sociological sense used by Strauss (1978). Through their talk, stakeholders try to arrive at collective interpretations of how they see the world. These interpretations form the basis for actions. Negotiation, therefore, refers to conversational interactions among collaborating parties as they try to define a problem, agree on recommendations, or design action steps. In this way they create a negotiated order . . .

Not all collaborations lead to agreements for action, but when agreements are reached, they are arrived at by consensus. Consensus is achieved when each of the stakeholders agrees they can live with a proposed solution, even though it may not be their most preferred solution. Both consensus building and negotiation . . . refer to the process of constructing agreements among the stakeholders.

Collaboration can occur with or without the assistance of a third party who serves as a mediator or facilitator. The task of the third party is not to render a decision (in the way that a judge does, for instance) but to help structure a dialogue within which the parties can work out their differences. The term *mediator* will generally be used here to refer to this third-party role.

Step into My Parlor: A Survey of Strategies and Techniques for Effective Negotiation

Terry Anderson

The idea of active negotiation is intimidating to most people. It conjures up images of smoke-filled rooms, raised voices, dirty tricks, and interminable haggling sessions encompassing a potential win-lose situation that could involve anything from personal relationships to nuclear warfare. Furthermore, most people are generally dubious of their own negotiating skills relative to those of other individuals. They consider encounters with blue-chip negotiators as perilous contests during which they stand a good chance of having the shirt talked right off their backs. Add to this the fact that the most significant negotiation activities are those associated with stressful, life-change events—the compensation package for a new job, custody rights in a divorce, the selling price of a new home—and it is no small wonder that most people have an instinctive aversion to the idea of negotiation. This fear of negotiation has made numerous lawyers, mediators, and professional arbitrators rich.

Like many things in life, negotiation is an aspect of reality that needs to be mastered rather than feared. In fact, skilled negotiators will only deliver a more thorough beating if they smell the fear of an opponent. As a result, it is important to learn effective negotiation techniques as a self-defense mechanism. Putting these techniques into practice and knowing when they are being used by others increase the probability of acquiring greater material rewards. Moreover, the likelihood of sustaining a productive relationship with others can be significantly improved. However, "despite its importance, the negotiation process is often misunderstood and badly carried out. Inferior agreements result, if not endless bickering, needless deadlock, or spiraling conflict" (Lax and Sebenius 1986).

SUBSTANTIVE AND RELATIONSHIP OUTCOMES

Of course, one of the primary incentives for negotiating is the pursuit of material, substantive outcomes: the raise, the promotion, or the rust-proofing option on a new car. However, because a crucial context for any bargaining session is the negotiators'

Reprinted from *Business Horizons*, May–June 1992, pp. 71–76. Reprinted with permission of JAI Press.

current and desired relationship with each other, the pursuit of these incentives is moderated by the pursuit of a positive relationship between the parties. Before rushing to secure the best possible substantive outcome, the negotiators must assess the impact of their respective negotiation strategies on the relationship that currently exists between them. Obviously, respective levels of power and conflict weigh heavily in this assessment.

The relative power of each negotiator is established by the extent of each party's dependence on the other. Individuals tend to assess the relative levels of power existing in a relationship and then choose whether to compete, accommodate, collaborate, or withdraw when negotiating with others. The level of conflict in a negotiation setting is established by how the negotiators perceive the effective dimension of their relationship—that is, its supportiveness or hostility. Indeed, the pursuit of a positive relationship between negotiating parties may be a primary motivation for continuing negotiation, even at the sacrifice of substantive outcomes, particularly if the relationship has deteriorated and is more highly valued than the issues on the table.

NEGOTIATION STRATEGIES

Only by appraising both their own and the other party's substantive and relationship priorities can negotiators effectively choose a negotiation strategy. To prevent reliance on intuition alone, researchers and academicians have developed formal models, such as simulation programs and decision trees, designed to train and assist individuals in selecting the most appropriate negotiation strategy. "Many people, due to their lack of awareness of any structured approach to the negotiating process, are forced to reuse self-taught methods that have merely appeared to work in the past—methods that were acquired, like diseases, from social contact. There is, however, an important and useful difference between merely knowing a few cunning homemade techniques and understanding the full cooperative human process of negotiation" (Nierenberg 1971).

Although formal approaches serve to add structure to the selection of negotiation strategies, they remain only barely perceptible outlines in a very foggy picture. For this reason, it is important not to be seduced into thinking that the process of negotiation is as simple as some of these models may imply, for the insight and intuition of the negotiator largely provide the musculature necessary to put these strategies into practice. With this in mind, it is useful to survey an entire spectrum of negotiation strategies in a structured yet realistic manner. Generally, negotiators and analysts tend to separate into two groups that are guided by conflicting conceptions of the bargaining process: symbiotic and predatory.

Symbiosis

This negotiation ideology is so named for its predisposition to create value by means of the bargaining process. Symbiotic negotiators tend to believe that mutual agreements are reached by being inventive, collaborative, and persistent in searching for substantial joint gains and the creation of value, relative to no-agreement possibilities. Stressing the importance of open communication and information sharing, symbiotic negotiators are sometimes apt to practice the immoderate strategy of open submission by conceding all but the barest substantive aspects of the negotiation in an attempt to build a productive relationship with the other party. The perception of relationship building as a positive outcome of such a negotiation yields the joint gains necessary for a symbiotic strategy. One side receives primarily substantive gains, while the other side receives the benefits of a strengthened relationship that could come to fruition in the form of future material rewards.

Another symbiotic bargaining strategy is often referred to as "win-win" negotiation, in which both sides win—or at least no one loses. Using this strategy, joint gains are achieved by avoiding actions that tend to worsen the relationship between the parties while increasing the substantive elements of the negotiation. This is accomplished through the bipartisan efforts of both parties to either make the value of the "pie" larger, or to find elements within it to satisfy both parties.

The Egyptian-Israeli peace treaty formulated at Camp David in 1978 illustrates the ideology behind this negotiation strategy:

> Israel had occupied the Egyptian Sinai Peninsula since the Six Day War of 1967. When Egypt and Israel sat down together in 1978 to negotiate a peace, their positions were incompatible. Israel insisted on keeping some of the Sinai. Egypt, on the other hand, insisted that every inch of the Sinai be returned to Egyptian sovereignty. People continuously drew maps showing possible boundary lines that would divide the Sinai between Egypt and Israel. Compromising in this way was wholly unacceptable to Egypt. To go back to the situation as it was in 1967 was equally unacceptable to Israel.
>
> Looking at their interests instead of their positions made it possible for Israel and Egypt to develop a solution. Israel's interest lay in security; they did not want Egyptian tanks poised on their border ready to roll across at any time. Egypt's interest lay in sovereignty; the Sinai had been part of Egypt since the time of the Pharaohs. After centuries of domination by Greeks, Romans, Turks, French, and British, Egypt had only recently regained full sovereignty and was not about to cede territory to another foreign conqueror.
>
> At Camp David, President Sadat of Egypt and Prime Minister Begin of Israel agreed to a plan that would return the Sinai to complete Egyptian sovereignty and, by demilitarizing large areas, would still assure Israeli security. The Egyptian flag would fly everywhere, but Egyptian tanks would be nowhere near Israel (Fisher and Ury 1981).

Creating Value via the Negotiation Process

In their highly publicized best-seller, *Getting to Yes* (1981), Roger Fisher and William Ury outline four points, each dealing with a basic element of negotiation. These comprise the foundation of a symbiotic negotiation strategy which they call "principled negotiation," or "negotiation on the merits." These four points are as follows:

- *Separate the people from the problem.* The first step in reaching a mutually agreeable solution is to disentangle the substantive elements of the negotiation from the relationship between the parties and deal with each set of elements separately. Negotiators should perceive themselves as working side by side, attacking the problem instead of attacking each other.

- *Focus on interests, not positions.* People's egos tend to become identified with their negotiating positions. Furthermore, focusing on positions often obscures what the participants really need or want. Rather than focusing on the positions taken by each negotiator, a much more effective strategy is to focus on the underlying human needs and interests that had caused them to adopt those positions.

- *Invent options for mutual gain.* Designing optimal solutions under pressure in the presence of an adversary tends to narrow people's vision. Searching for the one right solution inhibits creativity, particularly when the stakes are high. These constraints can be offset by establishing a forum in which a variety of possibilities are generated before deciding which action to take.

- *Insist on using objective criteria.* By discussing the conditions of the negotiation in terms of some fair standard such as market value, expert opinion, custom, or law, the discussion steers away from what the parties are willing or unwilling to do. By using objective criteria, neither party has to give in to the other, and both parties defer to a fair solution.

Symbiotic strategies tend to emphasize open channels of communication, separating the substantive aspects of the negotiation from the people involved in the discussion. By allowing negotiators to deal directly and empathetically with each other as human beings, these strategies increase the probability of reaching an amicable agreement. By focusing on the underlying human interests of each negotiator, they avoid the transactional costs associated with participants locking themselves into positions and then trying to dig their way out. Finally, by focusing on basic interests, mutually satisfying options, and objective standards, these strategies have the potential to produce an agreement that meets the legitimate interests of each side to the extent possible, resolves conflicting interests fairly, and takes into account the interests of associated third parties.

Predation

In direct contrast to their counterparts, predatory negotiators see the notion of a bargaining session characterized by openness, information sharing, clear communication, creativity, and an attitude of cultivating common interests as being naive and weak-minded. According to the predatory ideology, a pie of fixed size is being divided between negotiators, and each slice that each party receives must be taken away from the other. Hardball is the name of the game as each negotiator tries to claim as much of the value of the pie as possible by giving the other party as little as possible. At the extreme end of the spectrum, predatory negotiators try to devise Machiavellian ways to manipulate individuals in such a manner as to claim the entire pie.

Predation, as a negotiation ideology, is based on the view that negotiation is a hard, tough bargaining process in which neither participant cares about the needs of the other. In all cases, the relationship elements of the negotiation are perceived as subservient to the substantive gains achieved in an adversarial contest.

The object here is to persuade other parties that they want what you have to offer while you are only marginally interested in what they have to offer. Negotiation is a game to be won or lost. The outcome depends on each participant's ability to concede slowly, exaggerate the value of concessions, minimize the benefits of the other's concessions, conceal information, argue forcefully on behalf of principles that imply favorable settlements, wait out the other participant, and make commitments to accept only favorable settlements.

The toughest bargainers will make intransigent demands and threaten to walk away or retaliate aggressively if those demands are not met. Ridiculing, attacking, or intimidating adversaries is perceived simply as part of the game. For example, Lewis Glucksman, once the volatile head of trading activities at Lehman Brothers, utilized a very aggressive predatory strategy to seize control of Lehman from then-chairman Peter G. Peterson after being promoted to co-CEO status with Peterson. As co-CEO, Glucksman made a thinly veiled threat that unless he were granted full control of Lehman, he would provoke civil war within the firm and take the entire trading department elsewhere. When Peterson and others desperately sought less damaging accommodation, Glucksman refused to budge by indicating that "his feet were wet in cement," even at the cost of destroying the firm. Ultimately, Peterson left with a substantial money settlement and Glucksman presided briefly over the shaken firm until it was sold at a bargain price to American Express.

Claiming Value via the Negotiation Process

In his book *Negotiate Your Way to Financial Success* (1987), Ronald J. Posluns details his "Seven Golden Rules" of negotiating:

- *Negotiate tough.* Negotiators are not necessarily popular individuals, but there is nothing wrong with getting the edge in any deal. However, do not confuse "tough" with arrogant, rude, bullheaded, or ruthless. "Tough" means sticking to your guns, letting the other side know that you mean business, and being unafraid to ask for extra concessions.

- *Scrutinize the details.* The success of a negotiation strategy lies in the details of the final agreement. Go through each of them, point by point, and wherever an item is not settled, try to gain an advantage. Assume nothing, ask for everything, and consider no item insignificant. Negotiate hard on every specific item, especially the smaller ones, in an attempt to wear down your opponents' stamina and weaken their ability to negotiate for the major issues at stake.

- *Focus on the rewards.* Maintain a myopic view of those things you want to take away from the bargaining table, and learn to counter your opponents' negotiating strategies. For example, emotional outbursts should be perceived as merely part of the game, not as personal attacks. The best thing to do when your opponents exhibit extreme emotion is to simply let them rant, rave, and pound on the table. Once they play their emotional card to no avail, you will have gained the advantage.

- *Avoid ultimatums.* Give your opponents choices instead of ultimatums. Backing someone into a corner is similar to cornering a wild animal—predicting their reactions becomes impossible. When your opponents give you an ultimatum, the best thing to do is walk away from the deal. A good negotiator will not become committed to a deal that cannot survive another day of indecision.

- *Anything goes.* Negotiation is not a game with established rules. You can stall for time, cloud the issues, or use facial expressions to indicate that the concessions your opponents desire are painful ones (whether or not they actually are). Another strategy is to purposely drop your briefcase, or make a mess with a fountain pen. As you lull your opponents into underestimating you, set them up for the kill.

- *Find your opponents' pressure points.* If you discover that your opponents are facing a deadline, you can stall the negotiations by focusing on details until, as the final hour nears, your opponents are eager to agree on your main goals. Probe your opponents for vulnerabilities, then structure your negotiating stance to take full advantage of them.

- *Control the negotiation.* Get your opponents to follow your game plan, not theirs. For instance, if there is a choice between "your place or mine," consider that you have a turf advantage at home, but when you are "away" you have the option of leaving the table in mock outrage. Another ploy is to let the other party prepare the working document under discussion. Mistakenly believing that this will give them an edge, the other party will happily draft a document that itemizes their substantive priorities and the numbers they attach to those items.

THE NEGOTIATOR'S DILEMMA

In reality, symbiotic negotiation strategies designed to create value through cooperation and collaboration directly conflict with predatory strategies intended to claim value. That is, no matter how creative and collaborative the negotiators are, and no matter how successful they are at creating value by means of the bargaining process, reality dictates that at some point each negotiator must claim part of the pie. Moreover, the use of tactics for claiming value necessarily impedes its creation, and the use of tactics for creating value is vulnerable to predatory negotiation strategies.

First, predatory negotiation strategies intended to claim value tend to impair efforts to satisfy the interests of both parties through symbiotic, value-creating strategies. Exaggerating the value of concessions and minimizing the benefit of others' concessions presents a distorted picture of each negotiator's relative preferences and thereby inhibits the communication process. Making threats or intransigent demands is not conducive to effective listening or understanding the interests of the other party. Concealing information will likely result in leaving joint gains on the table. In fact, excessively using predatory strategies may well sour the relationship between the parties to the point at which conflict escalates and the prospects for arriving at a settlement are virtually eliminated.

Second, openly sharing information required to discover and satisfy joint interests makes symbiotic negotiators more susceptible to being victimized by value-claiming strategies. Revealing information about one's relative preferences is risky, and the willingness to make a new, creative offer can often be taken as a sign that its proponent is able and willing to make further concessions. As a result, these offers, which may satisfy joint interests and provide each negotiator with benefits that could not be attained otherwise, typically remain undisclosed. Even purely shared interests can be held hostage in exchange for concessions on other issues.

A Matrix of Outcomes

Although both negotiators may realize the importance of cooperatively creating value by means of the negotiation process in a symbiotic manner, they must also acknowledge the fact that each must eventually claim value through some degree of predation. The negotiator's dilemma lies in the fact that tactics to claim value tend to repel moves to create it. While an optimal solution normally results when both parties openly discuss the problem, respect each other's substantive and relationship needs, and creatively seek to satisfy each other's human interests, reality dictates that such behavior cannot always be expected to occur.

The legitimate attempts by one negotiator to employ symbiotic strategies will necessarily disclose information that makes that negotiator vulnerable to the predatory strategies of his opponent. As a result, the problem-solving atmosphere created by two symbionts is inevitably replaced by a competitive atmosphere of gamesmanship to the degree that at least one negotiator begins to utilize predatory strategies.

In a negotiation between a predator, who sees the bargaining process as competitive, and a symbiont, who sees the bargaining process as cooperative, the symbiont is highly vulnerable to the value-claiming strategies employed by the predator. For this reason, negotiators develop an inherent apprehension toward the use of symbiotic strategies to the degree that they expect their opponents to use predatory strategies. This mutual suspicion causes negotiators in many settings to leave joint gains on the table. Moreover, after being skewered in several encounters with experienced predators, the pull toward value-claiming tactics becomes insidious and symbionts often "learn" to become predators.

Finally, however, if both negotiators choose to employ predatory strategies, the probability of value being created through the negotiation process is virtually eliminated. This will likely result in both parties receiving only mediocre rewards, in terms of both substantive outcomes and building productive relationships with the other party. If the spectrum of negotiating strategies previously discussed is placed along vertical and horizontal axes, then for negotiating parties A and B, respectively, a matrix of possible outcomes emerging from the bargaining process can be developed to illustrate the negotiator's dilemma (see Figure 1).

FIGURE 1 A Matrix of Negotiated Outcomes

Strategy of party A			
	Predation	*Outcome:* Great for party A, Terrible for party B	*Outcome:* Mediocre for party A, Mediocre for party B
	Symbiosis	*Outcome:* Good for party A, Good for party B	*Outcome:* Terrible for party A, Great for party B
		Symbiosis	Predation
		Strategy of party B	

Operational Implications

The negotiator's dilemma may enhance the productivity of the bargaining process by providing insight into the mental metabolism of the negotiators. However, regardless of each negotiator's strategy preference, several actions may be taken at the operational level to increase the probability of achieving favorable outcomes while taking the relationship between the parties into account. The bases for these actions are found in the "middle ground" of the strategic spectrum, borrowing concepts from both the predatory and the symbiotic ideologies.

- *Do your homework.* Although it is the least glamorous aspect of the negotiating process, it is the most important. A good negotiator must realize the implications of each item on the table, the consequences associated with making various concessions, and what entails the "bottom line" of the negotiations.

- *Go to the top.* Unless you talk directly with individuals who have the authority to make the changes you propose, your success will hinge on someone else's ability to communicate, in minutes, what was discussed over several hours. In addition, dealing with unauthorized subordinates lessens accountability and may hinder the proceedings.

- *Build relationships whenever possible.* Even if you decide to employ a predatory strategy, remember that it is much easier to communicate with a friend than with a stranger, or even worse, an enemy. Relationship gains and losses are as much a part of the negotiated package as the substantive outcomes.

- *Avoid quick concessions.* Making a concession without having fully considered the issues opens you up to the risk of giving up something unnecessarily and compromising your own needs. Use discretion when conceding from your stated position.

- *Accentuate the positive.* By framing negative points in a positive way, you will be more likely to elicit a positive response. Couching controversial issues between positive points increases your chances of getting the other side to listen—and agree—to your demands.

- *Maintain your composure.* In any negotiation, but particularly in protracted ones, emotions may flare up and people may lose their tempers. Under these conditions, it is imperative to maintain composure, sift through emotions, and try to discern the other party's needs and wants.

- *Don't give up.* You may reach a point at which you do not like the proposed agreement, but still you do not see any alternatives. Remember that what seems like a dead end may actually be a corner. With a little perseverance, you can get around it.

At one extreme, the process of negotiation can be called a cooperative pursuit of joint gains and a collaborative effort to create value where none previously existed. At the other extreme, it can be described as a street fight. The negotiator's dilemma lies in determining where the cooperation ends and the street fight begins. Understanding this paradox more fully serves to reduce the anxiety associated with the process of negotiation by giving negotiators a structured approach to tailoring their strategies to both the substantive and relationship elements at stake.

Nevertheless, it is important not to be duped into believing that the bargaining process is as simple as any existing structured model may imply. The experience and intuition of the negotiator must inevitably provide the musculature necessary to put the structure into motion in a pragmatic and practicable manner. By taking a structured yet realistic approach to the negotiating process, and implementing established operational actions, the negotiator substantially increases the probability of acquiring substantive gains, as well as fostering a productive relationship with the other party.

REFERENCES

Asbrand, Deborah. "Games B-School Never Taught You." *PC Computing,* April 1989, pp. 153+.

Belzer, Ellen J. "The Negotiator's Art: You Can Always Get What You Want." *Working Woman,* April 1990, pp. 98+.

Brown, Paul B., and Michael S. Hopkins. "How to Negotiate Practically Anything." *Inc.,* February 1989, pp. 35+.

Fisher, Roger, and William Ury. *Getting to Yes.* Boston: Houghton Mifflin, 1981.

Ivancevich, John M., and Michael T. Matteson. *Organizational Behavior and Management.* Homewood, IL: Irwin, 1990.

Lax, David A., and James K. Sebenius. *The Manager as Negotiator.* New York: Free Press, 1986.

Legette, Cynthia. "How to Improve Your Negotiation Skills." *Black Enterprise,* October 1989, pp. 106–10.

Nierenberg, Gerard I. *Creative Business Negotiating.* New York: Hawthorn, 1971.

Posluns, Ronald J. *Negotiate Your Way to Financial Success.* New York: Putnam, 1987.

Willens, Michelle. "The Manly Art of Win-Win Negotiating." *Money,* February 1987, pp. 199–202.

Some Wise and Mistaken Assumptions about Conflict and Negotiation

Jeffrey Z. Rubin

CONFLICT SETTLEMENT AND RESOLUTION

For many years the attention of conflict researchers and theorists was directed to the laudable objective of conflict *resolution.* This term denotes as an outcome a state of attitude change that effectively brings an end to the conflict in question. In contrast, conflict *settlement* denotes outcomes in which the overt conflict has been brought to an end, even though the underlying bases may or may not have been addressed. The difference here is akin to Herbert Kelman's (1958) useful distinction among the three consequences of social influence: compliance, identification, and internalization. If conflict settlement implies the consequence of compliance (a change in behavior), then conflict resolution instead implies internalization (a more profound change, of underlying attitudes as well as behavior). The third consequence, *identification,* denotes a change in behavior that is based on the target of influence valuing his or her relationship with the source, and it serves as a bridge between behavior change and attitude change.

In keeping with the flourishing research in the 1950s on attitudes and attitude change, social psychological research on conflict in the 1950s and 1960s focused on conflict *resolution.* Only recently has there been a subtle shift in focus from attitude change to behavior change. Underlying this shift is the view that, while it is necessary that attitudes change if conflict is to be eliminated, such elimination is often simply not possible. Merely getting Iran and Iraq, Turkish and Greek Cypriots, Contras and Sandinistas to lay down their weapons—even temporarily—is a great accomplishment in its own right, even if the parties continue to hate each other. And this simple act of cessation, when coupled with other such acts, may eventually generate the momentum necessary to move antagonists out of stalemate toward a settlement of their differences. Just as "stateways" can change "folkways" (Deutsch and Collins, 1951), so too can a string of behavioral changes produce the basis for subsequent attitude change.

This paper is an expanded version of the presidential address, presented to the Society for the Psychological Study of Social Issues (SPSSI) in Atlanta, Georgia on August 12, 1988. Thanks to Walter Swap and J. William Breslin for helpful comments on an earlier draft of the manuscript.

Reprinted with permission of the *Journal of Social Issues,* Vol. 45, No. 2, 1989, pp. 195–206.

The gradual shift over the last years from a focus on resolution to a focus on settlement has had an important implication for the conflict field: It has increased the importance of understanding *negotiation*—which, after all, is a method of settling conflict rather than resolving it. The focus of negotiation is not attitude change per se, but an agreement to change behavior in ways that make settlement possible. Two people with underlying differences of beliefs or values (for example, over the issue of a woman's right to abortion or the existence of a higher deity) may come to change their views through discussion and an exchange of views, but it would be inappropriate and inaccurate to describe such an exchange as "negotiation."

Similarly, the shift from resolution to settlement of conflict has also increased the attention directed to the role of *third parties* in the conflict settlement process—individuals who are in some way external to a dispute and who, through identification of issues and judicious intervention, attempt to make it more likely that a conflict can be moved to settlement.

Finally, the shift in favor of techniques of conflict settlement has piqued the interest and attention of practitioners in a great many fields, ranging from divorce mediators and couples' counselors to negotiators operating in environmental, business, labor, community, or international disputes. Attitude change may not be possible in these settings, but behavior change—as the result of skillful negotiation or third-party intervention—is something else entirely. Witness the effective mediation by the Algerians during the so-called Iranian hostage crisis in the late 1970s; as a result of Algerian intervention, the Iranian government came to dislike the American Satan no less than before, but the basis for a quid pro quo had been worked out.

COOPERATION, COMPETITION, AND ENLIGHTENED SELF-INTEREST

Required for effective conflict settlement is neither cooperation nor competition, but what may be referred to as "enlightened self-interest." By this I simply mean a variation on what several conflict theorists have previously described as an "individualistic orientation" (Deutsch, 1960)—an outlook in which the disputant is simply interested in doing well for himself or herself, without regard for anyone else, out neither to help nor hinder the other's efforts to obtain his or her goal. The added word *enlightened* refers to the acknowledgment by each side that the other is also likely to be pursuing a path of self-interest—and that it may be possible for *both* to do well in the exchange. If there are ways in which I can move toward my objective in negotiation, while at the same time making it possible for you to approach your goal, then why not behave in ways that make both possible?

Notice that what I am describing here is neither pure individualism (where one side does not care at all about how the other is doing) nor pure cooperation (where each side cares deeply about helping the other to do well, likes and values the other side, etc.)—but an amalgam of the two.

Trivial though this distinction may seem, it has made it possible in recent years for work to develop that, paradoxically, creates a pattern of *inter*dependence out of the assumption of *in*dependence. Earlier work, focusing as it did on the perils of competition and the virtues of cooperation, made an important contribution to the field of conflict studies. However, in doing so, it also shifted attention away from the path of individualism—a path that is likely to provide a way out of stalemate and toward a settlement of differences. I do not have to like or trust you in order to negotiate wisely with you. Nor do I have to be driven by the passion of a competitive desire to beat you. All that is necessary is for me to find some way of getting what I want—perhaps even *more* than I considered possible—by leaving the door open for you too to do well. "Trust" and "trustworthiness," concepts central to the development of cooperation, are no longer necessary—only the understanding of what the other person may want or need.

A number of anecdotes have emerged to make this point; perhaps the most popular is the tale of two sisters who argue over the division of an orange between them (Fisher and Ury, 1981; Follett, 1940. Each would like the entire orange, and only reluctantly do the sisters move from extreme demands to a 50–50 split. While such a solution is eminently fair, it is not necessarily wise: One sister proceeds to peel the orange, discard the peel, and eat her half of the fruit; the other peels the orange, discards the fruit, and uses her 50 percent of the peel to bake a cake! If only the two sisters had understood what each wanted the orange for—not each side's "position," but rather each side's underlying "interest"—an agreement would have been possible that would have allowed each to get everything that she wanted.

Similarly, Jack Sprat and his wife—one preferring lean, the other fat—can lick the platter clean if they understand their respective interests. The interesting thing about this conjugal pair is that, married though they may be, when it comes to dining preferences they are hardly interdependent at all. For Jack and his wife to "lick the platter clean" requires neither that the two love each other nor care about helping each other in every way possible; nor does it require that each be determined to get more of the platter's contents than the other. Instead, it is enlightened self-interest that makes possible an optimal solution to the problem of resource distribution.

The lesson for international relations is instructive. For the United States and the Soviet Union, Israel and its Arab neighbors, Iran and Iraq, the Soviet Union and Afghanistan, the United States and Nicaragua to do well, neither cooperation nor competition is required, but rather an arrangement that acknowledges the possibility of a more complex mixture of these two motivational states—enlightened individualism. While the United States and Soviet Union will continue to have many arenas of conflict in which their interests are clearly and directly opposed, and will also continue to find new opportunities for cooperation (as in the management of nuclear proliferation, hazardous waste disposal, or international political terrorism), there are also arenas in which each side is not at all as dependent on the other for obtaining what it wants (e.g., the formulation of domestic economic or political policy). The world is a very big place; the pie is big enough for both of us, and for many others (as my grandmother might have said), to live and be well![1]

---

1. Two recent books (Lax and Sebenius, 1986; Susskind and Cruickshank, 1987) treat rather extensively the topic of enlightened self-interest, pointing out ways of expanding the resource pie, or finding uses for it that satisfy the interests of each side.

A COMMON PROCESS SUBSTRATE

It has been fashionable for several years now to observe that conflicts are fundamentally alike, whether they take place between individuals, within or between groups, communities, or nations. Nevertheless, conflict analysts in each of these domains have tended not to listen closely to one another, and have largely proceeded as if international conflict, labor disputes, and family spats are distinct and unrelated phenomena.

Within the last decade or so, with the advent of conflict and negotiation programs around the United States, a different point of view has begun to emerge: one that argues for a common set of processes that underlie all forms of conflict and their settlement. Third-party intervention—whether in divorce, international business and trade negotiations, a labor dispute, a conflict over nuclear siting or hazardous waste disposal, or an international border dispute—follows certain principles that dictate its likely effectiveness. Similarly, the principles of negotiation apply with equal vigor to conflicts at all levels of complexity, whether two or more than two parties are involved, negotiating one issue or many issues, with problems varying in difficulty, and so on.

Acceptance of this bit of ideology has had an extremely important effect on the field of conflict studies, for it has made it possible for conversations to take place among theorists and practitioners, at work in an extraordinarily rich and varied set of fields. Anthropologists, sociologists, lawyers, psychologists, economists, business men and women, community activists, labor experts, to name but a few, have now started to come together to exchange ideas, to map areas of overlap and divergence. This, in turn, has made it possible for the development of conflict theory and practice to take shape under a larger umbrella than ever before. In fact, the symbolic location of these conversations is more like a circus tent than an umbrella, with beasts of different stripe, size, and coloring all finding a place under the big top.

Most recently, yet another twist has appeared. Having engaged in fruitful preliminary conversations about the nature of conflict and negotiation in their respective fields and disciplines, scholars and practitioners are now turning to areas of *divergence* rather than *similarity*. Instead of homogenizing theory and practice in the different social sciences, analysts are now beginning to look beyond the areas of process similarity to the distinguishing features that characterize dispute management in different arenas.

At another but related level, conflict analysts are at last beginning to acknowledge that our pet formulations have been devised by, and are directed to, a community that is predominantly white, Western, male, and upper middle class. Now that fruitful conversations have begun to take place among members of our own intellectual community, it is becoming clear that some of our most cherished ideas may be limited in their applicability and generalizability. Other societies—indeed, other people within our own society—may not always "play the conflict game" by the set of rules that scholars and researchers have deduced on the basis of American paradigms.

As one example of what I mean, "face saving" has been an extremely important element of most conflict/negotiation formulations: the idea that people in conflict will go out of their way to avoid being made to look weak or foolish in the eyes of others and themselves. While face saving seems important in the United States and in countries such as Japan or Korea, less obvious is the extent to which this issue is of *universal* significance. Do Pacific Islanders, Native Americans, or South Asians experience "face," and therefore the possibility of "loss of face"? It is not clear. Do women experience face saving and face loss, or is this a phenomenon that is largely restricted to the XY genetic portion of the population?

Similarly, what does it mean to set a "time limit" in negotiations in different cultures? Do other cultures measure a successful negotiation outcome the same way we tend to in this country? Are coalitions considered equally acceptable, and are they like to form in much the same way, from one country to the next? Do different countries structure the negotiating environment—everything from the shape of the negotiating table to the presence of observing audiences and various constituencies—in the same way? The answers to questions such as these are not yet in, and we must therefore learn to be cautious in our propensity to advance a set of "universal" principles.

THE IMPORTANCE OF "RELATIONSHIP" IN NEGOTIATION

Much of the negotiation analysis that has taken place over the last 25 years has focused on the "bottom line": who gets how much once an agreement has been reached. The emphasis has thus largely been an *economic* one, and this emphasis has been strengthened by the significant role of game theory and other mathematical or economic formulations.

This economic focus is being supplanted by a richer, and more accurate, portrayal of negotiation in terms not only of economic, but also of relational, considerations. As any visitor to the Turkish bazaar in Istanbul will tell you, the purchase of an oriental carpet involves a great deal more than the exchange of money for an old rug. The emerging relationship between shopkeeper and customer is far more significant, weaving ever so naturally into the economic aspects of the transaction. An initial conversation about the selling price of some item is quickly transformed into an exchange of a more personal nature: Who one is, where one is from, stories about one's family and friends, impressions of the host country, and lots more. When my wife and I purchased several rugs in Turkey some years ago, we spent three days in conversation with the merchant—not because that is how long it took to "cut the best deal," but because we were clearly having a fine time getting to know one another over Turkish coffee, Turkish delight, and Turkish taffy. When, at the end of our three-day marathon transaction, the shopkeeper invited us to consider opening a carpet store in Boston that could be used to distribute his wares, I was convinced that this invitation was extended primarily to sustain an emerging relationship—rather than to make a financial "killing" in the United States.

Psychologists, sociologists, and anthropologists have long understood the importance of "relationship" in any interpersonal transaction, but only recently have conflict analysts begun to take this as seriously as it deserves. Although it seems convenient to distinguish negotiation in one-time-only exchanges (ones where you have no history of contact with the other party, come together for a "quickie," and then expect never to see the other again) from negotiation in ongoing relationships, this distinction is more illusory than real. Rarely does one negotiate in the absence of future consequences. Even if you and I meet once and once only, our reputations have a way of surviving the exchange, coloring the expectations that others will have of us in the future.

NEGOTIATION IN A TEMPORAL CONTEXT

For too long, analysts have considered only the negotiations proper, rather than the sequence of events preceding negotiation and the events that must transpire if a concluded agreement is to be implemented successfully. Only recently, as analysts have become more confident in their appraisal of the factors that influence effective negotiation, has attention been directed to the past and future, as anchors of the negotiating present.

Analysts of international negotiation (e.g., Saunders, 1985) have observed that some of the most important work takes place *before the parties ever come to the table.* Indeed, once they get to the table, all that typically remains is a matter of crossing the *t*'s and dotting the *i*'s in an agreement hammered out beforehand. It is during *prenegotiation* that the pertinent parties to the conflict are identified and invited to participate, that a listing of issues is developed and prioritized as an agenda, and that the formula by which a general agreement is to be reached is first outlined. Without such a set of preliminary understandings, international negotiators may well refuse to sit down at the same table with one another.

Prenegotiation is important in other contexts as well, something I discovered in conversation with a successful Thai businessman. He observed that Thais are extremely reluctant to confront an adversary in negotiation, or to show any sign whatsoever of disagreement, let alone conflict. Yet many Thais have succeeded admirably in negotiating agreements that are to their advantage. The key to their success is prenegotiation, making sure beforehand that there really *is* an agreement before labeling the process "negotiation," before ever sitting down with that other person. In effect, they use prenegotiation to arrange matters to their advantage, and they do so without ever identifying the relationship with the other party as conflictual, or signaling in any way that concessions or demands are being made.

At the other end of the temporal continuum lies the matter of follow-up and implementation. To reach an agreement through negotiation is not enough. Those partes who are in a position to sabotage this agreement, unless their advice is solicited and incorporated, must be taken into account if a negotiated agreement is to succeed. (Witness the failure of the Michael Dukakis campaign to consult sufficiently with Jesse Jackson and his supporters, prior to the 1988 Democratic Party Convention in Atlanta.) Note the trade-off here: The greater the number of parties to a negotiation, the more difficult it will be to reach any agreement at all. But only if the relevant parties and interests are included in the negotiations is the agreement reached likely to "stick."

As negotiation analysts have broadened the temporal spectrum to include pre- and postnegotiation processes, more work has been done toward devising creative options for improving upon the proceedings. To cite but one example, Howard Raiffa (1985) has proposed a procedure known as "postsettlement settlement," by which parties who have already concluded an agreement are given an opportunity—with the assistance of a third party—to improve upon their agreement. The third party examines the facts and figures that each side has used in reaching a settlement; based on this information, which is kept in strict confidence, the third party proposes a settlement that improves upon the agreement reached. Either side can veto this postsettlement settlement, in which case the status quo ante remains in effect. However, if both sides endorse the proposed improvement on the existing contract, then each stands to benefit from this proposal—and the third party, in turn, is guaranteed a percentage of the "added value" of the contract.

NEGOTIATING FROM THE INSIDE OUT

Conventional wisdom regarding effective negotiation calls for the parties to start by making extreme opening offers, then conceding stepwise until an agreement is reached. If you want to sell a used car, purchase a rug, secure a new wage package, or settle a territorial dispute with a neighboring country, you begin by asking for more than you expect to settle for, then gradually move inward until you and the other side overlap; at that point you have got a negotiated settlement.

A large body of negotiation analysis has proceeded in accordance with this conventional wisdom. Moreover, this way of negotiating "from the outside in" makes good sense for several reasons: It allows each negotiator to explore various possible agreements before settling, to obtain as much information as possible about the other negotiator and his or her preferences, before closing off discussion (Kelley, 1966). It also allows each party to give its respective constituency some sense of the degree to which the other side has already been "moved," thereby maintaining constituency support for the positions taken in negotiation.

On the other hand, this "traditional" way of conducting the business of negotiation ignores an important and creative alternative: working "from the inside out." Instead of beginning with extreme opening offers, then moving slowly and inexorably from this stance until agreement is reached, it often makes sense to start with an exchange of views about underlying needs and interests—and on the basis of such an exchange, to build an agreement that both parties find acceptable. The key to such an approach is, as negotiation analysts have observed (e.g., Fisher and Ury, 1981), to work at the level of interests rather than positions—what one really needs and wants (and why), rather than what one states that one would like to have.

This was precisely what happened in October of 1978 at Camp David where, with the mediation of President Jimmy Carter and his subordinates, President Anwar Sadat of Egypt and Prime Minister Menachem Begin of Israel were able to settle the disposition of the Sinai Peninsula. The Sinai had been taken by the Israelis in 1967, and its complete and immediate return had been demanded by the Egyptians ever since. Had the discussions about the fate of the Sinai been conducted solely at the level of positions—with each side demanding total control of the land in question, then making stepwise concessions from these extreme opening offers—*no* agreement would have been possible. Instead, with assistance from President Carter, the Egyptians and Israelis identified their own respective underlying interests—and were able to move to an agreement that allowed the Israelis to obtain the security they required, while the Egyptians obtained the territory they required. "Security in exchange for territory" was the formula used here, and it was a formula devised not by moving from the outside in, but by building up an agreement from the inside out.

A useful variation on this inside-out idea is the "one-text" negotiation procedure (Fisher, 1981), whereby a mediator develops a single negotiating text that is critiqued and improved by each side until a final draft is developed for approval by the interested parties. Instead of starting with demands that are gradually abandoned, the negotiators criticize a single document that is rewritten to take these criticisms into account, and eventually—through this sort of inside-out procedure—a proposal is developed for which both sides have some sense of ownership.

THE ROLE OF "RIPENESS"

Although it is comforting to assume people can start negotiating any time they want, such is not the case. First of all, just as it takes two hands to clap, it takes two to negotiate. *You* may be ready to come to the table for serious discussion, but your counterpart may not. Unless you are both at the table (or connected by a telephone line or cable link), no agreement is possible.

Second, even if both of you are present at the same place, at the same time, one or both of you may not be sufficiently motivated to take the conflict seriously. It is tempting to sit back, do nothing, and hope that the mere passage of time will turn events to your advantage. People typically do not sit down to negotiate unless and until they have reached a point of "stalemate," where each no longer believes it possible to obtain what he or she wants through efforts at domination or coercion (Kriesberg, 1987). It is only at this point, when the two sides grudgingly acknowledge the need for joint work if any agreement is to be reached, that negotiation can take place.

By "ripeness," then, I mean a stage of conflict in which all parties are ready to take their conflict seriously, and are willing to do whatever may be necessary to bring the conflict to a close. To pluck fruit from a tree before it is ripe is as problematic as waiting too long. There is a *right* time to negotiate, and the wise negotiator will attempt to seek out this point.

It is also possible, of course, to help "create" such a right time. One way of doing so entails the use of threat and coercion, as the two sides (either with or without the assistance of an outside intervenor) walk (or are led) to the edge of "lover's leap," stare into the abyss below, and contemplate the consequences of failing to reach agreement. The farther the drop—that is, the more terrible the consequences of failing to settle— the greater the pressure on each side to take the conflict seriously. There are at least two serious problems with such "coercive" means of creating a ripe conflict: First, as can be seen in the history of the arms race between the United States and the Soviet Union, it encourages further conflict escalation, as each side tries to "motivate" the other to settle by upping the ante a little bit at a time. Second, such escalatory moves invite a game of "chicken," in which each hopes that the other will be the first to succumb to coercion.

There is a second—and far *better*—way to create a situation that is ripe for settlement; namely, through the introduction of new opportunities for joint gain. If each side can be persuaded that there is more to gain than to lose through collaboration— that by working jointly, rewards can be harvested that stand to advance each side's respective agenda—then a basis for agreement can be established. In the era of glasnost, the United States and Soviet Union are currently learning this lesson—namely, that by working together they can better address problems of joint interest, the solution of which advances their respective self-interest. Arms control stands to save billions of dollars and rubles in the strained budgets of both nations, while advancing the credibility of each country in the eyes of the larger world community. The same is true of joint efforts to slow the consequences of the "greenhouse effect" on the atmosphere, to explore outer space, and to preserve and protect our precious natural resources in the seas.

A "RESIDUE" THAT CHANGES THINGS

It is tempting for parties to a conflict to begin by experimenting with a set of adversarial, confrontational moves in the hope that these will work. Why not give hard bargaining a try at first, since if moves such as threat, bluff, or intimidation work as intended, the other side may give up without much of a fight? Moreover, even if such tactics fail, one can always shift to a more benign stance. The problem with such a sticks-to-carrots approach is that once one has left the path of joint problem solving, it may be very difficult to return again. It takes two people to cooperate, but only one person is usually required to make a mess of a relationship. The two extremes of cooperation and competition, collaboration and confrontation, are thus *not* equally valenced; it is far easier to move from cooperation to competition than the other way around.

In the course of hard bargaining, things are often said and done that change the climate of relations in ways that do not easily allow for a return to a less confrontational stance. A "residue" is left behind (Pruitt and Rubin, 1986), in the form of words spoken or acts committed, which cannot be denied and which may well change the relationship. The words "I've never really liked or respected you," spoken in the throes of an angry exchange, may linger like a bad taste in the mouth, even when the conflict has apparently been settled. Similarly, a brandished fist or some other threatening gesture may leave scars that long outlive the heat of the moment. Thus, the escalation of conflict often carries with it moves and maneuvers that alter a relationship in ways that the parties do not anticipate.

The implication of this point for conflict and negotiation studies is clear: Insufficient attention has been directed to the lasting consequences of confrontational tactics. Too often scholars, researchers, and practitioners have assumed cooperation and competition are equally weighted, when in fact cooperation is a slippery slope; once left, the path leading to return is difficult indeed. Required for such a return journey is a combination of cooperation and persistence—the willingness to make a unilateral collaborative overture, and then to couple this with the tenacity necessary to persuade the other side that this collaborative overture is to be taken seriously (Axelrod, 1984; Fisher and Brown, 1988).

REFERENCES

Axelrod, R. *The Evolution of Cooperation.* New York: Basic Books, 1984.

Deutsch, M. "The Effect of Motivational Orientation upon Trust and Suspicion." *Human Relations,* 13 (1960), pp. 123–39.

Deutsch, M., and Collins, M. E. *Interracial Housing: A Psychological Evaluation of a Social Experiment.* Minneapolis: University of Minnesota Press, 1951.

Fisher, R. "Playing the Wrong Game?" In J. Z. Rubin, ed., *Dynamics of Third-Party Intervention: Kissinger in the Middle East.* New York: Praeger, 1981.

Fisher, R., & Brown, S. *Getting Together.* Boston: Houghton Mifflin, 1988.

Fisher, R., and Ury, W. L. *Getting to Yes: Negotiating Agreement without Giving In.* Boston: Houghton Mifflin, 1981.

Follett, M. P. "Constructive Conflict." In H. C. Metcalf and L. Urwick, eds., *Dynamic Administration: The Collected Papers of Mary Parker Follett.* New York: Harper, 1940.

Kelley, H. H. "A Classroom Study of the Dilemmas in Interpersonal Negotiations." In K. Archibald, ed., *Strategic Interaction and Conflict: Original Papers and Discussion.* Berkeley, CA: Institute of International Studies, 1966.

Kelman, H. C. "Compliance, Identification, and Internalization: Three Processes of Attitude Change. *Journal of Conflict Resolution* 2 (1958), pp. 51–60.

Kriesberg, L. "Timing and the Initiation of De-escalation Moves." *Negotiation Journal* 3 (1987), pp. 375–84.

Lax, D. A., and Sebenius, J. *The Manager as Negotiator.* New York: Free Press, 1986.

Pruitt, D. G., and Rubin, J. Z. *Social Conflict: Escalation, Stalemate, and Settlement.* New York: Random House, 1986.

Raiffa, H. "Post-settlement Settlements." *Negotiation Journal* 1 (1985), pp. 9–12.

Russell, R. W. ed. Psychology and Policy in a Nuclear Age. *Journal of Social Issues* 17, no. 3 (1961).

Saunders, H. H. "We Need a Larger Theory of Negotiation: The Importance of Prenegotiating Phases." *Negotiation Journal* 2 (1985), pp. 249–62.

Susskind, L., and Cruikshank, J. *Breaking the Impasse.* New York: Basic Books, 1987.

SECTION FIVE

Communication and Cognitive Biases

One of the critical subprocesses at the heart of negotiation is communication. Without communication no additional information would be provided to support a bid or offer, nor would there be any information about the needs and interests of both parties. Without the transmission of information there would be no reason, other than the passage of time, for parties to make concessions. In short, there would be no negotiation. In addition, many negotiation breakdowns result from communication breakdowns. (Negotiation breakdowns are discussed in more detail in Section 12 of this book, Managing Difficult Negotiation Situations: Individual Approaches.) The readings in this section present three different views of the communication process in negotiation; all three, however, share the fundamental premise that communication is a central aspect of negotiation.

The first reading in this section is "Negotiating Rationally: The Power and Impact of the Negotiator's Frame," by Margaret Neale and Max Bazerman. The authors suggest that the quality of negotiation outcomes would improve if negotiators acted more rationally. One of the most important aspects of communication that negotiators should consider is the *frame* of the negotiation. In simple terms, frame determines what the negotiation is about. For instance, are we discussing how much we are going to win, or how much we are not going to lose? The exact same facts may exist in both negotiations (the win frame and the lose frame), but research has consistently shown that negotiation outcomes will be different depending on how the negotiation is framed. When people become lazy and consistently apply the same frame to different negotiations a cognitive bias is occurring. Neale and Bazerman discuss several negotiation frames and cognitive biases in their article, use examples throughout to illustrate these biases, and conclude the article with a discussion of the implications of framing for the strategies and tactics that negotiators use.

In the second article in this section, "The Power of Talk: Who Gets Heard and Why," Deborah Tannen examines how linguistic style influences conversations between people. Linguistic styles are culturally determined, and include all aspects of "how" a conversation occurs. For instance, linguistic style includes tones of voice, speed of speech, whether or not the other person interrupts the conversation, and so on. For Tannen, all conversations occur on two levels: (1) the content of the ideas and (2) the messages signaled by the way people speak. Although this article does not specifically focus on negotiation, a strong understanding of the topics discussed by Tannen is critical for every negotiator because negotiators use words and language to craft their agreements and relationships. Too many negotiators focus exclusively on the content or ideas in the negotiation and ignore the other aspects of communication.

Careful attention to this article will help negotiators improve their command of language and thereby become better negotiators.

The third reading in this section, "Communication Freezers," by Mary Tramel and Helen Reynolds, is a checklist of statements and phrases that act to shut down, or at the very least detract from, the communication process. To check whether or not you really think these are freezers, ask yourself what you would think or feel if someone you were negotiating with were to say some of these things to you. These communication freezers will not only detract from the quality of a negotiation conversation, but they may also lead to negative feelings. The best way to manage a counterpart who is using such freezers on you is to discuss the negotiation process with him or her.

Negotiating Rationally: The Power and Impact of the Negotiator's Frame

Margaret A. Neale

Max H. Bazerman

Everyone negotiates. In its various forms, negotiation is a common mechanism for resolving differences and allocating resources. While many people perceive negotiation to be a specific interaction between a buyer and a seller, this process occurs with a wide variety of exchange partners, such as superiors, colleagues, spouses, children, neighbors, strangers, or even corporate entities and nations. Negotiation is a decision-making process among interdependent parties who do not share identical preferences. It is through negotiation that the parties decide what each will give and take in their relationship.

The aspect of negotiation that is most directly controllable by the negotiator is how he or she makes decisions. The parties, the issues, and the negotiation environment are often predetermined. Rather than trying to change the environment surrounding the negotiation or the parties or issues in the dispute, we believe that the greatest opportunity to improve negotiator performance lies in the negotiator's ability to make effective use of the information available about the issues in dispute as well as the likely behavior of an opponent to reach more rational agreements and make more rational decisions within the context of negotiation.

To this end, we offer advice on how a negotiator should make decisions. However, to follow this advice for analyzing negotiations rationally, a negotiator must understand the psychological forces that limit a negotiator's effectiveness. In addition, rational decisions require that we have an optimal way of evaluating the behavior of the opponent. This requires a psychological perspective for anticipating the likely decisions and subsequent behavior of the other party. Information such as this can not only create a framework that predicts how a negotiator structures problems, processes information, frames the situation, and evaluates alternatives but also identifies the limitations of his or her ability to follow rational advice.

Rationality refers to making the decision that maximizes the negotiator's interests. Since negotiation is a decision-making process that involves other people that do not have the same desires or preferences, the goal of a negotiation is not simply reaching an agreement. The goal of negotiations is to reach a *good* agreement. In some

Reprinted from *Academy of Management Executive* 6, no. 3 (1992), pp. 42–51. Used with permission of the authors and publisher.

cases, no agreement is better than reaching an agreement that is not in the negotiator's best interests. When negotiated agreements are based on biased decisions, the chances of getting the best possible outcome are significantly reduced and the probabilities of reaching an agreement when an impasse would have left the negotiator relatively better off are significantly enhanced.

A central theme of our work is that our natural decision and negotiation processes contain biases that prevent us from acting rationally and getting as much as we can out of a negotiation. These biases are pervasive, destroying the opportunities available in competitive contexts, and preventing us from negotiating rationally. During the last 10 or so years, the work that we and our colleagues have done suggests that negotiators make the following common cognitive mistakes: (1) negotiators tend to be overly affected by the frame, or form of presentation, of information in a negotiation; (2) negotiators tend to nonrationally escalate commitment to a previously selected course of action when it is no longer the most reasonable alternative; (3) negotiators tend to assume that their gain must come at the expense of the other party and thereby miss opportunities for mutually beneficial trade-offs between the parties; (4) negotiator judgments tend to be anchored upon irrelevant information—such as an initial offer; (5) negotiators tend to rely on readily available information; (6) negotiators tend to fail to consider information that is available by focusing on the opponent's perspective; and (7) negotiators tend to be overconfident concerning the likelihood of attaining outcomes that favor the individual(s) involved.

Describing the impact of each of these biases on negotiator behavior is obviously beyond the scope of this article. What we will attempt to do, however, is to focus on one particular and important cognitive bias, *framing,* and consider the impact of this bias on the process and outcome of negotiation. The manner in which negotiators frame the options available in a dispute can have a significant impact on their willingness to reach an agreement as well as the value of that agreement. In this article, we will identify factors that influence the choice of frame in a negotiation.

THE FRAMING OF NEGOTIATIONS

Consider the following situation, adapted from Russo and Schoemaker:[1]

You are in a store about to buy a new watch which costs $70. As you wait for the sales clerk, a friend of yours comes by and remarks that she has seen an identical watch on sale in another store two blocks away for $40. You know that the service and reliability of the other store are just as good as this one. Will you travel two blocks to save $30?

Now consider this similar situation:

You are in a store about to buy a new video camera that costs $800. As you wait for the sales clerk, a friend of yours comes by and remarks that she has seen an identical camera on sale in another store two blocks away for $770. You know that the service and reliability of the other store are just as good as this one. Will you travel two blocks to save the $30?

In the first scenario, Russo and Schoemaker report that about 90 percent of the managers presented this problem reported that they would travel the two blocks. However, in the second scenario, only about 50 percent of the managers would make the trip. What is the difference between the two situations that makes the $30 so attractive in the first scenario and considerably less attractive in the second scenario? One difference is that a $30 discount on a $70 watch represents a very good deal; the $30 discount on an $800 video camera is not such a good deal. In evaluating our willingness to walk two blocks, we frame the options in terms of the percentage discount. However, the correct comparison is not whether a percentage discount is sufficiently motivating, but whether the savings obtained is greater than the expected value of the additional time we would have to invest to realize those savings. So, if a $30 savings were sufficient to justify walking two blocks for the watch, an opportunity to save $30 on the video camera should also be worth an equivalent investment of time.

Richard Thaler illustrated the influence of frames when he presented the following two versions of another problem to participants of an executive development program:[2]

> You are lying on the beach on a hot day. All you have to drink is ice water. For the last hour you have been thinking about how much you would enjoy a nice cold bottle of your favorite brand of beer. A companion gets up to make a phone call and offers to bring back a beer from the only nearby place where beer is sold: a fancy resort hotel. She says that the beer might be expensive and asks how much you are willing to pay for the beer. She will buy the beer if it costs as much as or less than the price you state. But if it costs more than the price you state, she will not buy it. You trust your friend and there is no possibility of bargaining with the bartender. What price do you tell your friend you are willing to pay?

Now consider this version of the same story:

> You are lying on the beach on a hot day. All you have to drink is ice water. For the last hour you have been thinking about how much you would enjoy a nice cold bottle of your favorite brand of beer. A companion gets up to make a phone call and offers to bring back a beer from the only nearby place where beer is sold: a small, run-down grocery store. She says that the beer might be expensive and asks how much you are willing to pay for the beer. She will buy the beer if it costs as much as or less than the price you state. But if it costs more than the price you state, she will not buy it. You trust your friend and there is no possibility of bargaining with the store owner. What price do you tell your friend you are willing to pay?

In both versions of the story, the results are the same: you get the same beer and there is no negotiating with the seller. Also you will not be enjoying the resort's amenities since you will be drinking the beer on the beach. Recent responses of executives at a Kellogg executive training program indicated that they were willing to pay significantly more if the beer were purchased at a "fancy resort hotel" ($7.83) than if the beer were purchased at the "small, run-down grocery store" ($4.10). The difference in price the executives were willing to pay for the same beer was based upon the frame they imposed on this transaction. Paying over $5 for a beer is an expected annoyance at a fancy resort hotel; however, paying over $5 for a beer at a run-down grocery store is an obvious "rip-off"! So, even though the same beer is purchased and we enjoy none of the benefits of the fancy resort hotel, we are willing to pay over three dollars more because of the way in which we frame the purchase. The converse of this situation is probably familiar to many of us. Have you ever purchased an item because "it was too good of a deal to pass up," even though you had no use for it? We seem to assign a greater value to the quality of the transaction over and above the issue of what we get for what we pay.

Both of these examples emphasize the importance of the particular frames we place on problems we have to solve or decisions we have to make. Managers are constantly being exposed to many different frames, some naturally occurring and others that are purposefully proposed. An important task of managers is to identify the appropriate frame by which employees and the organization, in general, should evaluate its performance and direct its effort.

The Framing of Risky Negotiations

The way in which information is framed (in terms of either potential gains or potential losses) to the negotiator can have a significant impact on his or her preference for risk, particularly when uncertainty about future events or outcomes is involved. For example, when offered the choice between gains of equal expected value—one for certain and the other a lottery, we strongly prefer to take the *certain* gain. However, when we are offered the choice between potential losses of equal expected value, we clearly and consistently eschew the loss for certain and prefer the risk inherent in the *lottery*.

There is substantial evidence to suggest that we are not indifferent toward risky situations and we should not necessarily trust our intuitions about risk. Negotiators routinely deviate from rationality because they do not typically appreciate the transient nature of their preference for risk; nor do they take into consideration the ability of a particular decision frame to influence that preference. Influencing our attitudes toward risk through the positive or negative frames associated with the problem is the result of evaluating an alternative from a particular referent point or base line. A referent point is the basis by which we evaluate whether what we are considering is viewed as a gain or a loss. The referent point that we choose determines the frame we impose on our options and, subsequently, our willingness to accept or reject those options.

Consider the high-performing employee who is expecting a significant increase in salary this year. He frames his expectations on the past behavior of the company. As such, he is expecting a raise of approximately $5,000. Because of the recession, he receives a $3,500 salary increase. He immediately confronts his manager, complaining that he has been unfairly treated. He is extremely disappointed in what his surprised manager saw as an exceptional raise because the employee's referent point is $1,500 higher. Had he known that the average salary increase was only $2,000 (and used that as a more realistic referent point), he would have perceived the same raise quite differently and it may have had the motivating force that his manager had hoped to create.

The selection of which relevant frame influences our behavior is a function of our selection of a base line by which we evaluate potential outcomes. The choice of one referent point over another may be the result of a visible anchor, the "status quo," or our expectations. Probably one of the most common referent points is what we perceive to be in our current inventory (our status quo)—what is ours already. We then evaluate offers or options in terms of whether they make us better off (a gain) or worse off (a loss) from (what we perceive to be) our current resource state.

Interestingly, what we include in our current resource state is surprisingly easy to modify. Consider the executive vice president of a large automobile manufacturing concern that has been hit by a number of economic difficulties because of the recession in the United States. It appears as if she will have to close down three plants and the employee rolls will be trimmed by 6,000 individuals. In exploring ways to avoid this alternative, she has identified two plans that might ameliorate the situation. If she selects the first plan, she will be able to save 2,000 jobs and one of the three plants. If she implements the second plan, there is a one-third probability that she can save all three plants and all 6,000 jobs, but there is a two-thirds probability that this plan will end up saving none of the plants and none of the jobs. If you were this vice president, which plan would you select (#1 or #2)?

Now consider the same options (Plan 1 or Plan 2) framed as losses: If the vice president implements Plan 1, two of the three plants will be shut down and 4,000 jobs will be lost. If she implements Plan 2, then there is a two-thirds probability of losing all three plants and all 6,000 jobs, but there is a one-third probability of losing no plants and no jobs. If you were presented with these two plans, which would be more attractive? Plan 1 or Plan 2?

It is obvious that from a purely economic perspective, there is no difference between the two choices. Yet managers offered the plans framed in terms of gains select the first plan about 76 percent of the time. However, managers offered the choice between the plans framed in terms of losses only select the first plan about 22 percent of the time. When confronted with potential losses, the lottery represented by Plan 2 becomes relatively much more attractive.

An important point for managers to consider is that the way in which the problem is framed, or presented, can dramatically alter the perceived value or acceptability of alternative courses of action. In negotiation, for example, the more risk-averse course of action is to accept an offered settlement; the more risk-seeking course of action is to hold out for future, potential concessions. In translating the influence of the framing bias to negotiation, we must realize that the selection of a particular referent point or base line determines whether a negotiator will frame his or her decision as positive or negative.

Specifically, consider any recurring contract negotiation. As the representative of Company A, the offer from Company B can be viewed in two ways, depending on the referent point I use. If my referent point is the current contract, Company B's offer can be evaluated in terms of the "gains" Company A can expect relative to the previous contract. However, if the referent point for Company A is an initial offer on the issues under current consideration, then Company A is more likely to evaluate Company B's offers as losses to be incurred if the contract as proposed is accepted. Viewing options as losses or as gains will have considerable impact on the negotiator's willingness to accept side B's position—even though the same options may be offered in both cases.

Likewise, the referent points available to an individual negotiating his salary for a new position in the company include (1) his current salary; (2) the company's initial offer; (3) the least he is willing to accept; (4) his estimate of the most the company is willing to pay; or (5) his initial salary request. As his referent moves from 1 to 5, he progresses from a positive to a negative frame in the negotiation. What is a modest *gain* compared to his current wage is perceived as a loss when compared to what he would like to receive. Along these same lines, employees currently making $15/hour and demanding an increase of $4/hour can view a proposed increase of $2/hour as a

$2/hour gain in comparison to last year's wage (Referent 1) or as a $2/hour loss in comparison to their stated or initial proposal of $19/hour (Referent 5). Consequently, the location of the referent point is critical to whether the decision is positively or negatively framed and affects the resulting risk preference of the decision maker.

In a study of the impact of framing on collective bargaining outcomes, we used a five-issue negotiation with participants playing the roles of management or labor negotiators.[3] Each negotiator's frame was manipulated by adjusting his or her referent point. Half of the negotiators were told that any concessions they made from their initial offers represented losses to their constituencies (i.e., a negative frame). The other half were told that any agreements they were able to reach which were better than the current contract were gains to their constituencies (i.e., the positive frame). In analyzing the results of their negotiations, we found that negatively framed negotiators were less concessionary and reached fewer agreements than positively framed negotiators. In addition, negotiators who had positive frames perceived the negotiated outcomes as more fair than those who had negative frames.

In another study, we posed the following problem to negotiators:

> You are a wholesaler of refrigerators. Corporate policy does not allow any flexibility in pricing. However, flexibility does exist in terms of expenses that you can incur (shipping, financing terms, etc.), which have a direct effect on the profitability of the transaction. These expenses can all be viewed in dollar value terms. You are negotiating an $8,000 sale. The buyer wants you to pay $2,000 in expenses. You want to pay less expenses. When you negotiate the exchange, do you try to minimize your expenses (reduce them from $2,000) or maximize net profit, i.e., price less expenses (increase the net profit from $6,000)?

From an objective standpoint, the choice you make to reduce expenses or maximize profit should be irrelevant. Because the choice objectively is between two identical options, selecting one or the other should have no impact on the outcome of the negotiation. What we did find, in contrast, is that the frame that buyers and sellers take into the negotiation can systemically affect their behavior.[4]

In one study, negotiators were led to view transactions in terms of either (1) net profit or (2) total expenses deducted from gross profits. These two situations were objectively identical. Managers can think about maximizing their profits (i.e., gains) or minimizing their expenses (i.e., losses). These choices are linked; if one starts from the same set of revenues, then one way to maximize profits is to minimize expenses and if one is successful at minimizing expenses, the outcome is that profit may be maximized. That is, there is an obvious relationship between profits and expenses. So, objectively, there is no reason to believe that an individual should behave differently if given the instructions to minimize expenses or to maximize profits. However, those negotiators told to maximize profit (i.e., a positive frame) were more concessionary. In addition, positively framed negotiators completed significantly more transactions than their negatively framed (those told to minimize expenses) counterparts. Because they completed more transactions, their overall profitability in the market was higher, although negatively framed negotiators completed transactions of greater mean profit.[5]

The Endowment Effect

The ease with which we can alter our referent points was illustrated in a series of studies conducted by Daniel Kahneman, Jack Knetsch, and Richard Thaler.[6] In any exchange between a buyer and a seller, the buyer must be willing to pay at least the minimum amount the seller is willing to accept for a trade to take place. In determining the worth of an object, its value to the seller may, on occasion, be determined by some objective third party such as an economic market. However, in a large number of transactions, the seller places a value on the item—a value that may include not only the market value of the item but also a component for an emotional attachment to or unique appreciation of the item. What impact might such an attachment have on the framing of the transaction?

Let's imagine that you have just received a coffee mug.[7] (In the actual demonstration, coffee mugs were placed before one-third of the participants, the "sellers," in the study.) After receiving the mug, you are told that in fact you "own the object (coffee mug) in your possession. You have the option of selling it if a price, to be determined later, is acceptable to you." Next, you are given a list (see Exhibit 1) of possible selling prices, ranging from $.50 to $9.50, and are told for each of the possible prices, you should indicate whether you would (a) sell the mug and receive that amount in return, or (b) keep the object and take it home with you. What is your selling price for the mug?

Another third of the group (the "buyers") were told that they would be receiving a sum of money and they could choose to keep the money or use it to buy a mug. They were also asked to indicate their preferences between a mug and sums of money ranging from $.50 to $9.50. Finally, the last third of the participants (the "choosers") were given a questionnaire indicating that they would later be given an option of receiving either a mug or a sum of money to be determined later. They indicated their preferences between the mug and sums of money between $.50 and $9.50. All of the participants were told that their answers would not influence either the pre-determined price of the mug or the amount of money to be received in lieu of the mug.

The sellers reported a median value of $7.12 for the mug; the buyers valued the mug at $2.88; and the choosers valued the mug at $3.12. It is interesting that in this exercise, being a buyer or a chooser resulted in very similar evaluations of worth of the mug. However, owning the mug (the sellers) created a much greater sense of the mug's worth. In this case, it was approximately 40 percent greater than the market (or retail) value of the mug.

The explanation for this disparity lies in the fact that different roles (buyer, seller, or chooser) created different referent points. In fact, what seems to happen in such situations is that owning something changes the nature of the owner's relationship to the commodity. Giving up that item is now perceived as a loss, and in valuing the item, the owner may include a dollar value to offset his or her perceived loss. If we consider this discrepancy in the value of an item common, then the simple act of "owning" an item, however briefly, can increase one's personal attachment to an item—and, typically, its perceived value. After such an attachment is formed, the cost of breaking that attachment is greater and is reflected in the higher price the sellers demand to part with

EXHIBIT 1   The Coffee Mug Questionnaire

For each price listed below, indicate whether you would be willing to sell the coffee mug for that price or keep the mug.

If the price is $0.50, I will sell _____ ; I will keep the mug _____ .

If the price is $1.00, I will sell _____ ; I will keep the mug _____ .

If the price is $1.50, I will sell _____ ; I will keep the mug _____ .

If the price is $2.00, I will sell _____ ; I will keep the mug _____ .

If the price is $2.50, I will sell _____ ; I will keep the mug _____ .

If the price is $3.00, I will sell _____ ; I will keep the mug _____ .

If the price is $3.50, I will sell _____ ; I will keep the mug _____ .

If the price is $4.00, I will sell _____ ; I will keep the mug _____ .

If the price is $4.50, I will sell _____ ; I will keep the mug _____ .

If the price is $5.00, I will sell _____ ; I will keep the mug _____ .

If the price is $5.50, I will sell _____ ; I will keep the mug _____ .

If the price is $6.00, I will sell _____ ; I will keep the mug _____ .

If the price is $6.50, I will sell _____ ; I will keep the mug _____ .

If the price is $7.00, I will sell _____ ; I will keep the mug _____ .

If the price is $7.50, I will sell _____ ; I will keep the mug _____ .

If the price is $8.00, I will sell _____ ; I will keep the mug _____ .

If the price is $8.50, I will sell _____ ; I will keep the mug _____ .

If the price is $9.00, I will sell _____ ; I will keep the mug _____ .

If the price is $9.50, I will sell _____ ; I will keep the mug _____ .

their mugs as compared to the value the buyers or the choosers place on the exact same commodity. In addition, we would expect that the endowment effect intensifies to the extent that the value of the commodity of interest is ambiguous or subjective, the commodity itself is unique, or not easily substitutable in the marketplace.

Framing, Negotiator Bias, and Strategic Behavior

In the previous discussion, we described the negotiator behaviors that may arise from positive and negative frames within the context of the interaction. In this section, we identify some of the techniques for strategically manipulating framing to direct negotiator performance.

Framing has important implications for negotiator tactics. Using the framing effect to induce a negotiating opponent to concede requires that the negotiator create referents that lead the opposition to a positive frame by couching the proposal in terms of their potential gain. In addition, the negotiator should emphasize the inherent risk in the negotiation situation and the opportunity for a sure gain. As our research suggests, simply posing problems as choices among potential gains rather than choices among potential losses can significantly influence the negotiator's preferences for specific outcomes.

Framing can also have important implications for how managers choose to intervene in disputes among their peers or subordinates. Managers, of course, have a wide range of options to implement when deciding to intervene in disputes in which they are not active principals. If the manager's goal is to get the parties to reach an agreement rather than having the manager decide what the solution to the dispute will be, he or she may wish to facilitate both parties' viewing the negotiation from a positive frame. This is tricky, however, since the same referent that will lead to a positive frame for one negotiator is likely to lead to a negative frame for the other negotiator if presented simultaneously to the parties. Making use of the effects of framing may be most appropriate when a manager can meet with each side separately. He or she may present different perspectives to each party to create a positive frame (and the subsequent risk-averse behavior associated with such a frame) for parties on both sides of the dispute. Again, if the manager is to effect the frame of the problem in such a way as to encourage agreement, he or she may also emphasize the possible losses inherent in continuing the dispute. Combining these two strategies may facilitate both sides' preference for the certainty of a settlement.

Being in the role of buyer or seller can be a naturally occurring frame that can influence negotiator behavior in systematic ways. Consider the curious, consistent, and robust finding in a number of studies that buyers tend to outperform sellers in market settings in which the balance of power is equal.[8] Given the artificial context of the laboratory settings and the symmetry of the design of these field and laboratory markets, there is no logical reason why buyers should do better than sellers. One explanation for this observed difference may be that when the commodity is anonymous (or completely substitutable in a market sense), sellers may think about the transaction in terms of the dollars exchanged. That is, sellers may conceptualize the process of selling as gaining resources (e.g., how many dollars do I gain by selling the commodity); whereas buyers may view the transaction in terms of loss of dollars (e.g., how many dollars do I have to give up). If the dollars are the primary focus of the participants' attention, then buyers would tend to be risk seeking and sellers risk averse in the exchange.

When a risk-averse party (i.e., the seller, in this example) negotiates with a risk-seeking party (i.e., the buyer), the buyer is more willing to risk the potential agreement by demanding more or being less concessionary. To reach agreement, the seller must make additional concessions to induce the buyer, because of his or her risk-seeking propensity, to accept the agreement. Thus, in situations where the relative achievements of buyers and seller can be directly compared, buyers would benefit from their negative frame (and subsequent risk-averse behavior). The critical issue is that these naturally occurring frames such as the role demands of being a "buyer" or "seller" can easily influence the way in which the disputed issues are framed—even without the conscious intervention of one or more of the parties.

It is easy to see that the frames of negotiators can result in the difference between impasse and reaching an important agreement. Both sides in negotiations typically talk in terms of a certain wage, price, or outcome that they must get—setting a high referent point against which gains and losses are measured. If this occurs, any compromise below (or above) that point represents a loss. This perceived loss may lead negotiators to adopt a negative frame to all proposals, exhibit risk-seeking behaviors, and be less likely to reach settlement. Thus, negotiators, similar to the early example involving the beach and the beer, may end up with no beer (or no agreement) because of the frame (the amount of money I will pay for a beer from a run-down grocery store) that is placed on the choices rather than an objective assessment of what the beer is worth to the individual.

In addition, framing has important implications for the tactics that negotiators use. The framing effect suggests that to induce concessionary behavior from an opponent, a negotiator should always create anchors or emphasize referents that lead the opposition to a positive frame and couch the negotiation in terms of what the other side has to gain.

In addition, the negotiator should make the inherent risk salient to the opposition while the opponent is in a risky situation. If the sure gain that is being proposed is rejected, there is no certainty about the quality of the next offer. Simultaneously, the negotiator should also not be persuaded by similar arguments from opponents. Maintaining a risk-neutral or risk-seeking perspective in evaluating an opponent's proposals may, in the worst case, reduce the probability of reaching an agreement; however, if agreements are reached, the outcomes are more likely to be of greater value to the negotiator.

An important component in creating good negotiated agreements is to avoid the pitfalls of being framed while, simultaneously, understanding the impact of positively and negatively framing your negotiating opponent. However, framing is just one of a series of cognitive biases that can have a significant negative impact on the performance of negotiators. The purpose of this article was to describe the impact of one of these cognitive biases on negotiator behavior by considering the available research on the topic and to explore ways to reduce the problems associated with framing. By increasing our understanding of the subtle ways in which these cognitive biases can reduce the effectiveness of our negotiations, managers can begin to improve not only the quality of agreements for themselves but also fashion agreements that more efficiently allocate the available resources—leaving both parties and the communities of which they are a part better off.

ENDNOTES

This article is based on the book by M. H. Bazerman and M. A. Neale, *Negotiating Rationally*. Free Press: New York, 1992.

1. Adapted from J. E. Russo and P. J. Schoemaker, *Decision Traps* (New York: Doubleday, 1989).
2. R. Thaler, "Using Mental Accounting in a Theory of Purchasing Behavior," *Marketing Science* 4 (1985), pp. 12–13.
3. M. A. Neale and M. H. Bazerman, "The Effects of Framing and Negotiator Overconfidence," *Academy of Management Journal 28* (1985), pp. 34–49.
4. M. H. Bazerman, T. Magliozzi, and M. A. Neale, "The Acquisition of an Integrative Response in a Competitive Market Simulation," *Organizational Behavior and Human Performance* 34 (1985), pp. 294–313.

5. See, for example, Bazerman, Magliozzi, and Neale (1985), op. cit.; Neale and Bazerman, (1985), op. cit.; or M. A. Neale and G. B. Northcraft, "Experts, Amateurs and Refrigerators: Comparing Expert and Amateur Decision Making on a Novel Task," *Organizational Behavior and Human Decision Processes* 38 (1986), pp. 305–17; M. A. Neale, V. L. Huber, and G. B. Northcraft, "The Framing of Negotiations: Context Versus Task Frames," *Organizational Behavior and Human Decision Processes* 39 (1987), pp. 228–41.

6. D. Kahneman, J. L. Knetsch, and R. Thaler, "Experimental Tests of the Endowment Effect and Coase Theorem," *Journal of Political Economy*, 1990.

7. The coffee mugs were valued at approximately $5.00.

8. Bazerman et al. (1985), op. cit.; M. A. Neale, V. L. Huber, and G. B. Northcraft (1987), op. cit.

The Power of Talk:
Who Gets Heard and Why

Deborah Tannen

The head of a large division of a multinational corporation was running a meeting devoted to performance assessment. Each senior manager stood up, reviewed the individuals in his group, and evaluated them for promotion. Although there were women in every group, not one of them made the cut. One after another, each manager declared, in effect, that every woman in his group didn't have the self-confidence needed to be promoted. The division head began to doubt his ears. How could it be that all the talented women in the division suffered from a lack of self-confidence?

In all likelihood, they didn't. Consider the many women who have left large corporations to start their own businesses, obviously exhibiting enough confidence to succeed on their own. Judgments about confidence can be inferred only from the way people present themselves, and much of that presentation is in the form of talk.

The CEO of a major corporation told me that he often has to make decisions in five minutes about matters on which others may have worked five months. He said he uses this rule: If the person making the proposal seems confident, the CEO approves it. If not, he says no. This might seem like a reasonable approach. But my field of research, sociolinguistics, suggests otherwise. The CEO obviously thinks he knows what a confident person sounds like. But his judgment, which may be dead right for some people, may be dead wrong for others.

Communication isn't as simple as saying what you mean. How you say what you mean is crucial, and differs from one person to the next, because using language is learned social behavior: How we talk and listen are deeply influenced by cultural experience. Although we might think that our ways of saying what we mean are natural, we can run into trouble if we interpret and evaluate others as if they necessarily felt the same way we'd feel if we spoke the way they did.

Since 1974, I have been researching the influence of linguistic style on conversations and human relationships. In the past four years, I have extended that research to the workplace, where I have observed how ways of speaking learned in childhood affect judgments of competence and confidence, as well as who gets heard, who gets credit, and what gets done.

Reprinted from *Harvard Business Review*, September–October 1995. Reprinted with permission of *Harvard Business Review* and the author.

The division head who was dumbfounded to hear that all the talented women in his organization lacked confidence was probably right to be skeptical. The senior managers were judging the women in their groups by their own linguistic norms, but women—like people who have grown up in a different culture—have often learned different styles of speaking than men, which can make them seem less competent and self-assured than they are.

WHAT IS LINGUISTIC STYLE?

Everything that is said must be said in a certain way—in a certain tone of voice, at a certain rate of speed, and with a certain degree of loudness. Whereas often we consciously consider what to say before speaking, we rarely think about how to say it, unless the situation is obviously loaded—for example, a job interview or a tricky performance review. Linguistic style refers to a person's characteristic speaking pattern. It includes such features as directness or indirectness, pacing and pausing, word choice, and the use of such elements as jokes, figures of speech, stories, questions, and apologies. In other words, linguistic style is a set of culturally learned signals by which we not only communicate what we mean but also interpret others' meaning and evaluate one another as people.

Consider turn taking, one element of linguistic style. Conversation is an enterprise in which people take turns: One person speaks, then the other responds. However, this apparently simple exchange requires a subtle negotiation of signals so that you know when the other person is finished and it's your turn to begin. Cultural factors such as country or region of origin and ethnic background influence how long a pause seems natural. When Bob, who is from Detroit, has a conversation with his colleague Joe, from New York City, it's hard for him to get a word in edgewise because he expects a slightly longer pause between turns than Joe does. A pause of that length never comes because, before it has a chance to, Joe senses an uncomfortable silence, which he fills with more talk of his own. Both men fail to realize that differences in conversational style are getting in their way. Bob thinks that Joe is pushy and uninterested in what he has to say, and Joe thinks that Bob doesn't have much to contribute. Similarly, when Sally relocated from Texas to Washington, D.C., she kept searching for the right time to break in during staff meetings—and never found it. Although in Texas she was considered outgoing and confident, in Washington she was perceived as shy and retiring. Her boss even suggested she take an assertiveness training course. Thus slight differences in conversational style—in these cases, a few seconds of pause—can have a surprising impact on who gets heard and on the judgments, including psychological ones, that are made about people and their abilities.

Every utterance functions on two levels. We're all familiar with the first one: Language communicates ideas. The second level is mostly invisible to us, but it plays a powerful role in communication. As a form of social behavior, language also negotiates relationships. Through ways of speaking, we signal—and create—the relative status of speakers and their level of rapport. If you say, "Sit down!" you are signaling that you have higher status than the person you are addressing, that you are so close to each other that you can drop all pleasantries, or that you are angry. If you say, "I would be honored if you would sit down," you are signaling great respect—or great sarcasm, depending on your tone of voice, the situation, and what you both know about how close you really are. If you say, "You must be so tired—why don't you sit down," you are communicating either closeness and concern or condescension. Each of these ways of saying "the same thing"—telling someone to sit down—can have a vastly different meaning.

In every community known to linguists, the patterns that constitute linguistic style are relatively different for men and women. What's "natural" for most men speaking a given language is, in some cases, different from what's "natural" for most women. That is because we learn ways of speaking as children growing up, especially from peers, and children tend to play with other children of the same sex. The research of sociologists, anthropologists, and psychologists observing American children at play has shown that, although both girls and boys find ways of creating rapport and negotiating status, girls tend to learn conversational rituals that focus on the rapport dimension of relationships whereas boys tend to learn rituals that focus on the status dimension.

Girls tend to play with a single best friend or in small groups, and they spend a lot of time talking. They use language to negotiate how close they are; for example, the girl you tell your secrets to becomes your best friend. Girls learn to downplay ways in which one is better than the others and to emphasize ways in which they are all the same. From childhood, most girls learn that sounding too sure of themselves will make them unpopular with their peers—although nobody really takes such modesty literally. A group of girls will ostracize a girl who calls attention to her own superiority and criticize her by saying, "She thinks she's something"; and a girl who tells others what to do is called "bossy." Thus girls learn to talk in ways that balance their own needs with those of others—to save face for one another in the broadest sense of the term.

Boys tend to play very differently. They usually play in larger groups in which more boys can be included, but not everyone is treated as an equal. Boys with high status in their group are expected to emphasize rather than downplay their status, and usually one or several boys will be seen as the leader or leaders. Boys generally don't accuse one another of being bossy, because the leader is expected to tell lower-status boys what to do. Boys learn to use language to negotiate their status in the group by displaying their abilities and knowledge, and by challenging others and resisting challenges. Giving orders is one way of getting and keeping the high-status role. Another is taking center stage by telling stories or jokes.

This is not to say that all boys and girls grow up this way or feel comfortable in these groups or are equally successful at negotiating within these norms. But, for the most part, these childhood play groups are where boys and girls learn their conversational styles. In this sense, they grow up in different worlds. The result is that women and men tend to have different habitual ways of saying what they mean, and conversations between them can be like cross-cultural communication: You can't assume that the other person means what you would mean if you said the same thing in the same way.

My research in companies across the United States shows that the lessons learned in childhood carry over into the workplace. Consider the following example: A focus group was organized at a major multinational company to evaluate a recently implemented flextime policy. The participants sat in a circle and discussed the new system. The group concluded that it was excellent, but they also agreed on ways to improve it.

The meeting went well and was deemed a success by all, according to my own observations and everyone's comments to me. But the next day, I was in for a surprise.

I had left the meeting with the impression that Phil had been responsible for most of the suggestions adopted by the group. But as I typed up my notes, I noticed that Cheryl had made almost all those suggestions. I had thought that the key ideas came from Phil because he had picked up Cheryl's points and supported them, speaking at greater length in doing so than she had in raising them.

It would be easy to regard Phil as having stolen Cheryl's ideas—and her thunder. But that would be inaccurate. Phil never claimed Cheryl's ideas as his own. Cheryl herself told me later that she left the meeting confident that she had contributed significantly, and that she appreciated Phil's support. She volunteered, with a laugh, "It was not one of those times when a woman says something and it's ignored, then a man says it and it's picked up." In other words, Cheryl and Phil worked well as a team, the group fulfilled its charge, and the company got what it needed. So what was the problem?

I went back and asked all the participants who they thought had been the most influential group member, the one most responsible for the ideas that had been adopted. The pattern of answers was revealing. The two other women in the group named Cheryl. Two of the three men named Phil. Of the men, only Phil named Cheryl. In other words, in this instance, the women evaluated the contribution of another woman more accurately than the men did.

Meetings like this take place daily in companies around the country. Unless managers are unusually good at listening closely to how people say what they mean, the talents of someone like Cheryl may well be undervalued and underutilized.

ONE UP, ONE DOWN

Individual speakers vary in how sensitive they are to the social dynamics of language—in other words, to the subtle nuances of what others say to them. Men tend to be sensitive to the power dynamics of interaction, speaking in ways that position themselves as one up and resisting being put in a one-down position by others. Women tend to react more strongly to the rapport dynamic, speaking in ways that save face for others and buffering statements that could be seen as putting others in a one-down position. These linguistic patterns are pervasive; you can hear them in hundreds of exchanges in the workplace everyday. And, as in the case of Cheryl and Phil, they affect who gets heard and who gets credit.

Getting Credit.   Even so small a linguistic strategy as the choice of pronoun can affect who gets credit. In my research in the workplace, I heard men say "I" in situations where I heard women say "we." For example, one publishing company executive said, "I'm hiring a new manager. I'm going to put him in charge of my marketing division," as if he owned the corporation. In stark contrast, I recorded women saying "we" when referring to work they alone had done. One woman explained that it would sound too self-promoting to claim credit in an obvious way by saying, "I did this." Yet she expected—sometimes vainly—that others would know it was her work and would give her the credit she did not claim for herself.

Managers might leap to the conclusion that women who do not take credit for what they've done should be taught to do so. But that solution is problematic because we associate ways of speaking with moral qualities: The way we speak is who we are and who we want to be.

Veronica, a senior researcher in a high-tech company, had an observant boss. He noticed that many of the ideas coming out of the group were hers but that often someone else trumpeted them around the office and got credit for them. He advised her to "own" her ideas and make sure she got the credit. But Veronica found she simply didn't enjoy her work if she had to approach it as what seemed to her an unattractive and unappealing "grabbing game." It was her dislike of such behavior that had led her to avoid it in the first place.

Whatever the motivation, women are less likely than men to have learned to blow their own horn. And they are more likely than men to believe that if they do so, they won't be liked.

Many have argued that the growing trend of assigning work to teams may be especially congenial to women, but it may also create complications for performance evaluation. When ideas are generated and work is accomplished in the privacy of the team, the outcome of the team's effort may become associated with the person most vocal about reporting results. There are many women and men—but probably relatively more women—who are reluctant to put themselves forward in this way and who consequently risk not getting credit for their contributions.

Confidence and Boasting.   The CEO who based his decisions on the confidence level of speakers was articulating a value that is widely shared in U.S. businesses: One way to judge confidence is by an individual's behavior, especially verbal behavior. Here again, many women are at a disadvantage.

Studies show that women are more likely to downplay their certainty and men are more likely to minimize their doubts. Psychologist Laurie Heatherington and her colleagues devised an ingenious experiment, which they reported in the journal *Sex Roles* (Volume 29, 1993). They asked hundreds of incoming college students to predict what grades they would get in their first year. Some subjects were asked to make their predictions privately by writing them down and placing them in an envelope; others were asked to make their predictions publicly, in the presence of a researcher. The results showed that more women than men predicted lower grades for themselves if they made their predictions publicly. If they made their predictions privately, the predictions were the same as those of the men—and the same as their actual grades. This study provides evidence that what comes across as lack of confidence—predicting lower grades for oneself—may reflect not one's actual level of confidence but the desire not to seem boastful.

These habits with regard to appearing humble or confident result from the socialization of boys and girls by their peers in childhood play. As adults, both women and men find these behaviors reinforced by the positive responses they get from friends and relatives who share the same norms. But the norms of behavior in the U.S. business world are based on the style of interaction that is more common among men—at least, among American men.

Asking Questions.   Although asking the right questions is one of the hallmarks of a good manager, how and when questions are asked can send unintended signals about competence and power. In a group, if only one person asks questions, he or she risks being seen as the only ignorant one. Furthermore, we judge others not only by how they speak but also by how they are spoken to. The person who asks questions may end up being lectured to and looking like a novice under a schoolmaster's tutelage. The way boys are socialized makes them more likely to be aware of the underlying power dynamic by which a question asker can be seen in a one-down position.

One practicing physician learned the hard way that any exchange of information can become the basis for judgments—or misjudgments—about competence. During her training, she received a negative evaluation that she thought was unfair, so she asked her supervising physician for an explanation. He said that she knew less than her peers. Amazed at his answer, she asked how he had reached that conclusion. He said, "You ask more questions."

Along with cultural influences and individual personality, gender seems to play a role in whether and when people ask questions. For example, of all the observations I've made in lectures and books, the one that sparks the most enthusiastic flash of recognition is that men are less likely than women to stop and ask for directions when they are lost. I explain that men often resist asking for directions because they are aware that it puts them in a one-down position and because they value the independence that comes with finding their way by themselves. Asking for directions while driving is only one instance—along with many others that researchers have examined—in which men seem less likely than women to ask questions. I believe this is because they are more attuned than women to the potential face-losing aspect of asking questions. And men who believe that asking questions might reflect negatively on them may, in turn, be likely to form a negative opinion of others who ask questions in situations where they would not.

CONVERSATIONAL RITUALS

Conversation is fundamentally ritual in the sense that we speak in ways our culture has conventionalized and expect certain types of responses. Take greetings, for example. I have heard visitors to the United States complain Americans are hypocritical because they ask how you are but aren't interested in the answer. To Americans, How are you? is obviously a ritualized way to start a conversation rather than a literal request for information. In other parts of the world, including the Philippines, people ask each other, "Where are you going?" when they meet. The question seems intrusive to Americans, who do not realize that it, too, is a ritual query to which the only expected reply is a vague "Over there."

It's easy and entertaining to observe different rituals in foreign countries. But we don't expect differences, and are far less likely to recognize the ritualized nature of our conversations, when we are with our compatriots at work. Our differing rituals can be even more problematic when we think we're all speaking the same language.

Apologies.   Consider the simple phrase *I'm sorry.*

Catherine:

How did that big presentation go?

Bob:

> Oh, not very well. I got a lot of flak from the VP for finance, and I didn't have the numbers at my fingertips.

Catherine:

> Oh, I'm sorry. I know how hard you worked on that.

In this case, *I'm sorry* probably means "I'm sorry that happened," not "I apologize," unless it was Catherine's responsibility to supply Bob with the numbers for the presentation. Women tend to say *I'm sorry* more frequently than men, and often they intend it in this way—as a ritualized means of expressing concern. It's one of many learned elements of conversational style that girls often use to establish rapport. Ritual apologies—like other conversational rituals—work well when both parties share the same assumptions about their use. But people who utter frequent ritual apologies may end up appearing weaker, less confident, and literally more blameworthy than people who don't.

Apologies tend to be regarded differently by men, who are more likely to focus on the status implications of exchanges. Many men avoid apologies because they see them as putting the speaker in a one-down position. I observed with some amazement an encounter among several lawyers engaged in a negotiation over a speakerphone. At one point, the lawyer in whose office I was sitting accidentally elbowed the telephone and cut off the call. When his secretary got the parties back on again, I expected him to say what I would have said: "Sorry about that. I knocked the phone with my elbow." Instead, he said, "Hey, what happened? One minute you were there; the next minute you were gone!" This lawyer seemed to have an automatic impulse not to admit fault if he didn't have to. For me, it was one of those pivotal moments when you realize that the world you live in is not the one everyone lives in and that the way you assume is the way to talk is really only one of many.

Those who caution managers not to undermine their authority by apologizing are approaching interaction from the perspective of the power dynamic. In many cases, this strategy is effective. On the other hand, when I asked people what frustrated them in their jobs, one frequently voiced complaint was working with or for someone who refuses to apologize or admit fault. In other words, accepting responsibility for errors and admitting mistakes may be an equally effective or superior strategy in some settings.

Feedback. Styles of giving feedback contain a ritual element that often is the cause for misunderstanding. Consider the following exchange: A manager had to tell her marketing director to rewrite a report. She began this potentially awkward task by citing the report's strengths and then moved to the main point: the weaknesses that needed to be remedied. The marketing director seemed to understand and accept his supervisor's comments, but his revision contained only minor changes and failed to address the major weaknesses. When the manager told him of her dissatisfaction, he accused her of misleading him: "You told me it was fine."

The impasse resulted from different linguistic styles. To the manager, it was natural to buffer the criticism by beginning with praise. Telling her subordinate that his report is inadequate and has to be rewritten puts him in a one-down position. Praising him for the parts that are good is a ritualized way of saving face for him. But the marketing director did not share his supervisor's assumption about how feedback should be given. Instead, he assumed that what she mentioned first was the main point and that what she brought up later was an afterthought.

Those who expect feedback to come in the way the manager presented it would appreciate her tact and would regard a more blunt approach as unnecessarily callous. But those who share the marketing director's assumptions would regard the blunt approach as honest and no-nonsense, and the manager's as obfuscating. Because each one's assumptions seemed self-evident, each blamed the other: The manager thought the marketing director was not listening, and he thought she had not communicated clearly or had changed her mind. This is significant because it illustrates that incidents labeled vaguely as "poor communication" may be the result of differing linguistic styles.

Compliments.   Exchanging compliments is a common ritual, especially among women. A mismatch in expectations about this ritual left Susan, a manager in the human resources field, in a one-down position. She and her colleague Bill had both given presentations at a national conference. On the airplane home, Susan told Bill, "That was a great talk!" "Thank you," he said. Then she asked, "What did you think of mine?" He responded with a lengthy and detailed critique, as she listened uncomfortably. An unpleasant feeling of having been put down came over her. Somehow she had been positioned as the novice in need of his expert advice. Even worse, she had only herself to blame, since she had, after all, asked Bill what he thought of her talk.

But had Susan asked for the response she received? When she asked Bill what he thought about her talk, she expected to hear not a critique but a compliment. In fact, her question had been an attempt to repair a ritual gone awry. Susan's initial compliment to Bill was the kind of automatic recognition she felt was more or less required after a colleague gives a presentation, and she expected Bill to respond with a matching compliment. She was just talking automatically, but he either sincerely misunderstood the ritual or simply took the opportunity to bask in the one-up position of critic. Whatever his motivation, it was Susan's attempt to spark an exchange of compliments that gave him the opening.

Although this exchange could have occurred between two men, it does not seem coincidental that it happened between a man and a woman. Linguist Janet Holmes discovered that women pay more compliments than men (*Anthropological Linguistics*, Volume 28, 1986). And, as I have observed, fewer men are likely to ask, "What did you think of my talk?" precisely because the question might invite an unwanted critique.

In the social structure of the peer groups in which they grow up, boys are indeed looking for opportunities to put others down and take the one-up position for themselves. In contrast, one of the rituals girls learn is taking the one-down position but assuming that the other person will recognize the ritual nature of the self-denigration and pull them back up.

The exchange between Susan and Bill also suggests how women's and men's characteristic styles may put women at a disadvantage in the workplace. If one person is trying to minimize status differences, maintain an appearance that everyone is equal, and save face for the other, while another person is trying to maintain the one-up position and avoid being positioned as one down, the person seeking the one-up position is likely to get it. At the same time, the person who has not been expending any effort to avoid the one-down position is likely to end up in it. Because women are more likely to take (or accept) the role of advice seeker, men are more inclined to interpret a ritual question from a woman as a request for advice.

Ritual Opposition.   Apologizing, mitigating criticism with praise, and exchanging compliments are rituals common among women that men often take literally. A ritual common among men that women often take literally is ritual opposition.

A woman in communications told me she watched with distaste and distress as her office mate argued heatedly with another colleague about whose division should suffer budget cuts. She was even more surprised, however, that a short time later they were as friendly as ever. "How can you pretend that fight never happened?" she asked. "Who's pretending it never happened?" he responded, as puzzled by her question as she had been by his behavior. "It happened," he said, "and it's over." What she took as literal fighting to him was a routine part of daily negotiation: a ritual fight.

Many Americans expect the discussion of ideas to be a ritual fight—that is, an exploration through verbal opposition. They present their own ideas in the most certain and absolute form they can, and wait to see if they are challenged. Being forced to defend an idea provides an opportunity to test it. In the same spirit, they may play devil's advocate in challenging their colleagues' ideas—trying to poke holes and find weaknesses—as a way of helping them explore and test their ideas.

This style can work well if everyone shares it, but those unaccustomed to it are likely to miss its ritual nature. They may give up an idea that is challenged, taking the objections as an indication that the idea was a poor one. Worse, they may take the opposition as a personal attack and may find it impossible to do their best in a contentious environment. People unaccustomed to this style may hedge when stating their ideas in order to fend off potential attacks. Ironically, this posture makes their arguments appear weak and is more likely to invite attack from pugnacious colleagues than to fend it off.

Ritual opposition can even play a role in who gets hired. Some consulting firms that recruit graduates from the top business schools use a confrontational interviewing technique. They challenge the candidate to "crack a case" in real time. A partner at one firm told me, "Women tend to do less well in this kind of interaction, and it certainly affects who gets hired. But, in fact, many women who don't 'test well' turn out to be good consultants. They're often smarter than some of the men who looked like analytic powerhouses under pressure."

The level of verbal opposition varies from one company's culture to the next, but I saw instances of it in all the organizations I studied. Anyone who is uncomfortable with this linguistic style—and that includes some men as well as many women—risks appearing insecure about his or her ideas.

NEGOTIATING AUTHORITY

In organizations, formal authority comes from the position one holds. But actual authority has to be negotiated day to day. The effectiveness of individual managers depends in part on their skill in negotiating authority and on whether others reinforce or undercut their efforts. The way linguistic style reflects status plays a subtle role in placing individuals within a hierarchy.

Managing Up and Down.   In all the companies I researched, I heard from women who knew they were doing a superior job and knew that their coworkers (and sometimes their immediate bosses) knew it as well, but believed that the higher-ups did not. They frequently told me that something outside themselves was holding them back and found it frustrating because they thought that all that should be necessary for success was to do a great job, that superior performance should be recognized and rewarded. In contrast, men often told me that if women weren't promoted, it was because they simply weren't up to snuff. Looking around, however, I saw evidence that men more often than women behaved in ways likely to get them recognized by those with the power to determine their advancement.

In all the companies I visited, I observed what happened at lunchtime. I saw young men who regularly ate lunch with their boss, and senior men who ate with the big boss. I noticed far fewer women who sought out the highest-level person they could eat with. But one is more likely to get recognition for work done if one talks about it to those higher up, and it is easier to do so if the lines of communication are already open. Furthermore, given the opportunity for a conversation with superiors, men and women are likely to have different ways of talking about their accomplishments because of the different ways in which they were socialized as children. Boys are rewarded by their peers if they talk up their achievements, whereas girls are rewarded if they play theirs down. Linguistic styles common among men may tend to give them some advantages when it comes to managing up.

All speakers are aware of the status of the person they are talking to and adjust accordingly. Everyone speaks differently when talking to a boss than when talking to a subordinate. But, surprisingly, the ways in which they adjust their talk may be different and thus may project different images of themselves.

Communications researchers Karen Tracy and Eric Eisenberg studied how relative status affects the way people give criticism. They devised a business letter that contained some errors and asked 13 male and 11 female college students to role-play delivering criticism under two scenarios. In the first, the speaker was a boss talking to a subordinate; in the second, the speaker was a subordinate talking to his or her boss. The researchers measured how hard the speakers tried to avoid hurting the feelings of the person they were criticizing.

One might expect people to be more careful about how they deliver criticism when they are in a subordinate position. Tracy and Eisenberg found that hypothesis to be true for the men in their study but not for the women. As they reported in *Research on Language and Social Interaction* (Volume 24, 1990/1991), the women showed more concern about the other person's feelings when they were playing the role of superior. In other words, the women were more careful to save face for the other person when they were managing down than when they were managing up. This pattern recalls the way girls are socialized: Those who are in some way superior are expected to downplay rather than flaunt their superiority.

In my own recordings of workplace communication, I observed women talking in similar ways. For example, when a manager had to correct a mistake made by her secretary, she did so by acknowledging that there were mitigating circumstances. She said, laughing, "You know, it's hard to do things around here, isn't it, with all these people coming in!" The manager was just saving face for her subordinate, just like the female students role-playing in the Tracy and Eisenberg study.

Is this an effective way to communicate? One must ask, effective for what? The manager in question established a positive environment in her group, and the work was done effectively. On the other hand, numerous women in many different fields told me that their bosses say they don't project the proper authority.

Indirectness.   Another linguistic signal that varies with power and status is indirectness—the tendency to say what we mean without spelling it out in so many words. Despite the widespread belief in the United States that it's always best to say exactly what we mean, indirectness is a fundamental and pervasive element in human communication. It also is one of the elements that varies most from one culture to another, and it can cause enormous misunderstanding when speakers have different habits and expectations about how it is used. It's often said that American women are more indirect than American men, but in fact everyone tends to be indirect in some situations and in different ways. Allowing for cultural, ethnic, regional, and individual differences, women are especially likely to be indirect when it comes to telling others what to do, which is not surprising, considering girls' readiness to brand other girls as bossy. On the other hand, men are especially likely to be indirect when it comes to admitting fault or weakness, which also is not surprising, considering boys' readiness to push around boys who assume the one-down position.

At first glance, it would seem that only the powerful can get away with bald commands such as, "Have that report on my desk by noon." But power in an organization also can lead to requests so indirect that they don't sound like requests at all. A boss who says, "Do we have the sales data by product line for each region?" would be surprised and frustrated if a subordinate responded, "We probably do" rather than "I'll get it for you."

Examples such as these notwithstanding, many researchers have claimed that those in subordinate positions are more likely to speak indirectly, and that is surely accurate in some situations. For example, linguist Charlotte Linde, in a study published in *Language in Society* (Volume 17, 1988), examined the black-box conversations that took place between pilots and copilots before airplane crashes. In one particularly tragic instance, an Air Florida plane crashed into the Potomac River immediately after attempting takeoff from National Airport in Washington, D.C., killing all but 5 of the 74 people on board. The pilot, it turned out, had little experience flying in icy weather. The copilot had a bit more, and it became heartbreakingly clear on analysis that he had tried to warn the pilot but had done so indirectly. Alerted by Linde's observation, I examined the transcript of the conversations and found evidence of her hypothesis. The copilot repeatedly called attention to the bad weather and to ice buildup on other planes:

Copilot:

> Look how the ice is just hanging on his, ah, back, back there, see that? See all those icicles on the back there and everything?

Pilot:

> Yeah.

[The copilot also expressed concern about the long waiting time since deicing.]

Copilot:

Boy, this is a, this is a losing battle here on trying to deice those things; it [gives] you a false feeling of security, that's all that does.

[Just before they took off, the copilot expressed another concern—about abnormal instrument readings—but again he didn't press the matter when it wasn't picked up by the pilot.]

Copilot:

That doesn't seem right, does it? [3-second pause]. Ah, that's not right. Well—

Pilot:

Yes it is, there's 80.

Copilot:

Naw, I don't think that's right. [7-second pause] Ah, maybe it is.

Shortly thereafter, the plane took off, with tragic results. In other instances as well as this one, Linde observed that copilots, who are second in command, are more likely to express themselves indirectly or otherwise mitigate, or soften, their communication when they are suggesting courses of action to the pilot. In an effort to avert similar disasters, some airlines now offer training for copilots to express themselves in more assertive ways.

This solution seems self-evidently appropriate to most Americans. But when I assigned Linde's article in a graduate seminar I taught, a Japanese student pointed out that it would be just as effective to train pilots to pick up on hints. This approach reflects assumptions about communication that typify Japanese culture, which places great value on the ability of people to understand one another without putting everything into words. Either directness or indirectness can be a successful means of communication as long as the linguistic style is understood by the participants.

In the world of work, however, there is more at stake than whether the communication is understood. People in powerful positions are likely to reward styles similar to their own, because we all tend to take as self-evident the logic of our own styles. Accordingly, there is evidence that in the U.S. workplace, where instructions from a superior are expected to be voiced in a relatively direct manner, those who tend to be indirect when telling subordinates what to do may be perceived as lacking in confidence.

Consider the case of the manager at a national magazine who was responsible for giving assignments to reporters. She tended to phrase her assignments as questions. For example, she asked, "How would you like to do the X project with Y?" or said, "I was thinking of putting you on the X project. Is that okay?" This worked extremely well with her staff; they liked working for her, and the work got done in an efficient and orderly manner. But when she had her midyear evaluation with her own boss, he criticized her for not assuming the proper demeanor with her staff.

In any work environment, the higher-ranking person has the power to enforce his or her view of appropriate demeanor, created in part by linguistic style. In most U.S. contexts, that view is likely to assume that the person in authority has the right to be relatively direct rather than to mitigate orders. There also are cases, however, in which the higher-ranking person assumes a more indirect style. The owner of a retail operation told her subordinate, a store manager, to do something. He said he would do it, but a week later he still hadn't. They were able to trace the difficulty to the following conversation: She had said, "The bookkeeper needs help with the billing. How would you feel about helping her out?" He had said, "Fine." This conversation had seemed to be clear and flawless at the time, but it turned out that they had interpreted this simple exchange in very different ways. She thought he meant, "Fine, I'll help the bookkeeper out." He thought she meant, "Fine, I'll think about how I would feel about helping the book-keeper out." He did think about it and came to the conclusion that he had more important things to do and couldn't spare the time.

To the owner, "How would you feel about helping the bookkeeper out?" was an obviously appropriate way to give the order "Help the bookkeeper out with the billing." Those who expect orders to be given as bald imperatives may find such locutions an-noying or even misleading. But those for whom this style is natural do not think they are being indirect. They believe they are being clear in a polite or respectful way.

What is atypical in this example is that the person with the more indirect style was the boss, so the store manager was motivated to adapt to her style. She still gives orders the same way, but the store manager now understands how she means what she says. It's more common in U.S. business contexts for the highest-ranking people to take a more direct style, with the result that many women in authority risk being judged by their superiors as lacking the appropriate demeanor—and, consequently, lacking confidence.

WHAT TO DO?

I am often asked, What is the best way to give criticism? or What is the best way to give orders?—in other words, What is the best way to communicate? The answer is that there is no one best way. The results of a given way of speaking will vary depend-ing on the situation, the culture of the company, the relative rank of speakers, their lin-guistic styles, and how those styles interact with one another. Because of all those influences, any way of speaking could be perfect for communicating with one person in one situation and disastrous with someone else in another. The critical skill for man-agers is to become aware of the workings and power of linguistic style, to make sure that people with something valuable to contribute get heard.

It may seem, for example, that running a meeting in an unstructured way gives equal opportunity to all. But awareness of the differences in conversational style makes it easy to see the potential for unequal access. Those who are comfortable speaking up in groups, who need little or no silence before raising their hands, or who speak out easily without waiting to be recognized are far more likely to get heard at meetings. Those who refrain from talking until it's clear that the previous speaker is finished, who wait to be recognized, and who are inclined to link their comments to those of others will do fine at a meeting where everyone else is following the same rules but will have a hard time get-ting heard in a meeting with people whose styles are more like the first pattern. Given the socialization typical of boys and girls, men are more likely to have learned the first style and women the second, making meetings more congenial for men than for women. It's common to observe women who participate actively in one-on-one discussions or in all-female groups but who are seldom heard in meetings with a large proportion of men.

On the other hand, there are women who share the style more common among men, and they run a different risk—of being seen as too aggressive.

A manager aware of those dynamics might devise any number of ways of ensuring that everyone's ideas are heard and credited. Although no single solution will fit all contexts, managers who understand the dynamics of linguistic style can develop more adaptive and flexible approaches to running or participating in meetings, mentoring or advancing the careers of others, evaluating performance, and so on. Talk is the lifeblood of managerial work, and understanding that different people have different ways of saying what they mean will make it possible to take advantage of the talents of people with a broad range of linguistic styles. As the workplace becomes more culturally diverse and business becomes more global, managers will need to become even better at reading interactions and more flexible in adjusting their own styles to the people with whom they interact.

Communication Freezers

Mary E. Tramel

Helen Reynolds

1. Telling the other person what to do—for example:

   "You must . . ."

   "I expect you to . . ."

   "You cannot . . ."

2. Threatening with "or else" implied:

   "You had better . . ."

   "If you don't . . ."

3. Telling the other person what he ought to do:

   "You should . . ."

   "It's your duty to . . ."

   "It's your responsibility to . . ."

4. Making unasked-for suggestions:

   "Let me suggest . . ."

   "It would be best if you . . ."

5. Attempting to educate the other person:

   "Let me give you the facts."

   "Experience tells us that . . ."

6. Judging the other person negatively:

   "You're not thinking straight."

   "You're wrong."

7. Giving insincere praise:

   "You are an intelligent person."

   "You have so much potential."

8. Putting labels on people:

   "You're a sloppy worker."

   "You really goofed on this one!"

Reprinted from Mary Tramel and Helen Reynolds, *Executive Leadership* (Englewood Cliffs, NJ: Prentice Hall, 1981), pp. 208–9. Used with permission of the authors.

9. Psychoanalyzing the other person:

   "You're jealous."

   "You have problems with authority."

10. Making light of the other person's problems by generalizing:

    "Things will get better."

    "Behind every cloud there's a silver lining."

11. Giving the third degree:

    "Why did you do that?"

    "Who has influenced you?"

12. Making light of the problem by kidding:

    "Think about the positive side."

    "You think *you've* got problems!"

SECTION SIX

Finding Negotiation Leverage

In writings about social dynamics, the concept of *power* is both captivating and elusive. This is also true when focusing on the context of negotiation. Whether one is discussing a "power lunch" with an important business figure, "empowerment" of blue-collar employees or minority groups, or the "abuse of power" by a public official, power and its use have fascinated students and practitioners of social influence for thousands of years. The writings of Machiavelli, who lived over 450 years ago, continue to stand as a definitive treatise on the effective use of power. More recently, political scientists, psychologists, economists, philosophers, ethicists, and politicians have had much to say about power and influence, their use and misuse.

There are several ways to account for the fascination with power. In society, the possession of power is often coupled with status and affluence. For some people, power itself is an intoxicant—even an addiction. Powerful people get attention, press coverage, and privilege. There is a certain mysticism about power that makes it hard to define clearly or that makes its dynamics hard to explain. Yet power must be defined and explained for it to be harnessed—and that is our purpose in this section. We are not going to explore the very broad range of power approaches and dynamics; rather, we will restrict ourselves to those articles that specifically address the types and sources of power commonly available to negotiators and most commonly used in negotiation interactions.

The first article in this section is by a distinguished, eminent social scientist whose name is frequently associated with the systematic study of power and influence—Kenneth Boulding. In the article "The Nature of Power" (an excerpt from Boulding's book *Three Faces of Power*), Boulding cuts through much of the semantic debate in the social sciences about the definition, scope, and parameters of power. Boulding proposes a simple, straightforward definition: power is the ability to get what we want. As Boulding notes, however, even this simple definition is not so simple, since we quickly get into questions such as, "Who are *we?*" or "How do *we* decide what we want?" Boulding considers the nature of power in conflict situations, the problems of measuring power, and the fact that power is unequally distributed in most civilized societies (where a few gather sufficient power to control many). In order to help us understand different sources of power—the ways powerful people derive their power—Boulding proposes a major trichotomy. Power may be distinguished first by its consequences, as destructive, productive, and integrative. Destructive power is the power to destroy things; productive power is the power to create new things; and integrative power is the power to bring things together into more unified wholes. Boulding then associates different characteristic patterns of behavior with each of these categories: threats are likely to lead to destructive power patterns, exchanges (transactions) are likely to lead to productive power patterns, and love or respect (positive affect) is likely to lead to integrative power patterns. Boulding also briefly explores power at the institutional level, examining how political, military, economic, and social power all relate to these categories. The Boulding reading provides excellent groundwork on which to base our discussion of power; as we have seen in earlier readings, threats and promises, exchanges, and relationships clearly form the foundation for the use of power and influence in most negotiation contexts.

In its more stereotypic forms, power and its use are associated with the extreme destructive and productive forms. Yet the most effective forms of power use occur in simple exchange transactions. The prescriptions for the strategy and tactics of power use in exchange are found in the article "Influence without Authority: The Use of Alliances, Reciprocity, and Exchange to Accomplish Work," by Allan Cohen and David Bradford. After defining the nature of exchange relationships, Cohen and Bradford propose some simple rules for using power in this context: (1) think about the person to be influenced as a potential ally, not an adversary; (2) know the world of our potential allies, the pressures on them, their needs and goals (so you can tailor your influence attempts to their worlds); (3) be aware of key goals and available resources that may be valued by potential allies; and (4) understand the exchange transaction itself so that win-win outcomes are achieved. The authors also outline a comprehensive list of "currencies," or things that are offered between people in exchange transactions in order to establish a successful deal. These include inspiration-related currencies (visions of the future, commitments to moral principles); task-related currencies (resources, goods, and services); position-related currencies (recognition, reputation, contacts); relationship-related currencies (acceptance and personal support); and personal-related currencies (gratitude, ownership, involvement, etc.).

While Cohen and Bradford describe the use of power as "currencies" within an exchange transaction, in the article "How to Become an Influential Manager," Bernard Keys and Thomas Case approach the subject of influence tactics more broadly. In a series of research studies, the authors asked practicing managers to identify tactics that they used in successful and unsuccessful influence attempts. Tactics were identified that exerted influence upward (toward a boss), laterally (toward peers), and downward (toward subordinates). The results indicate that there are some similarities in the way managers report their influence attempts upward, downward, and laterally—but also some strong differences. With bosses and peers, the first choice of influence strategy is to present a rational explanation of what they want. (Rational explanations are high among influence attempts with subordinates, but not first.) However, showing support of others, or arguing and persisting in what we want, were also commonly used tactics. Keys and Case also analyze the effectiveness and ineffectiveness of certain tactic profiles; they discover that not all tactics work (nor do all fail) in all circumstances. On the basis of these findings, they suggest five key steps to becoming an influential manager:

- Develop a reputation as a knowledgeable person or expert.
- Balance the time spent in critical relationships based on what the work requires, not on habit or personal preference.

- Develop a network of key resource persons who can be called upon for assistance.
- Tailor the combination of influence tactics to the nature of one's objective and to the particular target to be influenced.
- Implement influence tactics with sensitivity, flexibility, and adequate levels of communication.

Specific pointers and examples are offered to implement each of these five key steps.

The final article in this section, "How to Get Clout," by Dr. Joyce Brothers, presents several different tactics for gaining "clout" in a persuasion situation. Many of these points will be familiar to those who are already conversant with methods that other experts have suggested to gain and use "leverage":

- Act as if you already had something you want—have confidence, talk as though it was automatically going to happen, believe it will inevitably come true.
- "Go to the balcony"—that is, maintain your composure, demeanor, and focus in the face of distractions and events designed to sidetrack you.
- Listen carefully so that you understand what the other person really wants.
- Let everybody win—create win-win agreements.
- Have an ace up your sleeve—that is, have a backup plan.
- Don't gloat—maintain your compassion for others and do not rub in your successes.
- Do something surprising—throw your opponent off balance by doing the unexpected and the unpredictable.

The Nature of Power

Kenneth Boulding

POWER AS THE ABILITY TO GET WHAT WE WANT

Power, like most important words, has many meanings. Its widest meaning is that of a potential for change. It has a very special meaning in physics: the time rate at which energy is transferred or converted into work. The concept of power is not used very much in the biological sciences, but is of great importance in human and social systems, which is the main subject of this volume. For individual human beings, power is the ability to get what one wants. The term *power* is also used, however, to describe the ability to achieve common ends for families, groups, organizations of all kinds, churches, corporations, political parties, national states, and so on. In this human sense, power is a concept without meaning in the absence of human valuations and human decision. Decision is a choice among a range or set of images of the future that we think are feasible. Power of decision relates to the size of this agenda of poten tial images of the future. A bedridden person who is dying of cancer has a very small range of possible futures, and a very small agenda of decisions, restricted almost to what the patient is thinking about. A rich person in the prime of life, in good health, has a very wide range of possible futures. As we move up in the hierarchy of organization toward people like Mr. Gorbachev, the pope, or President Bush, the range of agendas of decision includes not only one's personal condition or surroundings but the condition or surroundings of very large numbers of other people; in the extreme case, decisions may affect the condition of the whole planet.

The general concept of power is often confused with the idea of "force," which is a much narrower concept. If an audience is asked to give a symbolic gesture illustrating the concept of "power," many of them will raise their fists, suggesting threat power or the power to do injury. This, however, as we will see later, is only one aspect, and by no means the most important aspect of the general concept of power. Force is linked to the concept of domination, which, indeed, is only a small part of the general nature of power. There is a certain tendency among humans to identify power with the capacity for victory, that is, overcoming some other person, will, or institution. This, again, is a very narrow concept of power and, indeed, by no means the most important aspect of it. In mechanics we have the concept of horsepower, which is what it takes to lift 550 pounds one foot in one second, and reflects the larger concept of power in terms of getting something done that we want. It is perhaps significant that

Reprinted from Kenneth Boulding, *Three Faces of Power* (Newbury Park, CA: Sage, 1989), pp. 15–33. Reprinted by permission of Sage Publications, Inc.

there is no concept of "horse force." The unit of force in the centimeter-gram-second system is the dyne, which is the force that applied to one gram will give it an acceleration of one centimeter per second per second. This might almost be described as "grasshopper force." It does have a certain implication of overcoming gravity by hopping. It is interesting that in electronics what overcomes resistance and produces current is called "potential," which is also a form of power. "Power lines" carry electric potential from one place to another.

There is a certain parallel between the concept of power and the economist's concept of a possibility boundary, which divides the total set of future possibilities into those that a person can do and those that a person cannot do. In the next 24 hours I could go to New York by air, I could not go to Antarctica, and I could certainly not go to the moon. This might be called the "ultimate power boundary." This ultimate boundary, however, may not be very significant, because within it there are other boundaries that limit our decisions. One is the "taboo boundary," which divides the ultimate power area into two parts: that part within the taboo boundary, things we can do and do not feel we have to refrain from doing, and that part beyond the taboo boundary, things we can do but refrain from doing. In virtually all societies, with the exception of nudist camps, there is a strong taboo against a lecturer taking all his or her clothes off while lecturing. I have never known this taboo to be broken, although in physical terms there is no obstacle to it at all. Then inside the taboo boundary there are a great many things we can do, but do not want to do. We arrange the various items of the possibility agenda by order of preference and, according to economists at least, we select the one that is highest on our preference order, that is, the thing we want most.

Economists generally assume that what we want most will be on the possibility boundary, implying that what we want most of all is not within our power, that is, it is beyond the boundary. There is no principle of human behavior that says this assumption has to be true. There are many examples of human decisions that let us stay well within the possibility boundary. Monarchs abdicate, rich people set up foundations and give their money away, monks vow "poverty, chastity, and obedience," saints suffer, and martyrs die. It is possible indeed that the freest exercise of the will is the renunciation of power. If we feel we must exercise the power that we have, then we are trapped in an almost deterministic situation. Economists frequently assume that human preferences cannot be analyzed or criticized. This flies in the face of human history and experience. Virtually everyone has experienced changes in their preference structures and their valuations. There is the "sour grapes" principle, that what we cannot get we decide we do not want, which can be very comforting. At the other end of the scale is the addiction principle—that what we cannot get we want all the more. Taboos are not merely what society imposes on us. We set up our own taboos. Some people become teetotalers or vegetarians. Chastity may be rare, but it is not unknown.

The simple definition of human power, the ability to get what we want, turns out to be quite complex, as we have just seen, even when we ask: How do we know what we want? It gets still more complex when we ask: Who are we? All decisions are made by individuals, but nearly always "on behalf" of a larger entity. This is true even of the most personal and individual choice. An individual is not a single mental system but may have a diversity of personalities. It was Bismarck, I think, who said, "I am a committee," and each person possesses a great variety of roles, some of which may conflict. Our decision as a parent, or as an employer, or as a church member, or as a citizen of a national state, or as a president of a national organization, or as a captain of a team, may be different in each role, and this can create internal conflict. Every decision is made on behalf of the committee that is us. As we rise in hierarchies, what we are deciding, and "on behalf of " whom, becomes ever larger and more complex. A decision by a parent to take another job affects the whole family. A decision by an executive officer of a corporation to shut down a factory affects very large numbers of families, communities, and other organizations. A decision on the part of the president of the United States may affect the whole human race. Decisions of the powerful have an agenda that sometimes includes a large part of the total state of the world, or nowadays even of the solar system. Should we leave garbage on the moon?

There is a strong belief that a role transcends and survives the person occupying it. The whole concept of the "national interest" (we might add "corporate interest" or "church interest") implies that no matter who occupies the powerful roles, the agenda of decision making and of the preferences involved do not change very much, although, of course, every occupant of the role changes the role somewhat. The whole concept of a "representative," whether this is a congressman or the president, implies that decisions have to transcend personal interest, for a representative is supposed to make decisions on behalf of his or her constituents. Power may be getting what you want, but this achievement depends on who "you" are and how you know what "you" want. It is clear this is by no means a simple concept.

POWER IN CONFLICT

Another element that complicates the concept of power in social systems is that the various possibility boundaries of one person are where they are because of some decisions and some power exercised by another person, persons, or organizations. Conflict arises when a shift in the possibility boundary between two parties in some sense reduces the power of one and increases the power of the other. Costly and protracted conflict takes place when A pushes the boundary toward B, B pushes it back toward A, A toward B again, and so on. Essential to the resolution of conflict is the establishment of property lines agreed upon by both parties, so that neither attempts to increase his or her power by pushing out the possibility boundary at the expense of the other. Third parties, especially in the form of legal systems and governments, often assist this process by imposing further boundaries in the form of threats on any party who violates the property lines. Law, however, can break down if one or another party attempts to seize the power of government or defy the law, which sometimes happens. This often leads to cultures of violence, like Ulster, Lebanon, or Sri Lanka, with tragic and widespread loss to the whole society.

A significant element in the total structure of power is the way in which individuals evaluate the power and well-being of others. We can first of all distinguish a scale ranging from benevolence, through selfishness as the zero point, to malevolence.[1] A is

---

1. Kenneth E. Boulding, *The Economy of Love and Fear: A Preface to Grants Economics* (Belmont, CA: Wadsworth, 1973), p. 94.

benevolent toward B if A's perception that B's welfare is increased increases A's own perceived welfare. A is selfish if a perception of an increase in B's welfare does not affect A's perception of A's own welfare. A is malevolent toward B if A's perception of an increase in B's welfare diminishes A's own perceived welfare. Both benevolence and malevolence are exhibited in varying degrees. We may feel very mildly benevolent toward the salesclerk at the store where we are buying something. We pass the time of day and exchange little courtesies. We may feel very highly benevolent toward our own children, other members of our family, close friends, people with whom we cooperate in various tasks and enjoyments. Similarly, we may feel mildly malevolent toward the slowpoke who is in front of us on a narrow road, driving well below the speed limit. We may feel moderately malevolent toward our opponent in an election, and highly malevolent toward our enemies during war. Selfishness, the mere zero point on the scale, is actually rather rare in regard to people with whom we are in actual contact. It is common toward people far away with whom we have no contact, but even there the news of a catastrophe in a faraway land easily induces people to pity. Such news often induces people to make contributions toward ameliorating the disaster. Benevolence seems easier to express than does malevolence. Smiles take fewer muscles than do frowns. It is often harder work to injure somebody than to assist them.

An offshoot, and sometimes a cause, of malevolence is envy and jealousy, a feeling of dissatisfaction with our relative position in the power structure. Envy need only involve two parties, and the envied may be quite unaware of its existence, although envy can be very corrupting to the envious, diverting their attention from increasing their own power toward an often fruitless attempt to diminish the power of the envied. Jealousy involves envy of a relationship between two other people, one of whom the envious person would like to displace. This, again, can be very destructive and can be damaging to all parties, although it is more likely to damage the envious than the envied.[2]

THE MEASUREMENT OF POWER

Another important but very difficult question is whether power can be measured both in regard to its aggregate in the total world system and in regard to its distribution among individuals, groups, and organizations. Because power is a multidimensional concept, it is difficult to quantify and to measure. Perhaps the closest we come to a measure of power is the monetary unit. This only measures certain aspects of power and cannot be used to measure power as a whole. Nevertheless, the concept of the quantity of power is important, even if it is bound to be a little vague and qualitative in character. It would be hard to deny that the power of the human race over its environment, mainly, of course, on earth, but now expanding to the solar system and even beyond, has increased pretty steadily and at an accelerating rate over the course of human history. Certainly in the history of the 40,000 years or so of the Paleolithic period, human power was not very great. Probably the earliest acceleration in human power was the discovery of how to use fire, which may even have predated *Homo sapiens*.

---

2. Helmut Schoeck, *A Theory of Social Behavior* (from the German), trans. Michael Glenny and Betsy Ross (New York: Harcourt, Brace & World, 1969).

The use of fire almost certainly expanded the population that used it, but also introduced a new source of forest fires, which could affect the world's ecosystems over wide areas. There is little doubt that humans exterminated the mammoth and other large mammals, especially in North America, perhaps some 10,000 to 15,000 years ago.

With the development of agriculture, the human population expanded substantially, and human impact on the ecosystem and landscape became quite large, as forests and grasslands gave way to fields and farms. This led fairly rapidly to civilization and the rise of cities, coming out of the food surplus of storable foods from agriculture and improvement in the means of transportation, such as the development of wheeled vehicles, boats, and the domestication of horses, donkeys, and camels. Human power over the earth is reflected in the rise of Babylon, Rome, and so on, with dramatic local changes in the ecological pattern of the earth's surface. Human artifacts, which are just as much a part of the world ecosystem as are biological artifacts, have increased in complexity and number almost continuously, with occasional remissions and retreats.

Then comes the rise of modern science, beginning some 500 years ago. In the mid-19th century comes the application of science to technology of many kinds—chemicals, electricity, health and medicine, agriculture, transportation, and so on—producing the "modern world" and an enormous explosion of human population, which has more than doubled in the 20th century. The world has been mapped and charted, we have been to the highest peaks and the deepest depths, to the poles, and even to the moon. Messengers are going beyond the limits of the solar system. That this process represents an expansion of total human power could hardly be denied.

THE DISTRIBUTION OF POWER

We are also conscious of the fact that human power, especially since the rise of agriculture and civilization, has been very unequally distributed. In hunting-gathering societies there is not much power to distribute, but what there is is distributed fairly equally. The good hunters and the good gatherers do not eat much more than the poorer hunters and the poorer gatherers. There may be shamans and storytellers and leaders who have some power over the others, but all live very much alike. With agriculture and the rise of cities and empires, however, hierarchy develops with the development of organized threat systems, institutions for the collection of taxes, and so on. Then the human race tends to divide into a very small group of the powerful and a large group of the relatively indigent and powerless—the peasants, the soldiers, the servant class—and a small middle class of artisans, merchants, builders, and so on.

With the development of science-based technology after about 1850 (and even somewhat before this), we begin to get the rise of the middle class to a majority of the society, with political power limited by democracy, and economic power by progressive taxation and fluctuating markets, but still leaving a substantial body of the poor, powerless, and impotent, who cannot fit themselves into the society's expanding sectors.

We now have a situation where science-based technology is fairly widespread in the two temperate zones. Ironically enough, it is the Communist countries, with their ideology of equality, that probably have the greatest inequality of overall power—decision power being extremely concentrated at the top of the hierarchy, without the checks and balances that democratic institutions provide, although even this situation is now being modified. Most of the tropical societies, however, are still impoverished and have very small modern sectors. Hence, the overall distribution of power in the world still seems extremely unequal. Perhaps 25 percent of the human race is still in extreme poverty, frequently threatened by starvation and famine, constantly malnourished, and moving very slowly, if at all, into a better situation.

DESTRUCTIVE POWER

Along with the power to grow crops, build cities, fly airplanes, and have a worldwide communication system, the human race has also expanded its powers of destruction. This goes back a long way to the development of spears and bows and arrows in hunting-gathering societies, swords and catapults in early civilizations, and then gunpowder and the cannon, which really ended the feudal baron and established the national state. Now, of course, we have aerial bombings and the nuclear weapon, which has the potential at least to destroy the whole earth. The power of destruction can be used productively for the human race, as it is in hunting, in the use of explosives in building canals, dams, and so on, although even these structures, while often beneficial, can have disastrous, unexpected ecological and social consequences.

The dark side of the power of destruction is, of course, violence and war. This goes back a long way, as shown in the story of Cain and Abel. Up to now the increase in powers of destruction has not prevented an extraordinary expansion in the overall powers of production. There have been certain times and places where empires, for instance, have collapsed due to the use of the powers of destruction, with a temporary decline in the powers of production as a consequence, for instance, in Mesopotamia, in Europe after the fall of the Roman Empire, and so on. These episodes, however, have seldom lasted very long. In Europe, for instance, techniques of production, which had been fairly stagnant during the Roman Empire, began to improve within a century after its fall, as a result perhaps of the rise of monastic orders and new technologies creeping in from China. Warfare, which figures so prominently in history books, rarely occupies more than 10 percent of human time and energy. The other 90 percent or so goes into plowing, sowing, reaping, weaving, building, and making furniture and implements, utensils, and so on. It is ironic that the increase in the powers of destruction is in a sense a by-product of the strong tendency for the powers of production to increase. Agriculture produces a storable food surplus, which can feed armies; metallurgy produces weapons as well as plows; craftsmen produce chariots as well as carts, and nuclear fission can produce both electric power and bombs.

The future, however, remains in some doubt because of the enormous rise in the destructiveness of weaponry and the diminution in the cost of transport of the means of destruction, represented by the airplane, the missile, and, of course, the nuclear weapon. There have been a few occasions in human history when humans have abandoned some destructive power, as the samurai did in Japan in the 16th and 17th centuries when they gave up firearms introduced from Europe. One can only hope that the political institutions of the world will change in proportion to the powers of destruction.

THE DIFFERENT KINDS OF POWER:
DESTRUCTIVE, PRODUCTIVE, INTEGRATIVE

The structure of power is very complex. The first step to understanding it is to raise the question: How do we identify and categorize different sources of power? One of the greatest obstacles to human knowledge is the difficulty that we have in finding the right categories, that is, the right boxes to classify complex realities. We have to classify in order to be able to use language at all. We cannot talk about each of the 5 billion human beings separately. The same goes for the innumerable individual plants, rocks, clouds, and so on. There is always a danger, however, that when we classify we get the categories—that is, the boxes—wrong. We put unlike things together in one box and separate like things between several boxes. The failure of alchemy and the success of chemistry is a great tribute to the virtue of correct classification. As long as we thought earth, air, fire, and water were the elements, we got nowhere. These are not elements, but very heterogeneous collections of things. It was only when we identified the elements correctly, like hydrogen, oxygen, and carbon, that chemistry became possible. This problem is particularly acute in social systems, with their immense diversity of peoples, cultures, organizations, and structures of all kinds. So we are always putting people who are very diverse in the same box (like "race"), and we scatter things that are similar, like learning ability, among a lot of different boxes. When we move into abstract ideas, the classification problem becomes acute. There seems to be no formal theory about it; we can only rely on trial and error to see what works.

Figure 1 illustrates a set of categories of power that will be fundamental to the argument of this volume. None of these categories will be perfectly clear. They are all what the mathematicians call "fuzzy sets," for every example of power is in some sense unique, just as every human being is unique. Nevertheless, these categories are offered as a way of organizing an extremely complex reality in a way that perhaps will make for more realistic appraisals as to what kind of beliefs and actions really create power.

FIGURE 1   Categories of Power: Threat, Exchange, and Love

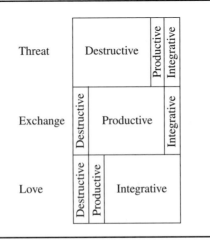

We first divide power into three major categories from the point of view of its consequences: destructive power, productive power, and integrative power. Destructive power is the power to destroy things. It has two very different aspects, reflected in the means of destruction. Some of these are weapons, whether directed toward killing people or destroying valued things. The means of destruction, however, also include such things as bulldozers, plows, furnaces, chain saws, knives, and so on, which are part of the productive process.

Productive power is found in the fertilized egg, in the blueprint, in the idea, in the tools and machines that make things, in the activity of human brains and muscles that sow and reap, weave and build, construct, paint, and sculpt.

Integrative power may be thought of perhaps as an aspect of productive power that involves the capacity to build organizations, to create families and groups, to inspire loyalty, to bind people together, to develop legitimacy. Integrative power has a negative sense, to create enemies, to alienate people; it has a destructive as well as a productive aspect.

THREAT POWER

The figure shows a rather similar tripartition involving characteristic behavior, roughly, but not exactly, corresponding to the first three categories. Behavior that is particularly associated with destructive power is threat. Threat originates when A says to B, "You do something I want or I will do something you do not want." For the threat to be carried out, of course, A must have control over some destructive power against persons or structures that B values. The dynamics of threat depend very much on how B responds to threat. The threat, of course, may be explicit or implicit, but it always involves some sort of communication. There are a number of possible responses from B. One is submission, that B does what A demands and the threat is not carried out. This is very common. This is why we pay our income taxes, why we stop our vehicle by the side of the road when the traffic cop says "Pull over." It explains in part, although only in part, why children obey parents, and students, teachers. Nations defeated in war submit to their conquerors; colonies submit to imperial powers. Without some element of threat-submission, social life would be very difficult to organize. But there are degrees of willingness to submit, or "grudgingness;" a highly grudged submission may be unstable.

Another possible reaction is defiance. B says to A, "I will not do what you want." This is probably less common than submission, but it is by no means unknown. Then the ball goes back to the threatener, who must then decide whether or not to carry out the threat. Sometimes carrying out a threat is very costly; sometimes the threatener does not have the destructive power that is professed and defiance may succeed, especially if it is widespread, persistent, and the defiers are willing to suffer. This indeed is the secret of success of nonviolent resistance, of which there are numerous examples in human history, Gandhi's being one of the most prominent.

A third reaction to threat may be counterthreat—"You do something nasty to me and I will do something nasty to you." In this case, the threatened party must also have, or convincingly pretend to have, means of destruction. This, again, throws the ball back into the camp of the original threatener, who may either try to carry out the threat or not carry it out, either of which will have a succession of subtle and often unpredictable consequences. Counterthreat leads into a situation of deterrence, the stability of which, as we shall see later, is very questionable, but it is highly characteristic of international systems and is the current justification for much military expenditure.

Another possible reaction to threat is flight, of which there are many examples. Indeed, the spread of the human race around the globe has flight as a very important element. Refugees throughout history, like the Pilgrim Fathers, have had a very profound effect on the geographical distribution of the human race. The success of flight depends on a principle that I have described as "the further, the weaker"—the further we go from the home base of the threatener, the harder it is for the threat to be carried out, simply because the carrying out of threat always has a cost of transport.[3] In the present day, with the enormous reduction in the cost of transport of threat in the form of weaponry, flight becomes very difficult because there may be nowhere to go out of range of the threat. But the very size of the current refugee problem suggests that flight is still with us.

A fifth reaction to threat might be called "disarming behavior." This is the "soft answer that turns away wrath." It involves an ability on the part of the threatened to integrate with the threatener into some sort of community or integrative structure.

Threat power has a productive component in the capacity to produce the means of destruction, like guns, and an integrative factor when the threat is made by a group, such as an army, which must have "morale" in order to function.

EXCHANGE POWER

Another major type of behavior, which like threat involves at least two parties, is exchange, which covers a range of activities, from formal and contractual trade to informal reciprocity. Exchange begins when A says to B, "You do something I want and I will do something you want." If B has a choice of either accepting or refusing the invitation, if B accepts then an exchange takes place. In the simple form of trade, A gives B something and B gives A something. The ratio of exchange—that is, how much one gives per unit of what the other gives—is an important quality of the transaction. Exchange, however, is a wider concept than trade. It involves such things as conversation, reciprocal service, and so on. The dynamics of exchange are much simpler than those of threat. If B accepts, the exchange takes place; if not, the exchange does not take place. There may, however, be more subtle dynamic consequences. If B accepts the exchange but then is not satisfied with what A gives, this may change the terms on which other exchanges may be made in the future. This might be called the "lemon principle."

Another complication is that exchange may or may not involve bargaining. Much exchange is conducted without bargaining under the custom of the fixed price. A the seller offers to exchange at a certain price, or ratio of exchange, and B the buyer either accepts the offer or does not. If A is asking too high a price, of course, A will not be

---

3. Kenneth E. Boulding, *Conflict and Defense: A General Theory* (New York: Harper, 1962; reprinted, Lanham, MD: University Press of America, 1988).

able to find people with whom to exchange. A may then lower the asking price. If A asks too low a price, he may be deluged with potential buyers, at which point he is likely to raise the price. Under some circumstances, however, B may offer to bargain—"I will accept the exchange, but at a lower price." A may respond, offering to exchange at a slightly higher price than B asks, and so on, until a bargain either is reached or is not.

Exchange is closely related to productive power simply because unless there is production there is not very much to exchange. Also, as Adam Smith pointed out so well, the development of exchange increases productive power through specialization and the human learning process.

Exchange has an integrative component, simply because without some sort of trust and courtesy exchange is very difficult. Exchange, however, is enough of a positive-sum relationship, in which both parties benefit, that the possibility of exchange may actively create the kind of integrative structure within which it becomes possible. There are old stories of "silent trade," in which two hostile tribes with different resources exchanged without even seeing each other, with one tribe putting out its specialized product in a mutually approved place, and the other coming and picking it up and leaving their own product, which the first tribe then came and took away. It is not quite clear whether this ever really happened, but, if it did, it was clearly a step toward the establishment of a market in which people would meet each other on the basis of mutual trust and courtesy. This is the integrative factor in exchange.

There may also be a little bit of a destructive element underlying exchange in the development of a system of law, organizing punishment for failure to live up to contracts and also punishment for failure to obey the principles of property, that is, for theft. Theft is very destructive of the integrative relationship. Trust is necessary for exchange to flourish. Often there is also a destructive element in producing the goods for exchange, simply because production involves the transformation of less valued things into more valued things, which involves the destruction or alteration of the less valued things, as, for instance, when wheat is ground into flour and flour baked into bread, when quarriers destroy hillsides, when miners extract ores, and so on.

THE POWER OF "LOVE"

Beyond threats and exchange, there are relationships that can be identified by the word *love,* in spite of its many meanings, and using it in the widest possible sense as an aspect of the integrative structure. In the love relationship, essentially, A says to B, "You do something for me because you love me." This may be one spouse to another; a leader talking to a follower; a monarch, especially a constitutional one, talking to his or her subjects; a state, to its citizens; a general, to his soldiers; or a religious leader, to his flock. If the word *love* seems too strong, substitute *respect.* There are degrees of love, as in everything else. Here again, the response and reaction may be important. If A demands too much, B may say, "Well, I do not love you that much." Then A may say, "Look what I do for you," and the situation edges back toward exchange. Love is also closely related to the integrative structures of pride and shame and perhaps guilt. A may say to B, "If you do not do something for me, you will be ashamed of yourself, you will feel guilty." These are subtle, but very important, relationships and they explain a great deal of human behavior. Destructive power—the power to hurt—may also play a small but complex part in the love relationship.

Love, of course, has its negative aspects in hate, and the capacity to create hatred is related to destructive power. A may say to B, "I am going to do this to you because I hate you." This is rather different from threat, although it may have somewhat the same structure of response. The complex dynamics of behavior that underlies the growth of love or of hatred is one of the real puzzles of social systems.

POLITICAL AND MILITARY POWER

A second set of categories of power, shown in Figure 2, relates more to institutions by which power is exercised, here again corresponding fairly closely to the first two sets of categories. We have political and military power, which is based primarily on threat systems and destructive power, although there is an element in it of productive and exchange power, simply because political and military institutions are virtually impossible, at least in any large scale, without something like money, for they have to purchase food, equipment, and buildings, as well as weapons, to feed, clothe, house, and arm their employees and their soldiers. Political institutions need some sort of income accounts, although they do not usually have much in the form of capital accounts. Even though they frequently use threat, for instance, in the form of conscription and the collection of taxes, there nevertheless remains a significant exchange element. There is also an element of love power, as suggested in the figure. Unless a ruler or a country is in some sense loved, or at least respected, his (her, or its) power to organize large threat systems will be very much diminished, as the history of revolution and the overthrow of rulers illustrates.

FIGURE 2   Categories of Power: Political-Military, Economic, and Social

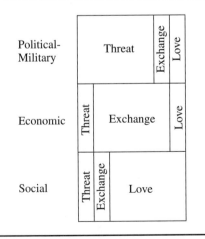

ECONOMIC POWER

Economic power is what the rich have a lot of and the poor, very little of. It has a good deal to do with the distribution of property. It is particularly characteristic of institutions such as the household, the firm, the corporation, the business, and the financial institutions—banks, insurance companies, stock markets, and so on. Its core is the productive and exchange power systems. Productive power and exchange are the basis of income, although the products of productive power do not always accrue to those who have produced them. There is a small element of threat in economic power, particularly noticeable in the institution of slavery. The slave owner in effect says to the slave, "You work for me or I will kill you, or at least make things very unpleasant for you." There is a certain element of threat in all property relations, and there is a good deal of it in the legal and police institutions. The law enforcement system is a public threat to those who privately threaten the existing allocation of property. Economic power also has a certain integrative component. Morale may not be quite so important to a corporation as it is to an army, but it is not insignificant. Unless existing economic institutions are generally accepted as legitimate, they will not be able to function very well.

SOCIAL POWER

It is hard to find a general name for those institutions that are based primarily on integrative power. The family certainly is one of them. Other examples are churches, religious and charitable organizations, the 10,000 or so international nongovernmental organizations, activists and reformist organizations, and so on. In Figure 2 I showed social power as the major characteristic of integrative institutions. Social power is the capacity to make people identify with some organization to which they give loyalty. One mark of such organizations is that they are often supported by grants rather than by exchange, that is, by one-way transfers from the loyal members or affiliates in terms of cash, goods, or labor, what might be called "voluntary grants." There are also involuntary grants that are made under threat, such as taxes or holdups. There may be some threat element in basically integrative organizations. Religious organizations may use the threat of hellfire; secular organizations may use the threat of disapproval, ostracism, and shame.

SOURCES OF POWER

A fourth set of categories of power might be described as the sources of power that underlie all the other forms. There are clearly physical, chemical, and material sources of power. The exercise of power always involves transformations of some kind, and many of these transformations are either physical or chemical, or both. People frequently equate energy with power, and certainly one aspect of energy is that which produces transformations. Energy is a very important condition of both destructive and constructive power. Without energy we cannot blow things up or move them around. Physical and chemical structures impose limits on power. We cannot make compounds out of helium or neon, although we can excite these gases to glow with light. There are only so many chemical compounds that are possible because of the principles of valency in spatial structure. Physical and chemical preconditions impose limits on power. These preconditions, however, should not be identified with human power. The structures and instruments of human power, whether guns, or houses and furniture, or persons or other living creatures, always originate in what might be called a genetic factor, whether this is an idea in the mind of a person or DNA in a fertilized egg. This genetic factor has the potential for power, whether destructive, productive, or integrative. Whether this potential is realized, however, depends on the capacity of the genetic structure to capture energy and to transport and transform appropriate materials into the product, whether a bombed city, an economic commodity, or a church. Energy and materials might be described as limiting factors, to which we might add space and time. The genetic factor fundamentally consists of knowledge, know-how, information, and the capacity for communication. These underlie all forms of power and they are particularly important in integrative power, which is mainly a matter of communication. Communication, of course, requires a physical and chemical medium, which can code the information that is communicated, and the absence of these certainly will limit communication. The physical-chemical structures of the human brain permit an immense amount of information and communication that the physical and chemical structures of a rock do not. Communication, however, may be coded in a great variety of physical and chemical structures—in light waves, sound waves, a printed page, a picture, a gesture or facial expression, and so on. As we move from destructive to productive and integrative systems, the amount of physical and chemical energy substratum probably declines, and knowledge, information, and communication increase.

One condition that underlies all forms of power in a limiting fashion might be described as "vulnerability" in relation to changing environments. Salt crystals are highly vulnerable when put in water; diamonds are not. Some rocks are soft and crumble easily; others are hard and can stand all sorts of environments. Some people are malleable, some are not. Some institutions are malleable, some are not. A suit of armor may render the wearer invulnerable to arrows, but not to cannon balls. Adaptability may lessen vulnerability in all the categories of power. A distinction related to vulnerability is that between defensive power, which is the capacity to prevent unwanted change, and the power to produce wanted change, which might be called "active" power. The general structure of power and the distribution of power often reflect the constantly shifting structures of defensive versus active power. This seems to be particularly important when it comes to threat and military power, but all forms of power are subject to this very fundamental, underlying condition. We even defend ourselves, at times, against being loved. Liquidity in economic organizations is a defense against the unexpected.

Influence without Authority:
The Use of Alliances, Reciprocity,
and Exchange to Accomplish Work

Allan R. Cohen

David L. Bradford

Bill Heatton is the director of research at a $250 million division of a large West Coast company. The division manufactures exotic telecommunications components and has many technical advancements to its credit. During the past several years, however, the division's performance has been spotty at best; multimillion-dollar losses have been experienced in some years despite many efforts to make the division more profitable. Several large contracts have resulted in major financial losses, and in each instance the various parts of the division blamed the others for the problems. Listen to Bill's frustration as he talks about his efforts to influence Ted, a colleague who is marketing director, and Roland, the program manager who reports to Ted:

> Another program is about to come through. Roland is a nice guy, but he knows nothing and never will. He was responsible for our last big loss, and now he's in charge of this one. I've tried to convince Ted, his boss, to get Roland off the program, but I get nowhere. Although Ted doesn't argue that Roland is capable, he doesn't act to find someone else. Instead, he comes to me with worries about my area.
>
> I decided to respond by changing my staffing plan, assigning to Roland's program the people they wanted. I had to override my staff's best judgment about who should be assigned. Yet I'm not getting needed progress reports from Roland, and he's never available for planning. I get little argument from him, but there's no action to correct the problem. That's bad because I'm responding but not getting any response.
>
> There's no way to resolve this. If they disagree, that's it. I could go to a tit-for-tat strategy, saying that if they don't do what I want, we'll get even with them next time. But I don't know how to do that without hurting the organization, which would feel worse than getting even!
>
> Ted, Roland's boss, is so much better than his predecessor that I hate to ask that he be removed. We could go together to our boss, the general manager, but I'm very reluctant to do that. You've failed in a matrix organization if you have to go to your boss. I have to try hard because I'd look bad if I had to throw it in his lap.
>
> Meanwhile, I'm being forceful, but I'm afraid it's in a destructive way. I don't want to wait until the program has failed to be told it was all my fault.

Bill is clearly angry and frustrated, leading him to behave in ways that he does not feel good about. Like other managers who very much want to influence an uncooperative co-worker whom they cannot control. Bill has begun to think of the intransigent employee as the enemy. Bill's anger is narrowing his sense of what is possible; he fantasizes revenge but is too dedicated to the organization to actually harm it. He is genuinely stuck.

Organizational members who want to make things happen often find themselves in this position. Irrespective of whether they are staff or line employees, professionals or managers, they find it increasingly necessary to influence colleagues and superiors. These critical others control needed resources, possess required information, set priorities on important activities, and have to agree and cooperate if plans are to be implemented. They cannot be ordered around because they are under another area's control and can legitimately say no because they have many other valid priorities. They respond only when they choose to. Despite the clear need and appropriateness of what is being asked for (certainly as seen by the person who is making the request), compliance may not be forthcoming.

All of this places a large burden on organizational members, who are expected not only to take initiatives but also to respond intelligently to requests made of them by others. Judgment is needed to sort out the value of the many requests made of anyone who has valuable resources to contribute. As Robert Kaplan argued in his article "Trade Routes: The Manager's Network of Relationships" (*Organizational Dynamics,* spring 1984), managers must now develop the organizational equivalent of "trade routes" to get things done. Informal networks of mutual influence are needed. In her book *The Change Masters* (Simon & Schuster, 1983) Rosabeth Moss Kanter showed that developing and implementing all kinds of innovations requires coalitions to be built to shape and support new ways of doing business.

A key current problem, then, is finding ways to develop mutual influence without the formal authority to command. A peer cannot "order" a colleague to change priorities, modify an approach, or implement a grand new idea. A staff member cannot "command" his or her supervisor to back a proposal, fight top management for greater resources, or allow more autonomy. Even Bill Heatton, in dealing with Roland (who was a level below him in the hierarchy but in another department), could not dictate that Roland provide the progress reports that Bill so desperately wanted.

EXCHANGE AND THE LAW OF RECIPROCITY

The way influence is acquired without formal authority is through the "law of reciprocity"—the almost universal belief that people should be paid back for what they do, that one good (or bad) deed deserves another. This belief is held by people in primitive and not-so-primitive societies all around the world, and it serves as the grease that allows the organizational wheels to turn smoothly. Because people expect that their actions will be paid back in one form or another, influence is possible.

In the case of Bill Heatton, his inability to get what he wanted from Roland and Ted stemmed from his failure to understand fully how reciprocity works in organizations. He therefore was unable to set up mutually beneficial exchanges. Bill believed that he had gone out of his way to help the marketing department by changing his staffing patterns, and he expected Roland to reciprocate by providing regular progress reports. When Roland failed to provide the reports, Bill believed that Ted was obligated to remove Roland from the project. When Ted did not respond, Bill became angry and wanted to retaliate. Thus Bill recognized the appropriateness of exchange in making organizations work. However, he did not understand how exchange operates.

Before exploring in detail how exchange can work in dealing with colleagues and superiors, it is important to recognize that reciprocity is the basic principle behind all organizational transactions. For example, the basic employment contract is an exchange ("an honest day's work for an honest day's pay"). Even work that is above and beyond what is formally required involves exchange. The person who helps out may not necessarily get (or expect) immediate payment for the extra effort requested, but some eventual compensation is expected.

Think of the likely irritation an employee would feel if his or her boss asked him or her to work through several weekends, never so much as said thanks, and then claimed credit for the extra work. The employee might not say anything the first time this happened, expecting or hoping that the boss would make it up somehow. However, if the effort were never acknowledged in any way, the employee, like most people, would feel that something important had been violated.

The expectation of reciprocal exchanges occurs between an employee and his or her supervisor, among peers, with higher-level managers in other parts of the organization, or all of the above. The exchange can be of tangible goods, such as a budget increase, new equipment, or more personnel; of tangible services, such as a faster response time, more information, or public support; or of sentiments, such as gratitude, admiration, or praise. Whatever form exchanges take, unless they are roughly equivalent over time, hard feelings will result.

Exchanges enable people to handle the give-and-take of working together without strong feelings of injustice arising. They are especially important during periods of rapid change because the number of requests that go far beyond the routine tends to escalate. In those situations, exchanges become less predictable, more free-floating, and spontaneous. Nevertheless, people still expect that somehow or other, sooner or later, they will be (roughly) equally compensated for the acts they do above and beyond those that are covered by the formal exchange agreements in their job. Consequently, some kind of "currency" equivalent needs to be worked out, implicitly if not explicitly, to keep the parties in the exchange feeling fairly treated.

CURRENCIES: THE SOURCE OF INFLUENCE

If the basis of organizational influence depends on mutually satisfactory exchanges, then people are influential only insofar as they can offer something that others need. Thus power comes from the ability to meet others' needs.

A useful way to think of how the process of exchange actually works in organizations is to use the metaphor of "currencies." This metaphor provides a powerful way to conceptualize what is important to the influencer and the person to be influenced. Just as many types of currencies are traded in the world financial market, many types are "traded" in organizational life. Too often people think only of money or promotion and status. Those "currencies," however, usually are available only to a manager in dealing with his or her employees. Peers who want to influence colleagues or employees who want to influence their supervisors often feel helpless. They need to recognize that many types of payments exist, broadening the range of what can be exchanged.

Some major currencies that are commonly valued and traded in organizations are listed in Exhibit 1. Although not exhaustive, the list makes evident that a person does not have to be at the top of an organization or have hands on the formal levers of power to command multiple resources that others may value.

Part of the usefulness of currencies comes from their flexibility. For example, there are many ways to express gratitude and to give assistance. A manager who most values the currency of appreciation could be paid through verbal thanks, praise, a public statement at a meeting, informal comments to his peers, and/or a note to her boss. However, the same note of thanks seen by one person as a sign of appreciation may be seen by another person as an attempt to brownnose or by a third person as a cheap way to try to repay extensive favors and service. Thus currencies have value not in some abstract sense but as defined by the receiver.

Although we have stressed the interactive nature of exchange, "payments" do not always have to be made by the other person. They can be self-generated to fit beliefs about being virtuous, benevolent, or committed to the organization's welfare. Someone may respond to another person's request because it reinforces cherished values, a sense of identity, or feelings of self-worth. The exchange is interpersonally stimulated because the one who wants influence has set up conditions that allow this kind of self-payment to occur by asking for cooperation to accomplish organizational goals. However, the person who responds because "it is the right thing to do" and who feels good about being the "kind of person who does not act out of narrow self-interest" is printing currency (virtue) that is self-satisfying.

Of course, the five categories of currencies listed in Exhibit 1 are not mutually exclusive. When the demand from the other person is high, people are likely to pay in several currencies across several categories. They may, for example, stress the organizational value of their request, promise to return the favor at a later time, imply that it will increase the other's prestige in the organization, and express their appreciation.

ESTABLISHING EXCHANGE RATES

What does it take to pay back in a currency that the other party in an exchange will perceive as equivalent? In impersonal markets, because everything is translated into a common monetary currency, it generally is easy to say what a fair payment is. Does a ton of steel equal a case of golfclubs? By translating both into dollar equivalents, a satisfactory deal can be worked out.

In interpersonal exchanges, however, the process becomes a bit more complicated. Just how does someone repay another person's willingness to help finish a report? Is a simple thank-you enough? Does it also require the recipient to say something nice about the helper to his or her boss? Whose standard of fairness should be used? What if one person's idea of fair repayment is very different from the other's?

EXHIBIT 1   Commonly Traded Organizational Currencies

Inspiration-Related Currencies

Vision	Being involved in a task that has larger significance for the unit, organization, customers, or society.
Excellence	Having a chance to do important things really well.
Moral/ethical correctness	Doing what is "right" by a higher standard than efficiency.

Task-Related Currencies

Resources	Lending or giving money, budget increases, personnel, space, and so forth.
Assistance	Helping with existing projects or undertaking unwanted tasks.
Cooperation	Giving task support, providing quicker response time, approving a project, or aiding implementation.
Information	Providing organizational as well as technical knowledge.

Position-Related Currencies

Advancement	Giving a task or assignment that can aid in promotion.
Recognition	Acknowledging effort, accomplishment, or abilities.
Visibility	Providing chance to be known by higher-ups or significant others in the organization.
Reputation	Enhancing the way a person is seen.
Importance/insiderness	Offering a sense of importance, of "belonging."
Network/contacts	Providing opportunities for linking with others.

Relationship-Related Currencies

Acceptance/inclusion	Providing closeness and friendship.
Personal support	Giving personal and emotional backing.
Understanding	Listening to others' concerns and issues.

Personal-Related Currencies

Self-concept	Affirming one's values, self-esteem, and identity.
Challenge/learning	Sharing tasks that increase skills and abilities.
Ownership/involvement	Letting others have ownership and influence.
Gratitude	Expressing appreciation or indebtedness.

Because of the natural differences in the way two parties can interpret the same activity, establishing exchanges that both parties will perceive as equitable can be problematic. Thus it is critical to understand what is important to the person to be influenced. Without a clear understanding of what that person experiences and values, it will be extremely difficult for anyone to thread a path through the minefield of creating mutually satisfactory exchanges.

Fortunately, the calibration of equivalent exchanges in the interpersonal and organizational worlds is facilitated by the fact that approximations will do in most cases. Occasionally, organizational members know exactly what they want in return for favors or help, but more often they will settle for very rough equivalents (providing that there is reasonable goodwill).

THE PROCESS OF EXCHANGE

To make the exchange process effective, the influencer needs to (1) think about the person to be influenced as a potential ally, not an adversary; (2) know the world of the potential ally, including the pressures as well as the person's needs and goals; (3) be aware of key goals and available resources that may be valued by the potential ally; and (4) understand the exchange transaction itself so that win-win outcomes are achieved. Each of these factors is discussed below.

Potential Ally, Not Adversary

A key to influence is thinking of the other person as a potential ally. Just as many contemporary organizations have discovered the importance of creating strategic alliances with suppliers and customers, employees who want influence within the organization need to create internal allies. Even though each party in an alliance continues to have freedom to pursue its own interests, the goal is to find areas of mutual benefit and develop trusting, sustainable relationships. Similarly, each person whose cooperation is needed inside the organization is a potential ally. Each still has self-interests to pursue, but those self-interests do not preclude searching for and building areas of mutual benefit.

Seeing other organizational members as potential allies decreases the chance that adversarial relationships will develop—an all-too-frequent result (as in the case of Bill Heatton) when the eager influencer does not quickly get the assistance or cooperation needed. Assuming that even a difficult person is a potential ally makes it easier to understand that person's world and thereby discover what that person values and needs.

The Potential Ally's World

We have stressed the importance of knowing the world of the potential ally. Without awareness of what the ally needs (what currencies are valued), attempts to influence that person can only be haphazard. Although its conclusion may seem self-evident, it is remarkable how often people attempt to influence without adequate information about what is important to the potential ally. Instead, they are driven by their own definition of "what should be" and "what is right" when they should be seeing the world from the other person's perspective.

For example, Bill Heatton never thought about the costs to Ted of removing Roland from the project. Did Ted believe he could coach Roland to perform better on this project? Did Ted even agree that Roland had done a poor job on the previous project, or did Ted think Roland had been hampered by other departments' shortcomings? Bill just did not know.

Several factors can keep the influencer from seeing the potential ally clearly. As with Bill Heatton, the frustration of meeting resistance from a potential ally can get in the way of really understanding the other person's world. The desire to influence is so strong that only the need for cooperation is visible to the influencer. As a result of not being understood, the potential ally digs in, making the influencer repeat an inappropriate strategy or back off in frustration.

When a potential ally's behavior is not understandable ("Why won't Roland send the needed progress reports?"), the influencer tends to stereotype that person. If early attempts to influence do not work, the influencer is tempted to write the person off as negative, stubborn, selfish, or "just another bean counter/whiz kid/sales-type" or whatever pejorative label is used in that organizational culture to dismiss those organizational members who are different.

Although some stereotypes may have a grain of truth, they generally conceal more than they reveal. The actuary who understands that judgment, not just numbers, is needed to make decisions disappears as an individual when the stereotype of "impersonal, detached number machine" is the filter through which he or she is seen. Once the stereotype is applied, the frustrated influencer is no longer likely to see what currencies that particular potential ally actually values.

Sometimes, the lack of clear understanding about a potential ally stems from the influencer's failure to appreciate the organizational forces acting on the potential ally. To a great extent, a person's behavior is a result of the situation in which that person works (and not just his or her personality). Potential allies are embedded in an organizational culture that shapes their interests and responses. For example, one of the key determinants of anyone's behavior is likely to be the way the person's performance is measured and rewarded. In many instances, what is mistaken for personal orneriness is merely the result of the person's doing something that will be seen as good performance in his or her function.

The salesperson who is furious because the plant manager resists changing priorities for a rush order may not realize that part of the plant manager's bonus depends on holding unit costs down—a task made easier with long production runs. The plant manager's resistance does not necessarily reflect his or her inability to be flexible or lack of concern about pleasing customers or about the company's overall success.

Other organizational forces that can affect the potential ally's behavior include the daily time demands on that person's position; the amount of contact the person has with customers, suppliers, and other outsiders; the organization's information flow (or lack of it); the style of the potential ally's boss; the belief and assumptions held by that person's co-workers; and so forth. Although some of these factors cannot be changed by the influencer, understanding them can be useful in figuring out how to frame and time requests. It also helps the influencer resist the temptation to stereotype the noncooperator.

Self-Awareness of the Influencer

Unfortunately, people desiring influence are not always aware of precisely what they want. Often their requests contain a cluster of needs (a certain product, arranged in a certain way, delivered at a specified time). They fail to think through which aspects are more important and which can be jettisoned if necessary. Did Bill Heatton want Roland removed, or did he want the project effectively managed? Did he want overt concessions from Ted, or did he want better progress reports?

Further, there is a tendency to confuse and intermingle the desired end goal with the means of accomplishing it, leading to too many battles over the wrong things. In *The Change Masters,* Kanter reported that successful influencers in organizations were those who never lost sight of the ultimate objective but were willing to be flexible about means.

Sometimes influencers underestimate the range of currencies available for use. They may assume, for example, that just because they are low in the organization they have nothing that others want. Employees who want to influence their boss are especially likely not to realize all of the supervisor's needs that they can fulfill. They become so caught up with their feelings of powerlessness that they fail to see the many ways they can generate valuable currencies.

In other instances, influencers fail to be aware of their preferred style of interaction and its fit with the potential ally's preferred style. Everyone has a way of relating to others to get work done. However, like the fish who is unaware of the water, many people are oblivious of their own style of interaction or see it as the only way to be. Yet interaction style can cause problems with potential allies who are different.

For example, does the influencer tend to socialize first and work later? If so, that style of interaction will distress a potential ally who likes to dig right in to solve the problem at hand and only afterward chat about sports, family, or office politics. Does the potential ally want to be approached with answers, not problems? If so, a tendency to start influence attempts with open-ended, exploratory problem solving can lead to rejection despite good intentions.

Nature of the Exchange Transaction

Many of the problems that occur in the actual exchange negotiation have their roots in the failure to deal adequately with the first three factors outlined above. Failure to treat other people as potential allies, to understand a potential ally's world, and to be self-aware are all factors that interfere with successful exchange. In addition, some special problems commonly arise when both parties are in the process of working out a mutually satisfactory exchange agreement.

- *Not knowing how to use reciprocity.* Using reciprocity requires stating needs clearly without "crying wolf," being aware of the needs of an ally without being manipulative, and seeking mutual gain rather than playing "winner takes all." One trap that Bill Heatton fell into was not being able to "close on the exchange." That is, he assumed that if he acted in good faith and did his part, others would automatically reciprocate. Part of his failure was not understanding the other party's world; another part was not being able to negotiate cleanly with Ted about what each of them wanted. It is not even clear that Ted realized Bill was altering his organization as per Ted's requests, that Ted got what he wanted, or that Ted knew Bill intended an exchange of responses.

- *Preferring to be right rather than effective.* This problem is especially endemic to professionals of all kinds. Because of their dedication to the "truth" (as their profession defines it), they stubbornly stick to their one right way when trying to line up potential allies instead of thinking about what will work given the audience and conditions. Organizational members with strong technical backgrounds often chorus the equivalent of "I'll be damned if I'm going to sell out and become a phony salesman, trying to get by on a shoeshine and smile." The failure to accommodate to the potential ally's needs and desires often kills otherwise sound ideas.

- *Overusing what has been successful.* When people find that a certain approach is effective in many situations, they often begin to use it in places where it does not fit. By overusing the approach, they block more appropriate methods. Just as a weight lifter becomes muscle-bound from overdeveloping particular muscles at the expense of others, people who have been reasonably successful at influencing other people can diminish that ability by overusing the same technique.

For example, John Brucker, the human resources director at a medium-size company, often cultivated support for new programs by taking people out to fancy restaurants for an evening of fine food and wine. He genuinely derived pleasure from entertaining, but at the same time he created subtle obligations. One time, a new program he wanted to introduce required the agreement of William Adams, head of engineering. Adams, an old-timer, perceived Brucker's proposal as an unnecessary frill, mainly because he did not perceive the real benefits to the overall organization. Brucker responded to Adams's negative comments as he always did in such cases—by becoming more friendly and insisting that they get together for dinner soon. After several of these invitations, Adams became furious. Insulted by what he considered to be Brucker's attempts to buy him off, he fought even harder to kill the proposal. Not only did the program die, but Brucker lost all possibility of influencing Adams in the future. Adams saw Brucker's attempts at socializing as a sleazy and crude way of trying to soften him up. For his part, Brucker was totally puzzled by Adams's frostiness and assumed that he was against all progress. He never realized that Adams had a deep sense of integrity and a real commitment to the good of the organization. Thus Brucker lost his opportunity to sell a program that, ironically, Adams would have found valuable had it been implemented.

As the case above illustrates, a broad repertoire of influence approaches is needed in modern organizations. Johnny-one-notes soon fall flat.

THE ROLE OF RELATIONSHIPS

All of the preceding discussion needs to be conditioned by one important variable: the nature of the relationship between both parties. The greater the extent to which the influencer has worked with the potential ally and created trust, the easier the exchange process will be. Each party will know the other's desired currencies and situational pressures, and each will have developed a mutually productive interaction style. With trust, less energy will be spent on figuring out the intentions of the ally, and there will be less suspicion about when and how the payback will occur.

A poor relationship (based on previous interactions, on the reputation each party has in the organization, and/or on stereotypes and animosities between the functions or departments that each party represents) will impede an otherwise easy exchange. Distrust of the goodwill, veracity, or reliability of the influencer can lead to the demand for "no credit; cash up front," which constrains the flexibility of both parties.

The nature of the interaction during the influencer process also affects the nature of the relationship between the influencer and the other party. The way that John Brucker attempted to relate to William Adams not only did not work but also irreparably damaged any future exchanges between them.

Few transactions within organizations are one-time deals. (Who knows when the other person may be needed again or even who may be working for him or her in the future?) Thus in most exchange situations two outcomes matter: success in achieving task goals and success in improving the relationship so that the next interaction will be even more productive. Too often, people who want to be influential focus only on the task and act as if there is no tomorrow. Although both task accomplishment and an improved relationship cannot always be realized at the same time, on some occasions the latter can be more important than the former. Winning the battle but losing the war is an expensive outcome.

INCONVERTIBLE CURRENCIES

We have spelled out ways organizational members operate to gain influence for achieving organizational goals. By effectively using exchange, organizational members can achieve their goals and at the same time help others achieve theirs. Exchange permits organizational members to be assertive without being antagonistic by keeping mutual benefit a central outcome.

In many cases, organizational members fail to acquire desired influence because they do not use all of their potential power. However, they sometimes fail because not all situations are amenable to even the best efforts at influencing. Not everything can be translated into compatible currencies. If there are fundamental differences in what is valued by two parties, it may not be possible to find common ground, as illustrated in the example below.

The founder and chairman of a high-technology company and the president he had hired five years previously were constantly displeased with one another. The president was committed to creating maximum shareholder value, the currency he valued most as a result of his MBA training, his position, and his temperament. Accordingly, he had concluded that the company was in a perfect position to cash in by squeezing expenses to maximize profits and going public. He could see that the company's product line of exotic components was within a few years of saturating its market and would require massive, risky investment to move to sophisticated end-user products.

The president could not influence the chairman to adopt this direction, however, because the chairman valued a totally different currency, the fun of technological challenge. An independently wealthy man, the chairman had no interest in realizing the $10 million or so he would get if the company maximized profits by cutting research and selling out. He wanted a place to test his intuitive, creative research hunches, not a source of income.

Thus the president's and chairman's currencies were not convertible into one another at an acceptable exchange rate. After they explored various possibilities but failed to find common ground, they mutually agreed that the president should leave— on good terms and only after a more compatible replacement could be found. Although this example acknowledges that influence through alliance, currency conversion, and exchange is not always possible, it is hard to be certain that any situation is hopeless until the person desiring influence has fully applied all of the diagnostic and interpersonal skills we have described.

Influence is enhanced by using the model of strategic alliances to engage in mutually beneficial exchanges with potential allies. Even though it is not always possible to be successful, the chances of achieving success can be greatly increased. In a period of rapid competitive, technological, regulative, and consumer change, individuals and their organizations need all the help they can get.

How to Become
an Influential Manager

Bernard Keys

Thomas Case

A hospital department head attempted in vain to persuade physicians working in a large metropolitan hospital to bring patient medical records up-to-date. Although doctors consider this an abhorrent chore, hospitals cannot begin the billing process until each record is completed and signed by the physician. After many frustrating attempts, the department head describes how he proved equal to the challenge:

> Every month we served the doctors breakfast and lunch and organized games that would allow them to win prizes. Sometimes we would place balloons on a bulletin board and let them throw darts at the balloons. At other times we would do something ridiculously child-like such as hosting a watermelon seed spitting contest or playing pin the tail on the donkey. The sessions worked beautifully because the doctors knew that when they came in someone would be there to help them and they would even have a little fun. Once when we were really desperate we hired a popular entertainer. The room was full that day and we completed over 1,000 charts.

Influence is simply the process by which people successfully persuade others to follow their advice, suggestion, or order. It can be contrasted with power, which is a personal or positional attribute that enables one to influence others and which can be thought of as "continuing or sustained" influence.[1] A number of popular books have suggested that influence must replace the use of formal authority in relationships with subordinates peers, outside contacts, and others on whom the job makes one dependent.[2] The writers of these books attribute the need for greater influence to the rapidity of change in organizations, the diversity of people, goals and values, increasing interdependence, and the diminishing acceptability of formal authority.[3] Bennis and Nanus have suggested that leaders must empower themselves by empowering their subordinates. Kouzes and Posner agree with this conclusion, explaining that the more people believe they can influence and control the organization, the greater will be the effectiveness of the organization. Tichy and Devanna extend this thought even further by suggesting that today we need transformational leaders who will allow networks that funnel diverse views upward from the lower level of the organization where a need for change is often first detected. Similarly, John Kotter observes that the increasing diversity and interdependence of organizational role players is creating a "power gap"

Reprinted from *Academy of Management Executive* 4, no. 4 (1990), pp. 38–49. Used with permission of the authors and publisher.

for managers who often have knowledge and good ideas for organizations but who have inadequate authority to implement their ideas.

For example, effectiveness with subordinates has been found to depend heavily on the ability to develop upward influence with superiors.[4] Influence with the boss often depends on the ability to accomplish things through one's subordinates.[5] Laterally, managers must spend time in group meetings, interorganizational negotiations, and in bids for departmental resources.[6] This is a role replete with power gaps. Most assuredly lateral relationships require the ability to influence without formal authority representatives with unions, customers, and government, or highly autonomous professionals such as the physician in our introductory example.[7]

The concept of "linking groups" seems to drive the middle manager's work while both middle management and executive levels are heavily engaged in "coordinating" independent groups. In this latter role, they must persuade other organizational groups to provide information, products, resources needed, and negotiate working agreements with other groups. Additionally, executive levels of management must frequently maintain relationships with management-level vendors, consultants, and other boundary-spanning agents through outside meetings. Recent research suggests that the "ambassador role" of "representing one's staff" is vitally important to all levels of management. It consists of developing relationships with other work groups and negotiating for information and resources on behalf of the manager's own group.[8]

Building on the previous thoughts and the research of others, we conducted field studies to collect incidents, similar to the one describing the hospital department head, and used these to analyze how managers build and sustain influence. This article explains our research findings and those of related studies for managers who wish to become more influential with subordinates, superiors, peers, and other target groups.

INFLUENCE TACTIC RESEARCH

Only a few writers have identified influence tactics from research investigations. David Kipnis and his colleagues asked evening graduate students to describe an incident in which they actually succeeded in getting either their boss, a co-worker, or a subordinate to do something they wanted. Their analysis revealed that the tactics of ingratiation (making the supervisor feel important) and developing rational plans were the most frequently used methods to influence superiors. When attempting to influence subordinates, respondents most often used formal authority, training, and explanations. Only one tactic, that of requesting help, was frequently associated with influencing co-workers.[9]

Our studies were aimed at strengthening the previous research. Since the studies cited above utilized categories of influence tactics derived from research with MBA students, we developed categories from influence incidents collected from practicing managers. Our three studies used trained students from several universities and structured interview forms to collect a wide geographic dispersion of responses.

Attempts were made to collect one successful incident and one unsuccessful incident from managers in a wide variety of both large and small businesses. One study focused on lateral influence processes, another on upward influence processes, and a third study examined downward influence. The primary question asked of each manager

EXHIBIT 1   Rank of Frequency with Which Each Influence Tactic Was Reported by Target Groups

	Boss	Peers	Subordinates
Presenting a rational explanation	1	1	3
Telling, arguing, or talking without support	2	0	0
Presenting a complete plan	3	0	0
Using persistence or repetition	4	0	0
Developing and showing support of others (employees, outsiders, etc.)	5	2	12
Using others as a platform to present ideas	6	0	0
Presenting an example of a parallel situation	7	3	5
Threatening	8	4	10
Offering to trade favors or concessions	9	5	0
Using manipulative techniques	10	6	7
Calling on formal authority and policies	0	8	6
Showing confidence and support	0	0	1
Delegating duties, guidelines, or goals	0	0	2
Listening, counseling, or soliciting ideas	0	0	4
Questioning, reviewing, or evaluating	0	0	9
Rewarding with status or salary	0	0	7
Developing friendship or trust	0	7	11

was, "Please think of a time when you successfully/unsuccessfully tried to influence a (superior, peer, or subordinate) toward the attainment of a personal, group, or organizational goal. . . . Please tell exactly what happened."

Exhibit 1 presents the summary of findings from these studies.[10] The numbers to the right of each tactic portray the rank order of the frequency with which influence tactics were reported for each target group.

Influencing Superiors

In influence attempts with superiors and peers, rational explanations were the most frequently used tactic. Often these techniques included the presentation of a complete plan, a comparative or quantitative analysis, or documentation of an idea or plan by way of survey, incidents, or interviews. In a few isolated cases, subordinates challenged their superiors' power, tried to manipulate them, bargained for influence, or threatened to quit. When these more assertive techniques were used, the subordinate was successful about 50 percent of the time—not very good odds for the risks which they were taking. In most narratives we found that the subordinates using these methods had discovered a powerless boss, or had developed an unusual position of power themselves by becoming indispensable. In a few cases they had simply become frustrated and thrown caution to the wind.

Upward influence tactics were characterized by numerous supporting tactics such as mustering the support of a variety of other persons (both internal and external to the organization) or by choosing appropriate timing to approach the boss. Only two tactics appeared with significant enough frequency differential to be clearly distinguished as a successful or unsuccessful tactic. Subordinates using the tactic of "talking to or arguing with the boss without support" were more likely to fail. On the other hand, those who continued persistently or repeated an influence attempt continuously were likely to succeed. Caution is in order, however, in interpreting the use of persistence and repetition; this was usually a secondary tactic used in combination with others such as presenting facts and rational plans.

The rational persuasion technique was used by a plant manager to prevent a cutback in his workforce when the army phased out one of its tanks:

> First the plant manager sold a new product line to divisional staff who reported to his boss. In the meantime he developed a presentation in the form of a comparative analysis showing the pros and cons of taking on the new product line. Ideas presented included such things as the reduced burden on other products, risk reward factors, and good community relations from the layoff avoided. The presentation was polished, written on viewgraphs, and presented in person. The plant manager made certain that his technical staff would be at the meeting ready to answer any questions that might damage the strength of the presentation.

Not only did the plant manager succeed with this influence attempt, he felt that his boss and peers were easier to convince on subsequent attempts.

Influencing Subordinates

When dealing with subordinates, of course, the manager may simply tell an employee to do something. But our research suggests that managers who rely on formal authority alone are greatly limiting their options. The power gap noted earlier exists with subordinates as well as with other groups. Today more than ever, it must be filled with methods of influence other than authority. The following incident presents an interesting view of a furniture manufacturer trying to persuade his upholstery foreman to accept the position of plant superintendent:

> The manager met with Foreman Z in the foreman's office for short periods to talk about the promotion. Anticipating resistance, he covered small increments of the superintendent's responsibilities and allowed the foreman time to think about each session. The manager made sure that each session ended on a positive note. He pointed out the many tasks and skills required of the superintendent's job were already inherent in the foreman position. He downplayed the more complex responsibilities, relying on his commitment to future training to resolve these. Several such meetings took place in a five-day period. On one occasion the foreman alluded to resentment from fellow foremen. This prompted the manager to enlist the help of some of the other foremen—several hunting buddies—to talk favorably about Z taking the position. In the last meeting the manager outlined the responsibilities and cited the salary and prestige which accompanied the position.

The senior manager in this incident later commented that he had always had success at using this technique—that is, breaking down a complex influence task into incremental steps and attacking each step separately. While there is some merit in this process, most readers would agree that the major reason for success in this case was the persistence exerted by the senior manager to win in his influence attempt. The mild deception in oversimplifying the open position could merit criticism but must be moderated by the manager's willingness to train and support the foreman. In this case, the influence tactic had positive long-term consequences; the foreman became a very successful plant superintendent and later trained his own successor.

Frequently, subordinates were questioned, reviewed, evaluated, threatened, warned, reprimanded, or embarrassed to change their minds or to solicit compliance with plans of the superior. These more threatening and negative techniques were more frequently associated with failure than success. Occasionally subordinates were transferred or relocated to influence them, but usually with little success. The more assertive tactics were typically used in cases where subordinates were initially reluctant to comply with reasonable requests or had violated policies or procedures.

Influencing Peers

Only one tactic from our lateral influence study was noted significantly more often in successful influence attempts with peers—that of "developing and showing support of others." This tactic was most often used along with others and therefore represented a part of a multiple influence tactic. Often a peer in a staff department or a subordinate is used to support a proposal, as in the influence attempt described by a zone manager with a large tire and rubber company:

> During this time I was managing 25 company-owned stores in which I initiated an effective program to control the handling of defective merchandise. I wanted to see the method utilized by the other store managers throughout the country who were supervised by other zone managers, but I felt that they would consider me to be intruding if I approached them directly. Therefore, I asked my store managers to tell the store managers in other zones about the sizable savings to be had from the use of the method. The other store managers told their zone managers and soon they came to me for information about my program. The new program saved the company $90,000 per year, which increased our pay in bonuses at the end of the year.

When dealing with peers, managers made extensive use of rational facts or ideas. They often presented an example of another organization using their idea or proposal. Demonstrating that they had the support of others was a frequently used managerial influence tactic. Occasionally they threatened to go to higher-level management or called on formal authority or policies to support their case. Assertive and manipulative tactics were used more often when attempting to influence the boss or subordinates, but less frequently with peers.

INFLUENCE TACTIC EFFECTIVENESS

Our research on individual influence attempts somewhat simplifies the area of influence effectiveness. In the first place, the methods listed in Exhibit 1 are the ones that are most frequently used and not necessarily the ones which are most successful. In all three studies we found that techniques that succeed in some instances fail in others. The few exceptions to this finding are noted in Exhibit 1 when the ranks of tactics are underlined. These represent tactics that were reported significantly more often, for either successful or unsuccessful influence attempts. For example, unsuccessful influence attempts with the boss often consisted of simply telling the boss something, arguing, or presenting an idea or suggestion without support. While this technique occasionally succeeded, it was more likely to be associated with unsuccessful episodes. Similarly, the use of persistence or repetition was reported more often in successful influence attempts with the boss than with unsuccessful ones.

Judging from the incidents collected, subordinate influence tactics of "threatening or questioning, reviewing, or evaluating" are significantly more likely to lead to failure than to success. Consider the experience of a plant operations manager attempting to introduce quality circles in an area to improve productivity:

> The operations manager requested the assistance of the manager of organizational development, who warned that such implementation would take time, patience and the building of trust among his employees. Turnover in the operations area was high, and negative attitudes tended to prevail. The operations manager became impatient, viewing QC as a quick fix for morale problems. The OD manager made available several persons who had worked successfully with a QC implementation, but after conversing with them the operations manager elected not to listen. He chose two subordinates to be trained as QC facilitators and immediately upon the completion of their training, began to implement QC. The operations manager and facilitators subtly coerced employees to join the circles and directed them toward the projects that management wanted attacked. After several months employee interest fell sharply and several complaints were filed with employee relations, leading to abandonment of the power.

Contrast this occurrence with a less threatening attempt reported by a manufacturing manager in another part of the country:

> The manager first read numerous articles about QC programs and learned the pitfalls to avoid. QC Information handouts were given to the supervisors over a period of a couple of months. The supervisors were never pressured and gradually they approached their manager, asking how they could get quality circles started in their departments. The program was then implemented using recognized procedures and is still operating successfully several years later.

The analysis of influence attempts such as the quality circles incidents demonstrates the need for careful implementation of management processes.

STEPS IN BECOMING AN INFLUENTIAL MANAGER

Power, or sustained influence, may be accumulated and stored by a manager for future use. This allows one to call on existing strength to bolster influence tactics and often affects the future choice of influence tactic. Power may also be provided by the strategic position that one occupies in an organization, but position is often beyond the control of the incumbent. Fortunately, power may also be acquired through the development and exercise of certain skills by the manager within the organization. It is this skill-based power that we discuss throughout the rest of this article.[11]

Our research, and that of other writers reviewed in this article, indicates that there are five key steps to establishing sustained managerial influence:

- Develop a reputation as a knowledgeable person or an expert.
- Balance the time spent in each critical relationship according to the needs of the work rather than on the basis of habit or social preference.
- Develop a network of resource persons who can be called upon for assistance.
- Choose the correct combination of influence tactics for the objective and for the target to be influenced.
- Implement influence tactics with sensitivity, flexibility, and adequate levels of communication.

These steps in developing influence might be compared to the development of a "web of influence" (no negative implication intended). Unlike the web of a spider, the manager's web of influence can be mutually advantageous to all who interact within it. The web is anchored by a bridgeline of knowledge and expertise. The structure of the web is extended when invested time is converted into a network of resource persons who may be called upon for information and special assistance or support with an influence attempt. These persons—superiors, peers, subordinates, outside contacts, and others might be thought of as spokes in the web. Establishing the web, however, does not ensure influence attempts will be successful. An effective combination of influence tactics must be selected for each influence target and influence objective sought. Finally, the tactics chosen must be communicated well within the sector of the web targeted.

Our research suggests that the web of influence is continually in a state of construction. It is often broken or weakened by an ill-chosen influence attempt requiring patch-up work for a portion of the web. Some webs are constructed poorly, haphazardly, or incompletely, like the tangled web of a common house spider, while others are constructed with a beautiful symmetrical pattern, like the one of the orb weaver.

Develop a Reputation as an Expert

Of all the influence tactics mentioned by respondents in our interviews, the use of rational facts and explanations was the most commonly reported—although in isolation this method succeeded no more often than it failed. Managers who possess expert knowledge in a field and who continually build that knowledge base are in a position to convert successful attempts into sustained power. In the early stages of a career (or shortly after a move) power from expertise is usually tentative and fragile, like the first strands of a web. Hampton and colleagues explain how expertise is extended to become sustained influence with the following example of Bill, a young staff specialist, hired to provide expertise to a number of production managers:

> Initially, the only influence process available to the specialist is persuasion—gaining the rational agreement of the managers. To be effective he prepares elaborate, clear presentations (even rehearsing with a colleague to anticipate any questions). By data, logic, and argument, he attempts to gain the agreement of his superiors. After a year of this kind of relationship, he goes one day to talk with Barbara, one of the managers. An hour has been reserved for the presentation. He arrives and begins his pitch. After a couple of minutes, however, the busy manager interrupts: "I'm just too busy to go over this. We'll do whatever you want to do."[12]

But enhancing expert-based power involves publicizing one's expertise as well as acquiring it. For example, Kotter contrasts two 35-year-old vice presidents in a large research and development organization, who are considered equally bright and technically competent:

> Close friends and associates claim the reason that Randley is so much more powerful is related to a number of tactics that he has used more than Kline has. Randley has published more scientific papers and managerial articles than Kline. Randley has been more selective in the assignments he has worked on, choosing those that are visible and that require his strong suits. He has given more speeches and presentations on projects that are his own achievements. And in meetings in general, he is allegedly forceful in areas where he has expertise and silent in those where he does not.[13]

Balance Time with Each Critical Relationship

Managers who desire to become influential must strike a reasonable balance in the investment of their time. In another study using a questionnaire, we surveyed managers from the United States, Korea, Hong Kong, and the Philippines to learn how they spent their time. These managers say that they spend about 10 percent of their time interacting with the boss, approximately 30 percent interacting with subordinates, and about 20 percent interacting with peers. As one might expect, the pattern of outside relations varies with the job (i.e., sales, engineering, etc.), but the managers report, on the average, spending from 15 to 20 percent of their time with external contacts. Time spent alone varies from 15 to 28 percent.[14] Although we cannot argue that this pattern is descriptive of all managers, it is similar to the pattern of communication distribution discovered from a sample of United States managers by Luthans and Larson.[15]

Some popular writers are calling for a heavy rescheduling of time and communications efforts.[16] Peters argues that 75 percent of a middle manager's time must be spent on horizontal relationships to speed up cross-functional communications in the middle of organizations. Johnson and Frostman see this kind of communication as being so critical that it must be mandated by upper-level management. Peters emphasizes the argument that upper-level managers spend too little time visiting with customers or in face-to-face relationships with subordinates (management by walking around). The bottom line is that time should be spent where influence is most needed to accomplish organizational goals.[17]

During our seminars on influence over the years, managers have often told us that they failed to spend enough time with the boss or with peers, or in simply keeping up with organizational happenings. This may be due to the fact that many managers are uncomfortable spending time with those who have more formal power than they (superiors), or with those with whom they must compete (peers). Sayles believed that managers' uneasiness with peers grows out of the difference in values across departments and work groups, the ambiguities which exist in cross-organizational relationships, and the conflict often generated in lateral relationships.[18] Other things being equal, realigning from a narrow focus on subordinates to a bigger picture which includes lateral and upward relationships can often yield a stronger web of sustained influence and should provide the supporting spokes needed to launch influence tactics.

A strong web of influence may even be quite desirable from the boss's viewpoint. Schilit found that managers who had been working for the same upper manager for a

long period of time were quite capable of influencing the manager even on strategic issues facing the company. He concludes that [managers] should be encouraged to be
assertive in presenting their strategic thoughts because widespread strategic thinking
may have a positive impact on their division or organization."[19]

Develop a Network of Resource Persons

Although managers do not use other people in most influence attempts, the more
important attempts invariably involve others. For example, in the incident cited earlier
about the furniture manufacturer who wanted a foreman to accept the plant manager's
job, the assistance of other foremen (fishing buddies) was solicited. Similarly, in the
case of the plant manager who tried to avoid a cutback in his workforce after the
phaseout of a military contract, the manager sold his idea to division staff and ensured
that his own technical staff would be in attendance at the meeting in which he was
making a presentation to the boss. The ability to establish and exploit a network is
clearly demonstrated by a branch manager of a bank who used the following tactic
with his superior, a vice president, when he found his operation in need of additional
space:

> My strategy was to convince my immediate superior that the current facilities were too
> small to not only handle the current volume of business, but too small to allow us to in-
> crease our share of the market in a rapidly growing area. First, I persuaded my superior to
> visit the branch more often, especially at times when the branch was particularly busy. I
> also solicited accounting's help to provide statistical reports on a regular basis that commu-
> nicated the amount of overall growth in the area as well as the growth of our competitors.
> These reports showed that our market share was increasing. I then asked my superior to
> visit with me as I called on several customers and prospects in the area to let him know the
> type of potential business in the area. During this period of time, I kept pushing to increase
> all levels of business at the branch. Finally, I encouraged key customers in the bank to say
> favorable things about my branch when they visited with my senior managers. Eventually
> my superior got behind my proposal and we were able to build an addition to the building
> which allowed me to add several new employees.

Such influence attempts clearly illustrate the fact that many managers do not assume that achievement in traditional areas of management—selling, organizing, promoting customers—will inspire sufficient confidence by others. Rather than waiting
for good publicity and resources to come to them, they seek them out through influence approaches built on carefully planned networks and persistent effort. The findings of our influence studies are supported by the observations of Luthans and his
colleagues, who concluded that managers who are both effective (have satisfied and
committed subordinates and high performance in their units) and successful (receive
relatively rapid promotions) strike a balanced approach between networking, human
resource management, communications, and traditional management activities.[20]

To some extent, networking activities may affect the positional strength of managers. The more contacts a manager has with others and the more independent the position relative to others, the more control the manager has over the flow of information.
Positions that involve interaction with more influential managers of the organization or
control information on which they rely, will typically be ones of power.[21]

Kaplan compares the strengthening of lateral relationships in the organization to the establishment of trade routes in international trade. According to this writer, managers, unlike countries which trade products, often trade power and the ability to get things done. Their goal is to build strong reciprocal relationships with other departments so that when the manager has immediate needs sufficient obligation exists to ensure fast cooperation. Often positions on the boundary of an organization can be especially influential. Consider the example referred to by Kaplan when describing a newly appointed manager of corporate employee relations: "I wanted a base that was different from what the groups reporting to me had and also from what my superiors had, so I established a series of contacts in other American industries until I knew on a first-name basis my counterpart of IBM, TRW, Procter & Gamble, Du Pont, and General Electric, and I could get their input—input which the people in my organization didn't have."[22] Kaplan suggests that networks of trading partners can be built by rotating jobs frequently, establishing strong friendships (and maintaining them), and seeking commonality with other managers, such as a shared work history.

Choose the Correct Combination of Influence Tactics

Influence tactics are the threads that complete a web, hold the spokes of the webbed network in place, and in turn are supported by the network. They must be chosen carefully on the basis of influence targets chosen and objectives sought.[23] One of the studies by Kipnis and colleagues found, as did we, that considerably more approaches were used to influence subordinates than were used to influence superiors or peers. Incidents in our studies suggested that most first influence attempts by managers involved soft approaches such as requests or reason, but later attempts included stronger tactics when the target of influence was reluctant to comply. This notion was confirmed statistically in the Kipnis study. Both superior and subordinate target groups in the Kipnis sample tended to use reason to sell ideas and friendliness to obtain favors. These authors also emphasize that influence tactics must vary with the target and objective of influence attempts: "only the most inflexible of managers can be expected to rely rigidly on a single strategy, say assertiveness, to achieve both personal and organizational objectives. It may be appropriate to 'insist' that one's boss pay more attention to cost overruns; it is less appropriate to 'insist' on time off for a game of golf."[24]

Taking a cue from the fact that few tactics were found to be associated more frequently with success than failure in any of our studies, we began to examine combinations of influence tactics. In each of the three influence studies (upward, downward, and lateral), managers who used a combination of approaches tended more often to be successful than managers who relied on a single tactic.

We noted that in many incidents short-term success seemed to lead to enhanced influence in the long term; therefore, we sought ways to measure sustained influence over time. Consequently, in our downward influence study, we asked managers about the nature of the subordinate-superior relationship that occurred two months following an influence attempt. As we expected, successful influence attempts led the managers to perceive that their relationships had improved and to believe they had expanded their potential for future influence. For example, the bank branch manager who was able to enlarge his building reported that because of his success with the influence attempt his profile at the bank was raised, that he was given a promotion and a raise, and that he was transferred to the main office.[25]

Although we cannot be certain that the managers experiencing short-term influence success derived power with their boss from these episodes, the fact that managers believed this to be so caused them, in most cases, to plan additional influence attempts. These findings are supported by a study by Kipnis and his colleagues which found that managers who perceive that they have power are more likely to select assertive influence tactics.[26] Failures at influence attempts may cause managers to plan fewer future attempts and to experience a period of weakened relationships with the boss. Frequently when a subordinate attempts to influence upper-level management in a manner where his or her intention is clearly for the advantage of the organization, failure is not damaging to future influence. When the purpose of an influence attempt is clearly seen as a personal goal, failure may be more serious. Such a case was reported by a supervisor of security services dealing with a vice president of operations:

> I wanted an assistant so that I could have some help in managing my department and would not have to handle petty problems of my employees. I tried to convince my boss that I was overworked since my staff has almost doubled and I was having a lot of people problems. I failed because I was just trying to make it easier on myself and wanted an assistant to do the job that I was supposed to be doing. I was also asking to increase the payroll of the company with no plans to increase revenue or profits. After my boss turned me down, I pouted for a few weeks and later learned that my boss thought I was immature. I then decided to forget about past disappointments and only worry about the future.

Communicate Influence Tactics Effectively

It is very difficult to separate influence tactic choice with the communications process itself. Cohen and Bradford stress the importance of knowing the world of potential allies—the needs, values, and organizational forces working on them. For example, they suggest that setting the stage for an influence attempt by wining and dining influence targets at a fancy restaurant may work well for a public relations director, but may appear to be a buyout attempt when directed toward the head of engineering.[27]

Many of our research participants mentioned the importance of their presentation or their manner of approaching the target. Managers who choose rational ideas based on the needs of the target, wrap them with a blanket of humor or anecdotes, and cast them in the language of the person to be influenced, are much more likely to see their influence objective achieved.

Effective communications become interwoven coils of silk in the web of influence that help ensure the success of tactics. Consider, for example, the combination of influence tactics and communication used by Lee Iacocca in his turnaround strategy of Chrysler. Kotter capsules these as follows: "He developed a bold new vision of what Chrysler should be . . . he (then) attracted, held on to, and elicited cooperation and teamwork from a large network . . . labor leaders, a whole new management team, dealers, suppliers, some key government officials and many others. He did so by articulating his agenda in emotionally powerful ways ("Remember, folks, we have a responsibility to save 600,000 jobs"), by using the credibility and relationships he had developed after a long and highly successful career in the automotive business, by communicating the new strategies in an intellectually powerful manner and in still other ways."[28]

Upward and lateral communications require more listening and more appreciation of the ideas and thoughts of others than dictated by subordinate relationships. Laborde suggests that a person who would master the communicator part of influence must see more and hear more than most people and must remain flexible to vary their behavior in response to what they see and hear.[29] Kaplan strongly emphasizes the importance of variation in the arsenal of communications skills—knowing when to meet with a person face-to-face, when to call group meetings, and when to use memos.[30]

Implications of Influence Research for Managers

No research is subtle enough to capture all of the relationships present between managers as they work together as peers, subordinates, and superiors. While incident- or questionnaire-type research may be subject to some self-report bias (if possible, managers try to make themselves look rational to the researcher), observers, even if they could remain long enough in an area, could never capture and connect all of the thoughts necessary to precisely determine motives, processes, and outcomes of managers attempting to develop long-term influence relationships. We have attempted to capture some of the pieces, reviewed the best of what other experts have said about the subject, and tried to establish some connections. While recognizing these limitations, our influence research over the past 10 years leads us to the following conclusions:

- Managers are continually in a state of building and extending webs of influence and repairing damaged threads. With every career change, new webs must be built. In the early part of a career or after a career move, a manager must establish a web of influence by developing a reputation as an expert, balancing this with key influence targets, networking to establish resources, and selecting and communicating appropriate influence tactics.

- No one influence tactic can be isolated as being superior to others. Tactics must be chosen on the basis of the influence target and objective sought. For more important influence objectives, a combination of influence tactics will be necessary.

- Frequency of reported tactic usage suggests that most contemporary managers initially try positive techniques with targets, but will quickly resort to threats or manipulation if necessary, especially if the target is a subordinate.

- The variety of approaches used to influence subordinates is wider than suggested by the traditional leadership models and wider than the variety used in upward and lateral influence attempts.[31] This appears to be due not only to the additional power bases available when dealing with subordinates, but also to the growing difficulty of obtaining subordinate compliance through traditional means.

- Contrary to traditional views that networking outside the hierarchy is disruptive, today's leaders must recognize the value of reciprocal influence relationships and must encourage them as long as they can be fruitfully directed toward organizational goals. Webs of influence may provide advantages for all involved.

- For these reasons, we are quite convinced that influential managers are ones who have developed and maintained a balanced web of relationships with the boss, subordinates, peers, and other key players; influence in each of these directions is banked for leverage to accomplish goals in the other directions. If knowledge alone and positional authority alone will not accomplish the manager's job, those who would be influential must fill power gaps with webs of influence.

ENDNOTES

The authors appreciate the helpful suggestions to an earlier draft of this manuscript by W. J. Heisler, manager, Management Development and Salaried Employee Training, Newport News Shipbuilding, and Fred Luthans, George Holmes professor of management, University of Nebraska. We especially appreciate the work of the anonymous reviewers who assisted us with the paper. Thanks also to the professors who participated in original research studies: Robert Bell, Tennessee Tech University; Lloyd Dosier and Gene Murkinson of Georgia Southern University; Tom Miller and Coy Jones, Memphis State University; Kent Curran, University of North Carolina, Charlotte; and Alfred Edge. University of Hawaii.

1. These definitions follow those of D. R. Hampton, C. E. Summer, and R. A. Webber, Chapter 3. *Organizational Behavior and the Practice of Management* (Glenview, Illinois: Scott, Foresman, 1987), Fifth Edition.

2. See Chapter 1 of A. R. Cohen and D. L. Bradford, *Influence without Authority* (New York: John Wiley, 1990). For a review of these thoughts, see W. Bennis and B. Nanus, *Leaders: The Strategies for Taking Charge* (New York: Harper & Row, 1985) and J. M. Kouzes and B. Z. Posner, *The Leadership Challenge* (San Francisco: Jossey-Bass, 1988). For a book that relates leadership influence to the way in which change is implemented in the American economy, see N. M. Tichy and M. A. Devanna, *The Transformational Leader* (New York: John Wiley & Sons, 1986). See also, Chapter 2 of J. P. Kotter, *Power and Influence—Beyond Formal Authority* (New York: The Free Press, 1985).

3. For the review of literature and our conceptualization of an influence model, see J. B. Keys and R. Bell, "The Four Faces of the Fully Functioning Middle Manager," *California Management Review,* 24 (4), Summer 1982, pp. 59–66; a condensed version of this article can be found in *World Executive's Digest,* 4 (7), 1983, pp. 25–31.

4. For the original research on the importance of upward influence to supervisory success, see D. C. Pelz, "Influence: Keys to Effective Leadership in the First Level Supervisor," *Personnel,* 29, 1959, pp. 209–17. For a later discussion with case illustrations, see F. Bartolomé and A. Laurent, "The Manager: Master and Servant of Power," *Harvard Business Review,* 64 (6), Nov/Dec. 1986, pp. 77–81. The ways in which managers, especially middle managers, acquire and sustain upward influence are outlined in D. H. Kreger, "Functions and Problems of Middle Management," *Personnel Journal,* 49 (11), November 1970, p. 935; P. D. Couch,

"Learning to Be a Middle Manager," *Business Horizons,* 22 (1), February 1979, pp. 33–41; R. A. Webber, "Career Problems of Young Managers," *California Management Review,* 18 (4), Summer 1976, pp. 19–33; H. E. R. Uyterhoeven, "General Managers in the Middle," *Harvard Business Review,* 50 (2), March–April 1972, pp. 75–85. For an article that has become a best selling classic on the subject, see J. J. Gabarro and J. P. Kotter, "Managing Your Boss," *Harvard Business Review,* 58 (1), January–February, 1980, pp. 92–100. For a recent article on maintaining loyalty and developing an initial relationship with the boss, see R. Vecchio, "Are You In or Out with the Boss?" *Business Horizons,* 29 (6), November–December 1986, pp. 76–78.

5. For the review of the way in which managers create influence downward see Uyterhoven Endnote 4 and S. H. Ruello, "Transferring Managerial Concepts and Techniques to Operating Management," *Advanced Management Journal,* 38 (3), July 1973, pp. 42–48. For a discussion of the importance of defending and supporting subordinates, see Bartolomé and Laurent Endnote 4.

6. For a discussion of how managers develop political skills, see Ruello, Endnote 5 and Uyterhoeven, Endnote 4. To review the integrative role of middle managers, see J. L. Hall and J. K. Leidecker, "Lateral Relations: The Impact on the Modern Managerial Role," *Industrial Management,* June 1974, p. 3.

7. For a discussion of external relationships, see D. W. Organ, "Linking Pins between Organizations and Environment," *Business Horizons,* 14 (6), December 1971, pp. 73–80.

8. A. I. Kraut, P. R. Pedigo, D. D. McKenna, and M. D. Dunnette, "The Role of the Manager: What's Really Important in Different Management Jobs," *The Academy of Management Executive,* 3 (4), pp. 286–93.

9. For other studies on influence tactics see: D. Kipnis, S. M. Schmidt and I. Wilkinson, "Interorganizational Influence Tactics: Explorations in Getting One's Way," *Journal of Applied Psychology,* 65 (4), August 1980, pp. 440–52. This study differed from our field study in that it surveyed evening MBA students and allowed them to describe any successful influence episode in which they had been involved. W. K. Schilit and E. A. Locke, "A Study of Upward Influence in Organizations," *Administrative Science Quarterly,* 27 (2), 1982, pp. 304–16 found that Kipnis and Schmidt's 14 tactic categories were not sufficient to categorize upward influence incident accounts collected from undergraduate and graduate business students and full-time employees or supervisors. They found evidence supporting the use of 20 types of upward influence tactics. Because these previous investigations relied so heavily on unchallenged global categories derived from a relatively small sample of evening MBA students which might not be representative of managers, we began our studies from scratch and collected narrative accounts of incidents from practicing managers. Each study focused on only one type of target and at least 250 influence tactics were collected. Flanagan's critical incident method was used to develop categories and to content analyze the responses. (J. C. Flanagan, "Defining the Requirements of the Executive's Job," *Personnel,* 28, July 1951, pp. 28–35.) Our findings for upward influence were more similar to those of Schilit and Locke than to those of Kipnis et al. Over 46 distinct tactics were observed across the three types of targets. Of course, tactics used to influence some targets are rarely, if ever, used to influence other types of targets. The description of managerial influence tactics which emerges from our three studies is much more detailed and therefore more suited to management applications than that provided by the previous investigations. Of equal importance, unlike the previous studies, our investigations also addressed the use of combinations of tactics vis-à-vis single tactics, and the long-term consequences of the influence attempt for the initiator and the organization.

10. For a more complete description of the research methods and statistical findings of the three studies reported here, see J. B. Keys, T. Miller, T. Case, K. Curran, and C. Jones, "Lateral Influence Tactics," *International Journal of Management,* 4 (3), 1987, pp. 425–31; L. Dosier, T. Case, J. B. Keys, G. Murkinson, "Upward Influence Tactics," *Leadership and Organizational Development Journal,* 9 (4), 1988, pp. 25–31; T. Case, J. B. Keys, and L. Dosier, "How Managers Influence Subordinates: A Study of Downward Influence Tactics," *Leadership and Organizational Development Journal,* 9 (5), 1988, pp. 22–28.

11. For an interesting theoretical discussion of these and other power producing factors see D. Mechanic, "Source of Power of Lower Participants in Complex Organizations," *Administrative Science Quarterly,* 7 (3), 1962, pp. 349–64. For an excellent case study of how a middle manager combines expertise, networking and the other techniques noted see D. Izraeli, "The Middle Manager and the Tactics of Power Expansion: A Case Study," *Sloan Management Review,* 16(2), 1975, pp. 57–69.

12. See Endnote 1, p. 35.

13. See Kotter in Endnote 2, p. 35.

14. B. Keys, T. Case, and A. Edge, "A Cross-National Study of Differences between Leadership Relationships of Managers in Hong Kong with Those in the Philippines, Korea, and the United States," *International Journal of Management,* 6 (4), 1989, pp. 390–404.

15. For a look at the pattern of managerial communications and time investment see F. Luthans and J. K. Larson, "How Managers Really Communicate," *Human Relations,* 39 (2), 1986, pp. 161–78.

16. For a discussion of the need for middle managers to spend time in lateral and external relationships, see also T. Peters, *Thriving on Chaos: Handbook for a Management Revolution* (New York: Harper & Row, 1987); T. Peters and N. Austin, *Passion for Excellence* (New York: Random House, 1985); and L. Johnson and A. L. Frohman, "Identifying and Closing the Gap in the Middle of Organizations," *The Academy of Management Executive,* 3(2), pp. 107–14.

17. R. E. Kaplan, "Trade Routes; The Manager's Network of Relationships," *Organizational Dynamics,* 12 (4), 1984, pp 37–52, and J. Kotter, *The General Managers* (New York: The Free Press, 1983).

18. For an excellent guide to handling lateral relations complete with case illustrations, see Chapter 5 of L. Sayles, *Leadership: Managing in Real Organizations,* second ed. (New York: McGraw-Hill).

19. For a discussion of why managers should encourage their subordinates to influence them, see W. K. Schilit, "An Examination of Individual Differences as Moderators of Upward Influence Activity in Strategic Decisions," *Human Relations,* 30 (10), 1986, p. 948. The author's findings from this empirical study lend support to the suggestions about transformational leaders by Tichy and Devanna, and Kotter, in Endnote 2.

20. For a further discussion of the activities of successful and effective managers, see F. Luthans, R. M. Hodgetts, and S. A. Rosenkrantz, *Real Managers* (Cambridge: Ballenger, 1988).

21. For a review of network theory, see J. Blau and R. Alba, "Empowering Nets of Participation," *Administrative Science Quarterly,* 27, 1982, pp. 363–79. See also Endnote 18.

22. See Kaplan, Endnote 17, above.

23. For an excellent treatment of the objectives and targets of influence, see D. Kipnis, S. Schmidt, C. Swaffin-Smith, and I. Wilkinson, "Patterns of Managerial Influence: Shotgun Managers, Tacticians, and Bystanders," *Organizational Dynamics,* 12 (3), 1984, pp. 58–67, and Kipnis et al., 1980, Endnote 9, above. These studies and the Erez et al.

study noted below also used a common questionnaire and a similar factor analysis to find broader categories of influence in which individual influence tactics (similar to those in Exhibit 1) fall. The categories derived include: Reason: The use of facts and data to support logical arguments. Manipulation: The use of impression management, flattery, or ingratiation. Coalitions: Obtaining the support of other people in the organization. Bargaining: The use of negotiation and exchange of benefits or favors. Assertiveness: Demanding or acting in a forceful manner. Upward appeal: Making an appeal to higher levels of management in the organization to back up requests. Sanctions: Threatening to withhold pay or advancement, or to impose organizational discipline. M. Erez, R. Rim, and I. Keider, "The Two Sides of the Tactics of Influence: Agent vs. Target," *Journal of Occupational Psychology,* 59, 1986, pp. 25–39.

24. See D. Kipnis et al., Endnote 23, above, p. 32.
25. For a discussion of the use of manipulation as an influence, and/or managerial approach, see Erez, Endnote 23, above, and A. Zalesnik, "The Leadership Gap," *The Academy of Management Executive,* 4 (1), 1990, pp. 7–22.
26. See D. Kipnis et al., in Endnote 23, above, p. 32.
27. A. R. Cohen and D. L. Bradford, "Influence without Authority: The Use of Alliances, Reciprocity, and Exchange to Accomplish Work," *Organizational Dynamics,* 17 (3), 1989, pp. 5–17.
28. J. P. Kotter, *The Leadership Factor* (New York: The Free Press, 1988), 18.
29. G. Laborde, *Influencing Integrity: Management Skills for Communication and Negotiation* (Palo Alto: Syntony Publishing, 1987).
30. See Endnote 17, above, p. 32.
31. For a discussion of power and influence as a leadership approach, see G. Yukl, "Managerial Leadership: A Review of Theory and Research," *Journal of Management,* 15 (2), 1989, pp. 251–89.

How to Get Clout

Dr. Joyce Brothers

One of the most powerful female executives in America can't reach President Clinton by phone or cause ripples on Wall Street with a press conference. But make no mistake, Dorothy Roberts, CEO of the scarf maker Echo Design Group, has clout. Her secret: she treats employees like something more than employees.

Roberts's staff numbers 100-plus, yet she calls every employee on his or her birthday. When a colleague had cancer, she visited him in the hospital and continued sending a full paycheck for nearly four months—rather than putting him on disability. When another employee was going through a messy divorce, Roberts gave her the summer off. In other words, Roberts makes her employees feel like family.

In return, she gets loyalty. "I've seen people here work around the clock to get out orders and do the job well," says Charles Williams, co-president of the company. Since Roberts took over the business in 1978, Echo's sales have grown to $30 million.

Dorothy Roberts proves a point: increasingly, clout belongs to people who treat others well. To achieve it, you must create and maintain positive relationships.

In the past, clout belonged to wily politicians and overbearing bosses. Fortunately, that's no longer true, says Bob Dilenschneider, head of the Dilenschneider Group, a public relations firm: "Power is much softer today. To get clout, you don't yell at people, you don't criticize them openly, and you don't use fear. You inform them and try to get them to endorse your ideas."

True clout, then, is available to us all—which is fortunate, because everyone needs it. Only with clout can we make a difference in our churches, our places of work, our communities, even our families.

1. Here's how to get clout: *Act "as if . . ."* Psychologist William James developed a theory he called his "as if" principle. "If you want a quality, act as if you already have it," he used to say. His point? The ability to influence others, or wield clout, is a state of mind.

That's what Jean Stryjewski discovered. From the time that Stryjewski, a doting grandmother and president of her neighborhood council in southeast Washington, D.C., moved into public housing seven years ago, she worried about the safety of the children straying from the complex's tiny unfenced yard into its busy parking lot. When a three-year-old boy was struck by a car one summer day in 1990, Stryjewski and her neighbors complained to officials, but no fences appeared.

Reprinted from *Reader's Digest,* Vol. 144, April 1994. Reprinted with permission of *Reader's Digest.*

The accident coincided with the capital's mayoral campaign. Stryjewski steeled herself to begin a campaign of her own. "Every time candidates went on the stump," she recalls, "I was there to look them in the eye and say, 'When you get elected, I need my fences.' "

When the election was over, Stryjewski's relentless crusade paid off. The city installed four-foot fences around her building, and now children can play safely.

"I knew I'd get those fences eventually," says Stryjewski. Her spearheading of a neighborhood campaign forced local politicians to respond. "If you project confidence, then you have clout," says William Ury, director of Harvard Law School's Negotiation Network.

2. *Go to the balcony.* Many people suppose that the one who yells loudest will emerge the victor. In fact, bullying rarely works. "When you're angry, you communicate in an ineffective way," says Ury. "A boss who screams at subordinates may get temporary results, but in the long run his employees will lose their respect for him."

Joseph Vittoria, the affable CEO of Avis, is famous for keeping his cool—and employees love him for it. When he left Avis in the mid-1970s to join chief competitor Hertz, nearly 50 employees left Avis to go with him. Five years later, Avis rehired Vittoria as president. This time, even more employees came with him.

"I believe in treating people the way I want to be treated," he says. "As a result, they give me loyalty, support, and extra effort."

Whenever the challenge to keep your cool seems insurmountable, try a technique Ury calls "going to the balcony." "Tell those you are meeting with that you have to make a phone call and leave the room for a few minutes," he suggests. "Then concentrate on your goals. Ask yourself what you really want to accomplish."

By giving yourself a brief time-out, you should be able to regain composure and reapproach your disagreement rationally and constructively. Then, like Vittoria, you'll gain the respect of others for your emotional maturity.

3. *Listen carefully.* An old Hindu proverb says, "Help thy brother's boat across and lo! thine own has reached the shore." To gain clout, you must pay close attention so that you can learn what others truly want.

When Steven Spielberg, director of *E.T., Jurassic Park,* and other modern film classics, was a skinny 13-year-old making movies at home and in school, he was tormented for months by the class bully. "This was somebody I feared," wrote Spielberg. "He was my nemesis. I dreamed about him."

Young Steven decided that since he couldn't beat the bully, he should join him. "So I said to him, 'I'm making a movie about fighting the Nazis, and I want you to play this war hero.' At first he laughed in my face, but later he said yes. I made him the squad leader in the film, with helmet, fatigues, and backpack. After that he became my best friend."

Spielberg recognized that what the bully really wanted was to be accepted by his classmates. Spielberg, the self-described "skinny wimp," now had an older, stronger ally—and, as a result, gained stature, or clout, among his teenage peers.

How did he establish the calm rapport necessary for empathizing? By keeping his ears open. "All effective communication starts with listening," says Bonnie Jacobson, director of the New York Institute for Psychological Change. When others aren't forthcoming, try saying, "Is this what you mean?" and then repeat what they've just said—or what you suspect they feel. The fact that you want to comprehend their position fully will help to establish trust.

Says Robert Conklin, author of *How to Get People to Do Things,* "To the degree that you give other people what they need, they will give you what you need."

4. *Let everybody win.* True masters of clout follow the dictum of the Italian diplomat Daniele Vare, who said, "Diplomacy is the art of letting someone have your way." Explains Ury, "Instead of pushing the other side toward an agreement, draw them in the direction you want them to move."

President Dwight D. Eisenhower well understood the importance of pulling instead of pushing. In one cabinet meeting, he demonstrated the art of leadership by placing a piece of string on a table. "Pull the string, and it will follow wherever you wish," he explained. "Push it, and it will go nowhere at all."

When Dorothy Brunson started her TV station WGTW in Philadelphia in 1990, she had to scramble to persuade advertisers to buy commercial time. She nabbed one of her early sponsors, a department store, by projecting good ratings by a certain deadline. When the station failed to attract the number of viewers forecast, the client threatened to pull out. Brunson convinced the store to extend its contract another 90 days in exchange for a 10 percent reduction in advertising costs.

When she again failed to get the anticipated viewership, she could not extend to her client the same discount. Instead, Brunson promised to increase its air time by 10 percent for 90 days *after* she reached the original goal. It was a perfect win-win solution. Brunson kept the account, and the client's free ads reached more viewers.

5. *Have an ace up your sleeve.* Image that your 15-year-old daughter is going out on her first date. You fear she might deliberately ignore her 11 P.M. curfew to assert her independence. If she disobeys you, losing your temper will only escalate the conflict; yet if you say nothing now, you'll fail to provide proper guidance.

Neither option offers you clout. But if you get her date's phone number, and let her know that if she hasn't arrived home by 11:15, you're going to call his mother, you've set up an appropriate fallback plan for misbehavior. With this in place, your daughter knows that disobedience will result in embarrassment.

"Clout comes most essentially from having a backup plan," says William Ury. It greatly increases your ability to persuade.

To develop a strong backup plan for any life situation, Ury suggests asking yourself, How can I best meet my needs if this interaction fails? For example, if you're requesting a raise, your backup plan might be another job offer. If you're fighting with a car mechanic over the price of repairs, plan B might be to complain to the Better Business Bureau and refuse to pay until the case has been resolved.

6. *Don't gloat.* Just as you need empathy and compassion to get others to listen to your ideas, you need compassion at the end of the process. If you make others lose face, you'll risk undermining all you've worked to achieve.

President John F. Kennedy understood this. In October 1962, after more than two weeks of tense negotiation, the Cuban missile crisis was resolved when Nikita Khrushchev, the Soviet leader, agreed to remove all missiles from Cuba, if Kennedy, in turn, promised not to invade the island. According to Kennedy adviser and biographer Theodore Sorensen, the president then "laid down the line for all of us. No boasting, no gloating, not even a claim of victory. We had won by enabling Khrushchev to avoid complete humiliation—we should not humiliate him now."

7. *Do something surprising.* No matter how sensitive your tactics, there will always be someone—a difficult boss, an insecure spouse, a jealous co-worker—who will try to undermine your clout. When this happens, your only option may be to throw him for a loop.

Lee Iacocca's forthright style often took people by surprise. When he became chairman and CEO of Chrysler at the height of the auto giant's problems in 1979, he knew he would have to ask employees to take a pay cut to keep the company out of bankruptcy. Although he persuaded Congress to guarantee the company loans, he was still deeply distrusted by Chrysler's union members. He knew that he had to find a way to persuade these workers that he had Chrysler's best interests at heart.

Iacocca called a meeting of key management and union executives. He announced that for the next year his salary would be $1. The gambit worked. By sacrificing his own salary, Iacocca proved that he placed the welfare of the company over personal gain.

"I discovered that people accept a lot of pain when everybody is going through the chute together," Iacocca later wrote in his autobiography. "If everybody is suffering equally, you can move a mountain."

But there is another reason Iacocca's gesture was so effective. By passing on his salary, Iacocca was following the most important tenet for getting clout—he was cementing relationships. In getting clout, no other single tactic can take its place.

Ethics in Negotiation

In this section we examine the role played by personal values and ethics in the negotiation process. If you have been participating in role-plays and simulations as part of a negotiation course, questions of ethics have no doubt already come up in discussion. Someone may have bluffed or even lied in a role-play, and won "unfairly" as a consequence. Someone else may have gained access to the other side's confidential briefing information and used it to (unfair) advantage. People may have been outraged, not because they lost but because they lost as a result of tactics that were somehow determined to be out of bounds. Your reactions to these events—whether you saw them as acceptable or unacceptable, fair or unfair, moral or immoral—are largely guided by your own personal ethics and values, and by the appropriate values and ethics that you believe should govern negotiation settings. The articles in this section focus on the ways we make these judgments.

Until recently the area of ethics in negotiation has received almost no formal attention from ethicists or researchers. Fortunately, several new articles have appeared in recent years. Perhaps this work has been spurred by what most social observers believe to be a significant "moral decline" in our society, and an increased frequency of ethical violations by businesspeople, politicians, and public figures. The nightly news regularly features stories on fraud, corruption, and violations of ethics and public trust. It may occur in the world of sports (violation of recruiting or eligibility rules, bribe taking); religion (televangelists misspending their funds); business (fraudulent practices in the stock market and in the banking industry, or environmental abuse); or politics (political favoritism, misuse of campaign funds, or simply making false campaign promises). In the academic world, incidents of cheating on examinations, falsifying research studies, or falsifying personal backgrounds and credentials on a résumé have been frequent occurrences. It seems appropriate to define the ethical issues likely to arise in negotiation and the boundaries (if they exist) that commonly separate ethical from unethical conduct.

In the first article, "The Ethics and Profitability of Bluffing in Business," Richard Wokutch and Thomas Carson focus on a controversial negotiation tactic: bluffing. A bluff is common in negotiation, particularly in distributive bargaining. A negotiator asking $1,300 for a used car argues that $1,000 would never be acceptable; yet after 20 minutes of hard bargaining with a neighbor, the negotiator walks away with $1,000 in cash. The authors point out that a bluff is a lie—a false statement, an untruth—and is thus prima facie wrong. Thus, to engage in it, we need some special justification or reason to commit this "immoral action." The authors then explore (and rebut) the common "excuses" that people use to justify bluffing, lying, and deception. First, some lying and deception are necessary to be economically profitable; for example, if the negotiator "told the truth" and only asked for $1,000 for the car, and then engaged in the give-and-take of negotiation over the car's price, he or she would most likely wind up settling for less than $1,000! Second, some lying and deception may be necessary in "extreme" situations, where personal or corporate survival is at stake, such as avoiding bankruptcy or financial ruin. Third, some lying and deception may help the party being lied to; thus, advertising that inflates the advantages of a new drug might result in people being more convinced that the drug "works," and this strengthened faith in the product itself will make the drug more successful. Finally, some deception in negotiation is necessary because the other side has no "right" to know our true bargaining position, or because it is "common practice" and most people are already using these tactics. In evaluating these common arguments and justifications, Wokutch and Carson evolve a set of clear-cut principles for determining when bluffing and deception are appropriate behaviors in business conduct.

In the second article in this section, "Shrewd Bargaining on the Moral Frontier: Toward a Theory of Morality in Practice," J. Gregory Dees and Peter Cramton point to the critical role played by trust in defining whether a negotiator will or will not use deceptive tactics. According to the authors, mutual trust in the other negotiator usually embraces the expectation that he or she will "play by the same rules" when negotiating. Hence, when one trusts the other, one is more likely to be honest and straightforward about one's preferences and desires in negotiation; this trust creates the "defining morality" for acceptable and unacceptable actions. However, a lack of information about the other's true preferences, combined with short-term incentives derived from deceptive actions, contributes both to an absence of trust in the other and to poor communication. These factors enhance the likelihood that one might be more deceptive about one's true preferences and intentions, which may lead one to a superior outcome but also to a damaged relationship with the other. Dees and Cramton argue both the philosophical and economic aspects of this reasoning process, as well as alternative ways to account for dishonest conduct in negotiation, and suggest several mechanisms for developing trust in order to minimize the likelihood of deceptive behavior.

In the final article in this section, "Deception and Mutual Gains Bargaining: Are They Mutually Exclusive?", Raymond Friedman and Debra Shapiro explore whether deception has a role in integrative or "principled" negotiations. The authors state that most writers on win-win or mutual gains negotiating (e.g., Walton and McKersie, Fisher and Ury, Susskind and Cruikshank) have suggested (but not explicitly stated) that any form of deception or ethically ambiguous tactic is inconsistent with the win-win approach. Friedman and Shapiro note that this admonition is based on the assumption that deceptive tactics make integrative negotiating less effective because parties would not be representing their true interests (i.e., the admonition is not based on moral grounds). Moreover, the authors point out that most negotiations are not exclusively integrative but are often a mixture of distributive and integrative motives and issues. In many contexts, such as labor relations, experienced negotiators often use deception, but there also appears to be strong mutual expectations about when deception might be useful and essential, and when it is highly inappropriate and not likely to be useful. The moral, therefore, is threefold:

- Mutual gains negotiating has beneficial, practical effects; it is not just a "moralistic" strategy.

- Mutual gains negotiating does not imply that one must disclose all of one's positions and interests; selective and careful disclosure is both necessary and desired.

- Negotiators-in-training should learn how to use both tough bargaining tactics, including deception, as well as more interest-based, cooperative tactics.

The Ethics and Profitability
of Bluffing in Business

Richard E. Wokutch
Thomas L. Carson

Consider a standard case of bluffing in an economic transaction. I am selling a used car and say that $1,500 is my final offer, even though I know that I would accept considerably less. Or, suppose that I am a union representative in a labor negotiation. Although I have been instructed to accept $10 an hour if that is the highest offer I receive, I say that we will not accept a wage of $10 an hour under any circumstances. This sort of bluffing is widely practiced and almost universally condoned. It is thought to be morally acceptable. It is our contention, however, that bluffing raises serious ethical questions. For bluffing is clearly an act of deception; the bluffer's intent is to deceive the other parties about the nature of his bargaining position. Furthermore, bluffing often involves lying. The two examples of bluffing presented here both fit the standard definition of lying: they are deliberate false statements made with the intent of deceiving others.[1]

Common sense holds that lying and deception are prima facie wrong. One could also put this by saying that there is a presumption against lying and deception: that they require some special justification in order to be permissible.[2] Almost no one would agree with Kant's view that it is wrong to lie even if doing so is necessary to protect the lives of innocent people. According to Kant it would be wrong to lie to a potential murderer concerning the whereabouts of his intended victim.[3]

Assuming the correctness of the view that there is a moral presumption against lying and deception, and assuming that we are correct in saying that bluffing often involves lying, it follows that bluffing and other deceptive business practices require some sort of special justification in order to be considered permissible. Businesspeople frequently defend bluffing and other deceptive practices on the grounds that they are profitable or economically necessary. Such acts are also defended on the grounds that they are standard practice in economic transactions. We will argue that these standard justifications of bluffing are unacceptable. Then we will propose an alternative justification for lying and deception about one's bargaining position.

There are those who hold that lying and deception are never profitable or economically necessary. In their view, honesty is always the best policy. One incentive for telling the truth is the law, but here we are referring to lying or bluffing which is not illegal, or for which the penalty or risk of being caught is not great enough to discourage the action.

Reprinted from the *Westminster Institute Review,* May 1981, pp. 77–83. Used with permission of the authors.

Those who hold that honesty is always in one's economic self-interest argue that economic transactions are built on trust and that a violation of that trust discourages an individual or organization from entering into further transactions with the lying party for fear of being lied to again. Thus, some mutually beneficial transactions may be foregone for lack of trust. Moreover, word of deceitful practices spreads through the marketplace and others also avoid doing business with the liar. Thus, while some short-run profit might accrue from lying, in the long run it is unprofitable. If this argument were sound, we would have a nonissue. Lying, like inefficiency, would be a question of bad management that would be in one's own best interest to eliminate.

Unfortunately, there are some anomalies in the marketplace which prevent the system from operating in a perfectly smooth manner. The very existence of bluffing and lying in the first place suggests that the economists' assumption of perfect (or near perfect) market information is incorrect. Some transactions, such as buying or selling a house, are one-shot deals with little or no chance of repeat business. Thus, there is no experience on which to base an assessment of the seller's honesty, and no incentive to build trust for future transactions. Even when a business is involved in an ongoing operation, information flows are such that a large number of people can be duped before others hear about it (e.g., selling Florida swampland or Arizona desertland sight unseen). Other bluffs and lies are difficult or even impossible to prove. If a union negotiator wins a concession from management on the grounds that the union would not ratify the contract without it—even though he has reason to believe that this is untrue—it would be extremely difficult for management to prove later that ratification could have been achieved without the provision. By the same token, some product claims, such as the salesman's contention that "this is the best X on the market," are inherently subjective. When the competing products are of similar quality, it is difficult to prove such statements untrue, even if the person making the statements believes them to be untrue. Another exception to the assumption of perfect information flows is the confusion brought on by the increasing technological complexity of goods and services. In fact, a product information industry in the form of publications like *Consumer Reports, Canadian Consumer, Consumer Union Reports, Money,* and *Changing Times* has arisen to provide, for a price, the kind of product information that economic theory assumes consumers have to begin with.

These arguments suggest not only that the commonly cited disincentives to bluffing and lying are often ineffective, but that there are some distinct financial incentives for these activities. If you can convince consumers that your product is better than it really is, you will have a better chance of selling them that product and you may be able to charge them a higher price than they would otherwise be willing to pay. It is also obvious that in a negotiating setting there are financial rewards for successful lies and bluffs. If you can conceal your actual minimal acceptable position, you may be able to achieve a more desirable settlement. By the same token, learning your negotiating opponent's true position will enable you to press toward his minimal acceptable position. This is, of course, why such intrigues as hiding microphones in the opposing negotiating team's private quarters or hiring informants are undertaken in negotiations—they produce valuable information.

An individual cannot, however, justify lying simply on the grounds that it is in his own self-interest to lie, for it is not always morally permissible to do what is in one's own self-interest. I would not be justified in killing you or falsely accusing you of a crime in order to get your job, even if doing so would be to my advantage. Similarly, a businessman cannot justify lying and deception simply on the grounds that they are advantageous, that is, profitable, to his company. This point can be strengthened if we remember that any advantages that one gains as a result of bluffing are usually counterbalanced by corresponding disadvantages on the part of others. If I succeed in getting a higher price by bluffing when I sell my house, there must be someone else who is paying more than he would have otherwise.

Economic necessity is a stronger justification for lying than mere profitability. Suppose that it is necessary for a businessman to engage in lying or deception in order to insure the survival of his firm. Many would not object to a person stealing food to prevent himself or his children from starving to death. Perhaps lying in an extreme situation to get money to buy food or to continue employing workers so that *they* can buy food would be equally justifiable. This case would best be described as a conflict of duties—a conflict between the duty to be honest and the duty to promote the welfare of those for/to whom one is responsible (one's children, one's employees, or the stockholders whose money one manages). However, it is extremely unlikely that bankruptcy would result in the death or starvation of anyone in a society which has unemployment compensation, welfare payments, food stamps, charitable organizations, and even opportunities for begging. The consequences of refraining from lying in transactions might still be very unfavorable indeed, involving, for example, the bankruptcy of a firm, loss of investment, unemployment, and the personal suffering associated with this. But a firm which needs to practice lying or deception in order to continue in existence is of doubtful value to society. Perhaps the labor, capital, and raw materials which it uses could be put to better use elsewhere. At least in a free-market situation, the interests of economic efficiency would be best served if such firms were to go out of business. An apparent exception to this argument about economic efficiency would be a situation in which a firm was pushed to the edge of bankruptcy by the lies of competitors or others. It seems probable that the long-term consequences of the bankruptcy of a firm which needs to lie in order to continue in existence would be better, or no worse, than those of its continuing to exist.

Suppose, however, that the immediate bad consequences of bankruptcy would not be offset by any long-term benefits. In that case it is not clear that it would be wrong for a company to resort to lying and deception out of economic necessity. One can, after all, be justified in lying or deceiving to save individuals from harms far less serious than death. I can be justified in lying about the gender of my friend's roommate to a nosy relative or boss in order to protect him from embarrassment or from being fired. If the degree of harm prevented by lying or deception were the only relevant factor, and if bankruptcy would not have any significant long-term benefits, then it would seem that a businessman could easily justify lying and deceiving in order to protect those associated with his business from the harm which would result from the bankruptcy of the firm. There is, however, another relevant factor which clouds the issue. In the case of lying about the private affairs of one's friends, one is lying to others about matters about which they have no right to know. Our present analogy warrants lying and deception for the sake of economic survival only in cases in which the persons being lied to or deceived have no right to the information in question. Among other things, this rules out deceiving customers about dangerous defects in one's products, because customers have a right to this information; but it does not rule out lying to someone or deceiving them about one's minimal bargaining position.

We have argued that personal or corporate profit is no justification for lying in business transactions, and that lying for reasons of economic necessity is also morally objectionable in many cases. But what about lying in order to benefit the party being lied to? There are certainly many self-serving claims to this effect. Some have argued that individuals derive greater satisfaction from a product or service if they can be convinced that it is better than is actually the case. On the other hand, an advertising executive made the argument in the recent Federal Trade Commission hearings on children's advertising that the disappointment children experience when a product fails to meet their commercial-inflated expectations is beneficial because it helps them develop a healthy skepticism. These arguments are not convincing. In fact, they appear to be smoke screens for actions taken out of self-interest. It is conceivable that consumers might benefit from it. For example, deceptive advertising claims may cause one to purchase a product which is of genuine benefit. While lying and deception can sometimes be justified by reference to the interests of those being lied to or deceived, such cases are very atypical in business situations. As was argued earlier, successful bluffing almost always harms the other party in business negotiations. The net effect of a successful bluff is paying more or receiving less than would otherwise have been the case.

A further ground on which lying or deception in bargaining situations is sometimes held to be justifiable is the claim that the other parties do not have a right to know one's true bargaining position. It is true that the other parties do not have a right to know one's position; that is, it would not be wrong to refuse to reveal it to them. But this is not to say that it is permissible to lie or deceive them. You have no right to know where I was born, but it would be prima facie wrong for me to lie to you about the place of my birth. So, lying and deception in bargaining situations cannot be justified simply on the grounds that the other parties have no right to know one's true position. However, other things being equal, it is much worse to lie or deceive about a matter concerning which the other parties have a right to know than one about which they have no right to know.

But what of the justification that lying and deception are standard practice in economic transactions? Certainly, lying and deception are very common, if not generally accepted or condoned. Bluffing and other deceptive practices are especially common in economic negotiations, and bluffing, at least, is generally thought to be an acceptable practice.[4] Does this fact in any way justify bluffing? We think not. The mere fact that something is standard practice or generally accepted is not enough to justify it. Standard practice and popular opinion can be in error. Such things as slavery were once standard practice and generally accepted. But they are and were morally wrong. Bluffing cannot be justified simply *because* it is a common and generally accepted practice. However, we shall now use the prevalence of bluffing involving lying and deception as a premise of an argument to show that there is a presumption for thinking that bluffing of this sort is morally permissible. If one is involved in a negotiation, it is very probable that the other parties with whom one is dealing are themselves bluffing. The presumption against lying and deception does not hold when the other parties with whom one is dealing are themselves lying to or otherwise attempting to deceive one. Given this, there is no presumption against lying or deceiving others about one's bargaining position in the course of an ordinary business negotiation, since the parties with whom one is dealing may be presumed to be doing the same themselves.

It is prima facie wrong to use violence against another person, but when one is a victim of violence oneself, it is permissible to use violence if doing so is necessary in order to prevent or limit harm to oneself. One is not morally required to refrain from self-defense. Similarly, other things being equal, if X is being harmed by the lies or deception of Y and if X can avoid or mitigate that harm only by lying to or deceiving Y, then it is permissible for X to lie to or deceive Y. These intuitions are captured by the following principle:

> (P) Other things being equal, it is permissible for X to do a to Y, even if a is a prima facie wrong, provided that X's doing a to Y is necessary in order to prevent or mitigate harm to X caused by Y's doing a to X.[5]

In business negotiations an individual can typically gain some benefit (balanced by corresponding harm to the other party) if he is willing to lie or deceive the other person about his own negotiating position. The other party can avoid or mitigate this harm only by being willing to do the same. In our society most people routinely practice this sort of lying and/or deception in business negotiations. Given this, (P) implies that one may presume that one is justified in bluffing (by means of lying and deception about one's negotiating position) in ordinary circumstances, unless either: (i) one has special reasons to suppose that the other party will not do the same (e.g., one might know that the individual with whom one is dealing is unusually scrupulous or naive), or (ii) one has special reasons for thinking that one will not be harmed by the bluffing of the other party, even if one does not bluff oneself.

Space does not permit an extended discussion or defense of (P). We would, however, like to forestall two possible objections. (i) (P) does not constitute a blanket endorsement of retaliation or the policy of "an eye for an eye and a tooth for a tooth." (P) would not justify my killing your child in retaliation for your having killed mine. (P) would justify my killing another person X only if my killing X is necessary in order to prevent X from killing me. (ii) It is standard practice for people involved in negotiations to misrepresent the terms they are willing to accept. In ordinary circumstances (P) will justify such actions. However, there are types of lying and deception which are not generally practiced in negotiations. For example, while meeting with a prospective buyer a person selling a house might have a friend pretend to make an offer to buy the house in order to pressure the prospective buyer. (P) does not imply that there is any presumption for thinking that such a ruse would be morally permissible.

NOTES

We are indebted to Thomas Beauchamp for comments on a previous version of this paper. Earlier versions of this paper were presented to a conference on Business and Professional Ethics at Kalamazoo College and Western Michigan University, November 1979, and to the Philosophy Department at Denison University.

1. For a much more thorough defense of the claim that bluffing involves lying, with an appeal to a somewhat different definition of lying, see our paper "The Moral Status of Bluffing and Deception in Business" in *Business and Professional Ethics,* ed., Wade L. Robison and Michael S. Pritchard (New York: Humana Press). Also see our paper "Bluffing in Labor Negotiations: Legal and Ethical Issues," with Kent F. Mursmann, *Journal of Business Ethics,* vol. 1, no. 1, January 1982.

2. The classic statement of this view is included in Chapter II of Sir David Ross's *The Right and the Good* (Oxford: Oxford University Press, 1930).

3. Immanual Kant, "On the Supposed Right to Tell Lies from Benevolent Motives," (1797), in *Moral Rules and Particular Circumstances,* ed. Baruch Brody (Englewood Cliffs, NJ: Prentice Hall, 1970), pp. 32 and 33.

4. In a well-known defense of bluffing, Albert Carr claims that it is permissible to make false statements in the course of business negotiations because doing so is "normal business practice," and part of what is involved in "playing the business game." See "Is Business Bluffing Ethical?," *Harvard Business Review,* January–February 1968.

5. It seems plausible to say that it would be permissible to do an act that is prima facie wrong to another person (X) if doing so were necessary in order to prevent X from harming a third party by doing the same act. For example, one would be justified in killing another person if doing so were necessary in order to prevent him from killing a third party. We accept the following stronger version of P:

   P′   Other things being equal, it is permissible for X to do *a* to Y, even if *a* is prima facie wrong, provided that X's doing *a* to Y is necessary in order to prevent or mitigate harm to *someone* caused by Y's doing *a* to that person.

   The weaker principle (P) is sufficient for the purposes of our argument.

Shrewd Bargaining on the Moral Frontier: Toward a Theory of Morality in Practice

J. Gregory Dees

Peter C. Cramton

Brer Rabbit had got himself caught by Brer Fox and was well on his way to becoming evening dinner. Brer Rabbit was in a great deal of deep trouble.

There didn't seem much he could do about this one, but he didn't seem concerned at all at being the Fox's dinner. He just said, "Brer Fox I don't mind if you eat me. But, oh, whatever you do don't throw me in that briar patch."

Now Brer Fox was surely looking forward to eating his old enemy, but he was mighty curious about Brer Rabbit's sweating and crying about being thrown into the briar patch.

And the more he questioned it the more Brer Rabbit wailed about how much he hated and feared that briar patch.

Pretty soon it did seem that Brer Rabbit would rather be eaten than be set among those briars. So Brer Fox threw Brer Rabbit into the heart of the briar patch. Brer Rabbit gleefully scampered away.

From the tales of Brer Rabbit[1]

One of the greatest frustrations of applied ethics arises when seemingly flawless logic fails to convince practitioners to take the morally superior course of action. The great temptation is for the ethicist to write off the practitioners as somehow morally or mentally deficient. For their part, the practitioners are likely to regard the ethicist as naively idealistic. This tendency to talk past one another must be resisted if academic ethicists are to avoid what Annette Baier has called "that arrogance of solitary intellect which has condemned much of moral theory to sustained self-delusions concerning its subject matter, its methods, and its authority" (Baier, 1985, p. 244).

This paper is written in an effort to move professional ethicists a notch closer to the world of practice. It uses a puzzle about a common form of deception in negotiation to stimulate the development of a perspective on morality that seems to be common in practice, but is underdeveloped in the literature of applied ethics. The deception that we are concerned with is illustrated in the story about Brer Rabbit, namely, deception about

Reprinted from *Business Ethics Quarterly,* Vol 1, No. 2, 1991, pp. 135–67. Reprinted with permission of the *Business Ethics Quarterly* and the authors.

one's settlement preferences. We choose this focus, not because we believe it to be one of the most pressing moral issues of the day, but because it is familiar to most readers, and it leads quite naturally to the perspective that we want to introduce in this paper. We call it the Mutual Trust perspective on morality.

To understand the Mutual Trust perspective, it is useful to distinguish between ideal morality and morality in practice. Ideal morality determines the practices, rules, values, virtues, and so on that might be derived a priori from an abstract moral point of view. This is the morality that concerns most philosophical ethicists. Morality in practice, by contrast, takes into account the fact that we live in a morally imperfect, often competitive, sometimes unjust world. The Mutual Trust account of morality in practice tempers ideal morality with concerns about prudence, fair play, and effectiveness, offering a pragmatic approach to moral responsibility. According to the Mutual Trust view, moral obligations rest, at least in part, on a foundation of mutual trust. When that foundation of trust is absent, the obligation is undermined. Specifically, to take risky or imprudent action on the basis of moral ideals, when others cannot be trusted to do the same, may be admirable, but it goes beyond the obligations of morality in practice.[2]

If we are correct that some form of the Mutual Trust perspective is widely accepted by practicing professionals and businesspeople, the implications go far beyond the issue of deception about settlement preferences. This approach to morality in practice could be used to justify a wide range of deviations from moral ideals. If we wish to correct those deviations, to move professional conduct closer to the ideals, it will not be sufficient to offer more arguments from an ideal moral point of view. To simply assert the logical dominance of idealistic moral reasoning begs the question. Standard moral arguments will fall on deaf ears. Either we need to convince practitioners to reject this view on less idealistic grounds, or we need to provide more practical advice. Our primary task changes from a purely philosophical one to the more pragmatic job of helping practitioners to minimize the risk of individual moral action, and to build and maintain trust.

In this paper, we offer a first cut at developing the Mutual Trust perspective on morality in practice. Our goal is to do what most practitioners are ill equipped to do for themselves, to present this view in a way that is philosophically coherent and defensible. We do not claim that it is the only defensible approach to morality in practice. It is not our intention to champion or promote it. In fact, we have concerns about it. We simply want to argue that it is a perspective that deserves more serious treatment than it has received to date.[3]

THE PUZZLE OF DECEPTION ABOUT SETTLEMENT ISSUES

Our thoughts about the Mutual Trust perspective developed largely in response to a puzzle that was born out of a frustrating clash between theory and practice. The puzzle concerns a form of deception that commonly occurs in negotiations, deception[4] about one's preferences regarding the terms, conditions, and timing of a settlement. Settlement-issue deception is so common that some see it as a defining characteristic of negotiation. As James J. White, writing in the *American Bar Foundation Research*

Journal, has put it, "To conceal one's true position, to mislead an opponent about one's true settling point, is the essence of negotiation" (White, 1980, p. 928). The puzzle is that, according to standard moral theories, this practice is objectionable, yet it is widely condoned in business and legal negotiations, and even praised, as "shrewd" bargaining when it is successful.

Consider a couple of examples. When the seller of a house coolly asserts that she is in no hurry to sell, even though she is in fact pressured by imminent employment and housing commitments a thousand miles away, she may be taking a negotiating risk, but few would condemn her as unethical in doing this. If this leads a motivated buyer to make a more attractive offer, we may think of her as shrewd. Contrast this attempted deception with her making an assertion that the house is in excellent mechanical condition when she knows that it has a very serious, but hard-to-detect plumbing problem. The latter is far more troubling, though both involve lies and both (if successful) may cause essentially the same degree of financial harm to the buyer. Second, consider a lawyer representing the plaintiff in an accident settlement case. She receives the following instructions from her client: "Try to get as much as you can, but I will accept anything over $50,000." When the defendant's lawyers open with a surprisingly high offer of $65,000, the plaintiff's lawyer coolly responds, "I do not think I can get my client to settle for that amount. I am hesitant to bring him anything under $75,000." Little negotiating risk is taken. She knows that if the other side does not budge, she can "reluctantly" return to the "disappointing offer" of $65,000. If the defendant's lawyers raise the offer, her ploy has worked. She has done a better job for her client. Compare misrepresentation of her client's settlement preferences with misrepresenting the extent and nature of her client's injuries. Why don't we condemn deception about settlement issues in the same way that we do other types of deception in negotiation? Why is it that we often applaud the shrewd bargainer who successfully bluffs the opposing party into a favorable agreement, while condemning the person who fraudulently misrepresents her product to the same end? Why do we tell stories such as the legend of Brer Rabbit to our children, when the moral seems to be that the shrewd use of deception is sometimes a good thing?

Using standard forms of ethical argument, a relatively strong prima facie case can be built against the general practice of settlement-issue deception. It raises concerns on Kantian, utilitarian, and justice grounds. Contributing to and capitalizing on a false belief in another, simply for personal (or parochial) gain, would seem to violate the Kantian injunction against treating others as means only. When outright lies are used, it violates one of the most common prohibitions found in deontological theories of ethics, and in most major religions. For the most part settlement-issue deception is done simply for private gain. Only in special circumstances are greater goods, such as innocent lives, at stake.

Deception about settlement issues is also hard to justify on consequentialist grounds. It is costly and inefficient. It can create unnecessary bargaining delays, increase anxiety, and cause lost opportunities as individuals walk away from deals based on the false impression that agreement is not possible. The very prospect of such deception can undermine trust and credibility. The costs may not be easy to identify and may be relatively minor in some individual cases, but they easily get magnified in serious business negotiations, such as collective bargaining. Third parties may be significantly harmed by these practices.[5] In any case, even when the costs are minor, they should not be neglected.[6] The cumulative effect of this practice may be quite significant. This is not to mention the potential spill-over effects that this deception might have on other aspects of an individual's life. Other than the pleasure that some (by no means all) negotiators get from this element of strategy, it is difficult to see any benefits to offset these costs.

Finally, we may be concerned about the fairness of the outcome when these sorts of deceptive tactics are used. The final settlement of a negotiation may be largely a function of which party is the best at deceiving the other. Some would not be troubled by this,[7] but many of us wonder whether this is a fair (or even efficient) way to allocate the gains from trade. It is hard to see how Rawlsian bargainers, behind their veil of ignorance, would embrace this convention. As for real people outside of that veil, there is experimental evidence that, when the gains to each side are known, many individuals refuse even a profitable deal, simply because they deem the division of gains to be unfair.[8] Furthermore, deception about settlement issues is likely to result in unequal treatment of like cases. For instance, a shrewd bargainer may extract a better salary from her employer than her less shrewd peers. This might be acceptable if shrewd bargaining is part of her job; but if it is not, the result seems unfair.

Despite general moral concerns, the use of these aggressive, deceptive bargaining tactics rarely arouses moral indignation, except in two situations; when there is a special bond of care or trust between the parties (as in a fiduciary relationship or a friendship), and when the party against whom the tactics are used is significantly disadvantaged.[9] Deception of the former constitutes a breach of trust; deception of the latter violates our sense of fair play and common decency. When the relationship is "arm's length" and neither party is particularly disadvantaged, we are rarely inclined to blame the deceiving party. If the deceived party finds out that she has been deceived in this way, she may object, but it is hard to tell whether this objection should be characterized as sour grapes, or whether it constitutes justified moral resentment. In some cases, with experienced negotiators, even the deceived party treats the other party's deception about settlement issues as fair game. Upon discovering that she really could have gotten better terms, her reaction may well be one of regret, possibly self-blame ("How could I have been so stupid?"), rather than one of moral resentment. She may even feel some grudging admiration for the deceiver. Our moral sentiments in practice often do not jibe with the conclusions from our abstract moral reasoning about this practice.

It is interesting to note that the moral toleration for deception about settlement issues is also reflected in the law governing negotiations (torts and contracts) and in the American Bar Association Model Rules of Professional Conduct (the only professional code of ethics that we have seen that explicitly addresses this issue). The law allows recourse against some forms of deception or concealment, but only with regard to "material facts." Settlement issues are not generally taken as material facts. As it is put in comments on Rule 4.1 of the ABA Model Rules, with regard to representing clients in a negotiation with third parties, "Under generally accepted conventions in negotiation, certain types of statements ordinarily are not taken as statements of material fact. Estimates of price or value placed on the subject of the transaction and a party's intention as to an acceptable settlement of a claim are in this category" (American Bar Association, 1987, p. 185, in the West Publishing edition). Barring the exceptions noted above, this observation seems to capture the spirit of tort and contract law as well. You generally cannot get a judgement against someone for fraud simply because she has deceived you about her true settling point, even if you could prove it.

This special legal treatment for settlement preferences is also a bit of a puzzle. The standard definitions of materiality in tort and contract law seem to turn on "the probability that the fact, if known, would alter the transaction in question. If the ignorant party might have behaved differently had the fact been known, then the fact can be said to be material" (Scheppele, 1988, p. 128). Surely the house buyer, or the defendant's lawyers in the two examples used above would bargain differently if they knew the settlement preferences of the other side. If this is the test, then settlement issues are often material. Why aren't they treated as such?

The puzzle gets deeper when we look at another factor that plays a major role in legal definitions of fraud, namely, whether one party has "superior means of knowledge."[10] "Superior means of knowledge" conveys a notion of epistemic advantage. It is not just that the person knows more, it is that she is in a position to know things that the other party would be hard pressed to discover.[11] A classic illustration of superior means of knowledge is provided by an art dealer who fails to inform a naive seller that the dusty old painting the dealer has just bought from her for $100 is a Monet worth a fortune. As Farnsworth points out, "A court is more likely to expect a party to disclose if that party has special knowledge, or a special means of knowledge not generally available to those in the position of the other party" (Farnsworth, 1990, p. 256). This point of common law is conveniently summarized in *American Jurisprudence 2d*, which states:

> There is abundant authority to the effect that if one party to a contract or transaction has superior knowledge, or knowledge that is not within the fair and reasonable reach of the other party and which he [the other party] could not discover by the exercise of reasonable diligence, or means of knowledge which are not open to both parties alike, he [the first party] is under a legal obligation to speak, and his silence constitutes fraud, especially when the other party relies upon him to judge the expedience of the bargain or transaction. (*American Jurisprudence 2d,* Fraud and Deceit, section 148)

Again, an individual always has a superior means of knowledge regarding her own (or her client's) settlement preferences. Why do these matters escape the strong disclosure requirement?[12]

One possible answer is that statements about settlement preferences are not statements of fact. The law typically treats opinions, predictions, and statements of intention as different from representations of "objective fact" (Shell, 1990, pp. 11–12). The former are often excluded from protection under the law of fraud. Settlement preferences may be characterized as either statements of intention, or as predictions, and thus not treated as facts. This is certainly a narrow conception of "fact." It is true that negotiators sometimes do not know their exact settlement preferences, that these preferences change over time, and that they are expressions of conditional intention. However, it is clearly wrong to say that, at any given time, there is no fact of the matter about a negotiator's settlement preferences. Some preferences will be firm and clear, but even when they are not, this is a fact. For an uncertain negotiator to represent herself as having a firm reservation price ("I'll take no less than $1,000") would be to misrepresent the uncertainty of her settlement preferences. These facts may be difficult to establish in a court of law, but that does not make them any less facts. In any case, the fraud law in most states does cover some intentions, under the heading of "promissory fraud" (Shell, 1990, pp. 12–13). If some intentions are covered, why not settlement preferences? To assert that these are not "objective facts" is merely verbal sleight of hand. It is not a satisfactory explanation of the special ethical status of deception about settlement preferences.

Some help is suggested by another legal distinction. This is the distinction between intrinsic and extrinsic facts. Intrinsic facts bear directly on the "nature, character, title, safety, use or enjoyment of the subject matter" under negotiation; extrinsic facts have only indirect, "accidental" bearing at best (Story, 1886, section 210, p. 232). Presumably settlement issues are extrinsic matters and thus of less concern in the law. However, the boundaries between intrinsic and extrinsic are fuzzy and the distinction has gone out of favor (Scheppele, 1988, p. 129). Nonetheless, it seems to be pointing in the right direction.

We find a related distinction in modern auction theory to be intuitively more appealing and to serve essentially the same purpose. This is the distinction between common-value uncertainty and private-value uncertainty.[13] Suppose S and B are negotiating the exchange of the property right X from S to B. Sharing information that influences the value both bargainers have for an item resolves *common-value uncertainty;* whereas, sharing S's knowledge that only affects S's value of X would resolve B's *private-value uncertainty* about S.[14] Preferences regarding settlement matters typically concern private rather than common value. However, because some facts that bear on S's settlement preferences also bear on the common value of X, we will count as pure settlement issues for S only those facts that bear on S's willingness to settle and her preferences regarding the terms of settlement, that are not also common-value facts about X. These facts do not bear on the value of X to B or anyone else other than S. This includes not only the traditional notion of S's reservation price, but also her negotiating aspirations, her resistance to specific concessions, time pressures, and the like.

This analysis suggests a useful matrix for thinking about legal requirements and moral judgments regarding deception and disclosure in negotiation. Assuming that we are talking only about "material" facts, in the sense of facts that if known would matter, the other two dimensions lead to the following categories:

Types of Deception in Negotiation

Negotiator Has:	Material Fact That Bears On:	
	Common Value	Private Value
Superior means of knowledge	1	3
No superior means	2	

The strongest obligation arises in cell 1, where disclosure is typically required. An example would be a homeowner who knows about a difficult-to-discover termite infestation in a house she is trying to sell. In cell 2 caveat emptor operates to some degree, in that there is no disclosure requirement. Each party must fend for herself in gathering information. Active deception or misrepresentation, on the other hand, is likely to be considered fraud. Think of an antique dealer selling an old chest that has some water damage on one of the legs. The damage is visible to anyone who examines the chest with a little care. With a careless buyer, the dealer is not required to point out the damage (though it might be good business to do so). However, if she tries to hide the damage, or makes the assertion that the finish is in perfect shape, she has gone too far. Cell 2 fraud is likely to be rare, given the lack of an epistemic advantage by either party, but it may occur when one party has not done her homework and is naive enough to rely on representations made by the other party. Cell 3, where settlement issues lie, has no prohibition on either concealment or deception, at least in evenly matched, arm's-length transactions. A seller of a house may well assert that she is in no hurry to sell, even though she is desperate.

To draw this matrix does not resolve our puzzle. It simply sharpens the definition. Both common-value and private-value uncertainty create frictions in bargaining due to the possibility of deception. It is easy to understand why deception about common-value facts is treated as more troublesome. With common-value uncertainty, the incentive to deceive can completely destroy all the gains from trade.[15] With private-value uncertainty, typically only a fraction of the gains from trade are lost as a result of bargaining costs (Cramton, 1984, and Kennan and Wilson, 1989, 1991). This accounts for some difference in treatment, but it does not explain why deception about settlement issues is not objectionable. The question remains: If S's settlement preferences matter to B, S has a superior means of knowledge about these preferences, and deception about them creates significant bargaining costs (not to mention, violates common moral rules), why do we tolerate, even admire, it in arm's-length business negotiations?

MUTUAL TRUST BASED MORALITY

At this point, we could consider a number of potentially promising answers. No doubt many readers will already have thought of their favorite candidate. We briefly discuss some other possibilities later. To explore all the possibilities, however, would take us off of our original track. Our stated objective is to examine in some depth one resolution to this puzzle, a resolution that was suggested by conversations we have had with practitioners (executives and lawyers). The resolution points to a general account of morality in practice that has implications beyond this particular issue.

The response that we have heard runs along the following lines. It is generally acknowledged that the practice of settlement-issue deception is less than optimal. In an ideal world, it would be minimized. This justification for engaging in it rests largely on a notion of defensive fair play in a morally imperfect world. Three conditions seem important in this justification: (1) a unilateral decision to refrain from this deception places one (or one's client) in a vulnerable position, exposed to exploitation by less scrupulous parties; (2) one typically has inadequate grounds for trusting the relevant others to refrain from this sort of deception (in fact, we expect that they will engage in it); and (3) it is unclear that unilateral honesty will have any positive effect, beyond possibly increasing the share of the gains from trade that go to the other, perhaps less scrupulous, party.[16]

These conditions seem to rest on two principles that blend prudence and morality. Together, they characterize the core of the Mutual Trust perspective. We offer the following as a rough cut at formulating them:

> *Mutual Trust Principle:* It is unfair to require an individual to take a significant risk or incur a significant cost out of respect for the interests or moral rights of others, if that individual has no reasonable grounds for trusting that the relevant others will (or would) take the same risk or make the same sacrifice.[17]

> *Efficacy Principle:* It is unfair to require an individual to take a significant risk, or incur a significant cost out of respect for the moral rights of others, if the action that creates the risk or cost is unlikely to have its normally expected beneficial effect, or if it would benefit only those who would not willingly incur the same risk or cost.

These two principles present only part of a comprehensive theory of morality in practice. Each points to a consideration about the specific social context in which actions are taken that can serve, other things being equal, to undermine obligations derived from ideal moral reasoning.

Philosophers will recognize that this argument, particularly the Mutual Trust Principle, has a distinctive Hobbesian flavor. It sounds as if these practitioners view themselves as operating in what Thomas Hobbes called the "state of nature," in which there are no solid grounds for trust. In such a state, each party is primarily concerned with her own preservation. It is a war of one against all. However, what the practitioners are describing is not a general state of nature, such as the one Hobbes envisioned (Hobbes, 1651, especially Chapters 13 and 14), but a highly restricted one. They are envisioning a state of nature with regard to this particular aspect of behavior in negotiations. This state of nature, specifically the absence of a basis for trust, provides the justification for defensive, self-interested behavior.

The requirement of Mutual Trust may be inspired by Hobbes's characterization of the state of nature, but it departs from Hobbes in many of its details. According to the Mutual Trust view, moral society has been incrementally carved out of a state of nature. In the state of nature, individuals have little reason to trust one another. Without trust, there can be only limited cooperation and, consequently, there is little room for putting moral ideals into practice. On the Mutual Trust view, this war of one against all is being held off by constant, sometimes creative, efforts on the part of individuals to "seek peace," to create a basis for mutual trust.[18] Individuals make truces in the war, by developing negotiating strategies, conventions, norms, legal systems, systems of political power, and religious systems to provide grounds for trusting others, so that they might cooperate with one another to pursue their independent, or commonly held notions of the good life and the good society. Thus, on the Mutual Trust view, taming the state of nature is an incremental, dynamic process. It may never be possible to declare complete victory. One may think of the process historically as starting within families and clans, extending to small, close-knit communities, then developing across different communities, as various forms of interaction and exchange develop. Progress has not been uniform and from time to time there may be a retreat. In Banfield's *Montegrano,* for instance, little progress is visible beyond moral bonds within the family (Banfield, 1958, especially Chapter 5). The progress is not purely geographic or demographic. Even within small, close-knit groups, some types of action (or transaction) remain insecure because of the practical difficulty of creating grounds for mutual trust. Some areas of the state of nature strongly resist taming. We call these pockets of resistance the "moral frontiers." At any place and any point in time, there will be such a frontier. The moral frontier marks the edge of civilized transaction space. Beyond this frontier, one is essentially back in the state of nature.

A major stream of social science research is devoted to understanding the ways in which individuals secure their agreements, act cooperatively, and pursue shared conceptions of the good. In fact, a number of mechanisms that fall short of centralized authority have been identified for pushing back the moral frontier. Potential mechanisms include reputational strategies (such as tit-for-tat), arrangements that create shared vulnerability, group discussion and multilateral promising, internalization of norms, development of private ethics codes, private institutional arrangements (arbitration systems, Better Business Bureaus, consumer research organizations), and so on.[19] This is not to say that we fully understand how these mechanisms work, but promising lines of research are underway.

The Mutual Trust view is not committed to a particular account of human nature. However, it presupposes that most human beings are not either pure egoists or pure altruists.[20] This allows for variety and complexity in human decision-making styles. For present purposes, these styles may be simplified into three categories.[21] At one extreme there are the opportunists, who are so constituted that they will seek their own fortune with guile, regardless of the behavior of others. The more other people behave morally, the greater the opportunity for the opportunists to take advantage of them. At the other extreme are the moral idealists, who unilaterally behave according to moral ideals, regardless of the behavior of others and the costs to themselves. On the Mutual Trust view, few people are solidly in either one of these categories; most are somewhere between the two extremes. Most are pragmatists, concerned with their own material welfare, but also with moral ideals. They are willing and able to constrain their self-seeking behavior for moral reasons, provided that they can be reasonably sure that others with whom they are interacting will do so as well.[22] Pragmatists are looking for reciprocal moral commitment. They behave like opportunists in the state of nature, not because they are inherently egoistic, but because they cannot trust others to constrain their opportunistic behavior. Pragmatists will gladly do their fair share to create a civil society, but not place themselves at a systematic disadvantage. Notice that all three types, the opportunists and moral idealists as well as the pragmatists have an incentive to lay a foundation for mutual trust.

In a Mutual Trust world, pragmatists must either be able to avoid the moral frontiers, or they must be psychologically prepared to handle the stress of shifting from one morality to another. The virtues in a morally civilized society are not necessarily virtues in the state of nature. Hobbes took an extreme view of this based on his account of the state of nature as a state of war. In war there is, according to Hobbes, a "generall rule of Reason, that every man, ought to endeavor Peace, as farre as he has hope of obtaining it; and when he cannot obtain it, that he may seek, and use, all helps, and advantages of Warre" (Hobbes, 1651, p. 190). He explicitly states, "Force, and fraud, are in warre the two Cardinall virtues." (Hobbes, 1651, p. 188). On the Mutual Trust view, this translates into a general obligation to attempt to push back the moral frontiers, when this seems feasible. When it is not feasible to establish grounds for trust and reciprocity, one is entitled to use otherwise immoral practices. This helps to explain why many are inclined to praise shrewd but deceptive bargaining. When used effectively, it is a virtue on the moral frontier.

THE MUTUAL TRUST RESOLUTION
OF THE SETTLEMENT-ISSUE PUZZLE

As the current norms of negotiation work, it seems clear that, with regard to information about settlement preferences, we are frequently operating along the moral frontier. With regard to the Mutual Trust Principle (outside of negotiations with close friends, relatives, and associates), we rarely have any assurance that the other party will refrain from attempts at deception regarding settlement preferences. In fact, we usually have general background reasons to believe that the other party will attempt some degree of deception.[23] To unilaterally refrain from deception in such circumstances would place one at a disadvantage. It would make one vulnerable to exploitation. A foundation of trust has not been created to support the moral ideal of honesty in this case.

With regard to the Efficacy Principle, honesty about settlement preferences is likely to be futile, in that the other party is probably expecting this sort of deception and, accordingly, is not likely to take such claims at face value. Honest disclosures may be misunderstood, or viewed with great skepticism. For instance, if an individual opens the negotiation by proposing a settlement at her reservation price and then refuses to make further concessions, this may be read as unwillingness to negotiate or stubbornness. In one theory of fairness in negotiations, negotiators expect each other to start at their aspirations (the best they could reasonably hope to get) and then seek out a compromise agreement that reflects equal resistance (Maser and Coleman, 1989). Firmness may easily be misread as an insistence on taking an unfair share of the gains. Opportunities may be lost because one is perceived as inflexible.

Furthermore, it is hard to invoke the standard rebuttal about setting an example for others, including those outside of this negotiation, to follow. Because honesty about these matters is especially difficult to demonstrate, few (if any) may ever know that one has been honest in a given negotiation. Without strong evidence, they may presume the opposite. Perhaps some highly visible individuals following a consistent practice over time may develop a reputation for honesty, but this is unlikely for most of us in most of our negotiations. As for other possible benefits from unilateral honesty, we do not have much data on which to base our conclusions. Defensive dishonesty about settlement preferences may cause some moral tension in the pragmatist, but it is unclear whether this tension outweighs the frustration and resentment that naturally accompany being "had" by a less scrupulous negotiator. One may even feel foolish for being unilaterally honest.

The combination of futility, vulnerability, and inadequate grounds for trust characterize a classic moral frontier. Using the Mutual Trust view, we can then see how it is possible to agree that settlement-issue deception is generally an undesirable practice, while condoning it on an individual level. Life in the state of nature has few redeeming features, but once in it one is free to act in a purely self-interested fashion. The Mutual Trust view even explains the fact that we sometimes admire clever deceivers, thinking of them as good negotiators. As noted above, virtues in a state of nature are quite different from virtues in a morally civilized state.

Why have we not tamed this particular portion of nature? The answer seems to lie in the difficulty of reinforcing or securing more honest behavior. It is extremely difficult to create the requisite degree of mutual trust when it comes to settlement issue deception, especially if the negotiating parties have a weak prior relationship and limited opportunities for future exchange. Possible foundations for mutual trust about settlement issues include each party being confident that (1) the other has certain personal characteristics that make her inherently trustworthy, for example, that the other party is a moral idealist; (2) there is a sufficiently close personal relationship between the parties that a special bond of mutual care has developed; or (3) external control methods are available to detect and punish any transgressions. In many business and legal transactions, conditions 1 and 2 are not readily available, or do not extend to settlement-issue deception. Granovetor (1985) has argued persuasively that economic transactions are embedded in social networks. Nonetheless, these social relations are rarely sufficient to create strong mutual trust. We are often dealing with relative strangers. With relative strangers, trust may need to be anchored in some form of external or institutional controls.

External control methods are weak in the case of settlement-issue deception for two related reasons. Settlement-issue deception is hard to verify in individual cases, and even if it is detected, it would be hard to deliver effective punishment. External control mechanisms depend on reasonably accurate detection of violations. Deception about settlement preferences typically falls into the category of "nonverifiable"[24] violations. To say that settlement preferences are typically "nonverifiable" in this sense is to say that it would be practically impossible for a third party to determine with any reasonable degree of confidence what an individual's settlement preferences were at a given point in time. Another way of putting this is that deception about settlement issues is not auditable.

There are some instances where deception about settlement preferences can be verified. For if the lawyer in our earlier example receives a letter (rather than verbal instructions) from her client stating, "You may settle at any amount above $50,000, but bargain for the highest settlement possible," the contents of the letter are verifiable. However, requiring lawyers to disclose this sort of information in order to detect attempts at deception would be useless. Doing so would serve only to alter the communication between the lawyer and her client. The client would have an incentive to communicate her true preferences secretly to the lawyer and then misrepresent her preferences in any verifiable communication (say demanding at least $75,000 rather than $50,000). Contrast this with a letter from a mechanic that reports that the car frame is cracked as a result of an accident. A key distinction between the mechanic's letter and the client's letter is that the information in the mechanic's letter can be verified, but it is not possible to verify the accuracy of the information in the client's letter.

Of course, we often have reason to suspect settlement-issue deception. In a given case, one may be able to gather some indirect evidence about settlement-issue deception. One could look at similar past transactions by this same party, at the deal the party finally accepts in this transaction, and at future transactions as they occur. Inconsistencies between verbal protestations and actual settlements may indicate some deception. There may even be clues in body language,[25] but all of this is highly imperfect. People change their minds, change their standards. Circumstances change.

To see the importance of independent verifiability for external control mechanisms, let's consider a few. Individual strategies for promoting cooperation, such as Axelrod's tit-for-tat (1984), work only in special circumstances. Not only is indefinite repeated play required, but each player must know what the other has done on the last play. This is the easiest epistemic hurdle; a negotiator need only satisfy himself that deception is going on. Still it is not always possible to get this information. This strategy has not been effective in conquering settlement-issue deception, because business situations rarely work out in such a way as to allow a consistent observable pattern of reinforcement to develop. General reputation can also serve to reinforce honesty, but here the epistemic hurdle is a bit higher. B not only has to have reason to believe S is trying to deceive him, but B must be able to demonstrate this to the satisfaction of others with whom S will deal in the future. These others need to be in a position to penalize S for indiscretions with B. Third-party adjudication and government enforcement are problematic for the same reasons. Investigations would be costly and rarely would produce the quality of information needed for action. Because detection would be rare, the punishment would have to be severe to provide an adequate ex ante incentive for honesty. Severe punishment for those unfortunate enough to get caught violates our sense of justice. It is simply too hard to detect and punish transgressions. Consequently, victims of this sort of deception have no legal recourse and private mechanisms (such as insurance and retribution) are rarely available. Until a mechanism is available that reasonably assures reciprocity, the Mutual Trust view of morality in practice would say that it is ethical to engage in the practice for defensive reasons.

ALTERNATIVE ACCOUNTS OF SETTLEMENT DECEPTION

The Mutual Trust account is not the only possible resolution of the puzzle regarding settlement-issue deception. In this section, we consider four alternative rationales for engaging in settlement-issue deception. Each has appeal and accounts for some cases. However, even taken together, they cannot account for the widespread and purposeful use of deception in negotiation that is captured by the Mutual Trust account.

It's Only a Game

Following Carr's (1968) famous suggestion, it can be claimed that negotiation is a game like poker. It has its own rules, and the rules allow for settlement-issue deception. Anyone who has chosen to play is free to engage in any tactic that is permitted by the rules.

What is it about the game analogy that gives this argument its moral force? Surely not all games are morally acceptable. Two people could invent a game of throwing knives out of a 10th-floor window onto a busy street. The rules may permit, even encourage, intentionally trying to hit pedestrians, but this does not justify throwing knives at pedestrians. People who use the game argument must have in mind certain morally relevant features of recreational games. Several features of recreational games seem morally relevant: such games are harmless to those who choose not to play, probable harm to the players is also limited, the rules are clear to all, entry to and exit from the game are fully voluntary, the players are relatively evenly matched (or given appropriate handicaps), and they freely consent to the rules (and to the limited harm that might be done them).[26] As some of these features are absent from games, moral questions can arise about whether and how one should play.

One source of appeal for this line of argument is that some practitioners do use the language of games to describe negotiation. Even the ABA Model Rules seem to rest the case for settlement-issue deception on nothing deeper than the "generally accepted conventions of negotiation." Furthermore, some negotiations are indeed very much like harmless parlor games. A prime example is bargaining over some souvenir in a bazaar. In such a case, strategic posturing, haggling, threatening to walk away from the deal, and bluffing are an important part of the fun. The availability of deceptive tactics is well known and often adds to the utility of the negotiators. It creates suspense, intrigue, and challenge. No one seems to be seriously harmed in the process. People who engage in this recreational negotiation typically know what they are getting into and freely choose to take the modest risks associated with it.

The difficulty is that many common business and legal negotiations lack the essential morally relevant features of recreational games. Think of labor negotiations, strategic arms reduction talks, the purchase of a car or a house, an accident settlement, plea bargaining, or initial contract negotiations with a major business supplier. Even if the negotiators in these situations are aware that settlement-issue deception is a common practice, and so expect it, it is stretching the truth to say that they somehow consented to a clear set of rules allowing it. Acquiescence is not the same as free consent. The absence of alternative institutional arrangements for coming to agreements on these matters raises questions about how fully voluntary the decision is to enter (and not to exit) from this sort of negotiating context. For most negotiators in these settings, the prevalence of settlement-issue deception is not a desirable feature of the negotiation "game." They are not looking for recreation, suspense, and intrigue. Regretfully accepting that deception is the norm does not carry the same moral weight as welcoming a rule because it makes the game more fun. The stakes are often significant and in many cases there are externalities. Third parties, who had no choice, may be affected. Think of small communities that are affected by labor negotiations with the community's major employer. The game analogy underestimates the morally problematic features of settlement-issue deception in a wide range of cases. It has a very limited range of application.

No Real Deception

People expect others to engage in some deception about settlement issues. One might argue then that no one is really deceived. They may guess wrong in a given case, but no one takes seriously the posturing and claims of the other negotiator regarding settlement issues. Experienced negotiators discount the claims of others to reflect this practice.[27]

Of course, that something is expected does not justify it, but the argument here is a bit more subtle. The claim is that, in effect, there is no deception. This is true only if the parties are fully rational and completely understand the situation they are in. Real negotiators rarely fall into this category. Even if they have unlimited abilities to calculate, they probably do not have the base of common knowledge that is needed to anticipate all deceptions. To guarantee that deception does not occur it must be that the negotiating strategies of all the parties are common knowledge. This may be a reasonable assumption in rudimentary games, where rationality leads to a unique prediction of behavior. But even the simplest negotiations are fraught with multiple equilibria when private information is introduced (Ausubel and Deneckere, 1989). We must acknowledge that expecting deception is not sufficient to prevent it, or to fully mitigate its effects.

Sometimes people are deceived about settlement issues because they are naive or gullible. Even a sophisticated negotiator can be deceived in a given case. What they know is that the other party *may* be attempting to deceive them. In any given case, negotiators face much uncertainty and have little information about the precise form any deception might take. The problem is that sometimes people attempt to deceive negotiation partners, and sometimes they do not. Truly clever negotiators will use this uncertainty to their advantage, overcoming the other party's skepticism, or using that skepticism to their advantage. Poker provides an example of a setting where the rules of the game are common knowledge and yet deception still frequently occurs. In poker, we expect people to bluff sometimes. With a good player, it is hard to tell when she is and when she is not. The expectation of bluffing does not prevent successfully using bluffing strategies. The strategies simply become more sophisticated. That is what makes poker interesting. Often the best gains come when you do have a strong hand, but you get others to believe you are bluffing. They stay in the game, calling, perhaps even raising your bets, creating a large pot. You bluff (perhaps even get caught), not so much to fool people about the quality of your hand, but to gain a reputation as someone who does bluff. That reputation allows you to confuse and mislead opponents in other hands. Skilled players are probably deceived less than beginners, but even a skilled player's expectations are not always consistent with the facts.

Even if we are willing to grant that the negotiators are fully rational, that they understand the "rules of the game," and that their negotiating strategies are common knowledge (so that, in a sense, deception does not occur), this does not imply that attempts at deception do not cause problems. Indeed, the inefficiencies caused by the *option* to deceive may well be greater when the parties rationally mistrust each other. The parties will have to take costly actions, such as risking impasse or delaying trade, in order to make claims credible.

We can easily imagine a negotiation in which the offers and counteroffers, threats, and promises are all choreographed. The two negotiators know each other well. They know where the settlement will be from the beginning. The negotiation is just a ritual. Neither takes the other's posturing seriously. In such a case, we should grant that there is no deception, but such cases are relatively rare. This argument does not dissolve the puzzle about widespread settlement-issue deception.

No Intentional Deception

Another tack would be to acknowledge that deception does occur but to claim that it is only an unintended but necessary side effect of the natural process of signaling and learning that characterizes negotiation. When a person approaches a negotiation, that person typically does not know whether a deal is possible and on what terms. A negotiator's initial settlement preferences are conditional and open to revision as she gains a better understanding of the settlement preferences of the other party. Because straightforward revelations of settlement preferences are problematic, the only reasonable way to elicit credible information from the other side is to make proposals or to send behavioral signals designed to find out where the other party stands on key issues. This often requires making proposals or conveying impressions that do not reflect one's actual settlement preferences at the time. The art of negotiation lies in eliciting information and signalling just enough about one's own position to efficiently determine whether a bargain is possible and, if so, to find a fair and reasonable settlement. If someone is deceived by ploys to elicit information, that is unfortunate, but given the complexities of gathering credible information in this context, it cannot be helped.

No one can deny that many maneuvers in a negotiation are attempts to gather information about the other side. The question is whether these attempts are simply innocent information eliciting devices, or whether they are at the same time deliberate attempts at deception. The answer probably varies from one negotiation to another. The negotiator's objective in making a proposal that misrepresents her settlement preferences may be to find out as much as possible about the preferences of the other side, while at the same time confusing or misleading the other side about her own settlement preferences. This strategy of trying to learn while preventing the other party from learning can (if successful) generate the best outcome in many negotiations, and it reflects the spirit of White's comment quoted earlier to the effect that misleading one's opponent is the essence of negotiation. In any case, this argument is largely compatible with the Mutual Trust account. Clever maneuvering is required to produce credible information from the other side just because trust is absent and verification is inherently difficult. The difference lies in the hypothesis about intentional deception. While it may be true that some negotiators are innocent information gatherers and signalers, content to achieve a settlement based on relatively equal information, our experience suggests that many are deliberately engaging in deception while they are gathering information. In such cases, the Mutual Trust perspective does a better job of accounting for the negotiators' behavior.

Right Not to Disclose

On this view, information about settlement preferences should be revealed only at the discretion of the party involved. B has no right to know A's settlement preferences, or the facts bearing only on those preferences. A may choose to disclose her eagerness to conclude a deal, or may reveal her real bottom line in hopes of saving time and fuss, forgoing the opportunity to strike a better deal. However, it would be wrong to require such disclosure.[28] It might be inappropriate to let settlement preferences determine the final terms of agreement. In many cases, we would like more objective factors to prevail in determining a fair settlement. Think of an academic whose spouse strongly prefers to be in a given city for career reasons. The academic finds only one suitable opening at a local college, and would accept the job at a substantial reduction in pay from the going rate at that school. Should she be required to reveal these family circumstances, and perhaps be offered a lower salary as a result? Should the school be permitted to take advantage of her situation? Many would say not.[29]

This argument is especially strong when one party is particularly desperate. To reveal the information about reservation price, aspirations, values, and so on should be optional. In such a case, revelation creates a risk of exploitation. It creates vulnerability, even when the other (less desperate) party is willing to disclose settlement preferences. The case is strengthened when the vulnerable party is in a class that has suffered economic discrimination. This line of argument also has some appeal, for different reasons, when one party has invested time and money in gathering information and the other party has not invested similar time and money.[30] If the investment has enabled the discovery of an attractive opportunity, it would seem inappropriate to require the party who made this discovery to disclose settlement preferences that are informed by this discovery. By revealing these settlement preferences, the investor might not be able to profit from, or even recoup the investment. Required disclosure would have the perverse effect of discouraging investment in the search for information.

We do not see this argument as a direct competitor to the Mutual Trust account of settlement issue deception. It does not answer the same question. It accounts for settlement-issue concealment, not settlement-issue deception. Presumably, deception would be permitted only as a last resort to protect private information, when releasing this information would have harmful effects. This argument may account for some settlement-issue deception, but it certainly does not explain the extensive settlement-issue deception that we observe in practice. At its heart, this argument seems to rest on some of the same concerns that motivate the Mutual Trust view, namely, the vulnerability created by candor in these competitive settings and the risk of being treated unfairly. The best way to understand this argument is as a supplement to the Mutual Trust account. It says that even if we could tame this part of the state of nature, we would still not want to require disclosure of settlement preferences in all cases. Mutual sharing of information about settlement preferences might generally be a good thing, but in some cases it would not be so good for all parties. Some vulnerability to exploitation will remain. In the absence of protective mechanisms, concealment (perhaps even deception) in such cases is morally justified.

CONCLUDING COMMENTS

We have considered a number of competing justifications for settlement-issue deception, each with a certain amount of validity. None of these accounts seems to capture the wide range of cases that could be explained by the hypothesis that a significant number of people, particularly lawyers and businesspeople in this country, accept something like the Mutual Trust perspective on morality in practice that we have presented in this paper. This perspective has been openly endorsed by some practitioners. As an explanation for the puzzle about settlement-issue deception, it allows us to account for moral regret about the general practice of settlement-issue deception, while at the same time seeing how it might be justified, even admired, in practice. It also helps to explain why some businesspeople see the law as providing a reasonable moral baseline. The law (if effectively enforced) can be instrumental, in the absence of more personal influences, in creating a basis for trust. The Mutual Trust account also helps explain the queer coincidence between the ease of detecting a given form of deception and our sense of moral outrage about it. Actual lies are regarded by many as inherently more objectionable than more subtle forms of deception, and deception about easily verified matters of fact is more objectionable than deception about more private matters. Trust is better established where detection is relatively easy.

Risks Inherent in the Mutual Trust Perspective

The Mutual Trust view clearly has its drawbacks. We would be remiss if we did not at least briefly discuss the potential problems. Most important, this may be a dangerous perspective to promote. A world of Mutual Trust pragmatists may be better than a world of selfish opportunists, but it is also a world fraught with moral problems. If a sufficient number of these pragmatists are risk averse, meaning that they have low risk and cost thresholds at which they invoke the Mutual Trust Principle, and that they initially distrust others until provided with grounds for doing otherwise, the problems of establishing and maintaining moral norms are likely to be severe. The problems are worse still when the boundaries at the moral frontiers are not clear. A mistake in judgment about whether or not grounds for trust are present can be quite costly to the individual involved and to others who are confused by this individual's behavior. It poses the prospect of moral regression. Trust may be eroded; downward spirals of more and more morally offensive behavior may occur. Only two forces work against this self-destruction of the Mutual Trust world, the commitment of the moral idealists to maintain high standards regardless, and the natural desire of individuals to "seek peace," as Hobbes would put it.

To the extent that we are faced with a world largely consisting of moral pragmatists and containing many pockets of distrust, it may even seem irresponsible to urge individual professionals to sacrifice personal and client interests for moral ideals. Rather, it may be more reasonable to place our emphasis on convincing them to integrate into their Mutual Trust perspective a third principle, which runs as follows:

> *Trust-Building Principle:* When mutual trust is absent or weak, individuals should be willing to take modest risks or incur modest costs, in an effort to build or reinforce the trust required to secure moral action in the future.

Of course, this principle will be appealing to pragmatists only if its demands are moderate and it is reasonable to believe that other pragmatists will commit to building trust. Fortunately, the benefits to be had from cooperative endeavors to improve on the state of nature are too great for most to ignore. They provide the impetus for peace-making experiments, for investments, for risk taking in hopes of reducing the undesirable features of the moral frontier. Nonetheless, even if the Mutual Trust view is supplemented with a Trust-Building Principle, a given amount of moral tension and confusion is inevitably created as people switch from the state of nature to more civilized transaction space, from one set of standards to another. This is likely to create spillover effects. These effects are the regrettable by-products of living in a morally imperfect world.

The Mutual Trust perspective is limited in what it justifies. It does not justify shrewd bargaining with parties known to be innocent or naive. Their very naivete provides a basis for trust. There can be some sense of decency even at the moral frontier. It also fails to justify shrewd bargaining in some special trusting relationships. And it does not justify escalation of the "war" beyond the edges of the moral frontier. In general, this perspective provides only a tentative and pragmatic justification for individual instances of deception, not a blanket justification of the practice. Nonetheless, there is a risk that the Mutual Trust line of argument will be abused, sloppily applied, or consciously misused to purportedly justify genuinely objectionable behavior. Opportunists may be happy to masquerade as pragmatists. We must encourage a critical approach.

Our point in this paper is not to promote moral pragmatism and its accompanying Mutual Trust perspective, but to recognize it as a feature of morality as it appears in practice. Those of us dedicated to understanding and enhancing professional ethics need to reckon with this perspective. We need to be fully aware of its features and its dangers. We also need to respond to it in a way that is likely to be effective in practice. Moral exhortation and abstract moral reasoning have their place, but they also have their limits.

Implications for Practitioners

In hopes of bringing practice closer to moral ideals, we could urge everyone to become moral idealists, carrying their ethical principles beyond the moral frontiers, indifferent to personal risk and cost. However, this would require imparting a high level of generalized benevolence, or moral commitment, higher than it seems reasonable to expect outside of particularly strong religious or moral communities. Until we can agree on an acceptable and effective program for doing this, it seems safe to remain skeptical about it. Without a more practical orientation, morally idealistic proposals are likely to be dismissed out of hand. What makes more sense is to urge people to exercise due care in assessing any negotiation situation and, especially where the social stakes are high, to experiment with methods for pushing back the frontier.

A separate paper is required to fully explore the issues and strategic options for practitioners. These would include guides for recognizing when one is at the moral frontier, methods for reducing the personal risks or costs of living up to moral ideals, possible avenues for creating trust, and techniques for minimizing the external costs of operating at the moral frontier. Here we can only sketch some of the general implications for negotiators.

In assessing whether there are sufficient grounds for trust, a negotiator should consider a number of factors concerning the basis of her relationship with the other party and the other party's incentives. Long-term relationships, empathy based on familiarity or common background, and common networks of relationships provide reasons for believing that trust is present. Trust is less likely to be present in one-shot negotiations with a relative stranger in which the stranger stands to gain a significant amount, or in adversarial negotiations where there is a history of mistrust or hostility.

If trust is absent and the transaction is large enough to justify the cost, trust may be built or reinforced through a variety of mechanisms. Because of verifiability problems, these mechanisms must not rely on independent access to the other party's settlement preferences. Potentially viable mechanisms fall into three categories: those that create opportunities to demonstrate trustworthy behavior, those that rely on external incentives, and those that attempt to create internal incentives. If the negotiation can be broken down into stages, the early stages may be structured so that the parties can each take some risks and demonstrate trustworthiness on issues that involve relatively low stakes. In one-shot transactions, reputations can be introduced by requiring each party to the transaction to provide a list of those they have dealt with recently. Honesty can also be motivated by external incentives, provided that arrangements can be made with a third party to pay a bonus, exact a penalty, or make an appraisal (Brams, 1990, Chapter 2). But for these procedures to work, strong assumptions about rationality and a base of common knowledge are required. Moreover, these procedures often do not avoid the inefficiencies created by the option to deceive. The internal mechanisms represent attempts to influence the preferences of the other party, making the other party more empathetic, more directly concerned not to take advantage. These are attempts to create mutual local benevolence, rather than relying on a more generalized benevolence. Mechanisms for doing this usually involve more frequent communications or more informal contact (increasing familiarity).

The best hope for building trust about settlement-issue deception among strangers or adversaries seems to lie not in standard external control mechanisms, but in relationship building and development of notions of group identity. Sometimes all that is needed is for the parties to get together on a regular basis to share concerns and other information relevant to an upcoming negotiation.[31] Some recent work on social dilemmas suggests that discussion and the creation of a sense of group identity can be a powerful tool in creating, at least in-group, trust (Dawes, 1990, and Orbell, Dawes, and van de Kragt, 1990). Negotiators should make reasonable efforts toward establishing an environment of trust and cooperation. We clearly need creative experimentation to find solutions to this problem. That creative solutions are often difficult to discover, does not justify the immediate use of cutthroat deceptive tactics, even on the Mutual Trust view.

All this said, in many cases of settlement-issue deception where the practice is widespread and the deception is hard to detect even ex post, trust building may not be viable. In many cases of negotiation, especially where the stakes are relatively small, caveat emptor may be the best advice.

Next Steps

Many questions remain about the Mutual Trust perspective. The theory clearly needs to be fleshed out in more detail. Empirical work is needed to provide a better understanding of how this perspective is reflected in practical decision making. We need to find out whether people actually think and act like moral pragmatists, as we characterize them. Are people willing to take risks or make genuine sacrifices when trust is present, that they would not make in the absence of trust? We also need to develop and refine the principles that constitute the Mutual Trust perspective. How do pragmatists think about appropriate thresholds of risk and cost? What sorts of risks and costs will they endure for the moral ideal of honesty, or for other moral ideals? How do they determine the "relevant others" in applying the Mutual Trust Principle? Are the relevant others always defined simply as direct competitors or adversaries? What about customers who may be affected by deceptive advertising, or rape victims who may be harmed by aggressive, harassing cross-examination? How do pragmatists determine whether sufficient trust is present in a given situation? How do they assess the efficacy of unilateral moral action? What are the other plausible candidates for moral frontiers, beyond settlement-issue deception? Are there moral frontiers that people have no desire to push back, that they wish to leave untamed? The reader could easily extend this list. However, in addition to descriptive questions, we also need to do some practical prescriptive research.

If the Mutual Trust account is a reasonable reconstruction of a view widely held, perhaps the most useful research that we can do for practitioners is research that helps them find strategies for bringing practice closer to moral ideals. We can share success stories, and provide problem-solving frameworks. This suggests that the most important work in business and legal ethics may not be the construction of arguments to appeal to moral idealists, but the creation of actionable strategies for the pragmatists. We may need to shift resources and energy from the construction of arguments to the effect that "It would be best if everyone did A," to concrete proposals for creating climates of trust in which our moral ideals might stand some hope of being implemented. This presents a challenge to philosophers to build closer ties to other disciplines and to actual practices, so that they might better address ethical concerns from a practical point of view.

NOTES

We are grateful to Warren Schwartz for urging us to look more closely at settlement-issue deception, and to Kenneth Andrews, Steven Brams, Frances Kamm, Susan Koniak, Lynn Paine, Seana Schiffrin, Howard Stevenson, Dennis Thompson, along with participants in the New York University Ethics Colloquium for their comments on earlier drafts.

1. The tales were originally written by Joel Chandler Harris in his Uncle Remus stories. This modern-language version has been adapted (with slight alterations) from Bellow and Moulton, 1981.
2. Someone holding the Mutual Trust view might construct her moral ideals using nearly any kind of moral theory. She simply questions the logical step in the deontological argument that moves from "It would be good if everyone in like circumstances did A" to "I should do A even though others similarly situated are not doing, or would do A." The parallel in the utilitarian argument would be to challenge the step from "A creates the greatest good for all, counting myself no more than anyone else" to "I should do A even though others are ignoring or would ignore my utility in making similar decisions."
3. Kavka (1983) presents a view similar to the Mutual Trust perspective in his treatment of defensive violations of moral rules, and Bok (1978) also looks at similar defenses in her treatment of lying, but we believe that neither gives adequate expression to, nor captures the appeal of, the full Mutual Trust perspective.

4. We will use the word *deception* narrowly to cover cases of deliberate actions taken, or statements made with the intention of creating or helping to perpetuate a false belief in another party. Common usage may allow for unintentional deception, but we are concerned only with the deliberate variety. For detailed treatment of some of the definitional complexities regarding deception and lying see Chisholm and Feeham (1977) and Fried (1978).

5. See the discussion of externalities in Lax and Sebenius (1986), pp. 152–53.

6. For a discussion of the complexities of consequentialist analysis when the harm from an individual action is not so readily visible or significant, see Parfit (1984), Chapter 3, pp. 67–86.

7. Libertarians would probably not see this as troubling. See, for instance, Nozick (1974), Chapter 7, pp. 149–82, for a theory of just transfer that does not concern itself with the distribution of gains.

8. Güth, Schmittberger, and Schwarze (1982) conducted an experiment where one bargainer makes a single take-it-or-leave-it offer to another. They find that if the offeror demands much over 50 percent of the gains from trade, the other tends to reject the offer and the gains are lost. This behavior suggests that bargainers have a preference for fairness. Kahneman, Knetsch, and Thaler (1986) also find that individuals will reject divisions that they regard as too lopsided, even if the rejection means that they get nothing. This preference for fairness is also found when the subjects can make many offers but delay is costly (Ochs and Roth, 1989).

9. For a discussion of fiduciary and confidential relationships in the law see Scheppele (1988), pp. 138–51 and pp. 171–75. On the topic of disadvantage and considerations of distributive justice, see Kronman (1980) and Lax and Sebenius (1986), pp. 150–52.

10. For a discussion of the role this factor plays in the law of fraud, see Scheppele (1988), pp. 134–60. We follow Scheppele's analysis throughout this discussion of the relevant law.

11. This distinction is more complex than it might first appear. The complexity is apparent when we consider the sticky issues raised by individual investment in superior knowledge. If one party makes a significant investment in gaining knowledge that allows her to identify a great opportunity, should she not have the right to use that knowledge for gain? To require disclosure of all superior knowledge would undermine any incentive to do one's homework. This suggests that we will want to be careful in distinguishing between superior *means* of knowledge (which presumably allows one access to superior information at low or no cost), and superior knowledge gained the hard way.

12. One possible explanation of the different treatment given to settlement preferences is that there is a certain symmetry. Each party has superior means of knowing her own settlement preferences. However, it is hard to see why symmetry should matter for these issues because it clearly does not matter for other material considerations. If both parties have superior means of knowledge regarding other important aspects of the item under negotiation, then presumably both have an obligation to disclose. The two obligations do not cancel each other out.

13. Note that this distinction is quite different from the distinction between creating common value and creating private value that is discussed by Lax and Sebenius (1986), pp. 88–116.

14. We do not claim that this distinction is perfectly clean. Some facts may predominantly affect S's value, only slightly bearing on B's value. In this case, it may seem inappropriate to classify it as a common-value fact. However, in many circumstances, we can sensibly distinguish between common and private value.

15. As an example, suppose S's value of X is v and B's value is $1.5v$. S knows the true value v, but B only knows that v is uniformly distributed from 0 to 1. In this case, despite the fact that gains from trade surely exist, if both S and B are rational and S cannot be trusted to honestly report v, then B will be unwilling to trade with S (Akerlof, 1970 and Samuelson,

1984). If B offered S a price of p, then S accepts if $v \le p$, so B's expected gain given acceptance by S is $E(v / v \le p) - p = 1.5(p/2) - p = - p/4$. Thus, any offer B makes results in a loss; B's best response is not to deal with S.

16. This argument should not be confused with the argument that because it is common practice, it is morally acceptable to go along with it. The argument presented is more specific and narrow in its claims. It should also be distinguished from most of the arguments that Bok (1978) rebuts in her chapters on lying to liars and enemies (pp. 130–53). It is not about revenge. The other may have done no wrong.

17. This principle resembles Elster's "norm of fairness." "The norm of fairness tells an individual to cooperate if and only if everybody else, or at least a substantial number of others, cooperate" (Elster, 1989, p. 187). While both appeal to the same notion of fair play, they are logically distinct. In content, the Mutual Trust Principle is concerned with moral behavior. Morality cannot always be reduced to a form of cooperation. Think of the original prisoners' dilemma example. The cooperative response is for two guilty prisoners to refuse to tell on each other. This is surely not the moral, or socially preferred, response. On many occasions in law and business, the moral (and the risky) thing is to compete when others would prefer you to cooperate (collude) for mutual gain, at the expense of some third party. In form, the Mutual Trust Principle is not posed as an "if and only if" decision rule. This principle provides only one consideration among many to be weighed in the final decision.

18. The Mutual Trust view, as we characterize it, rejects Hobbes's view that an all-powerful political ruler (a Leviathan) is required to provide grounds for moral constraint on self-seeking behavior. Perfect assurance of compliance is not necessary, only reasonable assurance is required, and this can be achieved incrementally through a variety of individual and social arrangements that fall far short of a Leviathan.

19. For a sampling of this literature, see Axelrod (1984), Kreps (1990), and Wilson (1985) on reputational strategies, Kronman (1985) on forms of mutual vulnerability (such as collateral, hostage taking, and hands-tying), Orbell, Dawes, and van de Kragt (1990) and Dawes (1990) on forms of multilateral promising and group discussion, and Arrow (1973) on ethics codes. Hirschleifer (1982) provides a wide-ranging discussion of the evolution of norms in groups. Taylor (1982) makes a case for the importance of small close-knit communities for nonpolitical, noncoercive mechanisms to work. Zucker (1986) provides an account of various mechanisms of trust formation in an economic setting. Coleman (1990) presents a comprehensive theory of the way authority, trust, and norms develop among individuals and organizations.

20. Hobbes, by contrast, is typically characterized as assuming that humans are by nature egoistic, personal utility maximizers. For an extensive discussion of both psychological and moral egoism in Hobbes, see Kavka (1986), Chapters 2 and 9. Kavka indicates the uncertainty and complexity of Hobbes's views on human nature and on morality.

21. A similar tripartite distinction has been made by Peter Koslowski in a talk on "Private Vices, No Public Virtues," at the Harvard Kennedy School of Government, February 26, 1990. These three types are clearly constructed as ideal-types. Real people are probably more complex than any one of these characterizations, being moral idealists on some things, pragmatists about other things, and opportunists about still others.

22. Our pragmatist is quite similar to Gauthier's "constrained maximizer." See his (1986) Chapter 6, pp. 157–89. However, our characterization is intended to be broader, less dependent on any specific theory of morality, such as Gauthier's bargaining-based conception.

23. The degree of deception is moderated by self-interest. As long as there is an incentive to reach a settlement and to do so in a timely fashion, individual negotiators will moderate their deceptive maneuvers.

24. By "verifiable" we do not mean the "in principle verifiability" of the logical positivists, but verifiability in the sense of credible independent verification.
25. See Ekman (1985). The implications of this way of imperfectly detecting dishonesty are discussed by Frank (1987).
26. For a discussion of these first two features and some general ethical tests regarding negotiation tactics, see Lax and Sebenius (1986), pp. 147–50.
27. This sort of argument is similar to the argument for permitting puffery in advertising.
28. This argument might be founded on the notion that settlement preferences are private matters, the personal property of their bearer. A similar argument regarding the privacy of ideas is presented in Paine (1990). However, it need not rest on the personal nature of these preferences. It might be founded on a desire to protect disadvantaged negotiators from exploitation, or socially undesirable discrimination.
29. This example and some of the language in framing this argument are due to Frances Kamm.
30. In keeping with the matrix presented earlier in the paper, we are assuming that this common-value information was available to both parties. Neither had a superior means, or special access to the information.
31. This practice has been used successfully in recent union contract negotiations. Labor contracts between CBS and IBEW now write into the contract that the parties "shall meet at least once every three months, unless waived by mutual consent, to discuss subjects of mutual concern or interest that may arise during the term of this Agreement or matters necessary to the implementation of this Agreement."

BIBLIOGRAPHY

Akerlof, George A.: 1970, "The Market for 'Lemons': Quality Uncertainty and the Market Mechanism." *Quarterly Journal of Economics* 84, 488–500.

American Bar Association Model Rules of Professional Conduct.: 1987, *Selected Statutes, Rules and Standards on the Legal Profession* (West Publishing, St. Paul).

American Jurisprudence 2d.: 1968, Vol. 37, *Fraud and Deceit* (The Lawyers Co-operative Publishing Company, San Francisco).

Arrow, Kenneth J.: 1973, "Social Responsibility and Economic Efficiency." *Public Policy,* 21, 303–17.

Ausubel, Lawrence M., and Deneckere, Raymond J.: 1989, "A Direct Mechanism Characterization of Sequential Bargaining with One-Sided Incomplete Information," *Journal of Economic Theory,* 48, 18–46.

Axelrod, Robert.: 1984, *The Evolution of Cooperation* (Basic Books, New York).

Baier, Annette.: 1985, *"Doing Without Moral Theory?" Postures of the Mind: Essays on Mind and Morals* (Methuen, London).

Banfield, Edward C.: 1958, *The Moral Basis of a Backward Society* (The Free Press, New York).

Bellow, Gary, and Moulton, Bea.: 1981, *The Lawyering Process: Negotiation* (Foundation Press, New York).

Bok, Sissela.: 1978, *Lying: Moral Choice in Public and Private Life* (Random House, New York).

Brams, Steven J.: 1990, *Negotiation Games: Applying Game Theory to Bargaining and Arbitration* (Routledge, New York).

Carr, Albert Z.: 1968, "Is Business Bluffing Ethical?" *Harvard Business Review,* January–February, 1968, 143–53.

Chisholm, Roderick, and Feehan, Thomas D.: 1977, "The Intent to Deceive," *Journal of Philosophy* 74, 143–59.

Coleman, James S.: 1990, *Foundations of Social Theory* (Harvard University Press, Cambridge, MA).

Cramton, Peter C.: 1984, "Bargaining with Incomplete Information: An Infinite-Horizon Model with Two-Sided Uncertainty." *Review of Economic Studies* 51, 579–93.

Dawes, Robyn M.: 1990, "Social Dilemmas, Economic Self-Interest, and Evolutionary Theory." Forthcoming in *Research in Psychology: Frontiers of Mathematics, Essays in Honor of Clyde Coombs* (Springer-Verlag, New York).

Ekman, Paul.: 1985, *Telling Lies* (W. W. Norton and Company, New York).

Elster, Jon.: 1989, *The Cement of Society: A Study of Social Order* (Cambridge University Press, New York).

Farnsworth, Allan.: 1990, *Contracts* (Little, Brown, and Co., Boston).

Frank, Robert H.: 1987, "If *Homo Economicus* Could Choose His Own Utility Function, Would He Want One with a Conscience?" *American Economic Review,* 77, 593–604.

Fried, Charles.: 1978, *Right and Wrong* (Harvard University Press, Cambridge, MA).

Gauthier, David.: 1986, *Morals by Agreement* (Clarendon Press, Oxford).

Granovettor, Mark.: 1985, "Economic Action and Social Structure: The Problem of Embeddedness." *American Journal of Sociology,* 91, 451–510.

Güth, W., Schmittberger, R., and Schwarze, B.: 1982, "An Experimental Analysis of Ultimatum Bargaining," *Journal of Economic Behavior and Organization,* 3, 367–88.

Hirschleifer, Jack.: 1982, "Evolutionary Models in Economics and Law: Cooperation versus Conflict Strategies." In P. H. Rubin and R. O. Zerbe, Jr. eds., *Research in Law and Economics* 4, 1–60 (JAI Press, Greenwich).

Hobbes, Thomas. 1651. *Leviathan.* All references are to the C. B. Macpherson edition, 1968 (Penguin Books, Baltimore).

Kahneman, Daniel, Knetsch, Jack L., and Thaler, Richard H.: 1986, "Fairness and the Assumptions of Economics," *Journal of Business,* 59, S285–S300.

Kavka, Gregory S.: 1983, "When Two 'Wrongs' Make a Right: An Essay on Business Ethics," *Journal of Business Ethics,* 2, 61–66.

Kavka, Gregory S.: 1986, *Hobbesian Moral and Political Theory* (Princeton University Press, Princeton).

Kennan, John, and Robert Wilson.: 1989, "Strategic Bargaining Models and Interpretation of Strike Data," *Journal of Applied Econometrics,* 4, S87–S130.

Kennan, John, and Robert Wilson.: 1991, "Bargaining with Private Information," *Journal of Economic Literature,* forthcoming.

Kreps, David M.: 1990, "Corporate Culture and Economic Theory." In James Alt and Kenneth Shepsle (ed), *Perspectives on Positive Political Economy* (Cambridge University Press, New York).

Kronman, Anthony T.: 1980, "Contract Law and Distributive Justice," *The Yale Law Journal* 89, 472–511.

Kronman, Anthony T.: 1985, "Contract Law and the State of Nature," *Journal of Law, Economics, and Organization* 1, 5–32.

Lax, David A. and Sebenius, James B.: 1986, *The Manager as Negotiator* (The Free Press, New York).

Maser, Steven M. and Coleman, Jules L.: 1989, "A Bargaining Theory Approach to Default Provisions and Disclosure Rules in Contract Law," *Harvard Journal of Law and Public Policy,* 12, 637–709.

Nozick, Robert.: 1974, *Anarchy, State, and Utopia* (Basic Books, New York).

Ochs, Jack, and Roth, Alvin E.: 1989, "An Experimental Study of Sequential Bargaining," *American Economic Review,* 89, 355–84.

Orbell, John, Dawes, Robyn, and van de Kragt, Alphons.: 1990, "The Limits of Multilateral Promising." *Ethics,* 100, 616–27.

Paine, Lynn.: 1990, "Trade Secrets and the Justification of Intellectual Property: A Comment on Hettinger." Mimeo.

Parfit, Derek.: 1984, *Reasons and Persons* (Oxford University Press, New York). Page references are to the 1985 corrected paperback edition.

Samuelson, William.: 1984, "Bargaining Under Asymmetric Information," *Econometrica,* 52, 995–1005.

Scheppele, Kim Lane.: 1988, *Legal Secrets: Equality and Efficiency in the Common Law* (University of Chicago Press, Chicago).

Shell, G. Richard.: 1990, "When Is It Legal to Lie in Negotiations?" *Sloan Management Review,* forthcoming.

Story, Joseph. 1886. *Commentaries on Equity Jurisprudence as Administered in England and America,* 13th ed. Revised by Melville M. Bigelow (Little, Brown, and Company, Boston).

Taylor, Michael.: 1982, *Community, Anarchy, and Liberty* (Cambridge University Press, New York).

White, James J.: 1980, "Machiavelli and the Bar: Ethical Limitations on Lying in Negotiation," *American Bar Foundation Research Journal,* 1980, 926–38.

Wilson, Robert.: 1985, "Reputations in Games and Markets." In Alvin Roth, ed., *Game Theoretic Models of Bargaining* (Cambridge University Press, New York).

Zucker, Lynne G.: 1986, "Production of Trust: Institutional Sources of Economic Structure, 1840–1920." *Research in Organizational Behavior,* 8, 53–111 (JAI Press, Greenwich).

Deception and Mutual Gains Bargaining: Are They Mutually Exclusive?

Raymond A. Friedman

Debra L. Shapiro

In the interest of being fair, a prospective car buyer goes to a car dealership with price-related information obtained from objectively valid sources, such as the American Automobile Association, *Consumer Reports,* and the "book" value (which reflects the car's model, year, and mileage). The car salesperson expresses an interest in reducing inventory *today* and the prospective buyer indicates that is possible, if they can agree on a price that is fair. The two parties share information regarding price-related criteria and their respective priorities with regard to car features, payment terms, and service-related concerns. In so doing, they learn that they have complementary needs, and only the issue of price seems competing (since the seller and buyer want a higher and lower price, respectively). Differences regarding price, however, seem resolvable when the parties focus their conversation on their mutual interests, these being a fair price and a long-term car service-based relationship. Two hours later, the parties have reached an agreement—at a price both deem fair.

The above scenario describes two parties engaged in problem-solving behaviors, such as focusing on being fair, basing proposals on objective (neutral) criteria, sharing information regarding priorities, discussing more than one issue as a means for determining possible concessionary trade-offs, and focusing on their shared interests, which results in a mutually satisfying agreement. This is a description of what has become commonly known as "integrative," "win-win," or "mutual gains" bargaining, or MGB (see, e.g., Walton and McKersie 1965; Fisher and Ury 1981; Susskind and Cruikshank 1987).

How would we characterize this scenario if the buyer was deceptive during the exchange—for example, by referring to a lower price obtainable from another, phantom dealership? Would such a tactic be considered distributive (win-lose) negotiation? No, because even in light of the deception created by referring to a nonexistent alternative, the car buyer and the salesperson have engaged in an exchange that is predominantly mutual gains bargaining. The modifier "predominantly" highlights the fact that the bargaining situation is *not* purely integrative. Indeed, many theorists have argued that no bargaining situation is purely integrative nor purely distributive, and thus all are "mixed-motive" (Lax and Sebenius 1986; Stevens 1963; Raiffa 1982; Walton and McKersie 1965).

Reprinted from Raymond A. Friedman and Debra L. Shapiro, "Deception and Mutual Gains Bargaining: Are They Mutually Exclusive?," *Negotiation Journal,* July 1995, pp. 243–53. Used with permission of Plenum Publishing Corporation and the authors.

Because of this duality, we believe negotiators can practice integrative bargaining effectively, even when this strategy includes deception (for example, the car buyer's phantom dealership). Yet negotiation scholars and trainers may leave the impression instead that anyone who wishes to be deceptive cannot engage in integrative bargaining, or MGB—that is, MGB and deception are presented as mutually exclusive. We arrived at this conclusion after a discussion among negotiation scholars at a recent national academic conference regarding what is ethical and unethical behavior in negotiations, and what we should be teaching students in our courses on negotiations. About an hour into the discussion, someone suggested that, in pursuit of being ethical teachers and promoting ethical behavior on the part of students, we should teach students integrative bargaining tactics only, and not traditional distributive bargaining tactics. This proposal created quite a debate among those attending, and an ensuing vote among the scholars showed that an overwhelming majority favored the proposal.

This turn of events was, for us, a great cause for concern. Should integrative bargaining really be promoted based on ethical arguments? Should we automatically label distributive bargaining as unethical? We were concerned because this equating of ethics and integrative, or mutual gains, bargaining had a familiar ring to it. In both training sessions and classrooms, it is not uncommon for MGB to be confused with being good, ethical, or nice. Moreover, confounding ethics and MGB can have negative effects—on our ability to understand ethical conventions in traditional negotiations, and on our ability to teach and implement MGB.

In this article, our goal is to clarify the *distinction* between ethics and MGB. In particular, our focus is on the one bargaining strategy—deception—that triggers many ethical discussions (Carr 1968; Lewicki 1983). We believe that negotiation teachers and trainers should be careful to keep ethics and integrative bargaining separate. It is obviously important to teach about ethics in bargaining, including the issue of deception, and to teach about integrative bargaining, but these are separate issues—both in theory and practice.

ETHICALLY AMBIGUOUS TACTICS

Many commonly used or taught negotiation tactics are fraught with ethical concerns. The types of tactics that are most often cited as being ethically ambiguous are ones involving deception (Dees and Cramton 1993; Carr 1968; Lewicki 1983; Shapiro and Bies 1994). For example, when a manufacturer is negotiating the price of a part, and no other supplier is available at the time, she or he would refrain from sharing that fact during negotiations. In addition to hiding this information, the manufacturer would probably try to lead the other side to believe that there were many suppliers to choose from, either by saying so explicitly or making statements that imply this. Negotiators commonly hide their true level of dependency, and commonly exaggerate the value of their options in the event of no agreement, their willingness and ability to choose other options, and the likelihood that their constituents (whose supposed demands may even be fabricated) will disapprove of concessions under discussion.

In such situations, the negotiator's goal is to shift the opponent's perception of the zone of possible agreement in one's favor. When this is done well, the opponent is left to decide whether s/he would rather risk having no agreement, or give in to the demands that have been made. Since the opponent has the same goal, if one listens to what is said early in negotiations one might believe that there is no zone of possible agreement at all when in fact there may be. The process of negotiating is at its core a process of shaping perceptions of reality (Berger and Luckman 1967). Deceptive tactics like hiding or exaggerating information often shape the perception of negotiators' power, which some have identified to be the most critical perception of all (Bacharach and Lawler 1988).[1]

Whether these behaviors are ethical is a great source of debate. People with absolutist moral positions might argue that misleading others is unethical in general and therefore should not be used in the context of bargaining. A more tolerant approach is to say that we should not do things that are acknowledged to be socially unacceptable. Using the test of whether people would want their actions told to their mother (Murnighan 1993) or described in a newspaper (Lax and Sebenius 1986), many would find it embarrassing for others to know that they acted deceptively. Others might counter that whether deception is considered ethical or not depends on the context, not the act of deceiving. For example, if one is negotiating with terrorists for the release of hostages and lives could be saved through deception, many would say the use of deception was ethical. Or, if one is acting as a negotiator for a relatively powerless community group trying to block the construction of a toxic waste dump, deception may be one of the few ways to create a balance of power in the negotiations, especially if the dump's owner has a history of misrepresenting data about the effects of toxins on drinking water. The ethically good "end" thus justifies the use of deception in some negotiation situations.

These are complex issues that are difficult to resolve on a philosophical level. It is not our goal in this article to make a definitive statement about the ethics of deceptive negotiating tactics. Rather, we shall examine the relationship between ethically ambiguous behaviors in negotiations and the use of MGB in negotiations. Our contention is that it is easy to confuse MGB with behaviors that are ethically pure, and that doing so may actually make it harder to teach MGB or get people to use it.

MUTUAL GAINS BARGAINING AND ETHICAL CLAIMS

MGB is an approach that helps negotiators produce the greatest joint gains possible. As noted earlier, it is also called "integrative bargaining," "win-win" or "principled" negotiation, and is often contrasted with "distributive" bargaining, that is, bargaining that is zero-sum or focused on getting more for oneself by forcing the opponent to take less. As explained by Fisher and Ury (1981), MGB is based on four principles: separating the people from the problem; focusing on interests, not positions; inventing options for mutual gain; and insisting on objective criteria.

There is nothing in these principles that directly addresses the issue of ethical behavior or deceptive tactics. However, there are several ways in which these principles can be inadvertently related to ethical behavior and trainees may come to believe that the primary reason for MGB is that it is more "honest" than traditional negotiations. It is possible that some trainers do frame MGB as the more ethical way to bargain, or that the "principled" and "mutual gains" labels themselves convey that message to trainees. More important, the connection between MGB and ethics may come from more deep-seated and fundamental misunderstandings of the ideas of MGB, especially the difference between interests and positions.

MGB suggests that negotiators explain to their opponent what their *interests* are, so that the opponent can propose actions that meet one's real needs at least cost. It does not, however, say anything about revealing one's alternatives to a negotiated agreement, what one's true reservation price is, or how much money is in the bargaining budget—all of which influence what final *position* will be acceptable. The problem is that the distinction is difficult for many negotiators to understand; even for trainers, the line between the two is frequently not completely clear. In fact, the distinction represents more of a continuum than an absolute difference. For example, a "5 percent pay raise" is a position in that it is one way to achieve the interest of "a better quality of life." From another perspective, it is an interest that may be achieved in various ways (such as 3 percent base wage increase and a 2 percent lump sum or via other "positions"). Therefore, some will tend to hear the MGB prescriptions as saying "reveal everything about oneself." MGB says only that you should not deceive the other party about your core underlying interests. And—this is worth emphasizing—the reason for this prescription is not that being honest about interests is inherently ethical. Rather, it is that being honest about one's interests can help you get more. If others do not know what really matters to you, they cannot help search for ways to meet your needs that are feasible for them.

Confusion is also likely to the degree that MGB is framed as an alternative to distributive bargaining. For pedagogical reasons it may be necessary at some stage of training to present MGB as a completely different model for negotiations, but few scholars would presume that many negotiations are wholly integrative. Rather, most negotiations are "mixed motive" (Stevens 1963); they include both opportunities for joint gain, and opportunities for grabbing more from the other side. Walton and McKersie (1965) call this the integrative and distributive dimensions of negotiation, while Lax and Sebenius (1986) write of the distinction between creating and claiming value in negotiation. There is indeed a tension between the two; strategies that are wise for creating are often opposite from those that are wise for claiming (e.g., deception about positions and power is necessary for claiming, while deception about interests is disruptive for creating). But all negotiations include both elements, and few negotiations occur where a wise negotiator would not employ at least some of each set of behaviors. Indeed, one of the more interesting challenges faced by negotiators is how to balance both of these elements.

Pruitt and Lewis (1977) have argued that the two approaches appear in the same negotiation by means of separating creating and claiming into distinct phases of the process, or by having different individuals on bargaining teams engage in creating or claiming. More recently, Friedman (1994) has argued that the two approaches coexist by having separate "stages" for each. While distributive tactics and deception occur front stage, integrative tactics and honest communication about interests occur backstage. In public, labor negotiators engage in a great deal of bravado, exaggeration, hiding, and, in general, attempts to deceive the other about what they want, what they are willing to accept, and what they are willing to fight over. But out of public view, negotiators engage in a well understood process of signaling to opponents, discounting information, and engaging in private sidebar meetings to clarify interests.

In sum, MGB does teach negotiators not to deceive the opponent—about their interests. But it makes this suggestion based on effectiveness, not ethics. And it does not presume that all parts of negotiations are integrative—there is a domain for distributive bargaining in most negotiations. This distinction can be easily lost if the interest–position distinction is not made clear, or if teachers express a preference for MGB because of its higher ethical status.

If, in these ways, ethics and MGB become conflated, several problems can occur. First, negotiators may miss the distinctions between ethical and unethical behavior that exist in traditional negotiations. Second, they may misunderstand the true benefits that MGB provides. And third, they may perceive MGB as naive and therefore avoid using it.

ETHICAL CONVENTIONS IN LABOR NEGOTIATIONS

Equating MGB with ethics overlooks the fact that there are ethical constraints on deception in traditional negotiations. We can see this by looking at the example of labor negotiations. During a study of labor negotiations (Friedman 1994), the first author studied 13 negotiations, including direct observations of eight cases and over 150 interviews, and in addition interviewed 19 experienced labor negotiators. the negotiators in that study talked extensively about their relationships with opponents and the kinds of tactics that they used and expected others to use. From these interviews and observations, it became clear that professional labor negotiators have a definite sense, in practice, of what is appropriate and inappropriate behavior. Experienced labor negotiators expect that opponents will hide information and try to build up false perceptions about their limits and determination. Negotiators on both sides expect their opponents to have "laundry lists" of demands, put exaggerated financial offers on the table, declare that constituents will not accept less, say that they and their constituents could and would weather a strike, and even put on displays of anger and resolve to show how tough they will be in defense of these demands.

Nonetheless, some types of deception are beyond the pale. The same negotiators who expressed tolerance for some levels of deception also reported that there was a limit to what was acceptable. Overtly inaccurate statements are considered unethical (and unprofessional) by lead bargainers. It is acceptable and expected for the company to say "we cannot pay a penny more for health care," while it is unacceptable to say "adding physical therapy to the benefit package will cost us an additional $100 a year per employee" when it is known it would only add $20 a year. The first statement is a general claim that can be readily interpreted as a bargaining stance; the latter is a factual claim that is either true or false. The first type of statement would be considered "bargaining" by experienced labor negotiators, and those who do it with cleverness and gusto are respected as savvy and skilled. The latter type of statement would be considered a lie, and the bargainer who was caught in such a lie would be deemed unprofessional and untrustworthy. In addition, for these negotiators it makes a difference if either statement is made in private between lead bargainers or in public across the main table. What is said across the table is expected to be exaggerated and not fully accurate; what is said in private is expected to be accurate. To claim inaccurately that the company cannot spend one penny more on health care across the table is expected and not deemed unethical; to make that same false claim in private would produce outrage if the lie was discovered.

Underlying this distinction is an understanding that some statements are *expected* to be untrue while others are not. When negotiators make statements that are expected to be untrue, the other negotiators are able to make appropriate adjustments, calculations, and predictions. These statements are interpreted, discounted, and treated with caution (Friedman 1994). Negotiators anticipate that these statements are made as bargaining stances, open to change, or that they are positions that need to be stated to look good to constituents and teammates. By contrast, when one negotiator makes statements that are expected to be true, the other party proceeds to act on them; this information is often represented to constituents as true, and major decisions are made based on it. The consequences of deception in those situations can be great: there might be an unnecessary strike, the negotiators could be hurt professionally if constituents find out that they were duped, and negotiators' ability to count on some truthful communication between the two sides is eliminated and their ability to manage the negotiations wisely is greatly diminished.

The ethical conventions that are common among labor negotiators ensure that both deception and honesty can occur, and that there is a common understanding of when and how deception is limited. These conventions are based not on some abstract moralism, but a very practical concern for enabling the negotiators to do their jobs, negotiate well for their side, and avoid an unnecessary strike. Negotiators still try to indicate that their side will stand tough against the opponent, and they still try to deceive (as one labor lawyer put it, even in sidebar meetings "I don't put all my cards on the table"). But there is also much trust and communication between opponents, particularly the lead bargainers. This lessens the personal nature of the conflict and makes integrative bargaining possible. While these negotiators would never want to be completely honest with their opponents, they do place limits on deception and will withdraw cooperation from those who cross the line.

The example from labor relations shows that there are ethical constraints on negotiations, regardless of whether one mentions mutual gains bargaining. And it shows that these ethical constraints operate despite the acknowledged presence of deception during much of negotiations. What might appear logically as mutually exclusive behaviors—being honest and deceiving—are not so in practice.

Thus, there are reasons to engage both in deception *and* honesty in negotiations, and there are enormous risks associated with either a purely honest or purely deceptive strategy. And negotiators have developed mechanisms to engage in both strategies. This mixture of tactics works exactly because negotiators recognize the need for both tactics, because the divide between them is well understood, and because an ethical system exists that ensures that negotiators act honestly when expected to and which keeps deception within some practical limit.

PUTTING THE MGB MESSAGE IN CONTEXT

If the message of mutual gains bargaining is not that integrative tactics alone should be used or that deception should be completely precluded, and if integrative tactics (including prohibitions against deception during integrative phases of negotiations) already exist in most negotiations, why have MGB training? We can identify three primary benefits to teaching MGB that do not depend on the "do-not-ever-be-deceptive" message. First, MGB training can help inexperienced trainees to discover that there is an integrative—and not only a distributive—side to bargaining. This discovery is especially likely among negotiators who may have been exposed only to the more public, high conflict aspects of bargaining.

Second, MGB can help negotiators anticipate times when their emotions make them forget what they know about integrative bargaining, and focus only on distributive bargaining. In this way, emotionally-triggered escalation traps are made less likely (Pruitt and Rubin 1986). Although professional bargainers usually know how to keep their emotions under control and "focus on the problem not the person," less experienced bargainers may not be as well prepared for the pressures of bargaining. And there may be times when relations between the two sides have become so difficult that even experienced bargainers have a difficult time sustaining the integrative side to bargaining that they know should exist. Third, MGB can encourage negotiators to be integrative bargainers somewhat more than they traditionally are. More specifically, MGB training may help negotiators lengthen the phase of negotiations that is more integrative, or to include more people in the backstage arena where integrative bargaining is done. While not eliminating hard bargaining, or telling negotiators to give up the deceptive tactics that are central to hard bargaining, MGB training may be able to shift the balance somewhat toward integrative bargaining.

THE DANGERS OF NAIVE MGB TRAINING

Not only is the "do-not-ever-deceive" message unnecessary in MGB training, it may also reduce the effectiveness of the training. The message "do-not-ever-deceive" does not recognize the fact that, even when integrative bargaining works well, there is still a need to engage in distributive tactics, nor the fact that being completely honest about one's fallback positions can diminish one's power. For these distributive elements of negotiations, tactics such as hiding information and shaping impressions are often necessary and do work. To teach that negotiators should abandon all impression management tactics would be unwise from an analytic perspective, would make the teacher appear naive, and ensure that the MGB approach would be seen as damaging to one's negotiating goals.

Moreover, these costs are not necessary; practicing mutual gains bargaining does not require that negotiators make themselves vulnerable through comprehensive revelations about their situation. It says only that it makes no sense to deceive the opponent about one's *interests*. Finally, to the degree that trainers signal an ethical priority (or allow trainees to read that into the training), trainees have a more difficult time seeing that MGB helps people to negotiate *smarter* and get better results. While some may believe that MGB helps make negotiations more ethical, that is unlikely to generate among trainees a true commitment to understand and use the MGB lessons.

That is not to say, however, that there are no ethical constraints. MGB does not free negotiators to be deceptive in ways that are traditionally unacceptable. If one is found to have lied, that would be a source of distrust during negotiations, it would engender uncooperative behavior by the opponent, and make him or her less likely to engage in integrative bargaining—with or without MGB training. To the degree that we might encourage people to use MGB techniques, or at least not to do less of it, negotiators should stay within commonly understood norms of acceptable behavior. Misrepresentations that cross the line have been found to interfere with negotiators' willingness to use MGB (Friedman 1993), just as those that cross the line make backstage interactions more difficult in traditional negotiations.

RECOMMENDATIONS FOR TEACHING MGB

From this analysis we suggest that those who teach mutual gains bargaining make clear that the benefits of MGB are practical, not ethical. Operationally, this means that MGB trainers may wish to consider the following three suggestions:

1. Given the degree to which it is easy for students to read into MGB training the message that they should "do MGB because it seems 'nicer' or more 'ethical', " special care must be taken to highlight the practical benefits of MGB, and to avoid moralistic statements that enhance this misreading.

2. Since MGB does encourage disclosure of one's interests, special care must be taken to clarify the distinction between interests and positions. Only then will it be possible for students to see that revealing one aspect of what a bargainer knows (i.e., his or her interests) does not imply that all information about one's strategies and fallback positions must be revealed.

3. MGB teachers and trainers should also teach their students about tough bargaining tactics, including deception, and acknowledge that there are benefits to hard bargaining. Moreover, students need to understand the "mixed motives" of negotiations and the need to be prepared for both integrative and distributive aspects of bargaining.

This advice does not mean that teachers should not teach ethics in bargaining. It is extremely valuable for students to evaluate both the ethical and practical costs of crossing the line. They need to understand what actions constitute fraud from a legal point of view (see, e.g., Shell 1991) and what actions are considered among negotiators to be excessive misrepresentation or lying. They also need to consider the effects that unethical behaviors can have on trust, and the effects that lack of trust can have on one's ability to negotiate effectively and one's ability to maintain a relationship with the opponent after negotiations are over. Teaching the effects of unethical behavior in negotiation does not require negotiation trainers to confuse MGB (and an understanding of the techniques and logic of integrative bargaining) with ethical concerns, nor does it require efforts to preclude all types of deception in negotiations. Indeed, we believe confusing ethics and MGB threatens a teacher's ability to teach effectively, and obtain a commitment to using MGB principles in practice. Such confusion diminishes the positive impact that MGB can otherwise have.

CONCLUSION

We have made great strides in recent years teaching more people—in classrooms, corporate training sessions, and actual negotiations—about negotiations, including how to be more ethical and how to ensure that integrative joint gains are not left on the table. The fact that we even need to write an article like this is an indication of the advances that have been made.

Yet exactly because of these advances, more care needs to be taken to ensure that the subtle distinction between what is ethical and what is integrative is maintained. Being ethical in negotiations is more complicated than producing greater joint utility, and the techniques that are helpful for producing greater joint utility should not be made more complicated by the addition of ethical concerns. Each issue—ethics and mutual gains bargaining—can stand on its own, and benefits by being considered on its own. By maintaining this distinction, we believe each will have greater clarity and greater impact, and our teaching and training will be both better received and more valuable to those we teach.

NOTES

1. Negotiators can actually reshape reality itself, not just perceptions of it. This is done by taking actions which really do tie one's hands so that compromise is impossible. Such commitment tactics are discussed by Schelling (1960) and Raiffa (1982). These tactics are not considered in this article since they are not instances of deception.

REFERENCES

Bacharach, S. B., and E. J. Lawler. 1988. *Bargaining: Power, tactics, and outcomes.* San Francisco: Jossey-Bass.

Berger, P. L., and T. Luckman. 1967. *The social construction of reality.* Garden City, NY: Anchor Books.

Carr, A. Z. 1968. Is business bluffing ethical? *Harvard Business Review,* January–February, 143–50.

Dees, J. Gregory, and P. Cramton. 1993. Promoting honesty in negotiation: An exercise in practical ethics. *Business Ethics Quarterly* 3(4): 44–61.

Fisher, R., and W. L. Ury. 1981. *Getting to Yes: Negotiating agreement without giving in.* Boston: Houghton Mifflin.

Friedman, R. A. 1994. *Front stage, backstage: The dramatic structure of labor negotiations.* Cambridge, MA: MIT Press.

_____. 1993. Bringing mutual gains bargaining to labor negotiations: The role of trust, understanding, and control. *Human Resource Management Journal* 32(4): 435–59.

Lax, D. A., and J. K. Sebenius. 1986. *The manager as negotiator.* New York: The Free Press.

Lewicki, R. 1993. Comments presented as part of the symposium "Ethical dilemmas in negotiating and getting people to 'yes'." Conflict Management Division, National Academy of Management meeting, Atlanta.

_____. 1983. Lying and deception. In *Negotiating in organizations,* edited by M. H. Bazerman and R. J. Lewicki. Beverly Hills, CA: Sage.

Murnighan, K. 1993. Comments presented as part of the preconference workshop "Ethical dilemmas in negotiating and getting people to 'yes'." Conflict Management Division, National Academy of Management meeting, Atlanta.

Pruitt, D. G., and S. A. Lewis. 1977. The psychology of integrative bargaining. In *Negotiations: Social psychological perspectives,* edited by D. Druckman. London: Sage.

Pruitt, D. G., and J. Z. Rubin. 1986. *Social conflict: Escalation, stalemate, and settlement.* New York: Random House.

Raiffa, H. 1982. *The art and science of negotiation.* Cambridge, MA: Harvard University Press.

Schelling, T. C. 1960. *The strategy of conflict.* Cambridge, MA: Harvard University Press.

Shapiro, D. I., and Bies, R. J. 1994. Threats, bluffs, and disclaimers in negotiation. *Organization Behavior and Human Decision Processes* 60: 14–35.

Shell, R. 1991. When is it legal to lie in negotiations? *Sloan Management Review* 32(3): 78–94.

Stevens, C. 1963. *Strategy and collective bargaining negotiations.* New York: McGraw-Hill.

Susskind, I., and J. Cruikshank. 1987. *Breaking the impasse.* New York: Basic Books.

Walton, R. E., and R. B. McKersie. 1965. *A behavioral theory of labor negotiations: An analysis of a social interaction system.* New York: McGraw-Hill.

Social Context

A critical change contributing to the dynamics of any complex negotiation occurs when there are more than two parties negotiating. Thus far, we have devoted almost all of our attention to negotiation as a dyadic process—the dynamic interaction between two negotiators. And some negotiations *are* exclusively conducted by two parties: a buyer and a seller, a husband and wife, or a boss and subordinate. But many more negotiations—particularly those that occur in organizations—involve more than two parties. The negotiators themselves may be representing groups of people who are not at the table but are affected by the outcome. A union leader represents the rank and file; a diplomat represents a country's government and leadership; a manager represents the senior leadership and owners of the company. Negotiators who represent these "constituencies" are usually given instructions about how to negotiate and what their objectives are; in addition, they are held accountable by their constituencies for achieving these objectives. In addition, there may also be people, such as third parties or audiences to the negotiation, who may or may not be directly affected by the negotiations themselves, and who may or may not be able to observe and participate in the process.

When constituencies, third parties, and audiences become involved in a negotiation, their very presence changes the nature of the negotiating dynamics. Experienced negotiators know how to assess the impact and consequences of these other actors on the negotiation process. Moreover, by understanding this impact, they can effectively employ constituencies, audiences, and third parties, either to protect themselves from undue pressures or to increase the pressures on the other negotiators.

The articles in this section outline the nature of this larger social dynamic. The first article, "When Should We Use Agents? Direct versus Representative Negotiation," by Jeffrey Rubin and Frank Sander, addresses a key question in the larger social dynamic of negotiation: When is it better for the key party to be represented by an "agent" rather than to be directly involved? The authors argue that using an agent inevitably complicates a negotiation, because the number of possible interactions (between the parties themselves, between party and agents, and between agents) increases from one to six. The advantages of using an agent are that an agent may have greater expertise (in a specific issue or in the negotiation process), may be more emotionally detached, and may offer an opportunity for the party to use various tactical ploys that could not be used on one's own. However, it is possible that each of these good reasons can backfire if the party is not careful about how the agent is chosen or used. The authors emphasize that parties do not often exercise enough control over how agents are selected or monitored, and that negotiations may actually suffer rather than prosper because of the use of agents. The article concludes by proposing some general principles describing when agents are desirable and when the parties ought to represent themselves in negotiation.

The second article, "Negotiating in Long-Term Mutually Interdependent Relationships among Relative Equals," by Blair Sheppard, clearly shows how the nature of negotiation must change significantly as one negotiates with someone of equal power within a long-term relationship. Sheppard argues that much of our theory of negotiation has been derived from assumptions derived from models of market and structural hierarchy in organizations. These models are largely transacted in nature, focusing on single exchanges in which both parties are most interested in only maximizing returns to self. Sheppard elaborates on the dangers of applying distributive bargaining strategies and tactics to negotiations in long-term relationships, and shows how the prescriptive nature of much of integrative negotiating theory may also be limited and myopic in its application to these negotiations. Sheppard stresses the key role of the long-term relationship in shaping and transforming what we know about negotiations, and points to a long agenda of issues that must be considered to understand relational negotiations.

The groundwork created by Sheppard's focus on relationships is expanded by Robert Kaplan in his article "Trade Routes: The Manager's Network of Relationships." Kaplan describes the network of relationships that constitute the life of most managers in modern complex organizations. Managers must maintain a complex web of relationships both inside their organizations (with bosses, subordinates, key co-workers, and representatives of other departments, divisions, and work units) and outside their organizations (with customers, suppliers, regulators, trade organizations, consultants, etc.). Kaplan describes the nature of that complexity, and shows that transactions within those relationships (both short-term and long-term) require a variety of influence skills and diplomatic qualities. Many of the tactics used along these trade routes will be found in the earlier articles by Cohen and Bradford, and Keys and Case, in Section Six, Finding Negotiation Leverage. Kaplan's article concludes with some excellent advice for handling some of the typical problems that arise in managing one's network, and offers the opportunity to consider strategies and tactics that go beyond advice given by traditional negotiation theory.

When Should We Use Agents? Direct versus Representative Negotiation

Jeffrey Z. Rubin

Frank E. A. Sander

Although we typically conceive of negotiations occurring directly between two or more principals, often neglected in a thoughtful analysis are the many situations where negotiations take place indirectly, through the use of representatives or surrogates of the principals. A father who speaks to his child's teacher (at the child's request), two lawyers meeting on behalf of their respective clients, the foreign service officers of different nations meeting to negotiate the settlement of a border dispute, a real estate agent informing would-be buyers of the seller's latest offer—each is an instance of negotiation through representatives.

In this brief essay, we wish to build on previous analyses of representative negotiation[1] to consider several key distinctions between direct and representative negotiations, and to indicate the circumstances under which we believe negotiators should go out of their way either to choose *or* to avoid negotiation through agents.

The most obvious effect of using agents—an effect that must be kept in mind in any analysis of representative negotiation—is complication of the transaction. As indicated in Figure 1, if we begin with a straightforward negotiation between two individuals, then the addition of two agents transforms this simple one-on-one deal into a complex matrix involving at least four primary negotiators, as well as two subsidiary ones (represented by the dotted lines in Figure 1). In addition, either of the agents may readily serve as a mediator between the client and the other agent or principal. Or the two agents might act as co-mediators between the principals. At a minimum, such a complex structure necessitates effective coordination. Beyond that, this structural complexity has implications—both positive and negative—for representative negotiation in general. Let us now review these respective benefits and liabilities.

Reprinted from Jeffrey Z. Rubin and Frank E. A. Sander, "When Should We Use Agents? Direct versus Representative Negotiation," *Negotiation Journal,* October 1988, pp. 395–401. Used with permission of Plenum Publishing Corporation and the authors.

1. See, in particular, the concise and insightful discussion by Lax and Sebenius (1986) in Chapter 15 of their *The Manager as Negotiator.*

FIGURE 1   Possible Relations among Two Principals (P1 and P2) and Their
Respective Agents (A1 and A2) (A solid line denotes an actual
relation, a dotted line a potential one.)

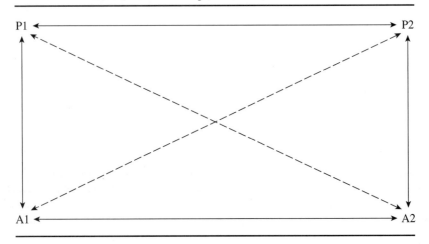

EXPERTISE

One of the primary reasons that principals choose to negotiate through agents
is that the latter possess expertise that makes agreement—particularly favorable
agreement—more likely. This expertise is likely to be of three different stripes.

Substantive Knowledge.   A tax attorney or accountant knows things about the
current tax code that make it more likely that negotiations with an IRS auditor will
benefit the client as much as possible. Similarly, a divorce lawyer, an engineering consultant, and a real estate agent may have substantive knowledge in a rather narrow domain of expertise, and this expertise may redound to the client's benefit.

Process Expertise.   Quite apart from the specific expertise they may have in particular content areas, agents may have skill at the negotiation *process,* per se, thereby enhancing the prospects of a favorable agreement. A skillful negotiator—someone who understands how to obtain and reveal information about preferences, who is inventive,
resourceful, firm on goals but flexible on means, etc.—is a valuable resource. Wise principals would do well to utilize the services of such skilled negotiators, unless they can
find ways of developing such process skills themselves.

Special Influence.   A Washington lobbyist is paid to know the "right" people,
to have access to the "corridors of power" that the principals themselves are unlikely
to possess. Such "pull" can certainly help immensely, and is yet another form of expertise that agents may possess, although the lure of this "access" often outweighs in
promise the special benefits that are confirmed in reality.

Note that the line separating these three forms of expertise is often a thin one, as in
the case of a supplier who wishes to negotiate a sales contract with a prospective pur-

chaser, and employs a former employee of the purchaser to handle the transaction; the former employee, as agent, may be a source of both substantive expertise *and* influence.

Note also that principals may not always know what expertise they need. Thus, a person who has a dispute that seems headed for the courts may automatically seek out a litigator, not realizing that the vast preponderance of cases are settled by negotiation, requiring very different skills that the litigator may not possess. So, although agents do indeed possess different forms of expertise that may enhance the prospects of a favorable settlement, clients do not necessarily know what they need; it's a bit like the problem of looking up the proper spelling of a word in the dictionary when you haven't got a clue about how to spell the word in question.

DETACHMENT

Another important reason for using an agent to do the actual negotiation is that the principals may be too emotionally entangled in the subject of the dispute. A classic example is divorce. A husband and wife, caught in the throes of a bitter fight over the end of their marriage, may benefit from the "buffering" that agents can provide. Rather than confront each other with the depth of their anger and bitterness, the principals (P1 and P2 in Figure 1) may do far better by communicating only *indirectly,* via their respective representatives, A1 and A2. Stated most generally, when the negotiating climate is adversarial—when the disputants are confrontational rather than collaborative—it may be wiser to manage the conflict through intermediaries than run the risk of an impasse or explosion resulting from direct exchange.

Sometimes, however, it is the *agents* who are too intensely entangled. What is needed then is the detachment and rationality that only the principals can bring to the exchange. For example, lawyers may get too caught up in the adversary game and lose sight of the underlying problem that is dividing the principals (e.g., how to resolve a dispute about the quality of goods delivered as part of a long-term supply contract). The lawyers may be more concerned about who would win in court, while the clients simply want to get their derailed relationship back on track. Hence the thrust of some modern dispute resolution mechanisms (such as the mini-trial) is precisely to take the dispute *out* of the hands of the technicians and give it back to the primary parties.[2]

Note, however, that the very "detachment" we are touting as a virtue of negotiation through agents can also be a liability. For example, in some interpersonal negotiations, apology and reconciliation may be an important ingredient of any resolution (see, e.g., Goldberg, Green, and Sander, 1987). Surrogates who are primarily technicians may not be able to bring to bear these empathic qualities.

TACTICAL FLEXIBILITY

The use of agents allows various gambits to be played out by the principals, in an effort to ratchet as much as possible from the other side. For example, if a seller asserts

---

2. Compare in this connection the unfortunate recent decision of the United States Court of Appeals for the Seventh Circuit to the effect that a federal district court judge has no power to compel principals with settlement authority to attend a settlement conference. *G. Heileman Brewing Co.* v. *Joseph Oat Corp.,* 848 F. 2d 1415 (7th Circuit 1988).

that the bottom line is $100,000, the buyer can try to haggle, albeit at the risk of losing the deal. If the buyer employs an agent, however, the agent can profess willingness to pay that sum but plead lack of authority, thereby gaining valuable time and opportunity for fuller consideration of the situation together with the principal. Or an agent for the seller who senses that the buyer may be especially eager to buy the property can claim that it is necessary to go back to the seller for ratification of the deal, only to return and up the price, profusely apologizing all the while for the behavior of an "unreasonable" client. The client and agent can thus together play the hard-hearted partner game.

Conversely, an agent may be used in order to push the other side in tough, even obnoxious, fashion, making it possible—in the best tradition of the "good cop/bad cop" ploy—for the client to intercede at last, and seem the essence of sweet reason in comparison with the agent. Or the agent may be used as a "stalking horse," to gather as much information about the adversary as possible, opening the way to proposals by the client that exploit the intelligence gathered.

Note that the tactical flexibility conferred by representative negotiations presupposes a competitive negotiating climate, a zero-sum contest in which each negotiator wishes to outsmart the other. It is the stuff of traditional statecraft, and the interested reader can do no better than study the writings of Schelling (1960) and Potter (1948), as well as Lax and Sebenius (1986). To repeat, the assumption behind this line of analysis is that effective negotiation requires some measure of artifice and duplicity, and that this is often best accomplished through the use of some sort of foil or alter ego—in the form of the agent. But the converse is not necessarily true: Where the negotiation is conducted in a problem-solving manner (cf. Fisher and Ury, 1981), agents may still be helpful, not because they resort to strategic ruses, but because they can help articulate interests, options, and alternatives. Four heads are clearly better than two, for example, when it comes to brainstorming about possible ways of reconciling the parties' interests.

Offsetting—indeed, typically *more* than offsetting—the three above apparent virtues of representative negotiation are several sources of difficulty. Each is sufficiently important and potentially problematic that we believe caution is necessary before entering into negotiation through agents.

EXTRA "MOVING PARTS"

As indicated in Figure 1, representative negotiations entail greater structural complexity, additional moving parts in the negotiation machinery that—given a need for expertise, detachment, or tactical flexibility—can help move parties toward a favorable agreement. Additional moving parts, however, can also mean additional expense, in the form of the time required in the finding, evaluating, and engaging of agents, as well as the financial cost of retaining their services. And it can mean additional problems, more things that can go wrong. For instance, a message intended by a client may not be the message transmitted by that client's agent to the other party. Or the message received by that agent from the other party may be very different from the one that that agent (either deliberately or inadvertently) manages to convey to his or her client.

At one level, then, the introduction of additional links in the communication system increases the risk of distortion in the information conveyed back and forth between the principals. Beyond that lies a second difficulty: the possibility that eventually the principals will come to rely so extensively on their respective agents that they no longer communicate directly—even though they could, and even though they might well benefit from doing so. In effect (see Figure 1), P1, in order to reach P2, now invariably goes through the A1–A2 chain, even though such maneuvering is no longer warranted. Consider, for example, the case of a divorcing couple who, in explicit compliance with the advice of their adversary lawyers, have avoided any direct contact with each other during the divorce proceedings. Once the divorce has been obtained, will the parties' ability to communicate effectively with each other (e.g., over support and custody issues) be adversely affected by their excessive prior reliance on their attorneys?

Yet another potentially problematic implication of this increasingly complex social machinery is that unwanted conditions may arise that apply undue pressure on individual negotiators. Thus A2, in performing a mediatory function between P2 and the other side (P1 and A1) may be prone to become allied with the opposing team—or at least to be so viewed by P2. Greater number does not necessarily mean greater wisdom, however, and the pressures toward uniformity of opinion that result from coalition formation may adversely affect the quality of the decisions reached.

In sum, the introduction of agents increases the complexity of the social apparatus of negotiation, and in so doing increases the chances of unwanted side effects. A related problem should be briefly noted here: the difficulty of asymmetry, as when an agent negotiates not with another agent but directly with the other principal. In effect, this was the case in 1978 when Egypt's Sadat negotiated with Israel's Begin at Camp David. Sadat considered himself empowered to make binding decisions for Egypt, while—at least partly for tactical purposes—Begin represented himself as ultimately accountable to his cabinet and to the Israeli parliament. While this "mismatched" negotiation between a principal (Sadat) and an agent (Begin) *did* result in agreement (thanks in good measure to President Carter's intercession as a mediator), it was not easy. The asymmetry of role meant that the two sides differed in their readiness to move forward toward an agreement, their ability to be shielded by a representative, and their willingness/ability to guarantee that any agreement reached would "stick."[3]

Different dynamics will characterize the negotiation depending on whether it is between clients, between lawyers, or with both present. If just the clients are there, the dealings will be more direct and forthright, and issues of authority and ratification disappear. With just the lawyers present, there may be less direct factual information but concomitantly more candor about delicate topics. Suppose, for example, that an aging soprano seeks to persuade an opera company to sign her for the lead role in an upcoming opera. If she is not present, the opera's agent may try to lower the price, contending that the singer is past her prime. Such candor is not recommended if the singer is present at the negotiation!

Problems of "Ownership" and Conflicting Interests

In theory, it is clear that the principal calls the shots. Imagine, however, an agent who is intent on applying the *Getting to Yes* (Fisher and Ury, 1981) approach by searching for objective criteria and a fair outcome. Suppose the client simply wants the best

---

3. Compare in this connection Rule 4.2 of the American Bar Association's Model Rules of Professional Conduct, which prohibits a lawyer from dealing directly with the opposing principal, if that principal is represented by an attorney.

possible outcome, perhaps because it is a one-shot deal not involving a future relationship with the other party. What if the agent (a lawyer, perhaps) *does* care about his future relationship with the other *agent,* and wants to be remembered as a fair and scrupulous bargainer? How *should* this conflict get resolved and how, in the absence of explicit discussion, *will* it be resolved, if at all? Conversely, the client, because of a valuable long-term relationship, may want to maintain good relations with the other side. But if the client simply looks for an agent who is renowned for an ability to pull out all the stops, the client's overall objectives may suffer as the result of an overzealous advocate.

This issue may arise in a number of contexts. Suppose that, in the course of a dispute settlement negotiation,[4] a lawyer who is intent on getting the best possible deal for a client turns down an offer that was within the client's acceptable range. Is this proper behavior by the agent? The Model Rules of Professional Conduct for attorneys explicitly require (see Rules 1.2(a), 1.4) that every offer must be communicated to the principal, and perhaps a failure to do so might lead to a successful malpractice action against the attorney if the deal finally fell through.

Another illustration involves the situation where the agent and principal have divergent ethical norms. Suppose that a seller of a house has just learned that the dwelling is infested with termites, but instructs the agent not to reveal this fact, even in response to specific inquiry from the buyer. How should these tensions be fairly resolved, keeping in mind the fact that the agent may be subject to a professional code of conduct that gives directions that may conflict with the ethical values of the client?[5] There may, of course, be artful ways of dealing with such dilemmas, as, for example, slyly deflecting any relevant inquiry by the buyer. But preferably these problems should be explicitly addressed in the course of the initial discussion between agent and principal. To some extent, the problem may be resolved by the principal's tendency to pick an agent who is congenial and compatible. But, as we pointed out before, principals are not always aware of and knowledgeable about the relevant considerations that go into the choice of an agent. Hence, if these issues are not addressed explicitly at the outset, termination of the relationship midstream in egregious cases may be the only alternative.

Differing goals and standards of agent and principal may create conflicting pulls. For example, the buyer's agent may be compensated as a percentage of the purchase price, thus creating an incentive to have the price as high as possible. The buyer, of course, wants the lowest possible price. Similarly, where a lawyer is paid by the hour, there may be an incentive to draw out the negotiation, whereas the client prefers an expeditious negotiation at the lowest possible cost.

While these are not insoluble problems, to be sure, they do constitute yet another example of the difficulties that may arise as one moves to representative negotiations. Although in theory the principals are in command, once agents have been introduced the chemistry changes, and new actors—with agenda, incentives, and constraints of their own—are part of the picture. Short of an abrupt firing of the agents, principals may find themselves less in control of the situation once agents have come on the scene.

---

4. See Sander and Rubin (1988) for a discussion of the differences between dealmaking and dispute settlement negotiation.

5. See, for example, Rule 4.1 of the ABA's Model Rules of Professional Conduct, prohibiting attorneys from making materially false statements.

ENCOURAGEMENT OF ARTIFICE AND DUPLICITY

Finally, as already noted, the introduction of agents often seems to invite clients to devise stratagems (with or without these agents) to outwit the other side. Admittedly, there is nothing intrinsic to the presence of representatives that dictates a move in this direction; still, perhaps because of the additional expense incurred, the seductive lure of a "killing" with the help of one's "hired gun," or the introduction of new, sometimes perverse incentives, representative negotiations often seem to instill (or reflect) a more adversarial climate.

CONCLUSION

It follows from the preceding analysis that, ordinarily, negotiations conducted directly between the principals are preferable to negotiation through representatives. When the principals' relationship is fundamentally cooperative or informed by enlightened self-interest, agents may often be unnecessary; since there is little or no antagonism in the relationship, there is no need for the buffering detachment afforded by agents. Moreover, by negotiating directly, there is reduced risk of miscoordination, misrepresentation, and miscommunication.

On the other hand, representative negotiation *does* have an important and necessary place. When special expertise is required, when tactical flexibility is deemed important and—most importantly—when direct contact is likely to produce confrontation rather than collaboration, agents *can* render an important service.

Above all, the choice of whether to negotiate directly or through surrogates is an important one, with significant ramifications. It therefore should be addressed explicitly by weighing some of the considerations advanced above. And if an agent *is* selected, careful advance canvassing of issues such as those discussed here (e.g., authority and ethical standards) is essential.

REFERENCES

Fisher, R., and Ury, W. L. (1981). *Getting to Yes: Negotiating agreement without giving in.* Boston: Houghton Mifflin.

Goldberg, S.; Green, E.; and Sander, F. E. A. (1987). "Saying you're sorry." *Negotiation Journal* 3: 221–224.

Lax, D. A., and Sebenius, J. K. (1986). *The manager as negotiator.* New York: The Free Press.

Potter, S. (1948). *The theory and practice of gamesmanship: The art of winning games without actually cheating.* New York: Holt.

Sander, F. E. A., and Rubin, J. Z. (1988). "The Janus quality of negotiation: Dealmaking and dispute settlement." *Negotiation Journal* 4: 109–113.

Schelling, T. (1960). *The strategy of conflict.* Cambridge, MA: Harvard University Press.

We thank Michael Wheeler for the many constructive comments, suggestions, and conversations that preceded this article; and we gratefully acknowledge the helpful comments of Stephen B. Goldberg on an earlier draft of this manuscript.

Negotiating in Long-Term Mutually Interdependent Relationships among Relative Equals

Blair H. Sheppard

For somehow this is tyranny's disease, to trust no friends.

Aeschylus, 525–456 B.C., *Prometheus Bound,* 1. 224

INTRODUCTION

In U.S. business theory and practice, market and hierarchy have dominated as mechanisms for organizing economic activity (Arrow, 1974; Barnard, 1938; Ouchi, 1980). Consider the decision about how to source a part or service. The sourcing decision has typically been thought of as a make-or-buy decision in which a firm has the choice between building or servicing internally to the firm using traditional hierarchical controls, such as budgeting, accounting, and performance appraisals processes, so that the production of a part or service can be planned and integrated into other aspects of a firm's performance, or buying that part or service on the open market and depending on competition to ensure good value and innovation. Until recently, alternatives to making it internally or buying in a market have gone largely unheeded in modern thought and practice. However, many firms are now experimenting with a plethora of alternative means for better sourcing a part or service, such as developing long-term relationships with a given set of suppliers rather than buying on the spot market, building alliances with competitors to produce the part or service, or building peer-based organizations within a firm to codesign and manufacture the part. Each of these models represents a radical departure from market or hierarchy as a way of organizing economic activity. The central argument of this chapter is that such alternative means of organizing work are evolving rapidly and that our models of management are being outstripped by these changes in the marketplace.

In particular, it will be argued that market and hierarchy have been assumed as the backdrop against which our models of Micro-organizational Behavior have been developed. Thus, much management research has been about the exercise of power or control within a hierarchical organization or managing exchanges in the marketplace (see Sheppard and Tuchinsky, in press). Nowhere is the purity of our view of eco-

Abridged version, originally appearing in *Research on Negotiation in Organizations,* Vol 5, 1995, pp. 3-44. Reprinted with permission of JAI Press.

nomic activity better expressed than in the dominant model of negotiation in academic research. Most negotiation research is concerned with how to engage in transactional, one-time negotiations in a relatively pure market (compare Lewicki, Litterer, Minton, and Saunders, 1994). The premise of this chapter is that unless we can develop models of negotiation that incorporate alternative models of economic exchange we are, in the extreme, doomed to irrelevancy . . .

NEGOTIATING IN A RELATIONSHIP

For some, negotiation is considered a key skill for effectively managing within these emerging forms of business relationship (see Greenhalgh, 1987; Sheppard and Tuchinsky, in press). It follows that long-standing relationships among relative equals require bargaining, as formal controls and sanctions do not exist as a means of getting others to do what we wish. In relationships it is necessary to discuss, quibble, exchange, and engage in quid pro quo as a way to get someone over whom one does not have power to do what is desired. Partially based on this observation, research on negotiation has been conducted to help fill in the void. This research has taken as its model either the bargaining model developed in labor relations (see for example, Lewicki, Litterer, Minton, and Saunders, 1994); game theory (see for example, Murnighan, 1991); or decision theoretic models of negotiation (for example, see Bazerman and Neale, 1992). Each of these points of view is primarily transactional. They have as their model maximizing return to self in each negotiation. They do not address, as their primary focus, negotiation as a means of establishing and growing long-term relationships nor how the context of a given relationship changes the nature of a negotiation.

Recent research methodologies are also limited. For example, a fairly typical study involves two relative strangers engaging in a simulated negotiation over a few dimensions where each has been given a set of information outlining the returns to them for a set of settlement points on each dimension. The most frequently used simulation is a variant on the two-person, three-issue negotiation developed by Dean Pruitt for the study of integrative bargaining (Pruitt, 1972). These are poor proxies for at least three reasons: (1) the negotiation is not in the context of a relationship, (2) the simulation entails a predefined, highly stylized problem, and (3) there is no past and no future. Negotiations among long-term cross-functional team members, strategic allies, and parties to a long-term customer–supplier relationship have a past and a future, occur in the context of a very elaborate relationship, and involve messy problems. Therefore, the field has attempted to address a very important question: how negotiations occur within the context of an ongoing relationship among relative equals. But given the limiting set of perspectives and methodologies, it really has not. Research has concentrated on transactional exchanges, not relationships. It has ignored the temporal element that colors ongoing bargaining. Up to this point, research has inadequately addressed issues unique to relational negotiations. To make this case, however, it is necessary to illustrate how negotiations in the context of ongoing relationships differ significantly from transactional negotiations. Let us turn to that question now.

The Relational Context for Negotiation

Sustaining effective ongoing relationships in which there is an investment in mutual development is a very difficult enterprise. Some marriages end in divorce. Some strategic alliances fail. Some teams splinter. Some friendships break up. With even greater frequency we find ourselves in unsatisfying relationships from which there is no obvious escape. The challenge of maintaining a cooperative relationship is illustrated no place better than in the consideration of negotiations within marriages. They entail greater emotion. They are more complicated. They frequently do not end. They cannot be easily separated from other ongoing discussions. It is with good reason that transactional, decontextualized negotiations have been the primary topic of study. At least it is possible to understand them. But for all their trouble, negotiations within a partnership, marriage, alliance, or team are fun, interesting, important, and a defining aspect of what it means to be human. The challenges of distributive and integrative negotiation in an ongoing relationship are somewhat different. Thus, we will take them one at a time.

Distributive Negotiation in a Relationship

A recently married couple are discussing whose parents they will be spending Christmas vacation with. Procter & Gamble and Wal-Mart are discussing who will own the inventory in their new relationship. Price Waterhouse is discussing a cost overrun with an extremely important audit client. Members of a new task force are determining their new roles only to discover that the two wish to serve the same function. Each of these discussions could be modeled quite well as a single-issue, distributive-negotiation problem. There are two parties—a single critical dimension and opposing positions. A great portion of each of these discussions will entail a search for the other's walkaway point and hiding of one's own. But the discussions are also more complicated than the simple distributive problem.

Transforming Distributive to Integrative Bargains.   Most obviously, because a history and a future exist in each of these discussions, there exist ways of identifying integrative potential not likely to be found in a simple transaction. A one-time distributive problem does not permit introducing other issues into a discussion. However, because within relationships there exists a past and a future, it is possible to transform a single-issue distributive discussion into a multiple-issue integrative discussion. One spouse cares a great deal about where to spend their first married Christmas, while the other harbors strong preferences about where to spend their summer vacation time. Procter & Gamble wishes Wal-Mart to own any inventory, Wal-Mart wishes to establish a mechanism to ensure a quick response on any future issues arising in the relationship. The customer is very concerned about paying additional costs, while the accountant is concerned about changing client procedures and practices during future audits. Existing procedures result in a slow, unprofitable audit. One member of the task force truly wishes to be the initial point of contact with a critical group, the other may really wish to be central in the final presentation to that group. In each of these examples, a difficult distributive negotiation problem becomes less difficult as the parties are allowed to logroll over time. Consider a husband and wife, one of whom wishes to vacation in the mountains and the other at the beach. If all else fails, it is possible to go to the mountains one year and the beach the next. To do so, however, there needs to be a next year. In transactional negotiation, a future does not exist, or it exists very tentatively and with no assurances. Thus, a bird in the hand is worth two in the bush. In an ongoing relationship, however, birds in the bush are much less likely to get away.

Not only is there an incentive to shift from distributive to integrative solutions without relationships, there is also an incentive to shift away from distributive processes. Because partners see future interaction, they are unlikely to wish to use the most problematic of distributive tactics. Knowing that the other can get them back and that cooperation is undermined by the tone created with the sorts of tactics typical of distributive negotiations, marital negotiators are less likely to use them. Similarly, revealing critical information is more likely as we come to believe that our partners are less likely to use that information unfairly. The abused partner has many chances to get the other partner back.

Distributive Negotiations within a Relationship Are Hot.   But the future is a two-edged sword. While integrative potential is raised by the possibility of introducing a second issue into the discussion there is also potential for the discussion to become very heated and focused on the single issue at hand. Frequently, distributive discussions in ongoing relationships are precedent establishing. Discussions over precedent are very important discussions, as the stakes entail all future such problems. The couple may not only be determining where to go at Christmas, but where to go for all future Christmases, whose family matters more and the relative priority of parents and in-laws versus the members of the couple themselves. Thus, a simple little distributive problem takes on great new importance. Who owns the inventory for one P&G product line has clear implications for who owns the inventory for all product lines and all future products. Thus, the discussion is not over just toothpaste for this year, but potentially the allocation of profits across all brands. A solution for determining payment in overruns frequently becomes the baseline for all future discussions. Simple allocation questions become questions of precedent and thus more important and more heated. A clear implication of this point is that negotiators within relationships need to be able to handle well emotion-laden or very important issues.

Emotion is likely to arise for several other reasons as well. The most important, although not the most obvious, reason that negotiations within relationships are likely to be more emotional and conflict filled than transactional negotiation is that distributive negotiations within relationships frequently serve to define the partners. We know from social psychology that a central means through which people develop an identity is through the people they interact with most intimately (Linville and Carlston, 1994). I, for example, define my sense of self very much through my relationship with my wife, children, mother, father, siblings, and close friends and colleagues. Who I am is to a large degree who I am for them. Distributive negotiation issues within these relationships are self-defining in two ways. First, the roles the other assumes are not me. Second, the things I do and the roles I assume are me. Of course, it is also true that identity emerges from considering ourselves in light of our competitors (see, for example, Sherif et al., 1961). In the terminology of social psychologists, our sense of self derives both from those we consider members of our in-group and our out-group. The difference is that elements of self and long-term capacity are negotiated with in-group members. With competitors, direct conversation about who one is and what one will do are not frequent; instead, the market is the field through which identity and comparative competencies are established.

Teams are a setting in which the negotiation of self occurs frequently. The roles each member of a team assumes influences the skills each will become better at, the roles others see them fulfilling, and how they come to think of themselves. I recently spoke to a member of a design team who recounted that she started out thinking of herself as a design engineer, but now considers herself the quality guru in the company. Others have come to think of her the same way as well. Interestingly, at the time it happened she was upset that another team member drove the design components of the project she was working on, while she was left with quality. But, since the emerging importance of quality in her firm, she is glad she lost the initial battle. Another business example can be found in strategic alliances. Two companies come together in the development of a long-term joint design and production relationship. The discussion at hand concerns who is to perform what function. Writing on strategic alliances suggests that it is important to retain control over and delivery of those things which are a firm's core competencies. Those things a firm does better than the competition should be done by that firm. Good alliances entail firms with complementary core competencies. In such instances the allocation of work between allies has the character of an integrative discussion. But there always exist gray areas in which both sides wish control or primary responsibility. The outcome of those instances matters a great deal. Who performs which roles has implications for the competencies each firm is going to develop or accentuate over the course of the alliance. Even sticking to one's core competence is not all that desirable if an objective of a strategic alliance is to learn how to do other things well (cf. Sitkin and Stickel, in press).

The methods and vocabulary presently used in the study of negotiation do not lend themselves well to the study of emotion in negotiations. First, the use of simulated negotiations with relative strangers does not evoke deep conflicts, critical future dependencies, or threats to one's sense of self. Second, the absence of a past does not permit the study of patterns of emotion management that naturally emerged between related others over time. Finally, the fields from which we borrow our theoretical models may need to expand. Marital research (e.g., Gottman, 1979), research on friendship and social relationships (e.g., Putallaz and Sheppard, 1992), and even facets of organizational development have much to offer us (for example, Brown, 1985). The predominant models entail a view that is somewhat too calculative, too cold, and too abstracted from relational contexts to help with the study of emotion in negotiation. I do not mean to argue that laboratory or rigorous theory be abandoned. John Gottman (1979), for example, has studied extremely well in the laboratory the negotiation patterns that serve as precursors to divorce. One very interesting device he has used is to ask married couples to begin describing a frequent conflict they have. Inevitably, that conflict reemerges in the discussion and can be studied. Another is to create proxies for negotiations parties are presently engaged in. In any instance, precedent, deeply interdependent outcomes, and implications for future competence need to be parameters incorporated into our research designs and theory.

Distributive Negotiations in Relationships May Never End.   All negotiations are performed with incomplete information. Parties' preferences are not entirely known. Critical uncertainties are not entirely understood. How others important to the negotiators will behave is not entirely known. For example, the newlyweds do not know how their families will react to the decision they reach. The audit partner and controller do not know how senior management or the audit committee will react to their decision. Procter & Gamble and Wal-Mart do not know how their method for establishing inventory levels will work, nor do they know if the new delivery arrangements are truly feasible. Task force members do not know if the anticipated work reflects what really needs to be done. Because a decision must be reached, however, settlements are reached on incomplete information. In a transactional environment settlements must attempt to anticipate all important contingencies and have specified the method for dealing with those. Stewart MacAulay (1963) outlined the type of planning typical of a buyer/seller negotiation in a transaction:

> (1) They can plan what each is to do or refrain from doing, e.g., S might agree to deliver ten 1963 Studebaker four-door sedan automobiles to B on a certain date in exchange for a specified amount of money. (2) They can plan what effect certain contingencies are to have on their duties; e.g., what is to happen to S and B's obligation if S cannot deliver the cars because of a strike at the Studebaker factory? (3) They can plan what is to happen if either of them fails to perform; e.g., what is to happen if S delivers nine of the cars two weeks late? (4) They can plan their agreement so that it is a legally enforceable contract—that is, so that a legal sanction would be available to provide compensation for injury suffered by B as a result of S's failure to deliver the cars on time (p. 57).

Sometimes such planning entails mutual negotiation between the parties. Sometimes it is done unilaterally in the form of fine-print boilerplate prepared by the house counsel of the seller or the buyer. Sometimes boilerplate is found on forms as they come from the printer. Sometimes typical industry practice is applied. In any instance, transactional negotiations often entail elaborate plans. However, in ongoing relationships these plans are frequently unnecessary and sometimes harmful. They are unnecessary because parties prefer to rely on a person's word, a handshake, or common honesty and decency. MacAulay (1963) quotes one purchasing agent who expresses this view:

> If something comes up, you get the other man on the telephone and deal with the problem. You don't read legalistic contract clauses at each other if you ever want to do business again. One doesn't run to lawyers if he wants to stay in business because one must behave decently (p. 61).

In the instance of this purchasing agent, the term *decently* means be open for further negotiation. Oliver Williamson (1975) best articulated the major reason for not depending on well-specified contracts: people are not infinitely smart. If we could anticipate and plan for all possible contingencies, then a contract could serve our needs. However, people have limited capacity, an especially important complication in today's increasingly complex, ambiguous world. For most interesting negotiations, neither all important contingencies, nor all important aspects of performance can be identified in advance. This is especially true as changes in products and services occur with increasing rapidity and the focus on customization increases. Moreover, even if we could anticipate all important contingencies, a contract covering them would be too cumbersome. Thus, more open-ended vehicles permit ongoing discussion as a method for responding to changes as they arise.

A second reason for leaving negotiations open is that binding, planful discussions can create antagonistic relations. The tactics and tone associated with a fine-tooth comb negotiation process tend to create a legalistic environment. Such an environment does not serve as a good basis for developing stronger ongoing relations.

Of course, there are times that extreme planning is called for in a relationship. When relations are faltering, a frequent tactic of behavioral therapists is to get parties to develop explicit contracts about things on which they can agree. Frequently, incomplete discussions or inaccurate implicit assumptions served as the basis for the relationship failing in the first place. To raise to discussion important little issues and create agreements on these can set the parties on the track to building a more solid base of understanding. Said differently, parties may act as if their relationship is more of a marriage than it is. In such cases, returning to market conditions for a while may be a good idea. A second instance is when coordination of activities is essential and communication either difficult or very disruptive. A large building project is one example. The client, engineers, architect, contractor, and subcontractors often cannot meet frequently enough to work through the details of a project. Moreover, detailed planning permits a level of coordination that ad hoc communication cannot. Thus, planning should take place. Even in such instances, however, it is wise to leave open the possibility of ongoing negotiation as all contingencies cannot be foreseen and it builds stronger relationships.

Enforcement of Distributive Settlements within a Relationship.   In a related vein, the mechanisms for the enforcement of an agreement tend to be much more informal for negotiations within a relationship than for transactional negotiations. One source of informal sanctions are those that come directly from the relationships between involved members. In interfirm relationships, personal relationships can be extensive. Again, refer to MacAulay (1963):

> At all levels of the two business units personal relationships across the boundaries of the two organizations exert pressures for conformity to expectations. Salesmen know purchasing agents well. The same two individuals occupying these roles may have dealt with each other from 5 to 25 years. Each has something to give the other. Salesmen have gossip about competitors, shortages, and price increases to give purchasing agents who treat them well. Salesmen take purchasing agents to dinner, and they give purchasing agents Christmas gifts hoping to improve chances of making sales. The buyer's engineering staff may work with the seller's engineering staff to solve problems jointly. The seller's engineers may render great assistance, and the buyer's engineers may desire to return the favor by drafting specifications which only the seller can meet. The top executives of the two firms may know each other. They may sit together on government or trade committees. They may know each other socially and even belong to the same country club. The interrelationships may be more formal. Sellers may hold stock in corporations which are important customers; buyers may hold stock in important suppliers. Both buyer and seller may share common directors on their boards. They may share a common financial institution which has financed both units (p. 63).

Executives, salespeople, and engineers do not like to hear that an important customer or supplier has been treated badly, or that an agreement with that customer or supplier has not been followed. To do so too often has clear career implications.

Other forms of enforcement hold as well. Most typically people who interact frequently with each other also interact with others important to one another. For example, an audit client probably knows many of the accounting firm's other clients. Wal-Mart personnel know people in similar positions at other retailers. Spouses know each other's parents, children, aunts, uncles, cousins, friends, and colleagues. The threat of lost reputation with important others is a very potent stimulus to following through on an agreement.

The dependence on the partner in a relationship is also a strong incentive to follow through on agreements. As indicated earlier, each member of a relationship comes to be dependent on the other for important services, advice, and help. The risk of losing those services is usually sufficient threat to follow through on an agreement.

Integrative Negotiation in a Relationship

In transactional negotiation, discussions are about the exchange of goods, services, or money. While these issues are central to discussions within ongoing business relationships, they take on a very different cast, one relating directly to the reasons why one would develop a close business relationship in the first place. Investment in an ongoing relationship permits the parties in that relationship to accrue real increases in efficiency, quality, and other forms of effectiveness. However, this is only true if investment occurs. Each side of the relationship should be learning about the other. Each side of the relationship should be working to improve their value to the other. Each side of the relationship should be developing plans that incorporate the other's interests into those plans. Without doing so, a long-term relationship entails the disadvantage of closing off options, without accruing the benefits of the longer-term commitment. Without mutual development, long-term relationships have no value. It is this quality of relationships that influences the meaning and form of integrative bargaining within them. Integrative bargaining within a relationship is where the seeds of mutual development are planted. Therefore, integrative bargaining within a relationship is directly about the people, or functions or firms, not about concepts that can be isolated from the parties to the relationship. Given the notion of mutual development as the cornerstone of effective relationship, how is integrative bargaining different within such a context?

Integrative Bargaining Entails Opportunities for Mutual Development.   As I just argued, within ongoing, interdependent relationships most discussions entail opportunities to discuss improving the relationship or each other in the context of the relationship. I do not mean to imply that pure exchange-based discussions never happen within a relationship. Clearly, they do. For example, a husband and wife in discussing house cleaning discover that one likes cleaning with water, while the other likes dusting, vacuuming, and tidying. The integrative deal entails giving the washrooms and kitchen to one spouse and the rest of the cleaning to the other. In a buyer–seller relationship the buyer may care about inventory levels, while the seller cares about delivery date. However, I do mean to imply that such pure exchanges are rare and to ignore the importance of mutual development is to miss opportunities for improving the value of each partner to the other. They have a static quality to them that minimizes growth. The couple may wish to talk about means for making cleaning easier. Sponging stains that have been allowed to dry is much harder than cleaning as spills occur. Tidying throughout the house is harder than tidying in a concentrated area. In other words, to separate the discussion of cleaning from the rest of their interchanges loses the real efficiencies that can accrue. If the buyer and seller restrict their discussion only to issues within the confines of existing business practice, they miss opportunities to think about whole new ways of doing ordering, methods for integrating information systems across partners, means for mutually reducing costs, identification of new strategic opportunities, product development possibilities, or identification of competitive threats.

I recently had a conversation with the chief operating officer (COO) of a large electronics firm (call it Firm X) who was very concerned about his company's efforts to improve relations with suppliers as a step in improving overall product quality. Like most of its competition, this firm reduced the number of suppliers of each part to manage better those that remain, increased the number of parts each supplier provided the firm to better tie the interests of the supplier to the firm, put suppliers through a rigorous supplier qualification program, trained suppliers in manufacturing quality processes, and raised dramatically the expected quality of supplied parts. This COO had just returned from a visit to his key supplier where he discovered that his company's program, while having some positive effect, was so poorly implemented that much of the potential benefit was lost. For example, the supplier ran a continuous improvement program in its plants. When a suggested improvement in process or product was made that had implications for Firm X, the supplier was required to submit a large set of drawings at its own expense and wait while its suggested changes underwent a lengthy review process. Often, the supplier did not hear back for six months, sometimes not at all. As a result of the cost and difficulty associated with this review process, the supplier just did not make many small but important improvements. This was in contrast to one of the Firm X's chief competitors, who for most suggestions required no drawings be submitted, and who provided an answer within a few days on all but the most complicated suggestions. Frequently, this competitor would fly someone down at its own expense to the supplier's plant site to clarify any questions. The supplier clearly admitted that this second firm received better and lower cost materials than did Firm X. In fact, the COO estimated that his parts were 30 percent more expensive and had far greater quality problems than his competitor. He was extremely concerned about his firm's ability to effectively manage adjustments in supplier relationships and within his own firm to meet the challenges this visit suggested.

In Many Relational Negotiations the Person Is the Problem.   A corollary of the notion of mutual development and negotiations in relationship is that in such negotiations, the person is the problem. Consider the husband and wife just discussed above. In many instances it behooves the couple to discuss messes throughout the house in a very depersonalized manner. In doing so, offense is not taken and the problem of multiple messes to tidy can be discussed without resulting in a long debate about character or personology. In other words, in relationships it is often important to separate the person from the problem. However, this is impossible or bad advice to follow in two particular instances. First, the problem of distributed mess may simply be part of a larger set of behaviors endemic to the other. The husband may not just leave trails of mess throughout the house, but also not turn his socks right side out before putting them in the laundry, leave paper, money and other assorted mess in his shirt pocket, bring the dog and children in all muddy and have them traipse throughout the house without concern for the new oriental rug, and leave coffee cups in every nook and cranny in the house. In sum, he may just be messy. Discussing his messiness, provided it is done with care for his feelings, permits a kind of conversation not permitted by separating the person from the problem. Discussing messiness provides an opportunity to diagnose why he is messy and thus potentially take action on the root cause. Discussing his messiness permits a broad-based discussion of the aspects of messy that cause his wife real concern and those that are not a problem or are even endearing. Discussing his messiness permits him and his wife to learn something about themselves and about each other. None of these could be easily done if a list of depersonalized local messes was brought up for discussion. Moreover, if the list is too long or different messes are discussed over frequent exchanges, the person has become the problem and in a much less direct passive-aggressive manner.

The example just given is clearly a limited one, not illustrating the full potential of making the person the problem. More important discussions may occur over issues such as self and career, orientation to family, personal values, or the role of one's childhood experiences in their present relationship. Consider an extreme example. Parents who were abused as children are much more likely to abuse their own children than are parents who were not abused as children. It appears that a critical determinant of whether or not abuse will be transferred from generation to generation is the ability for people who were abused as children to be able to confront their views and feelings about relationships with a trusted other. Good relationships are a context in which a person may be able to deal with her/his feelings about relationships and tendencies to abuse. Without recognizing that they are the problem, it is difficult for such abused people to develop truly effective relationships.

Equivalent business examples abound. Two people are going to be working together for a long time and one does not trust the other. A key supplier has adopted a long-term strategy inconsistent with a critical customer's needs. A colleague has become too arrogant to work with. A task force chair is lacking in confidence and is crippling performance. It is essential to have direct conversations about the other party as the problem in this situation.

Integrative Negotiations Have Implications for Power and Future Dependence.   A related aspect of integrative negotiations is that they entail implications for future power and dependence. In long-term relationships the members are and should be quite concerned about the nature of the dependency between them. Mutual development entails mutual dependence. Long-term commitment entails dependence. Dependence on others means that they wield power over you and they can take advantage of you. Consider the example of the supplier to the electronics company described above. One electronics company committed to the supplier over a very long term. In doing so, they shared critical information about their processes, strategy, and upcoming product design. They invested heavily in developing capabilities in that supplier so that the supplier could meet better and better the electronics company's material needs. They got to learn the processes of the supplier and incorporated their unique abilities into product development efforts. As a result, the electronics company has better, less expensive, and better integrated parts than their competitor described in the same example who did none of these things. However, they are also more dependent on the supplier. Because of information and abilities unique to their two-party relationship the supplier provides better, less expensive, and more integrated parts. As a result, the electronics company needs that supplier to sustain existing quality, cost, and integration. Williamson (1985) refers to this phenomenon as the development of firm-specific skills, that is, skills that only have value in relation to a particular company. The other electronics company has no such advantages, but they also are not as dependent. In the argot of 1950s teenagers, one firm is "going steady", while the other is "playing the field". The consequence is that both the supplier and the customer are at risk in this relationship. Negotiations when such potential for abuse exist are likely to be quite different from transactional discussions among relative strangers in a spot. They will likely be more tacit, focused on determining the appropriate level of involvement, and concerned with identifying protections against abuse. Negotiations when one side has taken advantage are especially likely to be quite different from one-off discussions.

Dependence can take many forms (Pfeffer and Salancik, 1978; Tichy, 1973). We can depend on others for information, goods, services, money, clout, personal support, or counsel. We can become dependent because of relationship-specific abilities. We can become dependent because of the development of a sense of attachment or identity. In each instance, dependence implies power. Where there exists power there is potential for abuse. This argument is a variant of Williamson's concern for opportunistic behavior. A solution is to develop mechanisms and relational qualities that permit trust.

Context Matters.   One mechanism that creates trust in an interdependent relationship is the social context in which the relationship is embedded. This point was alluded to earlier (see section on enforcement), but it deserves repeating and elaboration. Investment in another firm, or another function within the same firm is not just a relationship between people. It is a relationship between sets of people, systems, procedures, capital, and strategies. It is also a relationship that occurs in the context of a broader set of related economic relations of which this is just one. As such, a negotiation takes on a very new cast. For example, separating the dimensions of a problem from its broader context to permit effective problem solving must be done with great care. It is necessary to understand that any negotiated decision has implications for many other related decisions. I knew a dean once who made extremely sensible decisions, but without consideration of the interdependence among those decisions. The resulting chaos from inconsistencies, undermining of precedents, unanticipated consequences, and confusion of recipients of the decisions would have been amusing if some people I knew well were not affected by such local rationality.

But more important for the previous point, this context entails a set of social actors engaged in a set of exchanges entailing some obligation to monitor each other.

This set of interdependent actors is engaged in a network of relationships having what Alan Fiske would call jural qualities, meaning they "have intrinsic imperative force and are the source of moral, . . . customary, and traditional rules and practices" (Fiske, 1991, p. 172). The primary moral and social rules guiding an exchange derive from an interdependent network of relationships. For Fiske, "every social relationship entails moral obligations, and every moral obligation derives from the imputation of a social relationship." The potency of this notion of jural forms is clear when one considers the responsibilities of a person observing the violation of the obligation entailed in one of the social forms. Consider Ellen, who notices that her sister Mary is not satisfying the essential needs of Mary's newborn child (a violation of the need principle in a communal sharing relationship). Ellen would be found quite at fault by the broader community, such as her mother, husband, or children, if she did not speak to Mary about Mary's not meeting her obligations as a parent. It is the force on Mary by interested others that gives their network of relationships such jural status. In fact, being engaged in a network of interdependent relationships entails a moral obligation at three distinct levels: "First, the parties immediately and directly participating in the primary relationship have a duty to conform to the model (Mary should care for the needs of her child). Second, people with social links to the primary parties have a duty to react when the primary parties fail to meet their obligations—they must modify their social relationships with the primary parties in suitable ways (Ellen should speak to Mary about not caring for the needs of her child). Third, it is the duty of others with social links to the secondary parties to appropriately modulate their social relationships with the secondary parties if the latter fail to react to the primary parties' breach of duty (the community should remove support for Ellen if she does not deal with Mary's neglect of her child). In other words, people get sanctioned for failing to sanction" (p. 171: items in parentheses my addition).

From this discussion it should be obvious that much of the discourse of relational negotiations will be about parties' respective obligations as determined by the broader network of which they are members and that negotiations frequently are not just the business of the parties to that negotiation. Often, the broader community will consider it their business to know and influence the discussions of network members. This is in sharp contrast to the relatively isolated dyadic discussions implied by the methods and theory of most present negotiation research . . .

Hostile Context

Lastly, a given relationship will often have to learn to exist in a relatively hostile environment and often with conflicting motives. This problem exists in shifts from hierarchy and transactional exchanges. A cross-functional team will need to learn to live within a bigger hierarchy. Parties to a relationship between Ford and a critical supplier will need to learn to ignore others engaged in more predatory practices. However, the problem of a hostile environment and conflicting motives is most prevalent and perhaps most interesting in the context of alliances among competitors.

We cannot do it alone and frequently find that only a competitor has what we need to succeed. IBM and Apple shocked the world when they announced that they needed to join forces, at least temporarily, to achieve their business needs. General Motors is perhaps the most striking example. The independent, vertically integrated giant of business now finds itself in alliances of some form or another with nearly every other competitor in the automobile business. The reasons for creating alliances of convenience between hostile parties are many. Access to capital, access to new markets, access to critical technology or processes, completion of a product line, and assistance in the management of difficult international regulatory issues are among the many examples given for firms joining with the enemy. This need also arises inside firms among warring factions. The gurus of continuous improvement and the gurus of radical re-engineering occasionally discover they have a shared roadblock in driving effective organizational change. Egoists in competition for the same position recognize the need for an integrated corporate decision on an important issue likely to influence the existence of the job for which they are vying. Again, enemies discover that they need to cooperate in a local instance to succeed. Such discussions are very different from transactions between parties in a market exchange and very different from negotiations between partners. The motives are truly more mixed. I need you now, but will do what I can to undermine your long-term competitive posture in the process. As such, negotiations between competitors differ from other long-term negotiations in three critical ways: (1) the negative prior history has potential to undermine effective negotiations; (2) the exchange provides a dual opportunity: cut a good deal now, but use the situation to improve your own or undermine their long-term competitive posture; and (3) control over the implementation of the negotiated settlement is a critical consideration. Consider each briefly.

Negative Prior History.   It is long understood that a history of past competition makes collaboration difficult. Expectations entering a negotiation have a great deal of impact upon the negotiation. If one expects a negotiation partner to be competitive she or he will act so as to cause that partner to be competitive (Kelley and Stahelski, 1970). Parties with a history of hostile relations tend to make negative attributions about the other's behavior. A history of competition is often supported by an escalatory dance that is well programmed. For these reasons, it is especially likely that negotiations between competitors will be hot and negatively valent. Great care must be taken to build a sense of commonality, break stereotypes, and engage in the establishment of effective forms of communication. Mitigation of strong statements, explanation of difficult or easily misinterpreted issues, recognition of the need for deescalatory behavior, and efforts at consolidation all need be practiced in such circumstances. In addition to these points of negotiation process is the simple observation that it is most often necessary to separate the alliance from the two parents. Feuding parents have a way of spoiling children; so do feuding companies. This argument is supported by the number of allied efforts between competitors that take the form of independent joint ventures (Harrigan, 1988).

Negative Underside.   At the same time that the parties are learning to speak politely with one another, there is a negative underside to negotiations with competitors. Each side of the partnership is simultaneously attempting to maximize the value of the alliance and learn as much about the other party as possible so as to gain advantage in future competitive arenas. IBM is not just attempting to build a better chip with Apple and Motorola, they are also attempting to learn software skills from Apple, management practices from Motorola, and points of weakness of both. This learning is to be used in the broader competitive arena, including in direct competition with Apple and Motorola. Thus, the alliance is truly mixed motive and thus even more confusing to those engaged in efforts to make the local negotiation work well. This observation has obvious implications for how to conduct such negotiations and what the substance of the negotiation should be. For example, it is easier to steal hard knowledge, such as a type of technology, or manufacturing process, than it is to steal soft knowledge, such as manufacturing culture or management practices. Similarly, it is important to construct the deal so that there exists possibilities to observe that which a firm wishes to learn about an ally. However, less obvious but equally important are the implications for the capacities that need reside in the allying firms. Firms that have mechanisms for studying the partner and transferring that knowledge throughout the parent organization will benefit more than those that do not.[1]

Fight for Control.   A by-product of the two previous points is that alliances often become battles for control by the two parent companies. Like divorcing parents it is important whom the child is more loved by, who has more influence. This is not just an emotionally driven event, but has important value. Control means capacity to observe. Control means one's strategic objectives will be met. Control means one is more likely to end up with the child in the case of a divorce. Each of these is an important consideration. However, in such considerations of control, ownership is mistaken for control. For example, Ford and Volkswagen have been engaged in a long-term alliance in Brazil. Ford has majority ownership in this venture. However, managers from Ford have historically done two-year stints in Brazil, while managers from Volkswagen have moved to Brazil for at least five years. Ford recently discovered that although they owned controlling interest in the venture, it was their German partners who knew the language, local customs, regulations, market conditions, employees, and systems of the subsidiary venture. Ford owned the firm but did not have control.

This last point illustrates the subtlety of negotiation in relationships. Things are not always what they seem at first blush, and the application of traditional models of relationships be they the logic of contract, logic of ownership, or logic of competition will not do one well. I recently met a scientist from Japan who is responsible for helping transfer technology from Japanese companies to their U.S. subsidiaries. He made the observation that his experience with Japanese partners and American partners differed in many ways, but two struck him as especially interesting. One was that U.S. partners were generally not willing to admit that they could not do something and that a partner should look elsewhere for a particular type of assistance. The other was that in Japan it was not unusual for suppliers and customers to exchange equal amounts of stock (often the stock in question is of small quantities), while in the United States such stock exchanges were quite uncommon

---

1. For a more complete discussion of this issue, see Hamel et al., 1989, Ohmae in James, 1993.

and if they occurred the customer invariably bought stock in the supplier, but not the reverse. He was puzzled why a partner did not recognize the need to honestly admit limitations with the security that such admission would strengthen the relationship, and why partners did not recognize the symbolic value of the exchange of stock, much like the exchange of rings among newlyweds. He questioned if we knew how to get married.

REFERENCES

Agnew, J. (1986). *Worlds apart: The market and the theater in Anglo-American thought, 1550–1750.* New York: Cambridge University Press.

Aoki, M. (1988). *Information, incentives and bargaining in the Japanese economy.* New York: Cambridge University Press.

Arrow, K. (1974). *The limits of organization.* New York: Norton.

Barnard, C. I. (1938). *The function of the executive.* Cambridge, MA: Harvard University Press.

Bazerman, M. H., and Neale, M. A. (1992). *Negotiating rationally.* New York: The Free Press.

Bazerman, M. H., and Samuelson, W. F. (1983). I won the auction but don't want the prize. *Journal of Conflict Resolution, 27,* 618–34.

Brown, L. D. (1985). *Managing conflict at organizational interfaces.* Reading, MA: Addison-Wesley.

Finlcy, M. (1973). *The ancient economy.* Berkeley: University of California Press.

Fiske, A. P. (1991). *Structures of social life.* New York: The Free Press.

Gottman, J. M. (1979). *Marital interaction: Experimental investigation.* New York: Academic Press.

Greenhalgh, L. (1987). The case against winning in negotiations. *Negotiation Journal, 3*(2), 167–73.

Hamel, G., Doz, Y. L., and Prahalad, C. K. (1989). Collaborate with your competitor—and win. *Harvard Business Review, 67,* 133–39.

Harrigan, K. R. (1988). *Managing maturing businesses: Restructuring declining industries and revitalizing troubled operations.* Lexington, MA: Lexington Books.

Hergert, M., and Morris, D. (1988). Trends in international collaborative agreements. In F. J. Contractor & P. Lorange (eds.), *Cooperative strategies in international business.* Lexington, MA: Lexington Books.

James, H. S. (1993). *When businesses cross international borders: Strategic alliances and their alternatives.* Westport, CT: Praeger.

Kelley, H. H., and Stahelski, A. J. (1970). The inference of intentions from moves in the prisoner's dilemma game. *Journal of Experimental Social Psychology, 6,* 401–19.

Landes, D. S. (1966). *The rise of capitalism.* New York: Macmillan.

Larson, A. (1988). *Cooperative alliances: A study of entrepreneurship.* Unpublished doctoral dissertation, Harvard Business School.

Lewicki, R. J., Litterer, J. A., Minton, J. W., and Saunders, D. M. (1994). *Negotiation* (2nd ed). Burr Ridge, IL: Richard D. Irwin.

Lincoln, J. R. (1990). Japanese organization and organization theory. In *Research on Organizational Behavior* (vol. 12). Greenwich, CT: JAI Press.

Linville, P. W., and Carlston, D. (1994). Social cognition of the self. In P. G. Devine, D. L. Hamilton, and T. M. Ostrom (eds.), *Social cognition: Its impact on social psychology.* New York: Academic Press.

MacAulay, S. (1963). Noncontractual relations in business: A preliminary study. *American Sociology Review, 28,* 55–67.

Murnighan, J. K. (1991). *The dynamics of bargaining games.* Englewood Cliffs, NJ: Prentice-Hall.

Ouchi, W. G. (1980). Markets, bureaucracies and clans. *Administrative Science Quarterly, 25,* 129–41.

Parsons, T. (1960). *Structure and process in modern society.* New York: The Free Press.

Pfeffer, J., and Salancik, G. (1978). *The extended control of organizations.* New York: Harper & Row.

Polanyi, K. (1957). *The great transformation.* Boston: Beacon.

Porter, M. E. (1980). *Competitive strategy: Techniques for analyzing industries and competitors.* New York: The Free Press.

Powell, W. W. (1990). Neither market nor hierarchy: Network forms of organization. In B. M. Staw and L. L. Cummings (eds.), *Research in organizational behavior* (volume 12, pp. 295–336). Greenwich, CT: JAI Press.

Pruitt, D. (1972). Methods for resolving differences of interest: A theoretical analysis. *Journal of Social Issues, 28,* 133–54.

Putallaz, M., and Sheppard, B. (1992). Conflict management and social competence. In C. U. Shantz and W. W. Hartup (eds.), *Conflict in child and adolescent development.* New York: Cambridge University Press.

Sheppard, B. H., and Tuchinsky, M. (in press). Micro OB and the network organization. In R. Kramer and T. Tyler (eds.) *Trust in organizations.* Beverly Hills, CA: Sage.

Sherif, M., Harvey, D. J., White, B. J., Hood, W. R., and Sherif, C. W. (1961). *Intergroup conflict and cooperation: The robbers cave experiment.* Norman, OK: Institute of Group Relations.

Sitkin, S. B., and Stickel, D. (in press). The road to hell . . . The dynamics of distrust in an era of quality management. In R. Kramer and T. Tyler (eds.), *Trust in organizations.* Beverly Hills, CA: Sage.

Smith, Adam. ([1776] 1976). *An inquiry into the nature and causes of the wealth of nations.* Oxford: Clarendon Press.

Smitka, M. (1991). *Competitive ties: Subcontracting in the Japanese automotive industry.* New York: Columbia University Press.

Teece, D. (1986). Profiting from technological innovation: Implications for integration, collaboration, licensing, and public policy. *Research Policy, 15*(6), 785–805.

Thompson, J. D. (1967). *Organizations in action.* New York: McGraw-Hill.

Tichy, N. (1973). An analysis of clique formation and structure in organizations. *Administrative Science Quarterly, 18,* 194–208.

Wheelwright, S. C., and Clark, K. B. (1992). *Revolutionizing product development.* New York: The Free Press.

Williamson, O. E. (1975). *Markets and hierarchies.* New York: The Free Press.

_____. (1985). *The economic institution of capitalism.* New York: The Free Press.

Womack, J. P., Jones, D. T., and Roos, D. (1991). *The machine that changed the world.* New York: Harper Perennial.

Trade Routes: The Manager's Network of Relationships

Robert E. Kaplan

[B.J. Sparksman] had a good working relationship with his four bosses and a close mentor-protégé relationship with one of them. He had cordial-to-good relations with his peers, some of whom were friends and all of whom were aware of his track record . . . He also had a good working relationship with many of the subordinates of his peers (hundreds of people) based mostly on his reputation. B.J. had a close and strong working relationship with all but one of his main direct reports because they respected him, because he was the boss, and because he had promoted some of them into their current positions . . . B.J. also knew the vast majority of his subordinates' subordinates, if only by reputation, the fact that he was the boss, and the fact that he tried to treat them fairly and with respect. Outside the firm, B.J. maintained fairly strong relationships with dozens of top people in firms that were important clients for his organization . . . . He also had relationships with dozens of other important people in his local community.

John P. Kotter, *The General Managers* (Free Press, 1982)

Not all managers have a network that explodes in all directions like this one. But it is increasingly the fate of modern managers at all levels of today's institutions to work with a large and varied set of people in- and outside their organizations. A network is a reciprocating set of relationships that stabilizes the manager's world and gives it predictability.

Networks can stretch horizontally as well as vertically, as Exhibit 1 shows. The vertical sector of a network often includes not only boss and immediate subordinates, but also one's boss's superiors as well as one's subordinates' subordinates. The lateral sector encompasses people at the same level (peers) and at lower and higher levels (lateral subordinates and lateral superiors). The lateral relationship also includes people who are outside the organization (external contacts).

The literature on leadership and management has been preoccupied with superior-subordinate relationships and has paid much less attention to lateral relationships. Because of this and because most managers spend most of their time not with superiors and subordinates but with people outside of the vertical channel, this article will highlight managers' lateral relationships.

Lateral relationships are important to the manager, whatever the manager's line of work and station in organizational life. Take the case of a lower-level manager in an inner-city manpower agency who directed a program that taught job-search skills to

EXHIBIT 1   The Sectors of a Manager's Network

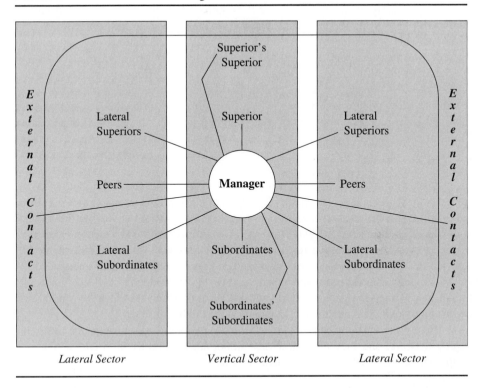

unemployed adults. In addition to his superior and his program staff, several peers were also indispensable to him and his program. To send participants to his program along with the appropriate paperwork, he depended on two managers who ran skill-training programs and another who was in charge of the agency's intake function. He also sorely needed the cooperation of the payroll clerks (lateral subordinates) to put the new participants who trickled into the program on the payroll, to pay both partici-pants and staff, and to clear up any payroll snafus promptly. Furthermore, he depended on the purchasing manager to authorize him to buy equipment and supplies—made difficult by the fact that it always took several calls to get through to the purchasing manager. The program manager could not function without recourse to his lateral rela-tionships. (*Note:* This example, and all other examples in the text not attributed to other authors, come from 55 interviews we conducted with managers and from infor-mal observations made during 10 management-development programs.)

From an entirely different walk of organizational life, the chief executive officer of Lockheed, Daniel Haughton, relied no less on lateral relationships. According to John Newhouse ("The Sporting Game," *The New Yorker,* July 5, 1982), in the late 1960s Lockheed Corporation began its program to build a wide-bodied plane, the L-1011, and in 1969 contracted with Rolls-Royce for the British aircraft engine com-pany to design and manufacture the huge jet engine, the RB211, for the aircraft. By early 1971 Rolls-Royce, with the job half completed and costs running far ahead of projections, nearly went under. To save the contract, Lockheed, itself in financial crisis, had to help Rolls-Royce secure renewed financial backing from the British government. This quest plunged Haughton into months of negotiations with lateral contacts, all of them external to Lockheed. These included Lord Carrington, the British Secretary of State for Defence; Edward Heath, the British Prime Minister; a syndicate of Lockheed's 24 bankers, who had to decide whether to save the L-1011 or put Lockheed into receivership; and the six U.S. airlines that had ordered L-1011s and were alarmed at the prospect of either not receiving their planes or being asked to agree to a higher price. The U.S. government, interested in supporting the aerospace industry during the 1971 recession, got involved through President Richard Nixon and Assistant Secretary of Defense David Packard.

After six months of feverish traveling and innumerable meetings, Haughton put together an agreement acceptable to his corporation and all the lateral parties involved. The British government pledged to pay for all further costs of supplying the engine; Lockheed agreed to pay $180,000 more for each engine; the six customer airlines agreed to pay $140,000 more for each airplane; Lockheed's creditor banks agreed to extend the corporation's line of credit, provided the U.S. government guaranteed repayment; and Congress narrowly approved a bill that guaranteed Lockheed's loans. As Newhouse wrote, Haughton is credited with accomplishing this feat "by tireless efforts, diplomatic skill, and the fact that he was trusted by all sides."

Both of these examples point up how important lateral relationships are in a manager's network, and they also show how important reciprocity is to lateral relationships. These relationships are the manager's trade routes.

WHY TRADE?

Managers enter trade relationships with lateral network members for one compelling reason: They depend on these people and literally can't get their jobs done without them. Like nations, managers are not self-sufficient and must engage in "foreign trade" to get what they need. Referring to large corporations, Rosabeth Moss Kanter, in *Men and Women of the Corporation,* observed that "Beyond the people in the most routine functions, no one has within a small domain all of the things he or she needs to carry out his or her job." Managers may be influential, but they cannot escape being dependent. An executive interviewed by John P. Kotter for *Power in Management* described the plight of the manager:

> My son, my wife, and many of my professional friends have very inaccurate conceptions of what I really do for a living . . . Most of these misperceptions are based on the implicit assumption that I somehow have control over all or most of the resources I need to do my job . . . In reality, of course, in addition to my direct subordinates, there are hundreds of people whom I have no direct control over but who can affect the performance of my job. At least two dozen of these people are crucial . . . All of this adds up, and leaves me in a much more vulnerable position than most people realize.

Managers open trade routes with their peers because without these informal arrangements managers are rendered powerless and ineffective. In an anthropological study of informal relationships—which he called cliques—many of which were horizontal, Melville Dalton (*Men Who Manage,* Wiley, 1959) found effective managers were "adroit at moving in and out of clique activities, [but less effective managers] . . . were unable to form cliques or to participate in clique behavior to win the informal strength eventually necessary for larger official action."

That managers have little or no formal authority over their counterparts in other spheres accentuates the need for managers to create some basis for cooperation. Because they are in no position to command cooperation or the resources they need, managers resort, in most cases, to trade: They obtain what they need by providing others with what they, in turn, require.

RECIPROCITY: THE FIRST PRINCIPLE OF TRADE

Unlike nations, managers usually do not trade goods; they trade services. Put another way: Managers trade power, or the ability to get things done. They provide services to others in exchange for the services that they themselves require.

What kinds of services do managers need from their lateral sector? They need people to provide accurate information, make technical expertise available, give advice, provide political backing, authorize changes, and lend moral support. Because managers are often pressed for time, they usually need these things quickly. As one manager told us: "I've worked at building my contacts in other departments so that when I need something done that involves another department, I have someone who will give me a fast, cooperative answer."

Managers obtain these services by setting up reciprocal relationships. They come to the lateral sector with "salable commodities." Dalton found that purchasing agents, for example, go to great lengths to learn about the products so that they can deal with company engineers on equal terms. As one manager in the health care field put it: "You persist and, hell, you make a lot of friends in this business. I do things for them and they do things for me." In her study of one corporation, Kanter found that:

> Peer alliances often worked through direct exchange of favors. On lower levels information was traded; on higher levels bargaining and trade often took place around good performers and job openings. In a senior executive's view, it worked like this: A good job becomes available. A list of candidates is generated. That's refined down to three or four. That is circulated to a select group that has an opportunity to look it over. Then they can make bargains among themselves. A manager commented, "There's lots of 'I owe you one.' " If you can accumulate enough chits, that helps you get what you need; but then, of course, people have to be in a position to cash them in.

Managers get what they want, provided they have what their fellow managers need. Commodities have value only if they are relevant to another person's needs. If manager A, for example, is responsible for succession planning and influences people's careers, but manager B, in his mid-40s, no longer yearns for rapid promotion, then A's power in this respect is lost on B.

Because managers can only get in proportion to what they can give, they work hard to accumulate valued resources. One executive told us how he built a knowledge base when he took over corporate employee relations:

> I wanted a base that was different from what the groups reporting to me had and also from what my superiors had so I established a series of contacts in other American industries until I knew on a first-name basis my counterpart at IBM, TRW, Procter & Gamble, Du Pont, and General Electric, and I could get their input—input which the people in my organization didn't have.

By developing exclusive sources of information, this executive operated on the principle that power accrues to the person with resources that are not readily available elsewhere.

When managers trade, they may sometimes give and get at the same time. Dalton described how a horizontal clique of managers coalesces to fend off a common danger—for example, a threatened reorganization or the introduction of an unwanted control system. These managers simultaneously lend each other support for the common cause.

But managers often do not reciprocate a service at the time that it is given. Because it is only over time that a balance has to be struck, managers can take turns being of service to each other. The giver obligates the receiver, who later discharges the obligation. A university administrator, lobbying for a state appropriation to support a construction project on campus, cashed in on a series of favors he had done for a former state official: "When he left state government, I had helped him get a job first as the head of a community agency and then as a staff member for a congressional committee. During the fight for the appropriation, he became a key guy for me. He was instrumental in getting the Catholic church to apply pressure to the governor." Managers will allow network members to open charge accounts so long as the debt is later repaid in needed services. They exchange help for the promise of future help.

In addition to promises, managers will also accept another kind of intangible return for services rendered: recognition. One party does another a favor, and the other party completes the exchange by expressing appreciation. Peter M. Blau (*Bureaucracy in Modern Society,* Wiley, 1964) found that law enforcement agents regularly exchanged intangible for tangible commodities by consulting on difficult cases:

> By asking for advice [an agent] implicitly pays his respect to the superior proficiency of his colleague . . . The consultant gains prestige, in return for which he is willing to devote some time to the consultation and permit it to disrupt his work . . . The expert whose advice was often sought by colleagues [also] obtained social evidence of his superior abilities.

Similarly, experienced managers who give advice and counsel to a junior manager get confirmation of their status as well as the satisfaction of bringing a promising individual along.

Managers also place a value on another sort of recognition—the kind that affects their reputation, job security, and careers. One manager stated flatly: "My performance rating depends on the feedback my superiors receive from my lateral contacts." It is well known that careers rise and fall with the impressions formed by higher-level managers. So if recognition seems an insubstantial form of payment now, it can translate into quite tangible returns later on.

The principle of reciprocity may seem obvious, but some managers don't have an instinctive appreciation of it. A manager from a Big Eight accounting firm, for example, attended a management training program because he had been told that he was, inexplicitly to him, "threatening" to other people. Because of this threatening quality, his relationships within the firm had suffered. He discovered in the training program that, being extremely ambitious, he single-mindedly pursued his own agendas to the exclusion of what anyone else might want or need. He didn't create reciprocal relationships: His relationships were long on take and short on give. He learned that to reduce the threat to others and to build connections, he needed to invest in other people's agendas.

A cautionary note: Giving is always, at some level, self-interested, done to tuck away an expectation of later return or to reap a psychic reward. None of this is objectionable or counterproductive, although it can slip into manipulation. A wry example is the cartoon showing a manager on the phone saying to a colleague (his hand over the mouthpiece): "It's the copier rep asking how my children are—must be contract time." When the psychic or social satisfactions one offers are self-serving and insincere, the attempt at giving backfires.

TRADE ADVANTAGES

When managers go after services from people in the lateral sector of their networks, they may bring power beyond their willingness to respond in kind. Four factors further empower managers vis-à-vis their trading partners: their reputation, their alliances, the importance of their position to the organization, and their favored standing with the network member.

Reputation

Power goes to those managers with a reputation for using power well—that is, for making things happen with the resources available to them. People are quicker to support individuals who consistently get results. The better a person's reputation, the more likely one's investment in that person will pay off.

Managers earn a good reputation to the extent that they have succeeded at extraordinary and visible assignments. Those managers who take on extraordinary projects—pulling an organization out of a tailspin, presiding over the development of a new product, redefining the organization's mission—win recognition that, in turn, makes it easier for them to mobilize support for their next undertaking.

Managers also earn and preserve their reputations by linking themselves, as much as possible, to winning causes. As one executive counseled:

> You have to know enough about your place in the organization that you don't take on the impossible task. Even if the idea is a good one, it may be an idea ahead of its time, or it may be beyond your scope in the organization.

By taking a realistic view of how much power they have and by gauging accurately a project's prospects for success, managers build a track record that enhances their attractiveness as trading partners, thus increasing their power.

A manager's opportunity for advancement, perceived or real, can also enhance his or her reputation. Other managers, on the lookout for powerful people to ally themselves with, are more than ready to hitch themselves to a rising star. In this case, managers moving up gain power because of the promise of future power accruing to themselves and to those who join forces with them.

Alliances

As managers enter a transaction with any one person, their power to get what they want derives, in part, from their connections to others. A glamorous example was Philip Graham, later the publisher of the *Washington Post,* who worked in a small group that President Franklin Roosevelt put together on the eve of World War II to mobilize American industry for the war effort. As David Halberstam described the activities of Philip Graham in his book *The Powers That Be* (Dell, 1979):

> He was brilliant at his job, cutting through red tape, getting things done, slipping past the bureaucracy which was in no way as passionate as he was about preparing America for war. He was smart and clever and fearless and dazzlingly well connected . . . He was also Frankfurter's protégé and Eugene Meyer's son-in-law and important people tended to take his phone calls as they did not take the phone calls of most twenty-five-year-olds.
>
> [Felix Frankfurter was at that time Chief Justice of the Supreme Court, and Eugene Meyer was a wealthy industrial magnate who later bought the *Washington Post* and made Graham publisher.]

Managers can operate laterally to the extent that they are well-connected elsewhere. In his study of gangs, William Whyte found that a gang leader's reputation in the community depended on his standing in the gang (the converse was also true). Managers launching innovative projects enjoy more success in recruiting peers as collaborators if they have won the support of top management for the project—and again the converse is also true.

Alliances help managers because they give potential trade partners an added incentive to help. If other powerful people support a project, then it looks like a better bet to someone being approached for help. In general, allies are a reason to go along with a request lest one lose favor with these people and hurt one's trading relationships with them.

Position

Managers are only as important as the positions they occupy. If the position is critical to the organization, then the manager acquires a kind of legitimate power to make demands on others for cooperation. As one manager said to us: "My peers are responsive to me because the functions that I manage are the lifeblood of the organization. I manage the people who provide readings on their vital signs, and consequently my presence in their office implies that there's a vital-sign concern . . . that needs to be dealt with."

Many times a critical position accrues power because the position is located in a function indispensable to the organization. This puts the manager in charge of a "critical contingency," as Gerald R. Salancik and Jeffrey Pfeffer put it (*Organizational Dynamics,* Winter, 1977). Kanter has noted that "For the system, the most power goes to those people in those functions that provide greater control over what the organization currently finds problematic: sales and marketing people when markets are competitive [and so on]." In a computer company like IBM, for example, the engineers who design new products and the production managers who get the products out are one-down to the marketing managers who, in the highly volatile computer industry, find and create the demand for new products. Managers in a function of strategic importance to the organization can make claims on the cooperation of their peers in the name of service to the organization.

Favored Standing

With some trading partners, managers achieve a sort of "favored nation status." Managers have an edge if they are on friendly terms with lateral contacts, share a common work history, or share similar demographic characteristics.

Several mayors in the study done by John P. Kotter and Paul Lawrence created cooperative relationships on the basis of friendship. Acquaintances also give the manager leverage, although mayors who cultivated numerous acquaintances spent many an evening at social and political functions. For the satisfaction and utility gained, managers develop personal as well as work connections with colleagues, Kotter has argued. A high-level manager in a hospital commented: "I spend a fair amount of time knowing the personal and professional side of the people I work with. I'll know that they play golf or that they are working on such and such system. It's never all business." In a study of the lateral relations of purchasing agents, George Strauss (*Administrative Science Quarterly,* June 1962) found that most agents prefer to deal with friends, that friendship gets proposals accepted more quickly, but that it is a mistake to rely on friendship alone.

Managers have a leg up if they share a common work history with the people on whom they must depend. A manager's track record is enhanced in the eyes of others when those others worked to achieve the same successes. This is power gained from "past cooperative victories," as Dalton put it. A financial manager explained the good response he gets from accountants in City Hall as follows: "For two years I worked closely with the current deputy controller and we had a good relationship. We still have. That's one reason he stayed here with me till midnight last week working on those audits." There is something almost romantically binding about accomplishing a difficult task together. A history of successfully working together creates a responsiveness that makes life easy for the manager. The program manager mentioned in the beginning of this article explained the good response he got from the payroll department in these terms: "The payroll manager and I have worked closely together for some time and know each other's styles. Usually she'll lean over backwards, and I'll do the same. She'll even respond to my secretary's requests."

A shared history one step removed—holding the same job at different times—can also pay dividends. A manager reported being on the same wavelength with a peer who succeeded him in a planning and development job: "Because I had his job before I got this one, I understand his problems in a way that I don't understand some of the other problems." This peer obviously gained an advantage with the manager, who identified so closely with the peer's situation. Herein lies the logic of job rotation, a common practice in some Japanese firms.

When a manager enters an exchange, it is more likely to go well if, other things being equal, the demographic characteristics of the other party match up with those of the manager. Similarities in skin color, gender, age, country of origin, and socioeconomic status smooth the way for each party to identify with and reach the other.

This is not to say that demographic differences inevitably raise barriers. In one case, a black manager formed a strong relationship with a white manager at his level because they both came of age during the same period. "We both went to college in the '60s and share enthusiasms from that time. We make references that go over most other people's heads." Their generational commonality overrode the racial difference.

Some factors that empower managers lie outside the relationship to the other individual—the manager's reputation, alliances, and position. Other factors lie within the relationship itself—favored standing with the other party stemming from friendship, shared work history, and similar demographic characteristics. Yet another asset, discussed next, is the skill that managers bring to interpersonal transactions.

DIPLOMATIC SKILL

As in foreign trade, trade among managers depends on the diplomatic ability of those involved. Managers strike deals and deliver services by making contact with one another, and they trade no more successfully than they handle the interpersonal medium. The requisite diplomatic skills all boil down to a talent for give-and-take accompanied by a sense of when to use which skill. One manager, adept at having brief, productive conversations, was described as having an "excellent quick-contact style." But invariably using the same mode of contact, no matter how adeptly, leads to ruin, or at least to impaired effectiveness. One high-level manager advised: "You have to have good communication skills, but you also have to know when to key in on some skills and when not to."

To trade successfully, managers need to call upon several skills, each of which entails versatility.

Varying One's Participation in Conversations

To achieve give-and-take in conversations, managers must be able to talk and to listen, as the occasion requires. Human beings seem to be divided into two categories— "producers," who in conversations specialize in producing words, ideas, information; and "elicitors" who specialize in bringing out other people. Managers who overspecialize in either of these roles hurt their effectiveness. They must be able both to hold up their end of a conversation and to take in the contributions of others.

One manager we know, for example, prided himself in being a good communicator. "KISS" was the way he put it: Keep It Short and Sweet. He had even developed his own ABCs of effective communication—A (for Accurate), B (for Brief), C (for Clear), D (for Direct), and so on. He was a skilled and, in spite of his credo, long-winded producer but not nearly as good an elicitor and listener. He had a habit of remaining impassive, giving no facial reinforcement, when other people spoke. And when someone disagreed with him, he either ignored the comment or bristled visibly. This deficiency hurt him as a conversational partner; he dealt out a good deal better than he took in.

Another dimension of conversational flexibility is the ability to vary the length of a conversation. Some managers favor a hit-and-run approach: Sit people down, hit them with your issue, and run off before they can respond. Others are notorious for lengthy conversations, no matter the issue. The trick is to be equally at ease in either mode. Frederick Richardson (cited by Leonard Sayles) offers the following words of wisdom: Beware of overly regular contact rhythms.

Apportioning Contact Time

How do managers distribute the time they can spend with other people? While, as we have seen, managers must invest in relationships, job demands should determine how the manager apportions contact time. Form should follow function. The 15 general managers that Kotter studied did invest most heavily in the relationships they needed most.

But, like conversational handicaps, distortions in contact patterns can hamper managers. Responding to their emotional needs instead of to job demands, managers may avoid relationships that make them uncomfortable. Managers who are phobic about people with greater power may neglect upward relationships. Managers of staff functions have jobs that dictate heavy contact with people at the same level, but they may choose instead to associate with their subordinates out of distaste for the conflict and tension touched off by lateral relationships. The rub is that neglected relationships won't produce any of the things that managers need.

Repertoire of Influence Tactics

As they go in quest of help, managers encounter a wide range of interpersonal situations that require a wide repertoire of behaviors for reaching people. In lateral relationships managers are not in a position to give orders, so they resort to persuasion, camaraderie, negotiation, bargaining. Lateral relationships put a premium on knowing when to act tough (for example, when conflict is built into the situation) and when to use softer methods (for example, when there is basic agreement). The program manager mentioned previously varied his approach according to how much resistance he ran into: "Depending on how other people respond, I can go from being pleasant to very dominating."

In Kotter's study of general managers, the better performers used a larger set of influence tactics and did so with greater skill. "The 'excellent' performers asked, encouraged, cajoled, praised, rewarded, demanded, manipulated, and generally motivated others with great skill in face-to-face situations." The managers' arsenal also typically included references to sports and family as well as liberal doses of joking and humor.

Mixing the Mode of Contact

In doing business, managers have a number of options available to them—the telephone, written communication (including, in some companies, electronic mail), and face-to-face contact, which can take the form of scheduled or unscheduled meetings held in groups or on a one-to-one basis.

Face-to-face contact is an immediate and powerful medium. Of the various forms of such contact, group meetings serve some important purposes, but there is evidence to suggest that one-to-one contact is the sine qua non of managerial life: Richardson found that the more effective research and development managers in his sample spent 45 to 65 percent of their time in one-to-one contact. On the other side of the coin, Peter Drucker has cautioned managers against spending more than 40 percent of their time in group meetings.

The smart money is on using the different mediums not singly but in happy combinations. Group meetings should be accompanied by premeeting huddles with key individuals to line up support and by post-meeting check-ins to clarify action taken and to smooth any ruffled feathers. Memos, when necessary, are more likely to get results when accompanied by a conversation to warn, clarify, explain, prod, sell, or soothe.

Fluency in a Number of Languages

On the international scene, it pays to know the languages of other countries. In organizational life, it helps to speak the specialized languages of the organization, however haltingly. A highly placed manager in a medical setting said: "With a systems person I talk a little differently than when I talk with a professor in obstetrics and gynecology or to a dean, or a clerk, or what have you. This is particularly important in this organization where we have an array of services all the way from housekeeping to neurosurgery." Among the 20 mayors whom Kotter and Lawrence studied, for example, the capacity to speak the different interpersonal languages of the community varied greatly. At one extreme was a mayor who always acted like a corporate executive, no matter what the setting. At the other was Richard C. Lee of New Haven, Connecticut, whose repertoire was extensive. Lee was described by Kotter and Lawrence as follows:

> When he is with the Irish, his ethnic background comes out and he looks like he grew up in Dublin. When he is at the university, he is a wise old man. Over at the Chamber he is a shrewd capitalist. With the unions he is a cigar-chomping tough guy. He's not just "acting" either. He really knows how to talk the language of each of those groups.

Lee didn't acquire this fluency out of thin air: It was born of a broad range of developmental experiences, including jobs in several different major institutions in the city and intensive contact with the city's major ethnic and racial groups.

Managers are only as interpersonally skilled as their organizations allow them to be. One organization we know of cramped the style of its managers by dealing heavily in one medium—the memo. Because of too much written contact and too little face-to-face contact, the pace of managerial work slowed to a crawl. Whatever the predispositions of the individual managers, they became captive to the overall pattern. In the next section, we look at other restraints of trade.

TRADE BARRIERS

In trying to establish lateral trade relationships, managers sometimes come up against formidable barriers. People don't get along; they are rivals; they work for different organizations; they are separated by potent demographic differences. Of the many possible barriers, we look at just three: functional differences, functional and level differences combined, and disparities in degrees of dependence.

Functional Differences

It is no mean task to transact business in the no-man's-land of interdepartmental relations," in Sayles's phrase. The parties to a cross-functional relationship belong to units with different goals, different interests, different cultures, and different languages. They often report to different people, further widening the gap. Finally, they may have little occasion to interact and therefore little opportunity to accommodate to each other's styles of working and relating. In an interview with the author, one executive described how key players at high levels assumed different organizational postures in the following way:

> Here you have a vice president of manufacturing whose performance is measured by the "numbers"—how many good pieces the factory gets into the tote box, rework and scrap figures, whether the production schedules are met at the end of the month. And then you have a human resources executive who is responding to a different set of measurements and whose accomplishments may or may not support the manufacturing executive. And then there is the sales executive pushing, as he should, for finished, high-quality units he can sell to the customers. So executives are people coming from different places, responding to different pressures. Whoever you are—the chief executive officer, the president, or a vice president—you have to build networks with all those people.

As we have already seen, the key to building networks across jurisdictions is to swap services—that is, to find a basis for reciprocal action.

Functional Plus Level Differences

Trade barriers climb higher when the functional difference inherent in lateral relationships is augmented by a hierarchical difference. The added difference is sure to make life difficult for the manager when it is charged with organizational significance. In a chemical plant, for example, second- and third-level supervisors were separated by an unwritten corporate rule that kept people from ascending beyond second-level management without an engineering degree, symbolized by a ring made of iron and worn on the right pinkie finger—thus the "iron ring syndrome." As a result, most second-level managers had worked their way up from the ranks of the workers and were going no further, and all third-level managers had college educations and varying degrees of opportunities to advance further. Thus lateral relationships between second- and third-level managers posed a particular challenge, and diagonal pairs of managers on the two levels had widely varying degrees of success in meeting this challenge.

Relationships with lateral superiors often give managers fits. The upward diagonal relationships can be troublesome for a number of reasons, itemized by Rosemary Stewart:

> [Lateral superiors] can be important to one's career, so making an unfavorable impression can matter more than with peers: They may be in a position to trim down a project that one is putting forward; they may be more demanding than peers in their service requirements; and they will probably be less familiar than one's own boss so that it will be harder to judge how they will react.

Lacking the immediate superior's responsibility to the individual, the lateral superior may be inaccessible and unresponsive. A woman manager in charge of her organization's affirmative action program desperately needed support and information from a lateral superior and his subordinate managers. She attributed his resistance to the notion that "He is one of the worst for resenting somebody who's not on his level communicating with him or feeling like they have a right to." Powerless because of a combination of gender, function, and level, she had no recourse with him. "I get practically nothing from his subordinates, either; any information I get from them has to be okayed by him."

In their attempts to build lateral upward relationships, managers are often hampered by scanty opportunities to interact. A manager in a food-service firm worried that his underdeveloped relationships with lateral superiors would hurt his chances for promotion: "I don't promote myself well. I don't mention casually that I've done something great. I don't joke or tell stories or give presentations to get visibility because those things are much less natural to me than personal relationships. But around what can I develop a personal relationship with them?"

The key to building relationships with lateral superiors is finding legitimate reasons for contact. If managers appear to be currying favor, they may only set the relationship back. It is best to cultivate such a relationship in the normal course of one's work by, for example, serving on the same task force or executing an assignment in the other manager's area. Special projects put the manager in touch with lateral superiors and give the manager a chance to shine. Kanter gives an example of how a relationship with a lateral superior might unfold:

> One salesman with a problem he wanted to solve for a customer described Indsco as "like the Army, Air Force, and Navy—we have a formal chain of command." The person who could make the decision on his problem was four steps removed from him, not in hierarchical rank but according to operating procedure. Ordinarily, he would not be able to go directly to him, but they had developed a relationship over a series of sales meetings, during which the more powerful person had said, "Please drop by anytime you're at headquarters." So the salesman found an occasion to "drop by," and in the course of the casual conversation mentioned his situation. It was solved immediately.

Unequal Dependence

Relationships with lateral superiors are a special case of relating to people who depend on the manager less than the manager depends on them. Managers can't readily set up a reciprocal relationship unless they are in a position to reciprocate. The manager's influence with someone is tied to how much the other person depends on the manager. Managers of staff functions that line managers regard as inessential run into this roadblock. As a result, they have to work harder at being acceptable personally. They also must find a way to sell their service to their unreceptive peers and thereby offset their own heavy dependence.

Consider the plight of a manager who, as a result of a reorganization, was assigned a new position designed to give the U.S. domestic organization greater control over operations in other countries. His job was to bridge a gap between headquarters and operations in South America. Because of the matrix arrangement, he had no direct control over the South American managers he had to work with. He recounted: "I made some friends, but basically I was as welcome as a skunk in church. They couldn't tell me not to come to Peru or Chile—but once I got there, they said: 'So what?' I fought the battle for two years, flying everywhere. But overall it was a very unhappy experience." In fact, he tried to overcome his peers' resistance by finding a way to be useful to them. "I had to get inside people's knickers by understanding their problems and bringing help. I was more welcome if I could bring something to the party." Unfortunately, this manager's sound strategy of trying to induce a need met with only limited success.

Building networks is tantamount to bridging gaps. The more differences that coincide in a relationship, the greater the gap and the harder a manager must work to form a relationship. Managers cross divides by doing the things described in the last three sections—setting up reciprocity, putting themselves in advantageous positions, and making good contact. No matter what the gap, the only alternative is to set about creating a successful history by getting down to work so that the bits of productive exchanges eventually add up to something worthwhile for the manager.

Growing Networks

Organizations cannot grant networks to managers. Managers must cultivate works. This is something that managers do deliberately and also something that happens naturally. Asked how he goes about cultivating relationships, one manager said:

> It depends on what you consider cultivating. I could argue that every time I answer the phone or every time someone drops in my office, I'm cultivating a contact.

As managers field requests, relationships develop almost on their own.

How long does it take to develop a network? If there are no big obstacles, relationships for getting routine things done can sprout almost like weeds. But relationships strong enough to stand up under heavy pressure are another story. Sturdy relationships take time to develop. Executives with many years in the same organization especially value their long-time contacts. An executive who has so far spent his entire 25-year career in one textile firm asserted: "I can't overestimate the importance of good interpersonal relationships. Growing up in the company, I have worked with all these guys. I know them; they know me. These relationships help tremendously in a crisis situation or when you need something quickly." History matters. Relationships gain strength as both parties show that they can and will come through for each other.

Managers have no choice but to keep growing their networks. They never have the luxury of sitting back and saying: "Now I can relax: I've got all the connections I need." Networks are dynamic, like the mobile society we live in.

Every time managers change jobs, as the upwardly mobile ones do every two years or so, they must rebuild their networks. Kotter found that general managers spend the first six months in a new job investing heavily in forming new bonds. The more different the new job is from the manager's previous experience, the more overhauling the network will need. When managers parachute into a different organization in a totally different field, they may need to rebuild their networks from scratch. On the other hand, when a manager moves to the next level or a neighboring function, he or she can get away with less network-building because large portions of the existing network then become portable.

If managers stay put, the world nevertheless changes around them. Faces change, with the rate of change linked to rates of turnover and mobility in that organization. The job of growing networks is never done.

Harvesting Networks

Networks aren't built to serve some vague global purpose, but to get help on the manager's specific tasks. To reap the full benefit of their networks, managers must excel not only at growing but also at harvesting. Managers get work done by activating their relationships selectively. Leaders call upon what Warren Bennis called their "executive constellations," by forming task forces for a particular assignment and reassembling others for a different assignment. John Friend, John Power, and C. J. L. Yewlett *(Public Planning: The Intercorporate Dimension,* Tavistock, 1964) stated that to make effective use of a network, managers mobilize their networks "in an intelligently selective way," which depends on knowing both the structure of the problem and the structure of the human relationships around the problem. A hospital administrator displayed this sense in talking about how he conceptualized the startup of a new project."

> I knew everybody that this project was going to impact in one way or another—systems, fiscal, the medical school, medical records, on down the line. I had to use my technical knowledge and the personal rapport that I had or didn't have with the individuals. I was kind of making a web of people and trying to bring them together to get something done.

To launch the project, he involved the people affected, calling upon relationships he already had and developing new ones he didn't have. Innovative projects in particular put a premium on the manager's ability to activate relationships—to define the project and to build a coalition of sponsors and collaborators to implement the project.

The notion of a network is simply another lens through which to view the work of a manager. Although fast becoming a cliché, the concept is nevertheless useful because it portrays the manager's relationships in context. It affords us a view that is faithful to the complex and richly textured setting in which most managers work.

CONCLUSION

A manager's connections often reach, like tentacles, throughout the organization (and outside it). The *number* of people is striking, but no less so than the diversity. Network members differ on organizational factors such as job, level, history, and future in the organization; on sociological factors such as age, sex, race, religion, ethnic background, education, and socioeconomic status; and on personal factors such as openness to influence, ability to communicate, and commitment to work. It is no small task to establish reliable relationships with so many different people. As a manager of packaging engineering put it, "The manager's role is to keep a friendly relationship with strange bedfellows."

Networks, with their emphasis on peer relationships, seem to have special relevance for middle managers, embedded as they are in a vertical channel and lateral work flow. Walter Tornow and Patrick Pinto *(Journal of Applied Psychology,* 1976), in a job analysis of 433 low-, middle-, and high-level managers, found that middle managers scored higher than the other two groups on "coordinating the efforts of those over whom one has no direct control" and "working across existing organizational boundaries." Middle managers develop a classic Hub-type network, in Stewart's terms; general managers exemplify this type (see the quotation at the beginning of this paper).

But networks are by no means the exclusive preserve of middle managers. According to Stewart, upper-level managers typically use Apex-type networks, which extend primarily downward in the organization and laterally into the outside world. The example of the Lockheed CEO given earlier played up his external relationships, leaving, however, his indispensable downward internal relationships in the background. Kotter found that over the course of their careers, high-level managers may accumulate hundreds, if not thousands, of contacts of varying degrees of importance. One management expert cited by Packard commented that the managers "who have really arrived will be spider-webbed off in several directions by a mysterious cross-hatching."

Lower-level managers may operate in a smaller sphere, both vertically and horizontally, but networks still figure prominently in their work lives. The program manager described in the introduction needed equally his staff to run the program and his peers to support the program, not to mention his boss to run interference. ("If my MasterCard doesn't work, I borrow his American Express card.")

Few managers function autonomously, having what Stewart called a solo network, and even these managers spend a sizeable chunk of their time interacting. Nowhere does John Donne's poetic dictum "No man is an island" apply with greater force than to the world of managers.

SELECTED BIBLIOGRAPHY

The work of four students of managerial relationships provided information for this article. Rosabeth Moss Kanter wrote about power and relationships in *Men and Women of the Corporation* (Basic Books, 1977) and about peer relationships in a *Harvard Business Review* article called "The Middle Manager as Innovator" (July–August 1982). John P. Kotter examined power and dependency in *Power in Management* (AMACOM, 1979), and he treated networks explicitly in the research reported in *Managers in Action* (Wiley, 1976) written with Paul Lawrence, and in *The General Managers* (Free Press, 1982). Leonard Sayles shed light on work-flow relationships and social contact in the manager's job in *Managerial Behavior* (McGraw-Hill, 1966). Finally, Rosemary Stewart in *Contrasts in Management* (McGraw-Hill, 1976) investigated types of networks as they vary with types of managers' jobs.

ACKNOWLEDGMENTS

I would like to thank Mignon Mazique for help as a collaborator at an early stage of the research, David DeVries and Michael Lombardo for their comments on an earlier draft, Bill Drath for his help in imposing conceptual order on a recalcitrant subject, and Alice Warren for indefatigably typing and retyping this paper.

Teams and Group Negotiations

A significant element contributing to the dynamics of any complex negotiation is whether there are more than two parties. Thus far, we have devoted almost all of our attention to negotiation as a dyadic process—the dynamic interaction between negotiator and opponent. Some negotiations *are* exclusively conducted by two parties: a buyer and a seller, a husband and wife, or a boss and subordinate. But many more negotiations—particularly those that occur in organizations—involve other parties. This is increasingly the case as individual organizations become leaner, flatter, less hierarchical, and less formal in an attempt to achieve greater efficiency, agility, and responsiveness.

The negotiators themselves may also represent stakeholders who are not at the table but who are interested in the negotiated outcomes. A union leader represents the rank and file; a diplomat represents a country's government and leadership; a manager represents the senior leadership and owners of the company. Negotiators who represent these "constituencies" are usually given instructions as to how to negotiate and what objectives are to be achieved; in addition, they are held accountable by their constituencies for achieving these objectives. There may also be other parties, such as interested third parties or audiences to the negotiation, who may or may not be directly affected by the negotiations themselves, and who may or may not be able to observe and participate in the process.

When constituencies, third parties, and audiences become involved in the negotiation, their very presence changes the nature of the negotiating dynamics. Experienced negotiators know how to assess the impact and consequences of these other actors on the negotiation process. Moreover, by understanding this impact, they can effectively employ constituencies, audiences, and third parties, either to protect themselves from undue pressures or to increase the pressures on their opponent. When this diversity is represented by negotiation teams, an understanding of the relevant dynamics and processes can improve the bargaining process by building on the strengths teams bring, while avoiding the pitfalls of faulty group process. The articles in this section address these social dynamics.

In the first article, "A Core Model of Negotiation," Thomas Colosi notes that while a great deal of the popular writing on negotiation depicts it as a one-on-one process, much of actual negotiation is, in fact, a rich and complex social interaction. Many negotiators function in teams rather than alone. Moreover, negotiating teams seldom agree among themselves as to their positions on issues. Individuals play different roles within these teams; these different roles often have the consequence of protracting a dispute rather than facilitating its resolution. Finally, as the negotiating team is often composed of organization members who have different job titles and levels of seniority, deliberations within and outside the team are likely to occur across organizational hierarchical levels. The reality, as painted by Colosi, shows how actual negotiations in organizations are often far more complex than the one-on-one dynamics described in textbooks or artificially simulated in class role-plays.

In the second article, "Get Things Done through Coalitions," Margo Vanover suggests that forming coalitions based on common interests can help us achieve negotiation objectives by providing "power through clout." These objectives can be achieved even if that clout tends to be highly issue- or situation-specific. Many of the elements of effective coalition management (commitment, expertise, preparation, etc.) are also those usually prescribed for effective negotiation in general, highlighting the strongly "negotiationlike" nature of the coalition process. Vanover's examples illustrate the importance of coalitions, and she offers a number of specific, useful suggestions for building broad support and for focusing this coalition of support on the key opponent. Her suggestions include ways to choose a leader, guidelines for making a coalition successful, and a valuable list of 20 tips for making coalitions work.

The third and final article in this section, "The Negotiation of Settlements: A Team Sport," by practitioner James Zack, builds on both Colosi and Vanover by providing both descriptive and prescriptive information in the rich, real environment of construction management. Of particular interest to readers is Zack's reminder of the importance of utility, compatibility, and issue clarity in assembling negotiating teams. Zack identifies team negotiation as an activity best suited to the integrative or collaborative approach of win-win negotiation. He contrasts this team orientation with what he labels "traditional" (chiefly competitive or distributive) negotiation, to the benefit of the integrative approach.

A Core Model of Negotiation

Thomas Colosi

THE CONVENTIONAL PERCEPTION OF BILATERAL NEGOTIATION

Negotiations are typically depicted as involving one group sitting across a bargaining table from a second. One side presents its demands or proposals to the other, and a discussion or debate follows. Counter-proposals and compromises are offered. When the offers are eventually accepted on both sides, the dispute is settled and an agreement is signed.

Within this model, all the interesting and relevant action is presumed to occur back and forth between the two sides. The model assumes that each party is monolithic, even if represented by bargaining teams. The way in which the participants are billed—labor versus management, prisoners versus guards, environmentalists versus industry—reflects the same monolithic assumption; that is, that all team members share the same set of demands, agree on a strategy for handling the opposition, and have come to the table with equal enthusiasm for the negotiating process.

Unfortunately, the conventional model of negotiation obscures much of the richness and complexity of the bargaining process. In practice, bargaining teams are seldom monolithic. Team members often have conflicting goals and values; some sort of consensus must develop internally before agreement can be reached with the other side. While some students of negotiation have recognized the importance of this internal bargaining, conventional models do not explain their relationship to the functioning of the larger process. By contrast, the model developed in this article attempts to incorporate this dimension and thus to present a richer and more realistic view of negotiation.

For the sake of simplicity, the model presented below assumes—at this point—just two bargaining teams. Later in the article it is expanded to incorporate multiparty situations; conceivably it might also be applied to cases involving just two individuals. In any event, the model is intended to describe the structure or core of negotiation, regardless of the particular issues at stake, the identity of the parties, or the sector (public or private) in which the dispute takes place.

STABILIZERS, NONSTABILIZERS, AND QUASI MEDIATORS

Within each team, negotiators usually hold quite different attitudes. Some negotiators tend to settle at any cost. They may be called *stabilizers*. They seek agreement with the other side to avoid the disruptive consequences of nonsettlement, particularly such lengthy, expensive, or disruptive alternatives as litigation, strikes, demonstrations, riots, and wars. A second general type, the *nonstabilizers,* do not particularly like the negotiation process. Nonstabilizers tend to disagree with most of the proposals of their own team and all of the counter-proposals of the other side. They would rather see disruption through raw contests of will and power than compromise on a given position. The terms nonstabilizers would accept are far more stringent than those to which the stabilizers would agree.

Finally, in the middle is a third type, the *quasi mediator,* who plays several roles. He or she is usually the spokesperson charged with the success of the effort. To those sitting across the table, the quasi mediator may simply look like another negotiator, but within a team he or she often acts as a kind of mediator between the stabilizers and the nonstabilizers. As will be shown later, the quasi mediator can also be a mediator between the team and its own constituents or clients.

HORIZONTAL, INTERNAL, AND VERTICAL NEGOTIATIONS

Although most conventional models limit their analysis to the bargaining that goes on across the table, relatively little true negotiating goes on horizontally. Instead, speeches are made, symbols and platitudes are thrown out, and emotions are displayed. If the communication is healthy, the two teams use this time constructively to educate each other: They explain proposals and counterproposals, compare data, show videotapes, share printouts, and present experts. Except for this opportunity to educate and to learn, however, all of this may be less important than the real activity going on internally.

The standard model also misses another important dimension of negotiation: the interchanges that occur between a bargaining team and its vertical hierarchy. A team is rarely independent of a larger constituency. It is at the bargaining table because it has been sent to accomplish something. In the context of private-sector labor negotiation, for example, management's vertical hierarchy is the company's leadership; for the union's bargaining committee, it is the international union and, most times, ultimately the membership who must vote on a proposed contract. Almost always, important negotiations must take place between a team and its vertical hierarchy at one point or another in the bargaining.

Since negotiators are continually being reeducated through the horizontal negotiations occurring at or near the bargaining table, they are frequently far more advanced in their thinking than are their constituents back home. The resulting gap can be a dangerous trap for all concerned. Part of the art and skill of being a negotiator is recognizing how far from the constituents the bargaining team has moved. The negotiator must also know when and how to go back and educate his or her own constituents.

Sometimes the vertical hierarchy will tell a negotiator what should be achieved at the bargaining table, but after several sessions with the other side, the negotiator may come to believe that these goals cannot be reached. It is within this context that negotiation between the team and its own vertical hierarchy takes place. The quasi mediator is often responsible for negotiating with the hierarchy of the team's parent organization. In labor–management negotiations, for instance, the spokesperson or quasi mediator on the union team may wind up intellectually positioned between the local's viewpoint on an issue and management's last known position. In such a case, the union spokesperson not only tries to get management to go along with labor's point of view but may also have to try to get the rest of the union team to accept management's view on some points.

INTERNAL TEAM NEGOTIATIONS

Resolving differences between the stabilizers and nonstabilizers may be a prerequisite for effective negotiation with the other side, as well as one for reaching accommodation with the team's own vertical hierarchy if settlement is the objective. Unless some means exist for coordinating positions and goals over time, there will be serious problems. When a team is considering making an offer, for example, the stabilizers likely will want to present a generous package, while the nonstabilizers will not want to offer anything. The quasi mediator must begin to explore with the stabilizers why the concessions might be excessive. At the same time, of course, the quasi-mediator must discuss with the nonstabilizers why the proposal may be good and why the team should not be so rigid. In the same way, when a team receives an offer from the other side, the quasi mediator must show the nonstabilizers why the team should not hold out for more while checking the stabilizers' tendency to grab the offer too quickly. Much like a neutral mediator, the quasi mediator may meet jointly and separately with the stabilizers and nonstabilizers. If the team is not well disciplined, these discussions unfortunately may take place at the table. Ideally, they should take place in a separate caucus, away from the other side.

RAISING AND MAINTAINING DOUBTS TO FOSTER SETTLEMENT

In a sense, this internal team negotiation process is a microcosm of the larger negotiations that occur across the table. Similar aspects of bargaining positions come into play; the same kinds of negotiation skills are required. As in across-the-table bargaining, the most important effects are those directed at changing the minds of parties who do not want to settle.

It is reasonable to ask why the focus should be on those who oppose settlement: Perhaps those who are anxious to settle—to sell the farm—should be challenged with at least as much force. The answer lies in the true essence of negotiation. Negotiations are not squabbles or battles between two sides. The goal of the process is not for one team to extract huge concessions from the other. Instead, the essence of negotiation is to provide an opportunity for parties to exchange promises through which they will resolve their differences with one another. A settlement thus is no more—and no less—than an expression of an exchange of promises. Because the emphasis in negotiations is on the resolution of differences through the exchange of promises, the process is oriented in favor of settlement. Attention is naturally focused on parties who seem to stand in settlement's way.

Settlement is fostered through the raising and maintaining of doubts. In all negotiations, parties that want to reach some settlement (e.g., the stabilizers and quasi mediators) work to raise or maintain doubts in the minds of others as to the viability of their particular positions, as well as doubts about the consequences of nonagreement. This effort is focused on nonstabilizers and the team across the table. The nonstabilizers are asked to consider the implications of nonsettlement, what it would mean to them personally, or to their organization, objectives, ideals, and reputations. Thus, the same techniques and strategies teams may use to raise and maintain doubts in the minds of parties across the table are also appropriate internally with the nonstabilizers. By the same token, of course, the nonstabilizers engage in a parallel effort to raise doubts in the minds of stabilizers and the quasi mediator about the consequences of settlement.

Because a particular settlement may not be in the interests of the nonstabilizer, he or she frequently must be convinced to accept a settlement through some method other than fostering doubts. Negotiators have an additional tool when dealing with a nonstabilizing teammate: the discipline of the parent organization. This discipline, which might rely upon power, title, prestige, or majority rule, operates within the team. The decision-making process is normally carried over from the parent organization through the chief spokesperson or team leader, which reinforces the roles and relationships of the vertical hierarchy. For instance, an organization that makes most of its important decisions by a majority vote will probably be represented in negotiations by a team that also makes its decisions by majority vote.

According to most practitioners, negotiation is a consensual process. The negotiators come to agreement precisely because they find settlement preferable to nonagreement. But it is erroneous to conclude, as some have, that everyone wins or gains from a negotiated agreement. The notion of "win-win" outcomes is another reflection of the limits of the conventional model of negotiation. Both sides across a table may appear to win, but within each team—where so much more bargaining goes on—there are often nonstabilizers who may view themselves as definite losers in the process.

TARGETING UNDERLYING CONCERNS

The creation and maintenance of doubts about the consequences of nonagreement (or one decision versus another) is central to inducing skeptics to settle. This is true whether they are nonstabilizers within a team or nonstabilizers across the table. But where should this effort be directed?

Fisher and Ury (1981) observe that a negotiator can move the opposite side closer to settlement by convincing it to participate in joint problem solving. This may be accomplished by separating the opposing side's *position* from its underlying *interests*.

Although positions are usually explicit, the interests that underlie them often are left unstated. For example, a community coalition might oppose the establishment of a home for mentally retarded adults in its neighborhood. Yet what is its true interest? Frequently, the community feels that the retarded adults would make the neighborhood less safe. Preserving safe streets may be the real interest at stake. A sophisticated advocate of the home would try to raise doubts about whether the community's stated position will actually satisfy its interests: "Might not additional numbers of sincere, capable adults contribute to community safety? Look at their abilities as well as their problems." An educational process showing that the retarded adults would pose no danger to neighborhood residents—and in fact might improve their security—could foster doubts in the minds of the neighbors about their flat refusal to consider the proposal. Even if opponents are not convinced on this particular score, identifying safety as their prime interest allows the parties to explore mitigating measures.

Education can be the most effective way to raise doubts. It is used, therefore, in every phase of negotiation: across the table, within a team, and between a team and its constituents. The plan of attack is to move the opponent to a more agreeable position.

As Fisher and Ury observe, the effective negotiator aims for the underlying interests that form the foundation of the adversary's position. What happens, however, if a negotiator cannot identify the opponent's interests? Where else can doubts be targeted to get others to adopt a more flexible stance? An answer requires a closer look at the different levels of concern that are often negotiated: issues, proposals, problem definitions, and assumptions.

ISSUES, PROPOSALS, PROBLEMS, AND ASSUMPTIONS

The negotiator's job is to raise and maintain doubts on all four levels of concern. Consider, for example, a proposal to site a hazardous waste management facility that requires the approval of a community board. If there is local opposition, it probably will be based on the assumption that such facilities are inherently dangerous. If that assumption cannot be questioned, no basis exists for negotiations between the community and the developer. As a consequence, the facility will be blocked.

Moreover, even if the project sponsors can convince the community that such facilities are not necessarily dangerous, they may encounter a different obstacle—that of problem definition. For example, the community might contend that its opposition is not to treatment facilities in general but to the proposed location of this particular plant. (It might be near a flood plain.) Casting the problem in these terms obviously would affect proposed solutions. The range of proposals could include the following: having no facility at all, putting the facility at another site, using control technologies to make the facility fit the site, or making the site more acceptable for the proposed use. The issues to be discussed in negotiation would be tied to such proposals. For example, discussion might focus on the need for such a facility, the reasons for (and against) this particular location, and the cost-effectiveness of various mitigating measures.

The task of the facility sponsor would be to raise doubts about the viability of any unacceptable proposals or issues. As assumptions and problem definitions are revealed—which is much more likely than the disclosure of an opponent's real interests—the sponsor would also question them. Since the issues and proposals are derived from the problems and assumptions, the sponsor would probably try to move the negotiations into discussions of the latter before considering specific issues and proposals. In short, the sponsor would focus on the underlying concerns.

EXPANDING THE CORE MODEL

Multilateral Negotiations

The core model that has been described above includes five axes of negotiation: one horizontal, two internal, and two with vertical hierarchies. This model was based on the simplifying assumption that only two teams are at the table. While there are many instances of two-party negotiation, in other cases—particularly those that arise in the public sector—many more parties may be involved. How must the core model be expanded to accommodate additional parties?

The most important difference between two-party and multiparty negotiation is that the latter opens up the possibility of coalition. For example, three parties—A, B, and C—may come to full agreement or no agreement, but they also may be able to forge alternative side deals. Any two parties may strike a deal that leaves the third out. Were A negotiating with just one other party, he could simply weigh any proposed settlement against the consequences of nonagreement. Here, however, he must also compare a possible settlement with both B and C with the advantages of different agreements with B alone or C alone. The addition of each new party at the bargaining table greatly increases the number of theoretical alliances. The introduction of additional parties, necessary as they might be, greatly complicates the negotiation process. Some coalitions may hold for the entire negotiation, but often alliances shift with various issues. Moreover, the lineup of coalitions may shift over time as events, personalities, and loyalties change. Consensus building is always a delicate balancing act.

Finally, the presence of so many parties at the table usually will mean that much more business must be transacted. The important education process usually requires much more time, as the negotiators at the table have the burden of carrying far more information back through their vertical hierarchy. Perhaps we should not be surprised that so many public disputes seem to take months—even years—to negotiate.

The Solitary Negotiator

When only two individuals are negotiating, each acting on his or her own behalf, the conventional model with its emphasis on two independent units bargaining across the table may afford understanding. Yet perhaps even here it is an oversimplification if we do not look at the negotiation that occurs within each of us. Individuals often have mixed feelings and competing priorities. People must admit (to themselves at least) that they sometimes vacillate between accepting a settlement and holding out for more.

Speculation as to whether stabilizing, nonstabilizing, and mediating impulses may exist in one mind is best left to psychiatrists, psychologists, behaviorists, neurologists, and theologians. It does seem true, however, that even in one-on-one bargaining, there can be distinct and contradictory attitudes toward a particular settlement. One strength of the model developed here is that it recognizes the stabilizing and non-stabilizing forces within each bargaining unit (be it a team or an individual), and attempts to understand the means by which they may be integrated.

Quasi Mediators and Mediators

Outside mediators enter disputes for a very specific reason: to fill a trust vacuum that exists at an impasse among and within the parties. The quasi mediator and mediator play separate, yet related, roles: Both use the creation and maintenance of doubts to move other negotiators closer to settlement. The quasi mediator, like the other negotiators, has personal, organizational, and institutional stakes in the outcome of the negotiation process. The truly neutral mediator does not. The quasi mediator also has some power to make decisions about substantive and procedural issues. Whatever power the mediator might enjoy is procedural.

Get Things Done through Coalitions

Margo Vanover

What do the American Paper Institute, National Coffee Association, Milk Industry Foundation, and American Council on Education have in common?

It may seem unlikely, but the answer is "an interest in sewer user charges."

These four associations and 11 others formed the Coalition for ICR Repeal to protect their members' interests in sewer user charges. Coalition members term industrial cost recovery (ICR) as "an unfair, unnecessary, and costly provision of the 1972 Federal Water Pollution Control Act."

This particular example of a coalition illustrates two very important points that you, a leader of your association, should be aware of. First of all, the coalition was successful. The industrial cost recovery provision was repealed on October 1, 1980, and coalition members frankly admit that they could never have done it alone. It took the efforts and—even more important—the clout of all 14 members to accomplish their goal.

The second point is this: Coalition members seemed like unlikely allies. Who would have thought they had anything in common?

"It's an interesting conglomeration of business groups with one similar interest," acknowledges Sheldon E. Steinbach, general counsel for the American Council on Education, Washington. "We all had one common problem—a proposed increase in sewer user charges.

"I remember the stunned look on the faces of the people at the first coalition meeting," he says with a chuckle. "They found out quickly that my association had the exact concern theirs did."

WHO ARE OUR ALLIES?

Right now, your association is probably a member of a coalition. But do you know what the coalition's purpose is? If you don't, ask your association's chief paid officer. He or she usually represents an association's interests in a coalition effort.

And while you are talking to your chief paid officer, ask what other associations comprise the coalition. You could be surprised. Like the Coalition for ICR Repeal, their names might not suggest a tie-in with your association's cause. In fact, they may be the names of associations that have been adversaries or competitors in the past.

It's not all that unusual, says Mr. Steinbach. "We look for common cause with other groups. We may be allies on one cause and enemies on another. It's happened time after time."

It's important to overlook past differences and concentrate on the present goal of the coalition, agrees Dr. Paul A. Kerschner, associate director for legislation, research, and programs at the National Retired Teachers Association/American Association of Retired Persons, Washington. "Two organizations can be in deep dissent on some issues," he says. "On those issues, we know we disagree. But on the issues where we do agree, it's much more powerful to speak in a unified voice."

Of course, sometimes your association's allies are obvious. Such was the case when the Distributive Services Committee was formed 17 years ago. Eighteen Ohio associations whose members were involved in distributing formed the coalition to reduce property tax on retail inventory. At the time, the tax was 70 percent of the value of the inventory. The coalition has successfully obtained several reductions since its formation, and the coalition's goal of a 35 percent inventory tax will go into effect in two years.

In this case, both the allies and the enemy were obvious. The allies: trade associations with retail merchant members. The enemy: the state legislature.

SO MANY SUCCESS STORIES

Case after case of association coalitions that have been successful in their pursuits can be cited. William T. Robinson, CAE, senior vice president of the American Hospital Association, Chicago, relates one coalition success story.

Several years ago, he says, the annual rate of increase in the level of expenditures for health care was out of control. Predictions were that if health care costs continued at the same rate it would be necessary to spend the entire gross national product on health care alone by the year 2010. In fact, the government's outlay for health care— Medicare and Medicaid—was beginning to compete with the defense budget.

Government officials, concerned, issued a challenge to the health care field to voluntarily control the rate of increase. A coalition called Voluntary Effort was created. It represented the interests of trade associations, commercial insurance companies, and others. Now, three years after the start of the coalition, "the rate of increase has been sufficiently retarded," Mr. Robinson says.

Edie Fraser, president of Fraser/Associates, Washington, has been involved in enough similar success stories to become a firm believer in their power. "Coalitions are the new trend in business relations on policy issues," she says. "I believe they are the most effective means of achieving results."

WHAT'S THEIR PURPOSE?

She explains that the basic purpose of a coalition is "to join forces together behind a mutual interest—generally a policy issue—and work together for common effectiveness and results."

"More and more associations are recognizing the power of coalitions," Ms. Fraser continues, "because they can achieve far more by integrating their resources and dividing the effort behind a common cause."

Paul Korody, director of public affairs for the National Meat Association, Washington, says coalitions are growing in numbers in response to a changing Congress. "Within the past 10 years, we have seen a decentralization of power on Capitol Hill. Today, every congressman is almost as important as another. They all have to be talked to."

That means, he says, that only the really large associations with members in every congressional district can tackle an issue alone. "The rest of us have to pool our memberships to be effective in Congress. Whereas we have a lot of meatpackers in the Northwest and Southwest, there are many congressional districts where we have no members at all. We would be less effective in those states [without a coalition]. By combining resources with a number of associations with different memberships but the same goals, you can cover the country."

He adds that, in most cases, congressional staffs appreciate a coalition's efforts. Why? Because it makes their jobs that much easier. They can get one document or have one conversation with a coalition leader and know who and how many are for or against an issue. That's in lieu of speaking with 50,000—a number that five association executives involved in a coalition can easily represent.

CHOOSING A LEADER

In order for any coalition to be successful, it has to have a leader or coordinator with a commitment to the cause and time to devote to it, says Sheldon Steinbach, American Council on Education. "The effectiveness of the ICR repeal was solely due to the continuous scrutiny and daily monitoring of one person.

"A coalition functions only when one person is given responsibility to make that issue move. Someone must call the shots. A leader must have ample time to spend on the issue, almost to the point of making it his or her primary preoccupation."

Because of the considerable time requirement, choosing a coalition coordinator is often simply a process of elimination. Who has the time to spend on it? Who was the expertise on the issue?

When these questions are answered, only a few eligibles are likely to remain. Usually it's the executive of the association which the outcome of the issue most affects.

Or as Ms. Fraser puts it, "The leader usually represents the one association that has the most to gain . . . or lose."

GUIDELINES FOR EFFECTIVENESS

Obviously, the selection of the leader can either make or break a coalition. But other factors also enter into the outcome of your association's coalition.

Here are just a few elements common to successful coalition efforts:

- A commitment by members to work, not in their own self-interest, but in the interest of the group.
- Expertise on the part of all members on the subject matter and its ramifications.

- Knowledge of how the legislature—either state or federal—works.
- Ability to plan a strategy and allow enough lead time to develop it detail by detail so nothing slips through the cracks and is left undone.
- Communication with members of the coalition—whether it's through meetings, newsletters, memos, or telephone calls.
- Keeping on the offensive, rather than the defensive. "Use facts, data, and public opinion to build on your important points," Ms. Fraser says. "It's not necessary to attack your opposition." She ticks off campaign after campaign that was lost because one side began to react defensively to the opposition.
- Member involvement. "If the issue is important to your members—and it should be or you shouldn't be part of the coalition—get them involved," Ms. Fraser urges. "The grassroots campaign is important. The work should really come from members; your association should serve as the catalyst."
- Latitude from you and your board of directors. "Our board sets broad policy," says John C. Mahaney, Jr., president of the Ohio Council of Retail Merchants in Columbus. "After that, my board leaves me alone. It doesn't tie the staff's hands."

A COMMITMENT TO GO

The last point, the latitude you give to your chief paid executive, can be a crucial item to your association's contribution to the coalition. "The board gives us a broad delegation of authority," Sheldon Steinbach says. "We are paid to exercise good judgment and proceed. If you are hamstrung, it will slow you down, if not completely cripple your coalition."

He explains that if he had to go back to his board of directors every time a decision was made in a coalition, he would lose valuable time—not to mention the confidence of other coalition members.

SURVEY OF MEMBERSHIP

To make sure his board of directors will agree with his decisions, Mr. Steinbach surveys his membership on major issues that concern the association. "If they think it is important, they tell us to go," he says. "But they don't tell us how to go."

Dr. Kerschner explains that the only time he goes back to his board for a coalition decision is when the issue is controversial and the association's stance involves a change in previous policy.

What do you do with dissent among coalition members?" asks Dr. Kerschner. "How do you handle it? Do you avoid the issue? Do you go with the majority?"

He explains that chief paid officers must answer these questions, and answer them adequately, for a coalition to work. He has found one possible answer for the coalitions he has been involved with: If there is a disagreement on one particular point of an issue, the dissenting party removes his or her name and endorsement from that specific letter but continues to endorse the remainder of the issue.

"Trade-offs are important because one small issue can divide the coalition," he says. "Before you say 'I will not sign that,' look at all sides. You might have to make a compromise. Internal negotiations are necessary to present a united front to those you are dealing with."

GOODWILL A KEY INGREDIENT

William Robinson advises associations to go into a coalition with the idea that there might have to be a trade-off. "Your pet ideas are going to be examined by others," he says. "You might have to accept the fact that the publicity will be given to the coalition and not to your association. A coalition takes goodwill by the participants. Sometimes the goodwill is there in the beginning; sometimes it takes time for it to grow."

Speaking realistically, Edie Fraser says it almost never happens that members of a coalition agree on every item, every detail of a coalition. "That's where the art of negotiation is important. The common end of the allies is more important than the priority of any one association."

SHARING IN THE GLORY

You may wonder why your association's past efforts in coalitions have not been more heavily publicized . . . why your association didn't take more credit for the outcome

"A coalition, to be effective, is without limelight or glory for the association involved," says Paul Korody. "The purpose is to get a particular job done. We're there to serve our members, and coalitions are the more effective means of doing that. Any glory is in the fact that we satisfactorily served our members."

Sheldon Steinbach admits that sharing the spotlight is a problem for some associations. Sometimes, they are so greedy for the recognition that they won't participate in a coalition—and risk losing the fight. Other times, they might participate in a coalition, but afterward they will attempt to garner all of the credit for their association alone.

When William Robinson was working on Voluntary Effort, he says, the businesses and associations involved had no qualms about giving complete credit to the coalition, not to themselves. "It would have been counterproductive to publish under any one member's name," Mr. Robinson says. "We wanted the coalition to become a familiar name . . . to have its own identity."

POTENTIAL PROBLEMS

Powerful though they may be, coalitions are not perfect. Problems arise, and they have to be alleviated before the cause can be won. Here are some snags that can occur. With negotiation, respect, and planning, all can be overcome.

1. *One member dominates.* Sometimes, when a coalition is composed of one or two large, domineering associations and a variety of small ones, representatives from the smaller associations are not given the chance to express their opinions. Or, if they are given the opportunity, they are not given priority. All members must listen to one another.

2. *Jealousy between members.* This usually occurs at the outset, Ms. Fraser points out, until coalition members realize that "they can achieve far more by integrating their resources and dividing the effort behind a common cause."

3. *Conflicting goals.* "You've got to go for the greatest good for the greatest number," Mr. Steinbach says.

4. *Conflicting strategy.* This occurs most often when two or more coalition members have considerable legislative experience. Because of their backgrounds, each thinks his own plan of attack is best.

5. *Minor disagreements.* Even though the association executives agree on the major issue, they sometimes bicker about a minor part of it. "You can't let a specific point divide and conquer the group," Dr. Kerschner says.

6. *Too formal.* Dr. Kerschner differentiates between organization, which you can never have enough of, and formalization, which you can. He says it's important to remember that each member of the coalition has an association to which he is responsible and that the coalition should not become a substitute for it.

7. *Too many meetings.* Some coalitions are permanent. Others are temporary— disbanded as soon as their cause is settled. Dr. Kerschner warns that members of permanent coalitions have to be careful not to call a meeting just to be calling a meeting. Unless a crisis has occurred or a new development has come up, he recommends meeting about once a month. Between meetings, he uses the phone for exchanges of information.

8. *Lack of follow-through.* Sometimes a coalition member will slip up, and the work assigned to him or her will not get done. If that happens, and it is not caught in time, all of the coalition efforts will be wasted.

EVERYONE'S DOING IT

Coalitions are not limited to associations. Business groups, consumer groups— just about any group you can think of is involved in some type of coalition. "On any side of any issue, you can find a coalition that has formed, is being formed, or will be formed," Mr. Korody says.

Whatever type of coalition your association may now be involved in, your chances of victory are better through unity. Mr. Mahaney firmly believes Ohio merchants would not have received inventory tax relief without the Distributive Service Committee. "We could not have done it alone," he states. "It took everyone in the coalition to do it."

"Sometimes a coalition is the only way to do something," he continues. "Especially now, as the problem becomes more complex. It seems like they are too big for any one—or even two—associations to handle." Paul Korody couldn't agree more. "A smart association executive seeks his peers and works through a coalition. The days of trying to do it all yourself are long gone."

Twenty Tips for Making a Coalition Work

If you aren't convinced of the value of coalitions, talk to Edie Fraser, president of Fraser/Associates, Washington, D.C. She's a firm believer in the effectiveness of coalitions and presents a persuasive argument on their behalf.

She asserts that coalitions are the wave of the future. "On most policy issues, a coalition is the only way to go—if you have a common interest," she says.

In her opinion, more and more association executives are recognizing the potential—and power—of coalitions, but they aren't sure how to proceed. "Carrying out the program is where they often fall down."

Here are her 20 rules for participating in an effective coalition:

1. Clearly define issues and strategy.
2. Determine a timetable and needs.
3. Identify both allies and opposition.
4. Build constituency and recruit allies.
5. Select leadership from within allies.
6. Devise a clear plan of action.
7. Determine resources, budget, and meet those needs.
8. Divide up tasks within the coalition.
9. Establish a working task force or executive committee.
10. Keep coalition members informed and involved.
11. Establish a communication program plan; clearly distribute tasks.
12. Build supportive case materials.
13. Develop an internal communication program, with each association involving its members.
14. Enlist experts to support the coalition's case.
15. Explain the issue in economic impact terms when possible; use appropriate public opinion.
16. Utilize all pertinent media for greatest impact.
17. Remember to keep all coalition constituents informed and involved.
18. If it's a legislative issue, review the congressional strategy on a regular basis.
19. Determine if the coalition leadership is serving as a catalyst for communication.
20. Prove the results and communicate them to the member constituencies.

The Negotiation of Settlements: A Team Sport

James G. Zack Jr.

TRADITIONAL NEGOTIATIONS

Negotiation is traditionally portrayed in a competitive or combative context. Analogies to competitive sports are frequent, and the terminology of war often slips into a traditional discussion of negotiation of settlements. For example, one author has stated, "[The] real act of negotiation lies in the exercise of power". In this traditional view, each party is depicted as single minded in its pursuit of the most favorable deal possible—almost always at the expense of the other party. Traditional negotiations can be summarized in the following four ways:

- The "win-at-any-cost" style, which allows pressure, threats, and intimidation, and results in a win-lose situation.
- The "maintain-the-relationship" style, which causes a negotiator to give anything to keep the other side happy, and results in a lose-win situation.
- The "conflict-avoidance" style, which causes you to take anything the other side offers, and results in a lose-win situation.
- The "compromise/find-an-acceptable-settlement" situation, which amounts to nothing more than bargaining, and results in no one winning or losing.

The last situation is frequently summed up with the expression "Neither side was happy with the settlement, but they agreed anyway."

NEW FORM OF NEGOTIATION

The traditional form of negotiation is often inefficient and wasteful of time and energy; it frequently leads to deadlock rather than agreement and dissatisfaction instead of accord and satisfaction. A new form of negotiation has been suggested, which is based on what is referred to as the win-win style. It has resulted from studies conducted over a number of years by the Harvard Negotiation Program and is most clearly articulated in Fisher and Ury's book *Getting to Yes: Getting to Agreement without Giving In*.

Reprinted from *Cost Engineering,* August, 1994 Vol. 36, No. 8, with permission of the publisher.

The win-win approach is premised on the concept that each party in the negotiation is a problem solver, and all of the parties share a need to solve the same problem. The problem is loosely defined as how to resolve the issue to the benefit of all parties. This is particularly true when two parties are trying to negotiate settlement of either a change or a dispute. In this new style of negotiation, each group is motivated to reach an agreement, although it is acknowledged that both parties may not be equally motivated.

Negotiators in this new style always keep the goal in mind and always focus exclusively on reaching the goal. In the win-win form of negotiation, the goal is to reach an agreement. In keeping with win-win negotiations, the new process of negotiating construction settlements is to first establish the contractor's position clearly and concisely, then establish the owner's position. This sets the stage for the remainder of the negotiation. The next step is to identify similarities and set them aside as agreements. This should be followed by a time when the negotiators explore alternatives concerning areas of disagreement. For example, in a change order situation, you may propose owner-furnished equipment or materials, or propose that the owner's staff do some of the changed work themselves. Long-duration change orders might become more palatable if agreement can be reached to include a price redetermination clause or a cost-escalation clause. The next step in the negotiation process is to choose among the alternatives identified and reach final agreement. Finally, formalize and finalize the settlement paperwork in an expeditious manner.

The general pattern of negotiations accomplished in the team format is modeled closely after the win-win style of negotiations. The first action in team negotiations is for both teams to meet with the specific objective of negotiating scope: either the scope of the changed work or the scope of the issue in dispute. The results of this first step should be recorded in writing and provided to both teams. Both teams are thus assured that they are focusing on the same work scope. This step should be followed by the time and cost estimating step, in which both the contractor and the owner should take the agreed-upon scope and perform independent analyses of the time and cost impact. Upon receipt of the contractor's time and cost proposal, the owner's negotiation team should analyze the contractor's proposal. This stage should be followed by joint meetings to negotiate a final settlement of the issue, and final agreement should be followed by the appropriate written documentation of the agreement.

TEAM NEGOTIATING—INTERNAL TEAMING

Experience indicates that teams almost always negotiate construction settlements better than individuals; therefore, settlement negotiations should always be planned as team events. Experience has shown that team negotiations bring more experience and knowledge to bear on a settlement situation, making it more likely that a rational, justifiable settlement can be reached. Teams generally have more skills and diverse talents than individuals. Finally, team negotiations not only allow the team to control individual members and help keep them focused on solving the problem, but also make it easier to keep written notes and documentation of the negotiation, since one team member can be specifically assigned at each session to take the meeting notes.

The procedure for establishing the internal team (for either the owner or the contractor) starts with the selection of team members. Selection of appropriate team members is critical to the success of team negotiations. Not only does the project manager have to select people with knowledge of the issue, but the members must bring the right mix of talents and skills. For example, a team may include a project manager, a superintendent for that portion of the work, a cost estimator, and a project scheduler, depending upon the issue in negotiation. After selection of the team members, the team must coalesce as a group and become motivated to solve the problem. Any team member whose motive is anything other than problem resolution (defined here as satisfactory settlement of the issue) should be removed from the team and replaced. There is no room on a tight-knit negotiating team for hidden agendas or conflicting egos.

After team selection and negotiation of scope, the team should meet to prepare independent time and cost estimates and/or perform a joint analysis and review of the time and cost proposal from the other side. The team should then meet to plan the negotiation. Planning the negotiation includes, at a minimum, drawing up a list of every issue needing resolution, establishing ranges of objectives (both time and cost), and determining which issues can be compromised, and to what extent, as well as those that cannot. The team needs to establish ground rules for the negotiation. Details such as who will lead the negotiations, when the lead will change hands, who will document the negotiations, what process will be used to develop alternatives, how the team's compromise offers will be presented, and when breaks will be taken need to be established in advance. This is the team's "game plan" and must be clearly understood and agreed to by all members.

The final action with respect to internal teaming is to raise the team's aspirations. Research has shown that teams entering negotiations with higher aspirations are more likely to achieve a settlement to their liking. This is a motivational activity, but it pays measurable dividends.

Upon achieving a settlement acceptable to both parties, the owner's team should draft the change order or settlement document, including full and final settlement language that waives further claims concerning the settlement. If all details of the issue being negotiated have been properly identified and fully explored, then there is no reason to object to the inclusion of such language. Finally, both teams need to conclude the agreement, follow up with the required paperwork, and pay or be paid promptly.

COMPARISON OF TRADITIONAL VERSUS TEAM NEGOTIATION TACTICS

Following is a comparison of the tactics recommended for use in traditional negotiations with team negotiation tactics using the win-win style, to draw a clearer distinction between the two approaches.

Trust

Traditional negotiators are advised to never trust the other side, and to "never let down your guard." Other negotiators are viewed as the enemy and as such should never be trusted. By contrast, in team negotiations you should begin negotiations on the basis of mutual trust. Unless something happens to destroy this premise, the team negotiator assumes the other party is both ethical and deserving of respect. Another way to express this new approach is that the team negotiator proceeds in the absence of trust. The team negotiator does not make trust an issue, but instead establishes that both parties have a mutual problem (the need to reach resolution of an issue) and that both parties are considered to be problem solvers. Focusing on the problem and a range of solutions potentially acceptable to both parties is more likely to lead to successful resolution.

Location

Advice concerning the tactics of traditional negotiations even addresses matters such as the location of each negotiation session. Traditionally, to be a successful negotiator you had to control the location of each negotiating session. In this way, the negotiator is advised, you can gain a psychological advantage over the other party that is similar to the vaunted home court/field advantage frequently discussed in sports. Alternatively, the traditional negotiator is told to find a neutral site for meetings where both parties are on a "level playing field." In team negotiations, location is irrelevant. The location selected simply needs to be comfortable and convenient and not used to either party's advantage.

Timing

Traditional negotiators are given advice on how to use tardiness or a planned late arrival at negotiating meetings to aggravate or shake the confidence of the other side and gain an advantage. Negotiators in the traditional style are often advised to "squeeze the time" of the negotiations with the strategy of finding out how long the other side can remain at the bargaining table before having to leave for the airport, for example, and then saving the most critical items of negotiation until very close to that time to apply pressure. Team negotiators are best advised to practice common business courtesy in all their dealings. This includes arriving on time and allowing sufficient time to conduct and complete the negotiations.

Obfuscation

Obfuscation tactics frequently described in traditional negotiation literature include the use of complaints about situations unrelated to the issue in negotiation to sidetrack or put the other side on the defensive. Advice concerning the use of general information versus detailed discussion of negotiation points, in a calculated effort to either hide information or cover up the fact that detailed information is unavailable, is often given. The concept is that withholding information or refusing to admit information does not exist puts the other party at a disadvantage. The information overload tactic is the converse of the above. This is the tactic of providing an inordinate amount of trivial information with the intent of distracting attention from areas of weakness. A team negotiator employing the win-win style seeks to clarify issues and facts rather than hide them and at all times proceeds in an open, honest manner.

Positioning

The use of "throwaway" positions is recommended to make the traditional negotiator seem conciliatory. These are contrived positions with no legitimate value to the outcome of the negotiation that are set forth solely to allow the other side to reject them and thus gain a victory. Traditional negotiators are told not to honor an initial high demand with an immediate counteroffer. Rather, the successful negotiator first gets the other side to lower their initial demand. Only then is it appropriate to set forth a reasonable counteroffer. Traditional negotiators are taught that the first goal of negotiation is to decrease the expectations of the other side. Regardless of how close the other side's position is, efforts must be made to convince them that they are far off the mark. Traditional negotiators are advised they should never accept a first offer even if it matches their own goal. The justification for this tactic is twofold; first, the belief is touted that the first offer is only an opening offer, or a "feeler," to sound out the other side, and the other negotiator is prepared to move off this position. The second justification offered is that if you accept the first offer, the other side leaves the bargaining table with a sense of disappointment. The team negotiator refuses to use throw away positions and won't use the "decrease their expectations" tactic since these methods are irrelevant to the objective of achieving settlement. The team negotiator is willing to accept initial offers if they meet the previously determined goal because this accomplishes settlement quickly.

Surprises

Traditional negotiators advise negotiating along the lines of "Perry Mason–style" courtroom tactics. Whenever possible, spring surprises on the other negotiator. The premise is that surprise is the enemy of a negotiator. The team negotiator recognizes that surprises are not an advantage but instead disrupt an otherwise orderly process.

Concessions

Traditional negotiators are given advice on making and receiving concessions during negotiations. Among the advice given are the following points: never make the first concession—research shows that losers in negotiations invariably are those who made the first concession. Make it clear to the other negotiator that all concessions offered are tentative and subject to withdrawal at any time if negotiations do not proceed satisfactorily. Never give a concession without getting one in return. When the other side offers a concession, take it. The traditional negotiator is advised to not feel compelled to offer one in return as this may establish a pattern of one-for-one trading. Traditional negotiators are cautioned not to "telegraph" moves by establishing a pattern of concessions during negotiations. Finally, traditional advice is to identify one last concession to terminate the negotiations and leave the other negotiator with the impression that he or she won the last round.

Team negotiators, on the other hand, only make and take concessions if they make sense in terms of the negotiation. They do not fear making the first or the last concession if it moves the negotiation toward the goal of acceptable settlement. Team negotiators only use concessions designed to move negotiations toward final settlement; anything else is considered a waste of time and effort. Team negotiators are cautioned to keep track of concessions by keeping a written list, not as you keep the box score during a baseball game, but as a way of recording agreements achieved on the way to the overall goal.

Aggression

Traditional negotiation tactics for those striving to become more aggressive negotiators include trying to make the other side appear unreasonable in an effort to put the other negotiator on the defensive. Use of any tactic whatsoever to place the other party "on the defensive" is fair in traditional negotiations. Throwing the blame for your "inability" to compromise on a third party is another strategy frequently recommended. For example, statements that "the city council will not approve . . ." or "the president of the company has told me not to . . ." are considered legitimate ways to avoid compromise, even if the statements are not true.

The "vinegar and sugar" approach is another plan whereby two members of the same team make offers at opposite ends of the spectrum. One is quite unreasonable and is offered only as a way to make the other side believe they can divide and conquer. The "good guy/bad guy routine" made so popular in the movies has long been standard procedure in traditional negotiations. The team negotiator maintains integrity at all times and has disdain for the use of such tactics because they waste time and do not contribute to the objective of reaching settlement.

Walkouts, Silence, and Asides

Traditional negotiators are often coached on the tactical use of the walkout to confuse the other negotiator, throw him or her off balance, or disrupt the flow of the negotiation. The agreement and rebuttal technique, wherein the traditional negotiator is advised to always say "Yes, but . . ." in an effort to seem reasonable, while at the same time not conceding anything, is usually recommended. Silence as a tactic also has often been written about. This is the tactic of not responding to any offer made and maintaining absolute silence in hopes that the other negotiator will feel uncomfortable and start talking (offering) more.

The aside meeting also is often recommended. This is a private meeting of the two chief traditional negotiators, outside the meeting room and beyond the hearing of the negotiating teams, in an effort to structure a side deal that may help make the main negotiating point more palatable. This tactic is adopted from international, diplomatic negotiations, "à la Henry Kissinger." Team negotiators only walk out when negotiations have utterly failed and need to be pushed to a higher level. Team negotiators rarely use the "Yes, but . . ." tactic since it is a charade, not open communication. Finally, the team negotiator does not hesitate to conduct business in an open environment, having no need for secret meetings or deals.

Authority and Bogeys

The use and abuse of higher authority in traditional negotiations is frequent. One practice is to have a high-ranking official on one side call a similar ranking official on the other to complain about the lack of cooperation of their negotiator. This is a legitimate tactic to increase pressure in traditional negotiations. Another use of higher authority is to get a high government or company official to sit in on a negotiating session with the idea of speaking directly to him or her, thus bypassing the negotiator. The idea is that higher authority is more likely to compromise because they lack detailed knowledge of the situation or because they are tempted to display their power and offer compromises others cannot agree to.

Finally, the "bogey" tactic is recommended, which is a tactic where the traditional negotiator, having received the other side's "best offer," says "I'd like to take the offer, but we've only budgeted $50,000. If you can come down to that, we've got a deal." Another form of the bogey in negotiations with government agencies is "Any agreement over $100,000 will delay settlement as we have to go back to the appropriation committee," or "We'll have to call in an auditor before we can sign any settlement above $100,000." Team negotiators using the win-win style recognize that pressure tactics are detrimental to the project in the long run. Higher authority should be involved only when it can legitimately contribute to the process, not as a tactic. Team negotiators do not use the bogey, since it works against open, honest communication.

Teamwork

Traditional negotiations are conducted as an "us versus them" exercise, much like a football game. The goal can only be attained at the expense of the other side. Team negotiations are instead structured as a team exercise. At the outset it is made clear that the sole purpose of the negotiation is to discuss a mutual problem, identify areas of agreement, identify areas of disagreement, understand why there is disagreement, identify and explore alternatives, and, finally, reach a mutually acceptable resolution. All those involved understand that both negotiating teams share an identical goal, which is defined as reaching settlement of the problem through negotiation. It is easier to reach settlement if both negotiating teams understand they share this joint goal. Team negotiators seek to turn adversaries into partners. Even though both teams enter negotiations with different outcomes in mind, they must understand that they share the same objective; by focusing on this objective, the teams cease to be adversaries and end up being partners. Instead of picturing themselves as opposing football teams on the field of contest, the idea prevails that the teams are working together to solve the same problem, albeit from different perspectives and with different motives.

Agenda

Traditional negotiators avoid meeting agendas, as they hinder obfuscation and other dilatory tactics. To team negotiators, agendas help establish the joint teaming framework needed for settlement negotiations. They help focus discussion and keep negotiations on track. The first item on the agenda is the simplest: the areas of agreement. This helps start the negotiation on a positive note and keeps it moving toward settlement. The second item should include the areas of disagreement. The contractor's time and cost proposal for each area should be discussed in enough detail so that both teams fully understand the contractor's position. The agenda should then proceed to development of alternatives, alternative selection, and settlement.

Basis of Negotiation

In settlement negotiations, traditional negotiators are advised to withhold all information concerning the owner's independent time and cost analysis, as if revelation of such information gives the other side a superior bargaining position. In fact, federal regulations verge on prohibiting government contracting officers from revealing their estimate. Team negotiators recognize that negotiations should be conducted on the basis of the owner's independent time and cost estimate. Having previously clearly established the contractor's position, the next logical step is to establish the owner's position. No better way exists to accomplish this than to provide the owner's independent estimate. The objective of joint-team negotiations is to remain positive in pursuit of the shared goal. Therefore, rather than attacking the contractor's estimate or trying to drive down the contractor's request, it is more positive to "build up" the owner's estimate. Once the owner's estimate is put on the table and thoroughly discussed, the contractor's team focuses on adjusting the estimate on an objective and rational basis.

Detailed Negotiations

Negotiators operating in the traditional mode generally pursue bottom-line negotiations. They seek to find a number that satisfies them and do not quibble about how to justify the settlement value. Team negotiators, however, concentrate on negotiating details and on letting the bottom line fall out as a logical consequence of detailed negotiations. Detailed negotiations allow fuller understanding of the issues and are less likely to lead to later disagreement of what was, or was not, included in the settlement. Bottom-line negotiations are more likely to lead to a later dispute if other things do not go well.

Emotions

Traditional negotiators do not hesitate to use emotions as a ploy during negotiations. The calculated use of emotional outbursts (including both anger and tears to create sympathy or empathy, the generation of fear, etc.) to gain an advantage is frequently discussed. Team negotiators strive to control their emotions as well as those of all team members on both sides. If an attack is made, it is deflected, and there is no counterattack, since that destroys joint teamwork and is less likely to result in achieving settlement. At all times, team negotiators should, as suggested by Ury in his recent book, *Getting Past No: Negotiating with Difficult People*, be prepared "to step to the other side." Team negotiators should conscientiously make an effort to understand what the other side is saying and why. You do not have to agree, but mutual understanding and respect are critical to team negotiations.

Reframing and Bridge Building

Traditional negotiators always reject and rebut all arguments from the other side, and rebuttal and counterattack are two of their main operating principles. Team negotiators, on the other hand, take another tactic from Ury; they do not reject positions asserted by the other side. Rather, they reframe them as attempts to deal with the problem. Questioning the position is more likely to lead to understanding and inventing options than direct rejection. Team negotiators build bridges to agreement by using the other team's ideas when identifying alternative solutions. Team negotiators concentrate on bringing the other side to their senses, not to their knees. They identify options that are mutually beneficial for both sides, and if these ideas are rejected, try to identify the cost of not reaching an agreement at the end of the negotiation. This is akin to the old adage of "keeping your eye on the ball," with the ball here being the mutually shared goal of reaching settlement.

Team negotiators also do not fall prey to the "settle at any cost" syndrome, which is an internalized pressure that causes people to stop acting in an objective, rational manner, and causes teams to agree to anything simply in order to reach any agreement. Almost without fail, teams arriving at settlements under these circumstances sooner or later conclude that they lost the negotiation and tend to become bitter toward the other team and look forward to opportunities to "get even."

Respect and Personal Relationships

Traditional negotiators view the other side as the enemy. They strive to maintain a cool, formal relationship, holding each other at arm's length. After all, it is easier to maintain the enemy image if you do not like the other negotiator. Team negotiators make an effort to understand and respect the other negotiators and their interests and fully explore these interests openly and honestly. Team negotiators take a personal approach during the negotiation process. They view the other negotiator as a problem solver who is helping to solve a mutual problem. Team negotiators take time to get to know the people on the other side and seek to separate the people from the problem. They do not take offense when the other negotiators represent their side with all the skill and talent they possess. Team negotiators are soft on people, but hard on the problem; they recognize that the opposition is simply trying to do a good job. Team negotiators also recognize and accept the emotions of the other team as a natural part of the process and use the personal and business relationships between themselves to facilitate negotiations.

Mutual Interests

Traditional negotiators make no attempt to understand the other side's interests. They represent their own interests, ignore everything else, and fail to recognize any shared interests. Thus, threatening the other side is a common traditional negotiation tactic. Team negotiators, by contrast, use offers to reach settlement, not threats. Team negotiators focus on mutual interests, not on positioning, which is a waste of time and energy. Team negotiators identify interests shared by both parties. One tactic frequently recommended along these lines is to ask "Why?" not "Why not?" Team negotiators attempt to understand the other side's interests before pressing their own.

Options

In the traditional form of negotiation there is an attitude of "my way or the wrong way." Traditional negotiators make no attempt to see beyond their own one-sided position. Having arrived at a position, the traditional negotiator spends the remainder of the time trying to force the other side to accept it. The team negotiator develops multiple options to choose from and then chooses from the options jointly suggested. Team negotiators try to "expand the pie" (i.e., "What if we also put in . . . ?") or change the scope of the issue being negotiated if it helps to reach settlement. Team negotiators are concrete in proposing options (they propose only specific options that can be accomplished) but flexible in thinking of options that can be legitimately considered. Team negotiation is based on the concept of inventing options for mutual gain through the use of creative, flexible, lateral thinking.

Option Selection

Traditional negotiators spend no time developing options for settlement, so there is no need to establish criteria for option selection. Team negotiators use objective criteria when choosing among options in order to reach settlement. Team negotiators make decisions based on objective standards, independent of will: they do not try to force the other side to accept something, nor allow themselves to be forced into settlement. Team negotiators go slowly, are patient during negotiations, and do not get angry or frustrated with the other side or the pace of negotiations. Team negotiators reason with the other side, and likewise, are open to reason. They yield to principle, not pressure, and avoid having a bottom line or negotiating the bottom line. Bottom-line negotiations, while frequently resulting in some sort of agreement, do not detail the settlement and frequently are the cause of future disputes.

THE MOST COMMON TRADITIONAL NEGOTIATION MISTAKES AND HOW TEAM NEGOTIATIONS HELP TO AVOID THEM

An excellent article appeared in the July 1992 issue of the *Journal of Management in Engineering,* entitled "Planning Your Negotiation". The author identified the 10 most common problems concerning negotiations, which are more likely to arise if a negotiator uses the traditional method rather than the team method of negotiation:

- The traditional negotiator uses a win-lose approach: "In order for me to win this negotiation, the other side will have to give up almost everything they demand." This approach inhibits a traditional negotiator from reaching rational settlements or even structuring compromises likely to lead to a settlement. Team negotiators use the win-win approach, which encourages settlements for the benefit of both parties.
- The traditional negotiator is unable to change negotiating styles and is so locked into a particular style of negotiation that he or she cannot adapt. This may result in a negotiation deadlocking or failing because of a breakdown of communication. Team negotiations are deliberately designed to be as flexible as possible to avoid deadlock and failed communication.

• Making concessions for the sake of a relationship is a problem more likely to be encountered with traditional negotiators. They may ignore their own needs in order to meet the needs of the other side, and as a result suffer a loss. Team negotiations focus on solutions that benefit both parties, precluding this sort of situation.

• Bargaining versus negotiating is a problem common in traditional negotiations. The traditional negotiator simply tries to drive the price up or down, similar to street-vendor negotiations. Emphasis is on the final cost, not on the scope of work, how the cost basis was established, or the elements of the cost proposal. Team negotiations use the detailed negotiation process to avoid this pitfall.

• Traditional negotiators establish objectives as a fixed point versus a range. Traditional negotiators who help prepare the proposal establish the goal for the negotiation as a fixed dollar amount ($178,500) rather than a range of values ($180,000 plus or minus 10 percent). It is then viewed as failure when the exact point is missed. Team negotiators use ranges of values to expand the probability of success and allow the negotiator to operate within a range rather than fixating on a specific point.

• Traditional negotiators often fail to choose their own team members properly and find they cannot control their own team. If a negotiator's own team members are "marching to the tune of a different drummer," the chances for success are substantially decreased. Team negotiators recognize this problem and pay attention to potential team members' personalities, knowledge of the situation, egos, ability to work as a team member, shared interest in reaching a reasonable settlement, past history with the other party, and so on.

• Traditional negotiators often fail to establish priorities for negotiations. In almost every negotiation, certain issues can be compromised, others can be compromised within specific limits, and some cannot be compromised at all. Traditional negotiators often don't recognize such differences and insist that all items be treated equally. Team negotiators understand this situation and establish priorities.

• Traditional negotiators also frequently fail to plan the negotiation and are so convinced that their position is right, they do not consider and plan for priorities, ranges of settlement values, an overall approach, negotiating tactics, and other details. The team negotiator knows these must be planned for and discussed in advance. Just as a sports team does not go onto the playing field without a game plan, a team negotiator does not begin without a negotiating plan.

• Traditional negotiators also often attempt to negotiate with unclear authority. This is especially true when negotiating a settlement with a public agency. All too frequently, the traditional negotiator reaches the point of settlement and then announces for the first time, "Of course, I'll need to clear this with the city engineer." Team negotiators understand the need to clearly establish the authority of both negotiators at the outset. Failure to do so means you may just be discussing something with a messenger.

• Traditional negotiators frequently do not take notes and debrief. This may be because they frequently negotiate on their own, without a team. Team negotiators know that taking notes during the negotiation is helpful in tracking the progress of negotiations and helps prevent the other party from changing arguments when it suits them. Team negotiators understand that documentation is absolutely critical to keep track of interim agreements and structure the final written agreement so that it properly covers all negotiated points. Finally, on publicly funded projects, the team negotiator knows that such documentation is critical to surviving the audit of the settlement.

The traditional form of negotiation is combative, wastes time and energy, sometimes verges on being unethical, and is less likely to achieve satisfactory resolution of issues. The team negotiation style outlined here is more likely to succeed than traditional negotiations. I hope this article convinces its readers that internal teaming and joint teaming are logical extensions of the win-win negotiation process. Joint teaming in the negotiation of construction settlements is more likely to keep both sides focused on a shared goal—finding a mutually acceptable settlement—rather than continuing the dispute. Team negotiations not only make achieving settlement easier but can help establish a more professional relationship on the project, which will pay dividends in numerous other ways.

REFERENCES

Bent, James A. "Implication of Contract Law on Cost/Claims/Extras." In *Advanced Skills and Knowledge of Cost Engineering,* Vol. 1. Morgantown, WV: AACE International, June 1989.

Department of the Navy, Naval Facilities Engineering Command. *Construction Management Technique: ROICC Field Manual.* Alexandria, VA: 1976.

Federal Acquisition Regulations, 48 CFR 36.203.

Fisher, R., and W. Ury. *Getting to Yes: Getting to Agreement without Giving In.* Boston: Houghton-Mifflin, 1982.

Glaser, Rollin, and C. Glaser. "The Negotiating Style Profile." In *Organization Design and Development.* Bryn Mawr, PA: 1982.

Karrass, C. L. *The Negotiating Game.* New York: Thomas Y. Crowell, 1970.

_____. *Give and Take: The Complete Guide to Negotiating Strategies and Tactics.* New York: Thomas Y. Crowell, 1974.

_____. *Effective Negotiating.* Santa Monica: 1986.

Smith, Michael L. "Planning Your Negotiation." *Journal of Management in Engineering.* 8 (July 1992): 254–60.

Ury, William. *Getting Past No: Negotiating with Difficult People.* New York: Bantam Books, 1991.

U.S. Army Corps of Engineers. *Construction Contract Negotiating Guide.* Huntsville, AL 1986.

Webster's New Collegiate Dictionary. Springfield, MA: G. & C. Merriam, 1977.

Zack, James G. Jr. "Claimsmanship—A Current Discussion." *1992 AACE Transactions.* Morgantown, WV: AACE International. D.6.1–D.69.

SECTION TEN
Individual Differences

Are some people born negotiators? Many observers of negotiation have argued that some negotiators, by virtue of their personality, are simply much more capable of winning a negotiation or getting the best outcome. They argue that if we can understand which dimensions of personality contribute to negotiation effectiveness, we would be able to select potentially good negotiators with greater accuracy or to better understand how to train people to adapt their behavior to situations that their personality style does not normally provide.

In spite of these assertions and a great deal of research that has been devoted to identifying the characteristics and personality styles of more or less effective negotiators, the exact role of a negotiator's personality and its impact on outcomes is not well known. Many of these studies have yielded inconclusive results, and others have often yielded contradictory findings. Nonetheless, some facts are known. The articles in this section examine individual differences among negotiators from two perspectives. The first two articles take a behavioral perspective and concentrate on the behavioral skills of successful negotiators. The final article in this section takes a dispositional perspective and examines the influence of gender on negotiation.

In the first article, "The Behavior of Successful Negotiators," Neil Rackham reports the results of a series of studies that identified the behaviors that distinguish between excellent and average negotiators. Rackham found that superior negotiators behaved differently than average negotiators during the planning, bargaining, and reviewing stages of negotiation. While many of the findings of this study echo common sense, there were a few surprises. For instance, Rackham found that superior negotiators used *fewer* arguments to make their point than average negotiators did. The article explains clearly how to interpret this and other surprising results, and it is quite easy for the reader to translate the findings into behaviors to add to their own repertoire of negotiation skills.

In the article "Six Basic Interpersonal Skills for a Negotiator's Repertoire," Roger Fisher and Wayne Davis describe six fundamental interpersonal skills that every successful negotiator should have. Fisher and Davis discuss three aspects of each of the interpersonal skills examined. First, they describe some of the dysfunctional symptoms that may occur if the negotiator is lacking in the particular interpersonal skill. Second, in their "diagnosis" section they discuss some of the possible reasons why people fail to master each interpersonal skill. Finally, clear, practical advice is offered about how to master each interpersonal skill.

In the third article in this section, "Our Game, Your Rules: Developing Effective Negotiation Approaches," Leonard Greenhalgh and Roderick Gilkey explore some of the differences between male and female negotiators. Greenhalgh and Gilkey draw their understanding of male–female differences in negotiation from over seven years of studying this topic in classroom, consulting, and laboratory situations. One of their most critical findings is that men and women begin negotiations with very different cognitive frames. Women tend to perceive negotiations as part of a long-term relationship with the other person where both sides seek a method of reaching the needs of both parties. In contrast, males tend to see negotiations as a single episode where both parties are trying to achieve their own goals. Greenhalgh and Gilkey present a comprehensive picture of the causes and consequences of male–female differences in negotiation and draw numerous implications for negotiators who want to expand their negotiation repertoire.

The Behavior of Successful Negotiators

Neil Rackham

BACKGROUND

Almost all publications about negotiating behavior fall into one of three classes:

1. Anecdotal "here's how I do it" accounts by successful negotiators. These have the advantage of being based on real life but the disadvantage that they frequently describe highly personal modes of behavior which are a risky guide for would-be negotiators to follow.

2. Theoretical models of negotiating which are idealized, complex, and seldom translatable into practical action.

3. Laboratory studies, which tend to be short-term and contain a degree of artificiality.

Very few studies have investigated what actually goes on face-to-face during a negotiation. Two reasons account for this lack of published research. First, real negotiators are understandably reluctant to let a researcher watch them at work. Such research requires the consent of both negotiating parties and constitutes a constraint on a delicate situation. The second reason for the poverty of research in this area is lack of methodology. Until recently there were few techniques available which allowed an observer to collect data on the behavior of negotiators without the use of cumbersome and unacceptable methods such as questionnaires.

Since 1968 a number of studies have been carried out by Neil Rackham of Huthwaite Research Group, using behavior analysis methods. These have allowed direct observation during real negotiations, so that an objective and quantified record can be collected to show how the skilled negotiator behaves.

THE SUCCESSFUL NEGOTIATOR

The basic methodology for studying negotiating behavior is simple—find some successful negotiators and watch them to discover how they do it. But what is the criterion for a successful negotiator? The Rackham studies used three successful criteria:

1. *He should be rated as effective by both sides.* This criterion enabled the researchers to identify likely candidates for further study. The condition that both sides should agree on a negotiator's effectiveness was a precaution to prevent picking a sample from a single frame of reference.

2. *He should have a track record of significant success.* The central criterion for choosing effective negotiators was track record over a time period. In such a complex field the researchers were anxious for evidence of consistency. They also wished to avoid the common trap of laboratory studies—looking only at the short-term consequences of a negotiator's behavior and therefore favoring those using tricks or deceptions.

3. *He should have a low incidence of implementation failures.* The researchers judged that the purpose of a negotiation was not just to reach an agreement but to reach an agreement that would be viable. Therefore, in addition to a track record of agreements, the record of implementation was also studied to ensure that any agreements reached were successfully implemented.

Forty-eight negotiators were picked who met all of these three success criteria. The breakdown of the sample was as follows:

Industrial (Labor) Relations Negotiators	
Union representatives	17
Management representatives	12
Contract negotiators	10
Others	9

Altogether the 48 successful negotiators were studied over a total of 102 separate negotiating sessions. For the remainder of this document these people are called the "skilled" group. In comparison, a group of negotiators who either failed to meet the criteria or about whom no criterion data was available, were also studied. These were called the "average" group. By comparing the behavior of the two groups, it was possible to isolate the crucial behaviors which made the skilled negotiators different.

THE RESEARCH METHOD

The researchers met the negotiator before the negotiation and encouraged her/him to talk about his/her planning and his/her objectives. For 56 sessions with the skilled negotiators and 37 sessions with the average negotiators, either this planning session was tape-recorded or extensive notes were taken.

The negotiator then introduced the researcher into the actual negotiation. The delicacy of this process can be judged from the fact that although most cases had been carefully prehandled, the researchers were not accepted in upward of 20 instances and were asked to withdraw.

During the negotiation the researcher counted the frequency with which certain key behaviors were used by the negotiators, using behavior analysis methods. In all of the 102 sessions interaction data was collected, while in 66 sessions content analysis was also obtained.

HOW THE SKILLED NEGOTIATOR PLANS

Negotiation training emphasizes the importance of planning. How does the skilled negotiator plan?

Amount of Planning Time

No significant difference was found between the total planning time which skilled and average negotiators claimed they spent prior to actual negotiation. This finding must be viewed cautiously because, unlike the other conclusions in this document, it is derived from the negotiators' impressions of themselves, not from their actual observed behavior. Nevertheless, it suggests the conclusion that it is not the amount of planning time which makes for success, but how that time is used.

Exploration of Options

The skilled negotiator considers a wider range of outcomes or options for action than the average negotiator.

	Outcomes/Options Considered during Planning (per negotiable issue)
Skilled negotiator	5.1
Average negotiator	2.6

The skilled negotiator is concerned with the whole spectrum of possibilities, both those which s/he could introduce himself and those which might be introduced by the people s/he negotiates with. In contrast, the average negotiator considers few options. An impression of the researchers, for which, unfortunately, no systematic data was collected, is that the average negotiator is especially less likely to consider options which might be raised by the other party.

Common Ground

Does the skilled negotiator concentrate during his/her planning on the areas which hold most potential for conflict, or does s/he give his/her attention to possible areas of common ground? The research showed that although both groups of negotiators tended to concentrate on the conflict areas, the skilled negotiators gave over three times as much attention to common ground areas as did average negotiators.

Skilled negotiators—38% of comments about areas of anticipated agreement
or common ground

Average negotiators—11% of comments about areas of anticipated agreement
or common ground

This is a significant finding and it can be interpreted in a variety of ways. It may be, for example, that the skilled negotiator has already built a climate of agreement so that undue concentration on conflict is unnecessary. Equally, concentration on the common-ground areas may be the key to building a satisfactory climate in the first place. A relatively high concentration on common-ground areas is known to be an effective strategy from other Huthwaite Research Group studies of persuasion, notably with "pull" styles of persuasion in selling.

In any event, a potential negotiator wishing to model himself on successful performers would do well to pay special attention to areas of anticipated common ground and not just to areas of conflict.

Long-Term or Short-Term?

It is often suggested that skilled negotiators spend much of their planning time considering the long-term implications of the issues, while unskilled negotiators concentrate on the short term. Is this in practice? The studies found that both groups showed an alarming concentration on the short-term aspects of issues.

	Percentage of Planning Comments about "Long-Term" Considerations of Anticipated Issues
Skilled negotiators	8.5
Average negotiators	4.0

With the average negotiator, approximately 1 comment in 25 during his/her planning met our criterion of a long-term consideration, namely a comment which involved any factor extending beyond the immediate implementation of the issue under negotiation. The skilled negotiator, while showing twice as many long-term comments, still only averages 8.5 percent of his/her total recorded planning comment. These figures must necessarily be approximate, partly because of the research methods (which may have inadvertently encouraged verbalization of short-term issues) and partly because our ignorance of individual circumstances made some comments hard to classify. Even so, they demonstrate how little thought is given by most negotiators to the long-term implications of what they negotiate.

Setting Limits

The researchers asked negotiators about their objectives and recorded whether their replies referred to single-point objectives (e.g., "we aim to settle at 83p") or to a defined range (e.g., "we hope to get 37p but we would settle for a minimum of 34p"). Skilled negotiators were significantly more likely to set upper and lower limits—to plan in terms of a range. Average negotiators, in contrast, were more likely to plan their objectives around a fixed point. Although one possible explanation is that the skilled negotiator has more freedom, which gives him the discretion of upper and lower limits, this seems unlikely from the research. Even where the average negotiator had considerable capacity to vary the terms of an agreement, s/he usually approached the negotiation with a fixed point objective in mind. The conclusion, for would-be negotiators, is that it seems to be preferable to approach a negotiation with objectives, specifying a clearly defined range rather than to base planning on an inflexible single-point objective.

Sequence and Issue Planning

The term *planning* frequently refers to a process of sequencing—putting a number of events, points, or potential occurrences into a time sequence. Critical path analysis and other forms of network planning are examples. This concept of planning, called sequence planning, works efficiently with inanimate objects, or in circumstances where the planner has real control which allows him to determine the sequence in which events will occur. The researchers found that average negotiators place very heavy reliance on sequence planning. So, for example, they would frequently verbalize a potential negotiation in terms like "First I'll bring up A, then lead to B, and after that I'll cover C, and finally go on to D." In order to succeed, sequence planning always requires the consent and cooperation of the other negotiating party. In many negotiations this cooperation is not forthcoming. The negotiator would begin at point A and the other party would only be interested in point D. This could put the negotiator in difficulty, requiring him/her to either mentally change gears and approach the negotiation in a sequence s/he had not planned for, or to carry through his/her original sequence, risking disinterest from the other party. In many negotiations, sequences were in themselves negotiable and it was ill-advised for the negotiator to plan on a sequence basis.

Typical Sequence Plan Used by Average Negotiators

A	then	B	then	C	then	D

in which issues are linked

Typical Issue Plan

Used by Skilled Negotiators

A

B

D

C

in which issues are independent and not linked by a sequence

They would consider issue C, for example, as if issues A, B, and D didn't exist. Compared with the average negotiators, they were careful not to draw sequence links between a series of issues. This was demonstrated by observing the number of occasions during the planning process that each negotiator mentioned sequence of issues.

	Number of Mentions Implying Sequence in Planning
Skilled negotiators	2.1 per session
Average negotiators	4.9 per session

The clear advantage of issue planning over sequence planning is flexibility. In planning a negotiation it is important to remember that the sequence of issues itself (unless a preset agenda is agreed) may be subject to negotiation. Even where an agenda exists, within a particular item, sequence planning may involve some loss of flexibility. So it seems useful for negotiators to plan their face-to-face strategy using issue planning and avoiding sequence planning.

FACE-TO-FACE BEHAVIOR

Skilled negotiators show marked differences in their face-to-face behavior, compared with average negotiators. They use certain types of behavior significantly more frequently while other types they tend to avoid.

Irritators

Certain words and phrases which are commonly used during negotiation have negligible value in persuading the other party but do cause irritation. Probably the most frequent example of these is the term *generous offer* used by a negotiator to describe his/her own proposal. Similarly, words such as *fair* or *reasonable,* and other terms with a high positive value loading, have no persuasive power when used as self-praise, while serving to irritate the other party because of the implication that he/she is unfair, unreasonable, and so on. Most negotiators avoid the gratuitous use of direct insults or unfavorable value judgments. They know that there is little to gain from saying unfavorable things about the other party during face-to-face exchanges. However, the other side of the coin—saying gratuitously favorable things about themselves—seems harder for them to avoid. The researchers called such words *irritators* and found that although the average negotiator used them fairly regularly, the skilled negotiator tended to avoid them.

	Use of Irritators per Hour Face-to-Face Speaking Time
Skilled negotiators	2.3
Average negotiators	10.8

It is hardly surprising that skilled negotiators use fewer irritators. Any type of verbal behavior which antagonizes without a persuasive effect is unlikely to be productive. More surprising is the heavy use of irritators by average negotiators. The conclusion must be that most people fail to recognize the counterproductive effect of using positive value judgments about themselves and, in doing so, implying negative judgments of the other party.

Counterproposals

During negotiation it frequently happens that one party puts forward a proposal and the other party immediately responds with a counterproposal. The researchers found that skilled negotiators made immediate counterproposals much less frequently than average negotiators.

	Frequency of Counterproposals per Hour of Face-to-Face Speaking Time
Skilled negotiators	1.7
Average negotiators	3.1

This difference suggests that the common strategy of meeting a proposal with a counterproposal may not be particularly effective. The disadvantages of counterproposals are

- They introduce an additional option, sometimes a whole new issue, which complicates and clouds the clarity of the negotiation.
- They are put forward at a point where the other party has least receptiveness, being concerned with his/her own proposal.
- They are perceived as blocking or disagreeing by the other party, not as proposals. (A study of 87 controlled-pace negotiation exercises by the researchers showed that when one side in a negotiation put forth a proposal there was an 87 percent chance that the other side would perceive it as a proposal. However, if the proposal immediately followed a proposal made by the other side (if in other words it was a counterproposal) the chance of being perceived as a proposal dropped to 61 percent, with a proportionate increase in the chances of being perceived as either disagreeing or blocking).

These reasons probably explain why the skilled negotiator is less likely to use counterproposing as a tactic than is the average negotiator.

Defend/Attack Spirals

Because negotiation frequently involves conflict, negotiators may become heated and use emotional or value-loaded behaviors. When such behavior was used to attack the other party, or to make an emotional defense, the researchers termed it *defending/attacking*.

Once initiated, this behavior tended to form a spiral of increasing intensity: one negotiator would attack, the other would defend himself, usually in a manner which the first negotiator perceived as an attack. In consequence, the first negotiator attacked more vigorously and the spiral commenced. Defending and attacking were often difficult to distinguish from each other. What one negotiator perceived as a legitimate defense, the other party might see as an unwarranted attack. This was the root cause of most defending/attacking spirals observed during the studies. Average negotiators, in particular, were likely to react defensively, using comments such as "You can't blame us for that" or "It's not our fault that the present difficulty has arisen." Such comments frequently provoked a sharp defensive reaction from the other side of the table.

	Percentage of Negotiators' Comments Classified as Defending/Attacking
Skilled negotiators	1.9
Average negotiators	6.3

The researchers found that average negotiators used more than three times as much defending/attacking behavior as skilled negotiators. Although no quantitative measure exists, the researchers observed that skilled negotiators, if they did decide to attack, gave no warning and attacked hard. Average negotiators, in contrast, usually began their attacking gently, working their way up to more intense attacks slowly and, in doing so, causing the other party to build up its defensive behavior in the characteristic defending/attacking spiral.

Behavior Labeling

The researchers found that skilled negotiators tended to give an advance indication of the class of behavior they were about to use. So, for example, instead of just asking "How many units are there?" they would say, "Can I ask you a question—how many units are there?" giving warning that a question was coming. Instead of just making a proposal they would say, "If I could make a suggestion . . . "and then follow this advance label with their proposal. With one exception, average negotiators were significantly less likely to label their behavior in this way. The only behavior which the average negotiator was more likely to label in advance was disagreeing.

	Percentage of All Negotiators' Behavior Immediately Preceded by a Behavior Label	
	Disagreeing	*All Behavior Except Disagreeing*
Skilled negotiator	0.4	6.4
Average negotiator	1.5	1.2

This is a slightly unusual finding and it may not be immediately evident why these differences should exist. The researcher's interpretation was that, in general, labeling of behavior gives the negotiator the following advantages:

- It draws the attention of the listeners to the behavior that follows. In this way social pressure can be brought to force a response.

- It slows the negotiation down, giving time for the negotiator using labeling to gather his/her thoughts and for the other party to clear his/her mind from the previous statements.

- It introduces a formality which takes away a little of the cut-and-thrust and therefore keeps the negotiation on a rational level.

- It reduces ambiguity and leads to clearer communication.

The skilled negotiator does, however, avoid labeling his or her disagreement. While the average negotiator will characteristically say "I disagree with that because of . . . ," thus labeling that she or he is about to disagree, the skilled negotiator is more likely to begin with the reasons and lead up to the disagreement.

Skilled Negotiators		
Reason/ explanation	Leading to	Statement of disagreement

Average Negotiators		
Statement of disagreement	Leading to	Reason/ explanation

If one of the functions of behavior labeling is to make a negotiator's intentions clear, then it is hardly surprising that the skilled negotiator avoids making it clear that s/he intends to disagree. S/he would normally prefer his/her reasons to be considered more neutrally so that acceptance involved minimal loss of face for the other party. But, if labeling disagreement is likely to be counterproductive, why does the average negotiator label disagreeing behavior more than all the other types of behavior put together? Most probably this tendency reflects the order in which we think. We decide that an argument we hear is unacceptable and only then do we assemble reasons to show why. The average negotiator speaks his/her disagreement in the same order as s/he thinks it—disagreement first, reasons afterward.

Testing Understanding and Summarizing

The researchers found that two behaviors with a similar function, testing understanding and summarizing, were used significantly more by the skilled negotiator. Testing understanding is a behavior which checks to establish whether a previous contribution or statement in the negotiation has been understood. Summarizing is a compact restatement of previous points in the discussion. Both behaviors sort out misunderstandings and reduce misconceptions.

	Percent of All Behavior by Negotiator		
	Testing Understanding	Summarizing	Testing Understanding and Summarizing
Skilled negotiators	9.7	7.5	17.2
Average negotiators	4.1	4.2	8.3

The higher level of these behaviors by the skilled negotiator reflects his/her concern with clarity and the prevention of misunderstanding. It may also relate to two less obvious factors.

1. *Reflecting*—Some skilled negotiators tended to use testing understanding as a form of reflecting behavior—turning the other party's words back in order to obtain further responses, for example, "So do I understand that you are saying you don't see any merit in this proposal at all?"

2. *Implementation concern*—The average negotiator, in his/her anxiety to obtain an agreement, would often quite deliberately fail to test understanding or to summarize. S/he would prefer to leave ambiguous points to be cleared later. S/he would fear that making things explicit might cause the other party to disagree. In short, his/her predominant objective was to obtain an agreement and s/he would not probe too deeply into any area of potential misunderstanding which might prejudice immediate agreement, even if it was likely to give rise to difficulties at the implementation stage. The skilled negotiator, on the other hand, tended to have a greater concern with the successful implementation (as would be predicted from the success criteria earlier in this document). S/he would therefore test and summarize in order to check out any ambiguities at the negotiating stage rather than leave them as potential hazards for implementation.

Asking Questions

The skilled negotiator asked significantly more questions during negotiation than did the average negotiator.

	Questions as a Percentage of All Negotiators' Behavior
Skilled negotiator	21.3
Average negotiator	9.6

This is a very significant difference in behavior. Many negotiators and researchers have suggested that questioning techniques are important to negotiating success. Among the reasons frequently given are:

1. Questions provide data about the other party's thinking and position.
2. Questions give control over the discussion.
3. Questions are more acceptable alternatives to direct disagreement.
4. Questions keep the other party active and reduce his/her thinking time.
5. Questions can give the negotiator a breathing space to allow him/her to marshal his/her own thoughts.

Feelings Commentary

The skilled negotiator is often thought of as a person who plays his/her cards close to the chest, and who keeps his/her feelings to her/himself. The research studies were unable to measure this directly because feelings are, in themselves, unobservable. However, an indirect measure was possible. The researchers counted the number of times that the negotiator made statements about what was going on inside his/her mind. The behavior category of "Giving Internal Information" was used to record any reference by the negotiator to his/her internal considerations such as feelings and motives.

	Giving Internal Information As Percentage of All Negotiators' Behavior
Skilled negotiator	12.1
Average negotiator	7.8

The skilled negotiator is more likely to give information about his/her internal events than the average negotiator. This contrasts sharply with the amount of information given about external events, such as facts, clarifications, general expressions of opinion, and so on. Here the average negotiator gives almost twice as much.

The effect of giving internal information is that the negotiator appears to reveal what is going on in his/her mind. This revelation may or may not be genuine, but it gives the other party a feeling of security because such things as motives appear to be explicit and aboveboard. The most characteristic and noticeable form of giving internal information is a *feelings commentary,* where the skilled negotiator talks about his/her feelings and the impression the other party has of him. For example, the average negotiator, hearing a point from the other party which s/he would like to accept but doubts whether it is true, is likely to receive the point in uncomfortable silence. The skilled negotiator is more likely to comment on his/her own feelings saying something like, "I'm uncertain how to react to what you've just said. If the information you've given me is true, then I would like to accept it; yet I feel some doubts inside me about its accuracy. So part of me feels happy and part feels suspicious. Can you help me resolve this?"

The work of psychologists such as Carl Rogers has shown that the expression of feelings is directly linked to establishing trust in counseling situations. It is probable that the same is true for negotiating.

Argument Dilution

Most people have a model of arguing which looks rather like a balance of a pair of scales. In fact, many of the terms we use about winning arguments reflect this balance model. We speak of "tipping the argument in our favor," of "the weight of the arguments," or how an issue "hangs in the balance." This way of thinking predisposes us to believe that there is some special merit in quantity. If we can find five reasons for doing something, then that should be more persuasive than only being able to think of a single reason. We feel that the more we can put on our scale pan, the more likely we are to tip the balance of an argument in our favor. If this model has any validity, then the skilled negotiator would be likely to use more reasons to back up his/her argument than the average negotiator.

	Average Number of Reasons Given by Negotiator to Back Each Argument/Case S/he Advanced
Skilled negotiator	1.8
Average negotiator	3.0

The researchers found that the opposite was true. The skilled negotiator used fewer reasons to back up each of his/her arguments. Although the balance-pan model may be very commonly believed, the studies suggest that it is a disadvantage to advance a whole series of reasons to back an argument or case. In doing so, the negotiator exposes a flank and gives the other party a choice of which reason to dispute. It seems self-evident that if a negotiator gives five reasons to back his/her case and the third reason is weak, the other party will exploit this third reason in their response. The most appropriate model seems to be one of dilution. The more reasons advanced, the more a case is potentially diluted. The poorest reason is a lowest common denominator: a weak argument generally dilutes a strong.

Unfortunately, many negotiators who had the disadvantage of higher education put a value on being able to ingeniously devise reasons to back their case. They frequently suffered from this dilution effect and had their point rejected, not on the strength of their principal argument, but on the weakness of the incidental supporting points they introduced. The skilled negotiator tended to advance single reasons insistently, only moving to subsidiary reasons if his/her main reason was clearly losing ground. It is probably no coincidence that an unexpectedly high proportion of the skilled negotiators studied, both in labor relations and in contract negotiation, had relatively little formal education. As a consequence, they had not been trained to value the balance-pan model and more easily avoided the trap of advancing a whole flank of reasons to back their cases.

REVIEWING THE NEGOTIATION

The researchers asked negotiators how likely they were to spend time reviewing the negotiation afterward. Over two-thirds of the skilled negotiators claimed that they always set aside some time after a negotiation to review it and consider what they had learned. Just under half of average negotiators, in contrast, made the same claim. Because the data is self-reported, it may be inaccurate. Even so, it seems that the old principle that more can be learned after a negotiation than during it may be true. An interesting difference between management and union representatives was observed. Management representatives, with other responsibilities and time pressures, were less likely to review a negotiation than were union representatives. This may, in part, account for the observation made by many writers on labor relations that union negotiators seem to learn negotiating skills from taking part in actual negotiations more quickly than management negotiators.

SUMMARY OF THE SUCCESSFUL NEGOTIATOR'S BEHAVIOR

The successful negotiator

- Is rated as effective by both sides.
- Has a track record of significant success.
- Has a low incidence of implementation failure.

Forty-eight negotiators meeting these criteria were studied during 102 negotiations.

Planning

	Negotiators	
	Skilled	Average
Overall amount of time spent	No significant difference	
Number of outcomes/options considered per issue	5.1	2.6
Percentage of comments about areas of anticipated common ground	38%	11%
Percentage of comments about long-term considerations of issues	8.5%	4%
Use of sequence during planning (per session)	2.1	4.9

Face-to-Face (Skilled Negotiators)

Avoid	Use
• Irritators	Behavior labeling (except disagreeing)
• Counterproposals	Testing understanding and summarizing
• Defend/attack spirals	Lots of questions
• Argument dilution	Feelings commentary

Six Basic Interpersonal Skills for a Negotiator's Repertoire

Roger Fisher

Wayne H. Davis

A well-rounded person has a large repertoire of interpersonal skills, and exercises them appropriately depending upon the circumstances. All of us, however, find ourselves stronger in some skills than in others. We naturally tend to use those skills in which we feel more adept and to avoid those in which we feel less comfortable or less competent.

A skilled negotiator not only has a broad repertoire of interpersonal skills but also uses those most appropriate to the circumstances of a particular situation. He or she recognizes that one's effectiveness within a given negotiation is likely to be enhanced by being able to change pace and approach.

There are an infinite range and variety in interpersonal skills. Many of these skills can be seen as attractive opposites, such as being independent and being cooperative, or being pragmatic and being imaginative, or being controlled and being expressive. We would like to be good at both but tend to be stronger in one than the other.

These desirable qualities can be visualized as lying on the circumference of a circle, so that becoming more skillful is seen as extending our skills in all directions. Improving our skills can then be recognized not as correcting a fault (such as "I am too flexible") but rather as becoming more skillful at its attractive opposite (e.g., "I want to become better at being firm when that is appropriate").

To broaden one's repertoire, it may help to think of these qualities as falling into six basic categories of interpersonal skills in which each effective negotiator enjoys some competence and confidence. We have tentatively identified these as follows:

- Expressing strong feelings appropriately.
- Remaining rational in the face of strong feelings.
- Being assertive within a negotiation without damaging the relationship.
- Improving a relationship without damage to a particular negotiation.
- Speaking clearly in ways that promote listening.
- Inquiring and listening effectively.

In use, these skills are often closely associated with each other, but in developing the skills and in practicing them it helps to focus on them one at a time. The following checklist can be used as a guide for negotiators who wish to develop a strong, well-balanced repertoire.

Reprinted from Roger Fisher and Wayne H. Davis, "Six Basic Interpersonal Skills for a Negotiator's Repertoire," *Negotiation Journal,* April 1987, pp. 117–22. Used with permission of Plenum Publishing Corporation and the authors.

Expressing Strong Feelings Appropriately

Disliked Symptoms.   Many negotiations take place as if the only effective mode of influence is the kind of rational dialogue that might take place between two computers. We may suppress or ignore flesh-and-blood feelings. In other negotiations, we may find our rational arguments overwhelmed by emotions such as anger, fear, insecurity, or hatred.

Possible Diagnoses.   Many of us learn as children that it is naughty to be angry. We may treat feelings as private problems best dealt with by suppressing them, or by denying their existence. Sometimes we may regard feelings as having less merit than reasoned argument—as something to be ashamed of.

At other times, we may contain feelings because we see no way to express them other than by losing our temper—a performance that our rational selves tell us is likely to appear ridiculous, damage our credibility, and at best prove ineffective.

General Prescriptive Approach

• *Recognize feelings.* A negotiator needs to recognize that feelings are a natural human phenomenon. They exist. There is nothing wrong with *having* emotions, although *expressing* them in particular ways may be costly or counterproductive.

• *Be aware.* It is a wise practice to become *aware* of the emotions—both our own and those of the other side—that are involved in any given negotiation. It appears to be true that if we suppress or deny our own feelings, we are likely to be unaware of the feelings of those with whom we are dealing. Before we can safely and appropriately express our feelings, we need to become aware of them, and to acknowledge them consciously.

In general, when some feeling inside seems to be growing larger and out of control, naming or identifying that feeling internally will, by itself, tend to reduce the feeling, make it more life-size, and help bring it under control.

• *Develop a range of expression.* When it comes to communicating feelings to someone else, it is well to recognize that there is a spectrum of ways to do so, ranging from talking rationally about them, through increasing the emotional content of verbal and nonverbal communication, to letting the emotions take charge.

Because of inhibitions, we often err on the side of insufficiently communicating our emotions. It is good to find a safe environment within which to experiment and practice. It is often useful to explore a range of possible expressions of emotion by deliberately overshooting. When we fear going too far, we are unlikely to learn how far we can, in fact, safely go.

• *Relate tone to substance.* Too often we fail to relate the emotional content of a communication to the substantive issue being discussed. It is far easier to be assertive—and certainly more effective—if we have something sensible to assert. Key to an effective communication of feeling is likely to be some well-prepared substantive content that identifies the purpose of the communication, justifies the feeling, and enlists its expression in the furtherance of that purpose.

Remaining Rational in the Face of Strong Feelings

Disliked Symptoms.   When others display strong emotions—particularly those hostile to us—we are likely to react and let emotions overwhelm our rationality. The cycle of emotional action and reaction is likely to preclude rational negotiation.

Possible Diagnoses.   We get caught up in the fray. We react to the last thing the other side said, and lose sight of the original purposes of talking. We may mistake their expression of strong feelings as a personal attack on us, so we feel obliged to respond in self-defense. If neither side acknowledges the existence or validity of the other's feelings, both may amplify their expression of feelings so that the underlying "message" will be heard. We may try to silence each other's expression of feelings, which compounds the frustration and felt need to be heard.

General Prescriptive Approach.   There are several different ways to deal effectively with displays of strong emotion in negotiation. Depending on the circumstances, any one of the following suggestions should prove useful:

• *Acknowledge their feelings.* When others begin to heighten the emotive content of their speech, they may not be fully aware of the feelings growing inside them. If we acknowledge that they *may* (don't attribute!) be feeling a certain way, that will usually help them to become more aware and in control of their feelings, and give us enough distance so that we don't react.

• *Step above the fray.* When the discussion turns so emotional that rational discussion seems pointless, we might withdraw from the discussion long enough for us and others to regain some composure. State frankly our reasons for withdrawing, and couple that with a commitment to return.

• *Step aside; let their emotions hit the problem.* If they're expressing an emotion, encourage them to express it fully and completely—so they can feel that they've "got it all out."

• *Separate the causes of their feelings from the substantive problem, and deal with them in parallel.* Once feelings have been fully expressed and acknowledged, it may be appropriate to analyze what engendered the feelings and take steps to alleviate those causes.

• *Be purposive.* At the outset, consciously consider and decide on the purpose of the negotiation. Then, when emotions run too strong, we can ask the parties to question whether or not the direction of the discussion serves the agreed-upon purposes of the meeting.

Being Assertive without Damaging the Relationship

Disliked Symptoms.   Often in a negotiation, we may refrain from being assertive (we fail to speak with conviction or tenaciously pursue a particular point) for fear that assertiveness will damage either the immediate or the long-term relationship. We may acquiesce when it ill serves our interests to do so.

Possible Diagnoses. When a relationship seems to be more important than any one substantive issue, some people tend to give in as soon as the other party's preference becomes clear. But giving in does not help the relationship: It may reward bad behavior or be mistaken for a lack of conviction or spinelessness—undesirable qualities for a partner in most relationships.

General Prescriptive Approach. With or without increasing the emotional content of our expressions, it is possible to be assertive without damage to a relationship. The suggested general strategy is as follows:

• *Disentangle relationship issues from substantive ones and work on them in parallel.* Although substantive disagreements can make a working relationship more difficult, and although a good working relationship can make it easier to reach agreement, the process of dealing with differences is usefully treated as a subject quite distinct and separate from the content and extent of those differences.

• *Be "soft on the people."* Avoid personal judgments. Acknowledge some merit in what the other side has said or done. Be open, polite, courteous, and considerate.

• *Have something to assert.* Know the *purpose* of the session in terms of some product that it is reasonable to expect. Focus on one or two points that we would like to communicate forcefully, such as the strength of our BATNA (best alternative to a negotiated agreement); the necessity of meeting some interest of ours; or our adherence to a particular standard of legitimacy unless and until we are convinced that some other standard is at least equally fair.

• *Be firm and open.* Be prepared to remain firm as long as that appears to us to make sense on the substance of the negotiation. At the same time, be open—both in words and thought—to alternative views that are truly persuasive.

Improving a Relationship without Damage to a Particular Negotiation

Disliked Symptoms. We often hesitate to be open and warm with people on the other side of a negotiation for fear that it will prejudice the outcome. We hesitate to acknowledge merit in what they say for fear that it will undercut what we say.

Possible Diagnoses. We may operate under a zero-sum assumption about ideas and arguments: To the extent that someone with whom we disagree is right, then we must be wrong. This assumption may stem from childhood fears of being pushed around, from formal high school or college debates, or from the general adversary nature of so much of our society. Some of us may assume that to develop a relationship in a negotiation, we must buy it with substantive concessions.

General Prescriptive Approach

• *Good relations help reach good outcomes.* It is important to recognize that relationship-building moves tend to strengthen rather than weaken our chances for achieving a good agreement.

• *Acknowledge merit in something they have done.* It is almost always possible to find something meritorious that the other side has done—perhaps in an area apart from what is being negotiated. By acknowledging that, we can communicate that we recognize and respect their worth as people.

• *Acknowledge a need on our part.* Relationships tend to be stronger when there is some interdependence: both sides feel and recognize their need or reliance on the other side in order to achieve mutually desired ends.

• *Take steps outside the negotiation to improve the relationship.* We can concentrate our relationship-building actions in temporally discrete segments of the negotiation, or when we are physically away from the table.

Speaking Clearly in Ways That Promote Listening

Disliked Symptoms.   They don't seem to be paying much attention to what we say.

Possible Diagnoses.   We may be including in what we say things that they know or believe to be mistaken. We often do so when we attribute particular intentions or motives to those on the other side. In the course of rejecting what they know to be wrong, they are likely to reject a lot of other ideas that are closely associated with them. Or something we say early in a long statement raises a red flag for them; they then tune out because they're busy thinking of a retort. Or we may be making unwarranted assumptions about what they know, when in fact they lack certain information needed to make our statements comprehensible.

General Prescriptive Approach

• *Speak for yourself.* Phrase statements about their behavior, motives, statements, and so on in first-person terms of our perceptions and feelings. They may deny the accusation "You're a bigot!" They can't deny the statement "I'm feeling discriminated against."

• *Avoid attribution and check assumptions.* Recognize when we make assumptions about their thoughts, feelings, motives, and so on, and try to verify those assumptions with the other side before acting on them. Inquire about their understanding of the background issues or information.

• *Use short, clear statements.* The longer any statement we make, the more they will edit it so they can respond. The more important our message is, the more succinct it should be. If the message is complex, break it down into small parts and confirm their understanding of each segment.

• *Ask them to repeat back what we've said.* In effect, encourage them to be active listeners by asking them to confirm in their own words what they've heard us say.

Actively Inquiring and Listening

Disliked Symptoms.   We don't learn as much as we should about the other side's interest and perceptions and the resources they could bring to bear on our joint problem. We may miss options and ideas that could lead to good solutions for us.

Possible Diagnosis.   We are often so concerned with our own interests that we ignore those of the other side. We are often bored or tired. When they say something that surprises or angers us, we may ignore the rest of what they have to say while we ready our response. We may fear that if we understand them, our resolve will weaken; or that if we show we've heard and understood, they will mistake that for acquiescence or agreement.

General Prescriptive Approach

• *Explicitly allocate time to listen and understand the other side.* Set portions of the agenda for them to explain their interests and ideas. That helps to put us into a "listening mode." An added benefit of this practice is that it establishes a precedent for reciprocal treatment of us by them.

• *Separate understanding their arguments from judging and responding to them.* Make sure that their full argument has been stated, and that we understand it before trying to respond.

• *Repeat back their statements in our own words.*

• *Inquire actively about the reasoning behind their statements.* Even if we repeat back what they said, often they haven't said all they were thinking. There will be some implicit reasoning or logic underlying their statements. It's helpful to ask them to make that reasoning explicit, and then to repeat back their explanation.

NOTE

Many of the ideas in this article were developed in collaboration with Richard Chasin, MD, and Richard Lee, PhD.

Our Game, Your Rules: Developing Effective Negotiating Approaches

Leonard Greenhalgh

Roderick W. Gilkey

Consider the following scenario: A female manager is having a discussion with a male counterpart. They are trying to reach agreement on some issue in dispute. The woman takes a flexible, friendly stance; the man is argumentative and holds firmly to his position. When they have made little progress toward agreement after some time, the woman makes concessions, telling the man she will give in on this issue and he can make it up to her next time. Some time after the negotiation is over, she learns that he did not disclose all the information he must have had, and that he even made some claims that subsequently proved to be untrue. But she gave him the benefit of the doubt on both these points; she figured he must have become a little confused while arguing for his position.

A couple of weeks later, they meet again to try to reach agreement on another issue in dispute. The woman politely reminds the man that she was generous on the last issue and therefore it is *his* turn to show some flexibility. He dismisses this reminder out of hand and proceeds to take a firm stand on the current issue. The woman, feeling angry and betrayed, now blames herself for being too unassertive.

The scenario is a familiar one. Assertiveness training, however, is not the answer to this woman's problem. Her poor short-term performance in this negotiation will show little improvement if all she learns are firmer ways of expressing herself. Instead, she needs to understand that there tends to be a fundamental difference in the way men and women view such interactions.

Women in organizations need to understand this difference because the ability to negotiate is a crucial skill in male-dominated organizational life. In theory, business decisions are rational conclusions drawn when problems are considered in the abstract. In practice, however, most significant decisions in organizations emerge from a process of negotiation; that is, reaching the decision involves reconciling the conflicting interests of the people who have some say in the matter. Making an organizational decision that is acceptable and can be implemented may require negotiating with a host of people—peers, subordinates, superiors, people in staff or control roles, customers, suppliers, regulators, news media representatives, perhaps even family members and others who may be indirectly affected by the decision. Most of the time, these

Reprinted by permission of the publisher from *Not as Far as You Think,* by Linda L. Moore (Lexington, MA: Lexington Books, D. C. Heath and Company). Copyright 1986, D. C. Heath and Company.

The authors gratefully acknowledge the contribution of Susan M. Pufahl and Lucy Axtell to the development of this chapter.

people are not conscious of the fact that they are negotiating. Nevertheless, negotiation is such a basic process in organizations that development of people's negotiating skills is as important as any other area of professional development.

During the past seven years of teaching negotiating skills to managers, executives, and MBAs in training for careers in organizations, we sensed a difference in the way men and women approach negotiation. We analyzed videotapes of simulated negotiation and found some of the differences reported in the popular press. For example, we saw that women are more likely to use powerless speech: instead of saying, "Your price is too high based on what your competitors are charging," they tend to say something like, "I don't suppose you'd consider a slightly lower price." Such hesitant, unassuming ways of making a point invite an uncooperative response if the other person is looking for a short-term gain. Women tended to demand less and concede more.

We weren't satisfied, however, that we really understood the nature and full implications of this difference in approach. We studied the relevant literature in social, personality, and developmental psychology, and saw a link between early developmental experiences, adult personality, and the negotiating behavior of young professionals. We then conducted a study to investigate the relationships we expected to find. As a result, we now have a better-informed idea of how to train men and women to reach agreements.

In this chapter, we will talk about what we have learned from our research and how this information is useful in developing women's skills as negotiators.

BACKGROUNDS

One of the most important factors affecting your approach to negotiation is your time perspective. If you view a negotiation as a single event, you will tend to focus on your immediate gain and probably will not make sacrifices in order to preserve and improve your relationship with the other person. This is known as an *episodic orientation:* you see the negotiation as a single episode whereby the history and future of your relationship with the other person are largely irrelevant. The contrasting time perspective is known as a *continuous orientation.* With such a perspective, you pay attention to the long-term relationship between you and the other person. The present negotiation is one event in a stream of interactions. Therefore, the history and future of the relationship are important—perhaps more important than immediate gain. Thus it is natural to expect that differences in time perspective will lead to differences in negotiating behavior. An episodic orientation should be associated with a competitive approach ("I need to come out ahead in this deal, and it's going to be at your expense"), whereas a continuous orientation should be associated with a more cooperative approach ("Let's find a way to meet both our needs").

Negotiators' different personalities are likely to affect whether they tend to perceive a bargaining situation as more episodic or more continuous. In particular, such differences in time perspective seem to result from a more fundamental difference in men's and women's orientations toward interpersonal relationships. This difference has been noted in a number of studies that have concluded that women tend to be concerned with their need to get along with others, cooperativeness, and fairness to both parties; men, by contrast, are concerned with their own interests, competing, and avoiding being controlled or dominated by others.[1]

One researcher attributes these contrasting orientations to differences in early developmental experiences.[2] Females develop their sex-role identity from an interaction *with* the mother that emphasizes interdependence, whereas males establish their sex-role identity through separation and individuation *from* their mothers. These differing experiences produce fundamental sex differences later in life that lead women to define themselves *in relation* to others and men *in contrast* to others.

A related factor is the difference in the way boys and girls approach games. Boys are brought up to play competitive games, in which the objective is to beat the opponent. It is acceptable to gloat about victory and deride the loser. Girls play games that focus less on winning and losing. In fact, if their games are progressing in such a way that someone is going to feel bad, girls are likely to stop the game or change the rules: girls don't sacrifice relationships in order to win games.

Carol Gilligan, in her now-classic book *In a Different Voice,* examines the consequences of such basic differences when those individuals become older children. She notes that the greater emphasis on interdependence and mutuality in women's development accounts for the difference between the sexes in their perspective on moral dilemmas: women tend to emphasize their long-term responsibilities and men their immediate rights.

Gilligan cites as an example the case of two 11-year-old children, a boy and a girl, who respond to questions about a moral dilemma. The boy, Jake, uses deductive logic to deal with what he sees as a conflict over rights and principles among three people, and he describes the solution that would quickly resolve the issues. The response of the girl, Amy, seems less clear and more equivocal. It is tempting to view Amy's response as being logically inferior to and less morally mature than Jake's, but on closer examination it becomes clear that she is viewing the conflict in very different terms. For her, the problem is one of trying to resolve a human-relations issue through ongoing personal communication. Jake, by contrast, views it as a conflict over rights that can be resolved through a morally informed legal system (the set of rules by which the "game" is played). Amy's response is actually based on a relatively sophisticated analysis of interpersonal dynamics. Her response calls for an ongoing series of interactions concerned more with preserving the relationships between conflicting parties than with deciding the parties' rights in the immediate situation.

Support for Gilligan's point of view can be found in studies that investigate the motivation of individuals to determine how they relate to other people. For example, some researchers have found a difference between boys and girls in the kinds of achievement toward which they aspire. Boys primarily strive to achieve success and therefore are more task-oriented; girls strive primarily to achieve praise and therefore are more relationship-oriented. Other studies have shown a tendency for males to be more competitive and women more cooperative in their interpersonal interactions.[3] Still other studies have examined whether males and females want different things from their jobs.[4] Those studies examine the view that women tend to be more concerned with interpersonal relationships in the work environment, whereas men appear to be more concerned with such factors as the opportunity for advancement (winning) and greater responsibility and influence (dominance).

One difficulty in conducting these studies is that women react to the experimental situation itself. A group of studies suggests that females appear to be more sensitive than males to a number of interpersonal cues that can influence their responses to the experiments. Such cues include the sex of the experimenter, whether communication is controlled or free in the experiment, and whether fairness issues are involved in the conflict.[5] These factors tend to affect women more than men and may indeed explain why research findings have been inconsistent.

Thus, some of the traits that tend to characterize women make it difficult for researchers to identify male–female differences accurately.

Taken as a whole, the diverse studies of gender differences show some general tendencies but are inconsistent in their specific conclusions. The inconsistencies are understandable when one takes into account that the behavior of adult negotiators is a function not only of biological sex but also of the effects of developmental experiences. The different childhood socialization experiences of males and females can result in different sex-role orientations, ranging from strongly masculine to strongly feminine. A strongly masculine person is concerned with power and prefers to dominate others rather than be dominated by them; a strongly feminine person is less concerned with dominance and more concerned with nurturance. Masculinity–feminity, however, does not correspond exactly to biological sex. Some boys are raised to have predominantly feminine orientations, and some girls are raised to have predominantly masculine orientations. All people fall on a continuum between these two extremes. Because sex role is expected to have greater effect on negotiating behavior, sex role rather than biological sex is used in the research reported here and in the discussion that follows.

THE STUDY

Having come this far in researching the literature, we were confident that there were masculine–feminine differences in negotiating approaches. As social scientists, however, we realized that our past observations could simply be hunches, that the studies we had read reported some inconsistencies, and that no one had yet directly studied masculine–feminine differences of adult negotiators. The burden of proof was on us to show that such differences really exist.

We decided to study masculine–feminine differences in a controlled, laboratory setting. Instead of observing everyday negotiations, we simulated the situations under controlled conditions and had young professionals role-play the negotiations. There was enough flexibility in the role instructions to allow masculine–feminine differences to emerge as expected. The use of a laboratory study had two advantages over observing naturally occurring negotiations: First, it allowed us to eliminate most extraneous factors that could contaminate the results; second, it would allow other researchers to replicate our study, thereby adding to its scientific value. (A description of the study can be found at the end of this chapter.)

The results of the study proved consistent with what we had hypothesized. Several differences between masculine and feminine negotiators emerged and are summarized

TABLE 1   Summary of the Different Tendencies of Masculine and Feminine Negotiators

Masculine Tendencies	*Feminine Tendencies*
Visualize a one-shot deal	Visualize the present transaction as one event in a long-term relationship
Seek a sports-type victory	Seek mutual gain
Emphasize rules of the game, precedents, and power positions	Emphasize fairness
Explain logic of their position	Inquire about other's needs and make personal appeals
Conceal or misrepresent their own needs	Be up front about their own needs
Speak in a dominating or controlling manner	Use "powerless" speech
Be intransigent about their position, perhaps trying to conceal their rigid stance	Be willing to compromise
Interrupt and deceive the other party	Avoid tactics that might jeopardize the long-term relationship

in Table 1. The most basic finding was that feminine negotiators tend to visualize the long-term relationship between the people involved when they think about negotiations. Their masculine counterparts tend to visualize a sporting event in which the other person is an opponent who has to be beaten.

Consistent with this basic difference in orientation, feminine negotiators were likely to be more empathic: that is, they had a natural tendency to try to see the situation from the other person's point of view. This put them in a position to meet mutual needs, which is an ideal outcome of negotiations when there is an ongoing relationship. Furthermore, in the absence of an urgency to "win," feminine negotiators sought fairness and were willing to compromise to achieve a fair outcome.

Finally, the feminine negotiators' concern with the long-term relationship seems to lead them to avoid using tactics that might jeopardize that relationship. Thus, we found that feminine negotiators were less likely to deceive the other person. Ironically, the stereotypical view of women's and men's relative trustworthiness is just the opposite. When social psychologists ask people whether women or men are more likely to use underhanded tactics, most people choose women as the less trustworthy. Our research shows that, in fact, women are likely to be more trustworthy than men.

IMPLICATIONS FOR NEGOTIATION RESEARCH

The time horizon makes a big difference in how a person approaches a negotiation. If the person visualizes a one-shot deal, any tactic that will produce an advantage is considered because there is no need to worry about future consequences. If, on the other hand, the person's focus is on the longer-term relationship, then immediate gain is less important than maintaining goodwill.

Two things determine whether a negotiator takes an episodic or a continuous orientation toward a particular transaction. The first is the objective situation: some transactions *are* one-shot deals in which the negotiators have never interacted beforehand and will probably never deal with each other again. Examples of such transactions include buying an item in a bazaar in a foreign country, or selling an automobile through a newspaper advertisement. The second determinant is the negotiator's personality, which may create *tendencies* to perceive the time horizon to be long-term or short-term, regardless of what the objective situation really calls for. We have seen that a person's sex-role orientation, arising from developmental experiences, has such an effect.

The results of this research help explain some of the inconsistencies in the literature on sex differences in interpersonal relations. In many studies, sex is defined in terms of biological gender; but that approach neglects the results of developmental experiences, which vary widely among individuals. If we are confident that sex-role orientation accurately measures the masculine-feminine perspective, it makes more sense to use this dimension rather than biological sex in our research.

This knowledge of masculine–feminine differences in negotiation approaches helps us understand the scenario we presented at the beginning of this chapter. The woman was willing to make concessions in the short term because she visualized a long-term relationship, in which present concessions would be reciprocated in the future. Her male counterpart had no such perspective. He was visualizing a one-shot deal in which the objective was to beat the other party. Because he saw the interaction as a game, any tactics were permissible—including withholding information and outright deception—as long as they did not violate the explicit rules of the game. The future was irrelevant once the game was over, and a victory in a past game did not obligate the man to try less hard in the next. Had the female negotiator realized that the man was approaching the interaction from this perspective, she could have imposed some rules on the game, or convinced the man not to think of it as a game and done a better job of emphasizing the long-term relationship between them.

IMPLICATIONS FOR DEVELOPMENT OF NEGOTIATING SKILL

Differences in socialization are among the many factors that explain personality differences among negotiators. There is no one best way to negotiate that is suitable for all personalities; rather, each person must develop an approach that capitalizes on unique strengths and compensates for weaknesses. Thus the development of individuals' negotiating approaches must be a highly individualized process that ideally begins with personality assessment.

Personality assessment, however, is not a process that can be taken lightly. The adage that "a little knowledge is a dangerous thing" can be particularly true in the case of understanding one's psychological makeup. Thus the personality-assessment phase of our approach to training negotiators is a comprehensive process, involving standardized self-report personality measures, projective tests, psychological histories, observation of negotiating behavior, and an in-depth interview conducted by a clinical psychologist. Only when we have a good understanding of the individual do we feed back the insights thus gained to the person to improve his or her self-understanding. This process also sensitizes the person both to improve his or her self-understanding and to start thinking about how others may be different, so that negotiating tactics can be somewhat tailored to the type of individual being dealt with. This aspect of our program for developing negotiators is very effective, but we caution individuals who may be undertaking their own self-development, as well as those seeking to develop others, to be sure that properly qualified people are involved in the assessment and that the analysis is comprehensive enough so that it does more good than harm.

Our next step is to help people valuate their effectiveness as negotiators, given their uniqueness as individuals. The best way to do this is to help people become good self-critics. They learn to assess the effectiveness of their negotiating approaches by analyzing a videotape of their own negotiation performance. We have found that people tend to downplay their mistakes and overlook important factors in a negotiation such as tone of voice, gestures, and body language. The videotape preserves such evidence for the purpose of constructive feedback.

Videotape feedback supervised by the instructor is extremely time-consuming, however. Therefore, it needs to be supplemented with supervised self-observation. A good way to accomplish this is to have students keep a journal of their negotiations inside and outside the classroom. They are encouraged to experiment with different approaches, and in the journal they analyze what tactics work well or poorly for them. After keeping a journal for a term, our trainees acquire the habit of constantly analyzing and critiquing their own performance in interactions. Finally, we expose them to a wide variety of negotiating situations—buying and selling, dealing with bosses and subordinates, negotiating and implementing a real estate contract, a corporate acquisition, collective bargaining, settling grievances, and various types of negotiations within and between groups.

Tailoring the learning experience to the unique needs of individuals provides the opportunity to address the special needs of women preparing for professional careers in organizations. For instance, the tendency for women to adopt a continuous time perspective can be a considerable asset in some bargaining situations and a liability in others. It is an asset when relationship-oriented, cooperative, and empathic behavior elicits similar behavior from the other party and leads to mutual accommodation. The liability of this time perspective is that it can make the negotiator vulnerable to exploitation by someone who seeks only short-term gain. In short, the woman who is too nice can be ripped off by an unscrupulous opponent.

The need to adapt to different approaches of the other party requires women to develop flexibility in their negotiating approaches. In practice this means that we encourage women to begin with a positive approach but to be ready to fight fire with fire if they encounter an exploitative, unyielding stance. Specifically, we hope to develop the woman's skill at expressing her commitment to a longer-term relationship and persuading the other person of the advantages of this predisposition. If this gentle persuasion doesn't work, she might interrupt the flow of the negotiation to comment on what is going on between the two people. She may approach this by trying to reflect back the position and assumptions of the other person. ("Let me see if I understand where you're coming from. You need to show your boss that you've gotten a good deal, and if you do that, I'm going to look bad to my boss. So why don't we brainstorm some ideas for how we can both look good?") If this positive approach does not work, the woman needs to have a more hard-line approach available, to use as a deterrent to the tactics of a chronically episodic-oriented opponent.

Another example of the ways in which women can constructively adapt their instinctive approaches to negotiation situations is to capitalize on their natural tendency to be empathic—that is, to be able to understand the perspective of the other party. Empathic tendencies give rise to empathy ("I'd like to learn what you would like to achieve by means of this agreement"), which can elicit a wealth of information about the interests of the other party. An empathic appeal is one of the most effective tactics that can be used to exert influence in a negotiation: it involves simply pointing out how settlements that are of benefit to oneself meet the other party's needs ("If we agree to what I suggested earlier, here's how *you'll* benefit").

We realize we may be coming close to suggesting ways to manipulate other people when we explain how to devise empathic appeals. Although it is true that information gained through empathic inquiries *could* be used exploitatively, such information also can be used in a way that ensures that both parties' needs are met and that both people feel good about the deal. Women's tendency to approach interactions from a continuous time perspective makes the manipulative use of information less likely.

The other feature of our development program that is worth mentioning attempts to undo some of the damage done during male socialization. Briefly, our mission is to help stamp out sports metaphors. This mission is as important to males whose thinking is distorted by these metaphors as it is to women who must suffer the effects.

Males become familiar with competitive games at an early age. When they encounter unfamiliar situations later on, they try to understand them in terms of what is familiar. As a result, many types of relationships are described in sports terms, from "making a big hit" in a business presentation to "scoring" on a date. Unfortunately, such metaphors shape the way males think about relationships in unhelpful ways. Sports contests are episodic by nature; they are either won or lost, so meeting mutual needs is inappropriate; any tactics that do not violate explicit rules are permissible; and the other person is defined as an opponent rather than a potential ally in solving a mutual problem.

It is very difficult to stamp out sports metaphors among negotiators. Because they so permeate the vocabulary of both men and women, they become invisible to those who are affected by them. Even some experts on negotiation cannot escape their effects. For example, some describe meeting mutual needs as a *win-win* solution, which stretches the metaphor beyond its logical limits: if there is a winner, someone else must be a loser; *both* people cannot win. Thus win-win imagery at best makes no sense and at worst perpetuates a view of the situation that fosters conflict rather than accommodation.

SUMMARY

Our professional development programs have been considerably enriched by the research we have conducted on masculine–feminine differences in negotiating. Improvement of negotiating skills, properly guided by research findings, is vital as women endeavor to become more influential in settings traditionally dominated by their male counterparts. Negotiation skills also are vital as organizations take new forms, such as matrix management, increasingly complex structures, team-centered workforces, and Japanese-style management. All these innovations emphasize agreement and coordination between people, which in turn call for effective negotiation skills. Thus, individuals should be strongly concerned with this aspect of their professional development, as should their higher-level managers.

A NOTE ON THE STUDY

The specific hypotheses we tested were based on our review of the literature and our experience in observing and training negotiators. We expected that individuals who are primarily feminine in their sex-role orientation would (1) tend to conceptualize interactions as continuous rather than episodic and (2) use negotiating tactics that strengthen the interpersonal relationship between the parties.

Our study used two different simulated business negotiations—an automobile purchase and a television advertising contract negotiation. Both were videotaped. The participants in the study (our experimental subjects) were 64 MBA students, all with previous business experience. Both men and women participated in the study, but the important variable was their sex-role orientation. As mentioned earlier, there is nothing in males' and females' genes or hormones that makes them negotiate differently; masculine–feminine differences arise from childhood socialization.

We measured sex-role orientation by means of a questionnaire.[6] Other personality characteristics were investigated in depth by a clinical psychologist, who used multiple measures to be sure to achieve a comprehensive assessment of each subject. Special instructions in the second simulation (the television advertising contract negotiation) informed subjects that they were in an episodic *situation.* Specifically, they were instructed that this was truly a one-shot deal; in fact, this was the last time they would be negotiating in this position for the company, and they would not be dealing with the other person again. This situation provided an opportunity to observe which subjects chose to respond to the situation by adopting an episodic *orientation* to their role and which subjects tried to maintain a continuous one.

The videotapes of the subjects' negotiating performance were analyzed by a trained observer, who was kept unaware of our hypotheses so that we could avoid possible biases to the analysis.

One of the clinical psychologist's specific tasks was to assess each subject's characteristic *tendency* to assume an episodic or a continuous orientation. In the one-hour, in-depth interview, he asked the subjects to describe various interactions they were having *outside* the laboratory study. From the patterns in the behavior they described, the psychologist was able to identify *general* tendencies to see situations as one-shot deals or as events within a long-term relationship.

In summary, then, we recruited 64 young professionals to participate in the study. Then we used a questionnaire to determine whether they had acquired a masculine or feminine sex-role orientation during their childhood socialization. Setting this information aside, we then asked the clinical psychologist to determine whether each person had a natural tendency to see negotiations as one-shot deals or as events in a longer-term relationship. Then we asked the participants to role-play two simulated negotiations each with a different (randomly assigned) partner. Videotapes of the negotiations were then analyzed to see what tactics were used. Finally, we put all the data together to see if, as we had hypothesized, the feminine negotiators had different time perspectives and used different tactics than their masculine counterparts.

NOTES

1. See, for example, the following studies: M. S. Horner, "Toward an Understanding of Achievement-Related Conflicts in Women," *Journal of Social Issues* 28 (1972): 157–75; N. Chodorow, "Family Structure and Feminine Personality," in M. Z. Rosaldo and L. Lamphere, eds., *Women, Culture and Society* (Stanford: Stanford University Press, 1974); J. B. Miller, *Toward a New Psychology of Women* (Boston: Beacon Press, 1976); C. Gilligan, *In a Different Voice* (Cambridge, MA: Harvard University Press, 1982).
2. See Chodorow, "Family Structure."
3. See E. E. Maccoby and C. N. Jacklin, *The Psychology of Sex Differences* (Stanford: Stanford University Press, 1974).
4. See K. M. Bartol and D. A. Butterfield, "Sex Effects in Evaluating Leaders," *Journal of Applied Psychology* 61 (1976): 446–54.
5. See J. Z. Rubin and B. R. Brown, *The Social Psychology of Bargaining and Negotiation* (New York: Academic Press, 1975).
6. The questionnaire was the Bem Sex-Role Inventory. For details of this measure, see S. L. Bem, "The Measurement of Psychological Androgyny," *Journal of Consulting and Clinical Psychology* 42 (1974): 155–62.

SECTION ELEVEN
Global Negotiations

More and more businesses conduct business across borders. Be it a joint venture in China, a technology transfer in Europe, outsourcing in the Pacific Basin, or new ventures in Africa or the former Soviet republics, American business is looking beyond its own borders more than ever before. Negotiating across national and cultural boundaries complicates the negotiation process. Obvious challenges such as logistics and language are just the tip of the iceberg of the special circumstances of global negotiations. More subtle issues such as the meaning of time, how concessions are made, who should be members of the negotiation team, and so on abound in global negotiations. To make this even more complex, our most basic assumptions about what negotiation is, how it works, why it is done, and where it is appropriate may or may not be shared by the other party with whom we are negotiating.

The literature on global negotiations has grown rapidly in the past 10 years. Both practitioners and academics have been studying global negotiations, and the size and complexity of this topic ensure that this research will continue well into the future. While a great deal has been written about global negotiations, until very recently much of it has been fragmented and impressionistic. Recent work has been more holistic, but it still remains a challenge to understand the nuances of even one culture in addition to our own. The first article in this section discusses the numerous special constraints involved in global negotiations, while the other two articles explore specific negotiation styles from America and abroad.

In "The Dynamics of International Business Negotiations," Arvind V. Phatak and Mohammed M. Habib review and discuss the numerous contexts that surround global negotiations. The authors suggest that there are two contexts under which all global negotiations occur: the environmental context and the immediate context. The environmental context includes things like political and legal pluralism, currency fluctuations, and cultural and ideological differences. The immediate context includes things like relative bargaining power, immediate stakeholder needs, and the extent of conflict between the negotiators. Phatak and Habib discuss the influence of several contextual factors on global negotiations and conclude their article with a discussion about how to use their model to improve global negotiations.

In the second article in this section, "American Strengths and Weaknesses," Tommy Koh, a former Singaporean ambassador to the United States, examines the strengths and weaknesses of American negotiators. Many of the strengths discussed by Koh will seem obvious to American negotiators, and include taking negotiation preparation seriously, the tendency to speak plainly, and pragmatism. What is illuminating about Koh's discussion, however, is that while these characteristics make sense, they are not necessarily those which American negotiators would recognize as defining them as "American negotiators." The remainder of Koh's article examines several weaknesses and idiosyncrasies of the American negotiation style, including factors that surround the immediate topic of the negotiation (e.g., the effects of the media) as well as individual-level characteristics (e.g., impatience). Koh concludes this article with a discussion of the attributes that should be considered when selecting someone to negotiate globally.

In the third article in this section, "Global Negotiating: Vive les Differences!," Sergey Frank presents his impressions of the negotiation styles of negotiators from several of the countries he has negotiated with. Frank writes from broad personal experience and gives tips for negotiating with people from Europe, Central and South America, Japan, and elsewhere. He offers practical advice for each of the cultures he discusses, and he suggests that people who are headed for global negotiations should seek advice from more experienced others before starting.

The Dynamics of International Business Negotiations

Arvind V. Phatak

Mohammed M. Habib

There can be no international business without the presence of at least two parties, each coming from different countries, sitting face to face and negotiating a business deal. Negotiations precede all international business transactions, whether they are the sale of a product to a foreign buyer, the formation of a joint venture between two companies of different nationalities to share distribution channels in a third country, an acquisition of a company by a foreign company, or the licensing of a technology by a company to a foreign producer. It is inevitable that negotiations between two or more sides will take place whenever a certain outcome is impossible to obtain unilaterally without incurring unacceptable political, legal, or economic consequences.

Negotiation is a process whereby two or more parties—be they individuals, groups, or larger social units—interact in developing potential agreements to provide guidance and regulation of their future behavior. Such negotiation can be conducted between nations, as in the tripartite negotiations between the United States, Canada, and Mexico to forge the North American Free Trade Agreement (NAFTA); between companies, as in the alliance between British Air and USAir to share routes, airport gates, and reservations systems; or between any two or more parties that need to cooperate or bargain to attain certain common or conflicting ends.

In any negotiation, the process and outcomes are influenced by contextual factors. Too often academics and the business press have focused on negotiating strategies without duly emphasizing context. Even when negotiation context is discussed, it is usually presented as a "cultural" issue. Only recently have some researchers examined and developed broad frameworks focusing on the context of international negotiation.

Using a similar approach, this article presents a comprehensive model of international negotiation describing the different contexts and their relationship to the negotiation process and outcomes. The proposed model should provide a practical framework for negotiators, assisting them in better preparing themselves for complex negotiations and recognizing the need for a broader perspective combined with the ability to comprehend details.

Whenever two parties negotiate, the entire process occurs under two umbrella contexts, *environmental* and *immediate.* The environmental context refers to forces in the environment that are beyond the control of either party involved in the negotiations.

Reprinted from *Business Horizons,* May–June 1996, pp. 30–38, with permission of the publisher.

The immediate context includes such aspects as the relative power of the negotiators and the nature of their interdependence—factors over which the negotiators have influence and some measure of control. Figure 1 shows the conceptual framework for international business negotiations and the various dimensions of these contexts. The environmental context, in the outer circle, consists of eight dimensions; the immediate context, in the middle circle, consists of five. Both jointly have an impact on the process and outcome of negotiations.

THE ENVIRONMENTAL CONTEXT OF INTERNATIONAL BUSINESS NEGOTIATIONS

We shall first explore the nature of the environmental context, the outermost circle in Figure 1.[1] The dimensions of the environmental context include legal and political pluralism, currency fluctuations and foreign exchange, foreign government controls and bureaucracy, instability and change, ideological and cultural differences, and the influence of external stakeholders.

FIGURE 1   The Contexts of International Negotiations

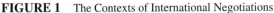

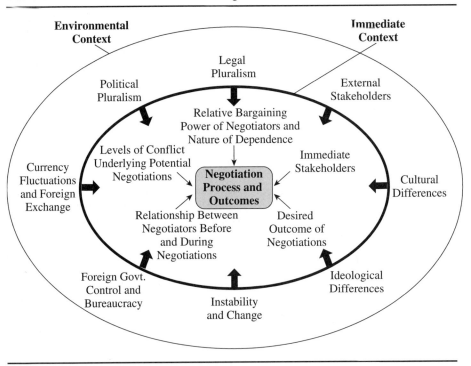

---

1. Some concepts for this section have been borrowed from Salacuse (1988).

Legal Pluralism

The principle of national sovereignty gives every nation-state the right to make laws that are supposedly in its national interests. An international business transaction must comply with the laws of the countries involved. Certain laws prohibit certain types of transactions. For example, the United States has legislation that lists the various types of technologies, particularly those with potential military applications, that are prohibited from being exported. When Cray Computer Company tried to sell a supercomputer to the Indian government, the United States disallowed the sale on the grounds that it was illegal because it hurt American national security interests.

In several countries, certain sectors of the economy, such as telecommunications and automobile manufacturing, are often kept off-limits to wholly owned foreign investments. For instance, a foreign company can enter the Indian and Chinese markets only by forming joint ventures with indigenous companies. General Motors, Ford, Volkswagen, and Mercedes have established manufacturing plants in India in joint ventures with Indian companies; Volkswagen, Citroën, and Peugeot have joint ventures in China. The joint venture requirement undoubtedly affected the negotiations between the two sides over other important aspects, such as managerial and quality control, global marketing rights, valuation of technology transferred, profit sharing, and royalty payments.

Negotiators should be forewarned about the legal traps that could transform a supposedly good agreement into a nightmare if the legal implications of the transaction are not carefully examined. It is imperative that negotiators be extremely careful in avoiding the risk of doing something illegal under the laws of either the home country or the host country.

Political Pluralism

The world consists of more than 100 countries, each with its own distinct political system and foreign policy. International businesspeople are often caught in the crossfire of sometimes conflicting foreign policies of two or more countries. For example, an American executive in a French subsidiary of a U.S. company must be aware of both French and American foreign policies as they apply to engaging in a business relationship with Cuba or North Korea. A business deal that may be in the political and economic interests of France may run counter to those of the United States.

An example of such a situation is the construction of the Trans-Siberian pipeline in the former Soviet Union in the 1980s. Several European subsidiaries of American companies had negotiated contracts to supply such equipment as transformers, generators, and construction services for the pipeline. When the Soviets invaded Afghanistan, however, American foreign policy turned quite hostile toward the Soviet Union, and the U.S. government demanded that American firms and their subsidiaries stop supplying the equipment and services. But the European governments demanded that the subsidiaries of American companies based in European countries be permitted to fulfill their contracts with the Soviets, claiming that the pipeline supply contracts were in the national interests of the host European countries. Only diplomacy at the highest level finally resolved the problem.

The foreign policy of the host country also affects the conduct of international business negotiations. For example, the Datuk Seri Mahathir Mohamad, Prime Minister of Malaysia, is noted for his anti-European, anti-British political stance. Thus, English companies engaged in negotiating a business transaction with Malaysian companies would have to try extra hard to get the deal. This is especially true if non-European companies from countries that are friendly with the Malaysian government are also in the fray.

It is vital to understand the constraints imposed on the process of international business negotiations by the foreign policies of countries that are directly or indirectly affected by the outcome of such negotiations. Parties involved should thoroughly study the potential political fallout of an international business deal before it is negotiated and the agreement is signed.

Currency Fluctuations and Foreign Exchange

When the Mexican currency crisis began in late 1994, *The Wall Street Journal* reported that within a week the peso had lost almost 36 percent of its value against the dollar, and 43 percent since the beginning of the year. This highlights the significance of the impact of currency value fluctuations on international business negotiations. International firms that negotiated business deals or operations in Mexico should have taken the risk of the peso devaluation into account during their negotiations with Mexican firms.

International business transactions take place in a world of multiple currencies, the values (foreign exchange rates) of which fluctuate daily. A business deal that is not effectively structured to compensate and protect against foreign exchange fluctuations is likely to be a prelude to a disaster if the underlying currencies in which payments are to be received precipitously decline in value—or a windfall if they appreciate in value—against the recipient company's home currency or other stable currencies. It would be prudent for negotiators of both companies to obtain realistic "most likely" forecasts of the exchange rates for the relevant currencies from such reliable sources as international banks and currency futures markets. They can thus build into the agreement contingency clauses that would protect either side from wild swings in the exchange rates of their respective currencies or engage in currency hedging contracts.

Foreign exchange controls by many governments also influence international business negotiations. The ability of a company to pay for imported raw materials, or to repatriate profits or dividends to a foreign parent, depends on the willingness of the host government to make the necessary foreign exchange available for such transactions. Negotiators for a foreign company must ensure that, in whatever agreement is negotiated, provisions are made that would avoid or blunt the effect of these controls. For instance, in the face of foreign exchange restrictions, an international company could negotiate a "countertrade" deal by which payment is made in goods, rather than cash.

Foreign Government Controls and Bureaucracy

The extent of governmental interference in business in many nations is extensive. Government agencies may have the authority to control the total output of an industry.

Or they may have absolute control over the granting of permits to expand production capacity. A company with the potential to increase market share is obligated to obtain the necessary license to expand capacity, a license that is often denied by government bureaucrats.

A company may also need a license to implement a strategy designed to expand its product line. As a case in point, in the mid-1980s the Indian subsidiary of Procter & Gamble had to plead with the Indian government for permission to market P&G's consumer products. Such pervasive intrusion into the "private" affairs of companies is quite routine in most developing countries, such as China, Indonesia, Egypt, and India. Efforts at liberalization and privatization in these countries have reduced this interference somewhat. However, the level of such interference is still far more than one normally encounters in the more economically advanced countries.

Government agencies control entire industries in many countries. Until recently, the entire telecommunications field was in the sole domain of government-owned enterprises in Brazil, Argentina, Chile, and India. Now, joint ventures are allowed in these sectors with government and private enterprises. In many countries, private enterprise is forbidden in such sectors as oil and gas, shipping, and airlines. In some industries, government firms compete with private enterprise, as is the case in India.

Negotiations in the sorts of business environment described above almost always include the government as one of the parties with whom a foreign firm is negotiating, directly or indirectly. The government agency may not be physically present at the negotiating table, but its silent presence is felt throughout the process because every issue negotiated has to be considered in light of the pertinent governmental regulations.

Instability and Change

Heraclitus said, "There is nothing permanent except change." Change is omnipresent. During the decade of the 1980s and the early 1990s, we have witnessed such unexpected events as the fall of the Soviet Union, the reunification of Germany, the Gulf War, significant peace prospects in the Middle East, and the economic liberalization and opening of markets to trade and foreign investments in China, India, and Russia. Each of these events has brought forth opportunities for international firms. However, such opportunities are also associated with risks in other areas. As Curran (1994) stated:

> A more immediate worry for investors is that if inflation is not checked, China's currency, the yuan, could be devalued. Investors only have to think back a few years to a period when China's government was devaluing the currency every few months. Growth is nice, but so is capital preservation.
>
> Political risks seem to be rising too. Can the market keep liberalizing without creating a strong desire among citizens for more freedom in other areas of life, leading to another bloody confrontation with the old line communist leaders? And what happens to China's power structure after Deng Xiaoping dies? Such concerns do not negate the long-term case for China, but they do make it less of a sure bet. Investors need patience, smarts, and a strong stomach for volatility.

To cope with volatility and risks, negotiators should be prepared with advice from experts on the probability of economic and political risks in the target country.

Armed with valid and reliable information on the most likely economic and political scenarios, international managers would be on a firmer footing to effectively negotiate the very best deal possible with their company counterparts in the host country.

International negotiators must have expertise in the target country as well as in the global business environment. Knowledge of global opportunities and risks for the company's product is most useful because it serves as a benchmark against which to evaluate the costs and benefits of doing business in a particular country. For example, a British company that is negotiating a joint venture with a Chinese enterprise to produce cars for the Chinese market would be in a much better bargaining position knowing that an equally good opportunity exists in India.

Ideological Differences

Ideology may be defined as the body of ideas on which a particular political, economic, or social system is based. International managers may be shocked to find that the ideologies—indeed, the very basis of life—they have always taken for granted may not exist in other countries. For example, political freedom is limited in Egypt, which allows only one political party to exist. It is almost totally absent in China. Equality does not exist among Saudi Arabians, especially between men and women. The right to own private property does not exist in communist countries like Cuba, North Korea, and China. And in segments of the economy where private enterprise does exist, that right is delegated to the individual by the state. These concepts all run quite contrary to the ideology of the United States, where individuals have the birthright to own property, exercise political freedom, and be treated equally.

Countries such as India, Nigeria, Malaysia, Egypt, and Indonesia, which were once Western colonies, have a history of antipathy toward foreign investment. It is mistakenly perceived as another form of foreign domination. Although these attitudes have changed dramatically since the beginning of the 1990s, left-wing political parties and labor unions continue to blame global companies for the countries' domestic problems. The conflict in political ideologies makes it necessary for negotiators to find a middle ground and frame the language and content of the negotiated contract in a pattern that is acceptable to both sides.

Cultural Differences

International business negotiations involve interactions between managers from disparate cultures. Cultural norms and differences between the negotiators have a significant influence on how they behave throughout the process. For instance, the building of trust and relationships is extremely important for the Japanese, Chinese, Mexicans, and most Latin Americans. In these cultures, it is considered essential to become acquainted with each other and to build a certain "comfort level" before sitting down at the negotiating table. "Japanese," says Foster (1992), "view negotiation as a collaborative process of 'mind-meeting,' which can mandate several meetings before substantive issues are even discussed." By contrast, Americans are known for their impatience to "get down to business" after a few pleasantries.

Cultural differences in the value placed on the use of time as a resource can influence negotiations. Americans are known to be meticulous about punctuality, getting things done when promised and not wasting time. They perceive time as a depleting resource that must be used efficiently. Mexicans and Chinese, on the other hand, see time as an endless continuum—a context rather than a constraint—in which we live.

During negotiations, Americans are inclined to make small concessions early to establish a relationship and to keep the negotiation process moving forward smoothly. In contrast, Japanese have a tendency to hold back major concessions until very late in the negotiations. Differences also exist on how much and what type of information is shared with the other side. American negotiators are inclined to share large amounts of significant information about their company's needs, limitations, and so on. The premise is that the other side will reciprocate upon seeing how open they are. Japanese, on the other hand, see no such need to provide meaningful information to the other side and so offer only the smallest crumbs of information in exchange.

To Americans, a contract signals the conclusion of negotiations; its terms establish the rights, responsibilities, and obligations of the parties involved. However, to the Japanese, a company is not forever bound to the terms of the contract. In fact, it can be renegotiated whenever there is a significant shift in the company's circumstances. For instance, an unexpected change in governmental tax policy, or a change in the competitive environment, are considered legitimate reasons for contract renegotiation. To the Chinese, a signatory to an agreement is a partner with whom they can work, so to them the signing of a contract is just the beginning of negotiations.

Most international business negotiations never fulfill their potential expectations because of cultural faux pas on one side or the other during the negotiations. International business negotiators would be better off to be well versed in the cultural nuances and unspoken language of the negotiators at the other end of the table.

External Stakeholders

The various people and organizations that have an interest or stake in the outcome of the negotiations are the external stakeholders. Examples include competitors, customers, labor unions, organized business groups such as chambers of commerce and industry associations, and the company's shareholders.

Competitors are likely to apply pressure by lobbying against a proposed business arrangement, such as a joint venture, if the outcome of the negotiation is the introduction of a formidable new competitor in the market. Lobbying strategies may include the launch of a public relations campaign against the deal, illustrating real or contrived harmful effects of the joint venture or trying to have key permits and approvals denied by the government.

Consumers that are affected by the outcome of the negotiations may become involved in ways that may help or hinder the negotiation process. For example, the United States has been negotiating for decades with Japan to provide greater access to the Japanese market for American goods and services. Japanese consumers are in favor of opening the market to foreign competition because it would result in their getting a cheaper and wider variety of goods. So they have been lobbying for it.

However, the various industry groups in the electronics, automobile, and agricultural sectors remain opposed to opening the market to foreign competitors, and to date have been quite successful at blocking any substantial market-opening measures.

Labor unions are generally opposed to any business transaction that is likely to reduce employment opportunities for their members. For example, unions have organized several strikes against Caterpillar, the American manufacturer of earth-moving equipment. One of their principal grievances against the company is the loss of manufacturing jobs in the United States resulting from the transfer of manufacturing jobs overseas by Caterpillar's management in search of low-cost production sites. Caterpillar has several manufacturing joint ventures abroad. The reaction of the labor unions in the United States must surely be having an impact on the negotiating process for any new foreign joint ventures.

For international joint ventures being set up in the home country, labor unions are concerned about such issues as union recognition, hiring, selection process, job classification, and seniority. A classic example is the role of the United Auto Workers in the NUMMI joint venture negotiations between General Motors and Toyota that occurred in the early 1980s.

The attitude of organized business groups, such as chambers of commerce, can influence the ambiance for international business negotiations. For example, with the opening of markets in China, India, and Russia, the U.S. Chamber of Commerce has organized several groups of top-level executives from major American corporations to visit these countries in search of joint ventures. The chambers of commerce in each country can help clear many hurdles, such as unnecessary bureaucratic red tape. The hundreds of joint ventures established in China, India, and Russia could never have materialized had it not been for the active stance of the chambers of commerce of the countries involved.

The progress of negotiations could be either stimulated or inhibited by the reaction of the shareholders. A company whose shareholders are opposed to a merger will either withdraw from the negotiations or try to change the attitude of other shareholders by making changes in their negotiating stance. Shareholders always maintain an "invisible" presence at the negotiating table, watching over the proceedings and signaling their approval or disapproval of the content of the negotiations.

THE IMMEDIATE CONTEXT OF INTERNATIONAL BUSINESS NEGOTIATIONS

In the middle circle of Figure 1 is the immediate context of international business negotiations. The immediate context consists of factors over which the negotiators have some measure of control and which have an impact on the negotiation process, including strategies and outcomes. It consists of five dimensions: the relative bargaining power of negotiators and the nature of dependence, the levels of conflict underlying potential negotiations, the relationship between negotiators prior to and during negotiations, the desired outcome of negotiations, and the immediate stakeholders.

Relative Bargaining Power of Negotiators and the Nature of Dependence

There can be no negotiations unless both sides cooperate with each other to achieve their respective goals. Consequently, there is some measure of interdependence between them. For example, many large global pharmaceutical companies have consummated joint ventures with small start-up biotechnology firms to develop breakthrough cures for a variety of diseases. The small firms need financial resources that only large companies are in a position to provide. In return, large pharmaceutical companies want to place their bets on the development of several risky projects by hooking up with as many promising small companies as possible. Such interdependence motivates both sides to negotiate.

In the context of negotiations, the nature of the dependence existing between the two sides determines the relative power of one side vis-à-vis the other. The negotiating strategies adopted by a company thus depend on that company's relative power in the negotiations. A company with greater power is more likely to adopt an aggressive "take it or leave it" stance, whereas a weaker firm will most likely adopt a far more submissive stance.

Levels of Conflict Underlying Potential Negotiations

The level of conflict on key issues underlying a potential negotiation establishes whether the relationship between the negotiators will be supportive or hostile. The more the negotiators agree on key issues—in other words, the more "common ground" both sides share—the less conflict there will be, and thus the more supportive of each other their relationship will be. On the other hand, the more they disagree on the key issues, the greater will be the conflict between them, resulting in a more hostile relationship.

The likelihood of a supportive relationship between negotiators is enhanced in a so-called win-win situation—also known as a non-zero-sum game, or integrative bargaining. The goals of the two sides are linked with each other in such a way that the extent to which one party attains its goals determines the extent to which the other does so. An example of a win-win situation is an agreement between a multinational company and a host country government that says the number of items the multinational can sell in the country market is equal to the number of items of the product exported by the host country. In this case, both parties win; exports help the host country earn foreign exchange, and sales in the host country allow the multinational company to increase its total revenue and market share.

Conflict between the two sides is inevitable in so-called win-lose situations. In such a situation—also known as a zero-sum game, or distributive bargaining—the gains of one side come at the expense of the other. For example, two companies negotiating the percentage of the total equity of each in a joint venture are involved in win-lose negotiations, because any increase in the equity over 50 percent for either side would result in the other getting less than 50 percent of the equity. One can observe a competitive business relationship between the two sides in which the purpose of negotiation is to maximize individual gains.

Relationship between Negotiators before and during Negotiations

The nature of the relationship between the two sides before the very first negotiating session would have a significant impact on their relations during the negotiations. If the two sides have had a harmonious relationship—perhaps a long and positive business relationship, or having engaged in mutually beneficial win-win types of negotiations—then the negotiating strategies adopted by each side would tend to be supportive of another win-win outcome. Prior relationships build expectations concerning the future of the current relationship that influence negotiation behavior.

The entire process actually consists of a series of negotiating sessions. So the experience—positive or negative—of each session serves as a backdrop for the next one, continuing to the culmination of the entire process. Consequently, each "positive" negotiation session serves to facilitate a favorable outcome at the next session; a "negative" session has the potential to do damage to the atmosphere of the next.

Desired Outcome of Negotiations

The outcome of negotiations can be both tangible and intangible. Tangible outcomes include agreement on such matters as profit sharing, technology transfer, royalty rates, laws for the protection of intellectual property, equity ownership, and other assets having real substance that can be appraised for value. Intangible outcomes include the goodwill generated between the two sides in the negotiations, the desire to make concessions to enlarge the stockpile of goodwill among the parties, and the overall desire to attain win-win outcomes through collaboration and compromise.

The strategies and outcomes of negotiations will be conditioned by the short-term versus long-term relationship emphasized by the two sides. For instance, it would be reasonable to expect both sides to compromise on tangible outcomes in favor of intangible ones if indeed the longer-term relationship is the preeminent objective of both sides. On the other hand, if a short-term relationship is all that is desired, the negotiators are likely to aim for tangible results that do not require goodwill between the two sides for their fulfillment. The U.S.–Japan trade negotiations are an example of negotiations in which the longer-term relationship between the two sides is even more important than the immediate tangible results of opening up the Japanese market and, especially, to reduce America's yearly trade deficit of approximately $60 billion with Japan.

It must be emphasized that most tangible outcomes in international business negotiations require goodwill and long-term relationships for them to become a reality. For example, the transfer of technology by an international company to a foreign enterprise is a tangible outcome. However, this transaction generally becomes effective after months or years of making goodwill and harmonious relations between the two sides a vital commodity.

Impact of Immediate Stakeholders

The immediate stakeholders in a business negotiation process are (1) the negotiators on each side and their characteristics; and (2) the companies' managers, employees, and boards of directors. The characteristics of the negotiators include such aspects as their cumulative experience in past international business negotiations and their cultural background. People who have negotiated numerous international business deals in the past will have a body of knowledge in their repertoire that could be quite an asset in impending business negotiations. For instance, a negotiator who has negotiated with the Chinese in the past will be far more adept at reading their "unspoken language" than someone who is a novice. Choosing which approaches and strategies work and which do not, in the context of a given negotiation, is an art that is acquired through the long practice of negotiations.

The negotiator's cultural background has perhaps the most profound impact on the negotiation process. After all, there can be no international negotiations without the interaction between at least two people of different cultural backgrounds. And culture, which is the amalgam of a set of values, beliefs, and norms that have been internalized by people in a society, has a definite role to play in how and why people behave the way they do, even in the context of international business negotiations.

The personal stakes of the managers, the employees, and the boards of directors in the outcome of the negotiations have a bearing on the strategies chosen and on any offers and counteroffers made during the process. All three groups may have one or more of the following stakes in the outcomes of the negotiations: financial, career advancement, ego and prestige, personal power, wages and employment, or economic security. Managers are likely to think twice before negotiating an agreement that would erode any of their personal stakes, or those of the employees or the board of directors. For example, as mentioned above, Caterpillar has suffered numerous breakdowns in labor-management negotiations and several strikes at its Peoria, Illinois, plant because the company has been negotiating with foreign firms to transfer several cost-sensitive operations to low-wage locations. Caterpillar's labor union is unhappy because of potential job losses at the Peoria plant caused by the exports of jobs. But Caterpillar's management was forced to follow this strategy because it had to make significant productivity and labor efficiency improvements to remain competitive against such global competitors as Komatsu.

Negotiation—a process in which one party tries to change the attitudes, beliefs, or behavior of another party—is essential in conducting international business. This comprehensive model views negotiations as occurring within two umbrella contexts: an environmental context of forces beyond the control of either party to the negotiations, and an immediate context consisting of controllable attributes and relationships that characterizes the negotiations process.

The proposed model should be applied from the outside in. Negotiators should start with the environmental context and study its impact on the immediate context and on the negotiation process and outcome. Then the direct impact of the immediate context on negotiations should be studied.

The model should be treated dynamically. Any changes in the environmental and immediate contexts will bring subsequent changes in the negotiation process and outcome. As the negotiation moves from one stage to the next, negotiators must reevaluate their initial needs, motivations, positions, and strategies under changing contextual circumstances.

It is also important to reevaluate the other party's situation. Negotiators should remain on the lookout for new and emerging needs of the other party and try to communicate openly with them for generating feasible solutions. International business negotiations are seldom restricted to a single issue, nor are both sides necessarily negotiating for the same outcomes. The model provided here should assist managers in identifying the potential sources of change, the issues brought forth by them, and the ramifications for outcomes.

It is imperative that negotiators obtain as much data as possible on the contexts of negotiation. Data at all three levels—national, industry, and company—should be targeted. Many sources are available. Most countries have trade officials in their embassies and consulates who may offer advice. The United States has trade officials based in the Commerce Department who are responsible for keeping tabs on the changing economic and political climates of other countries. International banks and organizations such as the International Monetary Fund (IMF) and the World Bank publish country reports containing volumes of data that are relevant to the current negotiations.

Because of these dynamic contexts, negotiators will have to be flexible. They must stay calm in the face of surprises and discontinuities. They should be prepared to accept new conditions and incorporate new agendas as long as they are credible and productive. Flexibility is important because it can generate creative solutions rather than traditional compromises. It certainly helps if the negotiators have a good knowledge of the potential obstacles in the host country. One should remain especially aware of the host country negotiator's pace of negotiation, the formality of the presentation, possible government official involvement, and so on. Interviews of individuals who have negotiating experience with the host country could be of help in this respect.

Above all, negotiators will have to practice patience in international negotiations. It usually takes a long time to reach an agreement between the parties because of all the complexities involved. Patience is vital because it sends a signal of the negotiator's commitment to the project, helping to build trust and a long-term relationship with the other party. It is also important because it ensures that possible contingencies resulting from changing contexts are planned and taken into account. Only a well-prepared, highly adaptive strategy will ultimately guarantee success in international negotiations.

REFERENCES

Martin Crutsinger, "Clinton-Murayama Downplay Trade Gap," *Philadelphia Inquirer,* January 12, 1995, p. A3.

John J. Curran, "China's Investment Boom," *Fortune,* March 7, 1994, p. 117.

Dean A. Foster, *Bargaining across Borders: How to Negotiate Business Successfully Anywhere in the World* (New York: McGraw-Hill, 1992).

John L. Graham and Roy A. Herberger, Jr., "Negotiators Abroad—Don't Shoot from the Hip," *Harvard Business Review,* July–August 1983, pp. 160–68.

Paul A. Herbig and Hugh E. Kramer, "Dos and Don'ts of Cross-Cultural Negotiations," *Industrial Marketing Management* 21 (1992), pp. 287–98.

"Mexico's Woes Accelerate as Peso Falls Further 2.26 Percent," *The Wall Street Journal,* December 8, 1994, p. A3.

D. G. Pruitt and J. Z. Rubin, *Social Conflict: Escalation, Stalemate, and Settlement* (New York: Random House, 1986), pp. 33–34.

D. Ricks and V. Mahajan, "Blunders in International Marketing: Fact or Fiction?" *Long Range Planning* 17 (1984), pp. 78–83.

Jeswald W. Salacuse, "Making Deals in Strange Places: A Beginner's Guide to International Business Negotiations," *Negotiation Journal,* January 1988, pp. 5–13.

Jack Sawyer and Harold Guetzkow, "Bargaining and Negotiation in International Relations," in Herbert C. Kelman, ed., *International Behavior: A Social-Psychological Analysis* (New York: Holt, Rinehart and Winston, 1965).

R. Tung, "Toward a Conceptual Paradigm of International Business Negotiations," in R. D. Farmer, ed., *Advances in International Comparative Management* (Greenwich, CT: JAI Press, 1988), pp. 203–19.

Stephen E. Weiss, "Creating the GM-Toyota Joint Venture: A Case in Complex Negotiations," *Columbia Journal of World Business,* Summer 1987, pp. 23–37.

Stephen E. Weiss, "Analysis of Complex Negotiations in International Business: The RBC Perspective," *Organization Science,* 4, 2 (1993), pp. 269–300.

American Strengths and Weaknesses

Tommy T. B. Koh

AMERICAN STRENGTHS AND QUALITIES

Two caveats are appropriate for any discussion of national negotiating styles. First, there may not necessarily be a definable negotiating style for each country or people. Good and effective negotiators, irrespective of their national or cultural background, have certain common skills. Second, although it is probably possible to say impressionistically that the American people possess certain character and personality traits, there are many exceptions to the rule, and a person's negotiating style is inevitably affected by his character, temperament, and attitude toward people.

American negotiators have many strengths and qualities. If distance makes the heart grow fonder, my perception of Americans may be unrealistically favorable and idealized, since Singapore is located 12,000 miles away from the United States.

First, U.S. negotiators are usually well prepared. They arrive at negotiations with their homework completed, and they are armed with facts, figures, maps, and charts. They usually know what their national interests are and what their negotiating objectives are. This is not always the case among Third World negotiators.

Second, American negotiators tend to speak clearly and plainly. As someone who was educated in the Anglo-Saxon legal tradition, I regard this as a virtue, not a liability. However, the American preference for plain speaking can sometimes cause unintended offense to other negotiators whose national culture prefers indirectness, subtlety, and avoidance of confrontation. There are, of course, exceptions to this rule.

Third, U.S. negotiators tend to be more pragmatic than doctrinaire. They focus on advancing their country's interests rather than principles which they cherish. The Reagan administration, however, was a clear exception to this rule, and at the Third U.N. Conference on the Law of the Sea, decided, for rational and arguable reasons, that principles were more important than interests.

Fourth, American negotiators generally do not regard negotiations as a zero-sum game. A good U.S. negotiator is even prepared to put himself in the place of his negotiating adversary. A good U.S. negotiator is prepared to admit that his adversary, like himself, has certain irreducible, minimum national interests. A good U.S. negotiator is prepared to engage in a process of give and take, and he believes that the successful outcome of a negotiation is not one in which he wins everything and his adversary loses everything, but rather one in which there is a mutuality of benefits and losses, in which each side has a stake in honoring and maintaining the agreement.

Reprinted from *International Negotiation,* 1996, Vol. 1, pp. 313–317.

Fifth, a U.S. negotiator's opening position is never his final position. He expects his opponent to make a counterproposal or a counteroffer. He is anxious to reach an agreement and will, therefore, make concessions to his opponent, expecting—not unreasonably—that his adversary will behave in like manner. Americans are sometimes completely exasperated at international forums when their adversaries do not behave as they do.

Sixth, the American people are very candid and straightforward, and this is reflected in their negotiating style. Americans are not usually perceived as cunning or devious. In only one incident have I found American negotiators to be devious, and that was shocking. This incident occurred in July 1981 when the United Nations sponsored an international conference on Cambodia. The conference was initiated by the ASEAN (Association of Southeast Asian Nations) countries, which proposed a framework for the resolution of the Cambodian situation. All Cambodian factions were invited to participate in the conference, including, of course, the Khmer Rouge. Vietnam was invited, but boycotted the meeting. At the conference, General Alexander Haig, then U.S. Secretary of State staged a dramatic walk-out, accompanied by the entire U.S. delegation, when the Khmer Rouge leader approached the rostrum to speak. The picture of this walk-out appeared on the front page of the *New York Times.*

On a subsequent day, the ASEAN countries and the People's Republic of China (PRC) were locked in a ferocious confrontation over the future role of the Khmer Rouge in any post-settlement Cambodia. The ASEAN countries argued that in light of the massacres and atrocities that the Khmer Rouge had committed, it would be morally and legally impermissible to allow them to return to power. We demanded a public election to be organized and supervised by the United Nations. To ensure free elections, we insisted that all armed elements be disarmed or sequestered in camp. The Chinese fought against all these points. The negotiating group was composed of 25 delegations, but the dynamics of the discussions revolved around the PRC, the ASEAN countries, and Pakistan as a middleman. Pakistan, however, was not an honest broker and basically submitted a series of amendments to dilute the ASEAN position. I assumed that Pakistan, because of its proximity to the PRC, was "fronting" for the Chinese, and was shocked to learn later that they were actually fronting for the Americans. Although the American delegation had publicly walked out of the negotiations, they were privately supporting China for geostrategic reasons. This is the only example of devious behavior by American negotiators of which I am aware, but I will remember it.

WEAKNESSES AND IDIOSYNCRASIES

One problem in negotiating with Americans is that American delegations usually suffer from serious interagency rivalries. During the U.N. Law of the Sea Conference, the American delegation met every morning and sometimes their internal meetings lasted longer than the other meetings in the conference.

A second problem in negotiating with the United States is the separation of power between the administration and the Congress. One has to be very careful if one is negotiating an agreement that is subject to ratification by the U.S. Senate. It is important to always keep in touch with U.S. senators as the negotiating process continues in order to obtain their independent inputs, be aware of their sensitivities, and recognize vested domestic interests and blocking constituencies.

A third special characteristic is the influence of the U.S. private sector and private interest groups on negotiations. During the Law of the Sea Conference I made it a point to meet not only with the official U.S. delegation and members of the Congress, but also to meet with representatives from the seabed mining industry, the petroleum industry, fishing industry, the marine scientific community, the environmental lobby, and individuals who have an affection for marine mammals. The reality of political life in America is that even one of these many lobbies can block ratification of a treaty. Foreign negotiators must understand the domestic political process in the United States and must, in some way, interfere in American internal affairs to ensure the success of their mission.

A fourth problem—the role of U.S. media—is a problem more for U.S. negotiators than for their counterparts. This is a problem because somehow the good nature of Americans and their propensity to candor makes it very difficult even for negotiators to keep confidences. And, in the midst of a sensitive negotiation it is sometimes very counterproductive for the media to report on issues that are under negotiation. In a speech to the House Foreign Affairs Committee, Secretary of State George Shultz recounted with great frustration an occasion when the U.S. and U.S.S.R. were engaged in bilateral negotiations. The negotiation had reached a critical point and he had that day drafted a cable giving his final instructions. He said he found to his horror at breakfast the next morning that the *New York Times* had reported the content of his cable. Members of the U.S. media should be asked whether they should exercise more discretion and self-restraint. Do they not feel an allegiance as American citizens to the advancement and protection of American national interests? Should not the right of the public to know and the freedom of the press sometimes be modulated by competing and larger interests? The extent to which the U.S. exposes its flank makes it easier for others to win at the negotiating table.

A fifth weakness is impatience. Americans suffer from an "instant-coffee complex." They do not have time, as Europeans and Asians do, to buy coffee beans, grind them every day, brew the coffee, enjoy the aroma, and savor every sip. Americans are always in a rush and are extremely frustrated when there is a lack of progress. Americans are result-oriented. Jeane Kirkpatrick had a shock several years ago when she visited the ASEAN capitals and met the foreign ministers of the six ASEAN countries. To each she asked, "Do you think there are prospects for settling the Cambodian conflict?" All six ASEAN foreign ministers said yes. She said, "Do you think it will be soon?" They all said, "Oh yes, very soon." She said, "Well, how soon?" They said, "Oh, about five years' time." She was shocked because to an American five years' time is certainly not soon.

A sixth weakness is cultural insensitivity. Everyone is guilty of this, not only Americans. Everyone assumes that others have similar cultures, customs, and manners. Singaporeans are "the barbarians of Southeast Asia." We are "the least sensitive and least subtle people in the region." But, if one is a professional negotiator, then part of the preparation for an effective negotiation is to learn enough about the culture of one's adversary to at least avoid simple errors of behavior, attribution, and body language.

Finally, it is surprising that in many recent multilateral forums the United States has been represented by amateur rather than professional negotiators. Given that the United States is so rich in human resources and has a foreign service studded by superstars, it is amazing how inadequately the United States is represented at important international negotiations.

CONCLUSION

In conclusion, a good negotiator, whether an Indian, an American, a Canadian, English, Ghanian, or whoever, is a person with certain definable skills, aptitudes, and temperaments. His character and personality have an impact on his effectiveness. Some American negotiators put people off; others readily win people's confidence. In choosing a negotiator, select someone who does not bristle like a porcupine but who can win the trust and confidence of his negotiating partners. What are these qualities that attract people's confidence and trust? These are moral qualities, qualities of leadership. If a negotiator is a leader, a person who acquires a reputation for competence, reliability, and trustworthiness, then others will trust him with leadership roles. The word *charisma* is not useful because it does not accurately portray the quality that bestows leadership on certain negotiators and not others. Henry Kissinger is not charismatic; he is dominating and impassive and has an exceptional intellect and a monotonous voice. In 1976, when the Law of Sea Conference was deadlocked between industrialized and developing countries, Kissinger, who was then Secretary of State and had no background in the law of the sea and knew nothing about seabed mining, spent one morning in New York meeting with the U.S. delegation. In the afternoon he met with other leaders of the Group of 77, and by the end of the day presented an innovative scheme for reconciling the competing ambitions and claims of the different countries.

There probably is an American negotiating style, and this partakes of the qualities, attitudes, customs, conventions, and reflexes that have come down through U.S. history, culture, and political institutions. On the whole, American negotiators have very positive qualities, being well prepared, reasonable, competent, and honorable. Even more than this, some, like Elliott Richardson, will take it upon themselves to be an honest broker and help to settle a conflict between two other groups in which they are a totally disinterested party. This graciousness and willingness to help is a positive attribute as well.

Global Negotiating:
Vive les Differences!

Sergey Frank

Japanese manufacturers are building plants in North America and Europe; U.S. companies are concluding cooperative joint ventures in Europe and Southeast Asia; West European companies are already active in most parts of the world. In addition, unprecedented political developments around the globe are opening doors and creating new markets and new demands at an exponential rate.

Events like the integration of the European Economic Market at the end of 1992, the dismantling of the Berlin Wall and the reunification of Germany, and the collapse and reorganization of the former Soviet Union all represent a time of great opportunity for the marketer willing to operate on a global scale.

Today there's a certain euphoria about globalization, not only in the United States but in Japan and Western Europe as well. Still, the company that attempts to jump into world markets indiscriminately—without tailoring its business, negotiating, and marketing approach to individual foreign markets—will suffer the same fate as other undifferentiated marketing efforts: a lot of time and money spent on mediocre results.

Given all this, marketers may find it advantageous to have some experienced insights on business transactions and negotiations as they're conducted in various areas of the world. This information will undoubtedly better prepare sales and marketing executives for doing business abroad, as well as reduce the number of negative surprises they're likely to encounter during international negotiations.

Keep in mind, however, that the nature of this article is somewhat personal and very limited in scope. It would be impossible in this space to cover every country in the world with the same degree of accuracy and comprehensiveness. If some countries and areas seem to get short shrift, blame it on my own limited business experience and make sure you find someone who knows about a particular area before you set out yourself. Take it from one who knows—you'll be glad you did.

EUROPEAN COUNTRIES

In Western Europe, as in the United States, personal relationships and the overall business and cultural climate are less important to a negotiation or business transaction than achieving the desired result.

Reprinted from *Sales and Marketing Management,* May 1992, pp. 64–69, with permission of the publisher.

Still, it's important in any negotiating situation to consider the organization, specific industry or service sector, competence, and personality (needs, constraints, etc.) of your business or negotiating counterpart, regardless of where it is or who is involved.

U.S. companies should feel at home dealing with most European trading partners, whose style often emulates the impersonal "time is money, let's get down to business" approach common to the States. To meet and deal with the European negotiator effectively, start with a well-prepared agenda and stick to a timetable.

Professionalism is also very important to Western European negotiators. You can make a good impression with good preparations and a well-structured agenda, and by leading the negotiation in a pragmatic, sober manner. (We'll be covering Eastern Europe—where business transactions are decidedly different—in conjunction with the former Soviet Union in a later section.)

Here are some business and negotiating tips for specific countries in Western Europe.

German-speaking Countries (Germany, Austria, and Parts of Switzerland).   Expect a rather sober, rigid business climate. The negotiating pattern of German businesspeople is often surprisingly close to some interpretations of the German character: thorough, systematic, very well prepared, but also rather dogmatic and therefore lacking in flexibility and compromise. Your partner will negotiate clearly, firmly, and assertively. You can interrupt the other side with counterarguments, however, without seeming impolite.

This, on the other hand, doesn't always apply to negotiations with Austrians, who because of their cultural background are far more influenced by South and Southeast European traditions. Thus, communications with Austrians are generally warmer and more relaxed.

In all cases, enter the negotiations well prepared. In addition, be sure to put your perspective and position across clearly during the opening stage, as well as during the exploration phases of your business negotiations. Also, don't be put off by the often intimidating impression created by German-speaking negotiators. There are some solid advantages when doing business with them, such as:

- Your partner is very reliable, keeps appointments to the minute, and expects the same from you.

- Great emphasis is placed on efficiency, not only in daily business operations but also within negotiations.

- Your partner is likely to speak good, or at least sufficient, English. Therefore, you're less likely to face potential language problems.

France and Belgium (Applies to the Walloons, the French-speaking, French-educated Belgians).   In these countries, it pays to start by putting forward a clear and well-structured agenda. If possible, decide jointly which language to speak. Keep in mind that partners from French-speaking countries will often insist on speaking French in business negotiations. Prepare in advance to provide an interpreter whom you know and who has your confidence.

In contrast to the usual American way of tackling a deal piece by piece, beginning with nitty-gritty details, your partner may prefer a different negotiating technique—the lateral style, which entails going from overall issues and general philosophies into more detailed matters.

Other points to keep in mind:

- The negotiation is likely to start with a mutual understanding of intents and purposes, then go via a master agreement to more specific headings, ending with the details. With this approach, it's important to try not to get sidetracked by minor points, but rather to concentrate on the important issues. Keep the overall picture in mind at all times.

- Rhetoric—the act and art of speaking—is very important in French-speaking countries. As a result, you should never interrupt your negotiating counterparts while they're presenting major statements.

- Don't get lost in your paperwork and files. Show them that you're well informed and confident.

- Avoid having heavy lunches with a lot of wine during the negotiations, even if they're purely social meals. Your partners might be used to it, but if big lunches aren't your normal practice, they're likely to hurt your concentration and performance in the afternoon negotiating session.

United Kingdom.   English negotiators are usually very kind, friendly, and show a lot of refined humor. They tend to be undogmatic and will more often be underprepared rather than overprepared for the negotiation. However, they're pragmatic and respect those who don't automatically take a defensive position when questioned.

Your counterpart from the United Kingdom will be flexible, cooperative, and responsive to initiatives. But don't try to use this as an opportunity to conclude too quickly. Instead, be sure to take all the time that's necessary. A negotiation with an "easy" partner may easily be underestimated, so try not to take too much advantage of the easygoing, gentlemanlike attitude of your English partner. If you do, the negotiation can quickly turn into a difficult, almost deadlocked situation.

Scandinavia.   Scandinavians commence negotiations less rigidly than the Germans and more quietly than Americans. The business climate will always be positive and polite.

They'll start rather low key and are often overwhelmed by strong and straightforward negotiating characteristics. Still, you should be careful in applying this tactic because your partners can become very stubborn once they've warmed up. The pace of the negotiation may then slow down, and much unnecessary time will have been wasted.

As a business relationship grows in intensity, the need to trust your partner becomes more and more important (this, of course, is true in any country, not just Scandinavia). A lot depends on him or her. The element of trust and professional friendship, the chemistry and business climate between the parties, should continuously be improved or at least maintained on a positive level. Remember: A successful relationship is like a bank account—you can't continue to draw on it without making a deposit or two.

THE MEDITERRANEAN/CENTRAL AND SOUTH AMERICA

In contrast to Western European negotiators, the business climate and the personal relationship are extremely important here. Try to make face-to-face, personal contact with your negotiating counterpart. In particular, avoid using the telephone or telex for important items of business. Other tips: Socialize first, work later. Convey your humanity, sincerity, loyalty, and friendship. Accept the pace and business practices of the region. And don't stress (short-term) profits too much.

Expect a certain amount of bargaining—don't expect everything to come off just as planned. Finally, try not to let your hands get tied by your own sense of organization.

Mexico. In addition to the advice given above, keep in mind the following when negotiating in Mexico:

- The decision-making process includes a great projection of individual personality. Take advantage of this by granting concessions that support the ego of the decision maker.
- The Mexican businessperson may prefer to address problems on a personal and private basis rather than on a business level. Be aware of this, and try to use recesses and other breaks during negotiations to talk privately with your negotiating counterpart.
- Mexican businesspeople will be rather flexible in bargaining trade-offs among different subjects and issues.

Remember that authority in these parts of the world tends to reside more in the person than the position, so do your homework by finding out as much as you can beforehand about the personality of the individual you'll be dealing with.

THE ARAB WORLD

Your counterparts in the Arab world will be very hospitable and favorably disposed toward you. Decisions there are frequently based on personal impressions supplemented by facts. The business climate and the tone of communication are very important. For Arabs, the negotiation or business transaction is considered a social event. Bargaining is an enjoyable and integral part of life.

Respect all religious and cultural customs of your Arab partners. Remember that during the course of negotiations they may not be available at all times because of their religious customs.

One thing that may be particularly aggravating to American businesspeople is that your Arab counterpart will never say no directly, a custom that avoids any loss of face on either side. You should be aware of this and respond accordingly.

At the end of the negotiation, your Arab counterpart will signal agreement orally and commit himself firmly by giving his word. If circumstances change, however, your new partner will feel free to renegotiate a modification of your agreement.

PEOPLE'S REPUBLIC OF CHINA

In China, great importance is attached to the personal relationship. Friendship means a lot here, and small courtesies and follow-up presents are essential to conducting business and reaching agreements. Communication, on the other hand, is often very difficult, since very few Chinese speak fluent English.

Here are some recommendations that may help:

- Your preparations should be meticulous. During the negotiating phase, one of your Chinese counterparts will be taking extensive notes. Therefore, be consistent in your attitude. Avoid radical changes in your proposals or in your negotiating strategy. Being too flexible may make it seem as if you're insincere. At the same time, be realistic in your approach. Unreasonable demands up front may destroy your credibility.

- In the course of your dealings, write out all numbers, make time available for translation and correction, and encourage your partner to repeat the agreed-upon understanding from time to time.

- In the concession-making phase, try not to impose upon or overpower your partner. Discuss concepts in terms of equality, mutual benefit, or reciprocity.

- Your Chinese counterpart believes that negotiations require a great deal of time and planning. Therefore, you should keep adequate time reserves.

You should also understand that due to the still-existing socialist system, your Chinese partners will often be unwilling to say publicly what they'll readily admit in private conversation. Therefore, it's very important to recognize and establish informal communications. For example, use the interpreter to exchange messages informally and thereby resolve a possible impasse that may have developed in the formal negotiations.

JAPAN

Your relationships and long-term considerations in negotiating with the Japanese are as important as the results of the negotiation itself. The business climate is very important.

Like the Chinese, your Japanese counterpart believes that negotiations require a great deal of time and planning. Again, you should keep plenty of extra time in reserve.

Communication is often difficult, since not many Japanese (at least in Japan) speak fluent English. So, as with the Chinese, write out all numbers, make time available for translation and correction, and encourage your partner to repeat the agreed-upon understanding from time to time.

Take into consideration that the decision-making process is "bottom-up" in Japanese companies. As a result, you have to make sure you reach agreement with all of the people involved, otherwise any agreement you come to will have to be renegotiated internally between your negotiating partner and colleagues who haven't been involved in the talks.

Again, your preparation should be meticulous. Your Japanese partner will ask for details about every aspect of the business you're negotiating and will be taking detailed notes. Therefore, be consistent in your attitude.

Due to cultural standards, your Japanese counterpart will also refrain from saying no. He'll either circumscribe the no or answer in terms of both yes and no.

Japan is another country where, should circumstances change after an agreement has been reached, your Japanese partner will feel free to renegotiate and alter all or part of the agreement.

THE SOVIET UNION, EASTERN EUROPE, AND THIRD-WORLD COUNTRIES

Despite essential differences between the former Soviet Union, its former satellites in Eastern Europe, and countries in the Third World, they share some very similar business problems: low productivity, poor-quality products, and in many cases, a physically run-down manufacturing location with a poor—or nonexistent—infrastructure.

Any form of cooperation with a Western partner is very attractive to businesspeople in these countries. In many cases, Western partners offer product and manufacturing knowledge; finance and experience in financial structures and credit sources; access to export markets; and, in particular, management skills and marketing expertise unavailable in their own country.

The Westerner, by contrast, expects low labor costs; local business knowledge; the understanding of the local legal, historical, and political system; and, possibly, marketing and distribution synergies.

Despite a seemingly advantageous position, however, Western business partners should be cautious and low key. The major disadvantage of a partnership with companies from the Soviet Union, the Eastern Bloc, or the Third-World countries is the problem of mixing two markedly different industrial, legal, political, social and, especially, economic cultures. Difficulties here can put unbearable strain on the cooperative effort. Therefore, the element of trust and the right choice of a partner are essential.

In addition, each party should clearly understand what the other side can—and cannot—provide. Any problems that arise should be solved jointly, with both parties prepared to mutually attack factual problems.

Expect a bureaucratic tone to the negotiating process itself, the methods applied, and the goals to be achieved. And remember that your partners from the other side may have a strong security concern. Their jobs—even their careers—may (still) depend on the success of the individual negotiation.

Since red tape can be an obstacle, expect to waste a lot of time when dealing with the bureaucracy. Even if there are progressive and liberal laws and regulations, the bureaucrats continue to use discretion in approving key questions of foreign investment activities. A significant delay, however, shouldn't necessarily jeopardize the whole transaction.

Settlements will usually be written in a highly detailed way (and this applies to everything from feasibility studies to multimillion-dollar equipment and construction contracts).

Also, don't expect the negotiation process to move quickly or smoothly. Negotiations are likely to continue right up to (and often through) the drafting of the final contract. Accept the possibility of a slow pace with a lot of attention given to what may seem like insignificant details.

Take into consideration that your partners have lived their lives in an economy governed by plan and not by free-market forces. Therefore, you may have to explain in detail certain economic and commercial mechanisms like depreciation, profit and loss accounts, and so on. Again, the trick is not to let your own hands be tied too much by your organizational proclivities. Try to remain as patient and flexible as possible.

One valuable weapon you may have at your disposal is that, due to their lack of management skills, East European managers desperately need training. You might be able to take advantage of this situation by offering certain types of training in exchange for valuable concessions.

It bears repeating here that patience is a considerable virtue and that business operations in Eastern Europe and Third World countries should be based on a long-term perspective.

Finally, because there are still many economic adjustments to be made in these countries, market conditions are not going to significantly improve overnight. Nonetheless, these regions will experience gradual growth well into the next century, which makes a long-term investment not only feasible but downright attractive.

Managing Difficult Negotiation Situations: Individual Approaches

It is inevitable that some negotiations go awry. Since the cost of a failed or faulty negotiation can be high in many different ways, a strong negotiator needs to try to understand why negotiations break down and to have a "tool kit" for repairing them when they do. The causes of negotiation breakdowns can be internal or external to the negotiation—that is, under the control of the participating negotiators or not. The focus of the present section is internal breakdown factors. Since many breakdowns are related to poor communication, readers should also refer to Section Five, on communication and cognitive biases.

The first article in this section, "Psychological Traps," by Jeffrey Rubin, explores the theme of mistakes and entrapment. A psychological trap is an outlook or mental set that works to our disadvantage and that we find difficult to stop. A common trap in negotiation occurs when people define a goal such as "to put the other party down" or "to win" by achieving some arbitrary standard. Some auto salespeople boast that they always sell a "loaded" car, that is, one with stereo, better-grade upholstery, and so on. What these salespeople do not mention is the number of people who do not buy a car from them because they left when they felt they were being pushed into something they did not want. It is all too easy in negotiation to want to get more than the other person yet in the process actually get less than might have been possible. There are other traps, such as wanting to complete a negotiation (at any cost) once it has been started. The personal determination to see something through is a virtue, but there are times when we continue with a process when it would be to our advantage to stop. The appearance of giving up is something that many people find difficult to cope with. It is hard to get out of a trap even when one is aware of it. Regrettably, we often are unaware of the traps we create for ourselves. Rubin identifies common traps and suggests some ways to prepare to avoid them.

While the first article in this section deals with what negotiators often do to themselves, the second and third articles address options when breakdown involves dealing with other parties. Len Leritz's article "Negotiating with Problem People" identifies five types of "difficult others" one is likely to meet in a variety of negotiation settings. The prescriptive advice Leritz offers is straightforward: "Get their attention," "Put their fears to rest," and "Put the ball in their court." Each general tactic is accompanied by examples in practice; while reading this brief article, you will likely be able to add specific applications that apply to your own unique settings and challenges.

The third and final article in this section, by Thomas Keiser, focuses on the thorny and often critical process of "Negotiating with a Customer You Can't Afford to Lose." Asking the question "What do you do when your customer turns into Attila the Hun?," Keiser examines several sales situations and applies eight key strategies for managing the sales negotiation more productively—for both parties. These remedial tactics will become increasingly important as the business world continues to become more competitive, and as the ability to establish and manage win-win business relationships becomes a more critical element of success and profitability. To the extent that all negotiations, indeed all attempts at interpersonal and interorganizational influence, are sales calls, readers should be able to glean many valuable insights to their choices and options in a broad range of settings.

Psychological Traps

Jeffrey Z. Rubin

You place a phone call and are put on hold. You wait. And then you wait some more. Should you hang up? Perhaps. After all, why waste another second of your valuable time? On the other hand, if you hang up you'll only have to call again to accomplish whatever business put you on the phone in the first place. Anyway, you've already spent all this time on hold, so why give up now? So you wait some more. At some point you finally resign yourself to the likelihood that you've been left on hold forever. Even as you hang up, though, your ear remains glued to the receiver, hoping to the bitter end that all the time spent waiting was not in vain.

Almost all of us have spent too much time caught in little traps like that. Even when it no longer makes sense, we continue to spend money on a failing automobile or washing machine, on an aging and decrepit house, a risky stock investment, or a doubtful poker hand. We simply do not know when to cut our losses and get out. And the same goes for more serious situations. Some of us remain longer than we should in a marriage or love relationship, a job or career, a therapy that is yielding diminishing returns. On a grander scale, entrapment is part of the dynamic in political controversies—Abscam, Watergate, the war in Vietnam.

A common set of psychological issues and motivations underlies all such situations, a process of entrapment that shares many of the characteristics of animal traps and con games and has been studied in a variety of laboratory and natural settings. As researchers, we are attempting to describe the properties of psychological traps: what they have in common, where they lurk, whom they tend to snare, and how they can be avoided.

When I was growing up in New York City there was a cunning little device that we called the Chinese Finger Trap—a woven straw cylinder about three or four inches long, with an opening at each end just large enough for a child's finger to be inserted. Once you put a finger into each end, the trap was sprung. The harder you tugged in opposite directions in an effort to get free, the more the woven cylinder stretched and pulled tight around each finger. Only by pushing inward, by moving *counter* to the direction in which escape appeared to lie, could you get free. So it is with entrapping situations. The tighter one pulls, the greater the conflict between the lure of the goal and the increasing cost of remaining in pursuit of it. And the tighter one pulls, the greater the trap's bite. Only by letting go at some point can the trap be escaped. Or, as the Chinese philosopher Lao-tzu put it: "Those who would conquer must yield; and those who conquer do so because they yield."

To understand psychological entrapment, we must first understand the simplest traps of all—physical traps for animals. Sometime rather early in the evolution of our species, human beings came to understand that the active pursuit of quarry by hunting was often impractical or undesirable. Thus, trapping was invented. A trap allows hunters to outwit their quarry, so offset any advantage that the quarry may have by virtue of its greater power, speed, or the limited destructive capacity of the hunters' weapons. An animal trap accomplishes these ends in a strikingly simple and clever way: it brings the quarry to the hunter rather than the other way around. Instead of continuing to hunt for quarry, often in vain and at considerable cost, trappers get the quarry to catch itself. Once set, the animal trap takes on a life of its own, a surrogate hunter waiting with infinite patience for the quarry to make an unwise choice. The consequence of having this surrogate is that hunters' limited resources can now be devoted to other pursuits, including the construction of additional traps.

Ingenious devices, these animal traps, devilishly clever and efficient—and utterly sinister in their effect on the victims who fall prey to them. What properties, then, make them work?

First of all, an effective trap must be able to lure or distract the quarry into behaving in ways that risk its self-preservation. Often this important first step is accomplished with some form of bait that is so tantalizingly attractive, so well suited to the quarry's particular needs, that the animal is induced to pursue it, oblivious to the trap's jaws.

Second, an effective animal trap permits traffic in one direction only. It is far easier for a lobster to push its way through the cone-shaped net into the lobster trap than, once in, to claw its way out. The bait that motivated the quarry to enter the trap in the first place obscures the irreversibility of that move. Doors that yield easily, inviting the quarry's entry, slam shut with a vengeance.

Third, an effective trap is often engineered so that the quarry's very efforts to escape entrap it all the more. The bear's considerable strength, applied in an effort to pull its paw from a trap, only sinks the traps' teeth deeper into its flesh. A fish's tendency to swim away from anything that constrains its free movement only deepens the bite of the hook. An effective trap thus invites the quarry to become the source of its own entrapment or possible destruction.

Finally, an effective animal trap must be suited to the particular attributes of the quarry it is designed to capture. One cannot catch a guppy with a lobster trap or a mosquito with a butterfly net. Consider the awful and awesomely effective 19th-century American wolf trap. The simplicity and frightening elegance of this trap is that it depends on the wolf's appetite for the taste of blood. A bloodied knife blade was left to freeze in the winter ice. While licking the knife, the wolf would cut its tongue and begin to bleed. It would then start to lick at the knife all the more, which in turn led to a greater flow of blood—and the wolf's ultimate undoing. The animal's blood attracted other wolves, who then attacked the victim and, eventually, one another. Thus a whole pack of wolves could be destroyed with just one trap.

Confidence games are psychological traps for capturing people and are remarkably similar to self-entrapment. Like animal traps, they rely for their effectiveness on the trapper's (con artist's) ability to lure the quarry (mark) into a course of action that becomes entrapping. The lure is typically based on the mark's cupidity; the fat, wriggling worm is the tempting possibility of getting something for nothing, a big killing that appears to happen at the expense of someone else.

The effective con also depends on the mark's willingness to cheat another person in order to reap large and easy profits. As a result, the mark's progressive pursuit of the lure tends to obscure the fact that the path taken is not easily reversible. With the con artist's kind assistance, the mark is increasingly rendered a coconspirator in a crime against another, a bit like Macbeth: "I am in blood / stepp'd so far that, should I wade no more, / Returning were as tedious as go o'er."

In addition, the mark's very efforts to escape—by making a quick, glorious, and final big killing before quitting once and for all—only lead to deeper entrapment. The more money the mark is persuaded to put up in this effort, the more carefully he or she is apt to guard the investment—and to justify it through the commitment of additional resources.

Finally, just as an animal trap is tailored to its quarry, so must a con be geared to the brand of avarice and dishonesty of the mark. "Different traps for different saps" is the rule.

There are two kinds of cons: so-called short cons, such as Three-Card Monte or the Shell Game, in which the mark is fleeced for a few dollars on the spot; and big cons, in which the mark is directed to a "big store"—a place where the con is played out. Big cons reached their heyday around the turn of the 19th century in this country and lined the pockets of skilled con artists with hundreds of thousands of dollars. Big cons include the Rag, the Pay-Off, and the Wire, the last of these made famous by Paul Newman and Robert Redford in *The Sting*. In that con, a mark was persuaded that horse-race results had been delayed long enough for him to place a bet *after* the race had been run, thereby betting on a sure thing. The con took place in a large ground-floor room, rented for the week as the big store. All the roles in the drama, save that of the mark, were played by confederates, creating an elaborate and complex ruse.

The steps or stages involved in most big cons are remarkably consistent:

1. "Putting the mark up"—finding the right person to fleece.
2. "Playing the con"—befriending the mark and gaining the mark's confidence.
3. "Roping the mark"—steering the victim to the "inside man," the person who is in charge of running the big store.
4. "Telling the tale"—giving the inside man an opportunity to show the mark how a large sum of money can be made dishonestly.
5. "Giving the convincer"—allowing the mark to make a substantial profit in a test run of the swindle.
6. "Giving the breakdown"—setting the mark up to invest a large sum of money for the final killing.
7. "Putting the mark on the send"—sending the mark home for that amount of money.
8. "The sting"—fleecing the mark in the big store.
9. "Blowing the mark off"—getting the mark out of the way as quickly and quietly as possible.

In psychological entrapment, one person may simultaneously play the role of roper, inside man, and mark. In so doing, we manage to ensnare ourselves. As with physical and psychological devices for capturing others, these traps only work when people are, first and foremost, interested in—and distracted by—the lure of some goal. Final victory in Vietnam, a happy marriage, a big killing at the gambling table, or simply the return of the person who pushed the hold button: all may be viewed as worthy goals—or as bait that conceals a dangerous hook. In entrapping situations, marks initially look in one direction only—forward—as they pursue the mirage of a goal that lies just beyond their grasp.

In their single-minded rush toward the objective, marks neglect the possibility that they are being sucked into a funnel from which escape may prove remarkably difficult. The first stage of entrapment—eager, forward-looking pursuit of one's goal—is thus followed by attention to the costs that have been unwittingly incurred along the way. The compulsive gambler's drive for a killing is inevitably followed by attention to the mounting costs of the pursuit, costs that in turn need to be justified by greater commitment. Similarly, when our personal or professional lives are disappointing—and our efforts to achieve a turnaround do not pay off quickly enough—we may decide to justify the high cost by renewing our commitment and remaining on the treadmill.

But notice that the more resources committed to attaining the goal, the greater the trap's bite. Each additional step toward a rewarding but unattained goal creates new and greater costs, requiring greater justification of the course of action than ever before. With each additional year that a person remains in a dissatisfying job, hoping it will take a turn for the better, he or she feels more compelled to rationalize the time invested by remaining in the job even longer.

In certain entrapping situations, those in which several people are competing with one another, reward pursuit and cost justification are followed by a third stage, in which people try to make sure that their competitors end up losing at least as much—if not more—than they. Like two children in a breath-holding contest or two nations in an arms race, many entrapping situations evolve to the point where each side's focus is no longer on winning or even on minimizing losses, but on getting even with the adversary who engineered the mess.

In the last major stage of entrapment, marks must finally let go, either because their resources are gone, because they are rescued by another person, or because they recognize the desperation of the pursuit. Just as the Chinese Finger Trap can be escaped only by pushing inward, entrapment can be avoided only by letting go.

One devilishly simple and effective example of entrapment is a game known as the Dollar Auction, invented about 10 years ago by Martin Shubik, an economist at Yale. As his proving ground Shubik allegedly used the Yale University cocktail-party circuit. Anyone can make some money—but perhaps lose some friends—by trying it out at a party.

Take a dollar bill from your pocket and announce that you will auction it off to the highest bidder. People will be invited to call out bids in multiples of five cents until no further bidding occurs, at which point the highest bidder will pay the amount bid and win the dollar. The only feature that distinguishes this auction from traditional auctions, you point out, is the rule that the *second-highest* bidder will also be asked to pay the amount bid, although he or she will obviously not win the dollar. For example, Susan has bid 30 cents and Bill has bid 25 cents; if the bidding stops at this point, you will pay Susan 70 cents ($1 minus the amount she bid) and Bill, the second-highest bidder, will have to pay you 25 cents. The auction ends when one minute has elapsed without any additional bidding.

If my own experience is any indication, the game is likely to follow a general pattern. One person bids a nickel, another bids a dime, someone else jumps the bidding to a quarter or so, and the bidding proceeds at a fast and furious pace until about 50 or 60 cents is reached. At around that point, the number of people calling out bids begins to decrease, and soon there are only three or four people still taking part. The bidding continues, at a somewhat slower pace, until the two highest bids are at about $1 and 95 cents. There is a break in the action at this point, as the two remaining bidders seem to consider what has happened and whether they should continue. Suddenly the person who bid 95 cents calls out $1.05, and the bidding resumes. Soon the two remaining bidders have escalated matters so far that both bids are over $4. Then one of the guests suddenly escalates the bidding by offering $5, the other (who has already bid $4.25 or so) refuses to go any higher, and the game ends. You proceed to collect $4.25 from the loser and $4 from the "winner."

Several researchers have had people play the Dollar Auction game under controlled laboratory conditions and have found that the participants typically end up bidding far in excess of the $1 prize at stake, sometimes paying as much as $5 or $6 for a dollar bill. The interesting question is, of course, why. What motivates people to bid initially and to persist in a self-defeating course of action?

Thanks primarily to the extensive research of Allan Teger, a social psychologist at Boston University, the question has been answered. Teger found that when Dollar Auction participants were asked to give reasons for their bidding, their responses fell into one of two major motivational categories: economic and interpersonal. Economic motives include a desire to win the dollar, a desire to regain losses, and a desire to avoid losing more money. Interpersonal motives include a desire to save face, a desire to prove one is the best player, and a desire to punish the other person.

Economic motives appear to predominate in the early stages of the Dollar Auction. People begin bidding with the hope of winning the dollar bill easily and inexpensively. Their bids increase a little bit at a time, in the expectation that their latest bid will prove to be the winning one. If the other participants reason the same way, however, the bidding escalates. At some subsequent point in the Dollar Auction, the bidders begin to realize that they have been drawn into an increasingly treacherous situation. Acknowledging that they have already invested a portion of their own resources in the auction, they begin to pay particular attention to the amount they stand to lose if they come in second. As the bidding approaches $1—or when the amount invested equals the objective worth of the prize—the tension rises. At this stage, Teger has found, the participants experience intense inner conflict, as measured by physiological measures of anxiety and nervousness; about half of them then quit the game.

People who remain in the auction past the $1 bid, however, typically stick with it to the bitter end—until they have exhausted their resources or their adversary has quit. Interpersonal motives come to the fore when the bid exceeds the objective value of the prize. Even though both players know they are sure to lose, each may go out of his or her way to punish the other, making sure that the other person loses even more, and each may become increasingly concerned about looking foolish by yielding to the adversary's aggression. Teger found that this mutual concern occasionally leads bidders to a cooperative solution to the problem of how to quit without losing face: a bid of $1 by one player, if followed by a quick final raise to $2 by the second, allows the first person to quit in the knowledge that both have lost equally.

If entrapping situations are as ubiquitous and powerful as I have suggested, how do people ever avoid getting into them? What, if anything, can people do to keep from getting in deeper? Over the past six years or so, I have been working with a research group at Tufts University to find some answers to these questions. We have conducted most of our research in the laboratory, using the Dollar Auction and several other procedures. We have begun to study entrapment in naturalistic settings, by holding contests in which residents of the Boston area, chosen at random, are invited to solve a series of increasingly difficult problems that require more and more of their time.

In one experimental model, people were invited to pay for the ticks of a numerical counter in the hope that they would obtain a jackpot—either by reaching a number that had been randomly generated by computer or by outlasting an adversary. A second laboratory paradigm challenged people to solve a jigsaw puzzle correctly within a limited period; if they succeeded, they received a cash jackpot, but if they failed, they had to pay for the number of pieces they had requested. Finally, in a third type of experiment, undergraduates were instructed to wait for an experimenter or another participant to arrive at the laboratory so that they could receive a research credit; naturally, the experimenter was always late, and the subjects had to continually decide how much longer they would wait.

In one such experiment, Tufts undergraduates were seated in individual rooms, given $2.50 in cash for agreeing to come to our laboratory, and invited to win an additional $10 jackpot by solving a crossword puzzle. The puzzle consisted of 10 words of varying difficulty, 8 or more of which had to be correctly solved in order to win the jackpot. Each student was given three "free" minutes to work on the puzzle; after that, 25 cents was deducted from the initial $2.50 stake for each additional minute. People could quit the experiment at any point and leave with their initial stake—minus 25 cents for each minute they remained in the study past the first three. If they remained in the study after 13 minutes had passed, they had to begin paying out of their own pockets, since their initial stake was exhausted at that point. The study was stopped after 15 minutes.

Almost everyone found the puzzle too difficult to solve without the aid of a crossword-puzzle dictionary, which they were told was available on request. Participants were also told that because there were two people working on the puzzle and only one dictionary, it would be available on a first-come, first-served basis. (No such dictionary was actually available.) When students requested the dictionary, they had to turn their puzzles face down, so they were not able to wait for the dictionary and work on the puzzle at the same time. Surprisingly, nearly 20 percent of the students stayed in the experiment the full 15 minutes.

We investigated several important influences on the entrapment process here. First, we created either a competitive or noncompetitive relationship between the participants by telling the students either that the $10 jackpot would be awarded to the first person who solved the puzzle or that it would go to anyone who was able to do so. We found that students who believed they were in a competition became more entrapped—they played the game far longer and spent more of their money—than those not in competition.

We also studied the nature of the investment process by giving participants different instructions about quitting the experiment. Some were told that they could quit at any time. Others were advised that the experimenter would ask them every three minutes if they wished to continue. We expected that the experimenter's intervention would serve as an indirect reminder of the cost of continued participation and that those students who were spoken to would become less entrapped than the others. That is exactly what happened. Students who were not asked if they wished to continue remained in the experiment far longer and, as a group, lost more than twice as much money.

In all of our experiments, as in the one described above, we encourage subjects to move toward some rewarding goal, while we increase the time or money they must invest in it and give them the option to quit at any time. Both our research and Teger's reveal certain repeating themes in the behavior of the participants, which I can summarize in the form of some advice on how to avoid entrapment.

- *Set limits on your involvement and commitment in advance.* We find that people who are not asked to indicate the limits of their participation become more entrapped than those who do indicate a limit, especially publicly. Depending on the entrapping situation you are in, you may wish to set a limit based on your past experience (for example, the average time you've spent waiting on hold); your available resources (the amount of time or money you have left to spend); the importance of reaching your goal on this occasion (you may be able to call later to make a plane reservation); and the possibility of reaching your goal in some other way (using a travel agent to make the reservation).

- *Once you set a limit, stick to it.* We all play little games with ourselves—we flip a coin to make a decision and then when we don't like the result, decide to make the contest two out of three flips. We set limits that are subsequently modified, shaded, and shifted as we get close to the finish. Each new investment, like the addition of an AM/FM radio to a new car that has already been decked out with extras, tends to be evaluated not in relation to zero (the total cost of the investment) but in relation to that inconsequential, minuscule increment above and beyond the amount we've already agreed to spend. If you're the sort of person who has trouble adhering to limits, get some help. Find a friend, tell him or her the limit you wish to set, and have your friend rope you in when you get to the end of your self-appointed tether. Ulysses used that method to resist the deadly temptation of the Sirens' wail.

• *Avoid looking to other people to see what you should do.* It's one thing to use a friend to rope you in, and it's another matter entirely to deal with your uncertainty about what to do by sheepishly following others. Given the uncertainty in entrapping situations, it is tempting to look to others for clues about the appropriateness of one's own behavior. Our research indicates that the presence and continued involvement of another person in an entrapping situation increases one's own entrapment, and that this occurs even when the behavior of each person has no effect on the other's fate. Proprietors of Las Vegas gambling casinos know what they're doing when they use shills to "prime the pump" and get the gambler's competitive juices flowing. Similarly, one is far more likely to continue waiting for a bus that has not yet arrived—and even wait for an outrageous, irrationally long time—if other people are also waiting.

• *Beware of your need to impress others.* Other people are not only a source of information about what to do in entrapping situations; they are also a critically important source of praise or disapproval for our behavior. We all want to be liked, loved, and respected by people whose opinions matter to us. This motive is perfectly healthy and often appropriate, but not in entrapping situations. Our research shows that people become more entrapped when they believe their effectiveness is being judged and scrutinized by others. This is particularly powerful when the perceived evaluation occurs early in the game, and diminishes in importance if evaluative observers are introduced later on. We also find that people who are especially anxious about their appearance in the eyes of others and who feel that they have something to prove by toughing things out get more entrapped than their less anxious counterparts.

• *Remind yourself of the costs involved.* Our research indicates that people are less likely to become entrapped when they are made aware early on of the costs associated with continued participation. Even the availability of a chart that depicts investment costs is sufficient to reduce entrapment. The net effect of such information about costs is to offset the distracting, shimmering lure of the goal ahead—especially if the cost information is introduced right away. If you don't start paying attention to the costs of your involvement until fairly late in the game, you may feel compelled to justify those costs by investing even more of your resources.

• *Remain vigilant.* Entrapping situations seem to sneak up on us. People who understand and avoid one brand of trap often manage to get caught in others with surprising frequency and ease. Just because you knew when to bail out of that lousy stock investment doesn't mean that you will have the good sense to give up on an unsatisfactory relationship or a profession in which you feel you have too much invested to quit. Obviously, people who are told about entrapment and its dangers are less likely to become entrapped. Our studies also show that being forewarned about one kind of trap, moreover, can put people on guard against other kinds of traps.

Although very little is known at this point about the kinds of people who tend to get entrapped, we have recently begun to study this issue and can therefore engage in a bit of informed speculation. First, people who go for bait are also likely to end up hooked. Those who are exceptionally ambitious or greedy or unusually self-confident and self-assured about their ability to reach a goal must tread warily. There may be icebergs lurking in those calm and glassy seas ahead. Second, the sort of person who believes that he should—indeed must—profit according to his efforts may also be ripe for the plucking. Those who tend to trust excessively in a just world, who think that people get what they deserve and deserve what they get, may end up caught in a version of the Chinese Finger Trap. They use their belief in justice to rationalize continued investments—and so tighten the noose all the more. Finally, the man or woman who tends to get swept up in macho ideology, who feels that nothing else applies, is also especially vulnerable to entrapment. Such people may be willing to invest more and more in order to avoid some small embarrassment—only to suffer greater humiliation in the final reckoning.

Despite cautionary advice, we all still manage to get ourselves entrapped. When the inevitable happens, when you find yourself asking "What have I done?" remember there are times when the wisest course may be to quit, not fight. There may just not be a way of salvaging the time, effort, money, even the human lives that have gone into a particular sinking ship. Know when to give it up, when to push rather than pull those fingers, when to yield and wait for victory another day. For there is almost always another day, despite our proclivity for ignoring that fact.

Negotiating with Problem People

Len Leritz

In the movie *Big* Tom Hanks stars as a kid locked inside an adult body. What makes the movie funny is that it strikes a chord with viewers. "I know someone like that," they think between fistfuls of popcorn.

There are a lot of people out there who look like adults on the outside but are thinking like kids on the inside. And when it's your job to negotiate with one of them, you've got trouble. Most of these problem people fall into one of five categories: Bullies, Avoiders, Withdrawers, High Rollers, or Wad Shooters.

- *Bullies* verbally or physically attack, use threats, demand or otherwise attempt to intimidate and push others around. They say things like: "That's a stupid thing to say!" "Do you expect me to respond to that?" "If you don't, I will . . . !" "I want it, and I want it now!" "Move it!" "You can't do that!" "You better shape up!"

- *Avoiders* physically avoid or procrastinate, hide out, or refuse to negotiate out of fear of losing. They say things like: "I'll do it tomorrow." "We don't have anything to talk about." "I don't have time." "That's not my problem."

- *Withdrawers* emotionally withdraw, get confused, go dumb and numb or become paralyzed with fear. You'll hear them say: "I don't understand." "That doesn't make sense." "I don't know."

- *High Rollers* attempt to shock and intimidate their opposition by making extreme demands: "You have until five o'clock to comply." "I want $50,000 for my car." "I want it all done by noon."

- *Wad Shooters* assume an all-or-nothing, take-it-or-leave-it stance: "That's my bottom line." "If you don't want it, forget it." "Either you agree to all five points or I'm leaving."

WHAT TO DO WITH THEM

The behavior of these different types of "enforcers" tends to be uncomplicated and obvious. Consequently, the following responses work effectively with most of them.

1. Get Their Attention. This step is especially important when you're up against bullies. Until you get their attention, you are wasting your time. You need to shock them out of their self-centered mindset and let them know with no uncertainty that you intend to be taken seriously. You need to make them feel your presence.

The way to get their attention is to draw a boundary. The intention is not to punish the other person but simply to let them know what you will and will not tolerate. You want to create a negative consequence that will outweigh whatever benefit they are deriving from their current behavior.

How you draw your boundary will differ in each situation. You need to ask yourself what it is that will get the other person's attention—what is important to them. You may do it by physical action, by shouting at them, by walking out, by initiating legal procedures or by telling them in a quiet and firm voice what you will and won't accept.

The key is that you have to mean it. The other person almost always knows whether you are serious about your boundary. No one crosses your boundary when you mean it.

Here is an example of what I call the "Skillet Approach" to dealing with enforcers. I once had a client who had been physically abused by her husband for years. She had threatened to leave him many times, but he knew that she didn't really mean it.

One night she finally decided to mean it. He had pushed her around earlier in the evening. She waited until he went to sleep and then went to the kitchen and got her biggest cast-iron skillet. She woke him up while holding the skillet over his head. "If you ever hit me again, I'll kill you in your sleep," she told him.

This time she meant it, and he believed her. Though he had trouble sleeping for a while, the abuse stopped. The woman had gotten her husband's attention by creating a consequence (the skillet), and she meant it.

Ask yourself what "skillet" you need to use—and mean it when you use it. When you don't mean it you are reinforcing the behavior you don't want.

2. Call a Spade a Spade. Identify the enforcer's behavior and invite her to do something more constructive. Explaining to a bully, for example, that she's being a bully helps her become conscious of what she's doing and will often take the power out of it. This is especially true if others are involved and the enforcer feels embarrassed.

Suggesting other options at this point will help the person save face and will keep the negotiations moving. For example, you might say something like: "Your repeated attacks are not getting us any closer to an agreement. I'd like to suggest that we each try to explain what we need, then work together to brainstorm some ways that we might both get what we need."

3. Put Their Fears to Rest. This step is particularly important when you're dealing with Avoiders or Withdrawers. You need to help them feel safer so that their capacities expand and they can move into more cooperative behaviors.

Here are some suggestions:

- Don't be defensive. Instead, look behind their behavior to their underlying needs and interests: "Would you be more comfortable if we met in your office?" "What conditions will make you willing to stay here and talk this out?"
- Respond to the needs of the internal kid: "I can see how you feel frustrated."
- Actively listen to them so they feel understood: "What I hear you saying is . . ."

- Be aware of who their constituency is, who it is they need to impress: "I want you to be able to go back to your department and feel proud of what we accomplished," you might say.
- Don't counterattack. When dealing with aggressive enforcers, such as bullies, the usual rule is: the more aggressive, the more frightened the internal kid. Helping bullies feel safer may seem counterintuitive, but it's exactly what you need to do to get them on your level.

4. Insist on Playing by the Rules. Bullies, High Rollers, and Wad Shooters will attempt to force you to accept unreasonable agreements. But you should refuse to be pressured. Instead, insist on fair criteria for both the process and the final settlement. You might say, "I refuse to be pressured into an agreement. I am only willing to continue the negotiation if we can agree to some fair procedures that we will both honor." Or if, for example, you feel a price the other person is asking is too high, you might say, "Let's check with some other suppliers and see what they are charging."

5. Put the Ball in Their Court. When the other person takes extreme stands and makes unreasonable demands, ask her to explain how she arrived at her position. Point out that you need to understand her underlying needs better. You might say, "In order to understand your demands, I need to hear more from you about how you arrived at those points." Or "Your price is a little higher than I expected. I want to pay you fairly for your work. Explain to me what you will need to do to complete the job." When she answers you, demands that cannot be justified lose their power.

6. Use the Silent Treatment. Silence can be one of your most powerful strategies, especially with Wad Shooters. When the other person is being aggressive or unreasonable, try just looking at them calmly. Silence gives them nothing to push against.

Calm silence communicates power. The other person will feel uncomfortable with the power of your silence and will probably begin to fill it in—often by backtracking and becoming more reasonable.

A variation of using silence is to walk away. "I'm willing to talk about this whenever you are willing to stop attacking me. Until then, we have nothing to talk about."

7. Do the Sidestep. Sidestepping or ignoring a statement can be an effective response if someone is making a personal attack, an extreme demand or a take-it-or-leave-it challenge. Instead of responding directly, act as if you didn't hear what it was the person said. Change the topic and/or refocus the discussion on the underlying problem or conflict at hand.

For example, a corporate attorney says angrily to an opposing attorney: "I can't believe they pay you a professional salary." The opposing attorney might calmly respond: "I think we still have four issues we have not settled. Let's look at them one at a time." Or a film supplier says to a production manager: "The price is $10,000 per segment. Take it or leave it." The manager would answer. "How many segments did you say you had?" or "Your tone of voice sounds angry. Do you feel as if we have not been fair to you in our past dealings?"

8. Meet the Enemy Head-on. Don't be defensive. Justifying your position or needs encourages the other party to step up their attack. If you become defensive, the other person knows that she has you on the run. Invite her to give her criticism, then refocus it as an attack on the problem at hand. Ask her to explain how her comments will help solve the problem.

For example, the account supervisor at an advertising agency says to the creative director: "If you were committed to this new ad, you would have been here last week." A defensive response from the creative director would be "I couldn't help it. I was burned out and needed the time off." A better reply would be: "I know you are under pressure and last week was frustrating. What do we need to do so we don't get caught in that kind of last-minute bind in the future?"

9. Refuse to be Punished. Anyone has a right to be angry from time to time, but no one has the right to punish you. You do not deserve to be punished. You will know that you are being punished when the other person keeps repeating her attack or the person vents her anger but refuses to tell you how she wants your behavior to change in response.

Draw a boundary by asking the other person what they want from you. If their response is "I don't know," inform them that you are willing to continue the discussion when they do know. In the meantime, you're not willing to be punished.

10. Ask Questions. Taking a stand may make the other person defensive. Instead, ask questions. Asking questions doesn't give them an object to attack; it invites them to justify their position or to vent their feelings. It gives you more information about them.

When asking your questions, ask "what" questions rather than "why" questions. "What" questions invite factual responses. "Why" questions are usually sneaky judgments that make the other party defensive. "What" questions will keep the negotiation moving. "Why" questions will tend to lead you to battle positions. For example:

- Why did you think you could do that? (attacking)
- What was your motivation for doing that? (information-seeking)
- Why did you do that? (attacking)
- What are the assumptions behind your actions? (information-seeking)

11. Point Out the Consequences. When the other person refuses to agree to a reasonable settlement, show them the ramifications of their actions. Try to present it as a statement of inevitable consequences rather than as a threat: "The reality is, if our company shows a loss again in the fourth quarter due to the strike, we will have no choice but to lay off 500 union workers."

Armed with the right approach, you can convince any Bully or Withdrawer on the block that a rational, well-negotiated settlement is in everyone's best interest.

Negotiating with a Customer You Can't Afford to Lose

Thomas C. Keiser

"I like your product, but your price is way out of line. We're used to paying half that much!"

"Acme's going to throw in the service contract for nothing. If you can't match that, you're not even in the running."

"Frankly, I think we've worked out a pretty good deal here, but now you've got to meet my boss. If you thought I was tough . . ."

"Tell you what: If you can drop the price by 20 percent, I'll give you the business. Once you're in our division, you know, you'll have a lock on the whole company. The volume will be huge!"

"I can't even talk to you about payment schedule. Company policy is ironclad on that point."

"Look here, at *that* price, you're just wasting my time! I thought this was a serious bid! Who do you think you're talking to, some green kid?"

This wasn't supposed to happen. You've invested a lot of time earning a customer's trust and goodwill. You've done needs-satisfaction selling, relationship selling, consultative selling, customer-oriented selling; you've been persuasive and good-humored. But as you approach the close, your good friend the customer suddenly turns into Attila the Hun, demanding a better deal, eager to plunder your company's margin and ride away with the profits. You're left with a lousy choice: do the business unprofitably or don't do the business at all.

This kind of dilemma is nothing new, of course. Deals fall through every day. But businesses that depend on long-term customer relationships have a particular need to avoid win-lose situations, since backing out of a bad deal can cost a lot of future deals as well. Some buyers resort to hardball tactics even when the salesperson has done a consummate job of selling. The premise is that it costs nothing to ask for a concession. Sellers can always say no. They will still do the deal. But many sellers—especially inexperienced ones—say yes to even the most outrageous customer demands. Shrewd buyers can lure even seasoned salespeople into deals based on emotion rather than on solid business sense. So how do you protect your own interests, save the sale, and preserve the relationship when the customer is trying to eat your lunch?

Reprinted from *Harvard Business Review,* November–December, 1988, pp. 30–34.

Joining battle is not the solution unless you're the only source of whatever the customer needs. (And in that case you'd better be sure you never lose your monopoly.) Leaving the field is an even worse tactic, however tempting it is to walk away from a really unreasonable customer.

Surprisingly, accommodation and compromise are not the answers either. Often a 10 percent price discount will make a trivial difference in the commission, so the salesperson quickly concedes it. But besides reducing your company's margin significantly, this kind of easy accommodation encourages the customer to expect something for nothing in future negotiations.

Compromise—splitting the difference, meeting the customer halfway—may save time, but because it fails to meet the needs of either party fully it is not the proverbial win-win solution. A competitor who finds a creative way to satisfy both parties can steal the business.

The best response to aggressive but important customers is a kind of assertive pacifism. Refuse to fight, but refuse to let the customer take advantage of you. Don't cave in, just don't counterattack. Duck, dodge, parry, but hold your ground. Never close a door; keep opening new ones. Try to draw the customer into a creative partnership where the two of you work together for inventive solutions that never occurred to any of your competitors.

There are eight key strategies for moving a customer out of a hardball mentality and into a more productive frame of mind.

1. *Prepare by knowing your walkaway and by building the number of variables you can work with during the negotiation.* Everyone agrees about the walkaway. Whether you're negotiating an arms deal with the Russians, a labor agreement with the UAW, or a contract you can't afford to lose, you need to have a walkaway: a combination of price, terms, and deliverables that represents the least you will accept. Without one, you have no negotiating road map.

Increasing the number of variables is even more important. The more variables you have to work with, the more options you have to offer; the greater your options, the better your chances of closing the deal. With an important customer, your first priority is to avoid take-it-or-leave-it situations and keep the negotiation going long enough to find a workable deal. Too many salespeople think their only variable is price, but such narrow thinking can be the kiss of death. After all, price is one area where the customer's and the supplier's interests are bound to be at odds. Focusing on price can only increase animosity, reduce margin, or both.

Instead, focus on variables where the customer's interests and your own have more in common. For example, a salesperson for a consumer-goods manufacturer might talk to the retailer about more effective ways to use advertising dollars—the retailer's as well as the manufacturer's—to promote the product. By including marketing programs in the discussion, the salesperson helps to build value into the price, which will come up later in the negotiation.

The salesperson's job is to find the specific package of products and services that most effectively increases value for the customer without sacrificing the seller's profit. For example, an automotive parts supplier built up its research and development capacity, giving customers the choice of doing their own R&D in-house or farming it out to the parts supplier. Having this option enabled the supplier to redirect negotiations away from price and toward creation of value in the product-development process. Its revenues and margins improved significantly.

Even with undifferentiated products, you can increase variables by focusing on services. A commodity chemicals salesperson, for example, routinely considered payment options, quantity discounts, bundling with other purchases, even the relative costs and benefits of using the supplier's tank cars or the customer's. Regardless of industry, the more variables you have, the greater your chances of success.

2. *When under attack, listen.* Collect as much information as possible from the customer. Once customers have locked into a position, it is difficult to move them with arguments, however brilliant. Under these circumstances, persuasion is more a function of listening.

Here's an example from my own company. During a protracted negotiation for a large training and development contract, the customer kept trying to drive down the per diem price of our professional seminar leaders. He pleaded poverty, cheaper competition, and company policy. The contract was a big one, but we were already operating at near capacity, so we had little incentive to shave the per diem even slightly However, we were also selling books to each seminar participant, and that business was at least as important to us as the services. The customer was not asking for concessions on books. He was only thinking of the per diem, and he was beginning to dig in his heels.

At this point our salesperson stopped talking, except to ask questions, and began listening. She learned a great deal—and uncovered an issue more important to the customer than price.

The customer was director of R&D for a large corporation and a man with career ambitions. To get the promotion he wanted, he needed visibility with his superiors. He was afraid that our professionals would develop their own relationships with his company's top management, leaving him out of the loop. Our salesperson decided to give him the control he wanted. Normally we would have hired freelancers to fill the gap between our own available staff and the customer's needs. But in this case she told him he could hire the freelancers himself, subject to our training and direction. The people we already employed would be billed at their full per diem. He would save money on the freelancers he paid directly, without our margin. We would still make our profit on the books and the professional services we did provide. He would maintain control.

Moreover, we were confident that the customer was underestimating the difficulty of hiring, training, and managing freelancers. We took the risk that somewhere down the road the customer would value this service and be willing to pay for it. Our judgment turned out to be accurate. Within a year we had obtained the entire professional services contract without sacrificing margin.

It was a solution no competitor could match because no competitor had listened carefully enough to the customer's underlying agenda. Even more important, the buyer's wary gamesmanship turned to trust, and that trust shaped all our subsequent negotiations.

When under attack, most people's natural response is to defend themselves or to counterattack. For a salesperson in a negotiation, either of these will fuel an upward spiral of heated disagreement. The best response, however counterintuitive, is to keep the customer talking, and for three good reasons. First, new information can increase the room for movement and the number of variables. Second, listening without defending helps to defuse any anger. Third, if you're listening, you're not making concessions.

3. *Keep track of the issues requiring discussion.* Negotiations can get confusing. Customers often get frustrated by an apparent lack of progress; they occasionally go back on agreements already made; they sometimes raise new issues at the last moment. One good way to avoid these problems is to summarize what's already been accomplished and sketch out what still needs to be discussed. Brief but frequent recaps actually help maintain momentum, and they reassure customers that you're listening to their arguments.

The best negotiators can neutralize even the most outspoken opposition by converting objections into issues that need to be addressed. The trick is to keep your cool, pay attention to the customer's words and tone, and wait patiently for a calm moment to summarize your progress.

4. *Assert your company's needs.* Effective salespeople always focus on their customers' interests—not their own. They learn to take on a customer perspective so completely that they project an uncanny understanding of the buyer's needs and wants. Too much empathy can work against salespeople, however, because sales bargaining requires a dual focus—on the customer and on the best interests of one's own company. The best negotiating stance is not a single-minded emphasis on customer satisfaction but a concentration on problem solving that seeks to satisfy both parties. Salespeople who fail to assert the needs of their own company are too likely to make unnecessary concessions.

The style of assertion is also extremely important. It must be nonprovocative. "You use our service center 50 percent more than our average customer. We've got to be paid for that . . ." will probably spark a defensive reaction from a combative customer. Instead, the salesperson should build common ground by emphasizing shared interests, avoiding inflammatory language, and encouraging discussion of disputed issues. This is a better approach: "It's clear that the service center is a critical piece of the overall package. Right now you're using it 50 percent more than our average customer, and that's driving up our costs and your price. Let's find a different way of working together to keep service costs down and still keep service quality high. To begin with, let's figure out what's behind these high service demands."

5. *Commit to a solution only after it's certain to work for both parties.* If a competitive customer senses that the salesperson is digging into a position, the chances of successfully closing the deal are dramatically reduced. A better approach is to suggest hypothetical solutions. Compare these two approaches in selling a commercial loan:

"I'll tell you what. If you give us all of the currency exchange business for your European branches, we'll cap this loan at prime plus one."

"You mentioned the currency exchange activity that comes out of your European branches. Suppose you placed that entirely with us. We may be able to give you a break in the pricing of the new loan."

The first is likely to draw a counterproposal from a competitive customer. It keeps the two of you on opposite sides of the negotiating table. The second invites the customer to help shape the proposal. Customers who participate in the search for solutions are much more likely to wind up with a deal they like.

Some salespeople make the mistake of agreeing definitively to an issue without making sure the overall deal still makes sense. This plays into the hands of an aggressive customer trying to get the whole loaf one slice at a time. It's difficult to take back a concession. Instead, wrap up issues tentatively. "We agree to do X, provided we can come up with a suitable agreement on Y and Z."

6. *Save the hardest issues for last.* When you have a lot of points to negotiate, don't start with the toughest, even though it may seem logical to begin with the deal killers. After all, why spend time on side issues without knowing whether the thorniest questions can be resolved?

There are two reasons. First, resolving relatively easy issues creates momentum. Suppose you're working with a customer who's bound and determined to skin you alive when it comes to the main event. By starting with lesser contests and finding inventive solutions, you may get the customer to see the value of exploring new approaches. Second, discussing easier issues may uncover additional variables. These will be helpful when you finally get down to the heart of the negotiation.

7. *Start high and concede slowly.* Competitive customers want to see a return on their negotiation investment. When you know that a customer wants to barter, start off with something you can afford to lose. Obviously, game playing has its price. Not only do you train your customers to ask for concessions, you also teach them never to relax their guard on money matters. Still, when the customer really wants to wheel and deal, you have little choice.

The customer too can pay a price for playing games. A classic case involves a customer who always bragged about his poker winnings, presumably to intimidate salespeople before negotiations got started. "I always leave the table a winner," he seemed to be saying. "Say your prayers." What salespeople actually did was raise their prices 10 percent to 15 percent before sitting down to negotiate. They'd let him win a few dollars, praise his skill, then walk away with the order at a reasonable margin.

A number of studies have shown that high expectations produce the best negotiating results and low expectations the poorest. This is why salespeople must not let themselves be intimidated by the customer who always bargains every point. Once they lower their expectations, they have made the first concession in their own minds before the negotiation gets under way. The customer then gets to take these premature concessions along with the normal allotment to follow.

A man I used to know—the CEO of a company selling software to pharmacies— always insisted on absolute candor in all customer dealings. He'd begin negotiations by showing customers his price list and saying, "Here's our standard price list. But since you're a big chain, we'll give you a discount." He broke the ice with a concession no one had asked for and got his clock cleaned nearly every time.

The key is always to get something in return for concessions and to know their economic value. Remember that any concession is likely to have a different value for buyer and seller, so begin by giving things that the customer values highly but that have little incremental cost for your company:

Control of the process.

Assurance of quality.

Convenience.

Preferred treatment in times of product scarcity.

Information on new technology (for example, sharing R&D).

Credit.

Timing of delivery.

Customization.

Service.

There's an old saying, "He who concedes first, loses." This may be true in a hard-ball negotiation where the customer has no other potential source of supply. But in most competitive sales situations, the salesperson has to make the first concession in order to keep the deal alive. Concede in small increments, get something in return, and know the concession's value to both sides. Taking time may seem crazy to salespeople who have learned that time is money. But in a negotiation, *not* taking time is money.

8. *Don't be trapped by emotional blackmail.* Buyers sometimes use emotion— usually anger—to rattle salespeople into making concessions they wouldn't otherwise make. Some use anger as a premeditated tactic; others are really angry. It doesn't matter whether the emotion is genuine or counterfeit. What does matter is how salespeople react. How do you deal with a customer's rage and manage your own emotions at the same time?

Here are three different techniques that salespeople find useful in handling a customer who uses anger—wittingly or unwittingly—as a manipulative tactic:

• *Withdraw.* Ask for a recess, consult with the boss, or reschedule the meeting. A change in time and place can change the entire landscape of a negotiation.

• Listen silently while the customer rants and raves. Don't nod your head or say "uh-huh." Maintain eye contact and a neutral expression, but do not reinforce the customer's behavior. When the tirade is over, suggest a constructive agenda.

• React openly to the customer's anger, say that you find it unproductive, and suggest focusing on a specific, nonemotional issue. There are two keys to this technique. The first is timing: don't rush the process or you risk backing the customer into a corner from which there is no graceful escape. The second is to insist that the use of manipulative tactics is unacceptable and then to suggest a constructive agenda. Don't be timid. The only way to pull this off is to be strong and assertive.

For example, imagine this response to a customer throwing a fit: "This attack is not constructive. (Strong eye contact, assertive tone.) We've spent three hours working the issues and trying to arrive at a fair and reasonable solution. Now I suggest that we go back to the question of payment terms and see if we can finalize those."

Of course, there is substantial risk in using any of these techniques. If you withdraw, you may not get a second chance. If you listen silently or react ineffectively, you may alienate the customer further. These are techniques to resort to only when the discussion is in danger of going off the deep end, but at such moments they have saved many a negotiation that looked hopeless.

The essence of negotiating effectively with aggressive customers is to sidestep their attacks and convince them that a common effort at problem solving will be more profitable and productive. Your toughest customers will stop throwing punches if they never connect. Your most difficult buyer will brighten if you can make the process interesting and rewarding. The old toe-to-toe scuffle had its points, no doubt. Trading blow for blow was a fine test of stamina and guts. But it was no test at all of imagination. In dealing with tough customers, creativity is a better way of doing business.

AUTHOR'S NOTE

I wish to acknowledge the ideas of Ann Carol Brown, David Berlew, John Carlisle, Greg Crawford, Richard Pascale, Mike Pedler, Neil Rackham, and my colleagues at the Forum Corporation.

Managing Difficult Negotiation Situations: Third-Party Approaches

In the earlier sections of this book we focused on the fundamentals of the negotiation process: planning and setting objectives, understanding the fundamental strategic approaches to negotiation, and procedures for developing tactics. We also explored the underlying components and processes of negotiation that lead to particular outcomes—persuasion processes, the use of power, the personality of the negotiator, and so on. These all help in assessing the types of negotiation situations we face, what resources we have to draw upon, how to set objectives and establish strategies—all things we do to prepare for negotiations.

At the center of any negotiation is conflict. The parties do not agree, and the negotiation that occurs is an effort to resolve that conflict. Even in integrative negotiating, while conflict may be transformed into a more muted and malleable form, it is still there. All parties want to affect and influence the final outcome—and some may want to contribute more than their fair share. Both parties want to benefit—but can they benefit equally? Tensions become heightened, positions become polarized, parties become deeply committed to their own points of view and no longer trust the other negotiators. If the parties do not recognize these dynamics while they are occurring, conflicts can grow and threaten to destroy the negotiated agreement they are seeking or even doom the negotiation process itself.

In this section, we examine methods of dealing with conflict when negotiators cannot manage it alone. Two of the articles examine the important process of mediation, the use of a neutral third party to facilitate the dispute resolution process. Mediation is particularly suited to this because it leaves the determination of the outcome *to the disputants.* In this sense, the mediator's role is limited to that of facilitator or "process mechanic" (thereby doing as little damage as possible to the ability of the negotiators to control their own outcomes). This is often a critical step to ensure that negotiators are committed to implementing the outcomes. The third article in this section goes a step further, looking at conflict from a managerial perspective, examining the managerial decision to intervene in conflicts as a third party and to the subsequent choices open to the intervenor.

In "The Role of the Mediator," Thomas Colosi describes the strategy and tactics that mediators use to help bring parties to agreement. Colosi suggests that mediators must follow several key steps in order to bring negotiating parties together. Basic to this process is the idea of trust: first, trust of the mediator; second, trust of the mediation process; and, finally, trust by the negotiators for each other. Colosi gives several examples of the ways effective mediators work to execute this process, and discusses how negotiation and mediation can each be an effective solution to problems traditionally resolved in court. Such litigation often involves prohibitive expenditures of time, money, and other resources, while resulting in a fatally damaged relationship between parties when a strong, healthy relationship would be in the best interests of both parties.

The second article in this section, " 'What Do We Need a Mediator For?': Mediation's 'Value-Added' for Negotiators," by Robert Baruch Bush, is a thorough, thoughtful answer to the question posed in its title. While focusing on the use of mediation in legal cases where attorneys represent clients, the answer that Bush constructs is a clear affirmation of the value of mediation in a broad range of situations. Asserting that mediation can be construed usefully as a form of "assisted negotiation," the author builds a solid case for mediation, first by identifying what negotiators typically want from a third-party process and second by specifying what mediation can provide to help negotiators achieve these aims. The first of Bush's two answers regarding the value of mediation is that it "can help cure inherent problems in the negotiation process by improving the quality of communication, information, and hence party decision making." His second assertion is that mediation not only can lead to improved negotiation outcomes but also "simultaneously increases the 'process control' that leads parties to prefer negotiation in the first place."

The last article in this section addresses the choices and options faced by managers when they are called upon to intervene in disputes between others in the workplace. A. R. Elangovan's "The Manager as the Third Party: Deciding How to Intervene in Employee Disputes," builds on work by others to develop a decision model to assist managers in making better intervention choices. This article represents the important idea that efforts at "assisted negotiation" are not limited professional or specialized interventions by mediators or other neutral facilitators, but are the daily fare of managers who are responsible for accomplishing organizational goals in an efficient, timely manner and who also want to engender disputant commitment to the settlement. Concentrating on the question of managerial control, Elangovan suggests that the intervening manager can choose to control (to a greater or lesser degree) the means of dispute resolution (the process), and/or the ends (the outcome). The ultimate choice is suggested by working through a specific application problem to a decision tree. While disputes and choices are often messy and not easily captured by decision trees, the process put forth in this article serves the critical purpose of reducing ambiguity and uncertainty, enabling intervenors to make these important decisions with much greater comfort and assurance.

The Role of the Mediator

Thomas Colosi

Because the essence of negotiations is to provide an opportunity for parties or disputants to exchange promises and thus resolve their differences, some measure of trust between the parties is critical. While some students of negotiation contend that trust is irrelevant to negotiations, it is hard to see how a serious exchange of promises can occur without trust. Each side must have some confidence that the other will keep its word once a promise is given (whether the promises involve benefits or threats). Trust need not be blind, of course. It may be supported by information that is uncovered and processed in the course of negotiation; it may rest on relationships that have strengthened in the course of negotiation; ultimately it may emerge even from the shared experience of coming to understand the negotiation process.

Parties can reach an impasse in negotiations, where no further discussion is possible because either their trust has run out or there was too little trust in the first place. Indeed, in the absence of trust, negotiations might never even begin. Parties with no trust between them can be said to be in a trust vacuum. This underlies their fears of each other. Moreover, it interferes with the very communication that might dispel such fears. Without open lines of productive communication, very little education can take place.

The necessary trust between the parties may be developed in three steps. First, a mediator must work to win the trust of the parties. Next, the mediator educates the parties about the negotiation process (not the mediation process) and works to encourage them to transfer their trust from him to it. Finally, the mediator persuades the parties to begin trusting each other, again using the negotiation process as a vehicle to demonstrate that trust.

THE EVOLUTION OF TRUST

Trust in the Outside Third-Party Mediator

The mediator wins the trust of the parties principally by demonstrating that he or she is truly neutral. The capacity of a mediator to win trust may be at its highest if intervention occurs when the situation is particularly polarized and trust between the parties is at its lowest.

Reprinted from "Negotiation in the Public and Private Sectors," *American Behavioral Scientist* (Newbury Park, Calif: Sage Publications, Inc., 1983), pp 237-47. Reprinted by permission of Sage Publications.

Others contend that a mediator should intervene before the parties are frozen into positions, but the particular mediator (and mediation in general) may very well be rejected early in the dispute. At best, the mediator may be underutilized or "bargained with" by parties, both of which make it difficult for him to determine their true objectives.

Just as nature abhors a vacuum, the negotiation process abhors the absence of trust. When parties are polarized, they also have a better idea of what they want the mediator to do. The issues and alternatives are better defined and, as a result, the disputants will be more likely to understand that it is they (and not the mediator) who must assume responsibility for the outcome of negotiations. This is, after all, a fundamental objective of the mediator. In addition, the more time the mediator is involved in the dispute, the less he or she will appear neutral to everyone involved. This perception, of course, can sabotage the mediator's effectiveness.

Mediators may use a number of techniques to demonstrate their neutrality and win the parties' trust. Mediators must learn, for example, how to listen and not say much; likewise, they cannot reveal their emotions and attitudes. Taking care to express only positive or neutral opinions of the groups involved in the dispute is one important approach. Mediators should listen to people's ideas with an open mind, not only to obtain a comprehensive view of the problem but to set an example by showing that there is little risk in entertaining other points of view. Mediators should emphasize that they are only there to help the parties, and have absolutely no decision-making authority regarding the substance or the issues. Mediators must also assure the parties that all conversations will be held in strict confidence. Additionally, a hard-won reputation for helping people in other cases provides a solid foundation for winning the parties' trust.

A mediator may also be able to use other processes for gaining trust. For example, parties who shy away from mediation nevertheless may be willing to engage in fact-finding. Viewed narrowly, fact-finding is a process of gathering information, understanding and organizing the issues in a dispute, and giving advice about a possible settlement; the parties are not bound by the fact-finder's recommendations. Sophisticated mediators, however, see broader potential in fact-finding: It can serve as a first step in negotiations, the mechanism by which the mediator gets to meet with all the parties and begins to win their trust.

The process of enhancing trust in the mediator is not without risk. Inexperienced mediators frequently feel empowered by the confidence and acceptance that the disputants may quickly show toward them. Mediators must keep in mind, however, that their perception of power comes from the parties' need to fill the trust vacuum. Furthermore, their perceived power is only an early stage in a developmental process that ideally should lead to the empowering of the negotiators themselves through the help of the mediator.

Trust in the Process

Having obtained the parties' trust, the mediator must next work to transfer it from himself to the negotiation process. The parties must be shown that the negotiation process is the way through their problem. They must become comfortable with the negotiation process, experiment with it, and use it to achieve success. In the early stages of a dispute, the best kind of intervenor often will avoid substantive issues and concentrate instead on procedural matters in order to educate the parties about negotiation and mediation. The parties should know that mediation is available if they want it, but they should not move into mediation until they really need it.

Because negotiating skills are not taught in our society to any great extent, there is very poor understanding about how the negotiation process works. People tend to concentrate on whether or not another *party* should be trusted, rather than on trusting the process itself. Learning to trust negotiations is a useful interim step between no trust and trust in another party. Disputants who do not take the interim step usually end up using alternative dispute resolution processes. In some cases, the alternative may be litigation; in others, a strike or a riot. The role of the mediator is to call attention to the need for establishing an understanding of, and confidence in, the negotiation process before trust in the other parties is sought.

Trust among the Parties

Once the interim steps have been taken and trust in both the mediator and in the negotiation process is established, the professional mediator must work hard to transfer that trust to the parties themselves. This can occur in two ways. First, the mediator acts as a role model: demonstrating good listening skills; showing respect for other people's opinions and constraints; and creating an atmosphere of trust by encouraging the negotiators to develop a statement of common goals. Second, trust is established among the parties through practice. The preliminary stages of negotiation involve some cooperation among the parties in relatively simple process decisions. These may involve minor procedural matters—"housekeeping issues" if you will—yet over time they provide a shared experience that allows the parties slowly to develop a more trusting relationship, one that is essential when more fundamental, high stakes issues are tackled.

The case that follows illustrates how these trust-building steps are implemented in practice.

Building Trust: An Example in Community Multilateral Negotiations

In 1973 a riot in a Rochester, New York, high school sent 16 students and teachers (8 blacks and 8 whites) to the hospital. I was one of two intervenors from the American Arbitration Association's National Center for Dispute Resolution in Washington, D.C., who entered the dispute as fact-finders. In truth, we borrowed from the public sector labor–management model to characterize our roles, using the Newman model of "mediators wearing fact-finders' hats." The particular intervenors were teamed because one is white and the other black.

About 18 different organizations, representing students, specific racial and ethnic groups, teachers, parents, and local citizens, were identified by the school board and one another as interested parties. They were invited by the American Arbitration Association to meet each other and the fact-finders. The purpose of the meeting was to determine what had caused the riot and to try to set up a process for avoiding future disruption. Once this group was assembled, one of the first questions that had to be answered was whether still other parties and organizations should be involved. Some groups already present voiced objections about inviting certain others, contending that they would ruin the process. Nevertheless, as mediator/fact-finders, we encouraged those who were involved to invite the threatening groups to participate on the ground that any outsiders who had enough power to stymie the process would likely be important to implementing any agreement. Ultimately, the original participants did decide who would be at the table and added several parties. In effect, the negotiators defined themselves.

Once the group's composition was established, the parties had to determine how decisions would be made. Two competing models of decision-making were offered: majority vote and full consensus. Some conservative groups supported the majority vote, while the minority organizations felt better protected by full consensus; indeed, they threatened to leave the table over this issue. The intervenors kept the parties together by observing that an effective solution to the high school problem would be possible only if all the groups present were involved in the negotiations. The intervenors pointed out that a settlement unanimously endorsed by a group as broadly based as those convened would carry a great deal of clout with the school board and the public. The parties remained at the table because they had begun to believe that some common goals and solutions were possible, even though these had yet to take concrete form.

Each group's attitudes on the decision-making issue were affected, in part, by the group's own internal structure and experience. Some groups that were accustomed to operating under an authoritarian model assumed that the mediator/fact-finders would make the decisions. Others thought that committees would be formed to discuss the issues and be given delegated powers. Majority rule, with and without minority opinion reports, were other suggestions. Before long, participants came to see how differently they all made decisions, and began to educate one another about the relative merits of each process.

The intervenors had to conduct side bar meetings (caucuses with groups in isolation from other groups) because of one minority group's flat refusal to participate under any process except full consensus. The mediator/fact-finder created doubts in the conservative camp as to the viability of the majority rule process by asking its members if they realized how much power was available to them through the full consensus process. The intervenors pointed out that a simple veto could be exercised by any group to prevent proposals and directions that were perceived to be inappropriate or undesirable from being adopted. After many internal discussions with the conservative group, full consensus decision-making was accepted.

Continuing the process discussions, we next suggested to the groups that they begin their negotiations by agreeing upon a common goal. The initial proposals were sweeping and often contradictory. Some said that the goal should be to stop busing. Others said that desegregation should be eliminated. One proposal was to abolish the school board. Even amendments to the U.S. Constitution were put forth. It was clear that the parties were still a long way from reaching a mutually acceptable goal.

We worked patiently in a variety of process configurations and settings to try to close the many gaps. Talks took place chiefly in informal meetings. Internal discussions took place within some of the parties; there was also direct talk between the parties, both with and without the mediators. In the course of these discussions, the mediators came to realize that despite the parties' obvious differences, they shared a common attitude: fear. They feared each other, but beyond that they feared what might happen in the schools and in the community if accommodation could not be achieved. Still, they were not ready to trust each other to be reasonable or to deliver on promises.

The parties met over a six-month period with the mediators and a local coordinator. A church basement was used as the formal meeting area. There was near-perfect attendance at all the weekly and biweekly meetings; no group pulled out of the process. Ultimately, the groups agreed on a common goal: to have *safe schools.* In retrospect, the goal may seem obvious, yet the fact that it eluded the parties for so long shows that polarization and lack of trust can keep disputants from recognizing their shared interests that, under other circumstances, might be easily perceived. Once the common goal was articulated, the parties tried to formulate an overall strategy for achieving it. Their initial strategy was to continue negotiations. Trust in the negotiation process and in each other was beginning to be established, and as the parties assumed greater responsibility for tasks, the mediators of course did less.

The outside neutrals entered this polarized situation as fact-finders, worked to establish trust—first in themselves and then in the negotiation process—by showing the parties how mediation could help them. By encouraging the parties to work together on small, seemingly procedural issues, the intervenors demonstrated how people with different priorities and outlooks could work cooperatively.

Once trust is established in the negotiation process and in each other, the negotiators will find that they no longer need a mediator. When this happens, the mediator should begin to leave the dispute, as his job may essentially be over. The mediator may make himself available for other process-management tasks, of course, or to resume mediation if the trust relationship breaks down for any reason.

THE MEDIATOR'S CAPACITY TO RAISE AND MAINTAIN DOUBTS

Effective mediators create and maintain doubts by raising questions about alternatives and implications that the negotiators may not have considered or fully appreciated. Like any good negotiator, the mediator avoids flat statements. If, for instance, a mediator wants a negotiator to think about the reaction of the negotiator's superiors to a certain proposal, the mediator is better off asking, "What would your boss say?" rather than declaring, "Your boss may not support you on that." The same axiom would apply in a situation in which a mediator and a negotiator are discussing a negotiator's decision to leave the bargaining table. Assuming that the negotiators are using full consensus in their decision-making process, the mediator might privately say to the reluctant negotiator, "The other parties might come to some decision in your absence. Have you considered the implications of your not being present to veto decisions that would hurt your side?" The use of questions rather than statements gives negotiators more room to respond and more freedom to consider what the mediator is saying. It also allows the mediator to play a more neutral, laissez-faire role as declarations tend to be more leading and value-loaded than questions. The negotiators are thus subtly encouraged to take maximum responsibility in the negotiation process.

As noted earlier, most important negotiating takes place in the internal team caucuses. As a consequence, this usually is where the mediator is most active as well. Private meetings are normally the best forum for the mediator to raise doubts.

During horizontal (across-the-table) negotiations, each team tries to educate the other about its position. The negotiators try to raise new doubts in the minds of their counterparts. As a result, a new set of assumptions and proposals may become plausible, and new issues and problems may arise as well. In this phase of negotiation, the stabilizers and nonstabilizers tend to open up to each other in the caucuses when these new concerns are discussed. If the quasi mediator is unable to create doubts in the nonstabilizer's mind, an outside, neutral mediator may be enlisted before the team resorts to autocratic decision making, or internal disciplinary measures to bring the dissenter along. Committed to stability, the mediator concentrates on internal team bargaining and similarly tries to raise doubts about the viability of nonsettlement in the mind of the nonstabilizer. Sometimes the emphasis is less on outcomes and more on process. If the nonstabilizer does not trust the negotiation process because of preconceived notions, the mediator must raise doubts about the competing process alternatives. By contrast, of course, effective mediators would not work to create doubt in the minds of the stabilizers, since this group wants settlement.

Parties Who Will Not Settle

The mediator's function is thus to create and maintain doubts in the minds of in dividual negotiators who oppose settlement. What can a mediator do if an entire team is composed of nonstabilizers?

Some negotiators enter the process quite committed to talking but not to settling. For them negotiation may only be a device to stall for time. They may be waiting for the other side to exhaust its strike fund or other resources. They may have calculated that in time public opinion will shift in their favor. Time may be needed to prepare a lawsuit, launch a media campaign, or use some other external pressure on the other side. It may simply be that these "negotiators" prefer the status quo to any foreseeable alternative.

When one team is negotiating just to buy time, the situation between the contending parties is similar in many respects to the internal process that occurs within a team between stabilizers and nonstabilizers. The nonstabilizers are the ones who must be convinced by the quasi mediator (and the stabilizers) to remain at the table, to listen to the other teams, to consider their arguments, and, ideally, to revise their positions to enable their negotiating team to offer deliverable proposals. The quasi mediator first tries to raise doubts in the mind of the uncooperative teammates about the consequences of nonsettlement. (What losses would have to be incurred: a strike, litigation, violence; can the group afford such losses?)

A team dedicated to nonsettlement occupies the same position in horizontal negotiations as does the nonstabilizer within his team. It, too, is uninterested in settlement. In this instance, however, it is the mediator rather than the quasi mediator who steps in. Although the person is different, the role is much the same. The mediator relies on the same basic technique of raising doubts about the team's decision to stall, probing to see if all the implications of nonsettlement have been evaluated.

In any case when it becomes obvious that a party has carefully considered its position and has determined that settlement is not in its interest, then, after appropriate probing, the mediator ultimately must accept the party's own judgment. When a party believes that it is better to stall than to settle, the mediator might reasonably continue with the process if the other party accedes.

NEGOTIATION AND LITIGATION

Deadlines are important monitors of the parties' success at reaching an agreement. Timing is a critical factor in a mediator's assessment of a party's willingness to settle. When there is no court-imposed or other "natural" deadline (for example, the expiration of a labor contract), the mediator can help the parties set the clock. He can warn the parties that if settlement is not reached by a certain time, then the parties may have to proceed without him. Mediators have to take care in using this tactic. The deadline should not be artificial; disputes are not poker games for bluffing. Instead, the mediator should use his general experience, combined with his knowledge of the specific dispute, to determine at what future point a failure to agree would show that his time was spent inefficiently.

The difficulty a mediator may have in getting negotiators to settle within a time limit gives much support to arguments that favor the deadlines imposed by the litigation process. In litigation, deadlines are perceived to be firmer and more believable. Disputes therefore can be settled within a set period of time. Although some proponents of negotiation extol it as an alternative to the courts, nothing settles a dispute better than the combined force of the strong arm of the court (or an arbitrator) and active negotiation.

Negotiation is often called an "alternative" dispute resolution process, a characterization that implicitly regards the judicial system as dominant. This view also seems predicated on a belief that negotiation and litigation represented entirely divergent paths, yet practice often reveals that the two can be inextricably bound.

This point is illustrated by a heated land-use dispute in New York State in which negotiation and litigation occurred in tandem. A group of Mohawk Indians occupied some open land, and town officials moved to have them evicted. Before the state police were deployed, however, help was sought from the National Center for Dispute Settlement. The center (a division of the American Arbitration Association) was contacted to serve as "Rumor Control Experts." (This term was carefully chosen to help the intervenors win the trust of all the parties, as rumors were potentially harmful to everyone.) Under that authority, representatives of the center began the delicate process of building trust. In time, the process came to be directed explicitly at negotiation. Prosecutorial actions were held in abeyance. Nevertheless, the specter of a court-imposed resolution kept the process on track. The mediators assured the parties that no action would be taken by the court so long as the negotiation process was reported as being fruitful. Neither side was confident what the judge would order if negotiation broke down.

In disputes that erupt spontaneously (such as the one just described), parties often find themselves simultaneously involved in lawsuits and negotiations. Usually their lawyers are likewise involved in both processes. But is a lawyer the best representative for a party in a negotiation process? Certainly, lawyers are assumed to be good negotiators. Yet the parties themselves may be just as good if they are educated properly about the process. Moreover, many lawyers are biased in favor of the judicial process and act with little enthusiasm for negotiation. Sophisticated clients could become knowledgeable about the negotiation process (using the mediator as a mentor, if necessary) and employ lawyers for advice on how the negotiations could influence the simultaneous litigation. In such a case, the lawyers should not take over the negotiation process, though their advice could be useful. The mediator, in turn, could help the negotiator and the lawyers coordinate their respective responsibilities. In a sense, this is just another example of building team cohesion: It is similar to the work a mediator does to produce greater harmony among the stabilizers and nonstabilizers.

"What Do We Need a Mediator For?": Mediation's "Value-Added" for Negotiators

Robert A. Baruch Bush

I. A FAMILIAR SCENARIO: "WHY DO WE NEED A MEDIATOR?"

A simple question inspires this lecture: What is the "value-added" of mediation for those trying to negotiate resolutions to conflicts? The question is one that mediators and proponents of mediation must be able to answer because it is one that parties to conflict—and their lawyers—frequently and justifiably raise.[1] To give the question sharper contours, let's imagine a scenario that, in some variation, is unfolding more and more often as ADR processes gain greater currency: Several parties were embroiled in a serious dispute—let us say, over land-use issues involved in a proposed development project and their environmental consequences. One party was on the verge of filing—or perhaps already had filed—legal papers to block the project. Before things proceeded further, however, one lawyer suggested that all sides consider the possibility of entering into some type of ADR process. After an initial round of client consultations to describe the variety of ADR options that might be used, the discussion began to focus on mediation as an option.[2]

Parenthetically, I note that . . . most of us will not spend the majority of our careers working directly as mediators, arbitrators or any other type of neutral third party. Rather, our primary involvement with ADR processes—other than negotiation itself—will be advising clients about them and representing clients in them. Thus, as in the scenario imagined here, the likelihood is that we ourselves, as lawyers, will be called upon increasingly to inform and advise our clients about ADR processes as a normal part of client counseling.[3] The obvious corollary is that law schools should prepare students for this task in the courses they offer on ADR.[4]

Once the discussion began to focus on mediation, the lawyers agreed that in order for everyone to feel fully informed about this option, they should call in an expert on mediation to explain its workings, advantages and limits, and answer questions that might arise, before recommending it to their clients. That expert was a mediator himself, though in this case he was being asked to "brief" everyone on the uses and limits

From *The Ohio State Journal on Dispute Resolution*, 1996, Vol. 12, No. 1, pp 1-36. Reprinted by permission of The Ohio State University Law School.

of mediation rather than to serve as mediator. The mediator began by explaining generally how mediation works and pointing out the differences between mediation and other, binding processes like arbitration. He then said that, although mediators take different approaches to the process, mediation is best understood as, in essence, a process of "facilitated or assisted negotiation" in which the mediator facilitates the parties' own negotiation process. Again, parenthetically, I think that many mediators would themselves endorse this description of the process and probably use very similar terms to explain the process to their clients.[5]

The parties and lawyers listened politely to the rest of the expert's presentation. However, when he finished, they seized on his description of the "essence" of mediation and asked bluntly:

> If mediation is simply, as you put it, assisted negotiation, then why do we need it at all? Why do we need a mediator? We ourselves, as businesspeople, are experienced negotiators; beyond that, we're all employing lawyers here who are expert negotiators. Surely, with all this expertise, we can negotiate by ourselves. What is added by a mediator? What is the value-added of the mediation process, compared to the negotiation process we can conduct for ourselves; and why should anyone pay for it, as well as spend the time to participate? Why should we consider this process a valuable product that we should pay extra for when we can accomplish the same thing ourselves?

II. "MEDIATION AS AN ALTERNATIVE": THE PROPER FRAMEWORK FOR COMPARISON

Thus far the scenario; now for some commentary. First of all, the imaginary exchange presented in the scenario is actually a very realistic one, in my experience. Parties and lawyers frequently cannot understand, without some good explanation, what a mediator will contribute to their case—besides another bill. As a former student of mine argued to me when we met at a conference in a state that had recently adopted court-ordered mediation:

> I enjoyed learning about mediation in law school. But now that I'm in the world of practice, I frankly don't see the point. I work for a major civil litigation firm, and almost all the cases we handle settle before trial—and they always have—whether or not there's a mediator involved. So what does having a mediator add? As far as I'm concerned, it's just another hoop you have to jump through and an additional expense. Tell me, am I missing something?

Before trying to answer the question posed by my student and the parties in our scenario, it is important to note that these questions themselves show an intuitive clarity about mediation's "place" in the dispute resolution universe that some scholars might envy. Many dispute resolution scholars, including myself, have presented and analyzed mediation as "an alternative to adjudication."[6] In fact, we are now coming to see that this comparative framework is itself misconceived. The "standard" method of case disposition, to which mediation or any other alternative process should be compared, is not adjudication or trial at all, but rather *settlement*—either by direct party negotiations or, where parties have lawyers, by negotiation between lawyers. A solid body of research tells us that throughout the country the vast majority of disputes are settled before a legal claim is ever filed; and of those cases that are brought to court, the large majority end in a negotiated settlement of some kind, and fewer than 10 percent are adjudicated to a verdict.[7] Given this context, if a process is being proposed as an "alternative" method of resolution, to what should it be compared?

The answer, clearly, is that it should be compared to the standard method of resolution, not to an exceptional method used in a tiny fraction of cases. Viewed in proper perspective, mediation and other third-party processes are alternatives not to court, but to unassisted settlement efforts, including party-to-party, lawyer-to-party, and lawyer-to-lawyer negotiation. Thus, the relevant question to be asked and answered about mediation is: How does it compare to, and what advantages does it have over, the negotiation process in its various configurations? This point has recently been articulated very clearly by one of this journal's own advisors, Dean Nancy Rogers, and her colleagues Craig McEwen and Richard Maiman.[8] Once made, the point seems obvious; but until now, it seems to have escaped many of us. However, as our scenario illustrates, it has not escaped the "consumers" of mediation—disputing parties and their lawyers. They see the true comparison and properly demand that mediators answer the question: "What do we need you for, since we can negotiate settlement for ourselves? In practice, you are providing an alternative to unassisted negotiation; what real value does this alternative have to offer us?"

III. SEARCHING FOR ANSWERS: RECENT SCHOLARSHIP ON "BARRIERS" TO NEGOTIATED SETTLEMENT

Redefining the comparative framework in this way not only helps clarify the question that is raised about mediation's value, it also points directly to a subject that may provide some answers. That subject is the negotiation process itself. Therefore, let me move away from the topic of mediation altogether for the moment and turn to some insights from the very rich literature on negotiation—including both research and theory—that has accumulated in recent years. This literature includes major contributions by scholars whose work you have probably encountered, such as Lax and Sebenius at Harvard;[9] Bazerman and Neale at Northwestern;[10] and Mnookin, Ross, and others at Stanford.[11]

These scholars and others have developed a body of work that uses the perspectives of many different disciplines to investigate a troubling and important question: Why do negotiations often fail to produce agreement, even when negotiators have the best training and skills available? Why is "getting to yes," in practice, not as easy as some have suggested? What are the barriers that make reaching agreement harder than we might think, even for skilled negotiators? I cannot do justice to this complex body of work in the brief time available here.[12] However, I want to mention a few of the major insights regarding the negotiation process—especially its limits—that this literature has produced, because they are directly relevant to the questions under discussion.

One theme that the negotiation scholars have developed is the "barriers" concept.[13] That is, they suggest that the most important factors in explaining failed negotiations are two kinds of "informational barriers" that impede negotiations and agreement. These barriers arise from structural and perceptual dynamics inherent in the negotiation process itself, and in this sense they represent "bugs" in the process that can undermine it despite the parties' skills and their desire to reach a settlement.

A. The Meaning of "Failed Negotiations"

Here we have an apparent contradiction: If, as noted above, the vast majority of cases (even those brought to court) do in fact settle, where is the problem the barriers literature describes? The explanation is that, for negotiation scholars—and probably for disputants themselves—a "failed negotiation" may mean either of two things.[14] First and most obvious, failure may mean impasse, the inability to reach any agreement. Second, even when agreement is reached, the negotiation may be considered a failure (or at least, not very successful) because the costs of reaching settlement (including time and indirect costs) were unnecessarily high or, more importantly, because the terms agreed we were "suboptimal"—they failed to realize all the gains that were actually available from exchange between the parties. Excessive bargaining costs or unrealized joint gains are common, the literature suggests, even where agreements are reached. Thus, negotiation often "fails," despite substantial settlement rates, both because some cases do not reach settlement at all and because many others reach settlement at undue cost or suboptimal terms.

B. Strategic Barriers

The question remains, Why is this kind of failed negotiation so common? As mentioned before, the negotiation scholars point to certain kinds of informational barriers as the cause. In general, two kinds of barriers are identified, with many variations of each type. The first kind are described as "strategic barriers." These arise because each negotiator usually holds certain private information, and each has a strategic incentive to hide this information or even mislead the other side about it, in order to win a larger share of the stakes. Even though this kind of strategic concealment will probably result in suboptimal outcomes, it is often quite rational, because openness and honesty could mean both giving up one's own advantage and creating one for an opponent who is ready and willing to exploit it.[15]

Looking at it differently, parties are (rightly) suspicious of each other in bargaining, and therefore not likely to put full and honest information on the table. Since everyone knows this is so, no one can rely upon the information put forth by the other. Thus, the barrier created by strategic behavior is informational poverty and unreliability. There is not enough reliable information on the table to enable the parties to identify possibilities for mutually beneficial exchange, and there is no way to improve the informational environment as long as strategic incentives exist.[16] As a result, deals are not made, or the deals that are made are suboptimal.

C. Cognitive Barriers

A second kind of informational barrier also arises, which impedes the use of whatever information parties do manage to put forth (despite strategic incentives), because of what negotiation scholars call "cognitive biases." The insight here is based on psychological research showing that, in the cognitive processes by which people assimilate information, there are regular and identifiable "departures from rationality" that lead to distortion and misinterpretation of the information received.[17] Negotiation scholars have shown that the same cognitive biases that operate elsewhere also affect the negotiation process.[18]

As an example, consider "loss aversion": In making decisions, individuals tend to give prospective losses more significance than prospective gains of actually equivalent value. Therefore, if taking an action would involve both getting something and giving something up, the object gained will seem less valuable than the object given, even if it is actually of equal or somewhat greater worth—because people tend to "feel the pain" of a loss more than they "feel the pleasure" of a gain. The action may therefore not be taken, despite its rational desirability, due to the cognitive distortion of value. In negotiation, loss aversion results in the reluctance of negotiators to make "trade-offs," even when an objective comparison shows that each side would gain more than it is giving up in the trade.[19]

The barrier created by this and other cognitive biases is informational distortion.[20] Even the information that is revealed by the parties gets distorted as it is received and processed. Because of cognitive biases, each party is incapable of reading the information provided by the other side—including offers and demands—accurately and objectively. Therefore, each is likely to analyze this information with a false and distorted perspective that, once again, leads them to miss opportunities for deals entirely, or make deals that fail to realize all possible joint gains.

Together, strategic and cognitive barriers help explain why reaching negotiated agreement is difficult, no matter how skillful the negotiators. Impasses and suboptimal bargains result because of decisions that are made with inadequate and unreliable information, which is further distorted through biased interpretive processes. And the strategic incentives and cognitive biases responsible for these informational barriers are very difficult for the parties themselves to change or transcend.[21]

IV. ONE ANSWER TO THE QUESTION: MEDIATION LOWERS THE BARRIERS TO SETTLEMENT

A. The Scholar's Answer

The obvious question that flows from the study of the barriers problem is: What can be done to eliminate or lower these barriers? What is striking is that negotiation scholars themselves place great hope in mediation as one potential solution to this problem. Their general suggestion is that mediators' interventions can somehow reduce both strategic and cognitive barriers to settlement: They believe that mediators can take steps that will improve the information flow between the parties and the parties' sense of confidence in the reliability of the information provided. They also suggest that mediators can do things that will remove or reduce the parties' cognitive distortions of this information as they process it and make decisions.[22] The negotiation scholars themselves do not go into much detail regarding the specific practices mediators might follow to achieve these effects; rather, they suggest some general ideas that mediation researchers and theorists might develop further.[23]

However, even without all the details, this accumulated body of negotiation scholarship does offer a general answer to the question at the heart of our discussion: What is the value-added of mediation to negotiators; what does the mediator add or facilitate that the parties could not accomplish on their own? The study of strategic and cognitive barriers suggests a powerful answer. First, *mediators can help parties put more information on the table and ensure that it is more reliable* and less suspect than would be the case if the parties negotiated alone. As a result, parties can enrich their informational environment, gain greater clarity and then go ahead as they would in negotiation and make decisions for themselves—but on an improved information base. Second, *mediators can help parties perceive each other*—including past and present actions, attitudes, motivations and positions—*more fully and accurately* than they would if left to themselves. The parties can thus avoid responses in negotiation that are based upon false assumptions about one another stemming from cognitive biases.[24] The implication of the theory is that, with better information and less interpretive distortion (i.e., with the barriers lowered) settlements will be reached more often and on terms that come closer to optimality.

B. Putting the Answer in Practitioners' Terms

What this discussion shows is that, according to one substantial body of scholarly work, mediation really does have added value for negotiators. It can help them achieve results that they cannot achieve for themselves by reducing the informational barriers that are inherent in unassisted negotiation. Thus, even good negotiators have something to gain from the assistance of a mediator.

As a practical matter, however, can this body of knowledge be conveyed to real-world disputants in a real case, who want to know why they need a mediator and why they cannot simply negotiate for themselves? To return to our scenario, how can the mediator respond to the questions posed there in a way that condenses this scholarly argument into a clear and concise answer for the parties and their lawyers?

The answer might run something like this:

> You ask what a mediator would add to your negotiation process. Fair question. The answer is that she can help you understand your situation—and your options and each other—better and more fully than you do now, and better than you will if you continue working on your own. I say this because research and experience have shown that gathering reliable information and analyzing it accurately is much easier when parties are working with a mediator than when they are working alone. And if you understand the situation, options and each other more completely and accurately, you will be able to make better decisions on what you want to do—to see if there is a deal that can be made; if there is one, to see how to move towards making it; and if not, to see what your other options are. All this would be easier to see because of the increased clarity that a mediator can help you attain about the situation and each other. The bottom line: a mediator's assistance will help you make the best possible decisions for yourselves—which means a better chance of reaching settlement, and on better terms.[25]

C. Yet Another Question

This answer—or something like it—gives the parties the basics of what negotiation theory says about mediation's value to negotiators. However, the answer itself immediately raises another question: Will disputants and lawyers really be impressed with this response? The gist of the answer is that a mediator will help improve the flow of information and reduce the effects of false or biased assumptions. Will the prospect of such assistance really be viewed as valuable by practical negotiators interested in reaching a deal?

To put the point more sharply: Isn't it more likely that the kind of "assistance" parties might value, if they want any at all, is something quite different? For example, if they were told that a mediator would help them by predicting what the court would decide if they went to trial, or by providing expertise in problem-solving and identifying a solution good for both sides, or by overcoming resistance on both sides and giving them a firm "push" toward settlement—aren't these kinds of help more likely to be what negotiators are looking for?[26] Explaining that mediation will "enrich the decision-making environment" is fine in theory, but will this explanation seem relevant to the parties—to put it bluntly, will it "sell"? If not, then regardless of what the negotiation literature shows, it will not satisfy negotiators demanding to know what a mediator will do for them.

V. SEARCHING FOR ANSWERS AGAIN: RECENT SCHOLARSHIP ON PARTY ATTITUDES TOWARD DISPUTE RESOLUTION PROCESSES

In effect, what we have just done is to shift the focus to a different question, although it is certainly related to the one with which we began. The new and broader question is: What are parties looking for, in general, when they are considering whether to bring an intervenor into their conflict? Even more broadly, what do parties most desire in a conflict handling process, with or without an intervenor? Or, to relate the broad question to our subject of mediation, what features do parties value in conflict handling processes that mediation can uniquely offer? These questions may seem to go beyond the scope of the topic at hand. However, a little reflection shows that this is not so. Indeed, the answers to these new questions will determine whether the above explanation of mediation's value to negotiators will have any salience to parties and lawyers, or whether it is just a nice piece of theory without practical relevance.

In looking for answers to this second set of questions, I want to point to another part of the literature of the field—the scholarship on party attitudes toward dispute resolution processes. There is a rich literature on this subject, including studies of party satisfaction with mediation and other processes, as well as research that tries to identify what *leads to* party satisfaction—what effects and features of processes parties value most. In numerous studies, researchers have interviewed and surveyed parties who have participated in different processes to determine levels of party satisfaction, rates of compliance with agreements or decisions and other post process attitudes and effects. As is well known, the consistent finding of these studies is that mediation produces high levels of satisfaction and compliance, and that these levels are typically much higher than those generated by court processing of similar cases.[27]

More important to our discussion here are the research findings and theory on *why* mediation tends to produce high levels of satisfaction and compliance, especially by comparison to court procedures. These findings on this question are consistent across two different kinds of studies.

A. Evaluation Studies

The first studies are evaluation studies of mediation itself, in which follow-up questions are asked of parties to elicit the reasons for their high satisfaction and compliance levels. Some of the most frequently given reasons are the following: mediation enabled the parties to deal with the issues they themselves felt important; it allowed them to present their views fully and gave them a sense of having been heard; it helped them to understand each other. Significantly, these and other commonly cited reasons relate to how the process worked rather than the outcome it produced.[28] Parties report high satisfaction levels with mediation, and for similar reasons, even in cases where no settlement was reached, and even when the parties "did worse" in mediation than they might have done in court—suggesting that settlement production per se, and even quality of outcome, are not what parties find most valuable about mediation.[29].

B. Procedural Justice Studies

The second group of studies is associated with "procedural justice" theory.[30] These studies use various research techniques to measure attitudes about consensual processes like negotiation, mediation, and nonbinding arbitration, by comparison to impositional procedures like adjudication or binding arbitration, in real and hypothetical situations. Their findings show that *parties usually prefer the consensual processes, even where the outcomes they receive in these processes are unfavorable.* Moreover, the main reason for this preference is the value that disputants place on "process control," a term that includes both the opportunity for meaningful participation in determining the outcome of the procedure (whatever it may ultimately be) and the opportunity for full self-expression. Consensual processes like mediation and negotiation offer a greater degree of process control, and hence they are seen by parties as "subjectively fairer" and are preferred, regardless of whether they ultimately lead to favorable outcomes.[31] In other words, procedural justice research shows that parties care as much about how dispute resolution is conducted as they do about what outcome results; and consensual processes provide the "how" that parties value most.

C. The Common Answer

Thus, when we examine why mediation generates high levels of party satisfaction and compliance, by comparison to court hearings, two distinct kinds of research— evaluation and procedural justice studies—tell us the same thing: Parties' favorable attitudes toward mediation stem largely from *how* the process works, and two features in particular are responsible. Those features are: (1) the greater degree of participation in decision making that parties experience in mediation; and (2) the fuller opportunity to express themselves and communicate their views, both to the neutral and to each other, that they experience in the process.[32] Because of these features, parties find mediation highly valuable, even when no settlement is reached, and even when a mediated settlement embodies a less favorable outcome than they could have obtained in court.

There is thus a substantial body of research that answers our question about what parties value in dispute resolution processes. The most remarkable thing is what the answer is *not*. Despite what we might have thought, parties do not place the most value on the fact that a process provides expediency, efficiency, or finality of resolution.[33] Not even the likelihood of a favorable substantive outcome is considered most important. Rather, an equally, if not even more highly, valued feature is "procedural justice of fairness," which in practice means the greatest possible opportunity for *participation* in determining outcome (as opposed to assurance of a favorable outcome), and for self-expression and *communication*.

D. The Answer in Practical Terms

To frame the importance of these findings for our topic—mediation's value to negotiators—let us return to our initial scenario for a moment. Imagine that we revised the scene as follows: Before answering the parties' question about what a mediator would add, the expert asked them a question of his own: "Tell me, first of all, what is it that you really want most from whatever process is used to handle this situation? Knowing that will help me to answer your question." Now, we might have assumed that the parties would respond by saying: "We want whatever it takes to get this dispute over with, as soon as possible and as cheaply as possible." Or perhaps, "I want my rights enforced so that this project _____ [is stopped for good] [is allowed to proceed full force] (with the blank completed differently by each party)."

However, the research just described suggests that their response is unlikely to be either of the above options. Instead, each party would probably say, in some fashion:

> Well, I do want to get this settled quickly, on reasonable terms. *But not* without my having real participation and control in the process—so that I am involved in making decisions, not just the lawyers and the judge; so that they're my decisions, and better decisions, and I'm more in control of the situation. Also, I want to be able to say what I want to say, and feel that I've really been heard—and hear something real from the other side as well. I want a chance to communicate, and not just hear legalese and debating points.

To this kind of clarification, the expert might then respond, "If this is what matters to you, then it's pretty clear that going to court or to arbitration will not meet your desires, because you won't get that kind of participation and communication in either forum. But now I can answer your question about mediation, because . . ." The expert would then continue with his explanation of mediation's value as described earlier—which would now resonate with the parties' own expression of their preferences.

E. Another Question

However, there is a weakness in this revised scenario: the party-attitude research described above, of both kinds, focuses on comparing adjudication, on the one hand, with consensual processes—including *both* mediation and negotiation—on the other. This research may help answer questions about why disputants would prefer to use mediation rather than go to court. But that is not the question we are asking today; rather, the question is, why should they use a mediator rather than negotiate on their own? In short, does the party satisfaction and procedural justice research tell us anything useful about the comparison between mediation and negotiation?

VI. WHAT MEDIATION HAS TO OFFER NEGOTIATORS: MORE OF WHAT THEY VALUE IN NEGOTIATION ITSELF

There are a number of ways to answer the above question. However, describing a recent study of "lawyered mediation"—mediation with both parties and lawyers present—seems a particularly good way to start because it offers some concrete answers that go right to the point.[34] This study looked at a court-ordered mediation program which allowed and encouraged lawyers to attend sessions with their clients, a somewhat unusual practice in such programs. Though some had predicted that lawyers would try to avoid attending mediations, it turned out that they attended willingly and regularly, and they seemingly found the process very productive.[35] In order to understand and explain these results, researchers studied the program and interviewed many of those involved, especially the lawyers who had participated in mediations.

One of the study's major questions was: Why had these lawyers decided that mediation was useful and worth participating in? The answers the researchers received are directly relevant to the questions we are asking today about mediation's value to negotiators. The study's main finding is striking: The lawyers decided that mediation was useful because they saw it as "an improvement on negotiation."[36] That is, these lawyers asked themselves the very same question we imagined parties asking in our scenario—"Can mediators add value to our negotiation process?"—and reached a positive conclusion.

The reasons they gave for this conclusion are even more striking. The lawyers valued mediation over unassisted negotiation because they found that:

- It structures the negotiation process in ways that lead to increased information becoming available to the negotiators, so that attorneys can better advise clients about what to do.[37]

- It increases clients' sense of participation in and control over their case, which is frequently attenuated in lawyer-lawyer negotiation.[38]

- It "provides a setting for communication between the parties that settlement [negotiation] does not, a setting in which parties can and do discuss and explain needs and problems and express anger and disappointment . . . , not just exchange demands and positions,"[39] in which clients can feel that "another person has heard their side of the story[,] that the other side . . . has heard their side[40] and in which "[suspicions and] misconceptions that clients tend to have about the other side" are cleared up.[41]

With these findings in mind, recall what the party satisfaction and procedural justice literature has shown about why disputants prefer consensual processes over impositional ones: the former offer greater opportunities for *participation* and *communication*. Both mediation and negotiation are preferred over court for this reason.[42] Here is the point: the lawyered mediation study shows that disputants find mediation "an improvement on negotiation" *for the very same reason*. That is, although both negotiation and mediation involve more and better party participation and communication than court proceedings, mediation provides even greater levels of both of these desired features than negotiation—and thus adds value to the negotiation process.

This same conclusion can be reached by a theoretical analysis, but the concrete findings of the lawyered mediation study make it very clear. They confirm that just as the party-attitude research explains why parties prefer both negotiation and mediation to trial, it also explains why parties will value mediation over unassisted negotiation: because mediation offers more of the "process control" that parties value in consensual processes generally.[43]

VII. MEDIATION AS "ASSISTED NEGOTIATION": THE COMMON LESSON OF THE NEGOTIATION AND PARTY-ATTITUDE SCHOLARSHIP

It is important to acknowledge a seeming inconsistency between the two bodies of work that we have discussed today, particularly as they offer answers to parties' questions about mediation's value. According to the negotiation literature, mediation's value lies in the fact that it can increase the likelihood and optimality of settlement. On the other hand, the party-attitude literature shows that what parties *themselves* will see as valuable about mediation is *not* primarily its effects on settlement production or quality but rather its mode of operation (i.e., its high degrees of party participation and communication).[44] The question is this: Given the findings of party-attitude research on what parties value—process control, even more than outcome effects—do the conclusions of negotiation scholarship, about mediation's value in "lowering barriers to settlement," still make sense as part of an answer to parties' questions about the value of mediation?

In fact there is no fundamental inconsistency between these two bodies of work, and both are important sources for an answer to the question about mediation's value to negotiators. First, the procedural justice literature does not look at party valuations of dispute resolution processes as an "either/or" matter—either parties value process quality, or outcome effects, but not both. The literature suggests instead that party valuations are "both/and" in character: outcome effects (i.e., settlement production and quality) are valued by parties—but not solely or primarily; and process quality (i.e., party participation and communication) is also valued—as much or even more so.[45] Therefore, parties should be responsive to explanations of mediation's value in terms of *both* outcome effects and process quality. The procedural justice and negotiation scholarship is thus consistent, although the emphasis of each is different. In particular, the important lesson of the procedural justice literature is that it makes no sense to frame explanations entirely in outcome terms and ignore or omit the process quality dimension—which is what some of the negotiation literature tends to do.[46]

Second, there are strong points of commonality between these two bodies of work, which teach an important lesson about mediation's value to negotiators. If we look at the specific kind of assistance that each body of work sees mediation as offering negotiators, there are strong correspondences between them.[47] For example, helping to lower strategic barriers by increasing information flow and quality corresponds in some degree to improving the quality of party participation and control. That is, when parties have minimal and unreliable information as a result of strategic maneuvering, this can be as destructive to the quality of party participation and decision making as any intrusion by an outside force or authority. Improving the informational environment simultaneously improves the quality of participation. In similar fashion, helping to lower cognitive barriers by reducing bias in interpretation corresponds to improving the quality of interparty communication. To put it differently, mediation's assistance in lowering barriers to settlement simultaneously enhances procedural justice, and vice versa.[48]

An important lesson can be derived from this commonality in the way two distinct bodies of scholarship conceptualize mediation's "added value" for the negotiation process. *Both* see mediators as adding value by *facilitating* and supporting the activities of the negotiators themselves—their information exchange, communication, deliberation and decision making—rather than by exerting pressure, offering evaluative judgments or engaging in other kinds of directive interventions. Thus both support the practice followed in our original scenario of explaining mediation as assisted negotiation; and together they help clarify just what constitutes the assistance and why it is valuable to negotiators.[49] At the same time, they support the view that mediation need not be directive or judgmental to be genuinely valuable—a point I will return to in my conclusion.[50]

VIII. THE CONCRETE MEANING OF "ASSISTED NEGOTIATION": THE IMPORTANCE OF "EMPOWERMENT AND RECOGNITION" TO MEDIATION PRACTICE

A. The Picture Thus Far

The foregoing discussion has focused on offering theoretical answers, based on research and scholarship, as to why negotiators should see mediation as valuable—with mediation defined, as in our original scenario, as facilitated or assisted negotiation. We have seen that the insights of two distinct bodies of scholarship are consistent and mutually reinforcing, and that they suggest two main theoretical answers to the question of mediation's value to negotiators:

1. The assistance mediation provides can help cure inherent problems in the negotiation process by improving the quality of information, communication and hence party decision making.

2. This kind of enhancement of negotiation is something that parties really value and want—not only or primarily because it produces better outcomes (though it probably will), but also because it simultaneously increases the "process control" that leads parties to prefer negotiation in the first place.

Thus, there is strong theoretical support for the statement that mediation as facilitated or assisted negotiation will be both genuinely useful and actually appealing to parties trying to negotiate resolution to conflict.

With the discussion of the lawyered mediation study, we moved from theory to reality. This study confirms that real-world negotiators see mediation as providing just the sort of "facilitation and assistance" the theory suggests it does. It also confirms that negotiators regard this assistance as a real added value. As other such studies are conducted, we can expect these conclusions to accumulate additional weight. Thus, looking back on our original scenario, and the mediator's explanation of what mediation has to offer, we see now that this explanation is based on a solid body of evidence about what negotiators need and want, and how mediation can provide it. It is not only a sound explanation, it is also one that should have real appeal to parties and lawyers.

B. Putting the Picture in a Different Light

Now I want to throw a different light on the picture presented today, by reframing somewhat the conclusions reached thus far. Suppose we put the question that we have been examining in a slightly different form, by asking: What is the most important product or effect that mediation *uniquely* offers, *as an alternative to negotiation,* that parties to conflict in fact value? Based on the material reviewed today, it is clear that the answer is not greater speed, lesser cost, increased likelihood of settlement or even improved quality of outcome.[51]

Instead, we can say that the most important product that mediation provides (that other negotiation alternatives do not) is *a twofold, qualitative improvement* over the way the negotiation process works when unassisted. One dimension of this improvement is an *increased level of party participation in and control over decisions* made in the process. This includes, for each party, greater ability to acquire and exchange information and to analyze it accurately, as well as greater direct involvement in decision making when lawyers or other agents are involved. The result is a qualitatively different deliberation and decision-making process, which enables parties to accept or reject terms of agreement with clarity, as they see fit, and thus to effectuate their desires in conflict situations more fully. Along with others, I have described this as the "value of self-determination" in mediation.[52] People value the experience of self-determination. They believe they know what is best for themselves and they want the opportunity to effectuate it, in conflict as in other aspects of their lives.[53] The evidence presented today shows that mediation provides that opportunity, to an even greater degree than negotiation.

The second way in which mediation improves negotiation is by *improving the character and quality of the communication that occurs between the parties* as human beings during the process. This includes an increased opportunity to present and receive a broad range of messages—verbal and nonverbal, rational and emotional—and, even more importantly, the reduction of all kinds of distortion and misunderstanding that otherwise tend to skew the interpretations that parties place on each other's statements and actions. In simple terms, conflict leads disputants to demonize each other, and mediation "de-demonizes" people to one another. Again, the evidence presented today suggests that parties value this "product" highly. People do not want to be regarded by each other, or even to regard each other, as demonic and ill-intentioned, and to relate to each other on the basis of such mutual negative characterization.[54] Mediation enables them to deal with a conflict without doing so, and even to find more positive ways of regarding each other, despite serious disagreement.

This way of describing the most valued products of mediation—in terms of the two important qualitative improvements it brings to the parties' experience of the negotiation process—raises one last set of questions. Mediation can increase self-determination and decrease mutual demonization in dispute handling better than any other process, including negotiation itself; and disputants value these effects so highly that they prefer processes that provide them. Therefore, why not design and practice an approach to mediation that aims at these valued effects *intentionally and directly,* instead of one that produces them accidentally, if at all? Why focus mediation practice solely on the objective of speedily and cheaply reaching a settlement—or reaching a good, creative, fair or optimal settlement? If these were the only valued products of mediation, it might make sense for mediators to focus on arm twisting, case evaluation, deal-making or problem-solving.[55] But the evidence suggests that there are other products of the process that parties value equally or even more highly. Therefore, why shouldn't mediators focus their practice on providing those products?

C. "Empowerment and Recognition" in Mediation Practice

These questions point to the importance of what my colleague Joe Folger and I have called "empowerment and recognition" in mediation practice.[56] These two concepts relate directly to what are described here as mediation's most valued products. The thrust of the work that Folger and I, and others, have been doing is to articulate an approach to mediation that is explicitly focused on providing these products. In that approach, mediators focus on two kinds of activities.[57]

First, they focus on supporting—and not supplanting—the parties' own deliberation and decision-making processes. That is, wherever opportunities arise for parties to think about and make choices—about participation, procedures, goals, issues, options, evaluative criteria, whether an agreement should be reached and on what terms—at all of these "party decision points," the mediator helps the parties enrich the informational environment, clarify and consider their own goals, options and preferences and make decisions for themselves. This is what we have called the practice of fostering empowerment in mediation.[58] It relates directly to the enhancement of participation, control and self-determination that the above discussion identifies as one of mediation's most valued products.

At the same time, in the approach we have been advocating, mediators focus on inviting, encouraging and supporting the parties' presentation to and reception from one another, of each other's perspectives and new and altered views of one another, at all points where the opportunity arises—with one important proviso. The proviso is that the parties themselves wish to engage in this dimension of the discussion. There are usually many points in a mediation where such opportunities are presented. We argue that mediation practice should include in its focus a constant attention to those points, and a conscious, intentional attempt to work with them whenever the parties are voluntarily interested in doing so. We have called this the practice of fostering recognition,[59] and it relates directly to the enhancement of interpersonal expression and communication, and de-demonization, that is also identified here as a highly valued product of mediation.

If mediation practice follows an approach centered around fostering empowerment and recognition, the effects or products of the process will be precisely the ones that research shows are valued most by disputants. First, parties will experience increased self-determination in dealing with the dispute at hand. We suggest also that this will contribute to an increased capacity for self-determined decision making in the future. Second, parties will experience improved, de-demonized communication with one another. Again, we believe that this experience will lead to an increased capacity for the same kind of enhanced communication in future situations. Finally, and primarily because of the first two effects, there will also be an increased likelihood that parties' specific concerns will be resolved on terms that they themselves see as fit and desirable, if such a resolution is at all possible. If it is not possible, it will be because the parties themselves have decided that their best options lie elsewhere. In other words, the parties may decide that they have a "BATNA" outside of mediation that they want to pursue—a decision which is itself a crucial exercise of self-determination.[60]

To return one last time to the imagined scenario of the parties and the mediation expert: The expert's statement that mediation is facilitated or assisted negotiation naturally evokes the question, "Exactly what kind of assistance or facilitation are you talking about?" A satisfying answer to this question must describe a form of help that is both valuable to and valued by negotiators. Based on all of the foregoing discussion, I suggest that *fostering empowerment and recognition is precisely the kind of assistance that negotiators need and value.* In other words, empowerment and recognition logically belong at the center of the practice of mediation as assisted negotiation.[61] When they are placed there, then the process will be as useful and attractive to its potential users as the theory suggests it should be.[62]

IX. WILL IT PLAY IN PEORIA AND ON PARK AVENUE?: THE VIABILITY AND VALUE OF DIFFERENT APPROACHES TO MEDIATION PRACTICE

This conclusion has direct relevance to a controversy that is going on within the mediation field today, over the viability and value of different approaches to practice. Within this discussion, supporters of an empowerment-and-recognition-centered approach have met with the criticism that this form of mediation ignores what disputants primarily need and want—which, the critics say, is the resolution of conflicts (on fair and optimal terms, some would add).[63] As these writers see it, in order to reach the desired goal of (fair and optimal) resolution, mediation practice necessarily and properly involves, in most contexts, a certain degree of evaluation, direction and even application of pressure by the mediator.[64] Moreover, in this view, this kind of "evaluative" practice is what parties expect and want from mediators.[65] Therefore, if mediators focus on merely "facilitating" party deliberation, decision making and communication—that is, on fostering empowerment and recognition—either they will have no clients, or they will be pushing upon clients a "service" that is neither needed nor wanted. Empowerment and recognition are thus portrayed as "an agenda" being pursued by some mediators, for various reasons, which is of no real interest to most disputants.[66]

The research and scholarly evidence reviewed today strongly suggest that this critique is misinformed and misguided. The evidence shows clearly that disputants place great value on the degree and quality of participation, expression and communication afforded them in mediation—as much or more value, in fact, than they place on substantive outcome. The evidence also shows that what negotiators need most, to overcome the kinds of information barriers that confront them, is help in acquiring reliable information and analyzing it accurately, so that they can make better informed and sounder decisions. All of this strongly suggests that mediators who focus on fostering empowerment and recognition will not only attract clients, but also send them away satisfied—whether or not a settlement is achieved. In other words, this approach to practice is both practically (and commercially) viable and substantively valuable; and those who would dismiss or marginalize it are simply ignoring a wealth of evidence about what negotiators need and value.[67]

Indeed, that evidence might even be read to suggest that it is the evaluative approach to practice that negotiators neither need nor want. To the extent that evaluation and other techniques can be and are used purely to enrich the informational environment—without any accompanying direction and pressure on parties—it is possible that these techniques could be useful ways to "assist negotiation."[68] However, evaluation can easily turn into direction and pressure, and there is considerable evidence that, in practice, it often does.[69] The literature reviewed here shows that, where this happens, the corresponding reduction of party control and self-determination will reduce satisfaction—even if settlement results—because of the value parties place on process control. In fact, the general implication of the research is clear: The more mediators use directiveness and pressure, and the less attention they give to enhancing party decision making and interparty communication, the less parties will be attracted to and satisfied by the process.[70]

Thus, mediation practice need not and should not focus on settlement production, and mediators do not have to "sell" their expertise as evaluators, deal makers or problem solvers. Instead, they can confidently advertise, and provide, the product that negotiators need and value most: assisted negotiation—in which fostering empowerment and recognition are central elements. In fact, for practitioners of empowerment-and-recognition-centered mediation, the evidence reviewed here suggests useful new ways to describe the assistance they can offer. In mediation with this approach, the value added for negotiators is clear and simply stated: it enhances the quality of both party decision making and interplay communication, which themselves lead to better quality outcomes—whether or not in the form of settlements.

In sum, those who support or engage in the practice of mediation as assisted negotiation need not be hesitant or doubtful about the value of the service they are providing. They have solid answers to the questions that may be asked about the value of their service—whether those questions come from parties, lawyers or others within and beyond the mediation field.[71]

ENDNOTES

1. This lecture focuses on the question of mediation's value to the parties themselves, not the social or public value that may be generated by its use. Demonstrating the social value of mediation is important in justifying its support or sponsorship by public authorities—for example, through rules requiring the use of mediation or public funding of mediation programs. For discussion of the social value of mediation, see Leonard L. Riskin, *Mediation and Lawyers,* 43 Ohio St. L.J. 29 (1982); Robert A. Baruch Bush, *Mediation and Adjudication, Dispute Resolution and Ideology: An Imaginary Conversation,* 3 J. Contemp. Legal Issues 1 (1989–90). *See generally* Nancy H. Rogers and Craig A. McEwen, Mediation: Law, Policy, Practice § 5:02 (2d. ed. 1994); U.S. Dep't of Justice, Paths to Justice: Major Public Policy Issues of Dispute Resolution, Report of the Ad Hoc Panel on Dispute Resolution and Public Policy (1984); Carrie Menkel-Meadow, *For and Against Settlement: Uses and Abuses of the Mandatory Settlement Conference,* 33 UCLA L. Rev. 485 (1985). However, regardless of whether disputants' use of mediation has social value, disputants must be convinced that using the process will be beneficial to them privately, or they will simply refrain from using it—and resist legal directives to do so. The discussion here tries to develop a sound answer to parties' questions about what private value mediation can provide them, particularly by contrast to the simple use of direct and unmediated negotiation.

2. This scenario is based on one used as part of the Mini-Workshop on Alternative Dispute Resolution at the 1996 Conference of the Association of American Law Schools. The opening session of the mini-workshop presented a "role play" of lawyers counseling clients about choosing among ADR options.

3. This is likely to become the case not only because clients seek this kind of advice, but also because legal authorities begin to require that lawyers provide it. Indeed, some jurisdictions already require lawyers to do this, as a matter of professional responsibility, and the issue is under consideration elsewhere. *See Colorado Adopts Ethics Rule,* 10 Alternatives to the High Cost of Litig. 70 (1992); Frank E. A. Sander and Michael L. Prigoff, *Should There Be a Duty to Advise of ADR Options?,* A.B.A. J., Nov. 1990, at 50, 51 (debate between authors).

4. To elaborate on the point made in the text, I think that our main obligation to our students, despite the value of skills training in specific processes like mediation, is to teach these future lawyers how to provide their clients with accurate helpful information and advice about when and how to use different ADR processes, what to expect from them and what to demand from ADR providers, as educated consumers. Some of the major texts on dispute resolution directly address this issue. *See, e.g.,* Leonard L. Riskin and James Westbrook, Dispute Resolution and Lawyers (1987): Stephen B. Goldberg et al., Dispute Resolution (2d ed. 1992). *See also* Frank E. A. Sander and Stephen B. Goldberg, *Fitting the Forum to the Fuss: A User-Friendly Guide to Selecting an ADR Procedure,* 10 Negotiation J. 49 (1994) (example of how the subject might be presented to not only future lawyers, but current practitioners).

5. However, other mediators might offer a different description. As discussed further on, different approaches to mediation practice are possible and currently in use. *See infra* notes 63–71 and accompanying text. They have been distinguished in a variety of ways, and a variety of terms have been used to express the distinctions. *See, e.g.,* Deborah M. Kolb and Kenneth Kressel, *Conclusion: The Realities of Making Talk Work, in* When Talk Works: Profiles of Mediators 459 (Deborah M. Kolb and Assocs. eds., 1994) [hereinafter When Talk Works] (settlement/communication distinction); Kenneth Kressel et al., *The Settlement-Orientation vs. the Problem-Solving Style in Custody Mediation,* 50 J. Social Issues 67 (1994) (settlement/problem-solving distinction); Susan Silbey and Sally E. Merry, *Mediator Settlement Strategies,* 8 L. and policy 7, 19–30 (1986) (bargaining/therapeutic distinction).

Recently, Professor Leonard Riskin suggested a framework that distinguishes between "evaluative" and "facilitative" approaches to mediation; this framework has attracted considerable attention. *See* Leonard L. Riskin, *Mediator Orientations, Strategies and Techniques,* 12 ALTERNATIVES TO THE HIGH COST OF LITIG. 111 (Sept. 1994); Leonard L. Riskin, *Understanding Mediator Orientations, Strategies and Techniques: A Grid for the Perplexed,* 1 HARV. NEG. L. REV. 7, 25, 35 (1996). In the evaluative approach, the mediator assesses the strengths and weaknesses of parties' claims, predicts court outcomes, develops and proposes a settlement and pushes the parties to accept settlement; the facilitative approach is essentially assisted negotiation, as the expert describes it in our text. The question of which framework for distinguishing approaches to mediation makes most sense is beyond the scope of this lecture. In fact, all of the frameworks have strong commonalities. For a discussion of this point, see ROBERT A. BARUCH BUSH AND JOSEPH P. FOLGER, THE PROMISE OF MEDIATION: RESPONDING TO CONFLICT THROUGH EMPOWERMENT AND RECOGNITION 59–68 (1994).

For the purposes of this lecture, I take the view that "assisted negotiation" defines and describes one possible approach to mediation practice. (Later on, I will suggest some of the specific practices that I believe this approach should encompass. *See infra* text accompanying notes 51–62.) Moreover, as the quoted scenario on the next page implies, the remainder of my discussion focuses on how to explain to negotiators the value of using a mediator who follows *this approach.* If an evaluative approach to mediation were the subject, some of the questions discussed in the text might even be raised, and the answers given might thus be irrelevant. However, my point here is specifically to demonstrate that "mediation as assisted negotiation" does indeed have value for negotiators—and to suggest what constitutes the core of such an approach—because I do not believe that mediation must be evaluative or directive to be useful and attractive to disputants. In fact, I suggest that just the opposite is true: mediation will be more valuable, and more attractive, to disputants when it facilitates and assists rather than supplants or directs the parties' negotiation. *See infra* text accompanying notes 63–71.

There is another reason for focusing this inquiry on the value of mediation as assisted negotiation. If we sought to explain why evaluative intervention is of value to negotiators, the question would apply well beyond the mediation process: we might equally ask, what value do processes like early neutral evaluation, advisory arbitration or summary jury trial, have to negotiators? That question is certainly worth answering, but it is not a question uniquely about mediation. And that is the point. When mediation follows an evaluative model, it is not very distinct from these other evaluative processes. Some argue that, for this very reason, it should not be called mediation at all. *See, e.g.,* Kimberlee K. Kovach and Lela P. Love, *"Evaluative" Mediation Is An Oxymoron,* 14 ALTERNATIVES TO THE HIGH COST OF LITIG. 31 (1996). Whatever one's view on this question, the point here is to examine whether mediation has value to negotiators even when—and perhaps precisely because—it is fundamentally *different* from other processes. This will help determine whether mediation has any unique value to offer negotiators that is not duplicative of other dispute resolution processes.

6. *See* Bush, *supra* note 1; Riskin, *supra* note 1; Warren E. Burger, *Isn't There a Better Way?,* A.B.A. J., Mar. 1982, at 274; Frank E. A. Sander, *Varieties of Dispute Processing,* 70 F.R.D. 111, 112–114 (1976); Jessica Pearson, *An Evaluation of Alternatives to Court Adjudication,* 7 JUST. SYS. J. 420 (1982); Jay Folberg, *Divorce Mediation—A Workable Alternative, in* ALTERNATIVE MEANS OF FAMILY DISPUTE RESOLUTION 11 (Howard Davidson et al. eds., 1982); Joshua D. Rosenberg, *In Defense of Mediation,* 33 ARIZ. L. REV. 466 (1991); Terri Garner, *Comment, Child Custody Mediation: A Proposed Alternative to Litigation,* 1989 J. DISP. RESOL. 139.

7. *See, e.g.,* Marc Galanter, *Reading the Landscape of Disputes: What We Know and Don't Know (and Think We Know) About Our Allegedly Contentious and Litigious Society,* 31

UCLA L. Rev. 4 (1983); Herbert M. Kritzer, *Adjudication to Settlement: Shading in the Gray,* 70 Judicature 161, 162–164 (1986) (of roughly 1,650 federal and state court cases, only 7 percent were tried to a verdict, 15 percent ended in another form of judicial determination, 9 percent settled following a ruling on a motion and the rest [69 percent] were otherwise settled); David M. Trubek et al., *The Costs of Ordinary Civil Litigation,* 31 UCLA L. Rev. 72, 89 (1983) (roughly 8 percent of civil suits filed in state and federal courts went to trial, 22.5 percent were resolved by judicial action such as summary judgment or dismissal, and the remainder were settled); Jonathan M. Hyman et al., Civil Settlement 26–27 (1995) (New Jersey lawyers surveyed about recently completed civil cases indicated that 75 percent were resolved by settlement).

8. *See* Craig A. McEwen et al., *Bring in the Lawyers: Challenging the Dominant Approaches to Ensuring Fairness in Divorce Mediation,* 79 Minn. L. Rev. 1317, 1373 (1995); Rogers and McEwen, *supra* note 1, §§ 4:04, 5:03.

9. *See* David A. Lax and James K. Sebenius, The Manager as Negotiator: Bargaining for Cooperation and Competitive Gain (1986).

10. *See* Margaret A. Neale and Max H. Bazerman, Cognition and Rationality in Negotiation (1991).

11. *See* Barriers to Conflict Resolution (Kenneth J. Arrow et al. eds., 1995) [hereinafter Barriers].

12. I note also that recent negotiation scholarship has generated many other important insights directed to other questions. *See, e.g.,* Barbara Gray, *The Gender-Based Foundations of Negotiation Theory,* 4 Research on Negotiation in Organizations 33 (1994); Roy J. Lewicki and Barbara Benedict Bunker, Developing and Maintaining Trust in Work Relationships (Max M. Fisher College of Business [The Ohio State University] Working Paper No. 94–49, 1994). These scholars are exploring alternative ways to conceptualize the negotiation process altogether, focusing on its significance as relationship-forming activity rather than as instrumental bargaining. My focus here on the "barriers" literature stems from its direct relevance to the questions at hand.

13. For a good introduction to this framework, see Robert H. Mnookin, *Why Negotiations Fail: An Exploration of Barriers to the Resolution of Conflict,* 8 Ohio St. J. on Disp. Resol. 235 (1993) (discussing his 1992 Schwartz Lecture on Dispute Resolution at The Ohio State University College of Law).

14. *See* Robert H. Mnookin and Lee Ross, *Introduction* to Barriers, *supra* note 11, at 3, 3–7.

15. *See id.* at 7–10; Lax and Sebenius, *supra* note 9, at 29–40. Lax and Sebenius, in their discussion of the problem of strategic behavior, articulate the now widely used concepts of "value claiming" and "value creation" to describe competitive and cooperative behavior by negotiators. In their framework, the tension between the opportunities to claim value and to create it leads to rational but ironically self-defeating strategic behavior. Dealing with this "negotiator's dilemma" is the task of the negotiator, but it is quite a difficult one, and the failure to "manage" the dilemma effectively often results in suboptimal bargains, if not impasse. Lax and Sebenius base their work on earlier work on strategic bargaining and game theory by Schelling and Raiffa, *see* Thomas C. Shelling, The Strategy of Conflict (1960); Howard Raiffa, The Art and Science of Negotiation (1982), and subsequent refinements of that work by Walton and McKersie, *see* Richard E. Walton and Robert B. McKersie, A Behavioral Theory of Labor Negotiations (1965). Related to the work of Lax and Sebenius is a growing body of work in the field of game theory that models negotiating behavior under conditions of imperfect information. *See, e.g.,* Peter C. Cramton, *Bargaining with Incomplete Information: An Infinite-Horizon Model with Two-Sided Uncertainty,* 51 Rev. Econ. Stud. 579 (1984); Kalyan Chatterjee, *Incentive Compatibility in Bargaining Under Uncertainty,* 97 Q.J. Econ. 717 (1982); Roger B. Myerson, *Analysis of Two Bargaining Problems with Incomplete*

Information, in GAME-THEORETIC MODELS OF BARGAINING 115 (Alvin E. Roth ed., 1985). This work in game theory, though more technical in form and presentation than that of Lax and Sebenius, suggests similar conclusions regarding the barrier effects of strategic behavior.

16. Some scholars argue that strikes and lockouts provide examples of the serious problems that arise from the inability of negotiators to transcend strategic barriers. They suggest that a strike or lockout often represents the only way that labor or management can convey to the other side the seriousness of a position, because every other kind of statement made within the negotiation process is seen as a strategic maneuver and therefore unreliable. Strikes and lockouts thus become the only reliable "signals" negotiators can use as a last-resort means of communicating serious positions. *See* ROBERT WILSON, NEGOTIATION WITH PRIVATE INFORMA-TION: LITIGATION AND STRIKES, 11–13 (Stanford Center on Conflict and Negotiation Working Paper No. 43, 1994).

17. NEALE AND BAZERMAN, *supra* note 10, at 41–43, point to the work of Kahneman and Tversky as the seminal work on "cognitive heuristics." *See* Daniel Kahneman and Amos Tversky, *Prospect Theory: An Analysis of Decision Under Risk,* 47 ECONOMETRICA 263 (1979); Amos Tversky and Daniel Kahneman, *Judgment Under Uncertainty: Heuristics and Biases,* 185 SCI-ENCE 1124 (1974); Amos Tversky and Daniel Kahneman, *The Framing of Decisions and the Psychology of Choice,* 211 SCIENCE 453 (1981). As Neale and Bazerman put it, "Kahneman and Tversky . . . provided critical information about specific, systematic biases that influence judgment; they also suggest that decision makers rely on . . . simplifying strategies, called cognitive heuristics, to make decisions, [whose] . . . use can sometimes lead to severe deci-sion errors." NEALE AND BAZERMAN, *supra* note 10, at 43.

18. Some of the major work translating the insights on cognitive biases to the negotiation con-text has been done by Neale, Bazerman, Ross, Tversky, and colleagues and students working with them. *See, e.g.,* NEALE AND BAZERMAN, *supra* note 10; Margaret A. Neale and Max H. Bazerman, *The Effects of Framing and Negotiator Overconfidence on Bargaining Behavior and Outcomes,* 28 ACAD. MGMT. J. 34 (1985); Max H. Bazerman and Margaret A. Neale, *The Role of Fairness Considerations and Relationships in a Judgmental Perspective of Ne-gotiation, in* BARRIERS, *supra* note 11, at 86 [hereinafter Bazerman and Neale, *Role of Fair-ness*]; Max H. Bazerman and J. S. Carroll, *Negotiator Cognition,* 9 RESEARCH IN ORGANIZA-TIONAL BEHAVIOR 247 (1987); Lee Ross, *Reactive Devaluation in Negotiation and Conflict Resolution, in* BARRIERS, *supra* note 11, at 26; Lee Ross and Constance Stillinger, *Barriers to Conflict Resolution,* 7 NEGOTIATION J. 389 (1991); Lee Ross and A. Ward, *Psychological Barriers to Dispute Resolution,* 27 ADVANCES IN EXPERIMENTAL SOC. PSYCHOL. 255 (1995); Daniel Kahneman and Amos Tversky, *Conflict Resolution: A Cognitive Perspective, in* BAR-RIERS, *supra* note 11, at 44; Russell Korobkin and Chris Guthrie, *Psychological Barriers to Litigation Settlement: An Experimental Approach,* 93 MICH. L. REV. 107 (1994).

19. *See* Mnookin and Ross, *supra* note 14, at 16–17; Kahneman and Tversky, *supra* note 18, at 54–59. In the literature, loss aversion is linked to a related cognitive bias called "framing." In this cognitive pattern, people have different attitudes when choosing between two out-comes of equal value, one certain and one contingent, depending on whether the outcomes are viewed as potential gains or potential losses. When both outcomes are seen as gains, people tend to choose the certain outcome, i.e., they are risk-averse; but when both are viewed as losses, they tend to choose the contingent outcome, i.e., they are risk-seeking. In other words, despite the fact that the choices are objectively fixed, they will be seen and compared differently depending on whether the choice is framed as "certain gain v. contin-gent gain" or "certain loss v. contingent loss." *See* NEALE AND BAZERMAN, *supra* note 10, at 44–48; Korobkin and Guthrie, *supra* note 18, at 109, 129–138. This difference of interpreta-tion cannot be explained in rational terms; rather, the process of cognition seems to "trick"

us into reacting differently to different frames—a point also evident in loss aversion. The consequences of the "framing effect" for negotiation can be very significant. For example, if a concession can be framed not as "giving up something of value," but rather "reducing a liability," loss aversion will be avoided. Likewise, if a settlement offer and possible verdict can both be framed as gains rather than losses, by comparison to the status quo, acceptance of the offer is more likely. *See* Mnookin and Ross, *supra* note 14, at 16–17.

20. The example given in the text, loss aversion, is only one of many cognitive biases that have been identified and shown to affect the negotiation process as "barriers to settlement." Some of the most important are: (1) framing, *see supra* note 19; (2) equity seeking (i.e., seeking outcomes that provide not merely gains but gains proportional to perceived past injustice done by others), *see* Mnookin and Ross, *supra* note 14, at 11–13; Bazerman and Neale, *The Role of Fairness, supra* note 18; Korobkin and Guthrie, *supra* note 18, at 142–150; (3) reactive devaluation (i.e., devaluing proposals or offers solely because they have been offered by an adversary), *see* Ross, *supra* note 18; Korobkin and Guthrie, *supra* note 18, at 150–160; (4) misattributional error (i.e., attributing others' actions or proposals to evil motives rather than situational constraints, while seeing one's own acts as wholly innocent), *see* Mnookin and Ross, *supra* note 14, at 13–15; and (5) judgmental overconfidence, (i.e., being overly optimistic about the likelihood of attaining outcomes that favor oneself), *see* Mnookin and Ross, *supra* note 14, at 17–18; Kahneman and Tversky, *supra* note 18, at 46–50. All of these biases can and do create barriers to negotiated settlement, in ways that can easily be imagined. Still other cognitive barriers are noted and discussed in NEALE AND BAZERMAN, *supra* note 10, at 12, 48–77.

21. With regard to the difficulty of negotiators overcoming strategic barriers by themselves, Gilson and Mnookin discuss the problem in the context of lawyers' incentives to exchange or conceal information in the litigation process. *See* Ronald J. Gilson and Robert H. Mnookin, *Cooperation and Competition in Litigation: Can Lawyers Dampen Conflict? in* BARRIERS, *supra* note 11, at 184, 192–211. Their discussion suggests that, in order to reduce strategic behavior in a particular negotiation, there must be some meta-framework surrounding the negotiation in which norms, rules or agreements are set regarding information exchange that everyone is confident will be followed by all sides. This might take various forms: a network of individual lawyer relationships, a "reputational market" for honesty, an unwritten code formed by large firms, judicial or professional rules and so on. What is obvious from the list itself is that these kinds of quasi-institutional frameworks are costly and difficult to establish, and defections from them difficult to police. As a result, it is unrealistic to expect negotiators to give up strategic behavior and rely on such frameworks to guarantee openness in information exchange. Lowering strategic barriers, in short, is hard for negotiators to do without a larger framework to rely on, and the larger frameworks are hard to create.

    Regarding the difficulty of negotiators overcoming cognitive barriers themselves, one of the most telling indicators of this is Neale and Bazerman's discussion of whether "negotiator experience and expertise" helps them to correct cognitive biases. *See* NEALE AND BAZERMAN, *supra* note 10, at 81–96. They review the evidence and conclude that it "paints a very pessimistic picture of the idea that experience will, in fact, eliminate decision biases." *Id.* at 86. Even training on how to avoid cognitive biases has not been much help: "Using extensive training to cure biases in decision making has met with only limited success." *Id.* at 94. Thus, negotiators, even after being made aware of cognitive biases and trained in how to avoid them, apparently find this very difficult to do for themselves.

22. *See* LAX AND SEBENIUS, *supra* note 9, at 172–176; Mnookin and Ross, *supra* note 14, at 22–24; NEALE AND BAZERMAN, *supra* note 10, at 136–140.

23. The fullest discussion is offered by LAX AND SEBENIUS, *supra* note 9, at 172–176. For example, they suggest that a mediator can: (1) facilitate information flow and communication "[b]y acting as a selective conduit of information"; (2) "help a negotiator understand the interests and predicaments" of the other side; (3) "foster each negotiator's creativity" in putting forward novel proposals; (4) "reduce [their] vulnerability" to perceptions of weakness by the other side that lead to "excessive claiming"; and (5) "blunt conflict escalation . . . by enhancing trust [and] convey to each negotiator a more sympathetic understanding of his counterparts." *Id.* at 172–174.

24. For suggestions along these lines by Lax and Sebenius, see *supra* note 23.

25. In the workshop role play on which our scenario is based, *see supra* note 2, the answer of the expert—played by Professor Leonard Riskin—followed very similar lines.

26. As noted above, *see supra* note 5, some mediators take an approach that involves this kind of prediction, advice-giving and even arm-twisting. *See, e.g.,* Kolb and Kressel, *supra* note 5, at 470–474, for one good summary of this approach. Presumably, one reason that some mediators follow this approach is that they believe this is what parties need and want. The view that this is so is indeed expressed by both mediators and by some lawyers. *See* Deborah M. Kolb, *William Hobgood: "Conditioning" Parties in Labor Grievances, in* WHEN TALK WORKS, *supra* note 5, at 149, 170–171 (citing comments by William Hobgood, a labor mediator, that "pretty early on, I get a feel for what a settlement will look like. You get a 'fix' on things because you've been there before. That's why the parties want you."); James J. Alfini, *Trashing, Bashing, and Hashing It Out: Is This the End of "Good Mediation"?,* 19 FLA. ST. U.L. REV. 47, 68 71 (1991) (citing comments by a mediation program that attorneys complain if "the mediator assigned to their case was 'not pushy enough.' . . . [T]he attorneys had come to expect mediators who would 'hammer some sense' into the other side.") *See also, e.g.,* JAMES C. FREUND, THE NEUTRAL NEGOTIATOR: WHY AND HOW MEDIATION CAN WORK TO RESOLVE DOLLAR DISPUTES (1994); DWIGHT GOLANN, MEDIATING LEGAL DISPUTES: EFFECTIVE STRATEGIES FOR LAWYERS AND MEDIATORS (1996). As discussed in the text below, *see infra* text accompanying notes 27–45, other evidence suggests that what parties value in mediation is quite different.

27. *See, e.g.,* Janice A. Roehl and Royer F. Cook, *Mediation in Interpersonal Disputes: Effectiveness and Limitations, in* MEDIATION RESEARCH: THE PROCESS AND EFFECTIVENESS OF THIRD-PARTY INTERVENTION 31, 33–37 (Kenneth Kressel and Dean G. Pruitt eds., 1989) [hereinafter MEDIATION RESEARCH] ("Disputing parties typically . . . feel satisfied with the process and would return if a dispute arose in the future. [One study] found that 80–89 percent of disputants . . . were satisfied with the mediator . . . and the mediation process. Similar or slightly lower satisfaction rates were found [in four other studies]."); Jessica Pearson and Nancy Thoennes, *Divorce Mediation: Reflections on a Decade of Research, in* MEDIATION RESEARCH, *supra,* at 9, 18–22 ("More than three-fourths of the . . . mediation clients [of two different programs studied] expressed extreme satisfaction with the process . . . In contrast, only 40 percent of . . . respondents [in one study] were satisfied with the court process, and only about 30 percent of the [other] sample . . ."); Craig A. McEwen and Richard J. Maiman, *Mediation in Small Claims Court: Achieving Compliance Through Consent,* 18 L. and SOC'Y REV. 11, 45–47 (1984) ("Our portrait of compliance and litigant satisfaction is much like that which emerges in other studies of small claims mediation, of custody mediation, and of mediation of neighborhood and interpersonal disputes. Rates of compliance and satisfaction are quite high in mediated cases and seem consistently higher than those reported in comparable adjudicated cases . . ."). *See generally* ROGERS AND MCEWEN, *supra* note 1, § 4:04, nn.28–29 and accompanying text (citing similar findings in studies of mediation of civil claims such as tort and contract actions). In most studies, the premise seems to be that

increased rates of compliance are themselves linked to higher satisfaction levels, although both may be linked to third variables such as perceptions of fairness, as discussed *infra* text accompanying notes 28–32. Many of the studies try to measure not only party attitudes but objective impacts of mediation, but those findings are not specifically relevant to the issue under discussion.

28. *See, e.g.,* Pearson and Thoennes, *supra* note 27, at 19 (noting that respondents cite all of these factors to explain their high satisfaction levels); Craig A. McEwen and Richard J. Maiman, *Small Claims Mediation in Maine: An Empirical Assessment,* 33 ME. L. REV. 237, 254–260 (1981) (linking high satisfaction levels to parties' perception of "processual advantages" including: opportunities for free expression of emotions and feeling, closer attention to a range of issues dividing the parties, full involvement of the parties in shaping the agreement and reduction of polarization between parties—all of which also tend to produce higher rates of compliance).

29. *See, e.g.,* Joan B. Kelly and Lynn L. Gigy, *Divorce Mediation: Characteristics of Clients and Outcomes, in* MEDIATION RESEARCH, *supra* note 27, at 263, 278 (finding "substantial satisfaction among those who try but are unable to reach agreement"); Kenneth Kressel and Dean G. Pruitt, *Conclusion: A Research Perspective on the Mediation of Social Conflict, in* MEDIATION RESEARCH, *supra* note 27, at 394, 395–396 ("User satisfaction with mediation is typically 75 percent or higher, even for those who fail to reach a mediated agreement."); ROGERS AND MCEWEN, *supra* note 1, § 4:04, n.29 and accompanying text ("Research . . . consistently shows that disputants come away well-satisfied with the experience even when mediation fails [to produce a settlement]."); McEwen and Maiman, *supra* note 28, at 254–260 (reporting that "winners" and "losers" both give mediation similar ratings on fairness); Michelle Hermann et al., The Metrocourt Project Final Report (Jan. 1993) (University of New Mexico Center for the Study and Resolution of Disputes) (finding that minority claimants, who seem to fare worse in mediation than in adjudication, nevertheless report greater satisfaction with mediation than with adjudication).

30. The term expresses the view that subjectively perceived fairness is an important factor in assessing social procedures of all kinds. *See* E. ALLAN LIND AND TOM R. TYLER, THE SOCIAL PSYCHOLOGY OF PROCEDURAL JUSTICE 3–5 (1988). The early procedural justice literature focused in large part on studying disputant preferences for adversarial as opposed to inquisitorial adjudicatory procedures and maintained that disputants preferred the former because it gave them more "process control"—i.e., greater opportunity to put what they felt was important information before the judge. *See generally* John Thibaut et al., *Procedural Justice as Fairness,* 26 STAN. L. REV. 1271, 1272–1273, 1287–1289 (1974); Stephen LaTour et al., *Procedure: Transnational Perspectives and Preferences,* 86 YALE L. J., 258, 250–262 (1976). Part of the thesis was the premise that the ultimate concern of disputants was obtaining a favorable outcome, and higher degrees of process control were valued because they seemed likely to improve the chances of such an outcome. Thus, procedural justice was valued because it helped produce substantive (or distributive) justice.

A "second generation" of procedural justice scholarship has challenged this premise, arguing that process control is valued not only because of its presumed benefit in attaining favorable outcomes, but also because the experience of participation and expression is itself valued highly by disputants. *See* LIND AND TYLER, *supra,* at 94–106, 206–217. Lind and Tyler, the foremost exponents of this view of procedural justice, describe numerous studies showing that, "the perception that one has had an opportunity to express oneself and to have one's views considered [i.e., process control] . . . plays a critical role in fairness judgments." *Id.* at 106. In fact, "virtually all of the studies of procedural fairness in dispute resolution" have shown that process control produces higher assessments of procedural fairness "even where subjects received negative outcomes." *Id.* at 97. Based on a wide array of research on procedure in areas ranging from management to governance to dispute resolution, Lind and Tyler conclude that high degrees of process control generate high levels of perceived fairness and satisfaction and that process control is valued because of the importance people place on being treated with dignity and having an opportunity to express themselves, independent of the ultimate outcome of the procedure. *See id.* at 206–217.

31. *See* LaTour et al., *supra* note 30, at 279–282; McEwen and Maiman, *supra* note 27, at 47; McEwen and Maiman, *supra* note 28; Tom R. Tyler et al., "Preferring, Choosing, and Evaluating Dispute Resolution Procedures: The Psychological Antecedents of Feelings and Choices" (American Bar Foundation Working Paper, 1993); Dean G. Pruitt et al., *Long-Term Success in Mediation,* 17 L. & Hum. Behav. 313 (1993); Stephen B. Goldberg and Jean M. Brett, *Disputants' Perspectives on the Differences Between Mediation and Arbitration,* 6 Negotiation J. 249 (1990); Dean G. Pruitt et al., *Goal Achievement, Procedural Justice and the Success of Mediation,* 1 Int'l J. Conflict Mgmt. 33, 42 (1990). In these and similar studies, disputants show a clear preference for processes with high levels of process control and prefer less autocratic, more consensual processes over those with the opposite character. *See generally* Tom R. Tyler, *The Psychology of Disputant Concerns in Mediation,* 3 Negotiation J. 367 (1987).

32. *See, e.g.,* Pearson and Thoennes, *supra* note 27, at 18–29, where the authors conclude that "the degree of disputant participation may be the key distinction between mediation and adjudication . . . [I]n mediation, disputants retain the opportunity to shape settlements and to accept or reject them." *Id.* at 29. By contrast, they report that "the degree of control exercised by lawyers and judges [in the court process] seemed shocking to many." *Id.* at 20. Moreover, several studies of mediation programs show that when the kind of mediation offered by the program *lacks* the features mentioned in the text—and thus lacks real process control—satisfaction levels are very low. *See, e.g.,* Nancy Thoennes et al., Evaluation of the Use of Mandatory Divorce Mediation (1991) (reporting high levels of dissatisfaction among clients where mediation involved perceived pressures to settle and narrow focus of issues); Pearson and Thoennes, *supra* note 27, at 18–21 (reporting much lower satisfaction rates, by comparison to other programs studied, for a program where practice was more concerned with "expediting the processing" of cases than with providing opportunities for participation or expression).

33. When explaining mediation to parties, placing emphasis on efficiency benefits is not only unnecessary—as pointed out in the text—but probably misleading. The reason is that while mediation and other ADR processes are often advocated on the grounds that they will provide the benefits of speed, cost savings, etc., there is still no clear evidence that this is the case. On the contrary, evidence is mounting that ADR processes have much more limited impact in these dimensions than originally expected. *See, e.g.,* John Barkai and Gene Kassebaum, *Using Court-Annexed Arbitration to Reduce Litigant Costs and to Increase the Pace of Litigation,* 16 Pepperdine L. Rev. 543, 557–564 (1989) (finding, based on one of the most extensive studies of a state court-ordered arbitration program, that time and cost savings, both public and private, were of limited and uncertain dimensions, even though settlements tended to occur earlier); Deborah R. Hensler, *What We Know and Don't Know About Court-Administered Arbitration,* 69 Judicature 270, 273–275 (1986) (reporting similar findings from studies of programs in three states).

Much of this evidence concerns court-ordered nonbinding arbitration, but the picture may not be too different for mediation when more evidence is accumulated. Thus far, the evidence on mediation's "efficiency" impact is mixed. *See* Kressel and Pruitt, *supra* note 29, at 394, 398–399 (1989); Rogers and McEwen, *supra* note 1, § 4:04 (accompanying text at nn.33–34), § 5:03 (accompanying text at nn.29–30), § 6:02; Marc Galanter and Mia

Cahill, *"Most Cases Settle" Judicial Promotion and Regulation of Settlements,* 46 STAN. L. REV. 1339, 1356–1366 and n.105. The discovery that ADR's efficiency impact may not be as great as expected is related to the realization that ADR processes are generally alternatives to negotiation, not trial—so that cost and time gains must be measured by reference to party negotiation. *See supra* notes 7–8 and accompanying text. Using this standard, the gains, even where they exist, may be modest rather than substantial.

34. *See* McEwen et al., *supra* note 8.

35. Some have argued that encouraging lawyer attendance at mediations is problematic because they believe that lawyers will strongly resist attending mediations, and that when they do attend they will obstruct the process. *See id.* at 1351–1355. In fact, this program had the opposite result: the lawyers attended mediation sessions willingly; and not only were the lawyers not obstructive, but mediators and lawyers found each other's contributions complementary and hence very productive. *See id.* at 1358–1373.

36. *See id.* at 1371.

37. *See id.* at 1369, 1381–1382.

38. *See id.* at 1381.

39. *Id.* at 1382–1383.

40. *Id.* at 1383–1384.

41. *Id.* at 1370.

42. *See supra* notes 27–32 and accompanying text.

43. Although this study concentrated on lawyers' views of mediation, it seems likely that the clients' views are very similar. It seems clear that lawyers found these features of mediation valuable because their clients place importance on having better information, greater participation and fuller communication. In fact, many of the specific comments reported in the study make it clear that the lawyers valued mediation because it helped them satisfy clients better. *See* McEwen et al., *supra* note 8, at 1364–1373, 1378–1385. A number of the studies of mediation cited earlier also demonstrate that the two features mentioned in the text—participation and communication or expression—are what make mediation so attractive and satisfying to participants. *See, e.g.,* Pearson and Thoennes, *supra* note 27, at 18–29; McEwen and Maiman, *supra* note 28, at 254–260. Both of these studies suggest that the more attention is given to these two dimensions of "process control," the more parties will value the process.

44. The reason for this inconsistency is not hard to see. Negotiation scholarship, looking at the parties' process from the *outside,* assumes both that parties value outcome effects (settlement production and quality) and see how mediation can enhance them by lowering the barriers that impede the negotiation process. Party-attitude scholarship, looking at how parties view dispute resolution from the *inside,* finds that outcome effects are less important to them than process quality, and sees how mediation can improve the process quality of unassisted negotiation.

45. *See* LIND AND TYLER, *supra* note 30, at 203–220.

46. In fact, in the major examples of the "barriers" literature cited earlier, *see supra* notes 9–14 and accompanying text, there is scarcely any reference to the notion that negotiators might value something other than obtaining an "optimal outcome." Indeed, some phenomena that might be seen, from the procedural justice viewpoint, as tied to the desire for process control—such as the desire to feel that one's grievance about a past injustice has been heard—are seen in the barriers literature primarily as obstacles to reaching an agreement. *See, e.g.,* Mnookin and Ross, *supra* note 14, at 11–13. The suggestion here is that a full explanation of how mediation can help with a phenomenon like "equity seeking" should mention how mediation can not only remove it as a barrier to settlement, but also satisfy it with the opportunity for expression and communication.

47. *Compare supra* text accompanying notes 15–21 *and supra* text accompanying notes 27–33.
48. Rogers and McEwen's discussion of how lawyers might explain mediation's value to clients implicitly confirms this point, by describing both kinds of potential impacts—barrier reduction and procedural justice enhancement—as benefits offered by mediation. *See* ROGER AND MCEWEN, *supra* note 1, § 4:04, text accompanying nn.1–32.
49. *See supra* note 5 and accompanying text.
50. *See infra* text accompanying notes 57–71; *see also supra* note 5 and accompanying text.
51. The emphasis here is on what mediation can offer that other negotiation alternatives cannot. So, for example, nonbinding arbitration or mini-trial may offer as much benefit as mediation in saving time and cost and in promoting settlement. If so, then these benefits are not unique products of mediation, and an explanation of mediation's value based on them would apply equally to other processes. Explaining mediation's value to negotiators means describing what mediation can *uniquely* offer them. *See supra* note 5.
52. *See* Robert A. Baruch Bush, *Efficiency and Protection, or Empowerment and Recognition?: The Mediator's Role and Ethical Standards in Mediation,* 41 FLA. L. REV. 253, 267–268 (1989); Bush, *supra* note 1, at 14; JAY FOLBERG AND ALISON TAYLOR, MEDIATION: A COMPREHENSIVE GUIDE TO RESOLVING CONFLICTS WITHOUT LITIGATION 245 (1984) (stating that the "overriding feature and redeeming value of mediation [is that] . . . it is a consensual process that seeks self-determined resolutions"); Joseph B. Stulberg, *The Theory and Practice of Mediation: A Reply to Professor Susskind,* 6 VT. L. REV. 85, 113–116 (1981). There is evidence that this value is gaining wider recognition. Recently, three major organizations—the American Arbitration Association, the Society for Professionals in Dispute Resolution and the American Bar Association—jointly adopted standards of conduct for mediators, the very first section of which declares: "Self-determination is the fundamental principle of mediation." MODEL STANDARDS OF CONDUCT FOR MEDIATORS Standard I (1995).
53. When presenting the ideas discussed in this section, I am often challenged on the grounds that it is unrealistic to think that disputants are really interested in achieving greater self-determination or, as discussed just below in the text, greater ability to view others positively rather than negatively. The realistic view, it is said, is that disputants simply want their problem solved and their case settled, as quickly and cheaply as possible. I sometimes respond to this question by pointing to the lists of best-selling books featured regularly in major newspapers, and noting that two categories of books appear with great regularity on these lists: books on self-help and self-improvement, and books on communicating better and improving relationships with others. Clearly, large numbers of people buy books on these two topics—clearly related to the values discussed in the text—of their own free choice and expense. Although this is certainly not a scientific demonstration, I suggest that it raises doubts about the "unrealism" of the views expressed here about how people value self-determination and relating positively to others.
54. *See supra* note 53.
55. There is considerable evidence that a large majority of mediation practitioners focus solely or primarily on these objectives and use one or more of the approaches to practice described in the text. *See* BUSH AND FOLGER, *supra* note 5, at 33–68, for a review of some of this evidence.
56. *See* BUSH AND FOLGER, *supra* note 5, at 84–112; Bush, *supra* note 52, at 267–275; Joseph P. Folger and Robert A. Baruch Bush, *Transformative Mediation and Third-Party Intervention: Ten Hallmarks of a Transformative Approach to Practice,* 13 MEDIATION Q. (forthcoming 1996).
57. The brief summary given in the following paragraphs is based on a much more extensive description and explanation of this approach to mediation—which we call the "transformative

approach"—published elsewhere. *See* BUSH AND FOLGER, *supra* note 5; Folger and Bush, *supra* note 56. The term "transformative" is meant to reflect that fact that, when mediation practice follows this approach, participants can experience changes and improvement not only in the situation that gave rise to the conflict, but also in their personal capacities for self-determination and relating positively to others. As noted above, *see supra* notes 53–54 and accompanying text, our view is that disputants are interested in both kinds of change or transformation. Others have also been striving to articulate and develop this sort of approach to mediation, whether or not using the exact same terms. *See, e.g.,* Sally Ganong Pope, *Inviting Fortuitous Events in Mediation: The Role of Empowerment and Recognition,* 13 MEDIATION Q. (forthcoming 1996); Trina Grillo, *Respecting the Struggle: Following the Parties Lead,* 13 MEDIATION Q. (forthcoming 1996); Albie Davis, *The Logic Behind the Magic of Mediation,* 5 NEGOTIATION J. 17 (1989). *See generally* Kolb and Kressel, *supra* note 5, at 466–468, 474–479.

58. The parties' exercise and strengthening of their capacity for self-determination, through making such choices, is what we mean by the empowerment effect of the mediation process. *See* BUSH AND FOLGER, *supra* note 5, at 85–89, 95–96; Folger and Bush, *supra* note 56. Mediators foster empowerment by supporting party deliberation and decision making throughout a mediation session. For concrete examples of the kinds of specific practices involved, in a case study, see BUSH AND FOLGER, *supra* note 5, at 139–188.

59. The parties' exercise and development of their capacity for self-transcendence, through giving consideration to the other party's diverse perspective, is what we mean by the recognition effect of the process. *See* BUSH AND FOLGER, *supra* note 5, at 89–94, 96–97; Folger and Bush, *supra* note 56. Mediators foster recognition by supporting party perspective-taking at all points in a mediation session where parties choose to engage in this effort. For concrete examples of the kinds of specific practices involved, in a case study, see BUSH AND FOLGER, *supra* note 5, at 139–188.

60. The term "BATNA" stands for "best alternative to negotiated agreement" and was popularized by Fisher and Ury. *See* ROGER FISHER AND WILLIAM URY, GETTING TO YES: NEGOTIATING AGREEMENT WITHOUT GIVING IN 97–106 (2d. ed. 1991). In effect, the BATNA represents a party's freedom to reject a proposed settlement, and this freedom represents the best guarantee that mediation will not be used to oppress parties in weaker positions. *See* BUSH AND FOLGER, *supra* note 5, at 275–276. Allowing and encouraging parties to pursue their BATNAs, where they think it appropriate, is one of the ways—among others—that empowerment-centered mediation avoids the risk of unfairness that some have rightly seen in mediation. *See, e.g.,* Trina Grillo, *The Mediation Alternative: Process Dangers for Women,* 100 YALE L. J. 1545 (1991).

61. For a more detailed discussion of what empowerment-and-recognition-centered mediation might look like, see BUSH AND FOLGER, *supra* note 5, at 99–226; Folger and Bush, *supra* note 56. In the second source, we identify 10 specific practices that mediators following this approach regularly employ and that mediators following a more evaluative or directive approach typically do not.

62. The dimensions of value described here are framed primarily in terms of "process control" benefits—participation, communication, self-determination and de-demonization—whose value to parties is evident from the party-attitude literature. However, it is important to realize that these dimensions relate very directly to other measures of value that have long been described as benefits to participants in mediation. For example, the ability to reach "creative solutions" to specific problems has long been cited as an important benefit of mediation. *See, e.g.,* Riskin, *supra* note 1, at 32–35. There is an obvious connection between the process-related value of participation and the benefit of creative solutions, which is likely to emerge from such participation.

Similarly, the ability to preserve or restore important relationships has also been cited as one of mediation's important benefits to parties. *See, e.g.,* Sander, *supra* note 6, at 33–35; Riskin, *supra* note 1, at 120–124. The process-related value of de-demonization is, again, clearly connected to the production of this benefit beyond the process itself. Thus, there is a direct correspondence and continuity between the explanation of mediation's value advanced in this essay, and other descriptions of mediation's benefits to parties. The advantage of the argument developed here is that it relates directly to "products" that disputants *themselves* have identified as highly desirable, rather than to benefits that seem to some outside observer to be things that parties "ought" to consider valuable.

Another point worth noting concerns the view advanced by some procedural justice theorists regarding *why* parties value process control so highly. Lind and Tyler argue that the reason is not related to parties' concern for instrumental gain, but rather to their desire for social connection and belonging. *See* Lind and Tyler, *supra* note 30, at 221–242. Although I concur with their view that individuals' values are not adequately explained by instrumentalist theories of human nature and motivation, I suggest that there may be another explanation beyond the desire for social connection. Folger and I have argued, based on work by others, including Gilligan, *see* Carol Gilligan, In a Different Voice: Psychological Theory and Women's Development (1982), that moral development is also a primary force in human motivation. *See* Bush and Folger, *supra* note 5, at 242–251. According to this view, people make choices, including choices about how they want to deal with conflict, out of a desire to develop and enact their capacities for morally superior forms of awareness and behavior. In short, people want, if possible, to act with both strength and compassion, and they value social processes that give the chance, and help them, to do so. *See id.* Mediation can be one such process, and this may explain its attractiveness.

63. *See* James Boskey, Book Review, The Alternative Newsletter, Mar. 1995, at 22, 23 (reviewing Robert A. Baruch Bush and Joseph Folger, The Promise of Mediation: Responding to Conflict Through Empowerment and Recognition (1994)); Carrie Menkel-Meadow, *The Many Ways of Mediation: The Transformation of Traditions, Ideologies, Paradigms, and Practices,* 11 Negotiation J. 217, 233–238, 240 (1995) (reviewing Robert A. Baruch Bush and Joseph Folger, The Promise of Mediation: Responding to Conflict Through Empowerment and Recognition (1994); Deborah M. Kolb and Assocs., When Talk Works: Profiles of Mediators (1994); The Possibility of Popular Justice: A Case Study of Community Mediation in the United States (Sally Engle Merry & Neal Milner eds., 1993)).

64. *See* Menkel-Meadow, *supra* note 63, at 225–230; Boskey, *supra* note 63, at 23. Menkel-Meadow includes "evaluative" and "activist or accountable" mediation within her description of viable "models of mediation" and "diversities of practice." *See* Menkel-Meadow, *supra* note 63, at 228–230. She also points approvingly to descriptions of the work of one particular mediator, Lawrence Susskind, who is profiled in When Talk Works, *supra* note 5, one of the books included in Menkel-Meadow's review. From the description of Susskind's work there, see John Forester, *Lawrence Susskind: Activist Mediation and Public Disputes, in* When Talk Works, *supra* note 5, at 309; Kolb and Kressel, *supra* note 5, at 470–474, 479–483, and indeed from Susskind's own writing, see Lawrence Susskind, *Environmental Mediation and the Accountability Problem,* 6 Vt. L. Rev. 1 (1981), it is clear that the kind of mediation he practices and advocates includes, at certain times, a considerable measure of evaluation, direction and pressure.

65. *See supra* note 5; *supra* note 26 and accompanying text.

66. Both of the critics cited above make these suggestions, implicitly or explicitly. *See* Boskey, *supra* note 63, at 23; Menkel-Meadow, *supra* note 63, at 235–237.

67. The claim that disputants will find this approach to mediation attractive and satisfying is not merely a theoretical proposition. Many of the studies cited earlier, in their detailed reports

of what parties to mediation find most valuable, describe practices and impacts that relate directly to either empowerment or recognition. *See, e.g.,* Pearson and Thoennes, *supra* note 27, at 19–21, 24, 29; McEwen and Maiman, *supra* note 28, at 254–260; McEwen et al., *supra* note 8, at 1364–1373, 1378–1385.

Those who claim that empowerment-and-recognition-centered mediation is not what disputants want may also claim that the evidence of party preferences reviewed here is not persuasive, because parties' subjective views of value are not necessarily objectively valid. That is, parties may suffer from a "false consciousness" that prevents them from realizing what is really of greatest value to them. *See* LIND AND TYLER, *supra* note 30, at 4; Galanter and Cahill, *supra* note 33, at 1357–1359. Such an argument, whatever its factual validity, would be ironic coming from the critics of the approach to mediation advocated here. One of their strongest objections to this approach has been that it imposes on the parties an outsider's view of what is important—empowerment and recognition rather than settlement. *See, e.g.,* Boskey, *supra* note 63, at 23; Menkel-Meadow, *supra* note 63, at 236–238. Once the evidence is put forth that parties themselves do value empowerment and recognition— which correspond to expressed procedural justice preferences—it would be ironic to dismiss this evidence itself on the grounds that parties do not really know what is good for them. Thus, the critics cannot have it both ways. If parties' preferences should count—as they indeed should—then so should evidence of what those preferences are.

68. A suggestion was made by Dean Nancy Rogers, in response to the argument presented here, that many parties may prefer a noncoercive evaluative approach to mediation to a facilitative, empowerment-and-recognition-centered approach. In fact, the findings of the party-attitude studies made thus far do not tell us which of these approaches parties find preferable, for two reasons. First, the studies made thus far have not distinguished between these two approaches in surveying or interviewing parties to mediation. Second, it is not clear that sufficient numbers of practitioners of both approaches could be found, so that a valid study of their clients' attitudes could be made. This argues for expansion of these approaches to practice, at least to the point where a broad enough base valid for study exists.

69. For a review of some of the literature related to this point, see BUSH AND FOLGER, *supra* note 5, at 63–75. *See also* Alfini, *supra* note 26, at 66–75; ROGERS AND McEWEN, *supra* note 1, §§ 7:04–7:05. The latter is an extended discussion of settlement pressure in mandatory mediation.

70. *See, e.g.,* THOENNES ET AL., *supra* note 32 (reporting high levels of dissatisfaction among clients where mediation involved perceived pressures to settle and narrow focus of issues); Pearson and Thoennes, *supra* note 27, at 18–21 (reporting much lower satisfaction rates, by comparison to other programs studied, for a program where practice was more concerned with "expediting the processing" of cases than with providing opportunities for participation or expression); McEwen and Maiman, *supra* note 28 (reporting high rates of perceived unfairness in sessions where parties felt heavily pressured by mediators to reach agreement).

71. As stated at the outset, this discussion has focused on how to explain to negotiators themselves the value of mediation as "assisted negotiation" has to offer. The value focused on here has thus been private value to the parties, as they themselves define it. The argument was developed that mediation's ability to foster empowerment and recognition, which directly relates to the kind of process control that parties demonstrably value in dispute resolution, is a benefit that negotiators will readily understand and appreciate when it is properly explained to them. The exclusive focus here on private benefit, however, in no way implies that the fostering of empowerment and recognition in mediation has no public benefits. For a discussion of the very important public benefits of an empowerment-and-recognition-centered approach to mediation, see BUSH AND FOLGER, *supra* note 5, at 28–32, 229–259; Bush, *supra* note 1.

The Manager as the Third Party: Deciding How to Intervene in Employee Disputes

A. R. Elangovan

Consider the following scenarios in an organization:

Two days before major contract work was to begin at an important client site, a dispute had erupted between the director of operations (DO) and controller of a small emission-testing (pollution control) company regarding hiring temporary workers. The DO argued that the extra workers were necessary to carry out the work, and as per company regulations she had the authority to do whatever was needed to complete a contract. The controller disagreed, saying that the company regulations allow the DO to purchase only equipment and materials and that adding employees to the payroll requires the final approval of the human resources department and the finance department. The dispute was brought to the attention of the president of the firm for a settlement.

The marketing manager and the production manager of a manufacturing company were at odds over the issue of design changes. The production manager was upset about the current procedures, which allowed marketing to make frequent changes to product design of new products right up to the commencement of production runs in order to appease customers. Each change meant three days of work to alter the specifications of all interacting components, loss of production line time reserved earlier, and lower cost-effectiveness. The production manager wanted to limit last-minute changes by setting two weeks before production as the deadline for final design. The marketing manager argued that last-minute alterations were necessary to cope with competitors' changes, meet customer demands, and maintain market share in the tough global environment. The conflict had escalated to an extent that coordination between the groups was suffering and morale was being affected, which prompted the executive vice president to step in.

If you were the president in the first example and the vice president in the second scenario, how would you intervene in the dispute? Would you facilitate the discussion and interaction between the two disputants but leave the final solution in their hands? Or would you listen carefully to both sides, analyze the issue, and come up with a good solution? Or would you impress upon the two disputants the importance of learning to handle such disputes on their own, and urge them to do so quickly? Of course, neither situation

Adapted from A. R. Elangovan, "Managerial Third-Party Dispute Intervention: A Prescriptive Model of Strategy Selection," *Academy of Management Review* 20 (1995), pp. 800–830.

would be a problem if there were an intervention strategy that worked well for all disputes. Unfortunately, research has been unable to pinpoint a "magic" strategy that would be effective in all disputes. Even the highly popular and much-touted approach of mediation has not lived up to its reputation under empirical scrutiny. Thus, managers are left with numerous options for interventions, and it is not always clear *how* they should intervene in a dispute between two subordinates to ensure maximum success in resolving it.

MANAGERS AS THIRD PARTIES

Conflict is an undeniable and pervasive feature of life in modern organizations. While the presence of conflict per se is not a problem, it is important that such conflict be managed properly to ensure that it is beneficial to achieving the goals of the organizations. Managed effectively, conflict can enhance performance by challenging the status quo, furthering the creation of new ideas, promoting reassessment of unit goals and activities, increasing the probability that the unit will respond to change, relieving tension, and serving as a medium for airing problems. But who is responsible for ensuring that conflict is managed successfully in organizations? At one level, it can be argued that it is every employee's responsibility to deal with daily conflict in a constructive rather than destructive manner. While an organization may aspire to this goal, the fact remains that employees or groups or departments are often unable to resolve disputes through established procedures or on their own. Often, the supervisor or manager at the next higher level intervenes in the dispute to help resolve it. Research has shown that managers frequently act as third parties in employee disputes concerning a wide range of issues such as failure to perform specified duties, usurpation of responsibility, disagreement over company policies, and discrimination.[1] Given the significance of these issues, it is important that the managers intervene in a manner that contributes to the effective functioning of the organization. But more often than not, these managers are informal third parties rather than highly trained professionals. Unlike professional "mediators" and "arbitrators," these managers are not external to the organization or the dispute but have an ongoing relationship with the disputants. Their effort at intervening is often part of their day-to-day managing of the work unit with a history of interactions and relationships among the parties involved. This not only limits the applicability of the prescriptions from professional third-party research to managerial intervention, but it also highlights the difficulties managers have in trying to identify the most appropriate form of intervention to use when handling a dispute between subordinates. What is needed is a framework that will help managers select the right intervention strategy in a given dispute situation. In developing this framework, however, it is necessary to identify what constitutes a successful intervention, the different intervention strategies available to the manager, and the key situational factors that would influence the selection of the appropriate strategy. Linking these three components, then, would produce a framework that indicates the kind of strategy to be selected in a given situation to achieve a successful resolution.

---

1. See (*a*) R. I. Lissak and B. H. Sheppard, "Beyond Fairness: The Criterion Problem in Research on Conflict Intervention," *Journal of Applied Social Psychology* 13 (1983), pp. 45–65; and (*b*) B. H. Sheppard, "Third-Party Conflict Intervention: A Procedural Framework." In B. M. Staw and L. L. Cummings, eds., *Research in Organizational Behavior* 6 (1984), pp. 141–190. Greenwich, CT: JAI.

CRITERIA FOR EVALUATING THE SUCCESS
OF AN INTERVENTION

What constitutes a successful intervention? Within the organizational context, research has identified a wide array of criteria for evaluating the quality of dispute interventions.[2] For example, it can be argued that for an intervention to be rated as successful it must address and resolve *all* the issues in the dispute. Similarly, a good case can be made for stating that a successful intervention should leave the disputants satisfied with the outcomes of the resolution. In addition, it is equally important that the intervention process be perceived as fair since that would affect the disputants' commitment to implementing the resolution. Although the criteria listed above are important, they focus on only part of the picture. For example, would an intervention that satisfies all these criteria be considered successful if it used up an inordinate amount of time and resources, and caused disruption? Probably not. In other words, the efficiency with which an intervention is undertaken also plays a role in determining the success of the intervention. Unfortunately, however, it is often extremely difficult, if not impossible, to have interventions that are concurrently high on effectiveness, efficiency, satisfaction, and fairness. Part of the problem lies with the counteracting nature of these criteria if taken together. For example, imposing a resolution on the disputants after quickly gathering information may increase efficiency but would negatively affect the satisfaction and perceived fairness criteria, since disputants may not accept or feel ownership of the resolution. Similarly, spending a lot of time seeking input and facilitating discussions to arrive at a consensus may lead to increased satisfaction and perceptions of fairness but does not guarantee a high-quality decision that effectively addresses all the problems in the best interest of the organization (effectiveness). This suggests that for developing a prescriptive model of intervention strategy selection, we need to first identify the criteria that are the most critical. But which of the criteria listed above are pivotal to the success of an intervention? And whose perspective should we adopt—the disputants', the intervening manager's, or the organization's?

Given the *prescriptive* nature of this model, it can be argued that it is the *organization's* perspective that matters rather than the personal interests of the disputants or third parties. After all, the aim here is to develop a set of prescriptions that will guide managers in successfully intervening in disputes so that it benefits and enhances organizational performance. Broadly speaking, therefore, a successful intervention would be one that satisfies three criteria: *settlement effectiveness, timeliness,* and *disputant commitment. Settlement effectiveness* refers to the extent to which the issues in the dispute are fully addressed to produce a settlement congruent with the goals of the organization. *Timeliness* refers to resolving the dispute before significant costs are incurred either in the form of resources, money, and time spent in squabbling and finger-pointing before actually dealing with the dispute, or in the form of a decline in productivity due to disruptions in operations or losses incurred due to missed deadlines. *Disputant commitment* refers to the extent to which disputants are motivated or determined to implement the agreed-upon settlement which, in turn, is contingent on their satisfaction with the resolu-

---

2. B. H. Sheppard, "Third-Party Conflict Intervention."

tion and perceptions of fairness. In sum, a successful intervention is one where (*a*) the issues are fully addressed to produce a settlement consistent with organizational objectives, (*b*) the resolution is timely, and (*c*) the disputants are committed to the resolution.

MANAGERIAL DISPUTE-INTERVENTION STRATEGIES

What are the various intervention strategies available to the manager acting as the third party? As noted in the introduction to this article, the manager has plenty of choice; the options range from imposing a settlement to encouraging the disputants to settle on their own, with numerous variations in between. Rather than compile a long, unwieldy list of the specific strategies that are available (some of which vary only by name), it is more useful and practical to identify the major *types* or categories of strategies that are significantly different from each other. This would also help in matching the different type of strategies to different disputes for achieving a successful resolution. One popular approach to classifying and understanding intervention strategies has been to use the degree of control wielded by the intervening third parties over the process (the procedures and activities involved in arriving at a settlement) and the outcome (the actual settlement to the dispute) of the resolution as two major dimensions.[3] Figure 1 presents a two-dimensional graph with the degree of third-party process control and the degree of third-party outcome control as the two axes.

FIGURE 1   Positioning of Managerial-Dispute Intervention Strategies

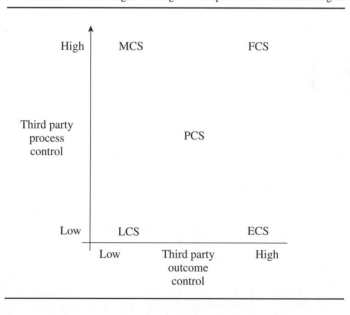

---

3. See (*a*) J. W. Thibaut and L. Walker, *Procedural Justice: A Psychological Analysis* (New York: Wiley, 1975), and (*b*) R. Lewicki and B. Sheppard, "Choosing How to Intervene: Factors Affecting the Use of Process and Outcome Control in Third-Party Dispute Resolution," *Journal of Occupational Behavior* 6 (1985), pp. 49–64.

Using these two axes, different intervention strategies can be identified by plotting various coordinates in the graph space. While numerous combinations varying by minute degrees of outcome and process control can be devised, for the sake of parsimony and applicability, only distinctly different combinations are considered here. Figure 1 shows five such combinations that are positioned into the corners and the center of the graph: *means control strategy* (MCS), *ends control strategy* (ECS), *full control strategy* (FCS), *low control strategy* (LCS), and *part control strategy* (PCS). These five combinations (intervention strategies) and the activities that are contained under each of these procedures are described in Figure 2. These descriptions capture

FIGURE 2   Description of Managerial Dispute Intervention Strategies

MCS	*Means control strategy:* Manager intervenes in the dispute by influencing the process of resolution (i.e., facilitates interaction, assists in communication, explains one disputant's views to another, clarifies issues, lays down rules for dealing with the dispute, maintains order during talks) but does not attempt to dictate or impose a resolution (though he or she might suggest solutions); the final decision is left to the disputants; high on process control but low on outcome control (e.g., mediation, conciliation).
ECS	*Ends control strategy:* Manager intervenes in the dispute by influencing the outcome of the resolution (i.e., takes full control of the final resolution, decides what the final decision would be, imposes the resolution on the disputants) but does not attempt to influence the process; the disputants have control over what information is presented and how it is presented; high on outcome control but low on process control (e.g., arbitration, adjudication, adversarial intervention).
LCS	*Low control strategy:* Manager does not intervene actively in resolving the dispute; either urges the parties to settle the dispute on their own or merely stays away from the dispute; low on both process and outcome control (e.g., encouraging or telling the parties to negotiate or settle the dispute by themselves, providing impetus).
FCS	*Full control strategy:* Manager intervenes in the dispute by influencing the process and outcome (i.e., decides what information is to be presented and how it should be presented and also decides on the final resolution); asks the disputants specific questions about the dispute to obtain information and imposes a resolution; manager has full control of the resolution of the dispute; high on both process and outcome control (e.g., inquisitorial intervention, autocratic intervention).
PCS	*Part control strategy:* Manager intervenes in the dispute by sharing control over the process and outcome with the disputants (i.e., manager and disputants jointly agree on the process of resolution as well as strive for a consensus on the settlement decision); works with the disputants to help them arrive at a solution by facilitating interaction, assisting in communication, discussing the issues, and so on; in addition, takes an active role in evaluating options, recommending solutions, persuading the disputants to accept them, and pushing for a settlement; moderate on managerial process and outcome control (e.g., group problem solving, med-arb).

the typical intervention procedures that fit under each combination. Variations of each combination can be included as long as they fit the basic description (e.g., mediation and conciliation are listed as examples under MCS).

So a manager using FCS to intervene in a dispute would control both the process and outcome of the resolution; that is, the manager would decide what information should be presented and how, ask specific questions, decide on a settlement, and impose it. When using MCS, however, the manager would control only the process and not the outcome. He or she would explain one disputant's views to the other, clarify issues, maintain order during talks, and lay down rules for dealing with the dispute. In contrast, under ECS, the manager would let the disputants control the process (e.g., decide what information to present and how to present it), but take full control of the outcome by deciding final settlement and imposing it on the disputants. A manager using LCS would urge or tell the parties to settle the dispute on their own but would not actively intervene in the dispute. Finally, when using PCS, the manager would share control over the process and outcome with the disputants. They would jointly work toward a resolution with the manager facilitating interaction, clarifying issues, evaluating options, recommending solutions, and persuading the disputants to accept them (e.g., group problem-solving).

KEY SITUATIONAL FACTORS THAT AFFECT STRATEGY SELECTION

Given the five strategies described above, when should each strategy be used? In other words, how would the manager be able to determine that a certain dispute calls for a specific strategy to maximize intervention success? Obviously this entails assessing each dispute to identify some key characteristics or situational factors which may, then, suggest that certain strategies are better suited for resolving that dispute than others. For example, if one of the distinguishing features of the dispute is time pressure (as in the first example in the introduction), it implies that speed is of essence and strategies that take longer to arrive at a settlement (e.g., PCS, MCS) may not be as appropriate as other strategies (e.g., FCS). Although one can focus on a plethora of factors to develop a profile of a dispute, it is both important and useful to zoom in on just the essential characteristics of the disputes that have significant bearing on the suitability and, hence, the probability of success of different intervention strategies. Described below are six factors that have been identified by prior research as being the critical ones, and their implications for strategy selection:[4]

1. *Dispute importance.* How important is the dispute? A dispute is important if it is central to the survival or functioning of a group or organization. From a prescriptive standpoint, the manager should be more concerned about the dispute when the dispute importance is high than when it is low. When dispute importance is high,

4. See (*a*) B. H. Sheppard, "Third-Party Conflict Intervention,"; (*b*) R. Karambayya and J. M. Brett, "Managers Handling Disputes: Third-Party Roles and Perceptions of Fairness," *Academy of Management Journal,* 32 (1989), pp. 687–704; (*c*) R. Karambayya, J. Brett, and A. Lytle, "The Effects of Formal Authority and Experience on Third-Party Roles, Outcomes and Perceptions of Fairness," *Academy of Management Journal* 35 (1992), pp. 426–38; and (*d*) R. Lewicki and B. Sheppard, "Choosing How to Intervene: Factors Affecting the Use of Process and Outcome Control in Third-Party Dispute Resolution," *Journal of Occupational Behavior* 6 (1985), pp. 49–64.

more care and control of outcome are needed, and therefore the intervening manager should not select a strategy that yields full outcome control to the disputants. This will ensure some managerial influence on the outcome and hence will lead to an organizationally beneficial solution. At the same time, however, to ensure commitment from the disputants, the manager should ensure that the process is orderly and not one-sided due to power and other differences between the disputants, and should make sure that the disputants feel that they have some influence in resolving the dispute (i.e., the manager should also retain some degree of process control).

2. *Time pressure.* Some disputes need to be settled more urgently than others. Since intervention strategies vary in how quickly they lead to a settlement, it is important to select the appropriate strategy to ensure intervention success. In general, when time pressure is high, the manager should not select a strategy that yields full control of the process and the outcome, in that order, to the disputants. Not acceding complete control of the process ensures that the manager can influence the speed at which the dispute is resolved. Not acceding complete control of the outcome ensures that the dispute will be resolved if disputants still cannot arrive at a settlement even when the process is speeded up.

3. *Nature of dispute.* Is the dispute about the interpretation, implementation, or execution of an existing rule, regulation, procedure, or operation within the existing organizational framework (dispute over "what is") or is it about creating a new or changing the existing procedures, operations, contracts or systems (dispute over "what should be or would like it to be")? The label *dispute over privileges* (DOP) is used here to identify the "interpretive" disputes (where misunderstandings or ambiguity is at the root of the dispute), while the label *dispute over stakes* (DOS) is used to distinguish the "change" disputes (where the focus is on altering the system). For example, the dispute between a financial controller and a marketing manager regarding the interpretation of an expenses reimbursement clause is a DOP dispute. A dispute between the same individuals about increasing the maximum amount for client entertainment expenses is a DOS dispute. In a DOP dispute, the disputants are generally more open to, and might even expect, a settlement from the third party because they were unable to, on their own, agree on an interpretation or application. This implies that an intervention strategy which gives the third party some degree of outcome control will be effective for a DOP dispute and therefore that the manager (third party) should not use strategies that limit his or her outcome control. In contrast, a DOS dispute reaches deeper to affect emotions and values, and it is imperative that disputants fully understand and accept any change in the system in order for them to be committed in the long run to the change. In such a situation, the manager should influence the process to ensure that it is orderly but leave the final settlement to the disputants; that is, for resolving a DOS dispute, the manager should not choose strategies that yield full process control but little outcome control to disputants.

4. *Nature of relations.* Are the disputants in a long-term relationship or are they not likely to interact with each other after the dispute is resolved? This factor addresses the work-group dynamics of the two disputants, and is important because different intervention strategies have different effects on the relations between disputants. Since it is in the best interests of the organization to have a normal or positive working relationship between the parties, an intervention strategy that will fur-

ther this objective should be selected for any given dispute. This implies that if the disputants are involved in a long-term relationship, then in the interest of long-term commitment and cooperation, the manager should ensure that the disputants have some degree of influence or control over the dispute settlement. So the manager should not choose an intervention strategy that limits the control disputants can have over the outcome. In addition, the manager should have some influence over the process to ensure that it is orderly and fair. On the other hand, when the disputants are not likely to interact with each other in the future on a regular basis, the manager can assume more control over the outcome, since the effect of the settlement on future relations is not much of a concern.

5. *Commitment probability.* This factor refers to the probability that the disputants will be committed to a settlement if it were to be decided unilaterally by the intervening manager. This, in turn, depends on the nature of the relationship between the manager and the disputants, including the degree of power the manager has and the subordinates' feelings of trust and loyalty. It is important to note that for long-term organizational effectiveness, it is not sufficient that the disputants merely indicate their acceptance of the settlement; they must honor the spirit of the settlement and not continue to harbor feelings of conflict or demonstrate reluctance in executing the resolution. This suggests that the manager must assess the commitment probability for imposing resolutions and select an intervention strategy accordingly. Low commitment probability implies that if the manager were to impose a settlement to a dispute then the disputants will not remain committed to it. In such cases, intervention strategies that do not accede control to disputants will be less effective than those that give disputants some control over the outcome. But if the manager perceives the commitment probability to be high, then he or she can assume more outcome control and impose a resolution whenever necessary (contingent on the status of the other attributes).

6. *Disputant orientation.* Disputant orientation addresses the question "What is the likelihood that the disputants will arrive at an organizationally appropriate settlement if given control over the resolution of the dispute (outcome control)?" If disputant orientation is high, then the probability that the disputants will arrive at an organizationally compatible settlement is high; if disputant orientation is low, then the probability is low. Regarding strategy selection, if the manager views the disputants' orientation as being low, then he or she should not select intervention strategies that yield full outcome control to the disputing subordinates. This would ensure that the manager has some control and input into the final settlement, and that the interests and goals of the organization are not compromised. On the other hand, if the disputant orientation is high, then the manager should select strategies that yield some degree of outcome control to the disputants to promote satisfaction and commitment.

In summary, the status of the six dispute factors discussed above have implications for the selection of strategies and help satisfy one or more of the three intervention success criteria identified earlier. Each of these factors can be represented by a question that has two response options (high/low); see Figure 3. A manager facing a particular dispute can diagnose the main situational demands by answering the six questions. The answers to the six questions provide the basis for selecting among the five intervention strategies.

FIGURE 3   Key Situational Factors Influencing Strategy Selection

Question A	How important is this dispute to the effective functioning of the organization? (High/Low)
Question B	How important is it to resolve the dispute as quickly as possible? (High/Low)
Question C	Does the dispute concern the interpretation/application of existing rules, procedures, arrangements, and so on, or does it concern the alteration/change of existing rules, procedures, arrangements? (DOP/DOS)
Question D	What is the expected frequency of future work-related interactions between the disputants? (High/Low)
Question E	If you were to impose a settlement on your subordinates (disputants), what is the probability that they would be committed to it? (High/Low)
Question F	If you were to let your subordinates (disputants) settle the dispute, what is the probability that they would come to an organizationally compatible settlement? (High/Low)

GENERATING DECISION RULES TO GUIDE STRATEGY SELECTION

Next, the recommendations for the use or avoidance of outcome and process control for each factor (discussed above) indicate when different intervention strategies should be selected for successful intervention. This logic can be captured in a set of decision rules to direct the strategy selection process. Figure 4 presents the seven rules that underlie the proposed model. These rules are a series of "if . . . then" statements that indicate for a certain status (high/low) of each factor the form of control (process, outcome) that should be retained by the intervening manager or given to the disputants to ensure the success of the intervention. This, in turn, implies that certain strategies may be dropped from the feasible full set of the five intervention strategies because of the risk they pose to a successful resolution of the dispute. For example, if the status of the commitment probability attribute is low (i.e., the likelihood that the disputants would be committed to a settlement imposed by the manager is low), then this suggests that the intervening manager should give the disputants some control over the outcome. For strategy selection purposes, this eliminates the two strategies that give the third-party full outcome control (i.e., FCS and ECS) from the feasible set (Rule 5). For any given dispute, using the first six rules will lead to a feasible set of intervention strategies that would be most successful in resolving the dispute. The last rule, Priority Rule, guides the choice within the feasible set based on efficiency maximization. Each rule also contributes to protecting one or more of the three success criteria. The Dispute Importance, Nature of Dispute, and Disputant Orientation rules focus on who controls the outcome, thus ensuring *settlement effectiveness;* the Time Pressure and Priority Rules focus on the need for expediency and the costs involved with delays, thus ensuring *timeliness;* and the Nature of Relations, Nature of Dispute, and Commitment Probability rules focus on ensuring acceptance and commitment of the disputants to the settlement, thus ensuring *disputant commitment.*

FIGURE 4   Rules Underlying the Model

1. The Dispute-Importance Rule

If the importance of the dispute is high, then the intervention strategy chosen should give the manager some degree of control on either or both dimensions. Accordingly, LCS is eliminated from the feasible set.

2. The Time-Pressure Rule

If the time pressure associated with settling the dispute is high, then the intervention strategy chosen should give the manager some degree of process control. Accordingly, LCS and ECS are eliminated from the feasible set.

3. The Nature of Dispute Rule

If the dispute between subordinates is a DOP dispute, then the intervention strategy chosen should give the manager some degree of outcome control. Accordingly, LCS and MCS are eliminated from the feasible set. The only exception to the rule is when time pressure is low, commitment probability is low but disputant orientation is high (MCS is the option). If the dispute between subordinates is a DOS dispute, then the manager should allow the subordinates some degree of control on either or both dimensions (process and outcome). Accordingly, FCS is eliminated from the feasible set. The only exception to the rule is when time pressure is high, commitment probability is high, and the disputants are not likely to interact frequently in the future.

4. The Nature of Relations Rule

If the subordinates (disputants) are likely to have a high frequency of interaction in the future, then the intervention strategy chosen should give the subordinates some degree of outcome control. Accordingly, FCS and ECS are eliminated from the feasible set. The only exception to the rule is when time pressure is low, commitment probability is high, and disputant orientation is low (ECS is the option).

5. The Commitment-Probability Rule

If the probability that the subordinates (disputants) would be committed to a settlement imposed by the manager is low, then the intervention strategy chosen should give subordinates some degree of outcome control. Accordingly, FCS and ECS are eliminated from the feasible set.

6. The Disputant-Orientation Rule

If the status of the dispute based on the five rules described above suggests choosing intervention strategies that yield full outcome control to subordinates (disputants), the manager should use disputant orientation as the final criterion. If the disputant orientation is low, the intervention strategy chosen should give the manager some degree of outcome control. Accordingly, LCS and MCS are eliminated from the feasible set. If the disputant orientation is high, the intervention strategy chosen should give subordinates some degree of outcome control. Accordingly, FCS and ECS are eliminated from the feasible set.

7. The Priority Rule

If the status of the dispute based on the previous six rules suggests more than one intervention as being equally effective, the following priority conditions must be observed to select one strategy. For high importance disputes, when time pressure is low and commitment probability is low, the manager should choose the intervention strategy that allows him/her maximum process control (so that by ensuring an orderly and fair process the commitment can be increased). When time pressure is low and commitment probability is high, the manager should select the strategy that allows him/her maximum outcome control (so that the best interests of the organization are always protected) while giving the disputants at least some control over the resolution. When time pressure is high, the manager should choose the intervention strategy that requires the least amount of time to resolve the dispute without endangering commitment. For low-importance disputes, the manager should select the strategy that requires the least amount of resources (skills, time, etc.).

FIGURE 5   A Model of Intervention Strategy Selection

DI   How important is this dispute to the effective functioning of the organization?
TP   How important is it to resolve the dispute as quickly as possible?
ND   Does the dispute concern the interpretation of existing rules, procedures, and
        arrangements or the changing of existing rules, procedures, and arrangements?
NR   What is the expected frequency of future work-related interactions between
        the disputants?
CP   If you were to impose a settlement on your subordinates (disputants), what is the
        probability that they would be committed to it?
DO   What is the orientation of the disputants? That is, if you were to let your subordinates
        (disputants) settle the dispute, what is the probability that they would come to an
        organizationally compatible settlement?

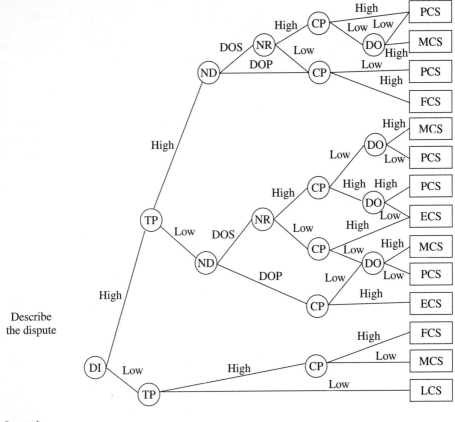

Legend:
MCS = Means-control strategy
ECS = Ends-control strategy
LCS = Low control strategy
FCS = Full control strategy
PCS = Part control strategy

A DECISION-TREE FOR SELECTING AN INTERVENTION STRATEGY

Figure 5 shows a decision tree developed using the five intervention strategies (Figure 2), the six questions pertaining to the situational factors of the dispute (Figure 3), and the seven rules with two status options (high/low) for each factor (Figure 4). To use the tree, a manager first identifies a dispute between subordinates that he or she has decided to help resolve. The manager starts at the extreme left of the decision tree and asks the first question. The answer, high or low, indicates the path to be taken to arrive at the next node signifying the next question. The process continues until the manager arrives at a terminal node or end point on the decision tree that indicates the optimal intervention strategy.

The model uses a choice-elimination approach to arrive at the right strategy. Choices or intervention strategies that are not likely to result in a successful resolution are eliminated, thus narrowing the choice to the most appropriate intervention strategy for that specific dispute. Although six factors were identified as key dispute attributes, all of them do not become relevant for all disputes. If the status of the attribute does not make a difference to the selection of an intervention strategy with regard to the success of the resolution for a particular dispute configuration, then it is not necessary to apply that rule. For example, when the dispute importance is low and time pressure is low, the manager need not be concerned with the status of the other attributes but can directly arrive at the appropriate intervention strategy without posing any risk to the dispute resolution success. Similarly, disputant orientation becomes relevant only when the status of other attributes suggest that the manager select an intervention strategy that yields full outcome control to the disputants. However, all six attributes are important and essential for the model as a whole to be valid and useful.

CONCLUSION

Managing disputes in organizations is an important part of a manager's job. Often, the success of the manager's interventions in these disputes has significant implications for the overall morale of the employees and their productivity. This article offers some guidelines for successful intervention by highlighting the key features of a successful intervention, classifying different intervention strategies, identifying the major situational factors that ought to be considered before selecting a strategy, generating a set of rules to guide the strategy selection process, and developing a decision-tree model that can be used by practicing managers.

Exercises

The Disarmament Exercise

INTRODUCTION

The purpose of this exercise is to engage you in working together in a small group, making decisions about the nature of your relationship with another group. Your group will be paired with another group. Each group will have the opportunity to make a decision about a series of "moves." The outcome of those moves (in terms of the amount of money that your team wins or loses) will be determined by the choice that your group makes, and the choice that the other group makes. Your group cannot independently determine its outcomes in this situation. The nature of your group's choices, and how well your group performs in this exercise, will be determined by (1) your group's behavior toward the other group, (2) the other group's behavior toward your group, and (3) the communication between groups when this is permitted.

ADVANCE PREPARATION

None.

PROCEDURE

Step 1: 5 Minutes

Divide the class into groups, or teams, of two to four people (your class leader will give you specific instructions). Pair off the teams so that all teams are paired. If there is more than one pair, the class leader may assign a referee to monitor each pair of teams. Designate a specific room or area of the classroom for each team.

The instructor may also collect money from each student at this time. How the money will be used is explained in the instructions (below).

Step 2: 15 Minutes

Read the following instructions—Rules for the Disarmament Exercise—carefully. When you have finished reading the instructions, the class leader will answer any questions you have. You will then be given time to discuss the rules with your teammates, and plan the strategy you will use.

Adapted by Roy J. Lewicki from an exercise developed by Noman Berkowitz and Harvey Hornstein. Reprinted from *Experiences in Management and Organizational Behavior,* by Douglas T. Hall, Donald D. Bowen, Roy J. Lewicki, and Francine Hall (Chicago: St. Clair Press, pp. 85–92, 1975). Used with permission.

RULES FOR THE DISARMAMENT EXERCISE

The Objective

You and your team are going to engage in a disarmament exercise in which you can win or lose money. You may think of each team as a country with weapons—some weapons are armed and others are not. There are at least two rounds of play in the exercise, and each round has up to seven moves. In this exercise your objective as a team is to win as much money as you can. The team opposing yours has the identical instructions and objective.

The Task

1. Each team is given 20 cards. These are your weapons; each card represents one weapon. Each card has one side marked *X* and an unmarked side. When the marked side of the card is displayed, this indicates that the weapon is armed; conversely, when the blank side of the card is displayed, this shows the weapon to be unarmed. Each team also has an A (attack) card; this will be explained later.

2. At the beginning of the exercise, each team places 10 of its 20 weapons (cards) in the armed position with the marked side up, and the remaining 10 in the unarmed position with the marked side down. All weapons will remain in your possession throughout the exercise; they must be placed so that the referee (group leader) can see them, but so that they are out of the sight of the other team.

3. During this exercise there are at least two rounds with up to seven moves each. Payoffs are calculated after each round (not after each move), and are cumulative.

   a. A move consists of a team turning two, one, or none of its weapons from armed (*X*) to unarmed (blank) status, or vice versa.

   b. Each team has three minutes to decide on its move and to make that move. There are 30-second periods between moves. At the end of three minutes, a team must have turned two, one, or none of its weapons from armed to unarmed status, or from unarmed to armed status. Failing to decide on a move in the allotted time means that no change can then be made in weapon status until the next move. In other words, failure to make a move by the deadline counts as a move of zero weapons.

   c. The length of the three-minute period is fixed and unalterable.

   d. The referee (instructor) will verify each move for both teams after it has been made.

4. Each new round of the exercise begins with all weapons returned to their original positions, 10 armed and 10 unarmed.

The Finances

If your referee chooses to use real money in this exercise, money will be distributed as described. If you use imaginary money, assume that each team member has made an imaginary contribution of $2.00, and that the money is also distributed as described.

Each member will contribute to the treasury. The money you have contributed will be allocated in the following manner:

1. Sixty percent will be returned to your team, to be used in the task. Your team may diminish or supplement this money depending on the outcomes during the exercise. At the end of the exercise your team's treasury will be divided among the members.

2. Forty percent will be donated to the World Bank, which is to be managed by the referee. This money will *not* be returned at the end of the exercise, and should be considered as no longer yours.

3. The opposing team's money will be allocated in the same way.

The Payoffs

1. If there is an attack during a round:

   a. Each team may announce an attack on the other team (by notifying the referee) during the 30 seconds following any three-minute period used to decide upon a move (including the seventh, or final, decision period in any round). To attack, you *must* display your A (attack) card to the referee. You may not attack without an A card. The moves of both teams during the decision period immediately *before* an attack count. An attack cannot be made during negotiations (see below).

   b. If there is an attack (by one or both teams) the round ends.

   c. The team with the greater number of armed weapons wins 5 cents per member for each armed weapon it has over and above the number of armed weapons of the other team. These funds are paid directly from the treasury of the losing team to the treasury of the winning team. If both teams have the same number of armed weapons, the team that attacked pays 2 cents per member for each armed weapon to the World Bank, and the team that was attacked pays 1 cent per member for each armed weapon to the World Bank. If both teams attacked, both pay the 2-cent rate.

2. If there is no attack by the end of a round:

   a. At the end of each round (seven moves), when there has been no attack, each team's treasury receives from the World Bank 2 cents per member for each of its weapons that is at that point unarmed, and each team's treasury pays to the World Bank 2 cents per member for each of its weapons remaining armed.

   b. When a team wins funds, they are awarded by the World Bank. When a team loses funds, they are paid to the World Bank.

3. Teams may run a deficit with the World Bank. If there is a deficit at the end of three rounds, the status of the deficit will be decided by the instructor.

The Negotiations

1. Between moves each team has the opportunity to communicate with the other team through negotiators chosen by the team members for this purpose. You may *not* communicate with the other team before the first move.

2. Either team may call for negotiations (by notifying the referee) during any of the 30-second periods between decisions. A team is free to accept or reject any invitation from the other team.

3. Negotiators from both teams are *required* to meet after the third and sixth moves.

4. Negotiations can last no longer than five minutes. When the two negotiators return to their teams, the three-minute decision period for the next move begins.

5. Negotiators are bound only by: (a) the five-minute time limit for negotiations, and (b) required appearance after the third and sixth moves. They are otherwise free to say whatever they choose, and to make an agreement which is necessary to benefit themselves or their teams. They are not required to tell the truth. Each team is similarly not bound by any agreements made by their negotiators, even when those agreements were made in good faith by the negotiators.

Reminders

1. Each move can consist of turning over two, one, or zero of your weapons to the unarmed side—or the armed side.

2. You have three minutes to decide which of the above moves you will choose.

3. If there is no attack, at the end of the round (seven moves) your team receives 2 cents per member for each unarmed weapon and loses 2 cents per member for each armed weapon.

4. If there is an attack, the team with the greater number of armed weapons wins 5 cents per member for each armed weapon it has over the number the other team has.

5. Remember that there is also a penalty if an attack is called and both teams have the same number of *X* cards displayed.

6. A team may call for negotiations after any move. Mandatory meetings of negotiators occur after moves 3 and 6.

Step 3: 15 Minutes

Once you have clarified and understood the rules, each team has 15 minutes to organize itself and to plan team strategy.

1. You must select people to fill the following roles (the persons can be changed at any time by a decision of the team): (1) A negotiator—activities as stated under "the Negotiations"; (2) a team spokesperson to communicate decisions to the referee about team moves, attacks, initiations or acceptances of negotiations, etc. The referee will listen only to the team spokesperson, and the spokesperson cannot also be the negotiator; (3) a team recorder to record moves of the team, and to keep running accounts of the team's treasury.

2. You should discuss with your team members the way that you want to play, what the other team might do and how that affects your strategy, the first move that you will make for the first round, whether or not you desire negotiations, and what you might say to the other team if you or they initiate them.

Step 4: 10–20 Minutes

Round 1.

1. The referee will signal that the first round begins.
2. Your team has three minutes to decide on its first move, and then to actually move zero, one, or two cards.
3. When the referee returns, show him or her your move. You may also attack at this point, and/or you may call for negotiations.
4. If neither team attacks or calls for negotiations, the referee will proceed to the second move.
5. Remember that there will be mandatory negotiations after moves 3 and 6. Also remember that the game will proceed for seven moves, unless there is an attack.
6. When the round ends, the referee will state how many missiles each team had armed, and whether either team attacked. Each team will calculate its financial status. Money (if used) will be transferred from one team's treasury to the other, or to/from the World Bank.
7. After accounts are settled, return the cards to their start-of-game position (10 X-side up and 10 X-side down).

Step 5: 5 Minutes

Evaluate your team's strategy and outcomes in round 1. Use your reactions to the Disarmament Exercise Questionnaire as a guide; then discuss the strategy you wish to pursue in round 2.

Step 6: 5–20 Minutes

Round 2. Proceed as in round 1 (Step 3).

Step 7: 5 Minutes (at the Referee's Discretion)

Complete the questions for round 2 on the questionnaire.

Step 8: 5–20 Minutes

Additional rounds may be played at the discretion of the referee.

DISCUSSION QUESTIONS

1. How effectively did your team work together?
    a. How did your team make decisions? (Did one or two persons make the decision for the whole team? A minority make decisions for the whole team? Always a democratic vote? Majority kept overriding the minority?)

Disarmament Exercise Questionnaire

For round 1, circle the appropriate number on each scale which best represents your feelings. (For subsequent rounds, use boxes or triangles or colored pencils to indicate the appropriate rating):

1. To what extent are you satisfied with your team's current strategy?

    highly satisfied   1   2   3   4   5   6   7   highly dissatisfied

2. To what extent do you believe the other team is now trustworthy?

    highly trustworthy   1   2   3   4   5   6   7   highly untrustworthy

3. To what extent are you now satisfied with the performance of your negotiator?

    highly dissatisfied   7   6   5   4   3   2   1   highly satisfied

4. To what extent is there now a consensus in your team regarding its moves?

    high consensus   1   2   3   4   5   6   7   very little consensus

5. To what extent are you now willing to trust the other people on your team?

    more than before   1   2   3   4   5   6   7   less than before

6. Select one word to describe how you feel about your team:

7. Select one word to describe how you feel about the *other* team:

Negotiators Only: Please respond to the following question:

How did you see the other team's negotiator?

authentic and sincere   1   2   3   4   5   6   7   phony and insincere

---

   b. Did your team make maximum use of information available? Did the team members really listen to each other? Why not? Were the opinions of the less vocal members sought? Why not? Did the team really try to obtain every piece of information from the negotiators, who were the team's only direct source of information about the other team?

2. Did your team have a *viable* strategy?

    a. Did your team have a *consistent* plan or was it "pushed around" by other teams?

    b. Was your team's plan *naive*? If so, why?

    c. To what extent was your team trying to "win a lot," but not risking anything to do that?

3. How did you team react to cooperation and competition?

    a. Why is cooperation so difficult to achieve?

    b. What are the barriers that stand in the way of developing trust?

    c. What assumptions did your team have about the other team which may have prevented trust and cooperation?

Disarmament Exercise Team Record Form

	Round 1		Round 2		Round 3		Round 4	
	Armed	Unarmed	Armed	Unarmed	Armed	Unarmed	Armed	Unarmed
Start	10	10	10	10	10	10	10	10
Move 1								
Move 2								
Move 3								
Negotiation								
Move 4								
Move 5								
Move 6								
Negotiation								
Move 7								
Net gain or loss in this round	My team:	Their team:	My team:	Their team:	My team:	Their team:	My team:	Their team:

At End of Round	Round 1	Round 2	Round 3	Round 4
Funds in own team treasury				
Funds in other team treasury				
Funds in World Bank				

    d. What happened to your team's morale and decision-making structure when it won? When it lost?

4. How did the negotiator get chosen? Delegated? Volunteered? Discussion of "qualifications"?

    a. How committed were you to your negotiator? Were you willing to stand by him or her through thick and thin, or did you abandon trust in your negotiator at some point?

    b. Did some of the negotiators lie? If they are not basically dishonest people, why did they? If they lied, how did they feel about this afterward?

Pemberton's Dilemma

INTRODUCTION

This exercise creates a situation in which you and the other person(s) will be making separate decisions about how to manage your firm. In this situation the outcomes (profits and losses) are determined not only by what you do, but also by a number of other factors such as the goals and motives that you and the other party have and the communication that takes place between you and them.

ADVANCE PREPARATION

None.

PROCEDURE

Step 1: 5 Minutes

The class will be broken into six-person groups; three people in each group will play the management team of the Country Market, and three will play the management team of the Corner Store. The teams should sit far enough from each other to allow private meetings.

Step 2: 10 Minutes

Read the background information for Pemberton's Dilemma on the following page. If you have any questions, clarify them with your instructor at this time.

In this exercise, you will represent your store in discussions with the other store about the hours that each store should open on Sundays. You and the other store will be making decisions simultaneously, and your profits will be directly affected by these decisions. How well you perform will depend in part on your goals, the other store's goals, and the communication between you.

Written in collaboration with Gregory Leck.

BACKGROUND INFORMATION

Pemberton is a quaint little town located in the heartland of our great country. Although it is only a 30-minute drive to a major metropolitan center, most of the town-folk prefer to do their shopping at one of the two general stores located in Pemberton. At these stores, one can buy a variety of goods, ranging from groceries to hardware equipment. Both establishments boast a soda fountain, which is quite popular among both the younger and older generations as well.

Like most small towns, Pemberton is proud of the fact that it has been able to preserve its many traditions, some of which date back to the 1890s. One of these grand traditions, which became official in 1923 when the Town Hall passed a resolution to this effect, is the cessation of all commercial activity on Sunday. Times have changed, however, and "Sunday shoppers" are becoming more and more prevalent. In fact, every Sunday there is a mass exodus to the nearby metropolitan center, where Sunday shopping has been permitted for years.

You are a member of the management team from one of the two general stores in Pemberton. Both the Country Market and the Corner Store have been consistently losing potential profit as Sunday shopping becomes more popular. Your management team, as well as the team from the competing general store, has recently contemplated opening the store on Sunday, in spite of the municipal resolution that prohibits this.

The ramifications of such decisions are important, since the profitability of such an action will depend on the decision made by the competing store. For instance, if neither store decides to open on Sunday, it will be business as usual, and both stores will make a profit of $20,000 in a given week.

If only one store decides to open on Sunday, that particular store would enjoy the patronage of all those Sunday shoppers and would manage to make a $40,000 profit for the week. Unfortunately, the store that decided to remain closed on that Sunday would actually incur a loss of $40,000 that week. This would be due to various reasons, most notably the preference of customers to continue to do their shopping throughout the week at the store that remained open on Sunday.

If both stores decided to stay open on Sunday, adverse consequences would be faced by both establishments. Although Town Hall may be able to turn a blind eye to one store violating the municipal resolution, two stores would be looked upon as a conspiracy against the traditionalists of Pemberton. Artemus Hampton, Pemberton's mayor and direct descendant of one of the town's founders, would no doubt pressure Town Hall into levying the highest possible fine allowable by law. In this case, the penalty would be so excessive that both stores would incur losses of $20,000 each for the week. While your lawyers have suggested that the municipal resolutions prohibiting Sunday shopping in Pemberton might be overturned in a court case, this too would be a costly option. In either case, if both stores open on Sunday, they will each incur losses of $20,000 for the week.

Keeping the above information in mind, your team is to decide each week, for the next 12 weeks, whether your store is to remain open on the Sunday of that week. The decision made for the first week must be made without prior consultation with the management team of the competing store. Subsequent decisions may be made after consulting with your competitors. Both teams shall reveal their decisions simultaneously. *Remember, the goal is to maximize profits over the next 12-week period.*

		Country Market			
		Close Sunday		Open Sunday	
	Close	Corner:	+$20,000	Corner:	−$40,000
Corner	Sunday	Country:	+$20,000	Country:	+$40,000
Store	Open	Corner:	+$40,000	Corner:	−$20,000
	Sunday	Country:	−$40,000	Country:	−$20,000

Step 3: 10 Minutes

Review the details of the situation and understand how you can make or lose money. Familiarize yourself with the profit chart above. Members of each management team should now plan their strategy. There may not be any communication between the teams before the first round.

There will be 12 one-minute rounds where the stores will either open or close. Each round represents one Sunday, and every *fourth* Sunday is part of a long weekend. A three-minute planning session separates each Sunday. *There may not be any communication between the stores during the planning sessions.*

Step 4: 30–45 Minutes

The exercise begins when representatives from the stores (one from each) meet and indicate with a card if their store will open or close on the first Sunday. There may be no communication between the stores before this decision is registered. After each Sunday, representatives from the stores *may* meet and negotiate for five minutes before each three-minute planning session. *Negotiations are optional, except after moves 4 and 8 when they are required.* If negotiations occur, they will be followed by a three-minute planning period. If there are no negotiations, the three-minute planning period will follow the sharing of the previous decision to open or close. Profits and losses are calculated after each Sunday and are cumulative for the 12 weeks.

Each team will record the outcome of each Sunday on their profit chart. The time periods between each Sunday are fixed, and may not be altered. Each team will complete a total of 12 moves.

Step 5: 30 Minutes

The instructor will record the total profit for each team in each negotiating group. Differences in performance will be noted and possible reasons explored. Participants should describe what happened, particularly in regard to their perceptions of and reactions to the other party. Some suggested questions and issues for discussion are given below.

DISCUSSION QUESTIONS

1. What were your basic objectives and strategy when you started the exercise? Did they change? What outcomes did you achieve as a result of these plans?
2. What did you talk about after the first round of negotiation?
3. Did the content of your negotiating discussion change? Why?
4. What were the most important things that led to the outcome of the exercise?

Profit Chart

	Corner Store's Choice	Country Market's Choice	Profit	
			Corner Store	Country Market
First 15-Minute Planning Period				
1.				
2.				
3.				
4. **Double** profit/loss, *this round only*				
Five-Minute Required Negotiation Period				
5.				
6.				
7.				
8. **Triple** profit/loss, *this round only*				
Five-Minute Required Negotiation Period				
9.				
10.				
11.				
12. **Quadruple** profit/loss, *this round only*				

The Used Car

INTRODUCTION

The scenario for this role-play involves a single issue: the price of a used car that is for sale. While there is a great deal of other information that may be used to construct supporting arguments or to build in demands and requests in addition to the price, the sale price will ultimately be the indicator used to determine how well you do in comparison to other role-play groups.

ADVANCE PREPARATION

1. The instructor is likely to assign preparation for this exercise in advance. If so read and review the Background Information section on the used car, and the buyer or seller position information that you have been assigned. *Read only your position,* as described in the information provided by the instructor.

2. If you are working with others as a team, meet with the team and prepare a negotiation strategy. If you are working alone, plan your individual strategy for your position.

3. Whether working in a small group or alone, make sure that you complete the section at the bottom of your confidential information sheet.

PROCEDURE

Step 1: 5 Minutes

The instructor will determine whether this exercise is to be conducted individually or in small groups. If it is individual, pairs of individuals will be assigned buyer and seller roles. Alternatively, groups of two or three persons will be assigned buyer and seller roles.

Step 2: 30 minutes

Read and prepare your negotiating position, if this assignment was not done as part of the advance preparation.

Revised version of an original role-play that was developed by Professor Leonard Greenhalgh, Dartmouth College. Used with permission.

Step 3: 30 Minutes or as Recommended by Instructor

Meet with the opposite side to negotiate a price for the used car. During this time, you may observe the following procedures:

1. Use any plan or strategy that will help you achieve your objectives.
2. If you are negotiating in a team, you may call a caucus at any time to evaluate your strategy or the opponent's strategy.
3. Reach an agreement by the end of the specified time period, or conclude that you are not able to agree and that buyer and seller will explore other alternatives.
4. Complete the Statement of Agreement form and submit it to the instructor. Be sure to write down any additional terms or conditions that were agreed to.

Step 4: 30 Minutes

Be prepared to discuss your settlement with the opposite side, and with other groups in the role-play.

BACKGROUND INFORMATION

You are about to negotiate the purchase/sale of an automobile. The seller advertised the car in the local newspaper. (Note: Both role-players should interpret "local" as the town in which the role-playing is occurring.) Before advertising it, the seller took the car to the local Ford dealer, who has provided the following information:

> 1994 Ford Escort two-door hatchback, four-cylinder, automatic transmission, power steering, air conditioning, front-wheel drive.
>
> White with red interior, power door locks, power sunroof, and AM/FM radio.
>
> Mileage 30,450 miles; steel-belted radial tires expected to last another 30,000 miles.
>
> Fuel economy 30 mpg city, 38 mpg highway; uses regular (87 octane) gasoline.
>
> No rust; dent on passenger door barely noticeable.
>
> Mechanically perfect except exhaust system, which may or may not last another 10,000 miles (costs $300 to replace).
>
> Blue book (1997) values: retail, $6,600; trade-in, $5,125; loan, $4,625.
>
> Car has been locally owned and driven.

DISCUSSION QUESTIONS

1. Did you reach an agreement in this negotiation? If so, how satisfied are you with the price? If not, are you satisfied that you did not agree? Why?
2. If you reached a settlement, how does the settlement price compare to your target price, to the buyer's opening offer, and to the lowest (highest) price that you were willing to accept? Who "won" in this exercise?

Statement of Agreement for Purchase of the Automobile _____

Price: _____

Manner of Payment: _____

Special Terms and Conditions: _____

_____

_____

_____

_____

We agree to the terms above:

_____   _____
           Seller   Buyer

****

Initial Settlement Proposals:

Seller: _____

_____

Buyer: _____

_____

Knight Engines/Excalibur Engine Parts

INTRODUCTION

The process of negotiation combines economic transactions with verbal persuasion. A great deal of what transpires during a negotiation is the verbal persuasion—people arguing for and supporting their own preferred position, and resisting similar arguments from the other party. At the same time, underlying this layer of persuasive messages is a set of economic transactions—bids and counterbids—that are at the economic core of the negotiation process.

The purpose of this exercise is to provide some experience with combining the economic transactions and the persuasive messages to support preferred economic outcomes.

ADVANCE PREPARATION

If assigned by the instructor, read the role-play briefing information (provided by the instructor) in advance.

PROCEDURE

Step 1: 20 Minutes

If your instructor has not already done so, you will be assigned the role of Knight Engines or Excalibur Engine Parts for this exercise. You will be told how to locate the appropriate information for your side. Read this information. You will also be assigned a partner (other party) for this exercise.

Step 2: 30–40 Minutes

Meet with the opposite side to negotiate a settlement to the issues in this scenario. Your objective is to negotiate a deal that is most advantageous to you and your company. During this negotiation, you may observe the following guidelines:

1. Use any plan or strategy that will help you achieve your objectives.

Written in collaboration with Gregory Leck.

2. Call a caucus at any time to evaluate your strategy or the other party's strategy.

3. Reach an agreement by the end of the specified time period, or conclude that you are not able to agree.

Step 4: 30–60 Minutes

Be prepared to discuss your settlement with the other party, and with other groups in the large-group setting.

DISCUSSION QUESTIONS

1. What goal did you set to be achieved in this negotiation? Your opening bid? Your bottom line?

2. Did you have a "Best Alternative" or "Option" if a deal was not struck? How good was this option? How did it affect your negotiations?

3. Did you reach an agreement in the negotiation? If yes, how satisfied were you with your agreement after you reached it? If not, were you convinced that it was a good idea not to agree?

4. How satisfied were you with your agreement after you heard other groups report in the general session? What was the impact of hearing other solutions on your own level of satisfaction?

5. In addition to a price for the pistons, what were the other elements of the deal that you agreed to? Did these factors help to make the negotiation more or less competitive?

6. What strategy and tactics did you use to help you achieve your objectives in this negotiation? Did your strategy and tactics "work"?

7. What strategy and tactics did the other party use? Did these tactics "work"? Why or why not?

8. As a result of these negotiations, what is the current state of your relationship with the other negotiator? Would you be more or less likely to do business with this person in the future? Why?

9. What did you learn from this exercise that you will want to continue (or change) in future negotiations?

Universal Computer Company I

INTRODUCTION

In this exercise you will play the role of a plant manager who has to negotiate some arrangements with another plant manager. You will be in a potentially competitive situation where cooperation is clearly desirable. Your task is to find some way to cooperate, when to do so might seem to put you at a disadvantage.

ADVANCE PREPARATION

Prior to class, read the Universal Computer Company Background Information section and the role information that the instructor has provided. Do not discuss your role with other class members. Plan how you will handle the forthcoming meeting with the other plant manager. Record your initial proposal on the Initial Settlement Proposal form. Do not show this to the other party you are negotiating with until after the negotiations are completed.

PROCEDURE

Step 1: 5 Minutes

The class will be divided into teams of two, with one person in each dyad representing the Crawley plant and the other representing the Phillips plant.

Step 2: 20–45 Minutes

Each dyad of plant managers will conduct its meeting and try to reach a solution. When an agreement is reached, both parties will record the outcome on the Final Settlement Agreement form.

Step 3: 10–20 Minutes

With your partner in the dyad, review the Initial Settlement Proposals you each prepared. What bargaining range did you have? What actions by either party led to the particular outcome you reached and recorded on the Final Settlement Agreement form?

Step 4: 15–20 Minutes

The instructor will poll each dyad for the Initial Settlement Proposals of the parties and the final agreement reached. The instructor will also ask any groups who have not reached an agreement where they were at the time negotiations were halted, and what might have prevented their reaching an agreement.

BACKGROUND INFORMATION

The Universal Computer Company is one of the nation's major producers of computers. Plants in the company tend to specialize in producing a single line of products or, at the most, a limited range of products. The company has considerable verti-

---

Initial Settlement Proposals

_____ Plant

How do you propose that the following expenses and repairs should be handled?

Expense of repairing all faulty modules _____

_____

Expense of repairing faulty modules other than the 12 types that fall below 95 percent

level _____

_____

Expense of repairing the faulty modules of the 12 types that fall below the 95 percent

level _____

_____

How to handle the repair of the faulty modules of the 12 types that fall below the 95 percent

level _____

_____

How to handle the repair of the modules other than the 12 types that fall below the 95 percent

level _____

_____

cal integration. Parts made at one plant are assembled into components at another, which in turn are assembled into final products at still another plant. Each plant operates on a profit-center basis.

The Crawley plant produces computer chips, modules, cable harnesses, and terminal boards which in turn are shipped to other company plants. In addition to numerous computer chips, the Crawley plant makes more than 40 different modules for the Phillips plant. The two plants are about five miles apart.

The Quality Problem

Production at the Phillips plant has been plagued by poor quality. Upon examination it has been found that a considerable portion of this problem can be traced to the quality of the modules received from the Crawley plant.

The Crawley plant maintains a final inspection operation. There has been considerable dispute between the two plants as to whether the Crawley plant was to maintain a 95 percent overall acceptance level for all modules shipped to the Phillips plant, or to maintain that standard for *each* of the 42 modules shipped. The Phillips plant manager has insisted that the standard had to be maintained for each of the 42 individual modules produced. The Crawley plant manager maintains that the requirements mean that the 95 percent level has to be maintained overall for the sum of modules produced. Experience at the Phillips plant shows that while some module types were consistently well above the 95 percent acceptance level, 12 types of modules had erratic quality and would often fall far below the 95 percent level. As a result, while individual types of modules might fall below standard, the quality level for all modules was at or above the 95 percent level. This raised serious problems at the Phillips plant, since the quality of its products is controlled by the quality of the poorest module.

The Interplant Dispute

The management of the Phillips plant felt that the quality problem of the modules received from the Crawley plant was causing them great difficulty. It caused problems with the customers, who complained of the improper operation of the products that contained the Crawley modules. As a result, the Phillips plant operation had earlier added secondary final inspection of its completed products. More recently it had added an incoming inspection of 12 poor-quality modules received from the Crawley plant. There were times when the number of modules rejected was large enough to slow or even temporarily stop production. At those times, to maintain production schedules, the Phillips plant had to work overtime. In addition, the Phillips plant had the expense of correcting all the faulty units received from the Crawley plant.

Ideally the management of the Phillips plant would like to receive all modules free of defects. While this was recognized as impossible, they felt that the Crawley plant should at least accept the expense of repairs, extra inspections, and overtime required by the poor quality of the parts.

Since installing incoming inspection procedures on the 12 modules, the Phillips plant had been rejecting about $8,000 of modules a week. For the most part, these had been put into storage pending settlement of the dispute as to which plant should handle

Final Settlement Agreement

___

How, exactly, did you agree that the following expenses and repairs would be handled?

Expense of repairing all faulty modules _____

___

Expense of repairing faulty modules other than the 12 types that fall below 95 percent

level _____

___

Expense of repairing the faulty modules of the 12 types that fall below the 95 percent

level _____

___

How to handle the repair of the faulty modules of the 12 types that fall below the 95 percent

level _____

___

How to handle the repair of the modules other than the 12 types that fall below the 95 percent

level _____

_____   _____

_____   _____
Representative, Phillips Plant   Representative, Crawley Plant

___

repairing them. Occasionally, when the supply of good modules had been depleted, repairs were made on some of the rejected units to keep production going. The Phillips plant had continued to make repairs on the remaining 30 types of modules as the need for repairs was discovered in assembly of final inspection.

From its perspective, the Crawley plant management felt that it was living up to its obligation by maintaining a 95 percent or better quality level on all its modules shipped to the Phillips plant. Further, they pointed out that using sampling methods on inspection meant that some below-standard units were bound to get through, and that the expense of dealing with these was a normal business expense which the Phillips plant would have to accept as would any other plant. They pointed out that when buying parts from outside suppliers it was common practice in the company to absorb the expenses from handling the normal level of faulty parts.

The Phillips plant management argued that the Crawley plant management was ignoring its responsibility to the company by forcing the cost of repairs on to their plant, where only repairs could be made—rather than to have the costs borne by the Crawley plant, where corrections of faulty processes could be made.

DISCUSSION QUESTIONS

1. What differences in strategy and tactics were followed in groups that reached negotiated settlements versus those that did not? Were relationships competitive or cooperative, conflicted, or problem solving?

2. What factors contributed most to the outcomes that various dyads reached?

3. Did the members of dyads change their feelings about the settlement after they learned how well they did relative to their initial goals for the negotiation? Why? What does this say about how we evaluate "good" and "bad" actions in negotiation?

Universal Computer Company II

INTRODUCTION

In this exercise you will play the role of a plant manager who has to negotiate the price of a new A25 computer chip. You will be in a potentially competitive situation where cooperation is clearly desirable. Your task is to find some way to cooperate, when to do so might seem to put you at a disadvantage.

ADVANCE PREPARATION

Prior to class, read the Universal Computer Company Background Information section and the role information that the instructor has provided. Do not discuss your role with other class members. Plan how you will handle the forthcoming meeting with the other plant manager.

PROCEDURE

Step 1: 5 Minutes

The class will be divided into teams of two, with one person in each dyad representing the Crawley plant and the other representing the Phillips plant.

Step 2: 20–30 Minutes

Each dyad of plant managers will conduct its meeting and try to reach a solution. When an agreement is reached, both parties should record the final outcome.

Step 4: 15–20 Minutes

The instructor will poll each dyad for the value of their final agreement. The instructor will also ask any groups who have not reached an agreement where they were at the time negotiations were halted, and what might have prevented their reaching an agreement.

BACKGROUND INFORMATION

The Universal Computer Company is one of the nation's major producers of computers. Plants in the company tend to specialize in producing a single line of products or, at the most, a limited range of products. The company has considerable vertical integration. Parts made at one plant are assembled into components at another, which in turn are assembled into final products at still another plant. Each plant operates on a profit-center basis.

The Crawley plant produces computer chips, modules, cable harnesses, and terminal boards, which in turn are shipped to other company plants. In addition to numerous computer chips, the Crawley plant makes more than 40 different modules for the Phillips plant. The two plants are about five miles apart.

The A25 Computer Chip

Phillips purchases over 30 different computer chips from Crawley. Computer chip A25 represents the most advanced engineering and manufacturing technologies available at the Crawley plant, and is an important advance in multimedia hardware design for personal computers. Phillips will integrate the A25 chip into its mother boards, and in turn will sell the mother boards to Universal Computer (the parent company) and to other computer companies. Since the prices on all purchases between Phillips and Crawley have been previously negotiated, the price of the A25 chip is currently the only computer chip up for negotiation.

DISCUSSION QUESTIONS

1. What differences in strategy and tactics were followed in groups that reached negotiated settlements versus those that did not? Were relationships competitive or cooperative, conflicted, or problem solving?
2. What factors contributed most to the outcomes that various dyads reached?
3. Did the members of dyads change their feelings about the settlement after they learned how well they did relative to their initial goals for the negotiation? Why? What does this say about how we evaluate "good" and "bad" actions in negotiation?

Twin Lakes Mining Company

INTRODUCTION

In this role-play, you will have the opportunity to negotiate a serious problem—a conflict between a mining company and the government of a small town regarding an environmental cleanup. While the issues in this scenario have been simplified somewhat for the purpose of this role-play, such conflicts between industry and governmental groups are typical throughout the country. Try to introduce as much realism into this situation as you can, based on your own personal experiences.

ADVANCE PREPARATION

The nature of advance preparation will be determined by your instructor. You may be required to read these materials and/or to meet with your other team members before the class session in which this problem will be negotiated.

PROCEDURE

1. You will be assigned to a small group to represent either the Twin Lakes Mining Company or the Tamarack Town Council in this negotiation.
2. Before meeting with your group, you should read the common Background Information section, and your own individual briefing sheet for either the company or the council. This information will be provided by your instructor.
3. When you meet with your group, review the issues and determine a strategy that you intend to pursue. Also assign group members realistic roles that might be represented if you were in an actual negotiation. These roles are described in your individual briefing sheets.
4. Negotiate for as long as you need to arrive at a solution, or follow the time limits set by your instructor.
5. When you arrive at an agreement, make sure you write down exactly what was agreed to. Have a representative of each side sign this document and either submit it to your instructor or bring it to class as instructed.

BACKGROUND INFORMATION

The Twin Lakes Mining Company is located in Tamarack, Minnesota, in the northern part of the state. It was established there in 1961. The town of Tamarack has a year-round population of approximately 12,000. Although there is a growing revenue that accrues to the town as a result of heavy summer tourism (summer homes, fishing, etc.) and several cottage industries, Tamarack is basically a one-industry town. Twenty-five hundred people, 60 percent of whom live within town limits, work for the Twin Lakes Mining Company; 33 percent of the town's real estate tax base of about $5 million consists of Twin Lakes Mining Company property and operations. Both in terms of direct tax revenue and indirect contribution to the economic stability of the local population, Tamarack is strongly dependent on the continued success of the Twin Lakes Mining Company.

The Twin Lakes Mining Company is an open-pit, iron ore mine. Open-pit mining consists of stripping the topsoil from the ore deposit with the use of power shovels. Train rails are then laid, and most of the ore is loaded into railroad cars for transportation to a central collecting point for rail or water shipment. As mining operations progress, rails are relaid or roads constructed to haul ore by truck. The ore is transported to a "benefication plant" located on the outskirts of Tamarack. Benefication of ore involves crushing, washing, concentration, blending, and agglomerating the ore. In the early days of ore production, such treatment was unnecessary; however, benefication is necessary today for several reasons. First, transportation costs of rejected material (gangue) are minimized. The crude ore may lose as much as one-third of its weight in grading, and, in addition, impurities are removed at a much lower cost than if removed during smelting. Second, ores of various physical and chemical properties can be purified and blended during this process. Finally, fine ore materials, which previously may have been rejected as a result of smelting problems, can now be briquetted and pelletized to increase their value. After the ore proceeds through this process of cleaning and agglomerating into larger lumps or pellets, it is shipped by railroad car to steel mills throughout the Midwest. Rejected materials are returned to "consumed" parts of the mine, and the land restored.

Twin Lakes' benefication plant is located approximately five miles outside of Tamarack. As a result of the expansion of the residential areas of the town, summer home development, and various Twin Lakes operations, the plant has become a major problem for local citizens. For years, the Tamarack Town Council has been pressing the company to clean up the most problematic operations.

While most of these discussions have been amicable, Twin Lakes has done little or nothing to remedy the major concerns. Now, as a result of more stringent environmental laws and regulations, Twin Lakes has come under pressure from both the state of Minnesota and the federal government for environmental cleanup. Both the state and the federal Environmental Protection Agency have informed Twin Lakes that the company is in major violation of water- and air-pollution quality standards, and that immediate action must be taken. Twin Lakes' estimates indicate that total compliance with the cleanup regulations will cost the company over $18 million. Because Twin Lakes is now mining reasonably low-grade ore and because foreign competition in the steel market has significantly eroded the demand for ore, environmental compliance may seriously influence the profitability of the company. Many local citizens, as individuals and through the local chapter of the United Mineworkers Union, are putting significant pressure on the Town Council to help the Twin Lakes Company in its environmental cleanup operations.

The imposition of the environmental controls on Twin Lakes, and the resulting pressure from all segments of the community, has led to renewed discussions between company officials and the Town Council. As a result of these discussions, the following environmental issues have emerged.

1. *Water quality.* The Twin Lakes plant requires large amounts of water to wash the crushed ore. In addition, much of the highest quality ore is reduced to an almost powderlike texture after washing, and is being lost in the washing operation. As a result, the company has built a series of settlement recovery ponds alongside Beaver Brook near the plant. Water that has been used for washing ore is allowed to stand in these ponds; they are periodically drained and the ore recovered. Nevertheless, granules of iron ore and other impurities continue to wash downstream from the plant. The environmental agents have insisted that the effluent from the plant and the ponds be cleaned up. Estimates for the cost of a filtration plant are $10 million. Twin Lakes claims that it cannot afford to build the plant with its own revenue. Since Tamarack has periodically talked about Beaver Brook as a secondary water source for the town (and residential development makes this a more pressing concern in two to three years), the Twin Lakes officials hope that they might interest Tamarack in a joint venture.

2. *Air quality.* The entire process of mining, transporting, and crushing ore generates large amounts of dust. This has significantly increased the levels of particulates in the air. In addition, during the dry summer months, the operation of many large trucks along dirt roads intensifies the problem considerably. Twin Lakes believes that it can control a great deal of the dust generated immediately around the plant at a cost of approximately $4 million. The most significant debate with the town has been over a series of roads around the outskirts of town. Approximately half of the roads are town owned; the rest have been specially constructed for the transportation of ore and material. Estimates for paving all the roads are $2.4 million, with a yearly maintenance cost of $300,000; periodic oil spraying of the roads, to keep down the dust, would run approximately $400,000 annually, but an agreement to do this as a short-term measure may not satisfy the environmental agencies.

3. *Taxation of company land.* The land for the mine itself is outside of town limits. However, the plant lies within township boundaries, and current taxes on the town land are $400,000 annually. The company has always felt that this taxation rate is excessive. In addition, several of the railroad spurs used to move ore into the plant, and out to the major railway line, cross town land. The town has continued to charge a flat rate of $200,000 annually for right-of-way use. It has occasionally offered the land for sale to the company at rates varying from $1.1 million to $1.2 million. Again, the company has felt that this rate is excessive.

Both the company and the town believe that if some resolution could be obtained on these three major issues, the remaining problems could be easily resolved, and Twin Lakes would agree to keep the mine open.

DISCUSSION QUESTIONS

1. How did you prepare for this role-play? What type of strategy did you decide to employ?

2. Did you set goals or targets that you wanted to achieve on each issue or the total package, and did you set "bottom lines" or resistance points? How did having these (or not having these) affect your negotiation effectiveness?

3. What roles did group members decide to play? How did this affect your team and the way it worked with the other group?

4. How satisfied are you with the final agreement (if you reached one)? What factors in your negotiation make you feel satisfied or dissatisfied with this outcome?

5. What did you learn from this situation that you feel you will want to continue (or try to change) in future negotiation situations?

Salary Negotiations

INTRODUCTION

In this simulation, you will play the role of either a manager or subordinate in a negotiation over the subordinate's salary. Both in securing employment as well as promotions, we are frequently in a position to negotiate with our superiors over salary. Moreover, once we achieve managerial rank, we do the same with subordinates. This is one of the most common and, at the same time, most personal forms of negotiation. For many people, it is also the most difficult. Since salary can be a means of satisfying many needs—economic, recognition, status, or competitive success measure—it naturally leads to complex negotiations.

PROCEDURE

Step 1: 5 Minutes

The class will be divided into groups of three; two will be assigned the roles of manager and subordinate, the other as an observer. Role-players will be assigned either an A or a B role in one of the Salary Simulations; your instructor will provide this information. Assemble with your trio in the place specified by the instructor. Each member of each triad should get a chance to play the supervisor once, the subordinate once, and to observe once.

Step 2: 5 Minutes

Read your assigned role and prepare a strategy. If you are an observer, review the Observer Reporting Sheet and make sure you understand what to look for.

Step 3: 10 Minutes

Carry out your discussion with your counterpart. If you finish before the allotted time is up, review the sequence of events with the other party and tell the other what he or she did that was productive or unproductive in the negotiation.

Developed from examples used by John Tarrant, *How To Negotiate A Raise.* Van Nostrand Reinhold, 1976.

If you are an observer, make brief notes during the role-play on your Observer Reporting Sheet. When the role-play is over, review the sheet and add further details where necessary.

Step 4: 10 Minutes

Discuss the outcome of the negotiation in your trio. The observer should report what he or she saw each party doing. Review what steps or positions seemed most and least useful.

At the end of the time for step 4, the observer should hand the Observer Reporting Sheet to the instructor.

Step 5: 5 Minutes

In your trio, change role assignments so that the person filling an A role now fills a B role, the person filling the B role now becomes observer, and the previous observer now fills an A role.

Step 6: 5 Minutes

Repeat step 2.

Step 7: 10 Minutes

Repeat step 3.

Step 8: 10 Minutes

Repeat step 4.

Steps 9, 10, 11, 12: 30 Minutes

Repeat steps 5, 6, 7, and 8.

Steps 13: 30 Minutes

The instructor will post the results from the three sets of role-plays. Examine the different outcomes and explore reasons why they occurred and their consequences.

DISCUSSION QUESTIONS

1. Were there any differences in the way negotiations were handled when:

   a. Both parties in a role-play were satisfied?

   b. One was satisfied?

   c. Both were dissatisfied?

Observer Reporting Sheet _____

Round_____

How did A open the meeting?_____

_____

_____

How did B respond to the way A opened the meeting? _____

_____

_____

Was an agreement reached? Yes _____ No _____

Was the salary agreed to, if there was an agreement? Yes _____ No _____

What, if any, added features were there in the settlement reached?_____

_____

Will future relations between A and B be better (+), worse (–), or about the same (=) as a result of this negotiation? List the opinions of A, B, and the observer:

A _____ B _____ Observer _____

2. Were some people playing the same role dissatisfied with an outcome that others in the same role found satisfying? Why? How do you account for this?
3. Poll quickly those who were satisfied with the outcome. Ask why they were satisfied.
4. Poll quickly those who were dissatisfied with the outcome. Ask why they were dissatisfied.
5. What was the effect of observing another's negotiation on how you negotiated? Did what you see as an observer affect how satisfied you felt with your own outcome?

Newtown School Dispute

INTRODUCTION

In this simulation, you will play a member of either a school board or teachers' association bargaining team. You and the other members of your team, and the members of the other team, are negotiators representing constituencies. You will deal with a complex mix of bargaining issues; these issues have differing preference functions for each side. Finally, you will be subject to a variety of pressures during the negotiations.

ADVANCE PREPARATION

Prior to class, read the Background Material on the Newtown School Dispute. You have been assigned to either the Board of Education or the Teachers' Association. Read the appropriate briefing information the instructor has given you.

Prior to class, meet with the members of your bargaining team, determine your objectives and strategy, and prepare your initial offer. Record this offer on the Initial Offer Form.

PROCEDURE

Step 1: 5 Minutes

The instructor will announce the team assignments and time schedules, and designate locations for negotiations and caucuses.

Step 2: 60–90 Minutes

Teams negotiate. Teams may negotiate as a whole or through spokespersons. Who makes the first offer, how time is used for caucus, and so on, are all controlled by the negotiators themselves. At the end, record your settlement on the Final Settlement Form and hand it to the instructor. If there has not been a complete settlement, note which items *have* been agreed upon.

Step 3: 30–60 Minutes

The instructor will post the initial offers and the final settlements.

Revised version of material originally developed by Frank W. Masters. Used with permission.

BACKGROUND INFORMATION

It is now September 10, the opening day of the school year in Newtown. The contract between Newtown School District and the Newtown Teachers' Association expired on June 30. Since then, the Board of Education and representatives of the Teachers' Association have met on several occasions in an attempt to finalize a contract, but these attempts have not been successful.

Prior to June 30 and during the summer months, there was increasing talk among the membership of the Teachers' Association of the desirability of calling a strike if the contract was not finalized by opening day. However, the leadership of the Teachers' Association agreed, for the benefit of the community, to resume normal operations throughout the system (without a contract) on opening day *on a day-to-day basis*. This is in response to parent pressures to resume normal operations. Parents have been placing pressure on both teachers and the board to keep the schools operating, but voters have twice defeated referendums for increased taxes to cover unavoidable budgetary increases. Due to decreases in enrollments and income from local taxes and state and federal aid, as well as increased costs, maintenance of the school budget at par with the previous year would produce a 4.08 percent budgetary shortfall, which the Board feels would begin to exhaust budgetary categories beginning in the coming April. Therefore, the Board feels that programs and personnel must be cut while, at the same time, productivity (workload) of teachers must be increased if the system is to function effectively within its budgetary constraints to the end (June 30) of the current fiscal year. The district is mandated by the state law to provide 190 instructional days during the school year.

The Board of Education is caught between the Teachers' Association and community pressure groups. The board believes that it must satisfy these pressure groups, while at the same time keeping the teachers on the job with a contract that is acceptable to the bargaining unit's membership. The board is concerned that if it fails to respond appropriately to community pressures for cost reductions, it may be removed. The board's primary objective, therefore, is to cut costs while retaining as many programs as possible. It hopes to do so through cutbacks in teaching personnel and increases in teacher productivity (workload). The board also wishes to eliminate certain existing agreements in order to increase productivity. In this connection, the board wants to negotiate a three-year contract that will "stabilize" the situation by creating orderly and predictable budgetary needs that will be less likely to be seen as excessive by various community groups. In contrast, the Teachers' Association wants to obtain a one-year contract to maintain flexibility.

The Teachers' Association also feels caught between community pressure groups, who want to avert a strike, and the board's apparent unwillingness to fight for increased budget allocations to run the system. The teachers feel the board has not faced up to the community's unwillingness to accept increased taxation to pay for education, and that the board is simply responding to community unwillingness by passing the burden along to teachers.

Newtown is a relatively settled and stable upper-middle-income community, with a strong interest in quality education, but is disinclined to increase its already burdensome tax rate. The Newtown School District consists of 12 schools: 9 elementary schools (K–8) and 3 senior high schools. The student population is 12,000, with 8,000 elementary and 4,000 high school students. The bargaining unit, representing 95 percent of all teachers, consists of 250 elementary teachers in all categories and 125 high school teachers in all categories.

Both sides wish to conclude an agreement to avert a strike. However, the Teachers' Association bargaining team is adamantly committed to improving the lot of its membership, and the board is just as committed to keeping its costs as low as possible. Nevertheless, each side feels it has some room to move on certain issues.

DISCUSSION QUESTIONS

1. The different sides in the negotiations should describe their initial strategies and positions, how well they worked together, and how their positions and strategies changed during negotiation.

2. The different sides should identify changes they made in their objectives during negotiations, what they saw to be the strengths and weaknesses of their own position, and of the opposing team's position.

3. Was there any discussion at the beginning of the negotiation about how the discussions were to be handled? If so, did they have any effect? If not, would some discussion have had an effect? How?

4. What was the bargaining range that existed at the beginning of negotiation?

5. Who made the opening offer? What effect did it have on the conduct of negotiations?

6. Were there attempts to use constituencies and /or bystanders? To what effect?

7. Who made the final offer? How was it structured?

Newtown School District Teachers' Salary Schedule

Step	Amount	Last Year's Number of Teachers	Cost	Current Year's Number of Teachers	Cost
Entry	$28,500	20	$570,000	0	0
1	29,000	20	580,000	20	$580,000
2	30,000	28	840,000	20	600,000
3	31,000	31	961,000	26	806,000
4	32,000	30	960,000	28	896,000
5	33,500	23	770,500	26	871,000
6	34,500	24	828,000	23	793,500
7	35,500	15	532,500	22	781,000
8	37,000	16	592,000	15	555,000
9	38,000	13	494,000	16	608,000
10	39,000	180	7,020,000	179	6,981,000
Totals		400	$14,148,000	375	$13,471,500

Current School Year
July 1–June 30
Projected Budget

1. Income

   1.1 Local Tax (same rate as last year will continue,
        $5.85 per $1,000. No significant increase in
        property values expected.) $22,767,700

   1.2 State (formula yield per pupil will remain the
        same. Legislature may meet and possibly
        raise formula for next year.)   8,470,000

   1.3 Federal   1,369,500

       Total $32,607,200

Note: This is a decrease of $696,037 (–2.09%) from the previous year's income.

2. Expenditures

   2.1 Administration

2.1.1	Professional salaries	$2,030,000
2.1.2	Clerical/secretaries	497,000
2.1.3	Other	470,000
	Total	2,997,000

   2.2 Instruction

2.2.1	Teacher	
	Salaries	$13,471,500[a]
	Fringes	2,640,450
2.2.2	Aides	2,047,000
2.2.3	Materials/supplies	2,053,400[b]
	Total	20,212,350

   2.3 Plant operation/maintenance

2.3.1	Salaries	$2,312,400
2.3.2	Utilities	2,023,000[c]
2.3.3	Other	500,000[d]
	Total	4,835,400

   2.4 Fixed charges

2.4.1	Retirement	$2,111,200[e]
2.4.2	Other	783,000
	Total	2,894,200

   2.5 Debt service $1,763,782[f]

   2.6 Transportation

2.6.1	Salaries	$631,060
2.6.2	Other	660,370[g]
	Total	$1,291,430
	Grand total	$33,994,162

Notes:
Total number of pupils=12,000
Total number of teachers=375
Per pupil expenditure=$2,833

	Percent of *Last Year's* *Total Expenditure*
a. Twenty-five teachers did not return to the system due to either retirement or other reasons.	−2.03%
b. Costs of materials and supplies will be up 46 percent over last year's cost based largely on the rising cost of paper.	+1.96%
c. Cost of utilities is expected to increase by approximately 65 percent due to rate increases and overdue, deferred maintenance.	+2.40%
d. Cost projections indicate a 13 percent increase in this category.	+0.17%
e. Teacher retirement is up 5 percent due to increases mandated by the legislature to pay for new benefits. This was partially offset by attrition.	+0.22%
f. Debt service is up 22 percent due to increased difficulty in floating bonds.	+0.96%
g. Other transportation costs are up 31 percent due to increases in operating and maintenance costs.	+0.23%
Total cost adjustments	+3.91%
Summary: Change in costs, including income decrease	+3.91%

Last School Year
July 1–June 30
Actual Audit

---

1. INCOME

  1.1 Local tax ($5.85 per $1,000 worth assessed real
      property. Assessment is at full value.) $23,459,716

  1.2 State (based on an equalization formula, improved
      during the last legislative session. Yielded $621.28
      per pupil in administration last year.)   8,475,354

  1.3 Federal   1,368,150

      Total $33,303,220

2. EXPENDITURES

  2.1 Administration

2.1.1	Professional salaries	$2,077,359
2.1.2	Clerical/secretarial	513,529
2.1.3	Other	454,972
	Total	3,045,860

  2.2 Instruction

2.2.1	Teachers	
	Salaries	$14,148,000
	Fringes	2,795,136
2.2.2	Aides	2,277,451
2.2.3	Materials/supplies	1,400,313
	Total	20,620,900

  2.3 Plant operations/maintenance

2.3.1	Salaries	$2,386,327
2.3.2.	Utilities	1,224,255
2.3.3	Other	441,788
	Total	4,052,370

  2.4 Fixed changes

2.4.1	Retirement	$2,039,280
2.4.2	Other	787,906
	Total	2,827,186

  2.5 Debt service $1,444,370

  2.6 Transportation

2.6.1	Salaries	$729,878
2.6.2	Other	582,656
	Total	$1,312,534
	Grand total	$33,303,220

Notes
  Total number of pupils = 12,800
  Total number of teachers = 400
  Per pupil expenditure = $2,602
  Last year, the year of the audit on this page, there were 12,800 students in the public school system.
  The current year's projected enrollment is 12,000.

Initial Offer Form

Board of Education _____   Teachers' Association _____

Item	Bottom-Line Position	Desired Settlement	Opening Offer
Salary	_____	_____	_____
Reduction in staff	_____	_____	_____
Workload	_____	_____	_____
Evaluation of teachers	_____	_____	_____
Binding arbitration	_____	_____	_____
Benefits	_____	_____	_____

Final Settlement Form

Board of Education _____   Teachers' Association _____

Item	Settlement
Salary	_____
Reduction in staff	_____
Workload	_____
Evaluation of teachers	_____
Binding arbitration	_____
Benefits	_____

Bestbooks/Paige Turner

INTRODUCTION

This situation involves a negotiation between two representatives: one for an author, Paige Turner, and the other for a publishing company, Bestbooks. This is clearly a competitive situation, but some cooperation is also required. Your challenge is to get the best contract possible for your side.

ADVANCE PREPARATION

None.

PROCEDURE

Step 1: 15 Minutes

The class will be broken into teams of two, one person representing Paige Turner and the other representing Bestbooks. Read the private material that your instructor has provided, and prepare your strategy for the negotiations.

Step 2: 20–30 Minutes

Each dyad of representatives will conduct its meeting trying to reach a new contract between Paige Turner and Bestbooks. When an agreement is reached, write down the settlement on the final settlement agreement form. Agreement must be reached on all eight issues in order for a final agreement to be struck. If you and your partner finish the negotiation early, review your strategies and the process of negotiations. What bargaining range did you have? What actions by either party led to the particular outcome reached?

Step 3: 15–20 Minutes

The instructor will gather the agreements reached by each dyad. Any groups who have not reached an agreement by the end of the negotiating period will be asked to record their final offers.

Written in collaboration with Gregory Leck.

Final Agreement Settlement Form

Issue	Settlement Point
Royalties	
Signing bonus	
Print runs	
Weeks of promotion	
Number of books	
Advance	
Countries distributed	
Book clubs	

DISCUSSION QUESTIONS

1. What tactics and strategies did the teams use to reach an agreement? Was there a difference in the approaches taken by those reaching agreement and those who did not settle?

2. Which team in the class reached the best settlement? What are the criteria for the best settlement in this exercise?

3. How were the issues structured in this exercise? What assumptions did people make about the structure of the issues? How did these assumptions influence the negotiation process? Outcome?

Elmwood Hospital Dispute

INTRODUCTION

In this exercise you will be dealing with a very complex negotiation situation. In contrast to earlier exercises, where there may have been a single opponent and one or two clearly defined issues, this simulation creates a negotiation between larger groups with less clearly defined issues—and perhaps stronger emotions. The key roles played by mediators are also introduced in this simulation.

ADVANCE PREPARATION

Read the Background Information section for the Elmwood Hospital Dispute in this exercise; then read the role information the instructor has provided. Prepare to play this role. Familiarize yourself with the facts and be prepared to act as you think you would act if you were a person in the situation described in this case.

BACKGROUND INFORMATION

The situation described below is a composite, with some data drawn from a number of similar disputes, and other information constructed specifically for this training exercise. The scenario is not to be interpreted as an account of any actual dispute. This simulation is one of several developed and tested by the Institute for Mediation and Conflict Resolution in New York, and adapted with permission by the Community Conflict Resolution Program.

Elmwood is a medium-sized, 450-bed private hospital in a southwestern city of approximately 600,000. It is well equipped for inpatient care, and has an open-heart surgery team that is a matter of special pride to the board of trustees and the hospital's director. None of the trustees live in the hospital's immediate neighborhood, though some of their parents once did. Most of them are professionals or business people, and one of their main functions as trustees is to help in fund-raising for the hospital.

Until 10 years ago, Elmwood was in the middle of a white, middle-class community. Now, however, it is on the eastern edge of an expanding low-income neighborhood, which has moved across the nearby expressway and is continuing to grow eastward. A

Adapted from an activity developed for the Institute of Mediation and Conflict Resolution, 1972.

good part of the low-income community is served by West Point Hospital, back on the western side of the expressway. People on the east, however, are turning to Elmwood. There are very few private physicians left in the Elmwood area, and the hospital, through its outpatient clinic, is the main source of medical care for the newer residents.

These newer residents, who now make up approximately 65 percent of the service area, are a mix of relatively recent newcomers to the city, some from other parts of the United States and others from various foreign countries. Most are in low-paying service jobs. Many are on public assistance. Infant mortality is three times as high as in the rest of the city. Malnutrition is a problem, as are tuberculosis, lead poisoning, and other diseases associated with a slum environment. Most of these new residents cannot afford to be admitted to the hospital when sick, and rely instead on outpatient treatment in what is now an overburdened facility at Elmwood.

Like most hospitals, Elmwood is in a financial squeeze. In addition, it has become increasingly difficult to attract new interns and residents and harder to retain present professionals. Although the hospital director is somewhat sympathetic to the medical care problems of the community, he sees his first priority as building the hospital's institutional strength by such measures as increasing intern- and resident-oriented research opportunities and adding facilities which would induce the staff to stay on rather than go elsewhere. He has apparently given some thought to sponsoring a neighborhood health center, but it has been put off by location problems. He has also heard about some heated conflicts over control of services at other hospitals in the state that took state and federal health grants. Right now, the director apparently intends to put these matters on the back burner until he gets the other things going.

Residents of the low-income community have organized a Concerned Community Coalition (CCC). The community has been asking the hospital to increase its almost nonexistent efforts in preventive medical care, improve and expand outpatient facilities, establish a satellite health center with day care facilities, and train a roving paraprofessional health team to administer diagnostic tests throughout the community. Elmwood is their neighborhood hospital and, to them, this is what a neighborhood hospital should be doing for the residents.

Two weeks ago, the CCC sent a letter to the director asking that the hospital initiate these efforts and requesting that he meet with them to discuss how the community and the hospital could work together. Although the community is deeply concerned about its medical problems and resents the fact that a city institution has not acted before this of its own volition, the letter was not unfriendly.

To date, the letter has not been answered.

Three days ago, the director and the chairman of the board announced the acquisition of a site about 15 blocks from the hospital on which it said it would build a heart research facility, a six-story nurses' residence, and a staff parking lot, with shuttle bus service to the hospital grounds.

On learning of the plans, the leaders and members of the CCC were incensed. They decided to sit in at the director's office until the hospital met their needs.

The day before yesterday, about 50 CCC supporters took over the director's office, vowing not to leave until the hospital agreed to meet the following demands:

1. Replacement of the board of trustees with a community-controlled board.
2. A 100 percent increase in outpatient facilities.
3. Establishment of a neighborhood health center and a day care facility on the newly acquired site.
4. Establishment of a preventive diagnostic mobile health team, consisting of neighborhood residents chosen by the CCC.
5. Replacement of the director by one chosen by the community.

While the hospital director indicated that he would be glad to meet with the group's leader to discuss the matters raised in its letter, he also stated quite forcefully that he considered the new demands arrogant and destructive and that, in any event, he would not meet under duress (i.e., as long as the sit-in continued).

The CCC said it would not leave until a meeting took place and the demands were accepted.

The sit-in began two days ago. This morning the hospital's lawyers moved to get an injunction against the sit-in. The CCC, aided by a legal services attorney, resisted.

The judge reserved decision, stating that to grant an injunction might only make the situation worse. He noted that both the hospital and the CCC would have to learn to live together for their own joint best interest. He therefore instructed the parties to meet to try to work out the problems between them, and has appointed a mediator to assist them. The mediator is a staff member of the city's Human Rights Commission, a unit of the municipal government.

At the judge's suggestion, the sides have agreed to meet with the mediator in the hospital library. The meeting has been scheduled for later today.

PROCEDURE

Step 1: 30 Minutes

Participants assigned to the same role, that is, board members and administrators, members of the Concerned Community Coalition, and the mediators will meet separately to plan how they will handle the upcoming meeting. If there are several sets of roles (i.e., if the class is so large that there are several Elmwood Hospitals), the role teams for each hospital will meet separately to plan strategy,

Step 2: 60 Minutes

The mediator(s) will call the parties together for the meeting. Discussion begins on the purpose of the meeting.

Step 3: 15–30 Minutes

At the end of the meeting, meet with your own team members and answer the following questions:

a. Review your original plans. Did you follow them? Meet your objectives? Why? Why not?

b. For those playing a board member or CCC member: Did having a mediator help or hinder you? How? For those filling the role of mediator: What strategy did you try to employ? What things did the other parties do that helped or hindered you in your work as mediator?

c. If you were in this position again, what would you do differently?

d. What things did you notice or think about that would have helped people in the other roles be more effective in dealing with you in your role?

e. For members of the CCC: What power tactics did you employ? How effective were they? For board members and mediators, what power tactics did the CCC employ? How did you react to these tactics?

f. What characteristics did this bargaining situation have that were different from those of other bargaining situations you have been in?

Step 4: 30–60 Minutes

Next, join the rest of the class and participate in the larger discussion of these six questions (a–f).

The Power Game

INTRODUCTION

The concept of "power" is a complex, elusive, and almost paradoxical one. It is complex because there is a wide variety of definitions of what constitutes power, and how it is effectively accumulated and used. It is elusive because there seems to be very little consensus about the definitions, or the best way to describe power and talk about it in action. Finally, power is paradoxical because it doesn't always work the way it is expected to; sometimes those who seem to have the most power really have the least, while those who may appear to have the least power are most in control.

This simulation offers an opportunity to experience power in a wide variety of forms and styles. During the activity, you may become aware of your own power, and the power of others. Your objective will be to determine who has power, how power is being used, and how to use your own power in order for you to achieve your goals. This type of analysis is essential to effective negotiations when power relationships have not been well defined.

ADVANCE PREPARATION

Your instructor will probably ask you to make a monetary contribution for this activity. Otherwise, no advance preparation is necessary.

PROCEDURE

Step 1

Your instructor will ask you for your monetary contribution. The instructor will then announce what will be done with the money.

Step 2

Your instructor will assign you to a group. You will become acquainted with the group you are assigned to, and the groups others are assigned to. You will be given a place to meet.

Adapted from exercise developed by Lee Bolman and Terrence Deal, Harvard Graduate School of Education, and published in *Exchange: The Organizational Behavior Teaching Journal.* Used with permission.

Step 3

Your instructor will give you descriptions of the duties and responsibilities of the group you are assigned to. Please read this information closely.

Step 4

You will have exactly one hour to conduct the exercise, unless your instructor gives you different instructions.

DISCUSSION QUESTIONS

1. What did you learn about power from this experience?
2. Did this experience remind you of events you have experienced in other organizations? If so, what were the similarities?
3. What did you learn about yourself personally, and the way that you react to power and its use?
4. What power events occurred in your own subgroup? Did you feel satisfied with the amount of power you had? With the way you used it? Why?
5. What did you or your group do to exercise power, or to gain more power? How did it work out?

Coalition Bargaining

INTRODUCTION

The word *coalition* may be loosely defined as a group of individuals or subgroups who assemble to *collectively* exert influence on another group or individual. In an environment where there are many individuals, there are often many different points of view. Each individual views things differently, and each individual would like to have the "system" represent his or her views. In a dictatorship, the system usually represents the views of the dictator, but in a democratic environment, the views that are represented are usually those of a subgroup who have agreed to work together and collectively support one another's views in exchange for having a stronger impact on the system than each individual could have alone.

Many of us are familiar with the work of coalitions. The patterns of influence in national politics, governments, and communities provide us with some excellent examples. Whether it be the coalitions that are formed along traditional party ties (Democrats or Republicans) or along the concerns of special interest groups (Common Cause, the Sierra Club, the AFL-CIO, the National Rifle Association, the National Organization for Women, or hundreds of others), each group is attempting to influence the direction of the larger system by effectively pooling its resources, working together as a team, and persuading those who have control of the current system.

Coalitions are a *common* phenomenon in organizations as well. The 1990s have seen a significant emergence of coalitions in the business sector. In earlier times, these may have been no more than cooperative agreements and licensing between companies, or efforts to work together to influence political and economic policy. But the demands for increased competitiveness in the 1990s have spawned a significant number of mergers, partnerships, and strategic alliances between companies, as they attempt to remain competitive in the international marketplace or move into new markets, product lines, and spin-off businesses. Organizations are a complex web of cross-pressures among various subgroups, each one striving to have its own priorities adopted as the primary goals of the total organization. Those who are initiating and leading these efforts must have excellent strategic skills to assess the "power dynamics" that each

Adapted from *Negotiation: Readings, Exercises and Cases,* first edition, by Roy J. Lewicki and Joseph Litterer (Richard D. Irwin, 1985), and from *Experiences in Management and Organizational Behavior*, second and fourth editions, by Donald D. Bowen, R. J. Lewicki, D. T. Hall, and F. Hall (John Wiley, 1996). Copyright © 1982 by John Wiley & Sons, Inc. Reprinted by permission of John Wiley & Sons, Inc.

party brings to this game, and sophisticated negotiating skills to forge and manage the relationships between the parties.

The purpose of this exercise is to help you understand the different sources and expressions of power, or "leverage," that individuals and groups can use in multiparty decision making. In this exercise, you will see people use power and influence in a variety of different ways. See if you can determine what kind of power is being used, and how effective it is at gaining the other's compliance or cooperation. In addition, this exercise will help you explore the dynamics of trust and cooperation in a strongly competitive situation.

ADVANCE PREPARATION

None.

PROCEDURE

Step 1: 5 Minutes

The instructor will break the class into three teams, with approximately an equal number of members on each team. In very large classes, two groups of three teams may be formed, or some class members may be designated as observers. You may be specifically assigned to a team by the leader in advance, or you may be selected randomly in advance. The teams will be randomly designated A, B, and C.

Each member should contribute funds to the "stake" or "prize" for the game. (The leader may choose to use "points" rather than real money.)

Step 2: 10 Minutes

Read the following rules.

RULES OF THE GAME

Objective

To form a coalition with another team, in order to divide the stake. The coalition must also decide on a way of dividing the stake so as to satisfy both parties.

The Stake

Each team has *unequal* resources. In spite of the fact that you each contributed $1.00, you will receive a different stake, depending on the coalition you form. The following table should be filled in with information provided by the group leader (the individual payoffs are determined by the number of participants in the activity):

If an AB coalition forms, it will receive a stake of $_____.

If an AC coalition forms, it will receive a stake of $_____.

If a BC coalition forms, it will receive a stake of $_____.

The Strategy

Each team will meet separately to develop a strategy before the negotiations. You should also select a negotiator.

Rules for Negotiation

1. All members on a team may be present for negotiations; however, only the negotiator may speak.
2. Notes may be passed to negotiators if desired.
3. A team may change its negotiator between conversations.
4. At the termination of the game, the stake will be allocated only if a coalition has been formed.
5. Only one formal coalition is permitted.
6. A coalition will be recognized by the group leader only if (*a*) no two teams are permitted to receive the same amount of money, and (*b*) neither team in the coalition is allowed to receive zero.
7. If no coalition is reached, no funds are allocated.
8. Negotiations will be conducted in the following fixed order, and for the following fixed periods of time:

Order of Negotiation	Time for First Round of Negotiation	Time for Second and Third Rounds of Negotiation
Teams A and B	5 minutes	4 minutes
Teams A and C	5 minutes	4 minutes
Teams B and C	5 minutes	4 minutes

9. The team *not* in negotiations—that is, while the other two teams are negotiating— must leave the negotiation room. Other members of the companies who are *not* in the negotiating teams may not speak with any of the negotiators.
10. There cannot be any conversation between team members and observers at any time.

Valid Coalitions

1. A coalition will be recognized by the group leader only if (*a*) no teams are permitted to receive the same amount of money, and (*b*) neither team in the coalition is allowed to receive zero.
2. After negotiations, all three teams are given the opportunity to submit a written statement in the following form: "Team X has a coalition with Team Y, whereby Team X gets $*X.xx* and Y gets $*Y.yy*." When written statements meeting the above requirements from any two teams agree, a valid coalition has been formed.

Step 3: 10 Minutes

Each team will meet in a separate area to plan its strategy. During the strategy session, you will want to decide which team you might want to coalesce with, how you might want to divide resources, what kind of offers the other team might make to you, and so on. You may also want to decide what sources of power you have and how you might take advantage of these sources of power in the upcoming negotiations. You must also select a negotiator.

Step 4: 20 Minutes (5 Minutes per Team Pair Plus Extra Time to Move Teams)

Each pair of teams will report to the "negotiation area" for five minutes to conduct its discussions. Only the negotiators will speak, but other team members can be present and pass notes. At the end of each five-minute block, the referee will stop the negotiations and move to the next pair. The team *not* in negotiations on a particular round *must leave the negotiating room.*

Step 5: 45 Minutes (4 Minutes per Team Pair Plus Extra Time to Move Teams)

Each pair of teams reports to the negotiating area for four-minute discussions for the *second* and *third* rounds (in the same sequence as above).

Step 6: 5 Minutes

The group leader will ask each team to meet separately, and to submit a ballot stating the coalition that they believe was formed. A blank ballot may be distributed by the referee, or should be written on a blank sheet of paper, in the following format:

> Team (your team) has a coalition with Team _____, whereby Team _____ receives _____ (dollars or points) and Team _____ receives _____ (dollars or points).

Put your own team letter (A, B, or C) on the ballot.

Each team brings its written statement to the negotiating room. The group leader will announce whether a valid coalition has been formed (two ballots agree); the money is then distributed as specified on the ballots. If a coalition has not been formed, or if the coalition that has formed does not use up all of the initial stake, a problem will arise as to what to do with the funds.

DISCUSSION QUESTIONS

1. What was the initial strategy that each team decided on?
2. How were strategies influenced by the resources (dollars or points) that each team could contribute to a coalition?
3. How did the sequence of conversations between teams influence strategy?

4. How did the prior "reputation" of people on your own team, or the other team, affect your strategy?

5. Was your strategy modified after you had talked to the other teams? How?

6. How were strategic decisions made within your team?

7. How was the negotiator chosen? In looking back on the negotiations, did you make the right choice? Why or why not?

8. What did the negotiators do that encouraged or hurt the development of trust between teams?

9. Were negotiators ever changed? If so, for what reason?

10. What factors most influenced the ultimate settlement between teams? Do you think you could have predicted this earlier? Why or why not?

Jordan Electronics Company

INTRODUCTION

In this simulation, you will play the role of a committee member on the New Products Committee of Jordan Electronics Company. The committee oversees the development of all new products. In particular, it approves the research and design of all new products and authorizes the release from R&D to begin the manufacturing process. At the moment, the committee is faced with a decision: whether or not to authorize the manufacture of a new model of the Jordan Auto Correlator Model 36, known as the JAC 36. As a member of the committee working on this problem, you will face some of the complex and tense deliberations that often confront senior management. You will have several levels of concern on the committee: your own job and the problems you may have in getting it done, representing the members of your unit whom you supervise, and worrying about the welfare of Jordan Electronics as a whole.

ADVANCE PREPARATION

Prior to class, read the Background Information section of the Jordan Electronics Company. Also read the information on the role that has been provided by your instructor. Plan what you are going to do in the forthcoming meeting.

PROCEDURE

Step 1: 5 Minutes

If this has not already been done, you will be assigned a role on the New Products Committee.

Step 2: 45 Minutes

The New Products Committee will meet and work toward settling the major issues.

Step 3: 15 Minutes

If you have not reached an agreement, stop the discussion at this point. Each member of the group should state the goals he or she was trying to achieve, the least-preferred solution that he or she would still accept for a settlement, and any other issues that must be included in a minimally acceptable deal. Then each member should state what factors in the group's decision blocked achieving a settlement within the time limits. If a settlement was reached, each member of the group should report what his or her minimally acceptable terms were and what factors helped the group reach a solution.

Step 4: 30 Minutes

The instructor will gather information from each New Products Committee on their outcome and the information assembled by each group in step 3. The exercise will then be reviewed and evaluated.

BACKGROUND INFORMATION

Jordan Electronics is a manufacturing company that produces two major lines of scientific measuring instruments: instruments for use in scientific laboratories (laboratory products) and industrial instruments for use in manufacturing processes (industrial products). The management of Jordan Electronics is currently confronted with a problem in authorizing the manufacture of a redesigned model of the Jordan Auto Correlator Model 36 (JAC 36).

The original measuring instrument was designed over 20 years ago by the current president of Jordan Electronics. The original mission of the company was to manufacture the auto correlator and other scientific instruments. (An auto correlator is a device used to monitor flow processes by measuring data at different points in the process. It might measure the rate of flow of chemicals through a pipeline as well as changes in temperature of the chemical at two different points along a pipeline and then correlate that information.) At the time, the instrument revolutionized the market. The JAC 36 (so-called because it was launched on the president's 36th birthday) permitted a researcher to make correlations simultaneously on 256, 512, or 1,024 channels (monitoring levels). This device was initially picked up by physicists doing research in diffraction and gradually was adopted by scientists from other fields and by manufacturing firms using complex chemical processes. The JAC 36 became the market leader in its field and maintained that position for over 15 years.

The past few years have brought changes. First, new, faster, and more powerful microprocessors are now in existence. The use of a 16-bit microprocessor chip has been made obsolete by superior 32-bit microprocessor chips. A leading Japanese microprocessor manufacturing company has just introduced a new 64-bit chip that would certainly overshadow the speed and capacity of its predecessors. Using these components would reduce the size and weight of the completed machine and would permit greater portability. The existence of flat LCD screens would enable the manufacturing of a portable JAC 36 unit that would resemble the very popular laptop computers. Although the hardware aspect was technically quite feasible, such a unit would be successful only if a special type of software was developed that would enable the smaller units to emulate the functions of the larger ones. Changeover to this manufacturing process is costly, but once the "bugs" are worked out, manufacturing cost per unit could be cut significantly.

Second, although the JAC 36 holds a strong share of the market, Jordan's competitors have been nibbling away at that market share by adding a variety of new features to their instruments. One addition has been to provide voice-activated command entry which enables one to control the auto correlator using verbal commands. This frees the user to perform other manual functions during the verbal command process. A second feature was the implementation of optical coupling. Although optical devices did not enhance the capacity or speed of the units, they did reduce the amount of heat that was emitted by the auto correlator. This aspect was appreciated by those who had to use the units in strict laboratory conditions. Although it was not perceived to be a widespread problem, the erratic behavior of some microprocessors was sometimes attributed to the excess heat generated by units that did not use optical coupling. Competing products with these features sell for $3,000 to $5,000 more than the present JAC 36. Finally, as mentioned above, some competitors are rumored to be working on a laptop design that would enhance the portability of such units. While the JAC 36 typically is used as a laboratory instrument, scientists now seem to want the flexibility of a lighter machine for field experiments and mobile laboratories. Lightness and ease of movement are even more attractive in industrial applications. Although use of the new technologies requires some change in the basic circuit design, it requires extensive change in the physical design of the instrument and in the manufacturing methods.

Six months ago, the sales vice president made a very strong pitch to management to encourage the production of a JAC 36 that incorporated reduced size, voice-activated control, and optical-coupling features. Jordan's sales representatives are becoming increasingly embarrassed by customer complaints about the outdated nature of the JAC 36 and their requests for a newer version similar to the competition. The sales vice president said there should be two versions of the JAC sometime in the future, a portable machine and a stationary one, but that the portable unit was clearly the second priority because strong demand was not anticipated for several years.

In response to this request, the president requested an intensive study of the market for an updated JAC 36 and an estimate for the manufacturing costs. The market study, conducted by an independent marketing research firm, reported that there was still a very strong market for the current JAC 36. In fact, many of the companies that had purchased auto correlators from competitors—machines that included the voice-activated command features—reported that they rarely used these features. In other words, many of the newer machines on the market were "overdesigned" for their customers' actual use. Market research on the portable versus nonportable units was inconclusive: Some purchasers clearly wanted it, but the overall demand for portability was not strong.

Cost estimates for an updated JAC 36 were developed by the senior electrical engineer, the vice president of manufacturing, and an electronics designer in the R&D department. They calculated that there would be a very high cost in changeover to the more advanced microprocessors as well as the associated costs in adapting the software used on the present JACs. Adding the voice-activated control mechanism to the present manual controls was the most simple and least costly change. Manufacturing the units with optical couplers would involve considerable redesign of the cabinet and manufacturing methods and would cost considerably less than if the new machine was adapted to the new microprocessors. Moreover, there were a few nagging technical problems in the electronic design of a portable unit; the longer it took to work these problems out, the higher the R&D costs would go and the longer it would take to put the portable JAC 36 on the market.

The president reviewed all of this information and decided that in spite of these reports, Jordan needed to come out with a new JAC 36 model, if only to satisfy the need to be competitive with other machines. Since the old standard JAC 36 units were holding their market share and since the development of the portable model was plagued with problems, the president decided to proceed with a redesign of the old JAC 36 unit that would include both the voice-activated command and optical coupling features. At the meeting announcing the decision, the president stressed that the new model should maintain Jordan's reputation for providing flexible, high-quality equipment. The sales vice president commented that the new JAC 36 should be offered at about the same price as the present model. Since the revised model was not designed to be portable, weight was not a problem for the new machine. The Research and Development department, after reviewing the design specifications, said the development work could probably be done in three to four months.

The Research and Development department finished the development work in early January. Production was sent the information it needed to set production methods and to estimate costs. After talking it over with his factory superintendent, the vice president of production described the production methods and costs in detail in a memorandum to the president. These estimates were considerably higher than anticipated. The current JAC 36 sold for $16,000, but the vice president of production estimated that it would be impossible to sell the new model for less than $20,000. The president and vice president of sales were very upset by this memorandum. They asked the vice president of production to review all of the figures and distribute them to all members of the New Products Committee, who would then make the decision whether to start manufacturing the revised JAC 36. It is now early March, and the meeting of the New Products Committee is about to occur. The revised figures from the vice president of production were not substantially different from the original estimates. The basic costs are presented in Exhibit 1. The committee has a real problem on its hands. In addition, the president, who normally chairs the meeting, will not be present because of a minor surgical procedure; the vice president of finance will chair the meeting. The purpose of this meeting is to determine if the revised JAC 36 should be put into production and, if so, at what price it should be marketed. In attendance will be

Vice president of finance (chair).

Director of research and development.

Vice president of sales.

Vice president of production.

Senior electrical engineer.

EXHIBIT 1   Jordan Electronics Company Cost Structures

	Present Cost Structure JAC 36	Estimated Cost Structure Revised JAC 36
Factory price	$16,000	$20,000
Costs:		
Direct labor	1,650	2,300
Raw materials	6,700	8,500
Factory overhead	3,700	5,200
Margin	3,950	4,000

	Variance Report Last Year JAC 36	
Labor:		
Metal shop	–2%	
Electronics components	+8%	
Other components	N.C.	
Assembly	+5%	
Test	+10%	
Materials:		
Metal	–3%	
Electronics	+10%	
Overhead	–11%	

DISCUSSION QUESTIONS

1. What were the most frequently cited obstacles to reaching an agreement?
2. What was or could be done to overcome these obstacles?
3. Were there any common features to the groups that did successfully achieve an agreement? That did not achieve an agreement?
4. Should this type of issue be handled by a committee in organizations? What are the pros and cons of this approach?

Third-Party Conflict Resolution

INTRODUCTION

In addition to being involved in their own conflicts, managers are often called upon to intervene and to settle conflicts between other people. The two activities in this section are designed to explore how third parties may enter conflicts for the purpose of resolving them, and to practice one very effective approach to intervention. In the first activity, you will read about a manager who has a problem deciding how to intervene in a dispute, and you will discuss this case in class. Part 2 of this exercise contains a Mediation Guide, which will be useful in completing the role-playing activity in Part 3, in which some of you will attempt to resolve a managerial dispute.

ADVANCE PREPARATION

The instructor will specify whether the case (Seatcor Manufacturing Company) or the Mediation Guide should be read in advance. Role-playing materials (The Summer Interns) may also be provided in advance.

PART 1

PROCEDURE

Step 1: 5 Minutes

Read the Seatcor Manufacturing Company case.

THE SEATCOR MANUFACTURING COMPANY

You are senior vice president of operations and chief operating officer of Seatcor, a major producer of office furniture. Joe Gibbons, your subordinate, is vice president and general manager of your largest desk assembly plant. Joe has been with Seatcor for 38 years and is 2 years away from retirement. He worked his way up through the ranks to his present position and has successfully operated his division for five years

---

Developed by Roy J. Lewicki. The Mediation Guide developed by Larry Ray, American Bar Association and Robert Helm, Oklahoma State University. "The Seatcor Manufacturing Company" and "The Summer Interns" developed by Blair Sheppard, Fuqua School of Business, Duke University. Used with permission.

with a marginally competent staff. You are a long-standing personal friend of Joe's and respect him a great deal. However, you have always had an uneasy feeling that Joe has surrounded himself with minimally competent people by his own choice. In some ways, you think he feels threatened by talented assistants.

Last week you were having lunch with Charles Stewart, assistant vice president and Joe's second in command. Upon your questioning, it became clear that he and Joe were engaged in a debilitating feud. Charles was hired last year, largely at your insistence. You had been concerned for some time about who was going to replace Joe when he retired, especially given the lack of really capable managerial talent on Joe's staff. Thus, you prodded Joe to hire your preferred candidate—Charles Stewart. Charles is relatively young, 39, extremely tenacious and bright, and a well-trained business school graduate. From all reports he is doing a good job in his new position.

Your concern centers on a topic that arose at the end of your lunch. Charles indicated that Joe Gibbons is in the process of completing a five-year plan for his plant. This plan is to serve as the basis for several major plant reinvestment and reorganization decisions that would be proposed to senior management. According to Charles, Joe Gibbons has not included Charles in the planning process at all. You had to leave lunch quickly and were unable to get much more information from Charles. However, he did admit that he was extremely disturbed by this exclusion and that his distress was influencing his work and probably his relationship with Joe.

You consider this a very serious problem. Charles will probably have to live with the results of any major decisions about the plant. More important, Joe's support is essential if Charles is to properly grow into his present and/or future job. Joe, on the other hand runs a good ship and you do not want to upset him or undermine his authority. Moreover, you know Joe has good judgment; thus, he may have a good reason for what he is doing.

How would you proceed to handle this issue?

Step 2: 5 Minutes

Before discussing this case with anyone else, answer the following two questions:

1. Assume you were the senior vice president of operations. Exactly what would you do in this situation regarding the conflict between Joe and Charles?
2. Why would you take this action—that is, what are your primary objectives by intervening in this way?

Step 3: 20–30 Minutes

The instructor will discuss this case with the entire class.

Step 4: 10–15 Minutes

The instructor will summarize the case discussion and present a framework for understanding how participants analyzed the case and decided to intervene.

DISCUSSION QUESTIONS

1. How much agreement was there within the class about the way that the senior vice president should approach the problem? How did this compare with your own preferred strategy?

2. Which style of conflict intervention do you use most frequently? Which one do you use least frequently? Are there other styles that are commonly used which are not listed here?

3. Which one of the four criteria (efficiency, effectiveness, participant satisfaction, and fairness) are typically most important to you when you intervene in someone else's dispute? Which one is most important when someone intervenes to settle a dispute you are having? If these are different, what are the implications of these differences for training managers in dispute resolution?

4. Do you use different styles in different situations? If so, what kind of situational factors affect which styles you use?

GENERALIZATIONS AND CONCLUSION

Compare your answers to the questions in step 2 with the ways that others approached the problem. To practice your own comprehension of third-party dynamics, answer the following questions:

1. What are four different criteria that managers can have when they intervene in disputes?

2. What are the various styles that managers use to intervene in disputes?

3. Which of these styles is most effective given each of the four criteria?

PART 2: THE MEDIATION GUIDE

This section presents a series of steps for effectively conducting a mediation. You may use this checklist and the flowchart depicted in Exhibit 1.

Step 1: Stabilize the Setting

Parties often bring some strong feelings of anger and frustration into mediation. These feelings can prevent them from talking productively about their dispute. You, as mediator, will try to gain their trust for you and for the mediation process. Stabilize the setting by being polite; show that you are in control and that you are neutral. This step helps the parties feel comfortable, so they can speak freely about their complaints, and safe, so they can air their feelings.

1. _____ Greet the parties.
2. _____ Indicate where each of them is to sit.
3. _____ Identify yourself and each party, by name.
4. _____ Offer water, paper and pencil, and patience.

5. _____ State the purpose of mediation.

6. _____ Confirm your neutrality.

7. _____ Get their commitment to proceed.

8. _____ Get their commitment that only one party at a time will speak.

9. _____ Get their commitment to speak directly to you.

10. _____ Use calming techniques as needed.

Step 2: Help the Parties Communicate

Once the setting is stable and the parties seem to trust you and the mediation process, you can begin to carefully build trust between them. Both must make statements about what has happened. Each will use these statements to air negative feelings. They may express anger, make accusations, and show frustration in other ways. But, with your help, this mutual ventilation lets them hear each other's side of the story, perhaps for the first time. It can help calm their emotions, and can build a basis for trust between them.

1. _____ Explain the rationale for who speaks first.

2. _____ Reassure them that both will speak without interruption, for as long as necessary.

3. _____ Ask the first speaker to tell what has happened.

      a. _____ Take notes.

      b. _____ Respond actively; restate and echo what is said.

      c. _____ Calm the parties as needed.

      d. _____ Clarify, with open or closed questions, or with restatements.

      e. _____ Focus the narration on the issues in the dispute.

      f. _____ Summarize, eliminating all disparaging references.

      g. _____ Check to see that you understand the story.

      h. _____ Thank this party for speaking, the other for listening quietly.

4. _____ Ask the second speaker to tell what has happened.

      a. _____ Take notes.

      b. _____ Respond actively; restate and echo what is said.

      c. _____ Calm the parties as needed.

      d. _____ Clarify, with open or closed questions, or with restatements.

      e. _____ Focus the narration on the issues in the dispute.

      f. _____ Summarize, eliminating all disparaging references.

      g. _____ Check to see that you understand the story.

      h. _____ Thank this party for speaking, the other for listening quietly.

5. _____ Ask each party, in turn, to help clarify the major issues to be resolved.

6. _____ Inquire into basic issues, probing to see if something instead may be at the root of the complaints.

7. _____ Define the problem by restating and summarizing.

8. _____ Conduct private meetings, if needed (explain what will happen during and after the private meetings).

9. _____ Summarize areas of agreement and disagreement.

10. _____ Help the parties set priorities on the issues and demands.

Step 3: Help the Parties Negotiate

Cooperativeness is needed for negotiations that lead to agreement. Cooperation requires a stable setting, to control disruptions, and exchanges of information, to develop mutual trust. With these conditions, the parties may be willing to cooperate, but still feel driven to compete. You can press for cooperative initiatives by patiently helping them to explore alternative solutions, and by directing attention to their progress.

1. _____ Ask each party to list alternative possibilities for a settlement.

2. _____ Restate and summarize each alternative.

3. _____ Check with each party on the workability of each alternative.

4. _____ Restate whether the alternative is workable.

5. _____ In an impasse, suggest the general form of other alternatives.

6. _____ Note the amount of progress already made, to show that success is likely.

7. _____ If the impasse continues, suggest a break or a second mediation session.

8. _____ Encourage them to select the alternative that appears to be workable.

9. _____ Increase their understanding by rephrasing the alternative.

10. _____ Help them plan a course of action to implement the alternative.

Step 4: Clarify Their Agreement

Mediation should change each party's attitude toward the other. When both have shown their commitment, through a joint declaration of agreement, each will support the agreement more strongly. For a settlement that lasts, each component of the parties' attitudes toward each other—their thinking, feeling, and acting—will have changed. Not only will they now *act* differently toward each other, but they are likely to *feel* differently, more positively, about each other and to *think* of their relationship in new ways.

1. _____ Summarize the agreement terms.

2. _____ Recheck with each party his or her understanding of the agreement.

3. _____ Ask whether other issues need to be discussed.

4. _____ Help them specify the terms of their agreement.

5. _____ State each person's role in the agreement.

6. _____ Recheck with each party on when he or she is to do certain things, where, and how.

7. _____ Explain the process of follow-up.

8. _____ Establish a time for follow-up with each party.

9. _____ Emphasize that the agreement is theirs, not yours.

10. _____ Congratulate the parties on their reasonableness and on the workability of their resolution.

EXHIBIT 1 Steps in a Mediation Process

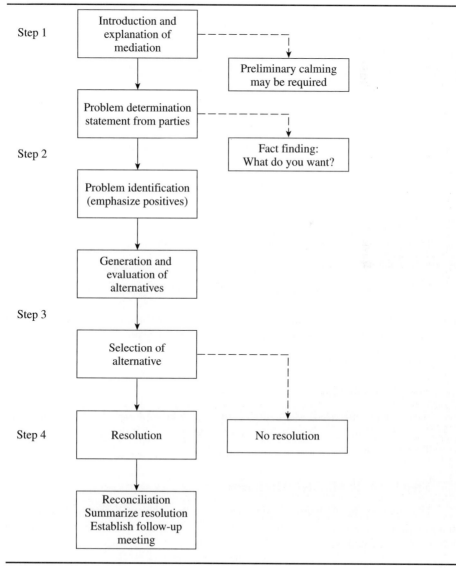

- Step 1: Introduction and explanation of mediation → Preliminary calming may be required
- Problem determination statement from parties → Fact finding: What do you want?
- Step 2: Problem identification (emphasize positives)
- Generation and evaluation of alternatives
- Step 3: Selection of alternative
- Step 4: Resolution / No resolution
- Reconciliation: Summarize resolution, Establish follow-up meeting

PART 3

PROCEDURE

Step 1: 15 Minutes

Read the Mediation Guide in Part 2 if it has not been previously assigned as advanced preparation.

Step 2: 5 Minutes

The instructor will divide the class into subgroups of three or four (the latter if an observer is to be used). One person should play the role of Samantha (Sam) Pinder, who will mediate the dispute. The other two parties will play the roles of Brenda Bennett (director of personnel) and Harold Stokes (vice president, engineering), who are having a dispute over the hiring of summer interns. The instructor will provide this information.

Step 3: 10 Minutes

Each party should read his or her role information and prepare to play the role. Remember to

1. Empathize with the role. Try to see the world as your assigned character sees it, and behave accordingly.
2. Do not add facts that are not in the case.
3. Stay in your role. Do not jump out of the role to comment on the process.
4. Try to make it realistic.

The person playing the third party will try to defuse the conflict and seek a resolution. Do not make it unnecessarily difficult for this person; "play along" to observe how third-party dispute resolution can work. On the other hand, you are not required to settle if you believe that your character's needs are truly not being met by the proposed agreement.

Step 4: 20–30 Minutes

Sam Pinder will "lead" each small group in an effort to resolve the summer interns' problem. When you have achieved a resolution, write it down so you can report it to the class later.

Step 5: 10–20 Minutes (Optional)

Discuss how the mediation session went in each of the small groups. Use the Mediation Guide. If you had an observer assigned, the observer can comment on the strengths and weaknesses of the mediator's efforts.

Step 6: 20–30 Minutes

Be prepared to report to the class on the outcome of the mediation session, and particular problems that may have occurred with the mediation session in your small group.

DISCUSSION QUESTIONS

1. What were some of the different settlements arrived at by different groups?
2. How did your group's specific settlement emerge? How much influence did Pinder have in shaping the final settlement? How much influence did Stokes and Bennett have?
3. Was the mediation process fair? Was the achieved outcome fair? What made them fair or unfair?
4. What tactics did the mediator use that were most effective? Least effective?
5. When would it be most useful to use mediation in an organization? When would it be least useful to use mediation?
6. What are some of the major problems and obstacles to using mediation as a manager?

The Connecticut Valley School

INTRODUCTION

In this situation you must allocate a limited capital budget among six or seven competing projects. Three parties are involved in the negotiation: the headmaster, the faculty budget committee, and the board of trustees. While the issues in this exercise appear straightforward, the parties do not necessarily perceive the budget process in the same manner.

ADVANCE PREPARATION

Read the Background Information section for the Connecticut Valley School in this exercise; then read the role information that the instructor has provided for you. Prepare to play this role. Familiarize yourself with the facts, and prepare to meet with your team and the other side.

Step 1: 30–45 Minutes

Participants who have been assigned to the same team (faculty budget committee, board of trustees, headmaster) will meet separately to decide how to manage the upcoming meeting. Each group should prepare a ranking and rating of the capital projects to be discussed.

Step 2: 45–60 Minutes

The different parties will meet together to negotiate an agreement about the capital projects that will be funded. The chairperson of the board of trustees will chair this meeting. Participants will leave this meeting with an agreement about the priority of the capital spending projects. If no agreement is reached then each team should have a record of their final rankings and where they are willing to make further concessions.

BACKGROUND INFORMATION

The Connecticut Valley School (CVS) is a private boarding school in Massachusetts. Headmaster John Loring has just submitted his annual recommendations for capi-

---

Written by Peter Nye, University of Washington at Bothell. Used with permission.

tal spending to the board of trustees. Capital spending will be funded from two sources, new debt and the accumulated interest on the school's endowment. Since the school is approaching its debt capacity and trustees are committed not to draw on the principal of the endowment, the school can afford to spend only $450,000 to $500,000 on capital improvements over the next year. The seven major projects under consideration are described briefly below.

1. *Swimming Pool*
   Cost: $320,000   Expected life: 15 years

   Currently the school rents a local facility for $30,000 per year. In addition, the school pays $5,000 per year to bus students to the facility. If the school owned its own pool, it could rent out pool time to local organizations for $15,000 per year. The headmaster feels that more students would use the pool if it were located on campus.

2. *Buses*
   Cost: $135,000 (3 buses)   Expected life: 6 years
   Salvage value: Nil

   CVS owns two campuses several miles apart. A private bus company transports students between campuses at a cost of $90,000 per year. If the school owns and operates its own buses, it will incur $40,000 in operating expenses each year.

3. *New Roof for Hockey Rink*
   Cost: $30,000

   A new roof is essential to prevent further damage to the rink and to the arena's infrastructure. The project could be delayed one year; but due to the additional damage that would result, total repair costs would jump to $60,000.

4. *Wood Chip Heating System*
   Cost: $400,000   Expected life: 15 years

   Cold New England winters and the high cost of fuel oil have been draining the school's operating funds. This new heating system could save the school between $70,000 and $80,000 per year over the next 15 years.

5. *Renovation of Fine Arts Building*
   Cost: $150,000

   The faculty and trustees agree that an improved fine arts program is critical to the school's liberal arts mission. The renovated fine arts building would include a photography lab, a pottery shop, and art studios, as well as a small gallery. The building would not generate any incremental revenues or cost savings. However, a wealthy benefactor (after whom the building would be named) has offered to contribute $75,000 to subsidize the project. In addition, the facility would provide some marketing benefits, as a strong arts program attracts quality students.

6. *Renovations to Women's Locker Room*
   Cost: $20,000

   The women's locker room has not been renovated since it was built 33 years ago for visiting men's teams. Many of the women have complained that the facility is dirty, depressing, and overcrowded. Some women refuse to use the facility. The headmaster insists that these complaints are unfounded. The renovations would generate no incremental revenues or cost savings.

7. *Upgrading the Computer Lab*
Cost: $60,000

Over the past eight years computer equipment has been purchased on a piecemeal basis with surplus operating funds. To support curricular goals, the school needs state-of-the-art computers and more workstations. The director of computing has proposed that the equipment be upgraded over three years. The first stage of this plan would require spending $60,000 on personal computers in the coming year. An additional $80,000 would be spent over the following two years.

The school uses a 12 percent annual discount rate to evaluate all cost-saving investment projects.

Since not all of these projects can be undertaken, they must be prioritized. In his report to the trustees, Headmaster Loring ranked the six projects as follows:

1. Swimming Pool $320,000
2. Hockey rink roof $30,000
3. Buses $135,000
4. Heating system $400,000
5. Fine arts building $75,000
6. Women's locker room $20,000
7. Computer lab $60,000

He recommended that this year's capital funds be spent on the construction of a swimming pool, repairs to the roof of the hockey rink, and the purchase of three buses. These projects would require a total expenditure of $485,000. Loring's rankings were based on his subjective evaluation of cost/benefit trade-offs.

While the trustees must make the final decision, they have solicited advice from the faculty. The faculty is in touch with the day-to-day operations of the school and with the needs of the students. In addition, many faculty members feel that they were closed out of the decision process last year and that the ultimate allocation of funds was inconsistent with the school's objectives. In an attempt to improve the decision process, the trustees appointed a faculty budget committee to advise them on capital spending priorities. A meeting of the trustees, the budget committee, and the headmaster has been scheduled. The purpose of this meeting is to prioritize capital spending projects. It is expected to be a lively and productive session.

Step 3: 30 Minutes

All group members will bring their final agreements (or within-team rankings) back to class. The instructor will share the final agreements with the rest of the class. The exercise will then be discussed and evaluated.

DISCUSSION QUESTIONS

1. Did the teams agree on appropriate decision criteria before debating the merits of the specific projects? Which party's decision criteria best promoted an integrative decision? A distributive decision?

2. What strategies and tactics were used to reach a solution? How were they similar or different from the strategies and tactics used during the within-team discussions?

3. Which group had the greatest power? How did the distribution of power across the groups influence the process of negotiations? The outcome?

4. Was this an integrative or distributive situation? Why? Was the outcome distributive or integrative? Why?

EXERCISE 17

Alpha–Beta

INTRODUCTION

In this situation you will negotiate a possible robot manufacturing and marketing agreement with another company. You will be a member of a team that represents either an electrical company in the nation of Alpha, or a manufacturer of electrical machinery in the nation of Beta.

ADVANCE PREPARATION

Read the Background Information section for Alpha–Beta in this exercise; then read the role information that the instructor has provided. Prepare to play this role. Familiarize yourself with the facts, and prepare to meet with the other members of your team to develop a strategy to negotiate with the other organization.

Step 1: 10–15 Minutes

Participants will read the common background information and the private role information assigned by the instructor.

Step 2: 25 Minutes

Participants will meet with other members of their team and develop a strategy for negotiating with the other organization.

Step 3: 20 Minutes

Representatives of the two organizations will meet and negotiate the remaining issues in the Alpha–Beta contract. Participants will leave this meeting with an agreement about all of the issues to be discussed. If no agreement is reached then each team should have a record of their final offers and where they are willing to make further concessions.

This exercise was first developed by Thomas N. Gladwin in 1984, and is copyrighted 1990–91 by Thomas N. Gladwin, Stephen E. Weiss, and Allen J. Zerkin. Used with permission.

BACKGROUND INFORMATION

Alpha

Alpha Inc. is a large, broadly diversified electrical company based in the nation of Alpha. The company is one of the leading makers of numerical control equipment and plans to become a leader in equipping the "factory of the future." It has recently spent hundreds of millions of dollars putting together a collection of factory automation capabilities ranging from robotics to computer-aided design and manufacturing. Alpha Inc. has been acquiring companies, investing heavily in new plants, and spending considerable sums on product development. Innovative robots, some equipped with vision, are being developed, but they have been a bit slow in making their way out of the company's R&D labs. To meet its objective of quickly becoming a major worldwide, full-service supplier of automation systems, Alpha Inc. has found it necessary to tie up, in various ways, with foreign firms that are further up the robotics learning curve.

Robotics in the Nation of Alpha

There are 30 robot manufacturers in Alpha, and big computer and auto firms have recently been entering the business. During 1980, use and production of robots in Alpha was only about 33 percent of what it was in the nation of Beta. One survey reported 4,370 robots in use in Alpha in 1980, mainly in the auto and foundry-type industries, and 1,269 produced. Robot sales in 1980 were estimated at $92 million, with a significant share accounted for by imports. The industrial automation market as a whole is growing at well over 20 percent a year, and the robotics portion of it is expected to become a $2-billion-a-year domestic market by 1990.

Beta

Beta Inc. is the leading manufacturer of integrated electrical machinery in the nation of Beta. Run by scientists since its founding, the company is Beta's most research-oriented corporation: it employs over 9,000 researchers, and its R&D spending equals 5.9 percent of corporate sales. Beta Inc. started producing robots only in 1979 but plans within a few years to become the world's largest robot producer. To do so, it must double its manufacturing capacity and strongly push exports (to date, nearly all of its output has been sold at home). The company's deep commitment to robotics is reflected in the recent formation of a 500-man technical task force to develop a universal assembly robot with both visual and tactile sensors. Beta Inc. expects to be using the new robots for some 60 percent of its in-house assembly operations within three years.

Robotics in the Nation of Beta

Beta Inc. is only 1 of 150 companies making or selling robots in Beta, a nation with "robot fever" and a government that has declared automation a national goal. An estimated 12,000 to 14,000 programmable robots are already on the job in the nation, representing 59 percent of those in use worldwide. In 1980, Betan firms churned out nearly $400 million worth of robots (approximately 3,200 units, or 50 percent of world production). The nation exported only 2.5 percent of its production and imported less than 5 percent of its robots. Industry analysts see robot production in Beta rising to $2 billion in 1985 and to $5 billion in 1990. Over the past five months, Alpha Inc. and Beta Inc. have held preliminary negotiations over a possible robot manufacturing and marketing tie-up. The two companies have reached the following tentative agreement:

1. The tie-up over seven years will proceed in two phases: (*a*) in years 1–4, Beta will supply Alpha with fully assembled Beta Inc. robots for sale under Alpha's brand name; (*b*) in years 5–7, Alpha will begin producing these robots themselves in Alpha, using Beta technology and key components.
2. The tie-up will focus on the robots that Beta Inc. currently has on the market.
3. The agreement will be nonexclusive; that is, Beta Inc. will be allowed to enter the Alphan market directly at any time and allowed to tie up with other Alphan firms.

The two companies' negotiation teams are now scheduled to meet for discussion of remaining issues. They include the following:

1. The number of different models involved.
2. The quantity of Beta Inc. units to be imported and/or produced under license by Alpha during each year.
3. The unit price to be paid to Beta.
4. Access to Alpha's vision technology.
5. The royalty rate to be paid to Beta.

Step 4: 30 Minutes

All groups will bring their final agreements (or final offers) back to class. The instructor will share the final agreements with the rest of the class. The exercise will then be discussed and evaluated.

DISCUSSION QUESTIONS

1. How did these negotiations feel? What did they feel like during the negotiations? How do they feel now?
2. What was it like negotiating with the other organization? How was their negotiating style similar to your own? Different?
3. How much did you adapt your negotiating style to match the other side's style? How much did you want to do this?

The New House Negotiation

INTRODUCTION

Many negotiations involve only two parties—a buyer and a seller. However, there are many other negotiations in which the parties are represented by agents. An agent is a person who is paid to negotiate on behalf of the buyer or seller and usually collects some fee or commission based on these services.

The purpose of this negotiation is to gain experience by negotiating through agents. The negotiation simulates the sale and purchase of a piece of real estate, a transaction which is normally conducted through agents. Some of you will play the role of agents; others will play the role of buyers and sellers. This experience should provide a simple but rich context in which to observe the ways that negotiation can very quickly become highly complex.

ADVANCE PREPARATION

None, unless your instructor assigns you to read and prepare your role in advance.

PROCEDURE

Step 1: 20 Minutes

Parties will be assigned one of four roles: seller of house, buyer of house, seller's agent, and buyer's agent. Observers may also be assigned to watch each foursome as they negotiate.

Each group of negotiators—parties, their agents, and an observer—will have a separate negotiation territory and operate on their own. Several groups may be operating in the classroom simultaneously.

If prior preparation has not occurred, each party should take 20 minutes to read and prepare roles. Your instructor will provide this information. Also study the following information, which is available to all sides.

The House. The house is a three-bedroom, two-bath, one-story. It was listed in the local real estate multiple listings service two weeks ago at $140,000. The house has the following features:

This simulation was developed by Conrad Jackson, College of Administrative Science, the University of Alabama at Huntsville. Adapted and used with permission.

- 2,100 square feet.
- Six years old (one owner prior to current owner).
- Two-car garage.
- Contemporary styling (back wall of house is basically all glass, with sliding draperies).
- Half-acre lot (no flooding problems).
- Brick exterior.
- Built-in range, dishwasher, garbage disposal, and microwave.
- Electric cooling and gas heat.
- Fireplace and ceiling fan in the family room.
- No fence.
- Assumable FHA loan.

EXHIBIT 1

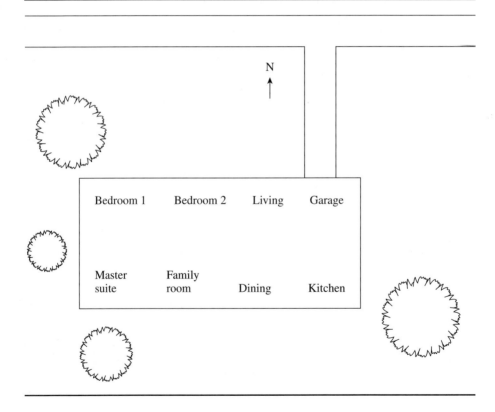

Step 2: 10 Minutes

Seller talks to seller's agent. Buyer talks to buyer's agent.

Step 3: 10 Minutes

Seller's agent and buyer's agent negotiate. Sellers and buyers may observe but not talk to agent.

Step 4: 5 Minutes

Seller confers with seller's agent; buyer confers with buyer's agent.

Step 5: 5 Minutes

Agents negotiate. Parties may observe.

Steps 6 and 7: 15 Minutes

Parties may confer with agents, and agents negotiate, until either a deal is struck or the agents agree that no deal is possible.

If a deal is reached, record exactly what was agreed to in the negotiation. Be prepared to report this to the instructor during class discussion.

DISCUSSION QUESTIONS

1. What goals (target price, opening bid, bottom line, etc.) did the seller(s) and buyer(s) set for themselves in the negotiation? Did they reveal these goals to their agent?
2. How did the meeting with the agents reshape or redefine any of these goals?
3. What did the agents tell each other about their clients' goals?
4. What new strategy and tactics were introduced into the negotiation as a result of using agents?
5. Did the instructor give either side additional information during the role-play? What effect did this additional information have?
6. Did the agents reach agreement ? How easy was it to achieve this agreement?
7. If the agents reached agreement, did their client support the agreement? Why or why not?
8. What are the advantages and disadvantages of negotiating through an agent rather than dealing with the opponent directly? Overall, does having an agent make the negotiation easier or more difficult? Why?

Eurotechnologies, Inc.

INTRODUCTION

This role-play brings three additional new features to your negotiating experience. First, the context of this negotiation is *inside* an organization. In this scenario, you will be asked to represent one of two groups: a management team or a group of scientists who are protesting against a major management decision. Second, this simulation is considerably less "structured" than others, in that there is a great deal more flexibility and opportunity for creative solutions. Finally the negotiation occurs in an international context, which may provide a new experience for many of you. We hope you find this simulation an interesting negotiating opportunity.

ADVANCE PREPARATION

Follow the instructor's requirements. You may be required to read the common background information below. You may also be required to read your own group's role information, which will be given to you by your instructor.

PROCEDURE

Step 1: 10 Minutes

This is a group negotiation. Your instructor will divide you into teams of two or three per side. Each team will be assigned to one of two roles: the management team of Eurotechnologies, Inc., or the scientist group.

If you have not already done so, you should read the common background information that begins below. You should then read the confidential information for either management or scientists, as assigned by your instructor.

EUROTECHNOLOGIES, INC. GENERAL INFORMATION

Eurotechnologies, Inc. (ETI), is a Munich-area firm that employs about 900 people. It is a high-technology division of Mentor, whose corporate offices are in Paris. ETI's primary product is an elaborate bioelectronic detection system developed and

---

This role-play was developed by Robert Reinheimer, adapted from a scenario developed by Robert Reinheimer and Roy Lewicki. Used with permission. The case and role-play have been prepared as a basis for class discussion rather than to illustrate either effective or ineffective handling of an administrative situation.

manufactured under contract with a consortium of European governments. This system is used for detecting various types of life forms through radarlike procedures. Because of the highly classified nature of the manufacturing process and the need for manufacturing to occur in a relatively pollution-free environment, ETI has chosen to separate its manufacturing facilities from its main offices.

The manufacturing facilities are located in a remote are near Wasserburg, approximately 40 miles from downtown Munich. ETI has purchased several hundred acres of land that provide the adequate security and air quality for manufacturing and full-scale test operations. While it is a picturesque area far away from the congestion of the Munich area, it is not without its faults. Access to the plant requires travel over 16 kilometers (km) of poor county-owned road; manufacturing employees constantly complain of worn brakes, tire wear, and strain on their cars. The road is often rain-slicked, muddy, and treacherous in the winter. Most of the 630 workers (450 hourly, 150 staff, and 30 R&D personnel) employed in this plant commute from a radius of 40–60 km over this road into the plant; traffic congestion, particularly around the times of shift changes, makes travel and access a highly undesirable aspect of working for this plant.

The manufacturing facility itself is not air-conditioned and, hence, frequently hot in the summer and stuffy in the winter. The closest town, Wasserburg, is 16 km away. The Wasserburg plant has a cafeteria, but the food is cooked elsewhere and reheated at the plant. The menu is limited and expensive.

There are two groups of support personnel at Wasserburg. One group (of approximately 110 employees) is directly connected with the manufacturing operations as supervisors, shipping and receiving, plant operation and maintenance, stock and inventory, clerical, and so on. The remainder (30 employees) are professional engineers who are responsible for providing technical support and quality maintenance for manufacturing. Facilities for this support staff are somewhat better than for hourly employees; office space and lighting are adequate and the building is air-conditioned. There is no separate cafeteria, and no place to entertain visitors; staff alternate between bringing their lunches, occasionally purchasing the cafeteria food and taking it back to their offices to eat, or carpooling for the 20-minute drive down to Wasserburg. Dissatisfaction and low morale are rampant among the professional staff.

The Downtown Location

The executive staff offices, the U.S. government liaison offices, and the research and development laboratory are located in suburban Munich, just north of the city. Also, there are test facilities on a one-tenth scale for ongoing research and development programs. All administrative services are conducted from here: employment, payroll, security, data processing and system analysis, and research engineering and design. The buildings are spacious, clean and air-conditioned, and boast two cafeterias: one for hourly workers and one for research personnel and executive officers. Employees can also go out for lunch, and many good restaurants are nearby. Working hours are more flexible, and the environment more relaxed with less visible pressure. While the normal starting time is 8:00 AM, professional staff drift in as late as 9:30 and often leave early in the afternoon; working at home is frequent. On the other hand, when deadlines or schedules have to be met, it is not unusual to find them working 60 hours a week. The work environment is more informal and displays a casualness similar to a university setting.

As the majority of the Munich-based employees are professional people, they consider themselves a cut above the manufacturing and technical service employees at Wasserburg. While they will acknowledge the value of the revenue generated by Wasserburg, they are convinced that it is really the Munich area group that carries the company. Without their high-level technical advances, ETI would not have the outside reputation it has for premium-quality products. Inside ETI, however, the rivalries between various engineering and scientific personnel had led to the creation of domains or kingdoms. The primary split is between Wasserburg and Munich, and over the years it has fostered extensive duplication of efforts. Each group (testing, maintenance, etc.) has been able to procure tools and equipment for itself that normally would be shared if the two locations were closer. The Munich Technical divisions have even subcontracted certain testing and development operations to suppliers who are competitors of ETI, due to their basic lack of respect for in-house capabilities at Wasserburg and due to the red tape and expense of having to work through their own planning and scheduling staffs. Additionally, the Munich R&D group has taken consulting contracts from other firms and has consistently failed to involve any Wasserburg personnel in those projects.

The Contract Bidding History

In recent years, ETI has put out numerous competitive bids for civilian and military contracts, but few projects have been forthcoming. Analysis of failures revealed that rejections have been due to excessive cost estimates rather than weak technical capabilities. ETI is considered to be one of the top 10 "quality-based" manufacturing firms of its kind in the country. However, the company's overhead costs are prohibitive. The cost of operating two sites, duplication of effort, overstaffing, and a blurring of goals for corporate growth and expansion have caused the overhead rate to be three times higher than that of competitors. For example, the air force had recently issued a request for bids on the development of a new bioelectronic system, similar to ETI's current product. The development contract alone was worth $15 million, and production of these units would be worth $90 million. ETI representatives were positive they would get the contract. When the government evaluated the bids from five different companies, however, ETI came in first in the technical aspect of the bidding and fifth in the cost aspect; the company did not get the contract.

The Alternatives

Top management's reaction to this setback was to propose a 20 percent cost reduction plan. Many high-salaried technical and engineering personnel were destined to be laid off. The housecleaning was overdue; some "deadwood" and duplication of effort was eliminated. But after six months, it became a hard, cold fact that further reductions in overhead costs would be necessary in order to continue to be competitive.

ETI owned the Munich-area facility, and top management believed the most obvious way to achieve the proposed reduction was to close it, move all of the Munich-area employees to the Wasserburg facility, and to lease out the vacated buildings. The leases would be excellent tax shelters and an additional source of revenue. This consolidation was expected to reduce much of the duplication of effort, as well as provide better coordination on existing and future projects.

In thinking through how the proposed move might be accomplished, they considered features designed to make it as palatable as possible. First, they proposed to spread the relocations over one full year. Each employee could either accept the move or reject it and accept termination from the company. ETI would go as far as possible with those employees who rejected the relocation. They would offer a liberal time-off policy to those involved so the employee could seek other employment, would provide a special bonus of one month's salary for relocation expenses, would notify other companies in the Munich area of the names and résumés of terminating employees, and set up employment interviews with these companies. They also would notify all placement agencies in the area and pay all placement agency fees.

It was clear to management that even with the generous plan they had outlined, the move would be hugely painful for the organization and would represent some very real costs in terms of overall effectiveness. Yet they saw no alternative but to proceed with studying the proposed consolidation.

When the details of the proposal leaked, the plan was met with a massive reaction of hostility and despair. Almost all the Munich-area professional employees felt that a transfer to Wasserburg would mean a sharp decline in status with their peers in similar industries. Most had their homes close to Munich, and the drive to Wasserburg would increase their commuting time and cause wear and tear on their automobiles. The company thus knew that a certain percentage of employees would terminate because of the relocation. It estimated that a "safe level" of termination was 22%; if it reached 35% in any occupational group, it could be considered a critical problem. Management informally surveyed employees and found that among the administrative staff, the termination rate was likely to be near 25%.

The strongest reaction came from the company's research and development staff. They had grown used to having their laboratory and test facilities in the Munich area and drew heavily on informal relationships with faculty at the area's most prestigious universities for ideas and information. Their view was that being forced to move to Wasserburg, in addition to being undesirable, would cripple their ability to function effectively because of their loss of contact with other professionals. Of the 11 members of the research and development staff, only two expressed a willingness to consider the move to Wasserburg. The others claimed they would avail themselves of the many other employment opportunities their specialties commanded. They formally expressed their resistance in a letter to the company president (Exhibit 1).

The letter was written by a committee of R&D personnel formed to represent the group's interests regarding the proposed move. In the letter, they outlined their concerns and volunteered to take 20 percent salary cuts to contribute to the reduction of

EXHIBIT 1

P. Jensen, President
Eurotechnologies, Inc.
300 Reinstrasse
Munich, Germany

Dear Mr. Jensen:

Our committee, representing your research and development personnel, wishes to express its serious concern about the recent events which have affected our company. We believe that ETI's survival depends on our retaining our technical excellence, and we are dismayed that you and your management team seem to be contemplating actions which would cripple that capability.

We have all been shocked by our recent loss of contracts. However, it is critical for you to note that we have never been faulted for our technical expertise. It is our cost structure that prevents us from winning these bids. But an action which addresses the cost problem while destroying our ability to compete technically simply trades one problem for a more disastrous one. Closing the Munich facility and consolidating operations at Wasserburg creates just such a trade, and that is unacceptable.

Although no formal announcement of management's response to the current situation has been provided, it is clear that consolidation is in the wind. We believe that forcing R&D to move to the Wasserburg location will ruin the professional network that is our (and the company's) most treasured asset. Some alternative must be found and, if it is not, the members of our department will seek individual solutions to their personal dilemmas.

It is time that management emerges from behind closed doors and asks vital members of the company team to become involved in this decision. If management intends to launch this consolidation effort, we believe it will have disastrous results and that it is unlikely that research and development personnel will remain with the company.

Our interest is in the company's survival. If it is necessary, the members of the committee would be willing to agree to a 20 percent salary reduction in return for being able to remain in the Munich-area network. We request an opportunity to speak with management about this vital decision which massively affects all of us.

Sincerely,

(signed by all members of the committee)

---

overhead costs. This reduction would total approximately DM 366,750. The committee members consisted of the following six employees:

- J. O'Hara, age 52. Oldest member of the group, but only one year at ETI. Previously worked with several enviromental engineering firms in the Munich area. Moved to ETI because of the quality of the other people in the research group and because of interest in the projects that were being considered.

- H. Loew, age 49. Most senior member of the ETI group (24 years), and a likely candidate to be the next vice president of research and development. Loew has always lived in Munich, and currently lives a block away from P. Jensen, the president.

- L. Berkowitz, age 42. Fifteen years with ETI, and the most "professionally aggressive" of the group. Most active in research with high professional visibility.

- A. Sharfstein, age 47. Twenty-two years with ETI. Also very professionally active, second to Berkowitz. Sharfstein has spent a number of years developing professional contacts in the Munich area, and has been the most articulate in defending the richness of the professional stimulation to be derived from the area.

- F. Jones, age 36. Five years with ETI. Worked for two years at Wasserburg before being assigned to the Munich group. A definite "up and comer" in this group.

- T. Black, age 32. Four years with ETI. Strong research orientation, a close collaborator with Berkowitz on several professional papers. Berkowitz also served as a mentor to Black while Black was completing a PhD at Munich University.

After reading the statement sent by the committee, the president of ETI, P. Jensen, conferred with the vice president for research and development (and the immediate superior of the scientists), and the vice president for human resources. The three discussed the statement that they had received, and agreed that the situation was serious. It was clear that the Wasserburg move created unforeseen legitimate problems for the vital R&D personnel and that management had erred in not seeking wider input in considering their cost reduction alternatives.

The management team debated the alternatives. They understood the frustrations of the research and development staff but were faced with having to cut almost DM 13,000,000 from annual costs in order for ETI to remain competitive. Consolidation still seemed the obvious answer, but the problems were mounting with this employee disclosure.

Jensen wrote a letter to the committee acknowledging their concerns and inviting the members of that group to come to a meeting with the president, the vice president of research and development, the vice president of human resources, and other senior company officials. Jensen was careful to make no commitments or promises in the letter; simply, the scientists were invited to come to a meeting (Exhibit 2).

Step 2 (Optional, May Be Done in Advance): 45–60 Minutes

If you have been assigned an individual role within your group, read your individual role information. Each management or scientist team should meet and plan their negotiation strategy.

Step 3: 90–120 Minutes

Teams meet to negotiate. Either team may call a caucus as necessary. If a deal is reached, record exactly what was agreed to in the negotiation. Be prepared to report this to the instructor during class discussion.

EXHIBIT 2

(addressed to all committee members)
Research and Development
Eurotechnologies, Inc.
300 Reinstrasse
Munich, Germany

Dear (names):

I have given my most serious consideration to the points you raised in your recent letter. We share your interest in doing what is best for ETI and welcome your interest in contributing to that goal.

It is clear that our technical expertise is one of our greatest assets and that your work in research and development is a vital contributor to that expertise. We have no wish to reduce our technical competitiveness. Nevertheless, our failure to produce cost-competitive contract bids is a problem which requires a painful solution, and we have only 18 months to produce an effective response.

We acknowledge that we have begun to examine the consolidation of our operations at the Wasserburg facility. Such a consolidation would reduce duplication of facilities, equipment, and personnel, and these reductions would contribute significantly to an overall cost saving. Page 2 of this letter is an exhibit of the cost savings we believe would result from such a move.

At the same time, we believe that this action would be unwise if it truly has the crippling effect on your effectiveness that you forecast. Our dilemma, as the management team for ETI, is to address the need for major, fast cost reduction while providing for the continuation of our technical excellence. We also believe that any proposal must be fair to the many employees who are a part of the Eurotechnologies family.

In response to your letter, I have ordered that further evaluation of the Wasserburg alternative be halted for the time being. I ask that your committee send some of its members to a meeting with myself and members of the management team to discuss the situation as it has evolved. We share an interest in ETI's survival if we can develop a plan that is mutually acceptable in achieving that goal. I look forward to meeting with you.

Sincerely,

(Signed, P. Jensen)

Step 4: Debriefing–60 Minutes (More if You Have More Than 4–5 Groups)

DISCUSSION QUESTIONS

1. What goals did management or the scientists set for themselves in the negotiation? What goals were actually achieved?

ETI Expense Statement (In Thousands of Deutschemarks)

Overhead	Wasserburg Separately	Munich Separately	Total Separately	Consolidated Facility
Manufacturing	36,071			36,071
Administration	5,325	10,812		12,103
R&D	965	8,685		9,063
Total	42,361	19,497	61,858	57,237
R&D expenses				
Utilities	163	408		245
Computer Lease		2,038		2,038
Supplies	425	897		983
Consulting		1,498		1,345
Total	588	4,841	5,429	4,611
Salaries and Benefits				
Professional	3,260	7,376		7,977
Benefits	489	685		880
Hourly	22,460	609		20,762
Benefits	1,627	61		2,655
Relocation				476
Total	27,836	8,731	36,567	32,750
Facilities				
Debt service	1,630	3,260		1,630
Insurance/maintenance/taxes	815	1,141		815
Total	2,445	4,401	6,846	2,445
Grand total: current versus consolidated	73,230	37,470	110,700	97,043

2. Did group members play individual roles—that is, did particular managers or scientists also try to play an indivdual character or pursue an individualistic strategy? Did this make the negotiation simpler or more difficult to resolve? Why?

3. What were the interests of each side? How could these interests be met in a joint solution?

4. What creative options were explored? Which ones were finally accepted?

5. How good was your solution to the problem? Is it practical? Easy to implement? Costly? Will it really help the company in reducing its overhead rates?

6. What would be the consequences if one or both sides pursued a distributive strategy in this negotiation?

7. After your negotiation, how would you describe the quality of the relationship between management and the scientists? Will you be able to work together effectively in the future? Why or why not?

8. How did the international aspects of this scenario change the negotiation process, the dynamics, and so on?

The Pakistani Prunes

INTRODUCTION

In many work settings it is not possible for people to work independently as they pursue their work goals. Often we find ourselves in situations where we must obtain the cooperation of other people, even though the other people's ultimate objectives may be different from our own. Getting things done in organizations requires us to work together in cooperation, even though your ultimate objective may be only to satisfy your own needs. Your task in this exercise is to learn how to work together more productively with others.

ADVANCE PREPARATION

None.

PROCEDURE

OPTION ONE

Step 1: 5 Minutes

Form the class in pairs. One person will play the role of Dr. Rubio Sanchez, and one will play Dr. Kim Wilson. Roles will be distributed by the instructor.

Step 2: 10 Minutes, Negotiation

At this point the group leader will read the following statement: "I am Mr. Cardoza, the owner of the remaining Pakistani Prunes. My fruit-exporting firm is based in the Middle East. My country does not have diplomatic relations with your country, although we do have stong trade relations."

The instructor will then tell you

- How long you have to meet with the other.

- What information the instructor will require from each pair at the end of your meeting.

Adapted by Roy J. Lewicki and John Minton.

You may then meet with the other person and determine whether you have issues you can agree to.

Step 3: 15 Minutes

Following the negotiation, each pair should report on the solution reached in each group and the process by which it was reached.

DISCUSSION QUESTIONS

1. Did you reach a solution? If so, what things were critical to reaching that solution?
2. Did you and the other negotiator trust one another? Why or why not?
3. Was there full disclosure by both sides in each group? How much information was shared?
4. How creative and/or complex were the solutions? If solutions were very complex, why do you think this occurred?

Planning for Negotiations

INTRODUCTION

This exercise asks you to focus on a real negotiation that will occur in your life within the next several weeks or months. In this exercise, your objective is to plan for that negotiation, and perhaps to share and discuss those plans with several other people. The sharing of information in groups illustrates the broad range of negotiations in which we engage. Presenting the plans to a small group, and then to the larger class, may help people shape and refine their plans. The posted results will illustrate the structure and direction a logical planning process can bring to any negotiation.

ADVANCE PREPARATION

None, unless the instructor directs you to accomplish Steps 1 or 2 (below) prior to class.

PROCEDURE

Step 1: 5 Minutes

The instructor will assign you to groups of four or five.

Step 2: 40 Minutes

Each person in the group will explain briefly an actual, personal negotiation he or she is facing within the next few weeks or months. After hearing all the individual examples, each group will pick the one they feel to be most interesting, instructive, and/or demanding; the "owner" of that negotiation will become the group's "client." Drawing on any readings, assignments, observations, and experiences the class has done or accomplished in the course thus far, each group must develop a plan for its client. The instructor may (or may not) provide a planning guide. In the report to your group or class, you should cover (but not necessarily be limited to) the following aspects, as appropriate:

Exercise developed by John W. Minton.

- Your understanding of the problem—that is, what is to be negotiated.
- Your understanding of the relationship and context—that is, your relationship with the other party, and the context factors that may affect that negotiation.
- Your intended strategies, tactics, and the tone you want to set.
- Your specific options/intentions for entry into the negotiation/initiation of the process.
- Your thinking about different scenarios—what the other might do, and how you would respond.
- Your plans for managing specific issues and parts of the process.
- Your specific options/intentions for reaching closure, completing the negotiation and assuring that they comply and follow through.
- Your desired guarantees, safeguards, assurances, and/or contracts.

One member of each group should record the results of the group's work, and designated to present the plan (see Steps 3 and 4, below).

Step 3: 10 Minutes

The designated presenter from each group will put on the board (or a flipchart page or overhead transparency), in outline form, the pertinent information regarding his or her group's chosen negotiation. Each group will be afforded roughly equal space to do this.

Step 4: 30 Minutes

Presenters will "walk" the class through their negotiation plans, as well as respond to any questions or comments that may arise.

Step 5: 30 Minutes

The instructor will lead the class through a debriefing after the exercise, and present summary points and observations.

Sanibel Island

INTRODUCTION

In this scenario, you will negotiate a set of environmental management issues. One of you will play the role of an environmental group, while the other will play the role of a land developer. Your objective is to negotiate three issues related to the development of a hotel/resort site on a particular piece of waterfront land.

ADVANCE PREPARATION

Read the Background Information section for Sanibel Island in this exercise; then read the role information that the instuctor has provided. Prepare to play this role. Familiarize yourself with the facts, and prepare to meet with the other party as the instructor will indicate.

Step 1: 15–20 Minutes

Participants will read the common background information and the private role information assigned by the instructor.

COMMON BACKGROUND INFORMATION

SANIBEL ISLAND

Sanibel Island is located off the western coast of central Florida in the Gulf of Mexico. Sanibel is known for its natural beauty and for its shape and position—many shells wash up on its beaches because it is longer east to west than north to south. It is estimated that about 400 different types of shells can be found by the knowledgeable collector. The island is dominated by private residences and is a popular vacation site.

A large portion of Sanibel Island's 11,000 acres is composed of freshwater wetlands, a unique feature in a barrier island. These are of benefit to the residents for many reasons, one of which is as a freshwater source. The island is home to the J. N. "Ding" Darling National Wildlife Refuge, a wetland system that covers 4,700 acres of habitat (about 40 percent of the island) and is home to more than 267 species of birds, including snakebirds,

---

This exercise was developed by Tim Poland, Craig Davis, and Roy J. Lewicki of the Ohio State University for classroom and research use.

egrets, and numerous species of ducks, and many plant species, including the epiphyte and the mangrove. The mangrove is of particular interest to the wetlands because it begins a food chain—its leaves and roots in the water create a habitat for microorganisms that get eaten by animals higher on the food chain, leading all the way up to shrimp and water-fowl. The roots of the mangrove are also partially responsible for binding up the shore.

Due to the popularity of the island as a vacation site, a causeway was built from the mainland, allowing cars direct access to the island for the first time. Although tourism is the island's main source of income, residents began to have many concerns about the effects of development and tourism on the island. Many residents rely on the waters for commercial catching of fish and scallops and were afraid of interference from increased population and traffic.

Tourists enjoy walking along the beach. Some collect the shells. This island's beaches are typical of many coastal areas in that there are cyclical periods of erosion and creation. In other words, the boundaries of the island are constantly in a state of flux—what was once dry land is now beach, and what were once coastal areas may become dry land.

Development of homes and hotels was also of concern to Sanibel's residents. In an effort to maintain Sanibel's aesthetics, a limit on building height was established. Other restrictions may include those requiring stilts and/or open first floors. This is more for safety than for any other reason. When the tide gets too high during a storm, the water can go right under the building without any hindrance, and the buildings remain intact.

The focus of this role-play will be the proposed development of a piece of Sanibel Island waterfront property into a hotel and beachfront recreation complex. The discussions will take place between the developer who wants to develop this property, and representatives of an environmental group who are concerned about environmental preservation. Additional information will be provided in your private role briefing information. You should also refer to two maps: a map of the undeveloped property (Exhibit 1) and a map of the developed property as proposed by the developer (Exhibit 2).

In an effort to protect wetlands, state and federal laws have been enacted that must be followed by land developers. Simply put, these laws require "no net loss" of wetlands. Ideally, this means no loss of existing wetlands; failing that, if any wetlands are lost through development, they must be recreated elsewhere.

Local enforcement of these wetland regulations is difficult. First, a commonly accepted definition of wetland has not yet been formulated. Basically, a wetland is any type of transitional area between dry land and open water, such as swamps, bogs, fens, and marshes. This leaves broad leeway for interpretation; in fact, many wetlands are not even "wet" during certain seasons. Second, because local regulations are more strict than state and federal wetland regulations, environmental conflicts are often played out at different political levels.

The current focus of attention is a proposed hotel development on Sanibel Island (see maps) and its possible environmental consequences. A developer has purchased a beachfront property and intends to create a resort, which includes a multistoried hotel building and a nature preserve.

In order to build this resort, the builder must apply for a permit from the U.S. Army Corps of Engineers. It is the task of the Corps to ensure compliance with existing

EXHIBIT 1

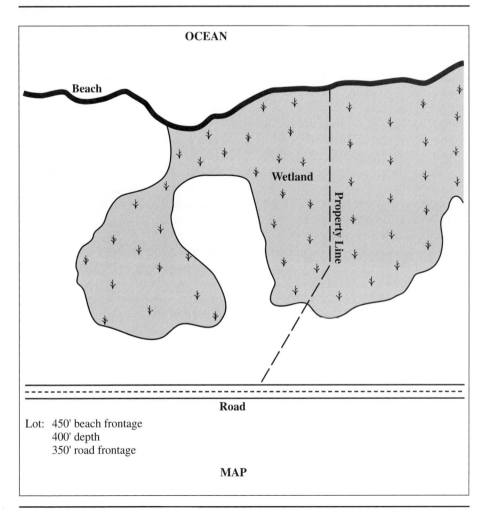

Lot: 450' beach frontage
      400' depth
      350' road frontage

MAP

laws, and to provide a forum in which interested parties can voice their concerns. Therefore, they have suggested bringing together the developers and environmentalists to negotiate the issues surrounding this development. The Corps hopes that this process will set a precedent that will balance the conservation of natural resources against further development on the island.

Step 2: 30–45 Minutes

Pairs of negotiators will meet together to negotiate an agreement about the three major environmental issues. You are not required to agree if you do not feel that the solution meets your needs. If no agreement is reached, then each person should make a record of his or her final rankings and where he or she is willing to make further concessions.

EXHIBIT 2

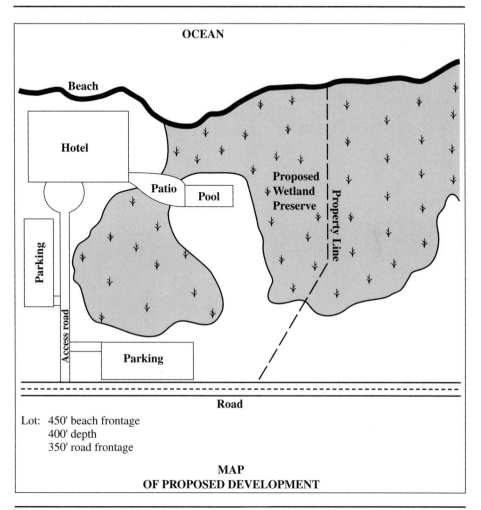

**MAP
OF PROPOSED DEVELOPMENT**

Lot: 450' beach frontage
        400' depth
        350' road frontage

DISCUSSION QUESTIONS

1. How did you prepare for this role-play? What type of strategy did you decide to employ?

2. Did you set goals or targets that you wanted to achieve on each issue or on the total package? Did you set bottom lines or walkaway points? How did having these (or not having these) affect your own negotiation effectiveness?

3. Were you presented with a specific viewpoint or perspective on the other party? How did this affect the way that you approached the negotiation? How did it affect the outcome?

4. Were you presented with a specific viewpoint or perspective on the issues? How did this affect the way that you approached the negotiation? How did it affect the outcome?

5. If you were presented with a specific viewpoint or perspective on either the issues or the other party, what did you learn about the influence of this "bias" on how parties approach disputes and the type of resolution strategies they prefer?

6. How satisfied are you with the final agreement (if you reached one)? What factors in your negotiation contributed most to your level of satisfaction?

EXERCISE 23

The Playground Negotiation

INTRODUCTION

This is a true-to-life case. Two elected local officials, one elected on a community involvement plank (herein referred to as the community volunteer representative) and the other elected because of a commitment to support the Parks Department (hereafter referred to as the Parks Department representative) comprise the Ithaca Special Projects Task Force. They have been charged with deciding whether to fund a playground for the community and, if so, how much of the city's limited special project funds they should spend. Other projects requesting funding will be presented to them later in the year. Both representatives share the common goal of bettering the community. However, the issue is complicated by a variety of potential intergroup conflicts that can threaten their position as elected officials, and that could jeopardize the harmony of the community that they are trying to help. Moreover, both representatives are aware that they, as well as their constituents, may have interests in both community volunteerism as well as in the well-being of the Parks Department; for example, Parks Department employees may also be community volunteers after work.

ADVANCE PREPARATION

Advance preparation will be announced by your instructor. You may be asked to read the Background Information in advance, and prepare for one of several roles in this case scenario.

BACKGROUND INFORMATION

You were elected as (either Parks Department representative or community volunteer representative) to the city council, a position in the local Ithaca government. Recently, you were appointed to the Ithaca Special Projects Task Force (ISPTF). This committee makes recommendations to the full council for funding special projects that will benefit the Ithaca community. The council then provides one-time funding for special projects that are not included in the budgets for any other department. ISPTF does not guarantee ongoing support for the projects it funds; thus, most projects are those that can be completed within one fiscal year.

Adapted from an exercise written by Jennifer J. Halpern and Dera L. Connelley and published in the *International Journal of Conflict Management*, 7, 3 (1996), pp. 247–74. Used with permission of the authors and publisher.

Each year the council considers three proposals. These proposals never arrive at the same time and are therefore considered independently from each other. The budget for ISPTF is fixed, and members of the task force must seriously consider the merits of each project as it is presented. Later projects may be more worthy of funding than the current project under consideration; alternatively, the current project may be more promising than either or both of the two later projects, but the ISPTF can't possibly know this at the time of its decision.

Your Task

You and your task force partner are to consider a proposal for an expanded playground at Titus Flats. This playground will require ISPTF funds, some Parks Department sponsorship (including human resources), and volunteer effort. Titus Flats is a low- to middle-income area across a four-lane street from the enormous Tops Supermarket at the southwest corner of Ithaca. Titus Flats is inland and on the opposite shore of the middle-income Inlet development and recreation area. Currently, Titus Flats is a recreation area with four softball fields, an outdoor basketball court, and a very small playground for children containing a tiny wooden climbing structure, a slide, and a tire swing.

The neighborhood around Titus Flats is home to a culturally diverse population. Across the street from the recreation area is a large public housing facility, Landmark Square. Its residents include welfare families with children and teenagers. These families have often borne the brunt of malicious stereotyping based on their socioeconomic status and their race, predominantly African American. They would prefer not to be seen as a source of trouble. At the same time, they do not wish to see their interests and needs ignored.

Adjacent to the park is a senior citizens' housing facility, Titus Towers. The residents here are functioning members of the community, doing their shopping and socializing in the neighborhood. Because of the proximity of the "Flats" to the "Towers," residents have come to view the area as an extension of their own grounds.

The surrounding neighborhood is low- to moderate-income single-family housing. These property owners pay more taxes than any of the other members of the neighborhood and expect to have a voice in how their neighborhood is managed. They are concerned about their liability for children playing in the streets and sidewalks in front of their homes, since Ithaca laws state that sidewalks in front of private homes are the owners' responsibility, and many children live in the area.

The different members of the community all make use of the existing park. The children of Landmark Square and the single-family property owners use the small playground. In addition, seniors from the Towers occcasionally bring visiting grandchildren to play. The playground gets overcrowded during peak after-school and weekend hours, and as a result, young children can often be found playing in the street. Although there has not yet been an automobile accident causing serious injury to a child, parents and City Council members are concerned about the possibility of such a tragedy in the future.

While there is support for a safe place for children to play, all parties are concerned that a larger playground could become a magnet for teenage gang activity and drug dealers. Some parents have already indicated that they keep their children away from the playground because of the "tough" teens on the basketball court. The Landmark Square teenagers and young adults use the basketball court heavily. It is rare when a game is not in progress.

Finally, impromptu ball games are sometimes organized by the residents at Landmark Square, but the fields are mainly used by citywide softball leagues and thus are unavailable throughout the season. In addition, many residents of Titus Towers complain that the playground is already too noisy and the basketball games are raucous and profane, and the residents say that they cannot enjoy sitting quietly on the benches that were provided for such use.

The Parks Department claims that it does not have enough money to build a new playground in an area where one already exists and that there are more pressing needs for its shrinking funds.

Ithaca is a town (some like to call it a small city) of about 30,000 year-round inhabitants. Students from the several colleges in the area almost double Ithaca's size during the school term, but very few of them choose to make Titus Flats their home. Ithaca also has several wealthy neighborhoods, two neighborhoods surrounding its largest colleges, and a downtown shopping are called The Commons that attracts tourists and well-to-do consumers. Each neighborhood has at least one children's playground. Two of these were built almost entirely by community volunteers, as was the Ithaca Science Center. The Commons also has a graceful wooden structure for children to play on while their parents shop or work downtown.

INSTRUCTIONS FOR EVERYONE

Playground Options

There are two options for building a playground and three options for a ground cover. These options can be implemented in a variety of ways, with costs depending on the particular elements chosen. Each option has advantages and drawbacks. You are to consider these options and negotiate with your task force partner in determining a recommendation for the City Council.

Keep in mind that you and your task force partner do not have vested interests in the options or alternatives you read about in the proposals. Also keep in mind that this playground is just one of three proposals that the city will ask you to consider funding during the year. The two representatives share a common goal: the betterment of community life in Ithaca through the wise and efficient use of ISPTF funds.

Goals

Your roles are intentionally vague. It is important for you to put yourself in the shoes of this task force member, to be creative and responsive as if you were actually in this situation. Experience has shown that role-players with detailed guidelines pay too much attention to what they should do rather than to what they could do.

The ISPTF is empowered to make recommendations about the funding of this playground only. It does not have the power to levy or even to depend on fines, fees, taxes, or large donations.

Budget Considerations

The budget for all three special projects for this year is $63,750. The first of the three projects to be proposed this year is a playground. You may choose to recommend that the City Council spend the entire $63,750 on this one playground project; not fund a playground at all; or recommend any other amount be granted, below, equal to, or above the amount requested.

Remember that the council considers three special projects a year, although at the present time you know nothing about the nature of the other two later proposals. These other projects may be more or less deserving of funding than this project. You cannot know for sure.

Money that is not used this year is returned to Ithaca's general budget and is not added to the ISPTF's budget the following year. In fact, moneys not used may be seen as superfluous, and may cause ISPTF to receive less money the next year.

You and your task force partner must make the best decision you can within these limitations, keeping in mind your responsibility to the public trust, the merits of this particular proposal, the limits of the special projects budget, and the unknown concerning other projects that will be proposed later this year. Over the past two years, the council funded special projects as follows:

Special Projects (Two Years Ago)

Project Title	Amount Requested	Amount Granted
Inlet exercise path	$31,675	$24,900
Lighting Improvements, The Commons	$59,100	$42,850
Seed money, Science Center	$10,000	$ 9,450
Total budget for the year		$77,200

Special Projects (Last Year)

Project Title	Amount Requested	Amount Granted
The Commons renovation	$68,976	$57,145
Landscaping, Stewart Park	$10,000	$14,300
Bike lanes, State Street	$26,800	0
Total budget for the year		$71,445

Descriptions of Past Projects

See Figure 1 for a map of Ithaca, highlighting the locations of past projects.

Inlet Exercise Path. The inlet area of Ithaca is a lovely greenway that sits astride a channel leading from Six Mile Creek to Lake Cayuga. It is home to two college crew teams, a community theater, a pool and skating rink, tennis courts, ball

FIGURE 1   Map of Ithaca, New York, Highlighting Areas Improved by the ISPTF

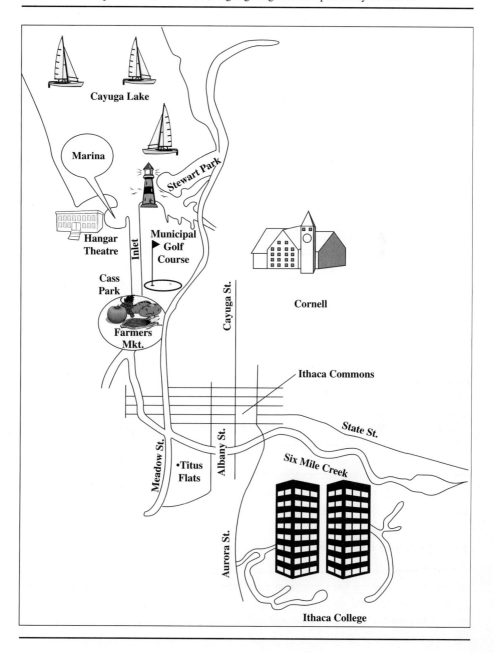

fields and picnic areas, a marina, and a covered outdoor market. The ISPTF provided funds for a cardiovascular exercise course that can also be used for bicycling, running, walking, and roller or in-line skating. It is open to everyone, without charge. It is most easily accessible by automobile.

Lighting Improvements and Renovations, Ithaca Commons. The Commons is an outdoor, downtown pedestrian mall featuring upscale boutiques, specialty shops, restaurants, and bars. When business proprietors suggested that customers would stay away in the evenings because of concerns about safety, the city installed new lights on the mall through ISPTF funding. The next year the ISPTF also made available funds to renovate a play structure for children, repair benches and other seating, and commission a public work of art.

Seed Money, Science Center. The Science Center is a highly visible organization in the Ithaca community that enjoys widespread support. After years of temporary quarters and mobile exhibits (including a regular one at a nearby covered market), the Science Center built a permanent home with seed money provided by the ISPTF. Located on the outskirts of a moderate-income area of private homes and small businesses, the building was erected with volunteer labor over several weekends.

Landscaping, Stewart Park. Stewart Park is a large park at the south end of Cayuga Lake, adjacent to the municipal golf course. Although the park is owned by the city, it is utilized by a regional population. The park is also home to part of the Ithaca Festival, a summer celebration of music and the arts that draws several thousand people every year. ISPTF funding helped with planting bushes and renovating flower beds, as well as reworking fences and decks around the ponds and pavilions.

State Street Bike Lanes. This project was not funded. The proposal called for bike lanes along a treacherous bus and automobile artery from Cornell University through a commercial district to the inlet exercise path. The proposal would have eliminated parking along the route, which is bordered by low-rent student apartments, inexpensive restaurants and bars, used furniture stores, and other businesses that make heavy use of on-street parking.

TITUS FLATS PLAYGROUND PROPOSAL

The proposal is summarized below. The parties proposing the playground have presented two options for equipment and three for ground covers. These options can be mixed and matched, and are presented as guidelines so that task force members will know what can be done at different levels of funding. See Figure 2 for a map of the existing park and playground.

Equipment

Option One. Price range: $40,360–$46,100. A ready-to-assemble metal-and-vinyl playground can be purchased from a supplier in Illinois. The unit is manufac-

FIGURE 2   Map of Titus Flats Park

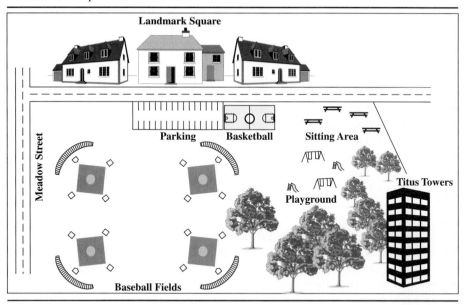

tured in Korea and imported to the United States. Assembly would be accomplished easily by Ithaca Parks personnel. This unit is estimated to last for 15 years, and maintenance would include paint touch-ups to prevent rust corrosion and replacement of vinyl parts after 7 years. Cost of replacement is estimated to be approximately $5,000–$6,500 (above the original purchase price), although it is difficult to foresee the effects of changes in inflation and exchange rates, oil prices (affecting the cost of the vinyl), and so on. At the present time, Ithaca has no playgrounds constructed of similar materials, although many other cities the size of Ithaca use these units extensively. There is some concern that these metal units are not as attractive as the wooden units used throughout the town, and one city council member has stated his opposition to erecting structures which are not in "harmony" with the other parks.

The cost of the structure ranges with size. The low estimate calls for one slide, one play platform, six swings, monkey bars, a fire fighter's pole, and an elevated crawl-through tunnel. The high estimate calls for two regular slides, one twisting slide, 10 swings, four platforms, monkey bars, a jungle gym, two elevated tunnels, a fire fighter's pole, and a climbing rope. Units of intermediate size can be ordered by omitting different parts.

Option Two. Price range: $34,600–$39,800. A custom-designed wood structure can be built on the spot. The plans would be drawn up by a local contractor who has designed and built several playground facilities in the city. Substantial savings could be achieved by using donated community labor. Even so, skilled carpenters would have to be hired and much of the materials purchased. Similar community efforts have been successful in renovating the playground at Belle Sherman School and building a new facility at Southside Community Center. However, each of those projects had a constituent community with a strong interest in contributing their time and efforts not only to construction activities, but also in providing food, child care for the workers, and a considerable amount of time in organizing the project and procuring labor and donated materials. You are not sure that the community surrounding Titus Flats would be as supportive as these other communities. One possibility is that a part-time coordinator may have to be hired for an additional cost of $3,000–$5,000.

Maintenance includes minor structural repair each year, easily accomplished by Parks personnel. Even so, wooden structures usually have nicked and rough boards which can inflict minor abrasions and splinters on the children. Every four to five years, major structural replacement would be required to replace rotting, loose, or broken boards and corroded or loose bolts. This maintenance could not be handled solely by Parks Department employees. Additional personnel from the community would be required for this work, involving periodic organizing of donated labor and resources. Because the extent of wear and tear on the facility cannot be anticipated, the cost of periodic maintenance cannot be estimated. The contractor calculates the life of such a unit, properly maintained, to be 20 years.

The range in cost depends on the size of the unit desired. The low estimate calls for four swings, a tire swing, a "suspension bridge" between two play platforms, a fire fighter's pole, monkey bars, and a small toddler's slide. The high estimate includes six swings, two tire swings, three suspension bridges between four play platforms, a tower with a turret, four seesaws, one toddler's slide, one twister slide, one large slide with three bumps, a balance beam, monkey bars, a climbing wall, and two fire fighter's poles. Units of intermediate size can be ordered by omitting different parts.

Ground Preparation

If you choose to recommend to the ISPTF that a playground should be constructed, you must recommend an appropriate ground cover for the area as well as the type of playground structure. Again there are several options, and you must consider such factors as additional cost, maintenance, and safety.

Option One. Price range: $4,580–$5,150. Pea gravel (small, rounded, smoothed stones) can be used to cover the playground. Advantages to this covering include the following: it is relatively permanent, it requires little maintenance, and it is clean because dirt and debris would sift through the gravel. Many Ithaca playgrounds use this for ground cover. One disadvantage, in addition to its relatively high cost, is that children who fall on it may get abrasions. Other concerns are that small children may swallow it, and it can be dangerous when thrown.

Option Two. Price range: $3,320–$3,700. Sand is a possible ground cover. It provides a soft medium that would reduce injuries if children fall from the structure. Sand also furnishes an additional play medium for children using toy dump trucks, shovels and buckets, and so on. Sand requires more maintenance than gravel, and additional sand would have to be spread each year. It is also not as clean as gravel, and some parents claim that cats and other animals would be attracted to the sand, thereby posing possible health and cleanliness risks.

Option Three. Price range: $850–$925. Following construction of the play structure, the ground could simply be leveled and grass could be planted. Maintenance would be minimal and could be handled by regular Parks maintenance crews. However, heavily trafficked areas would become hard-packed, and no grass would grow in those areas. Hard-packed ground would also yield more extensive injuries if a child should fall from the structure. Because of Ithaca's rainy climate, there is concern that the poor drainage qualities of this ground preparation would frequently reduce the park to a mud pit. This drawback could be dealt with by combining grass with chipped bark or shredded recycled tires in heavy traffic areas. This would result in an added cost of $1,000 initially and yearly replenishment costs. There is also a high probability that loose materials will get spread over grassy areas, creating mowing problems and giving the playground a messy appearance if not meticulously maintained.

PROCEDURE

Step 1: 15–20 Minutes

Read the Background Information and your own individual role information. This may be assigned in advance.

Step 2: 15–30 Minutes

Plan for your negotiation on your own, or with a partner, if you have been assigned one.

Step 3

Option 1: 60 Minutes. You have this time to negotiate a settlement with the other party, but this will be done in a "fishbowl" setting in which the audience may participate as members of various Ithaca community groups. Your final agreement should be written and should include:

a. A funding level (or recommendation not to fund the project).

b. If you decide to fund the playground, a description of which option to fund (including a description of specific equipment, maintenance arrangements, and ground cover).

c. A brief rationale of why you are recommending this particular course of action, including any objections or reservations that have not been resolved.

Please remember the role you have been assigned as you are negotiating. Attempt to reconcile your decision with your interests in making the best use of community volunteers or parks employees.

Option 2: 30 Minutes. You have this time to negotiate a specific agreement with *only* the other party concerning your joint recommendation to the ISPTF. Follow the same guidelines for the agreement as specified in Option 1.

DISCUSSION QUESTIONS

1. What is the overall goal of the ISPTF?

2. How would you describe the relationship between the Parks Department representative and the community volunteer representative?

3. Identify all persons or groups likely to have a stake in the outcome of the negotiation. What are their interests likely to be? Which interests are shared?

4. What decisions do the representatives face?

5. What are the social issues with which the representatives should be concerned in making the decision to fund or not to fund the playground?

6. What are the economic issues with which the representatives should be concerned in making the decision to fund or not fund the playground?

7. What are the political issues with which the representatives should be concerned in making the decision to fund or not to fund the playground?

8. What differences can you find between this low-conflict situation and a high-conflict negotiation?

9. If you did Option 1: What additional challenges are created when you negotiate in front of an audience who may participate and ask questions, and have their own preferences?

Collecting Nos

INTRODUCTION

In all work settings, there comes a time when we need something from someone else. It might be an approval, it might be resources, or it might be some form of assistance. Whatever it might be, it is virtually impossible for us to get our work done without the cooperation of others. And the best way to get what you want from others is to ask them for it. Yet many people would rather do it themselves than ask someone else. One reason people are hesitant to ask for things is because they do not want to get a no.

A similar problem exists in negotiations. On the one hand, inexperienced negotiators often are afraid to ask for what they want or need because they are afraid to get a no. On the other hand those who are asked will frequently *not* say no, in spite of their strong dislike of the request or having to fulfill it. Therefore, many negotiations are incomplete because the requester did not ask for enough, or the respondent actually gave more than they wanted to. Several negotiation experts have argued that negotiation only BEGINS when the other party says no; if you do not get a no, you probably have not asked for enough!

The purpose of this exercise is to give you experience in making requests and dealing with others' objections. Your task in this exercise is to collect nos.

ADVANCE PREPARATION

None. This exercise may be done in class or as homework.

PROCEDURE

Your are to make requests of people (ask them for things) subject to the following ground rules:

1. Requests must be legal.
2. You cannot tell people you are making the request as part of a class assignment.
3. The request is something that the person really could do, even though it might be unreasonable.
4. Each request must be different.
5. A minimum of 10 different people must be asked.

Developed by Professor Jeffrey Ford of the Fisher College of Business, the Ohio State University, for this volume. Used with permission.

PART A

Continue to make requests until you have collected 10 nos. Keep a verbatim written record of *each* request you make, the response you receive to each request, and what meaning or interpretation you gave to the response (what thoughts or feelings you had in reaction to the response). Create the following table:

Request I Made	*Response I Received*	*My Reaction to the Response*
1.		
2.		
3.		
etc.		

PART B

Pick one of the requests for which you received a no and make that same request of the same person a second time. If you receive another no, wait until later and make the same request yet a third time. Write down what the person says each time.

PART C

Pick at least one of the requests for which you received a no and ask the person who said no, "What would have to happen for you to say yes to my request?" Write down what the person says.

DISCUSSION QUESTIONS

PART A

1. How many requests did you have to make to get 10 nos? What does that say about the likelihood of being told no when you ask for something?
2. How many different ways did people tell you no? Did they actually say no, or did they say something else that you understood to mean no? Why do you think people don't actually say the word no? What do you think would happen in organizations if people were really straight about saying no?
3. How did you structure or phrase your requests to make it easier for people to say no? Do you think you "colluded" with people to help them say no? Why did you do that?

PART B

How willing were you to make the same request to someone who had already told you no? Do you consider a no to be forever, or only for the time you asked? What rules or policies do you have about getting and giving a no?

PART C

What did you learn when you asked people "What would have to happen for you to say yes to my request?" Would you be willing to do what they said would be necessary to get a yes?

EXERCISE 25

500 English Sentences

INTRODUCTION

This exercise involves a cross-cultural negotiation where there are several tangible and intangible factors at stake. You will play the role of either a Japanese teacher who is head of the English Department that is responsible for the publication of an English textbook, or an American assistant English teacher who has been asked to work on the book.

ADVANCE PREPARATION

Prior to the class you should read the articles in Section 11 of this text (Global Negotiations) so that you are familiar with some of the complexities of cross-cultural negotiations.

PROCEDURE

Step 1: 5 Minutes

You will be assigned to play the role of either the Japanese teacher or the American assistant English teacher.

Step 2: 15 Minutes

Read and prepare for the upcoming negotiation. Pay particular attention to deciding what each party considers to be the problem and its cause. Prepare your arguments so that the other party will be convinced that you are correct.

Step 3: 20 Minutes

Negotiate with the other party and try to reach an agreement. When an agreement is reached, record your agreement on paper. If you are unable to reach an agreement, be sure to note where each party was when the negotiation ended.

This exercise was written by Laura Turek. Copyright 1996. Used with permission.

Step 4: 30 Minutes

Be prepared to discuss your agreement with the other party and with other groups who did the role-play.

DISCUSSION QUESTIONS

1. What was this negotiation about? Was it about the same or different things for the two parties?

2. What strategies and tactics did you use to convince the other side? What seemed to be effective? Ineffective?

3. Was this a distributive or an integrative negotiation?

Sick Leave

INTRODUCTION

This exercise involves a cross-cultural negotiation where there are several tangible and intangible factors at stake. You will play the role of either a Japanese manager responsible for the supervision of several foreign assistant English teachers, or an American assistant English teacher.

ADVANCE PREPARATION

Prior to the class you should read the articles in Section 11 of this text (Global Negotiations) so that you are familiar with some of the complexities of cross-cultural negotiations.

PROCEDURE

Step 1: 5 Minutes

You will be assigned to play the role of either the Japanese manager or the American assistant English teacher.

Step 2: 15 Minutes

Read and prepare for the upcoming negotiation. Pay particular attention to deciding what each party considers to be the problem and its cause. Prepare your arguments so that the other party will be convinced that you are correct.

Step 3: 20 Minutes

Negotiate with the other party and try to reach an agreement. When an agreement is reached, record your agreement on paper. If you are unable to reach an agreement, be sure to note where each party was when the negotiation ended.

This exercise was written by Laura Turek. Copyright 1996. Used with permission.

Step 4: 30 Minutes

Be prepared to discuss your agreement with the other party and with other groups who did the role-play.

DISCUSSION QUESTIONS

1. What was this negotiation about? Was it about the same or different things for the two parties?
2. What strategies and tactics did you use to convince the other side? What seemed to be effective? Ineffective?
3. Was this a distributive or an integrative negotiation?

Town of Tamarack

INTRODUCTION

In this role-play, you will have the opportunity to negotiate a serious problem—a conflict between a mining company and the government of a small town regarding an environmental cleanup. Conflicts between community, government, and industry groups are very common, particularly around environmental management issues. The issues in this simulation may be similar to environmental cleanup, development, or management problems ongoing in your own community.

ADVANCE PREPARATION

The nature of advance preparation will be determined by your instructor. You may be required to read materials in advance (as distributed), and possibly to conduct the negotiation before class.

PROCEDURE

1. You will be assigned to represent either the Town of Tamarack or the Twin Lakes Mining Company.
2. Read the Background Information and the role briefing information assigned to you. All information will be given by your instructor.
3. Negotiate according to the time limits given to you by your instructor.
4. If you arrive at an agreement, make sure that you write down exactly what you agree to. Have a representative of each side sign an agreement form, and either submit it to your instructor or bring it to class as directed.

DISCUSSION QUESTIONS

1. How did you prepare for this role-play? What type of strategy did you decide to employ?
2. Did you set goals or targets that you wanted to achieve on each issue and on the total package? Did you set "bottom line" or resistance points? How did having these (or not having them) affect your negotiation effectiveness?

This exercise was written by Jeff Polzer. Used with permission.

3. What was the impact of having specific "points" allocated to particular settlement options on:

   a. Your ability to set goals and bottom lines?

   b. Your ability to propose "package" agreements to the other side?

   c. Your ability to achieve a settlement? What would have been the impact if you did not have these "points"?

4. How satisfied are you with the final agreement (if you negotiatied one)? What factors in the negotiation made you feel more or less satisfied with this outcome?

5. What did your learn from this situation that you might want to apply to future negotiation situations or problems?

Cases

Capital Mortgage Insurance
Corporation (A)

Frank Randall hung up the telephone, leaned across his desk, and fixed a cold stare at Jim Dolan.

> OK, Jim. They've agreed to a meeting. We've got three days to resolve this thing. The question is, what approach should we take? How do we get them to accept our offer?

Randall, president of Capital Mortgage Insurance Corporation (CMI), had called Dolan, his senior vice president and treasurer, into his office to help him plan their strategy for completing the acquisition of Corporate Transfer Services (CTS). The two men had begun informal discussions with the principal stockholders of the small employee relocation services company some four months earlier. Now, in late May 1979, they were developing the terms of a formal purchase offer and plotting their strategy for the final negotiations.

The acquisition, if consummated, would be the first in CMI's history. Furthermore, it represented a significant departure from the company's present business. Randall and Dolan knew that the acquisition could have major implications, both for themselves and for the company they had revitalized over the past several years.

Jim Dolan ignored Frank Randall's intense look and gazed out the eighth-floor window overlooking Philadelphia's Independence Square.

> That's not an easy question, Frank. We know they're still looking for a lot more money than we're thinking about. But beyond that, the four partners have their own differences, and we need to think through just what they're expecting. So I guess we'd better talk this one through pretty carefully.

COMPANY AND INDUSTRY BACKGROUND

CMI was a wholly owned subsidiary of Northwest Equipment Corporation, a major freight transporter and lessor of railcars, commercial aircraft, and other industrial equipment. Northwest had acquired CMI in 1978, two years after CMI's original

---

parent company, an investment management corporation, had gone into Chapter 11 bankruptcy proceedings.

CMI had been created to sell mortgage guaranty insurance policies to residential mortgage lenders throughout the United States. Mortgage insurance provides banks, savings and loans, mortgage bankers, and other mortgage lenders with protection against financial losses when homeowners default on their mortgage loans.

Lending institutions normally protect their property loan investments by offering loans of only 70 percent to 80 percent of the appraised value of the property; the remaining 20 percent to 30 percent constitutes the homeowner's down payment. However, mortgage loan insurance makes it possible for lenders to offer so-called high-ratio loans of up to 95 percent of a home's appraised value. High-ratio loans are permitted only when the lender insures the loan; although the policy protects the lender, the premiums are paid by the borrower, as an addition to monthly principal and interest charges.

The principal attraction of mortgage insurance is that it makes purchasing a home possible for many more individuals. It is much easier to produce a 5 percent down payment than to save up the 20 percent to 30 percent traditionally required.

CMI had a mixed record of success within the private mortgage insurance industry. Frank Randall, the company's first and only president, had gotten the organization off to an aggressive beginning, attaining a 14.8 percent market share by 1972. By 1979, however, that share had fallen to just over 10 percent even though revenues had grown from $18 million in 1972 to over $30 million in 1979. Randall attributed the loss of market share primarily to the difficulties created by the bankruptcy of CMI's original parent. Thus, he had been quite relieved when Northwest Equipment acquired CMI in January 1978. Northwest provided CMI with a level of management and financial support it had never before enjoyed. Furthermore, Northwest's corporate management had made it clear to Frank Randall that he was expected to build CMI into a much larger, diversified financial services company.

Northwest's growth expectations were highly consistent with Frank Randall's own ambitions. The stability created by the acquisition, in combination with the increasing solidity of CMI's reputation with mortgage lenders, made it possible for Randall to turn his attention more and more toward external acquisitions of his own. During 1978 Randall, with Jim Dolan's help, had investigated several acquisition opportunities in related insurance industries, with the hope of broadening CMI's financial base. After several unsuccessful investigations, the two men had come to believe that their knowledge and competence was focused less on insurance per se than it was on residential real estate and related financial transactions. These experiences had led to a recognition that, in Frank Randall's words, "we are a residential real estate financial services company."

THE RESIDENTIAL REAL ESTATE INDUSTRY

Frank Randall and Jim Dolan knew from personal experience that real estate brokers, who play an obvious and important role in property transactions, usually have close ties with local banks and savings and loans. When mortgage funds are plentiful, brokers often "steer" prospective home buyers to particular lending institutions. When funds are scarce, the lenders would then favor prospective borrowers referred by their "favorite" brokers. Randall believed that these informal relationships meant that realtors could have a significant impact on the mortgage loan decision and thus on a mortgage insurance decision as well.

For this reason, CMI had for many years directed a small portion of its marketing effort toward real estate brokers. CMI's activities had consisted of offering educational programs for realtors, property developers, and potential home buyers. The company derived no direct revenues from these programs, but offered them in the interest of stimulating home sales and, more particularly, of informing both realtors and home buyers of how mortgage insurance makes it possible to purchase a home with a relatively low down payment.

Because he felt that real estate brokers could be powerful allies in encouraging lenders to use mortgage insurance, Randall had been tracking developments in the real estate industry for many years. Historically a highly fragmented collection of local, independent entrepreneurs, the industry in 1979 appeared to be on the verge of a major restructuring and consolidation. For the past several years many of the smaller brokers had been joining national franchise organizations in an effort to gain a "brand image" and to acquire improved management and sales skills.

More significantly, in 1979, several large national corporations were beginning to acquire prominent real estate agencies in major urban areas. The most aggressive of these appeared to be Merrill Lynch and Company, the well-known Wall Street securities trading firm. Merrill Lynch's interest in real estate brokers stemmed from several sources; perhaps most important were the rapidly rising prices on property and homes. Realtors' commissions averaged slightly over 6 percent of the sales price; *Fortune* magazine estimated that real estate brokers had been involved in home sales totaling approximately $190 billion in 1978, netting commissions in excess of $11 billion (in comparison, stockbrokers' commissions on all securities transactions in 1978 were estimated at $3.7 billion).[1] With property values growing 10 to 20 percent per year, commissions would only get larger; where 6 percent of a $30,000 home netted only $1,800, 6 percent of a $90,000 sale resulted in a commission well in excess of $5,000—for basically the same work.

There were also clear signs that the volume of real estate transactions would continue to increase. Although voluntary intercity moves appeared to be declining slightly, corporate transfers of employees were still rising. One of Merrill Lynch's earliest moves toward the real estate market had been to acquire an employee relocation company several years earlier. Working on a contract basis with corporate clients, Merrill Lynch Relocation Management (MLRM) collaborated with independent real estate brokers to arrange home sales and purchases for transferred employees. Like other relocation companies, MLRM would purchase the home at a fair market value and then handle all the legal and financial details of reselling the home on the open market. MLRM also provided relocation counseling and home search assistance for transferred employees; its income was derived primarily from service fees paid by corporate clients (and augmented somewhat by referral fees from real estate brokers,

---

1. "Why Merrill Lynch Wants to Sell Your House," *Fortune,* January 29, 1979.

who paid MLRM a portion of the commissions they earned on home sales generated by the transferred employees).

Later, in September 1978, Merrill Lynch had formally announced its intention to acquire at least 40 real estate brokerage firms within three to four years. Merrill Lynch's interest in the industry stemmed not only from the profit opportunities it saw, but also from a corporate desire to become a "financial services supermarket," providing individual customers with a wide range of investment and brokerage services. In 1978 Merrill Lynch had acquired United First Mortgage Corporation (UFM), a mortgage banker. And in early 1979 Merrill Lynch was in the midst of acquiring AMIC Corporation, a small mortgage insurance company in direct competition with CMI. As *Fortune* reported:

> In combination, these diverse activities hold some striking possibilities. Merrill Lynch already packages and markets mortgages through its registered representatives . . . If all goes according to plan, the company could later this year be vertically integrated in a unique way. Assuming the AMIC acquisition goes through, Merrill Lynch will be able to guarantee mortgages. It could then originate mortgages through its realty brokerages, process and service them through UFM, insure them with AMIC, package them as pass-through or unit trusts, and market them through its army of registered representatives. (January 29, 1979, p. 89)

It was this vision of an integrated financial services organization that also excited Frank Randall. As he and Jim Dolan reviewed their position in early 1979, they were confident that they were in a unique position to build CMI into a much bigger and more diversified company. The mortgage insurance business gave them a solid financial base, with regional offices throughout the country. Northwest Equipment stood ready to provide the capital they would need for significant growth. They already had relationships with important lending institutions across the United States, and their marketing efforts had given them a solid reputation with important real estate brokers as well.

Thus, Randall, in particular, felt that at least he had most of the ingredients to begin building that diversified "residential real estate financial services company" he had been dreaming about for so long. Furthermore, Randall's reading of the banking, thrift, and real estate industries suggested that the time was ripe. In his view, the uncertainties in the financial and housing industries created rich opportunities for taking aggressive action, and the vision of Merrill Lynch "bulling" its way into the business was scaring realtors just enough for CMI to present a comforting and familiar alternative.

THE METROPOLITAN REALTY NETWORK

Frank Randall spent most of the fall of 1978 actively searching for acquisition opportunities. As part of his effort, he contacted David Osgood, who was the executive director of the Metropolitan Realty Network, a national association of independent real estate brokers. The association, commonly known as MetroNet, had been formed primarily as a communication vehicle so its members could refer home buyers moving from one city to another to a qualified broker in the new location.

Randall discovered that Osgood was somewhat concerned about MetroNet's long-term health and viability. Though MetroNet included over 13,000 real estate agencies, it was losing some members to national franchise chains, and Osgood was feeling increasing pressures to strengthen the association by providing more services to member firms. Yet the entrepreneurial independence of MetroNet's members made Osgood's task particularly difficult. He had found it almost impossible to get them to agree on what they wanted him to do.

One service that the MetroNet brokers *were* agreed on developing was the employee relocation business. Corporate contracts to handle transferred employees were especially attractive to the brokers, because the contracts virtually guaranteed repeat business in the local area, and they also led to intercity referrals that almost always resulted in a home sale.

MetroNet brokers were also resentful of how Merrill Lynch Relocation Management and other relocation services companies were getting a larger and larger share of "their" referral fees. Osgood told Randall that he had already set up a committee of MetroNet brokers to look into how the association could develop a corporate relocation and third-party equity capability[2] of its own. Osgood mentioned that their only effort to date was an independent firm in Chicago named Corporate Transfer Services, Inc. (CTS), that had been started by Elliott Burr, a prominent Chicago broker and a MetroNet director. CTS had been formed with the intention of working with MetroNet brokers, but so far it had remained relatively small and had not met MetroNet's expectations.

As Randall explained to Osgood what kinds of activities CMI engaged in to help lenders and increase the volume of home sales, Osgood suddenly exclaimed, "That's exactly what *we're* trying to do!" The two men ended their initial meeting convinced that some kind of working relationship between CMI and MetroNet could have major benefits for both organizations. Osgood invited Randall to attend the next meeting of MetroNet's Third-Party Equity Committee, scheduled for March 1. "Let's explore what we can do for each other," said Osgood. "You're on," concluded Randall.

THE THIRD-PARTY EQUITY BUSINESS

Randall's discussion with David Osgood had opened his eyes to the third-party equity business, and he and Jim Dolan spent most of their time in preparation for the March 1 committee meeting steeped in industry studies and pro forma income statements.

They quickly discovered that the employee relocation services industry was highly competitive, though its future looked bright. Corporate transfers of key employees appeared to be an ingrained practice that showed no signs of letting up in the foreseeable future. Merrill Lynch Relocation Management was one of the two largest firms in the industry; most of the prominent relocation companies were well-funded subsidiaries of large, well-known corporations. Exhibit 1 contains Jim Dolan's tabulation of the seven major relocation firms, along with his estimates of each company's 1978 volume of home purchases.

---

2. The term *third-party equity capability* derived from the fact that a relocation services company actually purchased an employee's home, freeing up the owner's equity and making it available for investment in a new home. Within the industry the terms *third-party equity company* and *employee relocation services company* were generally used interchangeably.

EXHIBIT 1 Major Employee Relocation Services Companies

Relocation Company	Parent Organization	Estimated 1978 Home Purchases	Estimated Value of Home Purchases*	Estimated Gross Fee Income†
Merrill Lynch Relocation	Merrill Lynch	13,000	$975,000,000	$26,800,000
Homequity	Peterson, Howell, & Heather	12,000	900,000,000	24,750,000
Equitable Relocation	Equitable Life Insurance	5,000	375,000,000	10,300,000
Employee Transfer	Chicago Title and Trust	5,000	375,000,000	10,300,000
Relocation Realty Corporation	Control Data Corporation	3,000	225,000,000	6,200,000
Executrans	Sears/Coldwell Banker	3,000	225,000,000	6,200,000
Transamerica Relocation	Transamerica, Inc.	3,000	225,000,000	6,200,000

*Assumes average home values of $75,000.
†Assumes fee averaging 2.75 percent of value of homes purchased.

EXHIBIT 2   Hypothetical Employee Relocation Company Pro Forma Income Statement

Key assumptions:

1. Annual purchase volume of 2,000 homes.
2. Assume average holding period of 120 days. Inventory turns over three times annually, for an average of 667 units in inventory at any point in time.
3. Average home value of $75,000.
4. Existing mortgages on homes average 50 percent of property value. Additional required capital will be 40 percent equity, 60 percent long-term debt.
5. Fee income from corporate clients will average 2.75 percent of value of properties purchased (based on historical industry data).
6. Operating expenses (marketing, sales, office administration) will average 1 percent of value of properties purchased (all costs associated with purchases, including debt service, are billed back to corporate clients).

   Calculations

Total value of purchases	
(2,000 units at $75,000)	$150,000,000
Average inventory value	50,000,000
Capital required:	
Existing mortgages	25,000,000
New long-term debt	15,000,000
Equity	10,000,000
Fee income at 2.75%	4,125,000
Operating expenses at 1%	1,500,000
Net income	$2,625,000
Tax at 50%	(1,312,500)
Profit after tax	$1,312,500
Return on equity	13.1%

Dolan also developed a pro forma income and expense statement for a hypothetical firm handling 2,000 home purchases annually (see Exhibit 2). His calculations showed a potential 13.1 percent return on equity (ROE). Dolan then discovered that some companies achieved a much higher ROE by using a Home Purchase Trust, a legal arrangement that made it possible to obtain enough bank financing to leverage a company's equity base by as much as 10 to 1.

Randall and Dolan were increasingly certain that they wanted to get CMI into the employee relocation services business. They saw it as a natural tie-in with CMI's mortgage insurance operations—one that could exploit the same set of relationships that CMI already had with banks, realtors, savings and loans, and other companies involved in the development, construction, sale, and financing of residential real estate. The two men felt that real estate brokers had a critically important role in the process. Brokers were not only involved in the actual property transactions, but in addition they almost always had local contacts with corporations that could lead to the signing of employee relocation contracts. Equally important, from Randall's and Dolan's perspective, was their belief that a close relationship between CMI and the MetroNet brokers would also lead to significant sales of CMI's mortgage insurance policies.

The March 1 meeting with MetroNet's Third-Party Equity Committee turned into an exploration of how CMI and MetroNet might help each other by stimulating both home sales and high-ratio mortgage loans. After several hours of discussion, Frank Randall proposed specifically that CMI build an operating company to handle the corporate relocation business jointly with the MetroNet brokers. As a quid pro quo, Randall suggested that the brokers could market CMI mortgage insurance to both potential home buyers and lending institutions.

The committee's response to this idea was initially skeptical. Finally, however, they agreed to consider a more formal proposal at a later date. MetroNet's board of directors was scheduled to meet on April 10; the Third-Party Equity Committee could review the proposal on April 9 and, if they approved, present it to the full board on the 10th.

As the committee meeting broke up, Randall and Dolan began talking with Elliott Burr and Thomas Winder, two of the four owners of Corporate Transfer Services, Inc. (CTS). Though Burr had been the principal founder of CTS, his primary business was a large real estate brokerage firm in north suburban Chicago that he operated in partnership with William Lehman, who was also a CTS stockholder.

The four men sat back down at the meeting table, and Randall mentioned that his primary interest was to learn more about how an employee relocation business operated. Burr offered to send him copies of contracts with corporate clients, sample financial statements, and so on. At one point during their discussion Burr mentioned the possibility of an acquisition. Randall asked, somewhat rhetorically, "How do you put a value on a company like this?" Burr responded almost immediately, "Funny you should ask. We've talked to an attorney and have put together this proposal." Burr reached into his briefcase and pulled out a two-page document. He then proceeded to describe a complex set of terms involving the sale of an 80 percent interest in CTS, subject to guarantees concerning capitalization, lines of credit, data processing support, future distribution of profits and dividends, and more.

Randall backed off immediately, explaining that he needed to learn more about the nature of the business before he would seriously consider an acquisition. As Jim Dolan later recalled:

> I think they were expecting an offer right then and there. But it was very hard to understand what they really wanted; it was nothing we could actually work from. Besides that, the numbers they were thinking about were ridiculously high—over $5 million. We put the letter away and told them we didn't want to get specific until after the April 10 meeting. And that's the way we left it.

Preparation for the April 10 Meeting

During the next six weeks Randall and Dolan continued their investigations of the employee relocation industry and studied CTS much more closely.

One of their major questions was how much additional mortgage insurance the MetroNet brokers might be able to generate. Frank Randall had CMI's marketing staff conduct a telephone survey of about 25 key MetroNet brokers. The survey suggested that most brokers were aware of mortgage insurance, although few of them were actively pushing it. All of those questioned expressed an interest in using CMI's marketing programs, and were eager to learn more about CMI insurance.

By early May a fairly clear picture of CTS was emerging. The company had been founded in 1975; it had barely achieved a break-even profit level. Annual home purchases and sales had reached a level of almost 500 properties, and CTS has worked with about 65 MetroNet brokers and 35 corporate clients. Tom Winder was the general manager; he supervised a staff of about 25 customer representatives and clerical support staff. Conversations with David Osgood and several MetroNet brokers who had worked with CTS suggested that the company had made promises to MetroNet about developing a nationwide, well-financed, fully competitive organization. To date, however, those promises were largely unfulfilled. Osgood believed that CTS's shortage of equity and, therefore, borrowing capacity, had severely limited its growth potential.

Jim Dolan obtained a copy of CTS's December 1978 balance sheet that, in his mind, confirmed Osgood's feelings (see Exhibit 3). The company had a net worth of only $420,000. Three of the four stockholders (Elliott Burr, William Lehman, and Michael Kupchak) had invested an additional $2 million in the company—$1.3 million in short-term notes and $700,000 in bank loans that they had personally guaranteed. While CTS owned homes valued at $13.4 million, it also had additional bank loans and assumed mortgages totaling $9.8 million. Furthermore, the company had a

EXHIBIT 3

CORPORATE TRANSFER SERVICES, INC.
Unaudited Balance Sheet
December 1978

Assets:	($ 000)
Cash	$ 190
Homes owned	13,366
Accounts and acquisition fees receivable	665
Other (mainly escrow deposits)	143
	$14,364
Liabilities:	
Client prepayments	$1,602
Notes payable to banks	4,161
Assumed mortgages payable	5,670
Loan from stockholders	700
Advance from MetroNet	300
Other liabilities	211
	$12,644
Capital:	
Subordinated debenture due stockholder (April 1981)	1,300
Common stock	450
Deficit	(30)
	$14,364

highly uncertain earnings stream; Frank Randall believed the current business could tail off to almost nothing within six months.

During late March both Randall and Dolan had a number of telephone conversations with Burr and Winder. Their discussions were wide ranging and quite open; the CTS partners struck Randall as being unusually candid. They seemed more than willing to share everything they knew about the business and their own company. On one occasion, Burr asked how much of CTS Randall wanted to buy, and how Randall would feel about the present owners retaining a minority interest. Burr's question led Randall and Dolan to conclude that in fact they wanted full ownership. They planned to build up the company's equity base considerably, and wanted to gain all the benefits of a larger, more profitable operation for CMI.

In early April, Randall developed the formal proposal that he intended to present to MetroNet's board of directors (see Exhibit 4). The proposal committed CMI to enter negotiations to acquire CTS and to use CTS as a base for building a third-party equity company with a capitalization sufficient to support an annual home purchase capability of at least 2,000 units. In return, the proposal asked MetroNet to begin a program of actively supporting the use of CMI's insurance on high-ratio loans.

Randall and Dolan met again with the Third-Party Equity Committee in New York on April 9 to preview the CMI proposal. The committee reacted favorably, and the next day MetroNet's board of directors unanimously accepted the proposal after discussing it for less than 15 minutes.

FORMAL NEGOTIATIONS WITH CORPORATE TRANSFER SERVICES

On the afternoon of April 10, following the MetroNet board meeting, Randall and Dolan met again with Elliott Burr and Tom Winder. Now that CMI was formally committed to acquisition negotiations, Burr and Winder were eager to get specific and talk numbers. However, Randall and Dolan remained very cautious. When Burr expressed an interest in discussing a price, Randall replied, "We don't know what you're worth. But we'll entertain any reasonable argument you want to make for why we should pay more than your net worth." The meeting ended with a general agreement to firm things up by April 25. Later, reflecting on this session, Jim Dolan commented:

> Our letter of agreement committed us to having an operating company by July 12, so the clock was running on us. However, we know that after the April 10 board meeting they would be hard pressed not to be bought, and besides they were obviously pretty eager. But at that point in time we had not even met the other two stockholders; we suspected the high numbers were coming from them.

Further Assessment of CTS

Even though the April 10 meeting had ended with an agreement to move ahead by April 25, it quickly became evident that a complete assessment of CTS and preparation of a formal offer would take more than two weeks. Other operating responsibilities

EXHIBIT 4

Board of Directors
The Metropolitan Realty Network
New York, NY

April 9, 1979

Gentlemen:

It is our intention to enter negotiations with the principals of Corporate Transfer Services, Inc., for the acquisition of the equity ownership of this Company by Capital Mortgage Insurance Corporation.

In the event Capital Mortgage Insurance Corporation is successful in the acquisition of Corporate Transfer Services, Inc., it is our intention to capitalize this Company to the extent required for the development of a complete bank line of credit. The initial capital and bank line of credit would provide the MetroNet association members an annual equity procurement of 1,500–2,000 units. In addition, we would be prepared to expand beyond this initial capacity if the MetroNet Association volume and profitability of business dictate.

We are prepared to develop an organizational structure and support system that can provide a competitive and professional marketing and administrative approach to the corporate transfer market.

Our intentions to enter negotiations with Corporate Transfer Services, Inc., are subject to the following:

1. The endorsement of this action by you, the board of directors of MetroNet, for Capital Mortgage Insurance Corporation to acquire this organization.

2. The assurance of the MetroNet Association for the continuation of their support and use of CTS. Upon completion of the acquisition, the MetroNet Association would agree to sign a Letter of Agreement with the new owners of Corporate Transfer Services.

3. The assurance of the MetroNet Association to cooperate in the development of a close working relationship with CMI for the influence and control they may provide when seeking high-ratio conventional mortgage loans using mortgage insurance.

Capital Mortgage Insurance will need the support of expanded business by the MetroNet Association, due to the heavy capital commitment we will be required to make to CTS to make this acquisition feasible. In this regard, CMI is prepared to offer the MetroNet nationwide members a range of marketing programs and mortgage financing packages that will help earn and deserve the mortgage insurance business and expand the listings, sales, and profitability of the MetroNet members.

Upon receiving the endorsement and support outlined in this letter from the board of directors of MetroNet, we will proceed immediately with the negotiations with Corporate Transfer Services, Inc. It would be our intention to have the acquisition completed and the company fully operational by the time of the MetroNet national convention in San Francisco in July 1979.

Sincerely,

Franklin T. Randall
President and Chief Executive Officer

prevented both Randall and Dolan from devoting as much time as they had intended to the acquisition, and the analysis process itself required more time than they had expected.

During the first week of May, Jim Dolan made a "reconnaissance" trip to Chicago. His stated purpose was to examine CTS's books and talk with the company's local bankers. He also scrutinized the office facilities, met and talked with several office employees, observed Tom Winder interacting with customers and subordinates, and generally assessed the company's operations. Dolan spent most of his time with Winder, but he also had an opportunity to have dinner with William Lehman, another of CTS's stockholders. Dolan returned to Philadelphia with a generally favorable set of impressions about the company's operations, and a much more concrete understanding of its financial situation. He reported to Randall, "They're running a responsible organization in a basically sensible manner." At the same time, however, Dolan also reported that CTS was under increasing pressure from its bankers to improve its financial performance.

Dolan's trip also provided him with a much richer understanding of the four men who owned CTS: Elliott Burr, William Lehman (Burr's real estate partner), Michael Kupchak (a private investor), and Tom Winder. Of these four, only Winder was actively involved in the day-to-day management of the company, although Elliott Burr stayed in very close touch with Winder and was significantly more involved than either Lehman or Kupchak. From their meetings and telephone conversations, Randall and Dolan pieced together the following pictures of the four men:

Elliott Burr, in his middle 50s, had been the driving force behind Corporate Transfer Services. He was a "classic" real estate salesman—a warm, straightforward, friendly man who enthusiastically believed in what he was doing. An eternal optimist, he had been an early advocate of MetroNet's getting into the employee relocation business. Burr knew the relocation business extremely well; he personally called on many of the large Chicago corporations to sell CTS's services.

Burr appeared to be very well off financially. Burr and Lehman Real Estate was one of the largest realty firms on Chicago's North Shore, and Burr was held in high regard by local bankers. One banker had told Dolan, "Burr's word is his bond."

William Lehman, Burr's real estate partner, was in his mid-60s. He appeared to be much more of a financial adviser and investor than an operating manager. Lehman personally owned the shopping center where Burr and Lehman Real Estate was located, as well as the office building where CTS was leasing space.

Dolan characterized Lehman as an "elder statesman—a true gentleman." Dolan recalled that when he had had dinner with Lehman during his visit to Chicago, Lehman had kept the conversation on a personal level, repeatedly expressing concern about Dolan's plane reservations, hotel accommodations, and so on. He had hardly mentioned CTS during the entire dinner.

Michael Kupchak was the third principal stockholder. Kupchak, about 50, had been a mortgage banker in Chicago for a number of years. Recently, however, he had left the bank to manage his own investments on a full-time basis.

Dolan met Kupchak briefly during his Chicago visit, and characterized him as a "bulldog"—an aggressive, ambitious man much more interested in financial transactions than in the nature of the business. He had apparently thought Dolan was coming to Chicago to make a firm offer, and had been irritated that one had not been forthcoming.

Frank Randall had not yet met Kupchak face to face, although they had talked once by telephone.

Thomas Winder, 44, had spent most of his career in real estate-related businesses. At one time he had worked for a construction company, and then he had joined the mortgage bank where Michael Kupchak worked.

Kupchak had actually brought Winder into CTS as its general manager, and the three original partners had offered him 25 percent ownership in the company as part of his compensation package.

Winder was not only CTS's general manager, but its lead salesperson as well. He called on prospective corporate clients all over the country, and he worked closely with MetroNet. That activity primarily involved appearing at association-sponsored seminars to inform member brokers about CTS and its services.

It was obvious to Jim Dolan that CTS had become an important source of real estate sales commissions for the Burr and Lehman partnership. Most of CTS's clients were in the Chicago area, and a large portion of the real estate transactions generated by CTS were being handled by Burr and Lehman Real Estate.

Dolan also inferred that the three senior partners—Burr, Lehman, and Kupchak—were close friends socially as well as professionally. The men clearly respected each other and valued each other's opinions. On one occasion Burr had told Dolan, "It's because of Bill Lehman that I have what I have today. I can always trust his word." Tom Winder was also woven into the relationship, but he was apparently not as closely involved as the other three. Randall and Dolan both sensed that Elliott Burr was the unofficial spokesman of the group. "I have the impression he can speak for all of them," commented Dolan.

In late April, Randall obtained a copy of a consultant's report on the employee relocation industry that had been commissioned by MetroNet's Third-Party Equity Committee. The report estimated that there were more than 500,000 homeowner/employees transferred annually, generating over 1 million home purchases and sales. However, fewer than 55,000 of these transfers were currently being handled by relocation services companies. Dolan's own analysis had projected a 10–15 percent annual growth rate in the use of relocation companies, leading to industry volume estimates of 60,000 in 1979, 67,000 in 1980, and 75,000 by 1981. The consultant's report stressed that success in the relocation business depended on a company's ability to provide services to its corporate clients at lower cost than the clients could do it themselves. In addition, profitability depended on a company's ability to turn over its inventory of homes quickly and at reasonable prices.

Dolan's own financial projections showed a potential return on equity of over 30 percent by 1983, assuming only an 8 percent share of the market. And that return did not include any incremental profits resulting from new sales of CMI mortgage insurance policies generated by MetroNet brokers. Randall in particular was confident that the close ties between CMI and MetroNet would result in at least 5,000 new mortgage insurance policies annually—a volume that could add over $400,000 in after-tax profits to CMI's basic business.

On May 10, Randall and Dolan attended a Northwest Equipment Corporation financial review meeting in Minneapolis. Prior to their trip west Randall had prepared a detailed analysis of the CTS acquisition and the employee relocation industry. The analysis, in the form of a proposal, served as documentation for a formal request to Northwest for a capital expenditure of $9 million. Randall had decided that he was willing to pay up to $600,000 more than the $420,000 book value of CTS's net worth; the remaining $8 million would constitute the initial equity base required to build CTS into a viable company.

The financial review meeting evolved into a lengthy critique of the acquisition proposal. Northwest's corporate staff was initially quite skeptical of the financial projections, but Randall and Dolan argued that the risks were relatively low (the homes could always be sold) and the potential payoffs, both economic and strategic, were enormous. Finally, after an extended debate, the request was approved.

FORMAL NEGOTIATIONS WITH CTS

When Randall and Dolan returned from Minneapolis, they felt it was finally time to proceed in earnest with the acquisition negotiations. Randall sensed that at present CTS was limping along to no one's satisfaction—including Elliott Burr's. The company was sucking up much more of Burr's time and energy than he wanted to give it, and its inability to fulfill MetroNet's expectations was beginning to be an embarrassment for Burr personally.

In spite of these problems, Randall remained interested in completing the acquisition. Buying CTS would get CMI into the relocation business quickly, would provide them with immediate licensing and other legal documentation in 38 states, and would get them an experienced operations manager in Tom Winder. More important, Randall knew that Elliott Burr was an important and respected MetroNet broker, and buying CTS would provide an effective, influential entry into the MetroNet "old boy" network. Though he couldn't put a number on the value of that network, Randall believed it was almost more important than the acquisition of CTS itself. Randall was convinced that the connection with the MetroNet brokers would enable him to run CTS at far lower cost than the established relocation companies, and he also expected to realize a significant increase in CMI's mortgage insurance business.

May 21, 1979

Now, as Randall and Dolan sat in Randall's office on May 21, they discussed the draft of a formal purchase offer that Dolan had prepared that morning (see Exhibit 5 for relevant excerpts). The two men had decided to make an initial offer of $400,000 more than the $420,000 book value of CTS's net worth, subject to a formal audit and adjustments depending on the final sales prices of all homes owned by CTS as of the formal purchase date. This opening bid was $200,000 below Randall's ceiling price of $600,000 for the firm's goodwill. The offer was for 100 percent of the ownership of the company. The $2 million in outstanding notes would pass through to the new company owned by Randall and Dolan. The offer also included a statement of intent to retain Tom Winder as CTS's general manager, and to move the company to CMI's home office in Philadelphia.

EXHIBIT 5 Excerpts from Draft of Purchase Letter

The Board of Directors and Stockholders
Corporate Transfer Services, Inc.
Chicago, IL

May 24, 1979

Gentlemen:

Capital Mortgage Insurance Corporation (the "Purchaser") hereby agrees to purchase from you (the "Stockholders"), and you, the Stockholders, hereby jointly and severally agree to sell to us, the Purchaser, 100 percent of the issued and outstanding shares of capital stock of Corporate Transfer Services (the "Company") on the following terms and conditions.

Purchase Price. Subject to any adjustment under the following paragraph, the Purchase Price of the Stock shall be the sum of $400,000.00 (four hundred thousand dollars even) and an amount equal to the Company's net worth as reflected in its audited financial statements on the closing date (the "Closing Date Net Worth").

Adjustment of Purchase Price. The Purchase Price shall be reduced or increased, as the case may be, dollar-for-dollar by the amount, if any, by which the net amount realized on the sale of homes owned as of the Closing Date is exceeded by, or exceeds, the value attributed to such homes in the Closing Date Net Worth.

Continuation of Employment. Immediately upon consummation of the transaction, the Purchaser will enter into discussion with Mr. Thomas Winder with the intent that he continue employment in a management capacity at a mutually agreeable rate of pay. Mr. Winder will relocate to Philadelphia, Pennsylvania, and will be responsible for the sale of all homes owned by the Company at the Closing Date.

Covenant-Not-to-Compete. At the closing, each Stockholder will execute and deliver a covenant-not-to-compete agreeing that he will not engage in any capacity in the business conducted by the Company for a period of two years. If the foregoing correctly states our agreement as to this transaction, please sign below.

Very truly yours,

CAPITAL MORTGAGE INSURANCE
CORPORATION

By _____
                    President

The foregoing is agreed to and accepted.

As Randall and Dolan reviewed their plans, it was clear that they were more concerned about how to conduct the face-to-face negotiations than with the formal terms themselves. In the telephone call he had just completed, Randall had told Elliott Burr only that they wanted to meet the other stockholders and review their current thinking. At one point during the conversation Jim Dolan commented:

> I really wonder how they'll react to this offer. We've been putting them off for so long now that I'm not sure how they feel about us anymore. And our offer is so much less than they're looking for.

Randall replied:

> I know that—but I have my ceiling. It seems to me the real question now is what kind of bargaining stance we should take, and how to carry it out. What do you think *they* are expecting?

DISCUSSION QUESTIONS

1. Prepare, and be ready to discuss, a negotiation strategy for Randall and Dolan.
2. What should CMI be expecting from CTS?

Pacific Oil Company (A)

For the session on Pacific Oil Company, please prepare the following:

1. As background information, read the appendix to this case: "Petrochemical Supply Contracts: A Technical Note" (p. 618).

2. After reading about the Pacific Oil Company, prepare the following questions for class discussion:

   a. Describe the "problem" that Pacific Oil Company faced as it reopened negotiations with Reliant Chemical Company in early 1985.

   b. Evaluate the styles and effectiveness of Messrs. Fontaine, Gaudin, Hauptmann, and Zinnser as negotiators in this case.

   c. What should Frank Kelsey recommend to Jean Fontaine at the end of the case? Why?

THE PACIFIC OIL COMPANY

"Look, you asked for my advice, and I gave it to you," Frank Kelsey said. "If I were you, I wouldn't make any more concessions! I really don't think you ought to agree to their last demand! But you're the one who has to live with the contract, not me!"

Static on the transatlantic telephone connection obscured Jean Fontaine's reply. Kelsey asked him to repeat what he had said.

"OK, OK, calm down, Jean. I can see your point of view. I appreciate the pressures you're under. But I sure don't like the looks of it from this end. Keep in touch— I'll talk to you early next week. In the meantime, I will see what others at the office think about this turn of events."

Frank Kelsey hung up the phone. He sat pensively, staring out at the rain pounding on the window. "Poor Fontaine," he muttered to himself. "He's so anxious to please the customer, he'd feel compelled to give them the whole pie without getting his fair share of the dessert!"

Kelsey cleaned and lit his pipe as he mentally reviewed the history of the negotiations. "My word," he thought to himself, "we are getting eaten in little bites in this Reliant deal! And I can't make Fontaine see it!"

BACKGROUND

Pacific Oil Company was founded in 1902 as the Sweetwater Oil Company of Oklahoma City, Oklahoma. The founder of Sweetwater Oil, E. M. Hutchinson, pioneered a major oil strike in north central Oklahoma that touched off the Oklahoma "black gold" rush of the early 1900s. Through growth and acquisition in the 1920s and 30s, Hutchinson expanded the company rapidly, and renamed it Pacific Oil in 1932. After a period of consolidation in the 1940s and 50s, Pacific expanded again. It developed extensive oil holdings in North Africa and the Middle East, as well as significant coal beds in the western United States. Much of Pacific's oil production is sold under its own name as gasoline through service stations in the United States and Europe, but it is also distributed through several chains of "independent" gasoline stations. In addition, Pacific is also one of the largest and best known worldwide producers of industrial petrochemicals.

One of Pacific's major industrial chemical lines is the production of vinyl chloride monomer (VCM). The basic components of VCM are ethylene and chlorine. Ethylene is a colorless, flammable, gaseous hydrocarbon with a disagreeable odor; it is generally obtained from natural or coal gas, or by "cracking" petroleum into smaller molecular components. As a further step in the petroleum "cracking" process, ethylene is combined with chlorine to produce VCM, also a colorless gas.

VCM is the primary component of a family of plastics known as the vinyl chlorides. VCM is subjected to the process of polymerization, in which smaller molecules of vinyl chloride are chemically bonded together to form larger molecular chains and networks. As the bonding occurs, polyvinyl chloride (PVC) is produced; coloring pigments may be added, as well as "plasticizer" compounds that determine the relative flexibility or hardness of the finished material. Through various forms of calendering (pressing between heavy rollers), extruding and injection molding, the plasticized polyvinyl chloride is converted to an enormous array of consumer and industrial applications: flooring, wire insulation, electrical transformers, home furnishings, piping, toys, bottles and containers, rainwear, light roofing, and a variety of protective coatings. (See Exhibit 1 for a breakdown of common PVC-based products.)

In 1979, Pacific Oil established the first major contract with the Reliant Corporation for the purchase of vinyl chloride monomer. The Reliant Corporation was a major industrial manufacturer of wood and petrochemical products for the construction industry. Reliant was expanding its manufacturing operations in the production of plastic pipe and pipe fittings, particularly in Europe. The use of plastic as a substitute for iron or copper pipe was gaining rapid acceptance in the construction trades, and the European markets were significantly more progressive in adopting the plastic pipe. Reliant already had developed a small polyvinyl chloride production facility at Abbeville, France, and Pacific constructed a pipeline from its petrochemical plant at Antwerp to Abbeville.

The 1979 contract between Pacific Oil and Reliant was a fairly standard one for the industry, and due to expire in December of 1982. The contract was negotiated by Reliant's purchasing managers in Europe, headquartered in Brussels, and the senior marketing managers of Pacific Oil's European offices, located in Paris. Each of these individuals reported to the vice presidents in charge of their company's European offices, who in turn reported back to their respective corporate headquarters in the States. (See Exhibits 2 and 3 for partial organization charts.)

EXHIBIT 1   Polyvinyl Chloride Major Markets, 1982 (Units Represented in MM Pounds)

Market	MM Pounds	Percent of Market Share
Apparel		
Baby pants	22	0.6
Footwear	128	3.2
Miscellaneous	<u>60</u>	<u>1.5</u>
	210	5.3
Building and construction		
Extruded foam moldings	46	1.2
Flooring	428	10.8
Lighting	10	0.3
Panels and siding	64	1.6
Pipe and conduit	720	18.5
Pipe fittings	78	2.0
Rainwater systems	28	0.7
Swimming pool liners	40	1.0
Weather stripping	36	0.9
Miscellaneous	<u>50</u>	<u>1.2</u>
	1,500	38.2
Electrical		
Wire and cable	390	9.9
Home furnishings		
Appliances	32	0.8
Miscellaneous	<u>286</u>	<u>9.8</u>
	318	10.6
Housewares	94	2.4
Packaging		
Blow molded bottles	64	1.6
Closure liners and gaskets	16	0.4
Coatings	16	0.4
Film	124	3.2
Miscellaneous	<u>80</u>	<u>2.0</u>
	300	7.6
Recreation		
Records	136	3.4
Sporting goods	46	1.2
Miscellaneous	<u>68</u>	<u>1.7</u>
	250	6.3
Transportation		
Auto mats	36	0.9
Auto tops	32	0.8
Miscellaneous	<u>164</u>	<u>4.2</u>
	232	5.9

EXHIBIT 1   (*continued*)

Market	MM Pounds	Percent of Market Share
Miscellaneous		
Agriculture (including pipe)	106	2.6
Credit cards	24	0.4
Garden hose	40	1.0
Laminates	44	1.1
Medical tubing	42	1.1
Novelties	12	0.3
Stationery supplies	32	0.8
Miscellaneous	12	0.3
	312	7.6
Export	146	3.7
Miscellaneous	98	2.5
	244	6.2
Total	3,850	100.0

EXHIBIT 2   Partial Organization Chart—Pacific Oil Company

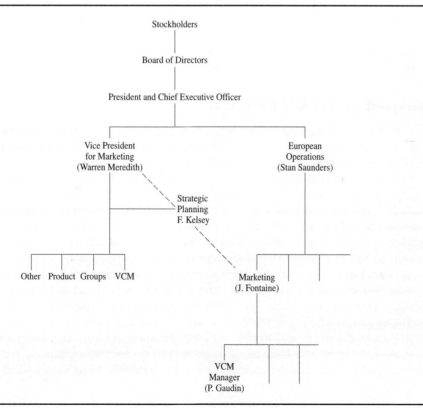

EXHIBIT 3   Partial Organization Chart—Reliant Chemical Company

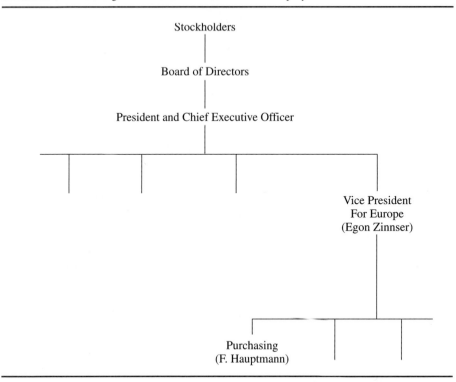

Stockholders

Board of Directors

President and Chief Executive Officer

Vice President
For Europe
(Egon Zinnser)

Purchasing
(F. Hauptmann)

THE 1982 CONTRACT RENEWAL

In February 1982, negotiations began to extend the four-year contract beyond the December 31, 1982, expiration date. Jean Fontaine, Pacific Oil's marketing vice president for Europe, discussed the Reliant account with his VCM marketing manager, Paul Gaudin. Fontaine had been promoted to the European vice presidency approximately 16 months earlier after having served as Pacific's ethylene marketing manager. Fontaine had been with Pacific Oil for 11 years, and had a reputation as a strong "up and comer" in Pacific's European operations. Gaudin had been appointed as VCM marketing manager eight months earlier; this was his first job with Pacific Oil, although he had five years of previous experience in European computer sales with a large American computer manufacturing company. Fontaine and Gaudin had worked well in their short time together, establishing a strong professional and personal relationship. Fontaine and Gaudin agreed that the Reliant account had been an extremely profitable and beneficial one for Pacific, and believed that Reliant had, overall, been satisfied with the quality and service under the agreement as well. They clearly wanted to work hard to obtain a favorable renegotiation of the existing agreement. Fontaine and Gaudin also reviewed the latest projections of worldwide VCM supply which they

EXHIBIT 4

MEMORANDUM

TO: All VCM Marketing Managers

FROM: F. Kelsey, Strategic Planning Division

RE: Worldwide VCM Supply/Demand Projections

DATE: January 17, 1982

CONFIDENTIAL—FOR YOUR EYES ONLY

Here are the data from 1980 and 1981, and the five-year projections that I promised you at our last meeting. As you can see, the market is tight, and is projected to get tighter. I hope you will find this useful in your marketing efforts—let me know if I can supply more detailed information.

Year	Total Projected Demand (in MM Pounds)	Supply Plant Capacities	Operating Rates to Meet Demand (Percent)
1980	4,040	5,390	75%
1981	4,336	5,390	80
1982	5,100	6,600	77
1983	5,350	6,600	81
1984	5,550	6,600	83
1985	5,650	7,300	75
1986	5,750	7,300	78

had just received from corporate headquarters. (See Exhibit 4.) The data confirmed what they already knew—that there was a worldwide shortage of VCM and that demand was continuing to rise. Pacific envisioned that the current demand–supply situation would remain this way for a number of years. As a result, Pacific believed that it could justify a high favorable formula price for VCM.

Fontaine and Gaudin decided that they would approach Reliant with an offer to renegotiate the current agreement. Their basic strategy would be to ask Reliant for their five-year demand projections on VCM and polyvinyl chloride products. Once these projections were received, Fontaine and Gaudin would frame the basic formula price that they would offer. (It would be expected that there would be no significant changes or variations in other elements of the contract, such as delivery and contract language.) In their negotiations, their strategy would be as follows:

a. To dwell on the successful long-term relationship that had already been built between Reliant and Pacific Oil, and to emphasize the value of that relationship for the success of both companies.

b. To emphasize all of the projections that predicted the worldwide shortage of VCM, and the desirability for Reliant to ensure that they would have a guaranteed supplier.

c. To point out all of the ways that Pacific had gone out of its way in the past to ensure delivery and service.

d. To use both the past and future quality of the relationship to justify what might appear to be a high formula price.

e. To point out the ways that Pacific's competitors could not offer the same kind of service.

Over the next six months, Gaudin and Fontaine, independently and together, made a number of trips to Brussels to visit Reliant executives. In addition, several members of Pacific's senior management visited Brussels and paid courtesy calls on Reliant management. The net result was a very favorable contract for Pacific Oil, signed by both parties on October 24, 1982. The basic contract, to extend from January 1983 to December 1987, is represented as Exhibit 5 (pages 605 through 608).

A CHANGED PERSPECTIVE

In December of 1984, Fontaine and Gaudin sat down to their traditional end-of-year review of all existing chemical contracts. As a matter of course, the Reliant VCM contract came under review. Although everything had been proceeding very smoothly, the prospects for the near and long-term future were obviously less clear, for the following reasons:

1. Both men reviewed the data that they had been receiving from corporate headquarters, as well as published projections of the supply situation for various chemicals over the next 10 years. It was clear that the basic supply–demand situation on VCM was changing. (See Exhibit 6.) While the market was currently "tight"—the favorable supply situation that had existed for Pacific when the Reliant contract was first negotiated—the supply of VCM was expected to expand rapidly over the next few years. Several of Pacific's competitors had announced plans for the construction of VCM manufacturing facilities that were expected to come on line in 20–30 months.

2. Fontaine and Gaudin knew that Reliant was probably aware of this situation as well. As a result, they would probably anticipate the change in the supply–demand situation as an opportunity to pursue a more favorable price, with the possible threat that they would be willing to change suppliers if the terms were not favorable enough. (Although rebuilding a pipeline is no simple matter, it clearly could be done, and had been, when the terms were sufficiently favorable to justify it.)

3. Fontaine was aware that in a situation where the market turned from one of high demand to excess supply, it was necessary to make extra efforts to maintain and "re-sign" all major current customers. A few large customers (100 million pounds a year and over) dominated the marketplace, and a single customer defection in an oversupplied market could cause major headaches for marketing and sales. It would simply be impossible to find another customer with demands of that magnitude; a number of smaller customers would have to be found, while Pacific would also have to compete with spot market prices that would cut profits to the bone.

EXHIBIT 5   Agreement of Sale

This Agreement, entered into this <u>24th</u> day of <u>October, 1982,</u> between <u>Pacific Oil Company,</u> hereinafter called Seller, and <u>Reliant Chemical Company of Europe,</u> hereinafter called Buyer.

WITNESSETH:

Seller agrees to sell and deliver and Buyer agrees to purchase and receive commodity (hereinafter called "product") under the terms and conditions set forth below.

1. Product: Vinyl Chloride Monomer

2. Quality: ASTM requirements for polymer-grade product

3. Quantity: 1983: 150 million pounds

    1984: 160 million pounds

    1985: 170 million pounds

    1986: 185 million pounds

    1987: 200 million pounds

4. Period: Contract shall extend from January 1, 1983, and extend until December 31, 1987, and evergreen thereafter, unless terminated with 180 days' prior notification at the end of each calendar year, but not before December 31, 1987.

5. Price: See Contract formula price.

6. Payment Terms:

    a. Net 30 days.

    b. All payments shall be made in United States dollars without discount or deduction, unless otherwise noted, by wire transfer at Seller's option, to a bank account designated by Seller. Invoices not paid on due date will be subject to a delinquency finance charge of 1 percent per month.

    c. If at any time the financial responsibility of Buyer shall become impaired or unsatisfactory to Seller, cash payment on delivery or satisfactory security may be required. A failure to pay any amount may, at the option of the Seller, terminate this contract as to further deliveries. No forbearance, course of dealing, or prior payment shall affect this right of Seller.

7. Price Change:

    The price specified in this Agreement may be changed by Seller on the first day of any calendar <u>half-year</u> by written notice sent to the Buyer not less than thirty (30) days prior to the effective date of change. Buyer gives Seller written notice of objection to such change at least ten (10) days prior to the effective date of change. Buyer's failure to serve Seller with written notice of objection thereto prior to the effective date thereof shall be considered acceptance of such change. If Buyer gives such notice of objection and Buyer and Seller fail to agree on such change prior to the effective date thereof, this Agreement and the obligations of Seller and Buyer hereunder shall terminate with respect to the unshipped portion of the Product governed by it. Seller has the option immediately to cancel this contract upon written notice to Buyer, to continue to sell hereunder at the same price and terms which were in effect at the time Seller gave notice of change, or to suspend performance under this contract while pricing is being resolved. If Seller desires to revise the price, freight allowance, or terms of payment pursuant to this agreement, but is restricted to any extent against doing so by reason of any law, governmental decree, order or regulation, or if the price, freight allowance, or terms of payment then in effect under this contract are nullified or reduced by reason of any law, governmental decree, order, or regulation. Seller shall have the right to cancel this contract upon fifteen (15) days' written notice to purchaser.

EXHIBIT 5 *(continued)*

8. Measurements:

Seller's determinations, unless proven to be erroneous, shall be accepted as conclusive evidence of the quantity of Product delivered hereunder. Credit will not be allowed for shortages of 1/2 of 1 percent or less of the quantity, and overages of 1/2 of 1 percent or less of the quantity will be waived. The total amount of shortages or overages will be credited or billed when quantities are greater and such differences are substantiated. Measurements of weight and volume shall be according to procedures and criteria standard for such determinations.

9. Shipments and Delivery:

Buyer shall give Seller annual or quarterly forecasts of its expected requirements as Seller may from time to time request. Buyer shall give Seller reasonably advanced notice for each shipment which shall include date of delivery and shipping instructions. Buyer shall agree to take deliveries in approximately equal monthly quantities, except as may be otherwise provided herein. In the event that Buyer fails to take the quantity specified or the pro rata quantity in any month, Seller may, at its option, in addition to other rights and remedies, cancel such shipments or parts thereof.

10. Purchase Requirements:

  a. If during any consecutive three-month period, Buyer for any reason (but not for reasons of force majeure as set forth in Section 12) takes less than 90 percent of the average monthly quantity specified, or the prorated minimum monthly quantity then applicable to such period under Section 12, Seller may elect to charge Buyer a penalty charge for failure to take the average monthly quantity or prorated minimum monthly quantity.

  b. If, during any consecutive three-month period, Buyer, for any reason (but not, however, for reasons of force majeure as set forth in Section 12) takes Product in quantities less than that equal to at least one-half of the average monthly quantity specified or the prorated minimum monthly quantity originally applicable to such period under Section 12, Seller may elect to terminate this agreement.

  c. It is the Seller's intent not to unreasonably exercise its right under (a) or (b) in the event of adverse economic and business conditions in general.

  d. Notice of election by Seller under (a) or (b) shall be given within 30 days after the end of the applicable three-month period, and the effective date of termination shall be 30 days after the date of said notice.

11. Detention Policy:

Seller may, from time to time, specify free unloading time allowances for its transportation equipment. Buyer shall be liable to the Transportation Company for all demurrage charges made by the Transportation Company, for railcars, trucks, tanks, or barges held by Buyer beyond the free unloading time.

12. Force Majeure:

Neither party shall be liable to the other for failure or delay in performance hereunder to the extent that such failure or delay is due to war, fire, flood, strike, lockout, or other labor trouble, accident, breakdown of equipment or machinery, riot, act, request, or suggestion of governmental authority, act of God, or other contingencies beyond the control of the affected party which interfere with the production or transportation of the material covered by this Agreement or with the

EXHIBIT 5   (*continued*)

supply of any raw material (whether or not the source of supply was in existence or contemplated at the time of this Agreement) or energy source used in connection therewith, or interfere with Buyer's consumption of such material, provided that in no event shall Buyer be relieved of the obligation to pay in full for material delivered hereunder. Without limitation on the foregoing, neither party shall be required to remove any cause listed above or replace the affected source of supply or facility if it shall involve additional expense or departure from its normal practices. If any of the events specified in this paragraph shall have occurred, Seller shall have the right to allocate in a fair and reasonable manner among its customers and Seller's own requirements any supplies of material Seller has available for delivery at the time or for the duration of the event.

13. Materials and Energy Supply:

If, for reasons beyond reasonable commercial control, Seller's supply of product to be delivered hereunder shall be limited due to continued availability of necessary raw materials and energy supplies, Seller shall have the right (without liability) to allocate to the Buyer a portion of such product on such basis as Seller deems equitable. Such allocation shall normally be that percent of Seller's total internal and external commitments which are committed to Buyer as related to the total quantity available from Seller's manufacturing facilities.

14. Disclaimer:

Seller makes no warranty, express or implied, concerning the product furnished hereunder other than it shall be of the quality and specifications stated herein. Any implied warranty of FITNESS is expressly excluded and to the extent that it is contrary to the foregoing sentence; any implied warranty of MERCHANTABILITY is expressed excluded. Any recommendation made by Seller makes no warranty of results to be obtained. Buyer assumes all responsibility and liability for loss or damage resulting from the handling or use of said product. In no event shall Seller be liable for any special, indirect, or consequential damages, irrespective of whether caused or allegedly caused by negligence.

15. Taxes:

Any tax, excise fee, or other charge or increase thereof upon the production, storage, withdrawal, sale, or transportation of the product sold hereunder, or entering into the cost of such product, imposed by any proper authority becoming effective after the date hereof, shall be added to the price herein provised and shall be paid by the Buyer.

16. Assignment and Resale:

This contract is not transferable or assignable by Buyer without the written consent of Seller. The product described hereunder, in the form and manner provided by the Seller, may not be assigned or resold without prior written consent of the Seller.

17. Acceptance:

Acceptance hereof must be without qualification, and Seller will not be bound by any different terms and conditions contained in any other communication.

18. Waiver of Breach:

No waiver by Seller or Buyer of any breach of any of the terms and conditions contained in this Agreement shall be construed as a waiver or any subsequent breach of the same or any other term or condition.

EXHIBIT 5   (*continued*)

19. Termination:

If any provision of this agreement is or become violate of any law, or any rule, order, or regulation issued thereunder, Seller shall have the right, upon notice to Buyer, to terminate the Agreement in its entirety.

20. Governing Law:

The construction of this Agreement and the rights and obligations of the parties hereunder shall be governed by the laws of the State of New York.

21. Special Provisions:

BUYER: SELLER:

_____   PACIFIC OIL CORPORATION
                 (firm)

By: _____   By: _____
Title: <u>Senior Purchasing Manager</u>   Title: <u>Marketing Vice President</u>
Date: _____   Date:_____

EXHIBIT 6

MEMORANDUM

TO: All VCM Marketing Managers

FROM: F. Kelsey, Strategic Planning Division

RE: Worldwide VCM/Supply/Demand Projections

DATE: December 9, 1984

CONFIDENTIAL—FOR YOUR EYES ONLY

This will confirm and summarize data that we discussed at the national marketing meeting last month in Atlanta. At that time, I indicated to you that the market projections we made several years ago have changed drastically. In early 1983, a number of our competitors announced their intentions to enter the VCM business over the next five years. Several facilities are now under construction, and are expected to come on line in late 1986 and early 1987. As a result, we expect a fairly significant shift in the supply/demand relationship over the next few years.

I hope you will give this appropriate consideration in your long-range planning effort. Please contact me if I can be helpful.

Year	Total Projected Demand (in MM Pounds)	Supply Plant Capacities	Operating Rates to Meet Demand (Percent)
1982	5,127 (actual)	6,600	78%
1983	5,321 (actual)	6,600	81
1984	5,572 (rev. 11/84)	6,600	84
1985	5,700	7,300	78
1986	5,900	8,450	70
1987	6,200	9,250	64
1988	6,500	9,650	67
1989	7,000	11,000	63

4. In a national product development meeting back in the States several weeks prior, Fontaine had learned of plans by Pacific to expand and diversify its own product line into VCM derivatives. There was serious talk of Pacific's manufacturing its own PVC for distribution under the Pacific name, as well as the manufacture and distribution of various PVC products. Should Pacific decide to enter these businesses, not only would they require a significant amount of the VCM now being sold on the external market, but Pacific would probably decide that, as a matter of principle, it would not want to be in the position of supplying a product competitor with the raw materials to manufacture the product line, unless the formula price were extremely favorable.

As they reviewed these factors, Gaudin and Fontaine realized that they needed to take action. They pondered the alternatives.

A NEW CONTRACT IS PROPOSED

As a result of their evaluation of the situation in December of 1984, Fontaine and Gaudin decided to proceed on two fronts. First, they would approach Reliant with the intent of reopening negotiation on the current VCM contract. They would propose to renegotiate the current agreement, with an interest toward extending the contract five years from the point of agreement on contract terms. Second, they would contact those people at corporate headquarters in New York who were evaluating Pacific's alternatives for new-product development, and inform them of the nature of the situation. The sooner a determination could be made on the product development strategies, the sooner the Pacific office would know how to proceed on the Reliant contract.

Gaudin contacted Frederich Hauptmann, the senior purchasing manager for Reliant Chemicals in Europe. Hauptmann had assumed the position as purchasing manager approximately four weeks earlier, after having served in a purchasing capacity for a large German steel company. Gaudin arranged a meeting for early January in Hauptmann's office. After getting acquainted over lunch, Gaudin briefed Hauptmann on the history of Reliant's contractual relationships with Pacific Oil. Gaudin made clear that Pacific had been very pleased with the relationship that had been maintained. He said that Pacific was concerned about the future, and about maintaining the relationship with Reliant for a long time to come. Hauptmann stated that he understood that the relationship had been a very productive one, too, and also hoped that the two companies could continue to work together in the future. Buoyed by Hauptmann's apparent enthusiasm and relative pleasure with the current agreement, Gaudin said that he and Jean Fontaine, his boss, had recently been reviewing all contracts. Even though the existing Pacific–Reliant VCM agreement had three years to run, Pacific felt that it was never too soon to begin thinking about the long-term future. In order to ensure that Reliant would be assured of a continued supply of VCM, under the favorable terms and working relationship that was already well established, Pacific hoped that Reliant might be willing to begin talks now for contract extension past December 31, 1987. Hauptmann said that he would be willing to consider it, but needed to consult other people in the Brussels office, as well as senior executives at corporate headquarters in Chicago. Hauptmann promised to contact Gaudin when he had the answer.

By mid-February, Hauptmann cabled Gaudin that Reliant was indeed willing to begin renegotiation of the current agreement, with interest in extending it for the future. He suggested that Gaudin and Fontaine come to Brussels for a preliminary meeting in early March. Hauptmann also planned to invite Egon Zinnser, the regional vice president of Reliant's European operations and Hauptmann's immediate superior.

MARCH 10

Light snow drifted onto the runway of the Brussels airport as the plane landed. Fontaine and Gaudin had talked about the Reliant contract, and the upcoming negotiations, for most of the trip. They had decided that while they did not expect the negotiations to be a complete "pushover," they expected no significant problems or stumbling points in the deliberations. They thought Reliant negotiators would routinely question some of the coefficients that were used to compute the formula price as well as to renegotiate some of the minimum quantity commitments. They felt that the other elements of the contract would be routinely discussed, but that no dramatic changes should be expected.

After a pleasant lunch with Hauptmann and Zinnser, the four men sat down to review the current VCM contract. They reviewed and restated much of what Gaudin and Hauptmann had done at their January meeting. Fontaine stated that Pacific Oil was looking toward the future, and hoping that it could maintain Reliant as a customer. Zinnser responded that Reliant had indeed been pleased by the contract as well, but that it was also concerned about the future. They felt that Pacific's basic formula price on VCM, while fair, might not remain competitive in the long-run future. Zinnser said that he had already had discussions with two other major chemical firms that were planning new VCM manufacturing facilities, and that one or both of these firms were due to come on line in the next 24–30 months. Zinnser wanted to make sure that Pacific could remain competitive with other firms in the marketplace. Fontaine responded that it was Pacific's full intention to remain completely competitive, whether it be in market price or in the formula price.

Zinnser said he was pleased by this reply, and took this as an indication that Pacific would be willing to evaluate and perhaps adjust some of the factors that were now being used to determine the VCM formula price. He then presented a rather elaborate proposal for adjusting the respective coefficients of these factors. The net result of these adjustments would be to reduce the effective price of VCM by approximately 2 cents per pound. It did not take long for Fontaine and Gaudin to calculate that this would be a net reduction of approximately $4 million per year. Fontaine stated that they would have to take the proposal back to Paris for intensive study and analysis. The men shook hands, and Fontaine and Gaudin headed back to the airport.

Throughout the spring, Gaudin and Hauptmann exchanged several letters and telephone calls. They met once at the Paris airport when Hauptmann stopped over on a trip to the States, and once in Zurich when both men discovered that they were going to be there on business the same day. By May 15, they had agreed on a revision of the formula price that would adjust the price downward by almost one cent per pound.

Gaudin, relieved that the price had finally been established, reported back to Fontaine that significant progress was being made. Gaudin expected that the remaining issues could be closed up in a few weeks, and a new contract signed.

MAY 27

Hauptmann contacted Gaudin to tell him that Reliant was now willing to talk about the remaining issues in the contract. The two men met in early June. Gaudin opened the discussion by saying that now that the formula price had been agreed upon, he hoped that Reliant would be willing to agree to extend the contract five years from the point of signing. Hauptmann replied that Reliant had serious reservations about committing the company to a five-year contract extension. He cited the rapid fluctuations in the demand, pricing structure, and competition of Reliant's various product lines, particularly in the construction industry, as well as what appeared to be a changing perspective in the overall supply of VCM. Quite frankly, Hauptmann said, Reliant didn't want to be caught in a long-term commitment to Pacific if the market price of VCM was likely to drop in the foreseeable future. As a result, Reliant wanted to make a commitment for only a two-year contract renewal.

Gaudin tried to give Hauptmann a number of assurances about the continued integrity of the market. He also said that if changing market prices were a concern for Reliant, Pacific Oil would be happy to attempt to make adjustments in other parts of the contract to ensure protection against dramatic changes in either the market price or the demand for Reliant's product lines. But Hauptmann was adamant. Gaudin said he would have to talk to Fontaine and others in Paris before he could agree to only a two-year contract.

The two men talked several times on the telephone over the next two months and met once in Paris to discuss contract length. On August 17, in a quick 45-minute meeting in Orly Airport, Gaudin and Hauptmann agreed to a three-year contract renewal. They also agreed to meet in early September to discuss remaining contract issues.

SEPTEMBER 10

Hauptmann met Gaudin and Fontaine in Pacific's Paris office. Hauptmann stressed that he and Zinnser were very pleased by the formula price and three-year contract duration that had been agreed to thus far. Fontaine echoed a similar satisfaction on behalf of Pacific, and stated that they expected a long and productive relationship with Reliant. Fontaine stressed, however, that Pacific felt it was most important to them to complete the contract negotiations as quickly as possible, in order to adequately plan for product and market development in the future. Hauptmann agreed, saying that this was in Reliant's best interest as well. He felt that there were only a few minor issues that remained to be discussed before the contract could be signed.

Fontaine inquired as to what those issues were. Hauptmann said that the most important one to Reliant was the minimum quantity requirements, stipulating the minimum amount that Reliant had to purchase each year. Gaudin said that based on the projections for the growth of the PVC and fabricated PVC products over the next few years, and patterns established by past contracts, it was Pacific's assumption that Reliant would want to increase their quantity commitments by a minimum of 10 percent each year. Based on minimums stipulated in the current contract, Gaudin expected that Reliant would want to purchase at least 220 million pounds in year 1, 240 million pounds in year 2, and 265 million pounds in year 3. Hauptmann responded that Reliant's projections were very different. The same kind of uncertainty that had led to Reliant's concern about the term of the contract also contributed to a caution about significantly overextending themselves on a minimum quantity commitment. In fact, Reliant's own predictions were that they were likely to take less than the minimum in the current year ("underlifting," in the parlance of the industry) and that, if they did so, they would incur almost a $1 million debt to Pacific. Conservative projections for the following year (1987) projected a similar deficit, but Reliant hoped that business would pick up and that the minimum quantities would be lifted. As a result, Hauptmann and Zinnser felt that it would be in Reliant's best interest to freeze minimum quantity requirements for the next two years—at 200 million pounds—and increase the minimum to 210 million pounds for the third year. Of course, Reliant *expected* that, most likely, they would be continuing to purchase much more than the specified minimums. But given the uncertainty of the future, Reliant did not want to get caught if the economy and the market truly turned sour.

Fontaine and Gaudin were astonished at the conservative projections Hauptmann was making. They tried in numerous ways to convince Hauptmann that his minimums were ridiculously low, and that the PVC products were bound to prosper far more than Hauptmann seemed willing to admit. But Hauptmann was adamant, and left Paris saying he needed to consult Zinnser and others in Brussels and the States before he could revise his minimum quantity estimates upward. Due to the pressure of other activities and vacation schedules, Gaudin and Hauptmann did not talk again until late October. Finally, on November 19, the two men agreed to a minimum quantity purchase schedule of 205 million pounds in the first year of the contract, 210 million pounds in the second year, and 220 million pounds in the third year. Moreover, Pacific agreed to waive any previous underlifting charges that might be incurred under the current contract when the new contract was signed.

OCTOBER 24

Jean Fontaine returned to Paris from meetings in New York and a major market development meeting held by senior Pacific executives at Hilton Head. After a number of delays due to conflicting market research and changes in senior management, as well as the general uncertainty in the petroleum and chemical markets, Pacific had decided not to develop its own product lines for either PVC or fabricated products. The decision was largely based on the conclusion—more "gut feel" than hard fact—that entry into these new markets was unwise at a time when much greater problems faced Pacific and the petrochemicals industry in general. Fontaine had argued strenuously that the VCM market was rapidly going soft, and that failure to create its own product lines would leave Pacific Oil in an extremely poor position to market one of its basic products. Fontaine was told that his position was appreciated, but that he and other chemical marketing people would simply have to develop new markets and customers for the product. Privately, Fontaine churned on the fact that it had taken senior executives almost a year to make the decision, while valuable time was being lost in developing the markets; but he wisely decided to bite his tongue and vent his frustration on 36 holes of golf. On the return flight to Paris, he read about Pacific's decision in the October 23rd issue of *The Wall Street Journal,* and ordered a double martini to soothe his nerves.

DECEMBER 14

Fontaine and Gaudin went to Brussels to meet with Hauptmann and Zinnser. The Pacific executives stressed that it was of the utmost importance for Pacific Oil to try to wrap up the contract as quickly as possible—almost a year had passed in deliberations, and although Pacific was not trying to place the "blame" on anyone, it was most concerned that the negotiations be settled as soon as possible.

Zinnser emphasized that he, too, was concerned about completing the negotiations quickly. Both he and Hauptmann were extremely pleased by the agreements that had been reached so far, and felt that there was no question that a final contract signing was imminent. The major issues of price, minimum quantities, and contract duration had been solved. In their minds, what remained were only a few minor technical items in contract language. Some minor discussion of each of these should wrap things up in a few weeks.

Fontaine asked what the issues were. Zinnser began by stating that Reliant had become concerned by the way that the delivery pipeline was being metered. As currently set up, the pipeline fed from Pacific's production facility in Antwerp, Belgium, to Reliant's refinery. Pacific had built the line, and was in charge of maintaining it. Meters had been installed at the exit flange of the pipeline, and Reliant was paying the metered amount to Pacific. Zinnser said that some spot-checking by Reliant at the manufacturing facility seemed to indicate that they may not be receiving all they were being billed for. They were not questioning the integrity of the meters or the meter readers, but felt that since the pipe was a number of years old, it may have developed leaks. Zinnser felt that it was inappropriate for Reliant to absorb the cost of VCM that was not reaching its facility. They therefore proposed that Pacific install meters directly outside of the entry flange of Reliant's manufacturing facility, and that Reliant only be required to pay the meter directly outside the plant.

Fontaine was astonished. In the first place, he said, this was the first time he had heard any complaint about the pipeline or the need to recalibrate the meters. Second, if the pipeline was leaking, Pacific would want to repair it, but it would be impossible to do so until spring. Finally, while the meters themselves were not prohibitively expensive, moving them would mean some interruption of service and definitely be costly to Pacific. Fontaine said he wanted to check with the maintenance personnel at Antwerp to find out whether they could corroborate such leaks.

Fontaine was unable to contact the operating manager at Antwerp, or anyone else who could confirm that leaks may have been detected. Routine inspection of the pipeline had been subcontracted to a firm which had sophisticated equipment for monitoring such things, and executives of the firm could not be reached for several days. Fontaine tried to raise other contract issues with Zinnser, but Zinnser said that this was his most important concern, and this issue needed to be resolved before the others could be finalized. Fontaine agreed to find out more about the situation and to bring the information to the next meeting. With the Christmas and New Year holidays approaching, the four men could not schedule another meeting until January 9.

JANUARY MEETINGS

The January 9 meeting was postponed until January 20, due to the death of Mr. Hauptmann's mother. The meeting was rescheduled for a time when Hauptmann needed to be in Geneva, and Gaudin agreed to meet him there.

Gaudin stated that the investigation of the pipeline had discovered no evidence of significant discharge. There were traces of *minor* leaks in the line, but they did not appear to be serious, and it was currently impossible to determine what percentage of the product may be escaping. The most generous estimate given to Gaudin had been 0.1 percent of the daily consumption. Hauptmann stated that their own spot monitoring showed it was considerably more, and that Reliant would feel infinitely more comfortable if the new metering system could be installed.

Gaudin had obtained estimates for the cost of remetering before he left Paris. It was estimated that the new meters could be installed for approximately $20,000. Tracing and fixing the leaks (if they existed) could not be done until April or May, and might run as much as $50,000 if leaks turned out to be located at some extremely difficult access points. After four hours of debating with Hauptmann in a small conference room off the lobby of the Geneva Hilton, Gaudin agreed that Pacific would remeter the pipeline.

Hauptmann said that as far as he was concerned, all of his issues had been settled; however, he thought Zinnser might have one or two other issues to raise. Hauptmann said that he would report back to Zinnser, and contact Gaudin as soon as possible if another meeting was necessary. Gaudin, believing that Pacific was finally beginning to see the light at the end of the tunnel, left for Paris.

JANUARY 23

Hauptmann called Gaudin and said that he and Zinnser had thoroughly reviewed the contract, and that there were a few small issues of contract language which Zinnser wanted to clarify. He said that he would prefer not to discuss them over the telephone, and suggested that since he was going to be in Paris on February 3, they meet at the Pacific offices. Gaudin agreed.

Fontaine and Gaudin met Hauptmann on February 3. Hauptmann informed them that he felt Reliant had been an outstanding customer for Pacific in the past, and that it probably was one of Pacific's biggest customers for VCM. Fontaine and Gaudin agreed, affirming the important role that Reliant was playing in Pacific's VCM market. Hauptmann said that he and Zinnser had been reviewing the contract, and were concerned that the changing nature of the VCM market might significantly affect Reliant's overall position in the marketplace as a purchaser. More specifically, Reliant was concerned that the decline in market and price for VCM in the future might endanger its own position in the market, since Pacific might sign contracts with other purchasers for lower formula prices than were currently being awarded to Reliant. Since Reliant was such an outstanding customer of Pacific—and Fontaine and Gaudin had agreed to that—it seemed to Reliant that Pacific Oil had an "obligation" to write two additional clauses into the contract that would protect Reliant in the event of further slippage in the VCM market. The first was a "favored nations" clause, stipulating that if Pacific negotiated with another purchaser a more favorable price for VCM than Reliant was receiving now, Pacific would guarantee that Reliant would receive that price as well. The second was a "meet competition" clause, guaranteeing that Pacific would willingly meet any lower price on VCM offered by a competitor, in order to maintain the Reliant relationship. Hauptmann argued that the "favored nations" clause was protection for Reliant, since it stipulated that Pacific valued the relationship enough to offer the best possible terms to Reliant. The "meet competition" clause, he argued, was clearly advantageous for Pacific since it ensured that Reliant would have no incentive to shift suppliers as the market changed.

Fontaine and Gaudin debated the terms at length with Hauptmann, stressing the potential costliness of these agreements for Pacific. Hauptmann responded by referring to the costliness that the absence of the terms could have for Reliant, and suggesting that perhaps the Pacific people were truly *not* as interested in a successful long-term relationship as they had been advocating. Fontaine said that he needed to get clearance from senior management in New York before he could agree to these terms, and said that he would get back to Hauptmann within a few days when the information was available.

FRANK KELSEY'S VIEW

Frank Kelsey was strategic planning manager, a staff role in the New York offices of the Pacific Oil Corporation. Kelsey had performed a number of roles for the company in his 12 years of work experience. Using the chemistry background he had achieved in college, Kelsey worked for six years in the research and development department of Pacific's Chemical Division before deciding to enter the management ranks. He transferred to the marketing area, spent three years in chemical marketing, and then assumed responsibilities in marketing planning and development. He moved to the strategic planning department four years ago.

In late 1985, Kelsey was working in a staff capacity as an adviser to the executive product vice president of the Pacific Oil Company. Pacific had developed a matrix organization. Reporting relationships were determined by business areas and by regional operating divisions within Pacific Oil. Warren Meredith, the executive vice president, had responsibility for monitoring the worldwide sale and distribution of VCM. Jean Fontaine reported to Meredith on all issues regarding the overall sale and marketing of

VCM, and reported to the president of Pacific Oil in Europe, Stan Saunders, on major issues regarding the management of the regional chemicals business in Europe. In general, Fontaine's primary working relationship was with Meredith; Saunders only became involved in day-to-day decisions as an arbiter of disputes or interpreter of major policy decisions.

As the negotiations with Reliant evolved, Meredith became distressed by the apparent turn that they were taking. He called in Frank Kelsey to review the situation. Kelsey knew that the VCM marketing effort for Pacific was going to face significant problems. Moreover, his dominant experience with Pacific in recent years had been in the purchasing and marketing operations, and he knew how difficult it would be for the company to maintain a strong negotiation in VCM contracts.

Meredith asked Kelsey to meet with Fontaine and Gaudin in Paris, and review the current status of negotiations on the Reliant contract. While Kelsey could act only in an advisory capacity—Fontaine and Gaudin were free to accept or reject any advice that was offered, since they were the ones who had to "live with" the contract—Meredith told Kelsey to offer whatever services the men would accept.

Kelsey flew to Paris shortly after New Year's Day 1986. He met with Fontaine and Gaudin, and they reviewed in detail what had happened in the Reliant contract negotiations over the past year. Kelsey listened, asked a lot of questions, and didn't say much. He felt that offering "advice" to the men was premature, and perhaps even unwise; Fontaine and Gaudin seemed very anxious about the negotiations, and felt that the new contract would be sealed within a month. Moreover, they seemed to resent Kelsey's visit, and clearly didn't want to share more than the minimum amount of information. Kelsey returned to New York, and briefed Meredith on the state of affairs.

When Fontaine called Meredith for "clearance" to give Reliant both "favored nations" and "meet competition" clauses in the new contract, Meredith immediately called Kelsey. The two of them went back through the history of events in the negotiation, and realized the major advantages that Reliant had gained by its negotiation tactics.

Meredith called Fontaine back and advised against granting the clauses in the contract. Fontaine said that Hauptmann was adamant, and that he was afraid the entire negotiation was going to collapse over a minor point in contract language. Meredith said he still thought it was a bad idea to make the concession. Fontaine said he thought he needed to consult Saunders, the European president of Pacific Oil, just to make sure.

Two days later, Saunders called Meredith and said that he had complete faith in Fontaine, and Fontaine's ability to determine what was necessary to make a contract work. If Fontaine felt that "favored nations" and "meet competition" clauses were necessary, he trusted Fontaine's judgment that the clauses could not cause significant adverse harm to Pacific Oil over the next few years. As a result, he had given Fontaine the go-ahead to agree to these clauses in the new contract.

MARCH 11

It was a dark and stormy night, March 11, 1986. Frank Kelsey was about to go to bed when the telephone rang. It was Jean Fontaine. Kelsey had not heard from

Fontaine since their meeting in Paris. Meredith had told Kelsey about the discussion with Saunders, and he had assumed that Fontaine had gone ahead and conceded on the two contract clauses that had been discussed. He thought the contract was about to be wrapped up, but he hadn't heard for sure.

The violent rainstorm outside disrupted the telephone transmission, and Kelsey had trouble hearing Fontaine. Fontaine said that he had appreciated Kelsey's visit in January. Fontaine was calling to ask Kelsey's advice. They had just come from a meeting with Hauptmann. Hauptmann and Zinnser had reported that recent news from Reliant's corporate headquarters in Chicago projected significant downturns in the sale of a number of Reliant's PVC products in the European market. While Reliant thought it could ride out the downturn, they were very concerned about their future obligations under the Pacific contract. Since Reliant and Pacific had already settled on minimum quantity amounts, Reliant wanted the contractual right to resell the product if it could not use the minimum amount.

Kelsey tried to control his emotions as he thought about this negative turn of events in the Reliant negotiations. He strongly advised against agreeing to the clause, saying that it could put Pacific in an extremely poor position. Fontaine debated the point, saying he really thought Reliant might default on the whole contract if they didn't get resale rights. "I can't see where agreeing to the right to resale is a big thing, Frank, particularly given the size of this contract and its value to me and Pacific."

Kelsey:

Look, you asked for my advice, and I gave it to you. If I were you, I wouldn't make any more concessions. Agreeing to a resale clause could create a whole lot of unforeseen problems. At this point I think it's also the principle of the thing!

Fontaine:

Who cares about principles at a time like this! It's my neck that's on the line if this Reliant contract goes under! I'll have over 200 million pounds of VCM a year to eat in an oversupplied market! It's my neck that's on the line, not yours! How in the world can you talk to me about "principle" at this point?

Kelsey:

Calm down, Jean! I can see your point of view! I appreciate the pressures on you, but I really don't like the looks of it from this end. Keep in touch—let me ask others down at the office what they think, and I'll call you next week.

Kelsey hung up the telephone, and stared out of the windows at the rain. He could certainly empathize with Fontaine's position—the man's neck was on the block. As he mentally reviewed the two-year history of the Reliant negotiations, Kelsey wondered how they had gotten to this point, and whether anyone could have done things differently. He also wondered what to do about the resale clause, which appeared to be the final sticking point in the deliberations. Would acquiescing to a resale clause for Reliant be a problem to Pacific Oil? Kelsey knew he had to take action soon.

Appendix: Petrochemical Supply Contracts

Supply contracts between chemical manufacturing/refining companies and purchasing companies are fairly standard in the industry trade. They are negotiated between supplier and purchaser in order to protect both parties against major fluctuations in supply and demand. Any purchaser wishing to obtain a limited amount of a particular product could always approach any one of a number of chemical manufacturing firms and obtain the product at "market price." The market price is controlled by the competitive supply and demand for the particular product on any given day. But purchasers want to be assured of a long-term supply and do not want to be subject to the vagaries of price fluctuation; similarly, manufacturers want to be assured of product outlets in order to adequately plan manufacturing schedules. Long-term contracts protect both parties against these fluctuations.

A supply contract is usually a relatively standard document, often condensed to one page. The major "negotiable" elements of the contract, on the "front side" of the document, include the price, quantity, product quality, contract duration, delivery point, and credit terms (see Exhibit 1A for a sample blank contract). The remainder ("back side") of the contract is filled with traditionally fixed legal terminology that governs the conditions under which the contract will be maintained. While the items are seldom changed, they may be altered or waived as part of the negotiated agreement.

The primary component of a long-term contract is the price. In the early years of the petrochemical industry, the raw product was metered by the supplier (either in liquid or gaseous form) and sold to the purchaser. As the industry became more competitive, as prices rose rapidly, and as the products developed from petrochemical supplies (called "feedstocks") became more sophisticated, pricing became a significantly more complex process. Most contemporary contract prices are determined by an elaborate calculation called a "formula price," composed of several elements:

1. *Feedstock characteristics.* Petrochemical feedstock supplies differ in the chemical composition and molecular structure of the crude oil. Differences in feedstocks will significantly affect the refining procedures and operating efficiency of the refinery that manufactures a product, as well as their relative usefulness to particular purchasers. While some chemical products may be drawn from a single feedstock, large-volume orders may necessitate the blending of several feedstocks with different structural characteristics.

2. *Fuel costs.* Fuel costs include the price and amount of energy that the manufacturing company must assume in cracking, refining, and producing a particular chemical stream.

3. *Labor costs.* Labor costs include the salaries of employees to operate the manufacturing facility for the purpose of producing a fixed unit amount of a particular product.

4. *Commodity costs.* Commodity costs include the value of the basic petrochemical base on the open marketplace. As the supply and demand for the basic commodity fluctuate on the open market, this factor is entered into the formula price.

EXHIBIT 1A   Agreement of Sale

This Agreement, entered into this _____ day of _____, _____, between Pacific Oil Company, hereinafter called Seller, and _____, hereinafter called Buyer. WITNESSETH:

Seller agrees to sell and deliver and Buyer agrees to purchase and receive commodity (hereinafter called "product") under the terms and conditions set forth below.

1. PRODUCT:

2. QUALITY:

3. QUANTITY:

4. PERIOD:

5. PRICE:

6. PAYMENT TERMS:

    (*a*) Net _____.

    (*b*) All payments shall be made in United States dollars without discount or deduction, unless otherwise noted, by wire transfer at Seller's option, to a bank account designated by Seller. Invoices not paid on due date will be subject to a delinquency finance charge of 1% per month.

    (*c*) If at any time the financial responsibility of Buyer shall become impaired or unsatisfactory to Seller, cash payment on delivery or satisfactory security may be required. A failure to pay any amount may, at the option of the Seller, terminate this contract as to further deliveries. No forbearance, course of dealing, or prior payment shall affect this right of Seller.

7. PRICE CHANGE:

    The price specified in this Agreement may be changed by Seller on the first day of any calendar _____ by written notice sent to the Buyer not less than thirty (30) days prior to the effective date of change. Buyer gives Seller written notice of objection to such change at least ten (10) days prior to the effective date of change. Buyer's failure to serve Seller with written notice of objection thereto prior to the effective date thereof shall be considered acceptance of such change. If Buyer gives such notice of objection and Buyer and Seller fail to agree on such change prior to the effective date thereof, this Agreement and the obligations of Seller and Buyer hereunder shall terminate with respect to the unshipped portion of the Product governed by it. Seller has the option immediately to cancel this contract upon written notice to Buyer, to continue to sell hereunder at the same price and terms which were in effect at the time Seller gave notice of change, or to suspend performance under this contract while pricing is being resolved. If Seller desires to revise the price, freight allowance, or terms of payment pursuant to this agreement, but is restricted to any extent against doing so by reason of any law, governmental decree, order, or regulation, or if the price, freight allowance, or terms of payment then in effect under this contract are nullified or reduced by reason of any law, governmental decree, order or regulation, Seller shall have the right to cancel this contract upon fifteen (15) days' written notice to purchaser.

8. MEASUREMENTS:

    Seller's determinations, unless proven to be erroneous, shall be accepted as conclusive evidence of the quantity of Product delivered hereunder. Credit will not be allowed for shortages of 1/2 of 1% or less of the quantity and overages of 1/2 of 1% or less of the quantity will be waived. The total amount of shortages or overages will be credited or billed when quantities are greater and such differences are substantiated. Measurements of weight and volume shall be according to procedures and criteria standard for such determinations.

EXHIBIT 1A   (*continued*)

---

9. SHIPMENTS AND DELIVERY:

Buyer shall give Seller annual or quarterly forecasts of its expected requirements as Seller may from time to time request. Buyer shall give Seller reasonably advanced notice for each shipment which shall include date of delivery and shipping instructions. Buyer shall agree to take deliveries in approximately equal monthly quantities, except as may be otherwise provided herein. In the event that Buyer fails to take the quantity specified or the pro rata quantity in any month, Seller may, at its option, in addition to other rights and remedies, cancel such shipments or parts thereof.

10. PURCHASE REQUIREMENTS:

(*a*) If during any consecutive three-month period, Buyer for any reason (but not for reasons of force majeure as set forth in Section 12) takes less than 90 percent of the average monthly quantity specified, or the prorated minimum monthly quantity then applicable to such period under Section 12, Seller may elect to charge Buyer a penalty charge for failure to take the average monthly quantity or prorated minimum monthly quantity.

(*b*) If, during any consecutive three-month period, Buyer, for any reason (but not, however, for reasons of force majeure as set forth in Section 12) takes Product in quantities less than that equal to at least one half of the average monthly quantity specified, or the prorated minimum monthly quantity originally applicable to such period under Section 12, Seller may elect to terminate this agreement.

(*c*) It is the Seller's intent not to unreasonably exercise its rights under (*a*) or (*b*) in the event of adverse economic and business conditions in general.

(*d*) Notice of election by Seller under (*a*) or (*b*) shall be given within 30 days after the end of the applicable three-month period, and the effective date of termination shall be 30 days after the date of said notice.

11. DETENTION POLICY:

Seller may, from time to time, specify free unloading time allowances for its transportation equipment. Buyer shall be liable to the Transportation Company for all demurrage charges made by the Transportation Company, for railcars, trucks, tanks, or barges held by Buyer beyond the free unloading time.

12. FORCE MAJEURE:

Neither party shall be liable to the other for failure or delay in performance hereunder to the extent that such failure or delay is due to war, fire, flood, strike, lockout, or other labor trouble, accident, breakdown of equipment or machinery, riot, act, request, or suggestion of governmental authority, act of God, or other contingencies beyond the control of the affected party which interfere with the production or transportation of the material covered by this Agreement or with the supply of any raw material (whether or not the source of supply was in existence or contemplated at the time of this Agreement) or energy source used in connection therewith, or interfere with Buyer's consumption of such material, provided that in no event shall Buyer be relieved of the obligation to pay in full for material delivered hereunder. Without limitation on the foregoing, neither party shall be required to remove any cause listed above or replace the affected source of supply or facility if it shall involve additional expense or departure from its normal practices. If any of the events specified in this paragraph shall have occurred, Seller shall have the right to al-

EXHIBIT 1A   *(continued)*

locate in a fair and reasonable manner among its customers and Seller's own requirements any supplies of material Seller has available for delivery at the time or for the duration of the event.

13. MATERIALS AND ENERGY SUPPLY:

If, for any reasons beyond reasonable commercial control, Seller's supply of product to be delivered hereunder shall be limited due to continued availability of necessary raw materials and energy supplies, Seller shall have the right (without liability) to allocate to the Buyer a portion of such product on such basis as Seller deems equitable. Such allocation shall normally be that percent of Seller's total internal and external commitments which are committed to Buyer as related to the total quantity from Seller's manufacturing facilities.

14. DISCLAIMER:

Seller makes no warranty, express or implied, concerning the product furnished hereunder other than it shall be of the quality and specification stated herein. Any implied warranty of FITNESS is expressly excluded and to the extent that it is contrary to the foregoing sentence: any implied warranty of MERCHANTABILITY is expressly excluded. Any recommendations made by Seller makes no warranty of results to be obtained. Buyer assumes all responsibility and liability for loss or damage resulting from the handling or use of said product. In no event shall Seller be liable for any special, indirect or consequential damages, irrespective of whether caused or allegedly caused by negligence.

15. TAXES:

Any tax, excise fee, or other charge or increase thereof upon the production, storage, withdrawal, sale, or transportation of the product sold hereunder, or entering into the cost of such product, imposed by any proper authority becoming effective after the date hereof, shall be added to the price herein provided and shall be paid by the Buyer.

16. ASSIGNMENT AND RESALE:

This contract is not transferable or assignable by Buyer without the written consent of Seller. The product described hereunder, in the form and manner provided by the Seller, may not be assigned or resold without prior written consent of the Seller.

17. ACCEPTANCE:

Acceptance hereof must be without qualification and Seller will not be bound by any different terms and conditions contained in any other communication.

18. WAIVER OF BREACH:

No waiver by Seller or Buyer of any breach of any of the terms and conditions contained in this Agreement shall be construed as a waiver or any subsequent breach of the same or any other term or condition.

19. TERMINATION:

If any provision of this agreement is or becomes violate of any law, or any rule, order, or regulation issued thereunder, Seller shall have the right upon notice to Buyer, to terminate the Agreement in its entirety.

20. GOVERNING LAW:

The construction of this Agreement and the rights and obligations of the parties hereunder shall be governed by the laws of the State of _____.

EXHIBIT 1A   *(continued)*

21. SPECIAL PROVISIONS:

BUYER: SELLER:

_____   _____

             (firm)   (firm)

By:_____   By:_____

Title:_____   Title:_____

Date:_____   Date:_____

A formula price may therefore be represented as a function of the following elements:

$$\text{Formula price} = \text{Feedstock cost} + \text{Energy cost} + \text{Labor cost} + \text{Commodity cost (per unit)}$$

If only one feedstock were used, the chemical composition of the feedstock would determine its basic cost, and the energy, labor, and commodity costs of producing it. If several feedstocks were used, the formula price would be a composite of separate calculations for each particular feedstock, or a weighted average of the feedstock components, multiplied by the cost of production of each one.

Each of the elements in the formula price is also multiplied by a weighting factor (coefficient) that specifies how much each cost will contribute to the determination of the overall formula price. The supplier generally sets a "ceiling price," guaranteeing that the formula price will not exceed this amount. Below the ceiling price, however, the supplier endeavors to maximize profits while clearly specifying the costs of production to the purchaser, while the purchaser attempts to obtain the most favorable formula price for himself. Since basic cost data and cost fluctuations are well known, negotiations typically focus on the magnitude of the coefficients that are applied to each element in the formula. Hence, the actual formula computation may be represented as follows:

$$\text{Formula price} = (\text{Weighting coefficient} \times \text{Feedstock cost})$$
$$+ (\text{Weighting coefficient} \times \text{Energy cost})$$
$$+ (\text{Weighting coefficient} \times \text{Labor cost})$$
$$+ (\text{Weighting coefficient} \times \text{Commodity cost})$$

A fairly typical ratio of the weighting coefficients in this formula would be 70 percent (0.7) for feedstock cost, 20 percent (0.2) for energy costs, 5 percent (0.05 for labor costs, and 5 percent (0.05) for commodity costs. Multiple feedstocks supplied in a particular contract would be composed of a different set of costs and weighting elements for each feedstock in the supply.

The computation of a formula price, as opposed to the determination of a market price, has a number of advantages and disadvantages. Clearly, it enables the supplier to pass costs along to the purchaser, which minimizes the risk for both parties in the event of rapid changes in cost during the duration of the contract. The purchaser can project directly how cost changes will affect his supply costs; the supplier is protected by being able to pass cost increases along to the purchaser. However, when the market demand for the product is very high, the formula price constrains the seller in the ceiling price he can charge, hence curtailing potential profit for the product compared to its value on the open marketplace. Conversely, when market demand is very low, the contract may guarantee a large market to the supplier, but at a price for the product that could be unprofitable compared to production costs.

QUANTITY

Formula prices are typically computed with major attention given to quantity. Costs will fluctuate considerably based on the efficiency with which the production plant is operated, number of labor shifts required, and so on. Hence, in order to adequately forecast demand, attain particular "economics of scale" in the manufacturing process, and plan production schedules, suppliers must be able to determine the quantities that a particular customer will want to acquire. (Because of the volumes involved, no significant inventory is produced.) Quantities will be specified in common units of weight (pounds, tons, etc.) or volume (gallons etc.).

Quantity specifications are typically treated as minimum purchase amounts. If a purchaser desires significantly more than the minimum amount ("overlifting") in a given time period (e.g., a year), the amount would be sold contingent on availability, and delivered at the formula price. Conceivably, "discount" prices or adjustments in the formula price could be negotiated for significant purchases over minimum quantity. Conversely, underpurchase of the minimum amount ("underlifting") by a significant degree typically results in penalty costs to the purchaser. These are typically referred to as "liquidated damages" in the industry, and may be negotiated at rates anywhere from a token fine of several thousand dollars to as much as 30 percent of the formula price for each unit underlifted. Faced with the possibility of underlifting (due to market or product demand changes that require less raw material in a given time period), purchasers typically handle underlifting in one of several ways:

a. Pay the underlifting charges ("liquidated damages") to the supplier, either as stated or according to some renegotiated rate.

b. *Not* pay the liquidated damages, under the assumption that the supplier will not want to press legal charges against the purchaser at the expense of endangering the entire supply contract.

c. Resell the commodity to another purchaser who may be in need of supply, perhaps at a discounted price. Such action by the purchaser could cause major instability in the market price and in supply contracts held at the original manufacturer or other manufacturers. For this reason, sellers typically preclude the right of the purchaser to resell the product as part of the "standard contract language."

QUALITY

The quality of the product is related to the particular feedstock from which it is drawn, as well as the type and degree of refining that is employed by the supplier. Standard descriptions for gradations of quality are common parlance for each major chemical product.

DELIVERY

Most contracts specify the method of delivery, point of delivery, and way that the quantity amounts will be measured as the product is delivered. Gases are typically metered and delivered by direct pipeline from the manufacturer to the purchaser; liquids and liquefied gases may be sold by pipeline, or shipped via tank truck, railroad tank car, tank barges, and tank ships.

CONTRACT DURATION

Most typical supply contracts extend for a period from one to five years; significantly longer or shorter ones would probably only be negotiated under extreme circumstances. Negotiations for contract renewal are typically begun several months prior to contract expiration.

PAYMENT TERMS

Payment terms are determined by the credit ratings and cash flow demands of both parties. Typical contracts specify payment within 30 days of delivery, although this time period may be shortened to payment on delivery, or lengthened to a period of three months between delivery and payment.

CONTRACT LANGUAGE

As can be determined from Exhibit 1A, there are a number of elements in the contract that delineate the conditions under which the parties agree to bind themselves to the contract, or to deviate from it. Terminology and agreements were typically standard, unless altered by negotiation prior to contract signing. These elements include the following:

1. *Measurements.* A mechanism for specifying how quantity amounts will be determined, and how disputes over differences in delivered quantity will be resolved.

2. *Meet competition.* The seller agrees to meet competitive market prices for the product if they become substantially lower than the current negotiated formula price.

3. *Favored nations.* The supplier agrees that if he offers a better price on the product to any of the purchaser's competitors, he will offer the same price to this buyer.

4. *Purchase requirements.* The purchase requirements govern the conditions and terms under which liquidated damages may be invoked.

5. *Force majeure.* The force majeure clause exempts the parties from contract default in the event of major natural disasters, strikes, fires, explosions, or other events that could preclude the seller's ability to deliver the product or the buyer's ability to purchase.

6. *Disclaimers.* The disclaimers protect both buyer and seller against unreasonable claims about the product or its quality.

7. *Assignability.* The assignability clause limits the right of either party to assign the contract to another purchaser or supplier if they so desire.

8. *Notifications.* The notifications section specifies the lead time during which one or both parties must notify the other party of any change in the contract or its renewal.

9. *Other clauses.* Other clauses include conditions under which the product may be assured delivery, application of taxes, provisions for resale, definitions of contract breach and termination, the legal framework used to enforce the contract (in the event of cross-state or cross-national agreements), and methods of notification of one party to the other.

CONTRACT MANAGEMENT AND MAINTENANCE

While a supply contract is a legally binding document that attempts to articulate the way two companies will work together, it more commonly stands as the cornerstone of a complex long-term social relationship between buyer and seller. This relationship requires constant monitoring, evaluation, and discussion by representatives of both organizations. Thus, while similar supply contracts may exist between a particular manufacturer and three different buyers, there may be major differences in the day-to-day interactions and quality of relationships between the manufacturer and each buyer. Experienced sales representatives have defined a "good" seller-buyer relationship as meeting the following criteria:

- *The purchaser can be counted on to live up to the terms and conditions of the contract as negotiated.* The purchaser accepts a fair formula price in price negotiations, and does not attempt to push the supplier into an artificially low price. The purchaser lifts as much of the product per time period as he agreed to lift under the contract. The purchaser is trustworthy, and follows a course of action based on sound business ethics.

- *The purchaser does not attempt to take advantage of fluctuations or aberrations in the spot market price to gain advantage.* He accepts the fact that a formula price has been negotiated, and that both parties agree to live up to this price for the duration of the contract. He does not seek contract price changes as the market price may drop for some time period.

- *When there is a mutual problem between seller and purchaser, it can be openly discussed and resolved between the two parties.* Problems resulting from the continued inability of the supplier to provide the product, and/or the continued inability of the buyer to consume the product, can be openly addressed and resolved. Problems in the quality of the product, labor difficulties resulting in problems in manufacturing, loading, shipping, unloading, cleanliness of the shipping equipment, and so on, can be promptly explored and resolved to mutual satisfaction. Finally, changes in the business projections of one or both parties can be shared, so that difficulties anticipated by the supplier in providing all of the product, or difficulties anticipated by the purchaser in consuming all of the product, can lead to amicable and satisfactory resolutions for both parties. Ability to resolve these problems requires mutual trust, honesty, open lines of communication, and an approach to problem solving that seeks the best solution for both sides.

A Power Play for Howard

Bill Brubaker
Mark Asher

Nothing less than the future of the Washington Bullets hung in the balance on the evening of July 11 when Juwan Howard, the club's all-star free agent forward, arrived at agent David Falk's headquarters in Chevy Chase Pavilion to solicit $100 million contract offers from National Basketball Association team executives.

Outside, on Wisconsin Avenue NW, the Bullets held a We-Love-Juwan rally for rabid fans desperate to keep their young star in Washington—a city that hasn't had a winning NBA team in nine years. Inside, in Falk's private office—adorned with Michael Jordan-autographed basketballs and other client memorabilia—Howard braced himself for a long night of high-stakes negotiating.

Bullets General Manager Wes Unseld got first crack at Howard—a courtesy Falk said he was extending to the club as "the incumbents." It soon became clear, however, that incumbency, like loyalty, had limited value in professional sports. Shortly after 7 PM Unseld offered a seven-year, $78.4 million contract. Lucrative as it was—the offer amounted to more than $136,000 per game through the 2002–2003 season—Howard considered the proposal far below his market value. He loved playing and living in Washington, and the thought of leaving brought tears to his eyes even as he dismissed Unseld's offer.

Yet leave he would. By dawn, Howard had begun seriously contemplating a move south to play for the Miami Heat which ultimately trumped the Bullets with a seven-year, guaranteed $100.8 million deal—the biggest in the history of team sports, garnished with luxury hotel suites and limousine service for the 23-year-old Howard during road trips. The Bullets' most promising player in a generation was gone, and with him hopes of resuscitating the club's fortunes.

But Howard's tears would prove premature and the Heat's huge offer only the opening gambit in one of the most intricate and controversial episodes in recent sports history. Over the next 30 days, Howard would sign with Miami only to have the contract invalidated by the league, triggering a bitter sequence of threats, legal maneuvers and shifting alliances. The final outcome would prove a colossal windfall for the Bullets: When Washington opens its 1996–97 season Friday in Orlando, Juwan Howard will be wearing his familiar No. 5 on a red, white, and blue Bullets uniform.

This turbulent saga—recounted here following extensive interviews with Howard, agents, league officials, union representatives, and team executives—illuminates the extent to which pro sports have become a tangle of emotion and fiscal logic; on-court talent and off-court financial calculation.

The unprecedented case also featured an unusual collaboration between two traditional adversaries, the NBA and the players' union, the National Basketball Players Association. It featured the repudiation, first by the league and then by Howard, of one of basketball's most charismatic, cunning and successful coaches, Pat Riley, who is also the Heat's president. By taking strong and decisive action against Riley and Heat owner Micky Arison, the NBA may have brought Washington's franchise back from the dead—a critical development for a club that will change its name to the Wizards next year and move into a new, 20,600-seat downtown arena, the MCI Center.

During a summer in which free agent bidding took the never-never land of NBA salaries to new heights, Howard's odyssey ultimately became the story of a favorite son who briefly sought his fortune elsewhere but ended up returning to the fold—perhaps wiser and certainly much, much richer. Buoyed with a nine-figure contract from the Bullets, Howard celebrated by buying a $230,000 Ferrari sports car and a luxury suite at MCI Center and by contemplating his dream house: a Washington-area mansion with eight bedrooms, indoor and outdoor swimming pools, a bowling alley, theater, and basketball court. "I want elevators inside my house," Howard would explain. "That's always has been a dream of mine."

"This was about bucks," Unseld said in his office next to USAir Arena, a computer printout of NBA player salaries by his side. "No matter how you want to put it, I think that's eventually what it came down to."

A SOUR START

Howard's summer of 1996 "fiasco," as he has called it, had its roots in the summer of 1994 when the Bullets drafted the 6-foot-9-inch University of Michigan junior. Howard wanted a six-year, $24 million deal, considered the going rate for the fifth player chosen in that year's draft. By agreeing, the Bullets could have locked Howard into a long-term contract.

But during negotiations in the sun room of Bullets owner Abe Pollin's house in Bethesda, John Nash, then the club's general manager, essentially told Howard he wasn't worth it. Nash (who resigned under pressure in April) later offered Howard an 11-year, $37.5 million deal with the option of becoming a free agent after his second season, in 1996. Howard considered the below-market offer "totally unfair," but he accepted it and soon established himself as a valuable NBA commodity, averaging 19.8 points, 8.3 rebounds and 3.6 assists per game over the two seasons.

Howard's game was more than statistics, however. With a positive attitude and strong work ethic, he became a guiding light for less disciplined teammates. Off court, he donated time and money to charitable causes and community projects. Polite and soft-spoken, Howard was untouched by controversy until this May when a Detroit woman filed a paternity suit alleging he is the father of her 4 1/2-year-old son. Howard has denied the allegation. A blood test taken by Howard indicated there is a greater than 99.99 percent probability he is the child's father, according to a lab report filed in court by the woman's attorneys.

Knowing that Howard would become a free agent this year, players from opposing teams playfully began recruiting him during games last season. "Grant Hill was recruiting me, telling me what Detroit had," Howard said in an interview earlier this month. "Alonzo [Mourning of the Heat] and Patrick [Ewing of the New York Knicks] were recruiting me at the All-Star Game. I just laughed, man. I just said, 'Yo, this seems like college recruiting all over again.' It felt good to feel wanted."

Howard insisted that he wanted to remain a Bullet. "He's theirs to lose," said agent Falk, 46, a George Washington University law school graduate whose client list at Falk Associates Management Enterprises (FAME) includes Jordan, Mourning and Ewing. In a half-page ad in The Washington Post, Pollin promised Bullets fans: "We will do everything we can to keep Juwan with us in Washington. . . . We love Juwan Howard." Howard and his agents could not open negotiations with clubs until a new collective bargaining agreement (CBA) was signed this summer. In early July, with the moratorium still in effect, Falk deliberately sent the Bullets a signal by telling a Washington Post reporter he expected Howard would sign for $15 million to $20 million a year ($105 million to $140 million over seven years, the maximum term allowed under the new CBA).

One minute after the new labor agreement was finalized at 4:59 PM on July 11, the NBA's free agent marketplace officially opened. So began a competition that in tone and tension resembled a cross between a television game show and a Turkish bazaar. That evening, a parade of free agents and team officials converged on FAME's eighth-floor headquarters at Chevy Chase Pavilion. Offers for various players were scrutinized by Falk's 36-year-old partner and fellow lawyer, Curtis Polk, in what the agents called their "War Room"—an inner sanctum with a computer mainframe, three laptops, and six telephone lines. But most of the action would unfold in Falk's private office, watched over by a framed *Sports Illustrated* magazine cover featuring Falk and Jordan.

Between 5 and 7 PM Falk quickly negotiated a one-year, $30 million contract that would keep Jordan playing for the Chicago Bulls. Then he turned to Howard.

Unseld, a wide-bodied, 6-foot-7 Hall of Famer who led Washington to its only NBA title in 1978, immediately notified Howard, Falk, and Polk that he alone would represent the Bullets. Howard and his agents asked for assurances that the Bullets' coaching staff, headed by Jim Lyman, would be retained. Unseld said it would. Howard also asked how the Bullets intended to improve a team that hadn't made the NBA playoffs for eight years. Unseld disclosed that he was trying to acquire Rod Strickland, one of the NBA's top point guards.

Unseld, who had replaced Nash as the Bullets' general manager only two months earlier, then offered Howard a seven-year, $78.4 million contract. The proposal stirred little enthusiasm among Howard or his agents, and after Unseld left Falk's office, Polk said there was no chance Howard would play again in a Bullets uniform. The assessment, with its ring of cold finality and implication of abrupt change, was upsetting to Howard, who began to cry.

But the press of business beckoned. Between 8 and 10 PM the Detroit Pistons' top basketball executive, Rick Sund, discussed his interest in Howard, followed at 11 PM by Knicks General Manager Ernie Grunfeld, who had flown to Washington in the team's Gulfstream jet. Neither made a firm offer that evening.

At 2 AM, Howard slipped off to take a nap. As he dozed, the Heat, represented by Riley, a club lawyer and two vice presidents, negotiated with Mourning, their prized, 6-foot-10, free agent center. Of 160 free agents on the market, the Heat rated Mourning and Howard third- and fourth-most desirable, respectively, after Jordan and the Orlando Magic's Shaquille O'Neal, who ended up with the Los Angeles Lakers.

Riley asked Mourning to sign a one-year contract at less than market value to help the Heat create more room under the salary cap. Mourning dismissed the proposal. Riley said he then assured Mourning that after "taking care of some business" with other players, "I will make you the highest-paid player on the team."

At that moment, the seeds of controversy were planted.

Under the CBA, club officials are forbidden to make undisclosed agreements, promises, "representations, commitments, inducements . . . or understandings of any kind" with players. The prohibition aimed to prevent clubs from circumventing the rules of the league's salary cap, which limits spending on players to keep teams competitive with one another; in general terms, the cap restricts teams' payrolls to $24.3 million for the 1996–97 season. The CBA also requires teams to report immediately all player contracts—oral or written—to the league.

Riley would later contend, bitterly, that his pledge to Mourning was proper because it contained no specific dollar figures—an interpretation of the CBA supported by the players' union but disputed by the league.

Shortly before 3 AM Mourning left the room and Howard walked in. "All the guys were very tired," Riley recalled, "and it was very, very serious in there. We all knew we were going to be talking about a lot of money." Riley tried to lighten the mood by recalling how his brother had represented him in his first negotiation as an NBA player in 1967. "Before going into the room, my brother looked me in the eye and said, 'Just think, Pat! You're going to earn $17,000 a year!' " Riley told Howard and his agents.

The Heat's opening bid for Howard was $84 million over seven years. For several hours the two sides haggled. By the time the session broke up around 6 AM on Friday, July 12, Riley had increased his offer to $91 million plus $3.5 million in bonuses and some perks. The Heat executives shuffled off to breakfast, then to their hotel, the ANA, on M Street NW.

At noon, Howard returned to Falk's office to review the offers. The Bullets initially were eliminated from consideration; Howard had been impressed by Riley, who had won four NBA championships as the Lakers' coach. But Howard could not easily shrug off his feelings for the Washington club and it was decided to give the team another chance, what Falk called "the court of appeals." Howard asked to meet Pollin at his house in Bethesda.

At 5 PM Howard, Falk and Polk joined Pollin, Unseld, and club president Susan O'Malley in the sun room where Howard had his first negotiation with the Bullets in

1994. Pollin announced to his guests that Unseld would make one last offer, and warned that the Bullets wouldn't exceed that "by a dime."

The Bullets executives left the room for a few minutes to confer. When they returned Unseld increased his seven-year offer from $78.4 million to $84 million. "Wes and Susan said they had studied the numbers and . . . this is what they could afford," Falk said. "They had given Juwan an ultimatum." (Pollin declined to be interviewed for this article.)

The meeting broke up before 6 PM. Back at FAME's offices Howard again cried as he considered the take-it-or-leave-it negotiation at Pollin's house, which echoed his first contract talks two years earlier. Regret gave way to irritation. "I couldn't believe this was happening again . . . despite that I gave 100 percent on and off the floor for the franchise," Howard said. "Abe Pollin had made that promise to the people that he would do anything it took—anything possible—to make sure Juwan Howard stays in Washington."

Howard told Falk and Polk that Miami was his top choice, but he wanted the Heat to up the ante. Within an hour Riley was back in Falk's office. The Heat now offered $95.2 million plus $6 million in bonuses, but Howard wanted more perks. Riley agreed to the hotel suites and limos, as well as an extra $5,000 to help Howard sponsor a summer basketball camp.

Still, Howard's agents pressed for more.

"You've got to stop this," an exasperated Riley finally demanded. "Every time I walk out of the room and come back in there is something else. Please. It's over with, okay? This is the final offer."

Riley left around 8:30 PM. Falk and Howard phoned Unseld at his Baltimore home. Do the Bullets have any room to compromise? Howard wanted to know. For three hours, Unseld floated various suggestions for increasing the value of his offer, such as deferred payments. But Falk would have none of it.

"Can you do any more?" Howard finally asked.

Unseld was out of ideas. "No," he said.

"Okay," Howard said, "I guess there's no more to talk about. Thank you for two great years. And good luck to you guys."

Howard hung up and turned to Falk. "Call Pat Riley," he told the agent.

MIAMI BOUND

Around 1 AM on July 13, the phone again rang in Riley's room at the ANA Hotel. Howard was on the phone.

"Coach," he told Riley. "I'm coming to Miami."

Howard reviewed the Heat's offer, point by point, with an elated Riley. The final deal would amount to $100.8 million in cash, plus perks. "Then they began to ask for a little bit more," Riley later recalled. "Silly things. I said, 'You need [more game] tickets? Okay, we'll give you a couple more tickets. But let's move on, okay?' "

In Falk's office, Howard exchanged champagne toasts with new teammate Mourning and FAME staffers. Falk declined to disclose FAME's cut for negotiating the Howard deal other than to say it was less than the maximum 4 percent agents can charge under the labor agreement.

Yet an apparently ironclad deal still seemed to have some wiggle room. Unseld talked to Falk by phone that afternoon.

"Is it a done deal?" the Bullets executive said he asked. Falk said no.

Later, Falk phoned Unseld again. "Falk gave me a figure and says, "If you guys did this . . .' " Unseld recalled. "And I thought that was strange because I thought it was finished with us."

Falk said later he never suggested Howard was open to new offers and Unseld concedes he may have misinterpreted Falk's signals. Nevertheless, Unseld phoned Pollin at his Virginia farm and the Bullets' owners agreed to increase the club's offer from $84 million to $94.5 million.

Unseld said he then phoned Falk only to have the new offer rejected. But Falk said he recalls no new bid on the afternoon of July 13, and he accused the Bullets of using "spin control . . . to make it look like they were really close" to signing Howard.

The next day, the Bullets renounced their rights to Howard—conditional on him having a valid contract with the Heat—in order to have room under the salary cap to sign free agent forward Tracy Murray. In the coming days the Bullets also would acquire free agent forward-center Lorenzo Williams and, in a trade with the Portland Trail Blazers, point guard Strickland and forward Harvey Grant. But the club was being lambasted by Washington fans and media for losing Howard.

On July 17, Howard flew to Miami in a private jet to sign his new contract. At a news conference that evening, Howard called his new contract a "blessing" and his relationship with the Heat "like a marriage." The signing, he said, was the most important day of his life, after graduation day in Ann Arbor, Michigan, last year.

THE UNRAVELING

Riley had little time to celebrate: NBA investigators were heading his way. In an interview on July 16 on ESPN, Mourning left the impression that he had an agreement with the Heat. Asked if his new deal was for $100 million plus," Mourning said, "Yeah, it is."

If Mourning had such an agreement, the Heat had not notified the NBA as required. A new Mourning agreement would have dramatically shrunk the room Miami had under the salary cap to sign Howard. And that would jeopardize the validity of Howard's contract. Riley and Falk again insisted no deal had been finalized. (Mourning declined to be interviewed for this story.)

The NBA hired Robert Del Tufo—a former New Jersey attorney general who also had once prosecuted mobsters and Russian spies as a U.S. attorney—to determine if the Heat had circumvented salary cap rules. Had the team made an undisclosed deal with Mourning, possibly as early as last November, when the club obtained him in a trade with the Charlotte Hornets?

Del Tufo and two other lawyers flew to Miami to interview Heat executives on July 24. Riley insisted there were no undisclosed deals. But a week later, on July 31, the NBA's chief legal officer, Jeffrey Mishkin, phoned Arison, the Heat's owner, to tell him the NBA had disapproved Howard's contract because the club could not fit Howard's first-year base pay of $9 million under the salary cap. Mishkin told Arison the Heat had improperly made an undisclosed agreement with Mourning and used his previous, less lucrative contract to calculate the room the club had available to sign Howard. The team also had miscalculated the portion of incentive bonuses in two other free agent deals—for guard Tim Hardaway and forward P. J. Brown—that should have been counted against the cap, Mishkin asserted.

Under the CBA, a club can offer a player performance bonuses that are unlikely, in the club's estimation, to be achieved. "Unlikely" bonuses ultimately are not charged against the cap. The CBA defines "unlikely" bonuses as those based on achievements not attained the previous season by a player or his team. The CBA also gives the NBA commissioner authority to contest any "unlikely" bonus he considers to be, in fact, probable.

Riley had given Brown and Hardaway "unlikely" bonuses. One incentive, for example, would pay Brown $1.5 million if the Heat won either 27 home games or 43 total games this season. The Heat deemed that "unlikely" because the franchise never had won more than 26 home games or 42 total games in its eight-year history.

But the league, noting that the Heat had significantly improved its prospects by signing Howard, disagreed. Mishkin told Arison that those bonuses, now deemed "likely," shaved $2.5 million from the Heat's payroll ceiling, thus invalidating the Howard deal.

Riley was stunned by the news. He denounced the ruling as "unconscionable," one that "dismantled" his team. As a "partner" of the Heat, he asserted that the NBA had a "fiduciary responsibility" to alert the club if the Howard deal was in jeopardy. "Every team in this league pushes the envelope a little," Riley said. "And then you talk to the NBA and they say, 'You can't go that far.'"

Owner Arison, who had tangled with the league before, was equally upset. In 1995, the league had fined him $1 million—and taken his top 1996 draft choice—for recruiting Riley while he was under contract to the Knicks. Miami officials speculated that NBA Commissioner David Stern may have disallowed the Howard contract to punish the Heat's relentlessness or to bail out Pollin's flailing franchise.

"We're not mistake-free," Arison, who also owns Carnival Cruise Lines, said in an interview. "I don't think we made mistakes greater than many teams have made, and we're being punished greater than any team's ever been punished for similar mistakes."

The NBA office was unmoved. The league could not alert Miami to potential problems with the Howard deal, an NBA official said, because it only learned of the Brown and Hardaway details after their contracts were signed.

Stern, in his first public comments on the Howard case, said he judged the case solely on its merits. "We took our action because that's what the facts before us required us to do. . . . If the Heat is unhappy, get on line," he said in an interview last month.

"At a meeting of 29 owners you would get unanimity that I have it in for all 29 owners," Stern added. "If you're not prepared to have all of the teams mad at you, you're not doing your job."

Over the Cap: The Dispute between the NBA and the Heat

	Miami's Version	NBA's Version
Salary cap	$24.3 million	$24.3 million
All other Heat players	$4.26 million	$4.26 million
Alonzo Mourning	$6.84 million*	$9.4 million**
Tim Hardaway	$2 million	$3 million
$2 million salary	$2 million salary	$2 million salary
$2 million bonuses	$2 million unlikely bonuses	$1 million likely bonuses, $1 million unlikely
P. J. Brown	$1.7 million	$3.2 million
$1.7 million salary	$1.7 million salary	$1.7 million salary
$1.5 million bonuses	$1.5 million unlikely bonuses	$1.5 million likely bonuses
Juwan Howard	$9 million	$9 million
Total	$23.8 million	$28.86 million
	($500,000 *under* cap)	($4.56 million *over* cap)

*Heat's figure—representing 150 percent of Mourning's salary last season, in accordance with new collective bargaining agreement—was based on its contention that it had not made agreement with Mourning before making agreement with Howard.

**NBA's figure—representing salary league believed Mourning would receive in 1996–97—was based on league's decision that Heat had made undisclosed deal with Mourning before it made deal with Howard.

◼ Areas of dispute.

THE HEAT IS OFF

In a news release on July 31, the NBA stated that issues raised by the Howard matter would be resolved by arbitrators jointly selected by the league and union. The Heat, however, had at least as much at risk under arbitration as Juwan Howard. Under a worse-case scenario for the Heat, if an arbitrator and appeals panel upheld the NBA's allegations regarding the alleged Mourning agreement, the league could void Mourning's contract, fine the club $5 million, suspend Riley for a year, take away draft picks—and still leave the Heat without Howard.

While the NBA was disapproving his contract, Howard was en route to Miami to shop for a house in Coconut Grove, a picturesque community on Biscayne Bay. Howard planned to visit a Mediterranean-style house on the water—a location that would even let him take a boat to practice. But as Howard stepped into the airport terminal, one of his agents told him of the latest trouble.

Howard rushed to the Heat's downtown offices, where Riley assured him the NBA's allegations were false. "We'll fight these charges like hell because we've been wronged here," Riley told Howard.

With Arison looking on, Howard hugged Riley. "Coach," he later quoted himself as saying, "I'm behind you guys 100 percent."

That evening, Howard joined Riley at Paulo Luigi's, a trendy restaurant in Coconut Grove. But in the next several days the warm relationship between new player and new team quickly cooled. Howard concluded after discussions with Polk that if he backed Miami and the team lost a protracted fight with the league, other NBA clubs might have as little as $40 million or $50 million to offer him for seven years. In effect, he would take a $50 million pay cut and become, he said, "a laughingstock."

That house on Biscayne Bay suddenly lost its appeal. Riley found he couldn't get Howard to return his calls.

"I mean, this is a business," Howard later explained. "Yes, indeed, I believe in loyalty. But I believe in loyalty in the sense that it has to be done right and make sure that I don't lose in no kind of fashion."

Falk had gone to Europe and Israel on a long-planned family vacation, leaving Polk to sort out Howard's future. Polk tried to sort through the key issues. Could the Heat prevail in arbitration? Possibly, Polk believed, but it might take two months. But if the Heat lost the arbitration, Howard stood to lose tens of millions.

The Bullets could sign Howard only if the league restored the team's "Larry Bird rights." The CBA provision, named after the former Boston Celtics star, allowed teams to exceed the salary cap in order to re-sign their own players. The Bullets had lost their "Bird rights" to Howard when they renounced him. But if the rights were restored, the Bullets would have no limit on the sum of money they could pay Howard.

On August 1, the NBA declared Howard a free agent. Howard instructed Polk: "Wait for word on the Bullets before coming to an agreement with any team."

The next day, Unseld phoned Pollin, who was in Atlanta for the Olympics.

"If we can get Juwan, we could be a very good team," Unseld said.

"Do what you want to do," Pollin responded. "Do what you have to do."

Unseld had tried not to second-guess himself over the earlier Howard negotiations—the media and irate fans had done plenty of that. But now he had a chance to make amends. "I'm sure if I looked back on it," he subsequently said, "I would find plenty of mistakes. . . . I choose not to do that because if I did I would drive myself crazy."

The league was driving the Heat crazy. On August 2, NBA Deputy Commissioner Russ Granik told Arison by phone that based on his understanding of the CBA the Heat would be unlikely to regain Howard's services through arbitration. "You will not get Juwan Howard," Granik declared, according to Heat officials.

Later that day, the Heat obtained a temporary injunction prohibiting Howard from signing another contract unless it recognized the validity of the Miami deal. The injunction named the NBA and Howard as defendants. Howard was angry at the Heat for not forewarning him. "Where's the loyalty there?" he demanded.

The players' union agreed with the Heat that the Hardaway and Brown bonuses were "unlikely" and that Mourning did not have an undisclosed agreement. But the union disagreed with Miami over whether Howard should be allowed to re-sign with the Bullets.

On August 3, as the league and union were completing an agreement to restore the Bullets' Bird rights, Unseld prepared to negotiate his second-chance contract with Howard. Polk, concerned that Miami would impose further legal obstacles, phoned

Howard in his hometown of Chicago and advised him to return to Washington. Howard arrived that night.

Monday, August 5 was triumphant for the Bullets, disastrous for the Heat. The league and union agreed that if a player signs a second contract after his first deal has been disapproved, the second contract is the valid one, making arbitration moot. The deal, which would apply first and foremost to Howard, was intended to protect players against financial losses in disputes between the NBA and its teams.

In Howard's case, the league and union also agreed to restore the Bullets' Bird rights and allow Murray and Williams to remain with the Bullets. If the club re-signed Howard, however, it would forfeit its 1997 first-round draft choice.

Riley, ever more furious, accused the league and union of "getting into bed together" in an "unholy alliance."

On the afternoon of August 5 Unseld phoned Polk. "We got our Bird rights restored. Why don't you come on over?" Unseld said, according to Polk.

Pollin agreed to match the terms of Howard's $100.8 million Miami deal—adding $4.2 million to cover Maryland taxes because Florida has no state income tax—even though Howard seemed to be in a decidedly weaker negotiating position. "We wanted a happy player," Unseld said.

Howard's seven-year, $105 million Bullets contract—contingent upon the resolution of the Heat's legal challenges—took but 30 minutes to negotiate. Unseld refused, however, to match Riley's offer of hotel suites and limos. "I didn't want him getting picked up in a limousine and everybody else getting on a bus. It's as simple as that," Unseld explained. "Everybody else in a regular room and one guy in a suite? I don't think it makes for the chemistry of a team."

Before signing the contract, Unseld took Howard aside. "He wanted to see where my head was at," Howard said. "He wanted to see: Did I have any grudges against him? . . . I told him, 'Hell, no.' Excuse my French. I said, 'No. You guys had to do what was best for the organization and make a bright business decision for yourselves. And I had to do the same thing for me.' "

Shortly after 10 PM, Riley called Polk at his Rockville home. Though arbitration was now a remote possibility, Riley still hoped for a final meeting with Howard. "We needed Juwan to tell us, 'If I go down the road with you and you win [arbitration] I will come to Miami,' " Riley said.

Polk refused and the conversation turned ugly. "Riley told me, 'You're a shrinking violet. . . . You're a coward,' " Polk said. Riley said he does not recall making those comments, but added, "We had some very, very heated discussions."

For Riley, the battle was over. Without Howard in his corner, he said, "we had nobody to fight for anymore. . . . And that's where you had to cut bait." Riley remained furious at the league for allowing Washington to recover from its mistake. "The league built a team in Washington, basically," he later charged.

Falk said the Heat fell victim to a league intent on "dealing very sternly, no pun intended" with clubs that pursued free agents too aggressively and to a union "not in a strong enough position to do battle with the league."

"The league had the whole thing wired; the league forced Miami to settle," Falk added. "The league presented the Heat with a plea bargain: If you go to an arbitrator, you'll go to jail for 100 years. If you don't, we'll let you off."

In the settlement, announced August 10, Howard's contract with the Bullets was approved. The NBA and Miami agreed to drop "the various legal proceedings between the parties," which meant the Heat would abandon its bid for a permanent injunction and the league would not pursue the alleged undisclosed Mourning agreement. The Heat signed Brown and Hardaway to new contracts, removing the issue of whether their bonuses were likely or not, and Mourning signed a seven-year, $105 million deal.

Two days later, Howard appeared at a news conference at USAir Arena.

"He's baaaaaack," Unseld said in introducing his once and future star.

"I look at this as a blessing—a blessing from God," Howard told reporters, echoing the same language he had used a few weeks earlier in Miami. "I could recall the time I graduated from college. That was the best day of my life, right there. I consider this behind that."

THE '$205 MILLION MAN'

In the end, Pat Riley said, he bears Howard no malice. "You know what? I wish Juwan the very best," Riley said one afternoon recently. "But I think deep down in his heart he will always wonder what it would have been like to play with Alonzo and this team down here. That's something he'll never know."

Riley paused, chuckling softly as he reconsidered. "Juwan will probably win championships in Washington," he said. "And he'll probably forget that this whole thing ever happened."

That, Howard said, is unlikely.

"I will never forget this," he said after a Bullets practice. "This is something I can tell my grandkids about. How I signed a $100 million contract. How I signed a $105 million contract. I'm the first guy this has ever happened to. This summer"—Juwan Howard had the look of a man who had just accomplished something really big—"I was a $205 million man."

Also contributing to this story were *Washington Post* staff writers George Solomon in New York and J. A. Adande at the Bullets training camp in Shepherdstown, West Virginia.

Creating the GM–Toyota Joint Venture: A Case in Complex Negotiation

Stephen E. Weiss

During the last four years, the joint venture between General Motors and Toyota Motor to assemble subcompact cars has become a symbol of international cooperation within the auto industry and beyond. Academics, managers, and government officials have all emphasized the parent companies' reputations and the joint venture's achievements in labor relations, production efficiencies, and product quality. Yet, as deserved as this attention to operations and performance may be, an important aspect of the venture has been neglected—its birth.

Creating an international joint venture is neither an easy nor a certain process. Like other negotiations, joint venture negotiations may, at worst, fail completely. Undertaking negotiations in an international context, moreover, adds obstacles as well as opportunities. Before its talks with GM, for example, Toyota negotiated with Ford (unsuccessfully as it turned out) for 13 months. Even the GM–Toyota talks were, in participants' words, "long," "hard," and "frustrating."[1] So the agreement leading to the establishment of the joint venture now known as New United Motor Manufacturing, Inc. (NUMMI), represents an important accomplishment.

The story of the GM–Toyota negotiations is also significant as an illustration of the complexity common to international business negotiations. They entail complicated issues, parties that are large organizations, and multiple, dynamic, and differing environments—all of which are given little attention in existing management research on negotiation.[2] This case study may stimulate future work. At the same time, it invokes concepts from existing literature on negotiation that further understanding of the GM–Toyota discussions. Finally, this article draws out strategic implications and guidelines for automakers and other firms considering international collaboration.

Stephen E. Weiss, a specialist in negotiation and conflict management, is currently Director of the International MBA Program and Associate Professor of Policy and International Business, York University, Faculty of Administrative Studies (Toronto). The assistance of the Faculty Editor, Susan Douglas, Thomas Gladwin, Stephen Kobrin, and especially the participants in the negotiations interviewed by the authors is gratefully acknowledged. Reprinted with permission of Stephen E. Weiss and the *Columbia Journal of World Business,* copyright 1987.

AN ANALYTIC APPROACH

News and other reports on the GM–Toyota negotiations have focused on only the two companies and their actions, but a number of factors describe and explain the negotiations. Other organizations, groups, and individuals took significant steps; their relationships as well as distinct actions deserve attention, as do the particular conditions and contexts in which those actions took place. In short, this study endeavors to enrich the understanding of the two companies' efforts by assuming an approach sensitive to most of these factors.[3]

With respect to the actors involved, the analysis that follows treats GM and Toyota as the two primary organizations. In addition to their intercompany (primary) talks, they met in critical ancillary negotiations with the United Auto Workers (UAW) and with the Federal Trade Commission (FTC). Chart 1, which guides this discussion, places the foursome at the center of activity as the most deeply involved organizational actors (Ring 1a).

Other actors also influenced and were affected by the negotiations. Chart 1 identifies and classifies several organizations by their degree of involvement (Rings 1a–4a). The chart also recognizes three levels of analysis for behavior: organizational wholes (a), groups such as negotiating teams (b), and individuals (c). The activities of each organization listed, which shaped conditions for the negotiations, could be analyzed at the two other levels. For clarity and brevity, only the groups and individuals representing the four major organizations appear in the chart (Box 1b, c).

The following account concentrates on the four main parties in Chart 1 and addresses their actions, relationships, and contexts. First, GM's and Toyota's motivations for a joint venture are considered. Then the discussion traces in detail the primary negotiations between GM and Toyota and the ancillary talks with the UAW and with the FTC. Each of the three negotiations is described according to the issues stemming from the parties' (organizations') relationship, the individual players involved, relevant conditions, the negotiation process (sessions held, proposals made), and the outcome.

MOTIVATING FACTORS

From late 1979 to late 1981, the General Motors Corporation and the Toyota Motor Company (as it was then called) were the largest car producers in their respective home countries and the first and third largest producers worldwide. They each saw the rise of several corporate needs, especially in the predominant U.S. market. Some of the needs, or interests, were straightforward and typical of firms that eventually seek the cooperation of another firm,[4] while other interests drawing less public attention also existed. All of these interests set the stage for the negotiations that followed.

The U.S. Market

February 1979 brought the second oil shock in six years to American consumers, and they reacted by postponing purchases and shifting preferences to small, fuel-efficient cars. During 1980, domestic subcompact and compact cars captured

CHART 1 Actors and Audiences in the GM–Toyota Negotiations*

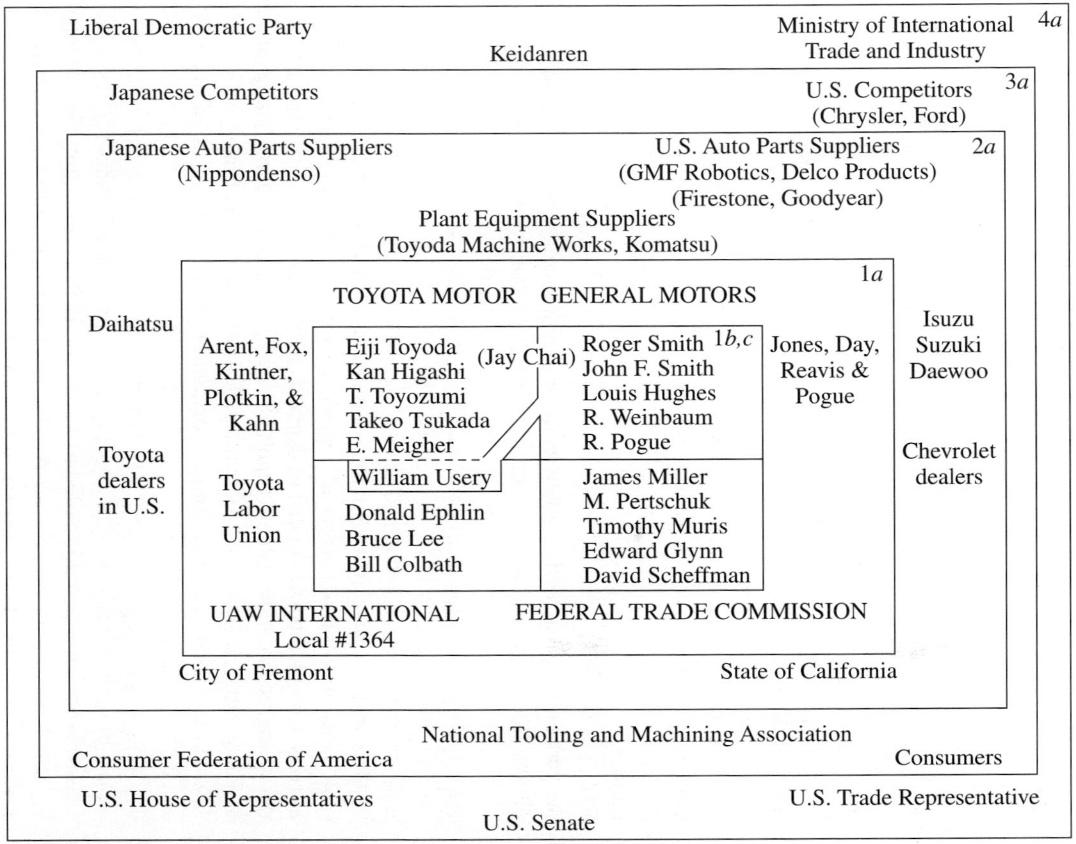

Liberal Democratic Party

Japanese Competitors

Japanese Auto Parts Suppliers
(Nippondenso)

Keidanren

Ministry of International
Trade and Industry *4a*

U.S. Competitors
(Chrysler, Ford) *3a*

U.S. Auto Parts Suppliers
(GMF Robotics, Delco Products) *2a*
(Firestone, Goodyear)

Plant Equipment Suppliers
(Toyoda Machine Works, Komatsu)

Daihatsu

Arent, Fox,
Kintner,
Plotkin, &
Kahn

Toyota
dealers
in U.S.

Toyota
Labor
Union

TOYOTA MOTOR   GENERAL MOTORS *1a*

Eiji Toyoda   (Jay Chai)   Roger Smith *1b,c*   Jones, Day,
Kan Higashi   John F. Smith   Reavis &
T. Toyozumi   Louis Hughes   Pogue
Takeo Tsukada   R. Weinbaum
E. Meigher   R. Pogue
William Usery
Donald Ephlin   James Miller
Bruce Lee   M. Pertschuk
Bill Colbath   Timothy Muris
                            Edward Glynn
                            David Scheffman

Isuzu
Suzuki
Daewoo

Chevrolet
dealers

UAW INTERNATIONAL
Local #1364

FEDERAL TRADE COMMISSION

City of Fremont

State of California

Consumer Federation of America

National Tooling and Machining Association

Consumers

U.S. House of Representatives

U.S. Senate

U.S. Trade Representative

*This structure was suggested by Ian Wise.

Notes

Larger rectangles (rings)
represent diminishing
degrees of involvement:
1—primary actors;
2—affiliates, network
   members, and supporting
   audiences;
3—industry and market
   actors (opponents)
4—environmental
   (political) actors.

Letters designate levels
of behavioral analysis:
a—organizations;
b—groups;
c—individuals.

With the exception of
the FTC, Boxes 1b,c contain
negotiating teams (excluding
CEO's Toyoda and Smith)
as well as primary individual
players.

36.37 percent of the U.S. car market. The subcompacts alone doubled their 1971 share of 7.42 percent.[5] In this segment of the market GM, like the rest of the U.S.'s Big Three, was confronted with highly competitive Japanese imports. In January of 1980, Japanese car imports jumped 86.5 percent over those of the previous January.[6] The U.S.'s Motor Vehicle Manufacturers Association reported 1,991,502 Japanese car imports in 1980, which translated into a 22.2 percent share of the market and a 23 percent increase over the 1979 total.[7]

General Motors' Performance

General Motors' position during this period was dramatically reflected in its net income for 1980—minus $763 million. The loss was the company's first since 1921. From 1979 to 1980, total sales dropped 20 percent, U.S. car (unit) sales dropped 17 percent, and U.S. car production fell 20 percent. (See Table 1.)

Toyota's Performance

Toyota did well. Ironically, the company earned almost as much as GM lost in 1980. From the 1979 to 1980 fiscal years, net sales increased 18 percent, and car production went up 9 percent. In fiscal year 1980, overseas (unit) sales of all motor vehicles as a percentage of world sales was 54.4 percent, and about 25 percent of total car production went to the United States. From 1979 to 1980, Toyota's car (unit) sales in the United States increased 15 percent, for a 6.5 percent share of the market.

Environmental Forces

As early as November 1979, however, environmental forces began to darken this picture for Toyota and other Japanese automakers. Politicians and other opinion leaders in the United States blamed the poor sales of domestic cars and layoffs not as much on the oil crisis, economic recession, and U.S. automakers' strategies as they did on Japanese industrial policy and export levels. The salience of the U.S. "road transportation" industry itself, which accounted for one out of five nonagricultural jobs and 18 percent of GNP in 1978 sustained attention on these problems; so did the U.S. deficit in trade with Japan. Forty-five percent of Japan's total exports to the United States were auto exports. Complaints culminated in demands for the production of Japanese autos within the United States, cutbacks of exports, liberalization of the Japanese market for autos and auto parts, and domestic content legislation in the United States.

In early 1980, Japan's Ministry of International Trade and Industry (MITI) pressured Toyota and other Japanese automakers to invest in the United States. Toyota, a conservative company historically reluctant to expand overseas, resisted. By early April, though, Honda and Nissan had each announced plans for U.S. production. These responses apparently failed to satisfy the U.S. government. Formal, intergovernmental negotiations commenced April 7 and continued until an agreement to restrict Japanese auto exports was reached 13 months later.[8]

TABLE 1 Financial and Competitive Profiles, 1979–1983

	General Motors		Toyota Motor		U.S. Total
Net Sales/Net Income[1]					
(U.S.$ mn.)					
1979	66,311.2	2,892.7	12,911.6	470.2	—
1980	53,173.0	(762.5)	15,212.2	659.8	—
1981	62,698.5	333.0	15,528.8	587.8	—
1982*	60,025.6	962.7	15,063.8	554.1	—
1983	74,581.6	3,730.2	20,450.0	841.7	—
Car Sales in U.S. (retail)[2]					
(units, % share)					
1979	4,931,726[a]	46.2	507,816	4.8	10,673,435
1980	4,116,482	45.8	582,195	6.5	8,979,194
1981	3,796,696	44.5	576,491	6.8	8,536,039
1982*	3,515,660	44.1	530,246	6.6	7,981,673
1983	4,053,561	44.2	555,766	6.1	9,182,067
Car Production in U.S.[3]					
(units, % change)					
1979	5,091,908	–3.6	0[b]	0	8,433,662[c]
1980	4,064,556	–20.2	0	0	6,375,506
1981	3,904,083	–4.0	0	0	6,253,138
1982*	3,173,145	–18.7	0	0	5,073,496
1983	3,975,291	25.3	0	0	6,781,184
Car Production in World[4]					
Overseas Car Sales[5]					**World Total**
(units, % of world [unit] sales)					
1979	—[d]	23.2[e]	2,174,202[f]	38.7[g]	30,774,627
1980	5,728,769	24.7	2,370,124	—	28,577,518
1981	5,497,052	25.2	2,337,471	50.8	27,457,792
1982*	4,869,672	28.9	2,347,293	46.6	26,626,660
1983	6,098,880	28.5	2,480,033	45.9	29,680,193

SOURCES
[1, 5]GM, Toyota Motor annual reports. For GM: consolidated figures, year end Dec. 31. For Toyota: unconsolidated, year end June 30, converted from yen by exchange rate in Tokyo on June 30 of each year.
[2, 3, 4]Motor Vehicle Manufacturers Association, U.S. For Toyota world production, Japan Automobile Manufacturers Association, Inc.
Notes
[a]Column figures include GM imports. In 1980, 514,396 from Canada.
[b]During the 1979–83 period, Toyota's only production in the U.S. was small-scale truck assembly (Toyota Long Beach Fabricators, California).
[c]For 1979–82, column figures include GM, Ford, Chrysler, AMC, VW of America (84,246 in 1982) and Checker Motor (2,000 in 1982). The 1983 figure drops Checker but includes Honda of America.
[d]Approximate figure for 1979 (based on factory sales) is 7,000,000.
[e]Retail sales. Canada excluded from calculations.
[f]Column figures include knock-down (KD) sets.
[g]Based on FY domestic sales and export statistics. KD sets excluded. For 1982, total motor vehicle KD sets: 297,282.
*Indicates main year of negotiation between GM and Toyota.

Thus, during this 1979–81 period both Toyota and GM faced significant threats. For GM there were changes in consumer preferences, a lingering inability to produce high-quality, low-cost subcompact and compact cars in the United States, and stiff competition in those segments of the market. Toyota had an increasingly hostile political environment to contend with, among other factors.

Toyota's Interests

More specifically, for Toyota, one can identify several strategic interests:

Placating the U.S. and Japanese governments.

Responding to U.S. and Japanese competition.

Determining the feasibility of U.S. car production.

Developing an internal consensus regarding U.S. plans.

And if go-ahead plans were made for production in the United States:

Minimizing financial costs and risk.

Building or obtaining a satisfactory plant.

Locating a good labor pool.

Finding suppliers for high-quality, cost-effective parts.

Placating the governments was probably the foremost of these interests, especially during the period preceding May 1981, when there was still the hope of avoiding export restraints. After this, however, other protectionist measures loomed, and pressure for responses specifically from Toyota, Japan's leading automaker, persisted. At the same time, Toyota officials considered subcompact demand in the U.S. market "explosive" and predicted in February 1980 that the "subcompact contest" would climax in 1983.[9] The company obviously wanted to be a major player. Setting up an assembly plant for annual production of 240,000 cars (the usual number for a profitable operation in the United States) was estimated to cost $800–$1,000 million overall and to take 3–4 years to reach startup.

General Motors' Interests

GM also had a number of specific interests during this period. They included the following:

A replacement for the aging subcompact Chevette.

Responding to Japanese and U.S. subcompact competition.

Responding to union complaints about layoffs.

Meeting fuel standards to protect profitable large cars.

And if a go-ahead decision was made for production of a new car:

Minimizing development costs and time.

Developing a broad, organizational commitment to the project.

Lowering the $1,500–$2,000 per car Japanese cost advantage (innovating in production and in the workplace).

Attracting customers back to GM products.

In 1981, the Chevette had been on the U.S. market six years, and it was selling poorly even at an $800 per car loss.[10] GM wanted to replace the car and to attract new, young buyers to Chevrolet products. Development and production of a new car would take up to six years and a heavy investment. The Chevette, borrowed from overseas operations in 1973, cost $1.5 billion; Ford's newer Escort, which debuted in 1980, ran $3.0 billion. GM also had to respond to federal regulations on corporate average fuel economy (CAFE) and, in the long run, to the competitiveness of Japanese automakers. This last concern went beyond mere replacement of the Chevette. It had the potential to call for new methods of production and management.

General Motors' Strategic Options

From a strategic perspective, GM and Toyota each had several possible courses of action. For GM, there was:

"Going it alone."

Joining up with one of several competitive subcompact automakers (e.g., Nissan, Volkswagen).

Given the size of the company (i.e., the use of "bigness" as a competitive tool), some well-defined combination of the first two.

In fact, in 1979, GM had begun a $40 billion, seven-year investment in new technology, new plants, and new cars. In compacts, the company reportedly moved two years ahead of domestic competitors with the introduction of its X-cars. For subcompacts, GM's existing "Asian strategy" called for captive imports. The company had acquired 34.2 percent of Isuzu in 1971 (later increased to 38–40 percent) and on August 12, 1981, bought 5.3 percent of Suzuki.[11]

Toyota's Strategic Options

Toyota seems to have had options as well. The company could have:

Continued producing from its massive plant-and-supplier complex in Toyota City, Japan.

Undertaken a wholly owned investment in the United States.

Joined a U.S. automaker for production in the United States.

Implemented some combination of the above.

Toyota had just built new plants in Toyota City in 1979–80. It could have exploited its superior productivity there, partly countering export restraints on units by shipping high value-added models to the United States and sending knock-down sets to overseas points for assembly and export to the United States. Restraints in other markets (e.g., Australia, Mexico, EEC) were compelling Toyota to build and expand foreign production facilities (its foreign plants in 1980–81 merely assembled kits), but it may have been able to postpone investment in the United States. On the other hand, the U.S. market (the world's largest) was growing rapidly for subcompacts, and Toyota had ample reserves to finance a wholly owned venture. Considering these options further would digress from the negotiation case study, but they offer clues as to Toyota's bargaining position, approach, and power.

In June 1980, Toyota ostensibly decided to pursue the joint venture route by contacting Ford Motor Company. Talks went on until July 1981, when they broke down completely.[12] In light of Chrysler's alliance with Mitsubishi Heavy Industries and AMC's with Renault, Toyota's only remaining prospective American partner was GM.

The Joint Venture Option—Bases for Collaboration

GM's decision to enter joint venture negotiations, like Toyota's, appears to follow naturally from the two companies' interests and complementary resources and skills. Through collaboration GM could learn production and management techniques from a company renowned for them, and Toyota could gain low-cost entry to the U.S. auto industry with the assistance of the industry leader. Other concerns and motivations are also worth noting.

On the skeptical side, one could speculate that each company could gain merely from the act of negotiating, regardless of the result. During the Toyota–Ford talks, after all, several American observers opined that Toyota was simply trying to demonstrate responsiveness to MITI and the U.S. government without intending to reach an agreement.[13] The same motivation coupled with gathering information about GM is conceivable here. GM too could benefit from "side-effects" such as learning more about its competitor and delaying Toyota's move to produce and to sell without restraints in the United States. The delays, expressed "worries,"[14] and actions that came up during the negotiations are consistent with these possibilities.

One GM participant who was interviewed mentioned that the possibility of Toyota's simply "buying time" did occur to the GM team and concerned them enough to ask Toyota about it. Toyota responded that they were negotiating in good faith and would go into the joint venture with an "open mind." GM itself had no desire to learn just from negotiating, according to another GM interviewee.

Other twists on the companies' motives include a UAW interviewee's assertion that GM simply wanted a replacement for the Chevette, not innovative techniques. One American news article reported that GM chairman and CEO Roger Smith called the joint venture a "stalling tactic,"[15] or otherwise put, a bridge between GM's product offerings. At one point during the negotiations, Vice Chairman Shigenobu Yamamoto of Toyota also cited his company's desire to *help* GM and the U.S. auto industry, likening this to the traditional Japanese idea of "offering salt to our enemy."[16] While these comments should be evaluated with regard to their sources and intended audiences, they do suggest additional factors for the negotiations.

In the main, however, the participants interviewed by the author and reporters felt that the companies' motivation for pursuing a joint venture was a shared interest in exploring the feasibility of profitable subcompact car production in the United States.

GM stood to gain working experience with Japanese techniques that neither licensing alone nor companies other than Toyota might effectively provide.[17] The prospective advantages included the demonstration to American labor that they could work in plants managed by Japanese techniques (a so-called "labor demonstration effect.") On the other hand Toyota could respond to political forces, enter the United States at low risk, and move more quickly up "the learning curve." These and other interests listed above were all reasons for the companies to try to reach an agreement.

In November 1981, Jay Chai, an executive vice president of C. Itoh and Company (America) and the adviser to the chairman (of GM) on Japanese affairs, broached with Toyota executives in Tokyo the possibility of a joint venture with GM. Then on December 21, 1981, Seishi Kato, chairman of Toyota Motor Sales, met with Roger Smith in Detroit. Language barriers made the visit "bewildering" in Smith's words,[18] but it got the ball rolling.

ISSUES

GM and Toyota faced a wide range of issues. The product, production site, financing, and target market segment had to be selected. The international context brought up issues such as foreign exchange rate fluctuations. And there were issues common to joint venture negotiations: ownership, organizational structure, and operational control (shared, dominant/passive).[19]

Some of the remaining issues were less typical. A car generally comprises 15,000–20,000 parts, so the companies faced a tremendous number of decisions about suppliers. Unionization of the workforce, which typified GM's but not Japanese automakers' (Honda, Nissan) U.S. plants, was on the agenda. Finally, a strategy would have to be formulated to meet any concerns about competition raised by the U.S. Federal Trade Commission.

PRENEGOTIATION PREPARATIONS

Toyota

Like many Japanese organizations, Toyota undoubtedly prepared assiduously for the negotiations.[20] In April 1980, as the U.S. and Japanese governments began auto export restraint negotiations, Toyota contracted one Japanese consulting firm, Nomura Research Institute, and two American firms, SRI International and Arthur D. Little, to study the feasibility of manufacturing in the United States. The intended effect then was probably to assuage government officials. After their completion in the spring of 1981, the studies probably also abetted preparations for the talks with Ford and with GM, although Nomura's study advised against a move to the United States while the two American studies supported it.

There was also dissent within Toyota on a move to the United States. According to one Toyota interviewee, those against it were concerned about UAW strikes and product quality. Eiji Toyoda, president of Toyota Motor Company, and others supporting the move thus had to negotiate internally as well as externally before and during the joint venture negotiations.

Shortly after the first formal intercompany contact in March 1982 (see below), Eiji Toyoda assembled a five-person project team consisting of representatives from production technology, finance, legal affairs, and overseas projects. Toshio Morita, executive vice president of production technology, led the team. One American insider who was interviewed revealed that Toyota's planning concentrated on the general relationship with GM; details were set aside. Plans were developed verbally and with little documentation in "numerous" meetings. One document, a draft memorandum of understanding for the joint venture, served as the centerpiece for those and subsequent internal efforts.[21]

In the legal realm, Toyota hired three American law firms. Their advice and "compatibility" with the company were assessed over several months. Toyota then narrowed its choice to Arent, Fox, Kintner, Plotkin, and Kahn, a prominent firm in Washington, D.C., among whose partners was a former FTC chairman.

General Motors

GM's preparations were also "very thorough" and "well-organized" in the words of non-GM observers. In January 1981, John F. Smith, Director of Worldwide Product Planning and a close associate of Roger Smith, went to Japan with Jay Chai to research Toyota's projects intensively. After his return GM concentrated on Toyota's Corolla, and the two Smiths, with some ideas perhaps from reports of the Toyota–Ford experience, outlined a proposal for joint production in the United States.[22]

Early in the process, a marketing group was put together to study the demand for a joint venture car. A design group looked into ways to differentiate a joint venture car from the common Corolla. A cost study for the venture was also undertaken.

Within the company a number of midlevel managers, operations people, and even executives resisted this plan. Perhaps they viewed it as an admission that GM could, or had to, learn from Toyota. That compelled Roger Smith, like Eiji Toyoda at Toyota, to devote a lot of energy during the negotiations to supporting the project and building organizational commitment to it.

Finally, GM continued to consult Chai on strategic and cultural matters since he knew the industry, the ways of Japanese business, and the Japanese language. For antitrust concerns, GM employed an outside law firm, Jones, Day, Reavis, and Pogue in Cleveland, Ohio, and an outside economist along with several antitrust lawyers within the company. The company also arranged to monitor carefully all negotiations with Toyota to ensure that parties avoided areas sensitive to the FTC.

THE PRIMARY NEGOTIATIONS

One approach to negotiations commonly taken in government and in business has been labeled "framework/detail."[23] The first phase entails the parties' development of a formula, or framework, of broad objectives and principles. In the second phase, the formula guides discussion toward a detailed agreement.

Although no interviewee cited explicit use of this approach, it provides a useful structure for a description of the negotiations between GM and Toyota. A memorandum of understanding signed on February 17, 1983, delineates two phases. Alternatively, one could refer to the company heads' agreement in principle in March 1982, not the memorandum, as the "framework." The memorandum was probably a more meaningful framework given the complexity of the overall agenda. Thus, the discussion below treats Phase 1 as March 2, 1982, to February 17, 1983; Phase 2 extends beyond that, through the drafting of the joint venture contract to the incorporation of the joint venture on February 21, 1984. Actions during the two phases are outlined in Table 2. As a comprehensive timeline of significant points during the primary and ancillary negotiations, the table serves as a reference for the detailed accounts that follow. Bear in mind that Chart 1 identifies the main actors.

Phase 1: Developing a Framework

The first formal intercompany negotiation concerning a joint venture occurred on March 1, 1982, in New York City, between Eiji Toyoda, president of Toyota Motor Company, and Roger Smith, chairman and CEO of GM. A GM source indicated that they discussed only the overall concept of a joint venture, not initial proposals. By the end of the month, he continued, the two company heads had agreed in principle to undertake a feasibility study for a joint venture. Interestingly, a Toyota interviewee read from an official company history of the talks that Smith had made a "very specific" proposal during March, namely a joint venture with equal capital contributions, use of an idle GM plant in California, production of a Corolla-class car beginning in fall of 1984, and an output of 200,000–400,000 cars.

Issues.   Whatever the actual circumstances, the issues for subsequent negotiation between the companies constituted a rather full agenda. (See the Issues section above.)

Players.   Responsibility for the day-to-day talks was given to John Smith, GM's director of worldwide product planning, and Kan Higashi, Toyota's general manager of overseas operations. The balance of both negotiating teams (Chart 1) was made up of representatives from finance (Hughes, Toyozumi) and legal affairs (Weinbaum and staff, Tsukada). Flavio Cella, an assistant to Hughes responsible for special projects, also participated. Each team included outside counsel (Pogue, Meigher), and interpreters were present. Louis Hughes, an assistant treasurer with responsibility for GM's overseas group, and Toyota's Higashi would become chief spokesmen.

Jay Chai officially participated as a member of the GM team but took a facilitating, intermediary role once talks got under way. At several points, he acted as an interpreter. More critically, at impasses Chai would carry and explain to Toyota representatives proposals written by Roger Smith and others.

In addition to this core negotiating group, there were several auxiliary "working groups" that communicated with counterparts across company lines and fed information to their companies' main negotiators.

TABLE 2 Chronology of GM–Toyota Negotiations

1981	Dec. 21	Kato visits R. Smith for the first time in Detroit.
1982	Mar. 1	R. Smith and E. Toyoda discuss the concept of a joint venture in New York City.
	Mar. (end)	Agreement in principle reached on undertaking a feasibility study for a joint venture.
	Apr. 5	GM board of directors informed of preliminary discussions with Toyota and their strategic implications.
	Apr. 14	First operational-level negotiations begin in Tokyo.
	May 17–20	Second operational-level negotiations held.
	June	Morita and other Toyota officials survey GM's U.S. plants.
	Summer (end)	Agreement reached on basic issues such as type of car, number to be produced, plant, site, sales channels.
	Sep. 20	Another round of operational level negotiations begins in Tokyo.
	Nov. 30	R. Smith makes proposal to break impasse on valuation of Fremont property and capitalization of venture.
	Dec. 23	Yamamoto and Iwasaki meet with R. Smith in Detroit (E. Toyoda visited the U.S. in Nov.).
	Dec. 27	E. Toyoda accepts Smith's proposal, and they resolve to finalize a memorandum of understanding quickly.
1983	Jan. 20–26	Last operational-level negotiations held in Japan.
	Feb. 7	GM board of directors approves final draft of agreement.
	Feb.	MITI announces extension of auto export restraints to a third year, April 1983–March 1984.
—	Feb. 16	GM and Toyota's in house and outside counsel inform Glynn at FTC of signing ceremony the following day.
—	Feb. 17	R. Smith and E. Toyoda sign "Memorandum of Understanding."
—	Feb. (end)	Hart-Scott-Rodino filing by GM and Toyota.
—	Mar. 3	Usery retained to assist in negotiations with UAW.
	Mar. 21	T. Toyoda named president and CEO of the joint venture.
	Mar. (end)	FTC makes "second request" for information from companies and begins investigational hearings that last till July.

———— GM–Toyota Talks: Phase One ————

Date	Event
Apr.	First negotiations between Toyota's counsel and FTC staff concerning release of requested information.
May 18	Bieber succeeds Fraser as president of the UAW.
May 25	Formal Toyota–UAW negotiations begin.
June	Toyota provides FTC with a number of company documents.
June 20	First deadline (120 days) for labor agreement stipulated in Memorandum of Understanding; extension granted.
Aug.	Toyota's counsel informs FTC that firm cannot release cost and profit data; Miller publicly demands the data.
Sep. 2	UAW Local #1364 (former GM Fremont workers) sue GM and UAW International for negotiating without them.
Sep. 22	UAW International reaches agreement in principle with GM and Toyota ("letter of intent").
Nov. 16	New FTC Commissioner Calvani begins term.
Nov. 24–27	FTC staff has access to depository of Toyota documents at offices of outside counsel, breaking two-month impasse.
Dec. 22	GM and Toyota sign consent accord with FTC.
1984 Feb. 21	Joint venture shareholders agreement executed, by-laws accepted, company established in California as New United Motor Manufacturing, Inc.
Apr. 11	FTC grants final approval to joint venture in 3–2 vote.
May	NUMMI begins hiring workers.
Dec. 10	Dedication of first NUMMI Nova (CL Sedan) off the line.

GM–Toyota Talks: Phase Two

UAW "Intent" Talks

FTC Talks — (FTC)

Conditions.   During the months of negotiation that ensued in 1982, several noteworthy events took place beyond the talks. During March, the same month of the E. Toyoda–R. Smith meeting, GM joined with Fujitsu Fanuc to establish GMF Robotics. In July, Toyota Motor Company and Toyota Motor Sales merged to become the Toyota Motor Corporation. On August 6, the U.S. Internal Revenue Service began an investigation of Toyota for underreporting taxable income. During the first week of February 1983, the Department of Justice actually sued Toyota for data on production costs, sales, and management.

Year-end statistics also reveal part of the broader picture during 1982. All of GM's production and sales figures dropped from 1981 totals, although net income improved (Table 1). Toyota's performance was mixed. Net sales in Japanese yen increased about 10 percent from 1981 (cf. dollar amounts in Table 1) but U.S. car (unit) sales declined. As a whole, Japanese imports increased their percentage share of the market in 1982 because overall U.S. demand was down. The value of imports also increased, notwithstanding the weaker yen in 1982, since Japanese automakers shipped more expensive models. No doubt one consequence was the passing in the U.S. House of Representatives of domestic content legislation, the Fair Practices in Automotive Product Act (HR 5133), on December 15, 1982. This was the context of the negotiations during Phase 1.

The Negotiation Process.   In April 1982, talks at the operational level began. (See Table 2.) The negotiating teams divided up the agenda and assigned pieces to working groups. The facility planning group, for example, comprised three to four engineers from Toyota and two from GM. Other groups were formed for costing, logistics planning, and labor. A schedule was charted; the target date for agreement was set for September 1982. According to two reports,[24] GM initially proposed a large venture involving two plants and production of some 400,000 subcompact cars. Toyota sought a limited venture based on one abandoned plant with a capacity of 200,000 cars. GM also may have become concerned about the antitrust ramifications of the larger venture, for the limited plan prevailed.

GM sought the Corolla, Toyota's best-selling car worldwide, as the product for the joint venture. Toyota offered instead the Sprinter, a sporty subcompact that had been produced since 1968 solely for domestic sale in Japan. One GM participant stated that GM was "very happy" with this offer because it obviated the investment needed to differentiate a Corolla-based joint venture car from the common Corolla.

Formal and informal negotiation sessions took place over several months, moving from discussion of the joint venture concept to feasibility studies to costing studies. (See Table 2.) By late summer 1982, news articles reported agreement on production volume, plant location, and sales channels as well as the type of product.

Sourcing of components had also been decided. Toyota would supply the engine and transmission, and all other parts would be procured through competitive bids. Most of the parts would be Japanese, and Toyota provided the list of bids from Japanese companies. They included affiliates (e.g., Nippondenso) and nonaffiliates (see Chart 1). GM provided the bids from its affiliates (e.g., Delco Products) and other American companies who would primarily supply parts such as radiators, glass, seats, and tires. Since just-in-time (*kanban*) inventory was integral to its production system,

Toyota sought explicit assurances from GM that supply decisions would be based on product quality and vendor reliability as well as cost.

The issues were more complicated and the discussion more arduous than either party had anticipated. Citing the number of parts to a car, one GM official reportedly stated, "dozens of decisions have to be made with practically every part . . . If any project ever required patience, this is it."[25] Participants interviewed by the author echoed that assessment for additional reasons.

Communication was difficult due to culturally based factors. For example, Japanese negotiators for Toyota addressed issues in ways that appeared "oblique" to the GM team. Some silences and affirmations at the negotiating table were mistaken for agreement. Translation also slowed the negotiation process considerably.

Negotiating and decision-making styles also contrasted. According to the participants interviewed, the Japanese tended to start talks with statements of general principles and usually did not respond to proposals before checking with their headquarters. The Americans preferred specific proposals and responses at the table. In fact, the GM team received so few proposals from Toyota initially that they wondered where they stood. Further, Toyota was struck by GM negotiators' ability to source information quickly from particular individuals within their organization; GM saw the Toyota team's ability as less clear-cut. In the end, the September 1982 target date for agreement passed, and the date was moved to December.

During the fall of 1982, unresolved issues included the licensing fee to Toyota for its car design, management of operations, prices of the cars (destined for GM), and exchange-rate fluctuations.

A major impasse developed on capitalization of the venture and the evaluation of the idle GM plant in Fremont, California, that the companies had selected. GM had reportedly renovated the plant at a cost of $280 million in the months before its closing in March 1982. Toyota, according to its written history of the talks, considered the equipment too old to be effective in increasing production. Toyota also must have figured that GM could at least write off much of that amount. On November 30, 1982, Roger Smith personally wrote to Eiji Toyoda softening GM's stand.[26] Toyoda accepted Smith's proposal on December 27. A final set of negotiations was held in January 1983 in Tokyo. Early in the month, Shoichiro Toyoda, president of Toyota said, "It is too early to predict the possibility of reaching a final agreement between our companies by the end of January."[27] Among other issues, the pricing of the joint venture car, which had been repeatedly set aside, remained unsettled. Even at the end of the month, as *The Wall Street Journal* reported the plan, a Toyota spokesman denied that the companies had an agreement.[28] By February 7, GM's board of directors had already twice authorized Roger Smith to sign an agreement. GM awaited Toyota.

The Outcome.   On February 14, 1983, only days after MITI notified the U.S. government that it would extend auto export restraints to a third year, GM and Toyota formally announced their agreement on a joint venture. Signed on the 17th, the 15-page "Memorandum of Understanding"[29] stipulated:

> Limited production of a car derived from Toyota's "new frontwheel Sprinter" for sale directly to GM.

Equal shares of capital from the parent companies (as it turned out, $100 million cash from Toyota; from GM, $11 million cash and the Fremont plant ($89 million); another $250 million was later raised.

Equal ownership by the parents.

Design of the Fremont manufacturing layout by Toyota.

Construction of a stamping plant.

A "reasonable" royalty to Toyota for the license to manufacture the car.

Technical assistance from GM and Toyota on a cost-plus basis.

Nominal annual production capacity of 200,000 cars.

Pricing joint venture cars on a market-basket standard.[30]

Startup for the 1985 model year.

Toyota would designate the president (who would serve as chief executive and operating officer) of the joint venture.

Several other clauses bear particular mention. One stipulated that an "acceptable labor relations structure" be established within 120 days. Both governments were also to review the agreement, and until the U.S. government approved it, either party could withdraw. The agreement did not prevent GM from establishing similar relationships with other companies and gave Toyota the opportunity to produce vehicles for itself at the new plant. Finally, the companies agreed to negotiate remaining issues in "good faith" and to use "best efforts" to complete details by May 15, 1983. How well this joint venture agreement would serve GM and Toyota's individual interests could only be partly assessed at that point. GM found a replacement for the Chevette, made an idle plant valuable without additional investment, created jobs for its laid-off workers, and gained access to a working model of the Toyota production system. Toyota eased government pressure (except for domestic content legislation in the United States), established a foothold from which to compete with Nissan and Honda (its Japanese forerunners in the U.S. auto industry) at a 50 percent savings, and gained access to the most extensive auto parts supplier network in the United States.

Some American observers complained in the American press that Toyota outnegotiated GM.[31] Toyota did gain operational control of the venture, although that could have been seen by GM as necessary for creating an accurate and didactic model of Toyota's system. Most of the components were to be Japanese. Toyota also had a built-in client, and royalties and other fees that considerably lowered its risk. Toyota clearly gained a great deal. But the achievement of each company's primary goal, learning from the other, depended on yet-to-be-designed mechanisms and on experiences of the joint venture well after startup.

Phase 2: Completing the Details

From the February 1983 signing of the memorandum to the May 15 target for a contract, and even up to the February 1984 incorporation of the joint venture, a number of additional issues required negotiation. Many concerned the United Auto Workers and the Federal Trade Commission, whose negotiations with the two companies will be discussed in the next section. There also remained detailed items for intercompany negotiations.

Issues.   The companies had previously agreed to establish the joint venture as a corporation, and that called for certain discussions and legal documentation. The names of the corporation and of the product were open. Furthermore, management structure and selection (except for the president) had to be decided and formulated, as did agreements on vehicle supply, component supply, service parts, technical assistance and license, realty, and "product responsibility" (liability).

Players.   For this phase Eiji Toyoda and Roger Smith assumed very limited roles. Some of the working groups (e.g., costing) had also largely completed their tasks. The core group of negotiators (Chart 1) stayed in place to work out the fine points.

Conditions.   The environment for the negotiations in 1983, like conditions throughout the joint venture talks, is again noteworthy. Commerce Secretary Malcolm Baldridge, among others, applauded the companies' February accord as "a significant development for the auto industry in the U.S. and in the world." Before that, however, opposition came from Ford, Chrysler, Toyota dealers in the United States, and others, and it continued throughout the year (Chart 1). Toyota itself continued to be pursued by the IRS. On March 14, a U.S. district court ordered the company to explain why it could not provide the IRS with cost and profit information.

In July, MITI hinted at ending the auto export restraints but relented, in October, to an extension. After bargaining with the U.S. Trade Representative to get a 10 percent increase, MITI announced a fourth year of restraints (April 1984–March 1985) on November 1. Two days later, the U.S. House of Representatives passed another bill on domestic content of autos (HR 1234).

The companies' activities beyond their joint talks in 1983 included Toyota's talks with the government of Taiwan for a joint venture in autos. The talks broke down in the fall. During the year, Isuzu and Suzuki built new plants to increase their export capacity, and on October 6, GM (who opposed Japanese auto export restraints) announced plans to import 200,000 subcompacts from Isuzu and 100,000 minicars from Suzuki. In November, GM also announced the establishment of the Saturn Project, an internal attempt to produce domestically a competitive small car. By year's end, GM's fortunes, and those of the U.S. auto industry, had clearly improved: Net sales and net income topped all four previous years. Toyota's net income rose 52 percent in dollars[32] (Table 1).

The Negotiation Process and Outcome.   Negotiations between the two companies during Phase 2 entered particularly sensitive areas, so information about meetings and proposals is scarce. A Japanese newspaper reported that the agreed licensing fee to Toyota was about 2.5 percent of factory shipments with no down payment.[33] A delivery system for American parts was also developed. Since California did not have a developed auto parts industry, nothing close to the hundreds of suppliers in Toyota

City, the logistic planning group looked to the Midwest's infrastructure. They set up a central supply point in Chicago and arranged for daily rail shipments to Fremont. Japanese supplies could be shipped right into the port of Oakland.

During this period, Toyota also moved ahead on its own. On March 21, 1983, Tatsuro Toyoda, a nephew of Eiji Toyoda, was informally named CEO of the yet-to-be-approved joint venture (Table 2). Having gained the right to lay out the plant and coordinate acquisition and installation of equipment, Toyota also requested bids from a number of suppliers and builders. By the summer of 1983, Toyoda Machine Works (a Toyoda Group member) and Komatsu, among others, had been selected as equipment suppliers for the new stamping plant. (Japanese suppliers provided most of the plant equipment for the venture, which all told ran about $450 million.)

When GM and Toyota began drafting the final joint venture contract, GM offered a version that, like many American companies' legal documents, covered numerous contingencies. Toyota's thinner initial draft came closer in size and form to the final contract. The joint venture was to be called New United Motor Manufacturing, Inc. (NUMMI), and its product would be sold as the Chevrolet Nova. NUMMI was incorporated in California on February 21, 1984.

ANCILLARY NEGOTIATIONS

To create their joint venture, GM and Toyota had to go beyond their intercompany negotiations. Talks were undertaken with suppliers; the State of California, which provided $2 million in training funds; the City of Fremont; and many other organizations, so that the overall process was generally complicated by having to negotiate several agendas with several parties in different arenas. Still, the talks with the United Auto Workers and the Federal Trade Commission, which went on largely during Phase 2 of the intercompany negotiations, were vital for the joint venture.

Negotiations with the UAW

In late 1979 and in 1980, a year that saw layoffs of 300,000 auto workers and twice that number in related industries, UAW president Douglas Fraser galvanized the American public to push for remedies. U.S. car production was still dropping in 1982. In this atmosphere, a venture that represented up to 3,000 direct jobs drew a lot of union attention.

Issues.   For the UAW, the primary issue to resolve with GM and Toyota was the rehiring of workers laid off when GM closed the Fremont plant in March 1982. (At its peak in 1978, the plant had employed 6,000.) Other issues included recognition of the UAW at the new plant, the hiring selection process, job classifications, and seniority. Toyota's concerns about production standards and compulsory overtime, among other points, would also come up in the talks.

A number of factors augmented the seriousness of these issues. The UAW had represented the Fremont workforce, as it did the rest of the GM system. At the same time, Toyota had very serious reservations about labor relations, cost, and quality in the United States. The reputation of GM-Fremont workers did not alleviate these concerns. In early 1982, there was absenteeism of 20 percent and a backlog of 1,000 grievances, while production costs and product quality were GM's worst.

Players.   Toyota took sole responsibility for working out a labor agreement for the new venture. The company could thereby pursue its concerns fully; the decision also set the venture somewhat apart from GM's existing bargaining agreement with the UAW. Takeo Tsukada, effectively Toyota's general counsel, led the negotiators' working group on labor.

On March 3, 1983, Toyota hired former U.S. secretary of labor William Usery as labor relations consultant to the still fetal joint venture[34] (Chart 1). He led the team that negotiated directly with the UAW. The team included one of his associates and an attorney hired by Toyota.

On the UAW side, Douglas Fraser played a supportive role in the early stages when he was president. The major union negotiators, however, were Donald Ephlin, a vice president of the UAW International and Director of the GM Department; Bruce Lee, a regional representative of the International in California; and Bill Colbath, a personal representative of Fraser's successor, Owen Bieber.

Conditions.   At least three conditions for the talks, conditions beyond the GM-Fremont community and the improving fortunes of the U.S. auto industry, deserve mention. First, the UAW International changed leadership on May 18, 1983, at its triennial conference. The new president, Bieber, was less enthusiastic than Fraser about the joint venture. He appointed Ephlin, who took on the primary role at the talks, but he sent Colbath as well. During the summer the International revoked the charter of the GM-Fremont local (#1364). Although it was ultimately unsuccessful, the local sued GM, Toyota, and the UAW International for depriving it of a voice in the negotiations.

During this period, GM was making Guaranteed Income Stream payments to some 828 former GM-Fremont workers. The 1982 national GM–UAW contract provided that workers with 10 years' seniority who were laid off because of a permanent plant closing would receive 50 percent of their wages until retirement. News reports suggested that as Fremont workers depleted other benefits, up to 2,100 workers might receive the GIS payments.

The third and most interesting condition was the UAW's legal position. The organization could not bargain or sign a contract because it had not been certified, and it could not be certified before the joint venture had a workforce. Thus, the negotiators had to consider and work toward an alternative form of agreement.

The Negotiation Process.   Beginning in March 1983, Usery met several times with Toyota executives in Japan and in the United States. He also met with Fraser and Bieber before the UAW election (Table 2). At a press conference on May 12, Usery announced his role and the willingness of Toyota to use former GM employees as the "primary source" for recruitment. Different interpretations of that statement and other issues underscored the need for negotiations.

Full-fledged talks began May 25. In addition to meetings between the Usery and UAW teams, there were several one-on-one sessions between Usery and Ephlin, among others. The talks went into mid-September, past the June 20 deadline set in the Memorandum and past even a second deadline.

One participant called these negotiations "very, very difficult." He cited conceptual and linguistic hurdles in conversations between Usery and the Japanese. With the UAW, the scope of the rehiring commitment was, as expected, a major issue. Job classifications also caused difficulty since the UAW had 100 different classifications at some GM plants, whereas Toyota had only a few classifications and rotated workers.

The Outcome.   On September 22, 1983, Usery announced an agreement between the joint venture and the UAW. The resulting "binding letter of intent" set forth general principles such as "undertaking this new proposed relationship with the full intention of fostering an innovative labor relations structure, minimizing traditional adversarial roles, and emphasizing mutual trust and good faith."[35] Specific points included the following:

Recognition of the UAW as the bargaining agent for workers once hiring began.

Using laid-off GM workers as the primary source of new hires.

Not preserving seniority rights from GM-Fremont.

Pegging wages at going industry rates.

Willingness of the UAW to be flexible on work rules.

Negotiating a contract with the UAW by June 1985.

This, then, provided the joint venture with an "understanding" with the UAW and a hiring pool of skilled workers.[36]

Negotiations with the FTC

The second critical ancillary arena for negotiation involved the Federal Trade Commission.

Issues.   The primary concern here was GM's and Toyota's compliance with antitrust regulations. From the FTC's viewpoint, the joint venture agreement potentially violated Section 5 of the Federal Trade Commission Act, which alludes to unfair methods of competition. If the agreement were consummated, the joint venture could violate Section 7 of the Clayton Act, which prohibits joint ventures that may substantially lessen competition. These were the bases for a complaint drafted by the FTC staff during the summer of 1983. A more immediate issue, however, was the type and amount of company information that GM and Toyota would provide for the FTC's deliberations.

Players.   The ultimate decision makers in this arena were the five FTC commissioners. James Miller, a Reagan appointee, chaired the commission. The other members were Michael Pertschuk (a Carter appointee); Patricia Bailey (Carter); George Douglas (Reagan); and, until his replacement in the fall of 1983, David Clanton (Ford).

For the GM–Toyota–FTC negotiations per se, though, other individuals were more involved; Eugene Meigher and Dennis Cuneo from Toyota's outside law firm, and Richard Pogue, from GM's outside law firm, participated actively along with their clients' in-house counsel (Chart 1). At the FTC, Edward Glynn, assistant director of international antitrust in the Bureau of Competition, and David Scheffman, deputy director of the bureau of economics, led day-to-day activities. In the late stages, Timothy Muris, director of the Bureau of Competition, drafted the final FTC staff position.

Conditions.   Within the FTC at that time, Chairman Miller and Commissioner Pertschuk, a former chairman, often led opposing viewpoints, and during this case, their differences again emerged. One of Pertschuk's allies, Commissioner Clanton, was scheduled to leave office on September 25, 1983. GM and Toyota thus faced the possibility that the swing vote in the final decision by the commission would be a new commissioner, a Reagan appointee.

The companies also had to contend with overt outside opposition to their plans. On February 21, 1983, days after the memorandum was signed, Lee Iacocca, chairman of Chrysler Corporation, stated, "I don't like it. I don't think the two biggest [auto companies] should make an assault on the U.S. market and carve it up."[37] For the next 14 months Chrysler maintained a "full court press" in the media, at the FTC, in Congress, and in the courts. On January 16, 1984, the company sued GM and Toyota in a U.S. district court, charging violation of antitrust laws and asking for compensation. Other opponents of the joint venture included Ford, Toyota dealers in the United States, the National Tooling and Machining Association, and the Consumer Federation of America (Chart 1). With this backdrop, GM and Toyota's efforts with the FTC staff must have been especially trying. The joint venture rested in the balance.

The Negotiation Process.   The companies concentrated on two steps: a favorable staff position, and the commissioners' ruling. The effort involved both companies. Because of the information available to the author, however, the account below highlights Toyota.

On February 16, 1983, the day before the signing of the Memorandum of Understanding, the companies' in-house and outside counsel met with Glynn at the FTC and informed him of the scheduled signing[38] (Table 2). Within the next two weeks, they made a Hart–Scott–Rodino filing, which basically entails notifying the FTC of certain merger or acquisition activities. A month later the FTC staff sent the companies a "Second Request" for company documents. The FTC also began investigational hearings that called in all the major auto companies. The hearings would go on for four months.

It was over the "Second Request" that the major negotiations occurred. In its first talks with a large FTC team in April, Toyota's outside counsel stated that Toyota would never fully comply with Hart–Scott–Rodino guidelines. Concerned about the confidentiality of cost and profit data, the company sent documents excluding that information to the FTC in June. Late in August, Chairman Miller publicly demanded the cost and profit data. Toyota reiterated its position, and negotiations came to a halt.

Some American observers felt Toyota awaited the departure of Commissioner Clanton, who allegedly opposed the joint venture. Others cited Toyota's interest in preventing company information from ultimately reaching the IRS, and still others speculated with little foundation that Toyota had lost interest in the venture because the improving U.S. auto industry had quieted protectionist voices.

In any event, Roger Smith said in October that GM was "anxious for Toyota to get their data in to get the so-called clock running."[39] The FTC's Muris wrote to Toyota, giving the company "one last chance."

The FTC staff and Toyota representatives resolved their two-month impasse over documents rather creatively. Documents on cost and profit were set aside in a depository at the company's outside law firm. Over the Thanksgiving weekend, a week after Terry Calvani replaced Clanton as the new FTC commissioner, FTC staff studied the documents in place. (GM also set up a depository for its documents.)

Throughout these negotiations, complications beyond the substantive issues arose. Ironically, FTC staff found that Toyota's documents, like those of many Japanese companies, were in a brief one-page format that offered them insufficient detail. Interviews became a more important source of information. Glynn took a staff team to Japan in September to take depositions from Toyota's negotiators, but only after the FTC had worked through the issue of extraterritoriality. Toyota's general expectations concerning legal matters also struck American observers as unusual, at least for American firms. For example, Toyota underestimated the amount of information needed by American attorneys before offering advice. Such were the international dimensions of legal and governmental affairs.

In mid-December, the FTC staff proposed that GM and Toyota sign a consent order, that is, that they agree to undertake certain obligations and limitations on their future conduct. From the FTC staff's point of view, the deal had been satisfactorily structured. Its main concern was that the companies follow through with the agreement as planned.

The Outcome.   On December 22, 1983, the companies signed the order, and a 60-day period for public comment began.

The consent order contains nine sections. The most significant features are prohibitions against exchanging nonpublic information about cars, parts, costs, marketing plans, sales forecasts, and model changes, and a requirement to maintain files on all communications. The FTC also limited the duration of the joint venture to 12 years after the start of production, but not beyond December 31, 1997. The order went into effect on April 11, 1984, when the commissioners approved the venture by a 3–2 vote. On that day, GM and Toyota surmounted the last major hurdle in the creation of their joint venture.

STRATEGIC IMPLICATIONS

From the initial Kato–Smith meeting to the consent agreement with the FTC, a 24-month period, GM and Toyota engaged in a complex process of negotiation. As Chart 1 illustrated, they each dealt with a number of actors in varied arenas: the intercompany talks, critical ancillary negotiations, interorganizational networks, the market and industry, and the political environment. Each party brought an agenda of issues.

Furthermore, several negotiations went on concurrently (recall Table 2), on more than one level of activity, in an environment that continually changed.

The two companies succeeded in reaching agreements that created, facilitated, and allowed a joint venture. An assessment of the contents of the intercompany agreement in particular is a subject for another study. This study delved into the process of negotiation, and from it one can draw five strategic implications for complex (specifically international joint venture) negotiations.

(1) Preparation and Monitoring

In light of the information and activity required in complex negotiations, careful planning seems especially important. Interests and options should be identified and evaluated for one's own company as well as the prospective partner(s). Assessment must continue through the negotiations. Moreover, the activities of a counterpart beyond the negotiating table and other forces in the dynamic multifaceted environment (recall Chart 1) may call for reevaluations of anticipated benefits and costs.

The timing of a venture and the expected duration of negotiations also deserve consideration. Restraints on Japanese auto exports are still in place today six years after the Kato–Smith meeting, but now products from even lower cost sources (Korea, Taiwan, Brazil, Mexico) have entered the U.S. market. Moreover, in July 1985, Toyota announced plans for its own assembly plants in the United States and in Canada, and in September 1986 began producing cars at NUMMI under its own nameplate. In late 1984, GM arranged to source from Korea's Daewoo, and in August 1986 set up a joint venture with Suzuki in Canada. Such factors must be monitored and anticipated without injuring the budding joint venture relationship.

(2) Top-Level Support

The GM–Toyota negotiations also illustrate the impact of top-level support on one's own organization and negotiators and on the counterpart. Both sides look for signals of commitment. At the same time, if too active, CEOs run the risk of diminishing the perceived authority of their more involved negotiators. Executive intervention may be most effective if used sparingly, for example, at major impasses.[40]

Leadership among the most involved negotiators also seems important given the diffusion of activity—the multiple negotiating arenas, internal and external negotiations—and dependence of resolution of issues in one arena on resolutions in other arenas; see also (5), next page. It was because of the "highly motivated" core group of negotiators, according to one participant, that the GM–Toyota talks succeeded.

(3) Intermediaries and Other Outside Experts

For negotiations involving a number of disparate issues and parties having different negotiating styles, outside experts may be especially helpful. The GM–Toyota talks entailed labor and antitrust as well as auto parts issues. Further, the two companies' predominantly domestic outlooks, ethnic differences and unknowns, and corporate cultures and attitudes based on being "number one" complicated the talks. GM employed Chai for strategic and cultural affairs, Toyota hired Usery for labor concerns, and both companies hired outside counsel for the antitrust issues. Intermediaries and other outside experts have facilitated other international auto negotiations as well (e.g., AMC and Beijing Automotive Works).[41]

(4) "Fractionating"[42] the Agenda and the Format

One way to handle very large agendas is to break them into manageable issue clusters. GM and Toyota, for example, formed working groups such as logistics planning to "feed" the main negotiation teams. Moreover, formal full team-on-team formats should probably not be the only venue for talks. Individuals can also accomplish a great deal in formal and informal one-on-one meetings.

(5) Referring to the "Big Picture"

For several reasons (the complexity and detail of the agenda, the various arenas of activity, the months of effort involved—(recall Table 2)—and strong partisan positions), key players should refer regularly to the basic relationship being sought and to the potential benefits of the companies' cooperation; see (2), previous page. Internally, Toyota seems to have done so by concentrating on a single draft memorandum of understanding. In joint sessions, the negotiators can also reframe in order to stimulate and sustain momentum as needed; this also counterbalances some of the drawbacks of (4), previous page. This tack is effective as long as the companies see more benefits than costs in the joint venture relationship.

Joint Ventures and Negotiation

By now, in 1987, each of the Big Three is allied with a Japanese automaker. Other international joint ventures and tie-ups are readily apparent elsewhere: AMC and Beijing Automotive Works, Ford and VW's formation of Autolatina, and Toyota and Kuozui Motors (Taiwan). Others have been attempted, but the negotiations failed: Saab and Volvo, GM and Leyland–Land Rover, and Ford and Fiat. And some are in progress: Ford and Nissan, Toyota and VW.

The reputations of GM and Toyota made their joint venture negotiations prominent. But aspects of the process will be similar for others. As alliances continue to be sought in the auto industry, their creation will entail a number of the challenges encountered by General Motors and Toyota Motor in the early 1980s.

NOTES

1. Those interviewed in structured and open-ended formats include 11 individuals from C. Itoh and Company, the Federal Trade Commission, General Motors, GM's outside counsel, NUMMI management, Toyota Motor, Toyota's outside counsel, and the UAW. Unless stated otherwise in the text, however, the views herein are the responsibility of the author.

2. See M. Bazerman and R. Lewicki, eds., *Negotiating in Organizations* (Sage, 1983), and J. Wall, *Negotiation: Theory and Practice* (Scott Foresman and Co., 1985). Cf. G. R. Winham, "Complexity in International Negotiation" in *Negotiations: Social Psychological Perspectives,* ed. D. Druckman (Sage, 1977).

3. For an elaboration of this approach, see S. E. Weiss, "Forests and Trees in International Business Negotiations: An Integrative Framework of Analysis," mimeo, New York University, 1987. [See now "Analysis of Complex Organizations in International Business: The RBC Perspective," *Organization Science,* 1993.]

4. K. R. Harrigan, *Strategies for Joint Ventures* (Lexington Books, 1985).

5. R. Phillips et al., *Auto Industries of Europe, United States, and Japan,* The Economist Intelligence Unit, 1982.

6. "Why Do Japanese Auto Makers Hesitate to Go to the United States?" *Oriental Economist,* April 1980.

7. Ward's Automotive Reports reported 1,908,000 Japanese car imports for 1980, and the Japan Automobile Manufacturers Association reported 1,819,092. Statistics vary by source, within and between countries.

8. See N. Fujii, "The Road to the U.S.–Japan Auto Crash: Agenda-Setting for Automobile Trade Friction," in *U.S.–Japan Relations: New Attitudes for a New Era,* The Program on U.S.–Japan Relations, Harvard University, 1984, and G. R. Winham and I. Kabashima, "The Politics of U.S.–Japanese Auto Trade" in *Coping with U.S.–Japanese Economic Conflicts,* eds. I. M. Destler and H. Sato (Lexington, 1982).

9. "Toyota Motor Co., Ltd.," *Oriental Economist,* February 1980.

10. According to a report in *The Asian Wall Street Journal* cited in *The Los Angeles Reporter,* February 14, 1983.

11. In contrast, during the 1970s, according to the MVMA, US, GM's non-Canadian imports dropped: in 1971, 88,535; in 1975, 39,730; and in 1980, none. In Canada, however, GM produced 406,186 cars in 1971 and 514,396 in 1980.

12. For more details, see S. E. Weiss, "One Impasse, One Agreement: Toyota's Joint Venture Negotiations with Ford and GM," mimeo, New York University, forthcoming.

13. L. M. Apcar, "Ford Is Likely to Reject Toyota Proposal for Joint Car-Production Venture in U.S.," *The Wall Street Journal,* July 14, 1980.

14. R. D. Hershey, Jr., "Toyota Warned by FTC," *The New York Times,* October 19, 1983.

15. "How the GM–Toyota Deal Buys Time," *Business Week,* February 28, 1983.

16. J. Holusha, "Toyota on G.M. Deal: Giving Aid to Opponent," *The New York Times,* March 22, 1983. Yamamoto also stated, "For a long time GM has sent staff to visit our manufacturing facilities, and I think GM has come to understand [our system] theoretically." See also New United Motor Manufacturing, Inc., UAW, and U.S. Dept. of Labor, "New United Motor Manufacturing, Inc., and the United Automobile Workers: Partners in Training," paper for the ILO/Turin Center, May 1986.

17. The Japanese held the largest cost advantage over other automakers. Of the Japanese companies that had the resources for a joint venture, Toyota was best known for production technology. That is presumably why Nissan and Honda were avoided as possible partners.

18. C. Reich, "The Innovator," *The New York Times Magazine,* April 21, 1985.

19. J. P. Killing, *Strategies for Joint Venture Success* (Praeger, 1983).

20. See N. B. Thayer and S. E. Weiss, "Japan: The Changing Logic of a Former Minor Power" in *National Negotiating Styles,* ed. H. Binnendijk, U.S. Dept. of State, 1987.

21. On the concept of a "single negotiating text," see R. Fisher and W. Ury, *Getting to Yes* (Houghton Mifflin, 1981). Toyota's draft agreement, which also contained notes on the company's internal discussions, would go through some 12 revisions before becoming the actual memorandum of understanding with GM.

22. Reich, "The Innovator."

23. F. C. Ikle, *How Nations Negotiate* (Harper and Row, 1964); I. W. Zartman and M. R. Berman, *The Practical Negotiator* (Yale University Press, 1982).

24. Based on an interview and cited in "GM, Toyota Agree to Explore Joint Output of Small Car, A Proposal Rejected by Ford," *The Wall Street Journal,* March 9, 1982.

25. J. Koten, "GM '90% Sure' of Joint Venture Accord with Toyota in U.S. as the Talks Drag On," *The Wall Street Journal,* January 24, 1983.

26. Based on an interview. See also *Nihon Keizei Shimbun,* February 16, 1983, as reported in J. Graham and Y. Sano, *Smart Bargaining* (Ballinger, 1984).

27. J. Hartley, "GM and Toyota Trying Too Hard?" *Automotive News,* January 24, 1983.

28. J. Koten, "GM, Toyota Pact Is Expected Soon on Joint Output," *The Wall Street Journal,* January 31, 1983.

29. As reprinted in *Federal Trade Commission Decisions,* 103.

30. According to a participant, the pricing of the car was settled only a couple of days before the signing on the 17th. The market-basket standard is a formula based on the weighted average of wholesale prices of 10 competitive small cars (including Toyota's Corolla).

31. One GM official said, "When you look at it closely, they [Toyota] really aren't giving up anything. All they can do is win on this," as quoted in J. Koten, "How Toyota Stands to Gain From the GM Deal," *The Wall Street Journal,* February 14, 1983.

32. According to the Dissenting Statement of FTC Commissioner Bailey, top shares in the subcompact segment of the U.S. market in 1983 were: Ford, 19.1%, Toyota, 16.06%, and GM, 14.41%.

33. "Toyota, GM Reach Rough Accord on Joint Car Production in US," *Japan Economic Journal,* February 8, 1983.

34. D. Henne et al., "A Case Study in Cross-Cultural Mediation: The General Motors–Toyota Joint Venture," *Arbitration Journal,* September 1986.

35. NUMMI, UAW, US DoL, op. cit.

36. As for the epilogue, contract negotiations began in April 1984. The talks went through the national GM-UAW negotiations during the fall of 1984 and reached agreement in mid-July 1985, seven months after the plant had begun production. A new UAW chapter, Local No. 2244, was established to replace No. 1364.

37. A. Fleming, "GM–Toyota: Blazing Topic," *Automotive News,* February 21, 1983.

38. One interviewee said Toyota's outside counsel informed the FTC of "discussions" between the two companies in March 1982. An interviewee at the FTC said he heard of the talks while in Japan in September 1982 then notified a contact at GM in October that the FTC would be looking into the negotiations.

39. Hershey, "Toyota Warned by FTC."

40. See J. Brooks and E. Brooks, "The Role of Top Management in Negotiations," *MSU Business Topics,* summer 1979.

41. See J. Rubin, ed., *Dynamics of Third-Party Intervention* (Praeger, 1981).

42. From R. Fisher, *International Conflict for Beginners* (Harper and Row, 1969).

Collective Bargaining at Magic Carpet Airlines: A Union Perspective (A)

HISTORY OF MAGIC CARPET AIR

Magic Carpet Air (MCA) began operations in 1961, serving 2 cities, and grew to serve 18 cities by 1987. River City Airlines (RCA) began in 1969 with service to 4 cities and grew to serve 12 cities by 1987. In January 1987, Magic Carpet Air purchased River City Airlines and merged the two operations. The joining of these two regional airlines created a small "national" airline (defined as a carrier with sales between $100 million and $1 billion) with sales of $140,265,000 in 1987. Even so, the firm competed primarily in only one region of the country and managers constantly compared it to other large regional airlines.

In May 1988, Magic Carpet Air entered into a marketing agreement with a major national carrier and became a "feeder" airline for that carrier (e.g., American Eagle is a feeder airline for American Airlines, United Express is a feeder for United Airlines). That is, MCA delivered passengers from small airports to larger ones, where passengers could make connections using that airline. Subsequently, no more reservations were given to the public as Magic Carpet Air; passengers believed that they bought tickets for the major carrier. The company also repainted all aircraft to make the public believe Magic Carpet Air was part of the major carrier.

Prior to 1989, the flight attendants at neither company were unionized. However, both MCA and RCA flight attendants worried about what they perceived as the arbitrary way that MCA management resolved personnel issues such as merging seniority lists. Such fears led several workers to contact the League of Flight Attendants (LFA), a union whose membership consisted solely of flight attendants. Despite opposition to unionization from MCA, the LFA won a union certification election with 82 percent of the vote.

This case was prepared by Peggy Briggs and William Ross of the University of Wisconsin–LaCrosse, and is intended to be used as a basis for class discussion rather than to illustrate either effective or ineffective handling of the situation. The names of the firms, individuals, and locations; dates; conversation quotations; and financial information have all been disguised to preserve the firm's and union's desire for anonymity.

An earlier version of this case was presented and accepted by the refereed Midwest Society for Case Research and appeared in *Annual Advances in Case Research, 1991*. All rights reserved to the authors and the MSCR.

PREVIOUS CONTRACT NEGOTIATIONS

Negotiations for the first MCA–LFA contract began in November 1989, and negotiators from both sides cooperated effectively. The committee borrowed language from other airline contracts (e.g., Piedmont Airlines). The committee also incorporated the past practices and working conditions that were used at River City Airlines. These rules had not been written down but had been mutually acceptable past practices. Negotiators signed the final contract in August 1990. The contract was effective until August 1994.

Negotiations for the second contract also went smoothly. In terms of contract provisions, the second contract was basically an extension of the first, with a modest pay increase and one additional paid holiday. The agreement was effective until August 31, 1997.

What follows is a synopsis of the 1997 contract negotiations from a union negotiator's perspective.

LEAGUE OF FLIGHT ATTENDANTS (LFA) NEGOTIATING TEAM

Whenever an LFA carrier began negotiations, the National Office of LFA sent a national bargaining representative (NBR) to the scene. Dixie Lee, the NBR assigned to the MCA negotiations, met with the flight attendants' Master Executive Council (MEC) to select a negotiating team. The negotiating team prepared for negotiations and conducted the actual bargaining sessions. Once at the table, Dixie spoke for the committee. Using an NBR as the spokesperson lessened the likelihood that a flight attendant who was emotionally involved with an issue might say something inappropriate while trying to negotiate. Dixie had 14 years' experience and had also assisted with the 1994 MCA contract negotiations. Although Dixie was the spokesperson, the negotiating team was formally chaired by Ruth Boaz, LFA MEC president at Magic Carpet Air. Other members of the team included local LFA union presidents Peggy Hardy, Marie Phillips, and Jody Rogers.

DETERMINING THE UNION'S BARGAINING OBJECTIVES

The LFA negotiating committee members first identified their bargaining objectives. For the 1997 contract, the LFA negotiating committee devised an opening offer based on the average working conditions and wage rates for flight attendants offered by other, similarly sized carriers. They looked at wage, unemployment, and cost-of-living data from government sources such as the *Monthly Labor Review*. The committee members knew the financial history of MCA and kept their proposals within financial reach of the company. They also used other employee groups (e.g., pilots, mechanics) within MCA as a guide—many of the LFA proposals were items that these other unions already had in their contracts. The LFA negotiating committee hoped to bring wages and work rules in line with the company's financial performance and industry standards (see Table 1). Finally, they looked at past grievances and arbitration cases to determine if contract wording needed changes.

   Committee members also considered the wishes of the rank-and-file members. To do this, the committee mailed a survey to the 115 LFA members asking questions regarding wages, working conditions, and issues of concern to flight attendants. They received a 75 percent response rate; results are shown in Table 2.

TABLE 1   1996–97 Regional Airline Industry Comparisons

	Starting Wage/Hour	Days Off Per Month	Duty Rig* as Airline (Percent of Time)
A	$17.00	11	60%
B	$15.00	12	62%
C	$15.00	12	none
D	$14.00	13	none
E	$14.00	10	none
F	$13.50	10	33%
Magic Carpet	$13.00	10	none

*Duty Rig is a pay calculation that is a certain percentage of the period of time which a flight attendant is on duty with the company. Duty time normally begins 45 minutes prior to first scheduled trip departure time and ends 15 minutes after final arrival time at the end of the day.

TABLE 2   Results of the Flight Attendant Survey

Questionnaires mailed: 115

Questionnaires returned: 86

Question: What was the flight attendant's top priority for the new contract?

Direct wages	40%
Job security	31%
Working conditions	26%
Other	3%

Question: How did the flight attendant want to receive her/his direct wages?

Duty rigs	47%
Hourly rate	34%
Holiday pay	15%
Other	4%

Question: How did the flight attendant want her/his job security?

Seniority protection	60%
Protection from layoffs	28%
Protection of contract	12%

After tallying the responses, negotiating team members discovered that the flight attendants' major concern was wage determination. MCA currently paid flight attendants for the time they were in the aircraft with it moving under its own power—they were not paid for the time spent sitting in airports waiting for flights. Union members wanted MCA to implement "duty rigs." A duty rig paid the attendant a fixed percentage of the period of time he or she was on duty with the company.

For example, suppose an attendant worked a 15-hour day, but worked in moving aircraft for only 6 hours. Under the current system, MCA paid wages for six hours, plus one hour for preparation time ("duty time") at the beginning of the day. However, if the duty rig pay rate was 67 percent, MCA would pay the attendant for 10 hours of work, plus 1 hour for duty time. Thus, duty rigs would require the airline to pay a percentage of the wage for all time at work, whether flying or sitting.

Flight attendants also voiced concern over job security and working conditions. When they analyzed the job security issue, team members found that in the event of any merger or buyout of MCA, the flight attendants wanted their seniority with the carrier to be continued by any new company. Second, flight attendants sought protection from layoffs in the event of a merger or acquisition.

The survey also had a section for employee comments. The area that members most frequently relayed as a concern was their current sick leave program. Many flight attendants complained that they were not allowed to use their accrued sick time when they were sick. Others complained that they had to give management a five-day notice whenever they wanted to swap routes with other MCA attendants.

From this information, union negotiating committee members identified two broad objectives: increased wages via a duty rig provision, and increased job security. They also decided that their initial package would be very close to their final objectives. The committee members proposed a duty rig clause with the same standards as the pilots, although the dollar amount was less important than just obtaining the provision itself. They also devised a "successorship clause" allowing attendants to arbitrate their seniority rights in the event someone bought MCA. In order to obtain these clauses, the union also proposed two "throwaway" clauses: an expensive health care package and "double-time" wages for working holidays.

STRATEGIES OF THE UNION

During planning sessions, the negotiating committee identified four strategies for achieving its objectives through bargaining:

1. Keeping union members informed of negotiation progress.
2. Getting union members involved.
3. Convincing the company that the union's demands were serious.
4. Settling an issue only with the unanimous consent of the negotiating committee.

Informing Union Members

The first strategy attempted to keep the union members informed. The negotiating committee mailed a short letter after each bargaining session, explaining the issues discussed and the general content of any agreed-upon sections. Members were also sent *Negotiation Update* newsletters every two weeks, telling flight attendants of their progress. These newsletters did not reveal any initial proposals because committee members knew that union members would be disappointed if the union did not receive what was initially requested.

Involving Union Members

The second strategy sought to get the union members involved. The negotiating committee printed the slogan, "We make the difference and they make the money" on pens, buttons, and T-shirts. These were distributed to all members and to all passengers on selected flights. This program was loosely modeled after the United Airlines' 1996–97 Create Havoc Around Our System (CHAOS) program, where the union sought to enlist the aid of the public and employed creative tactics (e.g., intermittent strikes, informational picketing) to pressure management to resolve their contract dispute. The union also invited any member in good standing to attend any negotiation session.

Convincing the Company

The third strategy attempted to convince the company to take the LFA seriously. In a widely publicized move, negotiation team members did extensive research on both economic picketing and informational picketing, inquiring at all of their domicile cities as to what permits would be needed to picket. The union mailed their *Negotiation Update* newsletters to each manager's home address, informing managers of the LFA's preparations in the event of a future strike. Committee members hoped these actions would convince management that the LFA made serious proposals—and would strike if those proposals were not met.

Settling Issues

The fourth strategy was that the team would not proceed with an item without the entire team being in total agreement. All planning meetings, and caucuses (meetings without the company team member present) during negotiations would involve every committee member.

COMPANY NEGOTIATING TEAM

The company negotiating team consisted of the following people:

- Bill Orleans, director of labor relations.
- Ross Irving, director of human resources.
- Kristine Lamb, director of inflight services.
- Christian Andrew, executive vice president.
- Willie Sanders, senior vice president of operations.
- Tom Windham, chief executive officer (CEO) and president.

The company team was in a state of transition, and consequently seemed to suffer from much confusion. Bill Orleans had recently been demoted from director of human resources to director of labor relations—a move he resented. Ross Irving, the new director of human resources, hired from another firm, avoided the sessions; he seemed uncomfortable sitting next to his predecessor, particularly since Mr. Orleans had negotiated most of the union contracts at MCA. Finally, Mrs. Lamb, who was used to giving orders to flight attendants, acted as if the negotiations reflected a lack of loyalty on the part of the workers and interference with her job on the part of management. Tom Windham was grooming Willie Sanders to take over upon Windham's retirement.

THE NEGOTIATING PROCESS: INITIAL POSITIONS

Airlines are governed under the Railway Labor Act of 1926, as amended. This act states that labor contracts never expire, but may be amended on their amendable dates. When the amendable date comes near, a letter is mailed by the party requesting changes in the contract to the counterparty in the contract. This letter allows contract talks to begin. Dixie mailed MCA such a letter on March 31, giving a full 60 days' notice of the flight attendants' intent to open talks for amending their current contract before September 1.

Inasmuch as the company would not meet in a neutral city, LFA negotiators agreed to an MCA proposal to meet at a hotel located near corporate headquarters. MCA paid for the meeting room. The first negotiation session was scheduled for May 29, 1997.

Everyone on the LFA committee had the jitters. It was the first time in negotiations for Marie, Jody, and Peggy. Dixie gave them some last-minute instructions:

> I don't want y'all to speak or use any facial expressions at the table. Instead, I want all of y'all to silently take notes. Draw a vertical line down the middle of each note page. Write whatever the managers say on the left side of the page and write whatever I say on the right-hand side of the page. Is it OK with y'all if I do the negotiating? I've found things go best if only one person talks at the bargaining table.

As the LFA negotiators filed into the conference room, they saw it was empty. Each of the managers arrived late. Twenty minutes later, Mr. Orleans still had not come. As everyone waited, CEO Tom Windham arrived. Small talk began as Mr. Windham glanced over his notes and spoke:

> You know that as a feeder airline we do not have full control over our own destiny; the marketing agreement with the major carrier restricts our flexibility. Even so, I am willing to give your flight attendant group a modest increase. I am not looking for any concessions. Also, my philosophy is that all the groups (pilots, agents, office personnel) should be treated equally. However, your union does have a good agreement right now—say, why don't we just agree to continue the present contract for another six years? It could save a lot of time!

As everyone chuckled at Mr. Windham's joke, Mr. Orleans arrived. The union negotiators could tell by the expression on his face that he was surprised and embarrassed to see Tom Windham there. Mr. Windham stood up, wished everyone good luck, and left.

THE UNION'S INITIAL POSITION

Dixie spent the first day describing problems with the current contract. At 4:15 PM, the union presented the company with its neatly typed contract proposal. Dixie had written "change," "new," "clarification," and so on in the margin next to each paragraph that had been changed in any way from the 1994 contract.

Orleans:

This is a "wish book"! Do I look like Santa Claus?

Lee:

Stop fidgeting, Mr. Orleans. Let me explain why we are insisting on these changes.

Dixie read only about one-third of the provisions in the union's contract proposal. Two additional sessions were necessary to read through the entire proposal. The major changes are summarized in Table 3.

MANAGEMENT'S INITIAL POSITION

On the fourth day, company representatives presented their initial offer to the union. Mr. Orleans handed each of the LFA committee members a book in a binder. As they leafed through the book, members were puzzled. They did not see any notations indicating changes from the current contract. Mr. Orleans talked quickly, summarizing the provisions in the contract; most of the proposed provisions included some type of union concessions, but he did not highlight these.

Lee:

Is this a serious proposal? The union presented a realistic proposal using industry standards, and your opener (opening offer) is totally unreasonable.

Orleans:

Don't get your panties in a wad. The party has just begun and there is lots of time to dance. Why, we didn't even list any wages in our proposal—we were hoping you would work for free, ha ha.

Mr. Orleans then gave a long, patronizing, sermon regarding MCA's poor financial health and how the company could be bankrupt at any time. However, in the history of Magic Carpet Air, the company had never shown a loss on its financial statement.

A recess was called for lunch. As the union members caucused, Peggy looked depressed. Marie sat with fists clenched.

Marie:

I can't eat anything! I am furious at Mr. Orleans—he has some nerve!

Jody:

The others were not much better. Did you hear their snide remarks about us when they went to lunch?

Peggy:

What are we going to do? They have asked for concessions on everything! And Mr. Windham promised us just the opposite.

TABLE 3   Changes in the Magic Carpet Air–League of Flight Attendants Contract

Contract Provision	1994–97 Contract	Union Proposal
Compensation		
Base wage	$13.00	$15.45
Wage after five years	$20.20	$25.55
Duty rig pay	None	1 hour pay per 2 hour duty (50%)
Daily guarantee	3.25 hours	4.5 hours
Holiday pay	None	8 holidays at "double-time" rate
Job Security		
Successorship	None	Contract will still be binding
Protection of seniority rights in the event of a merger	None	Arbitrator combines MCA seniority list with that of the other airline
Working Conditions		
Trip trading lead time	5 days	24 hours
Shoe allowance	None	$100/year
Winter coat	None	Total cost
Uniform maintenance	$16/month	$20/month

Dixie:

Now girls, just relax. It is still the first week of negotiations. I suggest that we just work from our initial contract proposal and ignore theirs. It can't be taken seriously anyway, in my opinion.

Marie:

Well, you'll have to carry on without me tomorrow; I have to work. Management won't let me rearrange my schedule to negotiate. At least I won't have to watch Mr. Orleans chain-smoke!

Talks resumed after lunch break. Dixie summarized each section of the LFA proposal. Mr. Orleans fidgeted and kept saying "No." Nothing was settled that day.

By noon the next day, it became obvious that not much was getting accomplished. Finally, the union moved to sections where it did not propose any changes and the managers tentatively agreed to keep those intact. It seemed like a mountain had been climbed just to get the company to agree to those "no changes." Negotiations were adjourned for the day.

Lee:

When can we meet? Monday, at 8:30?

Sanders:

No good for me. I have important meetings that day.

Lee:

How about Tuesday?

Andrew:

I can't make it. Every day next week is bad.

Orleans:

The following week I will be out of town. Sorry!

Lee:

OK, y'all tell us when y'all's schedules are free.

Orleans:

We'll have to caucus. We'll get back to you.

Instead of caucusing and deciding when they could next meet, the managers simply went home, leaving the union negotiating team to wonder when—or if—bargaining would continue.

ROUND 2

On Wednesday, July 16, Ruth Boaz got a letter from management asking for a meeting two days later. Ruth quickly scheduled a planning session for Thursday night, where the LFA team members reviewed their objectives and and the progress to date. Negotiations with MCA resumed Friday.

JULY 18: GRIEVANCES AND UNIFORMS

Mr. Irving proposed using the same language for a revised grievance procedure as that printed in the pilot's contract. The union caucused. Ruth telephoned the pilot's union and, once she was satisfied that the pilots were happy with their grievance procedure, convinced the union negotiating team to agree.

The discussion moved to the section on uniforms. After some countering back and forth on various issues, a winter coat was added as an optional item; however, who would pay the cost was still an issue. The union wanted MCA to pay the total cost.

Orleans:

Unacceptable. You'll have to buy your own coats. We already give $16 per month for uniform cleaning.

Lee:

But a winter coat is expensive. Surely y'all recognize that a poor little ol' flight attendant couldn't be expected to shoulder the entire cost of a new coat. Mr. Orleans, have a heart.

Orleans:

I do have a heart; fortunately, it is not attached to my wallet, ha ha. OK, we will allow $40 every five years to buy a coat.

Lee:

According to my research, a new cost costs $120. And it costs $10.00 per month to clean.

Orleans:

How often does someone dry-clean a coat she only wears three months of the year? She doesn't clean it 12 times! *(Pause.)* OK, if you drop this silly request for free shoes, then we'll raise the combined uniform and coat maintenance allowance to $16.50 per month.

Lee:

But, Mr. Orleans, shoes are a part of our uniform, too. You expect us to all wear the same type of shoes, don't you? You pay for the other parts of our uniforms, so it is only reasonable that MCA should also pay for shoes. Our research shows that two pairs of standard shoes cost, on average, $100.

Orleans:

However, you can wear the shoes when you are not on duty, too. You probably wouldn't do that with other parts of your uniforms. So we're not paying for shoes you can wear other places.

Boaz:

Mr. Orleans, I can assure you that we don't wear our uniform shoes when we go dancing on the weekends. (Everyone laughed.)

Orleans:

If we pay $25 for shoes and $45 for a coat, then we will pay $17.50 per month for uniform maintenance.

Lee:

Good, but not good enough.

(Both sides sat in silence for nearly four minutes. Mr. Orleans was obviously uncomfortable with this period of silence.)

Orleans:

Let's see . . . *(fumbling with a pen and paper)* we'll split the cost of the new coat, so that is $60 and we'll pay $25 for shoes. Good enough now?

Lee:

Raise the combined uniform and coat maintenance to $18 per month and you have a deal.

Lee:

(As they were writing the agreed-upon section.) Why don't we make it one new coat for the life of the three-year contract, instead of one new coat every five years? That makes it so much easier for everyone to keep track of.

Mr. Orleans rolled his eyes and nodded in acquiescence. The meeting then adjourned for the weekend. At last the union team felt that some progress was being made.

CASE 6

Vanessa Abrams (A)

Vanessa Abrams, executive vice president of sales and marketing, after nine years with Swanton & Gardner (S&G), found herself involved unexpectedly in a tense negotiation with her boss, Jerome Bailey, president and franchise owner of S&G's New York office. Hired in 1980 as director of sales and marketing, a position then new to S&G's office, Abrams had over the years turned in consistently excellent performances for the health care consulting firm, and she had been promoted to vice president and, later, executive vice president. She had been a member of the New York office's management committee since her promotion to vice president in 1983. S&G's 42-person New York office was one of a chain of 73 offices throughout the United States, each of which was owned locally.

As executive vice president of sales and marketing, Abrams participated in setting the office's yearly revenue goal and was responsible for meeting that goal with her staff of two account managers, one administrative person, and a number of consultants who reported indirectly to her. Some of the New York office's revenues came through other S&G offices (including corporate headquarters in Boston), and some originated in New York.

Historically, Abrams had herself brought in between 30 and 40 percent of the office's revenues each year. Her compensation package consisted of base salary plus commission. The commission that she and all members of her sales group received could total to about 16 percent on any one account. Each member of the sales group (including Abrams) received a 4 percent commission on any new business brought in and a 12 percent commission on any accounts managed. In addition, Abrams received a 2 percent override commission on all new business generated by her sales team. In fiscal 1989–90, her team had exceeded the total revenue goal of $4.7 million. (S&G's fiscal year ended on August 31.) In addition to her revenue-generation responsibilities, Abrams made all management decisions regarding pricing, assigning of consultants to accounts, and workloads. Abrams oversaw training for both new and existing staff and was responsible for the New York office's public relations needs.

Vanessa Abrams, who held a master's degree in psychology, had been a therapist prior to coming to S&G. Her training in her "first career," as she put it, came through

This case was prepared by Deborah Kolb and Cinny Little for the Institute for Case Development and Research, Simmons Graduate School of Management, Boston, MA 02215.

clearly in conversations with her. She listened attentively and well, often making notes in a small leather notebook that was always close at hand, bristling with pieces of paper. Though Abrams was persistent when pursuing a line of questioning or seeking information, she spoke in a quiet voice and frequently pushed her long hair gently back from her face as she paused for thought. An observer could not help but notice Abrams's appearance. She was very tall and strikingly slender. Her wardrobe was sophisticated, unusual, and elegant, and included bright colors and artful jewelry.

During the spring of 1990, Bailey came to Abrams and asked her to sign a "nondisclosure" agreement. It was very common for companies to protect themselves by having employees sign an agreement stating that they will not share company or client knowledge with other companies. Most such agreements would require that an employee not solicit former clients for business for a certain length of time after termination. It was particularly common for employees in positions with sales or bottom-line responsibilities as well as senior management to work under the terms of such an agreement. As she understood the S&G nondisclosure agreement, Abrams said, "It meant that if I ever left S&G, I couldn't work for a competitor or solicit any of my clients for a year. I couldn't solicit clients for *anything;* I mean if I had wanted, for whatever reason, to sell them recycling services or anything else, I couldn't do that. And he could do anything he wanted after I signed it."

This was not the first time that Bailey had asked her to sign the agreement, but Abrams had always refused to sign, since, she said, "I had been working for Jerry for years without a nondisclosure. He had asked me to sign it time and again, and I refused. There was absolutely no reason, in my mind, why I needed to sign it. It was the only way I had leverage over him."

But in May 1990, Bailey was insistent that this time she really had to sign the agreement. Corporate headquarters was pressuring him, he said, "and they just don't want anybody in the company without one." Somewhat confused by the sudden urgency of Bailey's request, Abrams decided to call Jim, a good friend of hers who was an attorney. Jim thought it might be a good idea for her to get someone to look over the S&G nondisclosure agreement, and he referred her to Nick, an attorney who worked in the same firm. Nick told Vanessa that S&G's nondisclosure agreement seemed to be a pretty standard. But, he told her, "Jerry can't *make* you sign the agreement." He suggested to Abrams that she should get some compensation for signing. "He said," Vanessa recounted, "that I should really get tough with Jerry; if Jerry really needed me to sign this, then I should be able to get something for it.

Vanessa thought about Nick's advice to "get tough," and she considered past situations in which she had negotiated with Jerry:

> I had always negotiated with him in a very psychological way, and it's always been very successful. I'm a therapist from my first career, and a lot of it was intuitive for me. I'd play to his ego, and I'd make him feel good. I'd put myself in his shoes and try to figure out what he thinks. He would huffle and buffle and try to make me feel sorry for him. That was his negotiating style. He acts out of his emotions.

Vanessa said that what she really wanted from Jerry at this point was for him to show her how much he valued her. She also decided to take Nick's advice about getting tough and seeking "compensation" for signing the nondisclosure. She wrote a memo to Jerry in early June 1990 in which she stated that in exchange for signing the nondisclosure, she wanted a contract with the following protections in place:

1. The right of first refusal should Jerry decide to sell the New York office franchise.

2. The continuation of reimbursement for all "customary and reasonable" professional expenses incurred (e.g., parking, mileage, car phone, client entertainment) and continuation of all customary S&G employee benefits.

3. A salary in the range that is equal to the compensation she had historically received, and which takes into account the revenues she had historically generated and places a value on the loss of mobility she would incur if she signed the nondisclosure.

4. A parachute clause that provides her with customary benefits in the event she is no longer employed by S&G. (Note: A "parachute" is an agreement that provides for payment after termination of employment.)

5. A signing bonus of 5 percent of her salary.

In the June 13 meeting they held to discuss her memo, Jerry said that he "really didn't have to do anything for" her. Vanessa said:

> Then I became much harder. Here I was the goose laying the golden eggs. I told Jerry that my attorney had advised me in this matter, and with that Jerry was just furious. He got enraged. He is a large man, on the stocky side and his broad face got redder than I have ever seen it. He said, "How did you get an attorney involved in this?" I said, "Jerry, if this were you, wouldn't you?" And he replied, "No! We've had a relationship for all these years!" I said, "But look what you're trying to do to me; you're going to take away all this." He said, "Well, look what you're doing to *me*. I got written up." "Written up" in our corporate lingo means that he was cited by corporate headquarters for having a senior member of management who is not covered by the agreement. So I understood about him having to have the agreement. I really did. But the feeling that he wasn't willing to give me a goddamn thing for signing was enraging. It was the feeling that was important to me. The one thing I had over him, in my mind, was the leverage of *not* signing the nondisclosure. The leverage was important to me, too.
>
> After the June 13 meeting, he brought a lot of pressure to bear on me. He took me off the management committee [which had been made up of Bailey, Abrams, and 2 others]. He told me that he couldn't let me be privy to management discussions if I didn't sign the nondisclosure. Nick was telling me that I had to be ready to walk out. But psychologically, I was not prepared to walk. I couldn't. I was making good money, and I knew that the next quarter was going to be big. Nick said, "Don't sign it, and then you can work for a competitor." And I even went so far as to speak to one of them. I flew to Baltimore and talked to them. But the money was nowhere near where it was at S&G. And the thing is, I *loved* S&G. I loved the people, loved the work.

In July 1990, Abrams decided to sign the nondisclosure agreement. She said:

> I succumbed to the pressure. Being taken off the management committee was public and it was embarrassing. So, I signed it, and I did get one consideration. I got the consideration that if he fired me, I would get one year's salary. In my mind, I didn't think this was worth a thing, but on the other hand, I figured he wouldn't fire me. After all, I was the major revenue-producer.

The thing was in all of this, I had negotiated from my attorney's style rather than the style I'd used over the years with Jerry. With Jerry, I *knew* I had to cajole him and just work things out, but when I took a much stronger stand and had this and that in writing, he was furious. And I ended up giving in. Taking a hard line just didn't seem to work.

As soon as Abrams signed the nondisclosure statement, S&G New York experienced a rush of new business. Abrams said, "We had six phenomenal months, which started with July 1990 and August 1990. Fiscal 1989–90 ended up with a bang and made it a great year for us." This high-level performance continued for the first months of fiscal 1990–91, and the sales group made their numbers in the first half of the fiscal year, which was very unusual. As Abrams said, "This meant that if we held even for the rest of fiscal year, we'd have the best year ever. We were staffed up on the service delivery side, and we took more space in our building to accommodate new people . . . and then things began to slow down."

All through the spring and summer of 1991, Abrams noticed empty offices and could see that S&G was spending more and more money on office equipment and other materials. Abrams told Bailey that she thought they needed to do something about the expenses. Her feeling was that, if sales slowed down and expenses were too high, profits would be unnecessarily low. Jerry replied that he wasn't terribly concerned and that July and August were always S&G's best months. Abrams said, "But Jerry, although that's usually true, this year is unusual. The market is shifting, and I don't see an August 1991 that looks good. I feel it in my bones. I don't see anything in the pipeline."

DISCUSSION QUESTIONS

1. At the conclusion of the noncompete negotiations, Vanessa Abrams said, "I ended up giving in." Do you agree?

2. How did Abrams get herself in this position? What other choices did she have? Why didn't she pursue them?

3. Have you had similar experiences? What were they and how did you handle them?

500 English Sentences

Scott sat looking out the window, watching a group of boys playing baseball in the school yard. Poor kids, he thought, they are the real losers in all of this. He looked down at a copy of *500 English Sentences* and the endorsement letter on his desk. He glanced at the clock and realized that he had to have an answer for Mr. Honda within the hour. He was feeling very frustrated and stressed from the events of the past 10 days. He decided that he would go to the karate school after work, something which always made him feel better. He sighed as he thought about what he had to do next.

SCOTT

Scott was 26 years old and had been living in Japan for 18 months. He was born in Auburn, Massachusetts, and had spent most of his life in the United States. Scott's father was a successful entrepreneur who believed that hard work and good old-fashioned principles were the ingredients to success. He always taught his children to stand up for what they believed in and to never sacrifice their values in order to get ahead. Scott's mother was a housewife who took care of the family home and the children. She loved to travel and encouraged Scott's father to take the family abroad every year so that their children would have a better understanding of the world around them.

Scott was a very disciplined student. He was an English major and had been on the dean's honor role for every semester throughout his four years at college. During his senior year, Scott worked as a teaching assistant, grading papers and tutoring students.

Scott started studying karate when he was a junior in high school. He enjoyed the physical workout and the disciplinary aspect of the sport and continued to train throughout his undergraduate years. By the time he was ready to graduate, Scott had earned a third-degree black belt.

> It was through karate that I first became interested in Japan. I thought it would be enlightening to experience Japanese culture and learn more about their ways of thinking. My goal was to one day go over to Japan and train in a Japanese karate dojo (school) and learn from a real karate sensei. My biggest problem was to figure out how to go about doing this. I knew that I didn't have the luxury of just moving to Japan to study karate and since I didn't speak the language I figured that my chances of working for a company in Japan were about nil.

This case was written by Laura Turek. Copyright © 1996 by Laura Turek. Used with permission. This case was prepared as a basis for classroom discussion, not to illustrate either the effective or ineffective management of an administrative situation.

In the fall of his senior year, Scott saw a poster for the Japan Exchange and Teaching (JET) Program at school that advertised teaching jobs in Japan. He had heard of other students going over to Japan to teach English but had never given any serious thought to a career in teaching, even if only for a short time. To work as an assistant English teacher on the JET program, applicants had to have a bachelor's degree and an interest in Japan. Knowledge of Japanese language or a degree in education were not listed as requirements. This was what Scott had been hoping for, an opportunity to go over to Japan to continue his karate under a Japanese instructor as well as a chance to put his English degree to good use. He wrote the address in his notebook and sent for an application that very night.

THE JAPAN EXCHANGE AND TEACHING (JET) PROGRAM

Before the JET Program

The origins of the JET program can be traced back to 1982. In that year, the Japanese Ministry of Education (Monbusho) initiated a project known as the Monbusho English Fellows (MEF) Program, which hired Americans to work at the local boards of education in order to assist Japanese English teaching consultants who acted as advisors to the Japanese teachers of English in the public schools. The task of the MEFs was to oversee the junior and senior high school English teachers and to assist them with their training. In 1983, the British English Teachers Scheme (BETS) was inaugurated by the Ministry of Education. However, from the outset the British teachers were stationed at schools, and the goals of the program did not only concern English instruction but also sought to increase mutual understanding and improve friendly relations between the peoples of Japan and Britain. While there were some differences between the two programs, both shared a common goal: inviting native English speakers to Japan to assist in improving foreign-language instruction.

The Birth of the JET Program

The realization that Japan must open itself more fully to contact with international society began to foster an awareness of the importance of promoting internationalization and international exchange at the local level. This brought about not only expanded English instruction, but also a rapid increase in exchange programs. Taking these new circumstances into account, the Japanese Ministry of Home Affairs in 1985 released a paper entitled "Plans for International Exchange Projects" as part of its priority policy of local governments for the following year. In the paper, the Ministry of Home Affairs proposed a definite course for the internationalization of local governments, which ideally would lead to smoothly functioning cultural exchanges. All of these ideas were finally implemented in a concrete project: the Japan Exchange and Teaching (JET) Program.

The Ministry of Home Affairs abolished the two projects currently in effect (MEF and BETS) and created a new one that was entrusted simultaneously to three ministries: the Ministry of Foreign Affairs, the Ministry of Education, and the

Ministry of Home Affairs. However, the concept of appointing local authorities to implement the program and act as host institutions was preserved. While discussions were held with each of the local authorities to work out the details and ensure the smooth implementation of such a massive program, the formation of a cooperative organization for all local governments was expedited.

The Creation of CLAIR

CLAIR, originally the Conference of Local Authorities for International Relations, was established in October 1986 by the *Todofuken* (the 47 prefectures of Japan) and the *Seireishiteitoshi* (the [then] 10 designated cities) as a cooperative organization responsible for implementing the JET program in conjunction with the three Japanese ministries named above.

CLAIR's Role in the JET Program

To ensure smooth implementation of the JET program, the three ministries, the local authorities, and CLAIR were all given specific functions. The functions that the conference attempted to fulfill for implementing the JET program were as follows:

1. Advice and liaison during recruitment and selection.
2. Placement of participants.
3. Participant orientation, conferences.
4. Guidance for local authority host institutions.
5. Participant welfare and counseling.
6. Travel arrangements for participants coming to Japan.
7. Liaison with related groups and institutions.
8. Publications and reference materials.
9. Publicity for the program.

The larger goal behind these functions of the conference was the promotion of international exchange at the local level. Independent of this development, the Council of Local Authorities for International Relations (a publicly endowed foundation) was inaugurated in July 1987. The council's main duty was to study and survey participating nations' local authorities overseas with the ultimate objective being to support local government programs for the promotion of internationalization. By fostering international exchange at the regional level, the council came to assume the same duties as the Conference of Local Authorities for International Relations. It was suggested that both organizations merge since they held information relevant to each other's work and shared the goals of improving work efficiency and performing their tasks more effectively. Moreover, the annual growth of the JET program led to an increased number of interrelated duties and tasks. Thus, it was necessary to strengthen the structure of the Conference of Local Authorities for International Relations.

It was decided that the operations and financial assets of the conference would be assumed by the council, and in August 1989 they were amalgamated, under the acronym of CLAIR, to form a joint organization of local public bodies in Japan to support and promote internationalization at the regional level.

SCOTT'S ACCEPTANCE

Scott reviewed the JET information he had received. There were two different positions available: (1) the coordinator for international relations (CIR) and (2) the assistant language teacher (ALT). The first position, although it sounded interesting, was out of the question since knowledge of Japanese was a requirement. Scott applied for the second position because as an English major he felt that he was qualified to assist in the teaching of English. Scott was chosen for an interview and was successful in obtaining an offer to teach English in Japan.

> The JET program and CLAIR were very good at trying to prepare the participants for their stay in Japan. I attended several workshops and orientations concerning my job in Japan as well as seminars on what to expect living in such a different culture from my own. I remember thinking some of the potential situations they were preparing us for seemed a bit unrealistic and that I would probably never encounter them, but I found out soon enough that Japan and the United States are culturally a world apart, and I was glad to have received the predeparture training. Without it, I would have thought that I had arrived in Wonderland with no idea on how to behave at the tea party.

SCOTT'S SITUATION IN JAPAN

Scott was sent to a small village on the northern island of Hokkaido, where he taught English at Naka High School. At first, Scott had some difficulties adjusting to living in such a remote place. The people were friendly, yet since they were not accustomed to seeing many foreigners, Scott always felt that he was on display, or that his every move was under scrutiny.

> It was strange being the only non-Japanese person living in the town. I was there to do my job, and study karate, but somehow ended up as the town celebrity. Everyone in town knew everything about me. They all knew where I lived, when I entertained guests. I felt like my every move was monitored. It got so bad that I even had to hang my wash inside my house because people started to tell me that they liked my colorful boxer shorts.
>
> People not only watched what I did, but how I did it. Everyone wanted to know how the American talked, walked, and how he ate. People asked me daily if I could eat with chopsticks. I made a conscious effort very quickly to blend in as much as I could. It was either that or get angry, and I don't think people were being malicious, they were just overly curious.

The biggest problem that Scott encountered from the start was feelings of incompetence and frustration. The only people in the whole village with whom he could speak without much difficulty were the Japanese English teachers at the high school. If he ran into problems at the bank or supermarket, he was forced to rely on a mixture of basic Japanese and English accompanied by an elaborate display of sign language which more often than not ended in frustration. To overcome the communication problems, Scott began studying Japanese every night at home. He also found a Japanese language teacher at the high school who agreed to tutor him.

> Until I moved to Japan, I never realized how frustrating life can be when you cannot even do the simplest tasks for yourself like read your electric bill or use an automated teller machine. I felt pretty helpless a lot of the time and no one seemed to understand what I was going through. Whenever I had a problem involving a language or cultural misunderstanding, I would go see Mr. Honda, the head of English, not only because his English was the best of all of the teachers, but also because he had lived abroad in England and Australia, and I figured that he would be able to understand what I was going through.

MR. HONDA

Mr. Honda was the head of English at Naka High School. He was 46 years old and had been teaching English at various schools in the prefecture for more than 22 years. In his youth, Mr. Honda had studied English at Oxford, and had spent two summers in Australia on homestays. His command of spoken English and his vocabulary were quite remarkable. Mr. Honda acted as a mentor to Scott. He considered Scott as his *kohai* (junior) and believed that as a good Japanese manager, it was his duty to guide the young foreigner throughout his stay in Japan. Mr. Honda showed this same kind of paternalistic concern for all of the junior English teachers and counseled them on everything from lesson planning to when they should think about marrying. None of the younger teachers in the English department made any decision without the approval of Mr. Honda. Scott thought that this was a waste of talent and initiative. He knew a couple of young teachers who were very dynamic and had some creative teaching ideas, yet were forced to use the dated teaching methods of Mr. Honda because he was their superior.

Although he never expressed it openly, Mr. Honda did not really like dealing with these young ALTs. He found it insulting to work with such young foreigners, who more often than not had no formal training as English teachers yet were hired to tell him how to do his job better. He did not share in the opinion that these foreign assistants were experts in English teaching just because they could speak the language fluently. Mr. Honda, as well as the other teachers on the staff, had trouble adjusting to the ALTs since they were hired on a yearly contract basis which was renewable only to a maximum of three years. This left the school barely enough time to get to know an ALT before he or she left and another took over. Mr. Honda also didn't like the fact that these young assistant teachers were earning nearly the same salary as he each month, despite his 22 years of experience.

In spite of his feelings for ALTs in general, Mr. Honda liked Scott. He not only felt that Scott was qualified to be doing the job but also thought that Scott was adapting very well to the Japanese style of management.

> Scott works very hard. He shows great enthusiasm for teaching English at our school. He is very pleasant to work with and is making a big effort to learn the Japanese language and ways. It is a pleasure to have such a good teacher on our staff.

ACCEPTANCE IN THE GROUP

Scott joined the local karate school and began training every night after work.

> I felt very much at ease at the karate dojo. Despite the fact that I had no idea what my karate teacher and the other men were saying to me, we seemed to get along very well because we were all there for a common goal: to study karate. I think the other members accepted me into their group because I showed them that I was serious about the sport and had a determination to learn. At first, I saw the other members only at the karate school, but after a few months, they started inviting me to dinners and other social gatherings. Sometimes we even went out drinking after practice. It was good to feel like I was a part of something. I was tired of being treated like the "funny *gaijin*" all the time.

For the first few months, Scott felt isolated at work. Excluding the English teachers, many of his co-workers did not talk to him at all, which made him feel unwelcome at the school. It wasn't until he asked a young English teacher about the situation that she told Scott how several of the teachers were afraid to speak to him because they felt that their English skills were too weak. Scott told the young teacher that it was he who should be embarrassed for not speaking Japanese. After that, Scott made an effort to speak in Japanese, even though his mistakes often made him feel ridiculous and self-conscious. The other teachers slowly began to warm up to Scott and started to converse more with him at school.

Scott went out of his way to get involved at school. He not only taught his courses but also became involved with many of the clubs after school. He ran the English-speaking club and helped coach the karate club. He was also willing to come in on weekends when there was a special event going on at the school.

> I got involved with extracurricular activities at school, not necessarily for altruistic reasons, but I guess because aside from karate, there was really not much for me to do in such a remote place where I could barely speak the language. I guess the other teachers thought that I was different from some of the other foreigners who had worked at Naka High because I was putting in extra time and work. What ever the reason, they began to treat me like one of the group.

THE MOVE

Scott had been in Japan almost a year and made the decision to renew for another. He asked to be transferred to Satsuki, the capital city of the prefecture, because his girlfriend back in the United States was thinking of coming over to Japan and there would be no work for her in such a small town as the one he was in. The teachers at Naka High were sad to see Scott leave and gave him a huge farewell party at which everyone made speeches saying how they would miss him.

> It was kind of sad to leave Naka High. Once I got to know them, the teachers at Naka were quite a down-to-earth group who treated me like I was one of the family. The problem was that life in such a small town no longer offered what I needed. My girlfriend wanted to come over to Japan and I knew that she could get a job in Satsuki. My karate sensei also told me that if I wanted to test for my fourth-degree black belt, I would get better training at one of the bigger karate dojos in the city, and this was the reason that I came to Japan in the first place.

The city was quite a change for Scott. Since many foreigners lived there—English teachers, university students, and businesspeople—he did not receive the same attention as he had in the village. Compared to the small town, it was like living back in the United States. Nishi High, the school where Scott was assigned, was not at all like Naka High. Instead, it was a large academic high school where there was a particular emphasis placed on preparing for the rigorous university entrance exam. Only students who scored in the very top percentile were admitted to the best universities in the country, and Nishi prided itself on the number of students who were accepted to Tokyo University, the best in the country.

Scott was not the only foreigner working at this school. John, a 22-year-old from Australia had just been hired to replace a Canadian woman who had spent two years teaching at the school. John had just graduated with a degree in chemistry but he had studied Japanese for about seven years before moving to Japan.

One surprise Scott encountered was that Mr. Honda had also been transferred to Nishi High to head their English department. Mr. Honda spoke very highly of Scott to the teachers at Nishi and, as a result, Scott was put in charge of the *advanced English* class, which was cramming for the university entrance exams.

The English department used a textbook entitled *500 English Sentences,* which had been written approximately 10 years before by members of Nishi's staff. The book had become a standard and was used by virtually every high school in the prefecture. The teachers who wrote it were all subsequently promoted to work as advisers at the Satsuki Board of Education. Scott had tried the book in his classes, but thought that it was an inferior text riddled with grammatical inconsistencies, spelling mistakes, and archaic usages of the English language. Although this book was part of the curriculum, Scott refused to use it and instead taught from the other texts. Scott assumed this was not a problem since none of the other teachers ever mentioned the fact that he did not use the text in his classes.

IN THE LIMELIGHT

After three months of working at Nishi, Scott found out that there was going to be a prefecturewide English teachers' convention held at the school. Scott was surprised when the English staff asked him to conduct a demonstration class for one of the seminars. He was told that, in total, about 200 teachers were expected to attend.

Despite initial misgivings and stage fright, Scott's demonstration class was a huge success and Nishi High received outstanding commendations from all the teachers who attended and from the board of education. The English teachers at Nishi praised Scott for bringing honor to their school. Scott was glad that everything had gone well, but he did not think that he deserved the only credit.

> For various reasons, I was awarded much of the credit for the outstanding commendations, though I felt most of the work had been done by the regular English staff. Anyway, at this point I had built an excellent relationship with the school's staff, and found that this made the whole working situation function much easier, made getting things done possible, and kept me "part of the loop" in decisions in the English department.

Scott began to receive more and more responsibilities at work. The English staff would consult with him on problems big or small concerning the teaching of English. Although Scott and John both arrived at Nishi High at the same time, Scott was considered *sempai* (the senior). Scott attributed this to a combination of his age and the fact that he had already worked one year at another school in Japan.

> It was a bit unnerving that I was given more authority than John, I had been in Japan one year longer than he had and was a few years older, but he was able to speak their language fluently and was a capable teacher. The Japanese English teachers treated me as though I were John's superior and often put me in an awkward position by making John answer to me.

THE DILEMMA

One afternoon while Scott was sitting at his desk in the staff room, he was approached by several of the Japanese English teachers, including Mr. Honda. Mr. Honda began by inquiring after Scott's health, and complimenting him on his students' recent test scores. After several minutes of small talk, Mr. Honda cleared his throat and got to the point. He laid a copy of *500 English Sentences* on Scott's desk and smiled at him. Scott thought that Mr. Honda and the other teachers had finally come to ask him to use the text in his class. "Yes, it's a textbook, and a humdinger at that," said Scott. Scott's comment was met with confusion, nervous laughs, and several coughs. "No," replied Mr. Honda, "We were hoping that you would be so kind as to help us in repairing any errors there might be in this text for republication by the prefecture." Mr. Honda continued saying that Nishi High had been assigned the duty of editing the text and resubmitting it to the publisher for printing. He said that Scott's help would be greatly appreciated since he had been an English major at university and the Japanese teachers already knew that he was a more capable teacher. Mr. Honda also said that they desired Scott's help because he was a native English speaker and he would have an excellent grasp of both current and colloquial usage of the language, something which none of the Japanese English teachers had.

Scott agreed to help them with the project and asked Mr. Honda how soon he wanted the manuscript returned. Again Mr. Honda cleared his throat and said, "Very soon."

"How soon is very soon?" asked Scott. Mr. Honda replied that the manuscript had to be into the publisher within 10 days. Ten days seemed unreasonably short to Scott, so he asked Mr. Honda how long he had known about the project. Mr. Honda replied that the school had been asked to do the project more than six months ago. Not wanting to ask why the English teachers took so long to begin working on the manuscript, Scott took the project and promised to have it back within a few days. Mr. Honda smiled and thanked Scott. Scott went home that night and started working on the project.

> I was glad to have the opportunity to do something productive and lasting. I had hated this text since I had first seen it and had secretly ridiculed the foolish foreigner whose name and recommendation graced its inner cover. I exalted in the opportunity to finally dismember the text and replace the reams of errors with actual functional English.

Scott worked on the manuscript every night for four nights, putting in an average of eight hours of work each night. He returned the text to Mr. Honda on the fifth day, full of red ink: corrections, sample replacement sentences, and explanations as to why the changes were necessary. To Scott's surprise, Mr. Honda did not thank him for the work. Instead, he looked very uncomfortable and smiled nervously as he flipped through the marked pages of the manuscript.

Two days later, Mr. Honda returned to Scott's desk. He praised Scott for his work and reminded him of their mutual indebtedness. He talked about the weather, asked Scott how his karate training was progressing, and inquired about Scott's girlfriend's health. Eventually, Mr. Honda turned the discussion to the manuscript. Apologetically, he said, most of the corrections could not be used. Scott was confused and asked why. Mr. Honda revealed that he had given the corrected manuscript to John to look at and that John had disagreed with some of the corrections. Scott became concerned and asked to see the manuscript to see the contended corrections. Upon reviewing the manuscript, Scott noted three places where John had marked disagreement. John had also noted that the differences with these three sentences were probably due to usage in Australia compared with the United States and that since he was not an English major, like Scott, Scott was probably correct. Mr. Honda agreed that Scott's corrections were valid and went back to his desk.

Mr. Honda returned an hour later to say that despite their earlier conversation all of the corrections could not be used because it was so late in the process, and that it would be very troublesome for the publisher to make so many changes.

> By now I was getting frustrated. I told Mr. Honda that he should have thought of this six months ago when he first learned about the project and then asked him which was more important to him, the publisher or the students?

That night, one of the junior members of the Japanese English staff offered Scott a ride home. They discussed various topics, including how much Scott liked living in Japan. The young teacher then told Scott a story involving a junior member of the staff who tried to be helpful by correcting a memo that his boss had written. Since the memo had already been circulated once, the subsequent recirculation with the corrections resulted in a great loss of face for the boss. This resulted in strained relations, even though no offense was intended. By the time the teacher finished his anecdote, they had already arrived at Scott's house. He thanked the teacher for the ride, then got out of the car.

The next day, Scott did not discuss the topic of the manuscript and the situation seemed to have resolved itself. He assumed that Mr. Honda would go ahead and not use his changes, but he was unsure of what he could do about it.

After a few days of silence between Scott and the English teachers, Mr. Honda and the same group of English teachers came over to Scott's desk. This time they looked extremely nervous and spoke in very polite *keigo* (extremely respectful Japanese) that Scott could barely follow. Upon reaching some sort of consensus among themselves, they presented Scott with a single sheet of paper. On it was the verbatim endorsement of the previous issue of *500 English Sentences* with a blank line and Scott's name typed under the blank. "Would you be so kind as to sign this?" asked Mr. Honda. Scott was shocked. He thought the issue was closed when he had made a fuss about the corrections.

I looked at the group and plainly and directly said that there was no way that I would sign such a statement since I felt that the text was substandard and that my integrity as a teacher would be compromised by signing the statement.

Scott suggested that Mr. Honda ask John to sign the endorsement, but Mr. Honda replied that due to his seniority, English degree, and good association with Nishi High, the board of education had personally asked for Scott's signature. Mr. Honda then added that he needed to send it in to the publisher by 5:00 P.M. that same day.

WHAT TO DO

Mr. Honda went back to his own desk and Scott sat thinking about what he should do. All he could think about was having his name endorsing a text that he considered to be substandard. He didn't see how he could knowingly sign his name to a project that he knew was flawed.

Sick Leave

Kelly tried to control her anger as she thought about her supervisor. She couldn't understand why he was being so unreasonable. Maybe to him it was only a couple days of paid leave and not worth fighting over, but to her it meant the difference between being able to go on vacation during Golden Week[1] or having to stay home. She looked at her contract and the phone number of CLAIR on her desk. She wasn't the only person in the office affected by this. She sat and thought about how she should proceed.

KELLY

Kelly was 22 years old and had been working for the past six months at the Soto Board of Education office in Japan. This was her first job after graduating from college with a degree in management, and she was really excited to finally be in the real world.

Kelly was born in Calgary and had spent most of her life in Alberta, Canada. Kelly's father was a successful lawyer in Calgary and her mother was a high school English teacher. Kelly had an older sister, Laurel, 27, who had just passed the bar exam and was working for a corporate law firm in Edmonton.

Kelly had studied Japanese in high school and in university and spoke and wrote the language quite well. When she was 15 years old, Kelly spent four months in Japan on a school exchange. She had enjoyed the time she spent there and always planned to return one day. Upon graduating from high school, Kelly went to the University of Alberta, in Edmonton, to study management.

During her final year at the university, Kelly heard some of her friends talking about the Japan Exchange and Teaching (JET) Program. She was told that it was quite easy to get accepted—all an applicant needed was a university degree and an interest in Japan—and that it would be a great way to make money and see another part of the world. Kelly would have her degree by the end of the year and thought that having lived in Japan and knowing the language showed enough interest to have her application

---

This case was written by Laura Turek. Copyright © 1996 by Laura Turek. Used with permission. This case was prepared as a basis for classroom discussion, not to illustrate either the effective or ineffective management of an administrative situation.

[1]Golden Week is the period from April 29 to May 5, in which there are four Japanese national holidays. Many Japanese employees and their families take advantage of this period to go on vacation.

considered. Kelly thought that a year or two in Japan after her management degree would improve her Japanese and give her more of a competitive advantage when she returned to Canada to begin her career. She also thought that it would be a great way to make money and have some fun before she came home to start a real job. She asked her friend how she could apply to the program and returned home that night to work on her résumé.

THE JAPAN EXCHANGE AND TEACHING (JET) PROGRAM

Before the JET Program

The origins of the JET program can be traced back to 1982. In that year, the Japanese Ministry of Education (Monbusho) initiated a project known as the Monbusho English Fellows (MEF) Program, which hired Americans to work at the local boards of education in order to assist Japanese English teaching consultants who acted as advisors to the Japanese teachers of English in the public schools. The task of the MEFs was to oversee the junior and senior high school English teachers and to assist them with their training. In 1983, the British English Teachers Scheme (BETS) was inaugurated by the Ministry of Education. However, from the outset the British teachers were stationed at schools, and the goals of the program did not only concern English instruction but also sought to increase mutual understanding and improve friendly relations between the peoples of Japan and Britain. While there were some differences between the two programs, both shared a common goal: inviting native English speakers to Japan to assist in improving foreign-language instruction.

The Birth of the JET Program

The realization that Japan must open itself more fully to contact with international society began to foster an awareness of the importance of promoting internalization and international exchange at the local level. This brought about not only expanded English instruction, but also a rapid increase in exchange programs. Taking these new circumstances into account, the Japanese Ministry of Home Affairs in 1985 released a paper entitled "Plans for International Exchange Projects" as part of its priority policy of local governments for the following year. In the paper, the Ministry of Home Affairs proposed a definite course for the internationalization of local governments, which ideally would lead to smoothly functioning cultural exchanges. All of these ideas were finally implemented in a concrete project: the Japan Exchange and Teaching (JET) Program.

The Ministry of Home Affairs abolished the two projects currently in effect (MEF and BETS) and created a new one that was entrusted simultaneously to three ministries: the Ministry of Foreign Affairs, the Ministry of Education, and the Ministry of Home Affairs. However, the concept of appointing local authorities to implement the program and act as host institutions was preserved. While discussions were held with each of the local authorities to work out the details and ensure the smooth implementation of such a massive program, the formation of a cooperative organization for all local government was expedited.

The Creation of CLAIR

CLAIR, originally the Conference of Local Authorities for International Relations, was established in October 1986 by the *Todofuken* (the 47 prefectures of Japan) and the *Seireishiteitoshi* (the [then] 10 designated cities) as a cooperative organization responsible for implementing the JET program in conjunction with the three Japanese ministries named above.

CLAIR's Role in the JET Program

To ensure smooth implementation of the JET program, the three ministries, the local authorities, and CLAIR were all given specific functions. The functions that the conference attempted to fulfill for implementing the JET program were as follows:

1. Advice and liaison during recruitment and selection.
2. Placement of participants.
3. Participant orientation, conferences.
4. Guidance for local authority host institutions.
5. Participant welfare and counseling.
6. Travel arrangements for participants coming to Japan.
7. Liaison with related groups and institutions.
8. Publications and reference materials.
9. Publicity for the program.

The larger goal behind these functions of the conference was the promotion of international exchange at the local level. Independent of this development, the Council of Local Authorities for International Relations (a public endowed foundation) was inaugurated in July 1987. The council's main duty was to study and survey participating nations' local authorities overseas with the ultimate objective being to support local government programs for the promotion of internationalization. By fostering international exchange at the regional level, the council came to assume the same duties as the Conference of Local Authorities for International Relations. It was suggested that both organizations merge since they held information relevant to each other's work and shared the goals of improving work efficiency and performing their tasks more effectively. Moreover, the annual growth of the JET program led to an increased number of interrelated duties and tasks. Thus, it was necessary to strengthen the structure of the Conference of Local Authorities for International Relations.

It was decided that the operations and financial assets of the conference would be assumed by the council, and in August 1989 they were amalgamated, under the acronym of CLAIR, to form a joint organization of local public bodies in Japan to support and promote internationalization at the regional level.

Counseling System of JET (Figure 1)

1. *Role of the host institution.* Basically problems which JET participants faced during their stay in Japan were addressed by the host institution. If a JET

FIGURE 1 Counseling System

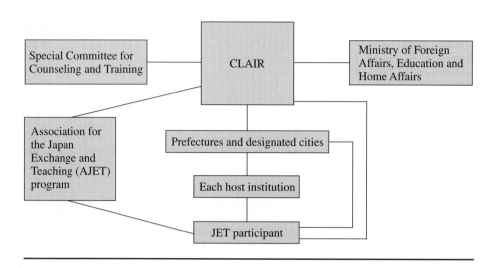

had a complaint or a problem at work or in his or her private life, the JET could alert his or her supervisor, who took up the matter and attempted to solve it.

2. *Role of CLAIR.* Problems or difficulties which JET program participants faced were as a rule dealt with by host institutions. However, if the issues were difficult to solve at this level, or if they concerned grievances between the JET participant and the host institution, CLAIR employed a number of non-Japanese program coordinators who would intervene and respond directly to participants' needs. CLAIR would then step in on behalf of the JET participant and work to solve the problems with the host institution.

3. *The Special Committee for Counseling and Training.* The Special Committee for Counseling and Training consisted of the staff members of the three ministries (Foreign Affairs, Home Affairs, and Education), embassies of the participating countries, and host institutions. It took charge of orientation, conferences, public welfare, and counseling. If necessary, it answered the questions and concerns of the JET participants.

AJET

The Association for the Japan Exchange and Teaching (AJET) Program was an independent, self-supporting organization created by JET program participants, whose elected officers were all volunteers. Membership in AJET was also voluntary. AJET provided members with information about working and living in Japan and provided a support network for members at the local, regional, and national levels. Many Japanese and JETs considered AJET to be the union of the JET program participants.

THE FIRST JOB

Kelly looked over the information she received from JET. There were two different positions available; (1) the coordinator for international relations (CIR) and (2) the Assistant Language Teacher (ALT). The first position sounded quite interesting to Kelly since applicants were required to have a functional knowledge of Japanese. ALTs, on the other hand, were not required to know any Japanese before arriving in Japan. She realized that her odds of getting accepted were greater if she applied to the second position since almost 600 ALTs were selected across Canada, compared with only 25 CIRs. Kelly was chosen for a CIR interview, but in the end was offered a position as an ALT. At first she was a little disappointed, but then she reminded herself that her original goal was to perfect her Japanese and she started to look forward to her trip to Japan.

Kelly received a lot of information about working and living in Japan from CLAIR. CLAIR also offered several predeparture training sessions and orientations about life in Japan and its potential problems, but she decided not to attend, because after four months in Japan she already knew what to expect.

THE PLACEMENT

Kelly was sent to Soto, a medium-sized city on the island of Shikoku. Kelly found the area a far cry from Osaka, where she had stayed the previous time she was in Japan. Soto was, in Kelly's opinion, "a small provincial town, stuck in the middle of nowhere." She had enjoyed the activity and night life of Osaka and, except for sports, her only entertainment options in Soto were one movie theater, several pachinko[2] parlors, and scores of karaoke bars. Kelly very quickly developed the habit of going away on the weekends to tour different parts of the island. She would also use her holidays to take advantage of visiting parts of Japan that she might never again get a chance to see. After a few months, Kelly decided that Soto was at least a good place to improve her Japanese since not many people spoke English very well, and only a few other foreigners lived there.

Kelly worked at the board of education office three days a week and visited schools the other two days to help with their English programs. There were three other JET participants who worked in the same office: Mark, 27, another Canadian; Andrea, 26, an American; and Suzanne, 25, from Britain. Like Kelly, Suzanne had been in Japan for only the past six months, while Mark and Andrea had been working there for a year and a half. Kelly was on good terms with the other JETs in the office, although she was closest with Suzanne since they had both arrived in Japan at the same time and had met at their orientation in Tokyo.

Although Kelly had lived in Japan before, this was the first time she had worked in a Japanese office. She had learned about Japanese work habits in a cross-cultural

---

[2]Pachinko is a Japanese-style game of chance that resembles a cross between pinball and a slot machine. It is a very popular pastime among certain groups and, like any form of gambling, can be quite lucrative.

management class at the university, yet she was still surprised at how committed the Japanese were to their jobs. The workday began each morning at 8:30 with a staff meeting and officially ended each night at 5:00 PM, yet no one left the office before 7:00 or 8:00 PM. The Japanese also came in on Saturdays, which Kelly thought was absurd since it left the employees with only one day a week to relax or spend time with their families.

Kelly and the other JETs in the office had a standard North American contract given to them by CLAIR which stipulated hours, number of vacation days, amount of sick leave and so on (Figure 2). The contract stated that the JET participants only worked from Monday to Friday until 5:00 PM and did not mention working on Saturdays. Neither Kelly nor the other foreigners ever put in extra hours at the office, nor were they ever asked to do so.

Kelly's supervisor was Mr. Higashi. At first Kelly thought that he was very kind and helpful because he had picked her and Suzanne up from the airport and had arranged their housing before they arrived in Japan. Mr. Higashi even took the two women shopping to help them buy necessary items like bedding and dishes so they did not have to be without, even for one night.

MR. HIGASHI

Mr. Higashi was born and had lived all of his life in Soto. He was 44 years old and had been teaching high school English in and around Soto for more than 20 years. Two years ago, Mr. Higashi was promoted to work as an adviser to all English teachers at the Soto Board of Education. This was a career-making move, and one that placed him on the track to becoming a school principal.

This new position at the board of education made Mr. Higashi the direct supervisor over the foreign JET participants in the office, as well as making him responsible for their actions. He had worked with them before when he was still teaching in the schools, but since they only came once a week to his school, he had never had the chance to get to know any of them really well.

Mr. Higashi found it very difficult to work with JETs. Since they were hired on a one-year contract basis, renewable only to a maximum of three, he had already seen several come and go. He also considered it inconvenient that Japanese was not a requirement for the JET participants because, since he was the only person in the office who could speak English, he found that he wasted a lot of his time working as an interpreter and helping the foreigners do simple everyday tasks like reading electric bills and opening a bank account. Despite this, he did his best to treat the foreign assistants as he would any other *kohai,* or subordinate, by nurturing their careers and acting as a father to them, since he knew what was best for them. Mr. Higashi was aware that his next promotion was due not only to his own performance but also to how well he interacted with his subordinates, so he worked hard to be a good mentor.

Mr. Higashi took an instant liking to Kelly because she spoke Japanese well and had already lived in Japan. Although she was the youngest of the four ALTs, he hoped that she would guide the others and assumed that she would not be the source of any problems for him.

FIGURE 2   Contract of English Teaching Engagement

Article 11: Paid Leave

Section 1

During the period of employment and with the approval of his/her supervisor, the JET participant may use 20 paid holidays individually or consecutively.

Section 2

When the JET participant wishes to make use of one of the above-mentioned paid holidays, he/she shall inform his/her supervisor three days in advance. Should the JET participant wish to use more than three paid holidays in succession, he/she is required to inform his/her supervisor one month in advance.

Article 12: Special Holidays

Section 1

The JET participant shall be entitled to special holidays under the following circumstances:

1. Sick leave—the period of serious illness or injury resulting in an acknowledged inability to work.

2. Bereavement—the period of 14 consecutive days, including Sundays and national holidays, immediately after the loss of father, mother, or spouse.

3. Natural disaster—the period the board of education deems necessary in the event of destruction of or serious damage to the JET participant's place of residence.

4. Transportation system failure—the period until the said problem has been resolved.

Section 2

Under the conditions of Article 12, Section 1 (1), above, the JET participant may take not more than 20 days of consecutive sick leave. Moreover, if the interval between two such periods of sick leave is less than one week, those two periods shall be regarded as continuous.

Section 3

The special holidays noted above in Article 12, Section 1, are paid holidays.

Article 17: Procedure for Taking (Sick) Leave

Section 1

When the JET participant wishes to make use of the special holidays/leave specified in Article 12, Section 1, he/she must apply and receive consent from his/her supervisor before taking the requested holidays. If circumstances prevent the JET participant from making necessary application beforehand, he/she should do so as soon as conditions permit it.

Section 2

In the event of the JET participant taking three or more consecutive days of sick leave, he/she must submit a doctor's certificate. The board of education may require the JET participant to obtain the said medical certificate from a medical practitioner specified by the board.

THE ALTS' OPINION OF MR. HIGASHI

At first, Mr. Higashi seemed fine. All of the ALTs sat in two rows with their desks facing each other, as they used to do in grade school, with Mr. Higashi's desk facing Kelly's. The foreigners all agreed that Mr. Higashi acted more like a father than a boss. He continually asked Kelly and Suzanne how they were enjoying Japanese life and kept encouraging them to immerse themselves in Japanese culture. He left brochures on Kelly's desk for courses in flower arranging and tea ceremony and even one on Japanese cooking. At first Kelly found this rather amusing, but she soon tired of it and started to get fed up with this constant pressure to "sign up" for Japanese culture. What she resented the most was that Mr. Higashi kept insisting she try activities that were traditionally considered a woman's domain. Not that she had anything against flowers, but if she had been a man, she knew that Mr. Higashi would not have hassled her this much to fit in. She knew that Japanese society was a male-dominated one. On her first day at the office, Kelly had looked around and noticed that there were no Japanese women who had been promoted to such a senior level within the board of education. The only women who worked there were young and single "office ladies" or secretaries. Although they were all very sweet young women, Kelly was not about to become one of them and "retire" if and when she found a husband.

Kelly had been very active in sports back in Canada and bought herself a mountain bike when she arrived in Japan so that she could go for rides in the country. At Suzanne's encouragement, Kelly joined a local Kendo club. She had seen this Japanese style of fencing before back in Calgary, and had always been attracted to the fast movements and interesting uniforms. Kelly hoped that Mr. Higashi would be satisfied that she was finally getting involved in something traditionally Japanese and leave her alone.

On top of his chauvinistic attitudes, Kelly didn't think much of Mr. Higashi as a supervisor. If Kelly or any of the other foreigners had a problem or question concerning living in Japan, he would either ignore them or give them information that they later found out was incorrect. Andrea told Kelly that she stopped going to Mr. Higashi when she had problems and instead consulted the office lady, since she was always able to help her. Andrea had even joked that the office lady should be their supervisor because she was by far more effective than Mr. Higashi.

As far as Suzanne was concerned, Mr. Higashi was utterly exasperating. He was forever arranging projects and conferences for the ALTs to participate in, then changing his mind and canceling at the last minute without bothering to tell them. He would also volunteer the ALTs to work on special assignments over the holiday periods and then get angry when they told him that they had previous plans and were unable to go. Suzanne recalled that one week before the Christmas vacation, Mr. Higashi announced that he had arranged for her to visit a junior high school. Suzanne informed him that while she would love to go, it was impossible since she had already booked the time off and had arranged a holiday to Seoul, Korea. Mr. Higashi got angry and told her that he and the board of education would lose face if she didn't attend. Suzanne told Mr. Higashi that losing face would not have been an issue if he had told her about the visit in advance so she could have prepared for it. As a result, Suzanne lost all respect for Mr. Higashi as a manager and continually challenged his authority. Whenever a problem arose, she was quick to remind him that things were very different and much better in Britain.

Mark also had difficulties with Mr. Higashi. Mark was not much of a group player and resented Mr. Higashi's constantly telling him what to do. He preferred to withdraw and work on his own. He didn't like Mr. Higashi's paternalistic attitude. He just wanted to be treated like a normal, capable employee and given free rein to do his work. As a show of his independence, Mark refused to join in on any of the "drinking meetings" after work.

THE JAPANESE OPINION OF THE ALTS

The other Japanese employees in the office found it difficult to work with the ALTs because, as far as they were concerned, the ALTs were never there long enough to become part of the group. It seemed like just after they got to know one ALT, he or she left and was replaced by another. Another problem was that since the foreigners usually did not speak Japanese, communication with them was extremely frustrating.

The biggest problem that the employees at the board of education office had with the ALTs was that they were so young and inexperienced. All of the men in the office had worked a minimum of 20 years to reach this stage in their careers, only to find themselves working side by side with foreigners who had recently graduated from college. To make matters worse, these young foreigners were also hired to advise them how to do their jobs better. The employees were also aware that the ALTs earned practically the same salary as their supervisor each month.

The Japanese employees did not consider the ALTs to be very committed workers. They never stayed past 5:00 PM on weekdays, and never came to work on the weekends even though the rest of the office did. It seemed as though the ALTs were rarely at the office. The ALTs also made it very clear that they had a contract that allowed them vacation days, and they made sure that they used every single day. The Japanese employees, on the other hand, rarely ever made use of their vacation time and knew that if they took holidays as frequently as the foreigners, they could return to find that their desk had been cleared.

THE INCIDENT

Kelly woke up one Monday morning with a high fever and a sore throat. She phoned Mr. Higashi to let him know that she wouldn't be coming in that day and possibly not the next. Mr. Higashi asked if she needed anything and told her to relax and take care of herself. Before he hung up, Mr. Higashi told her that when she came back to the office, to make sure to bring in a doctor's note. Kelly was annoyed. The last thing she wanted to do was to get out of bed and go to the clinic for a simple case of the flu. As she was getting dressed she thought she was being treated like a schoolgirl by being forced to bring in a note.

Two days later, Kelly returned to the office with the note from a physician in her hand. Andrea informed her that Mark and Suzanne had also been sick and that she had been by herself in the office. She also said that Mr. Higashi was suspicious that the three of them had been sick at the same time and had commented that he knew that foreigners sometimes pretended to be sick in order to create longer weekends. Kelly was glad that she had gone to the doctor and got a note so she could prove that she was really sick. Kelly said good morning to Mr. Higashi and gave him her note. He took it from her without so much as looking at it and threw it onto a huge pile of incoming mail on his desk. He asked her if she was feeling better and then went back to his work.

At midmorning, the accountant came over to Kelly's desk and asked her to sign some papers. Kelly reached for her pen and started to sign automatically until she noticed that she was signing for two days of paid leave and not sick leave. She pointed out the error to the accountant, who told her that there had not been a mistake. Kelly told the accountant to come back later and went over to speak with Mr. Higashi. To her surprise, Mr. Higashi said that there had been no mistake and that this was standard procedure in Japan. He said that typical Japanese employees normally did not make use of their vacation time due to their great loyalty to the company. If an employee became sick, he often used his paid vacation first out of respect for his employers.

Kelly responded that this was fine for Japanese employees, but since she was not Japanese, she preferred to do things the Canadian way. Mr. Higashi replied that since she was in Japan, maybe she should start doing things the Japanese way. Kelly turned away and looked at Andrea, not believing what had just happened.

The next day, both Mark and Suzanne returned to the office only to find themselves in the same predicament as Kelly. Suzanne called Mr. Higashi a lunatic and Mark chose to stop speaking to him altogether. Kelly was furious that they were being forced to waste two of their vacation days when they were guaranteed sick leave. She threw the JET contract on Mr. Higashi's desk and pointed out the section that stipulated the number of sick days they were entitled to and demanded that he honor their contract as written.

Mr. Higashi looked extremely agitated and said that he had to go to a very important meeting and would discuss the situation later. The accountant reappeared with the papers for the three ALTs to sign, but they all refused. Suzanne started to complain about Mr. Higashi's incompetence, while Mark complained about the Japanese style of management. Suzanne said that it was a shame that none of them had bothered to join AJET, for wasn't this the kind of problem that unions were supposed to handle? Kelly stared at the contract on her desk and said that they could take it to a higher level and involve CLAIR. Andrea said that things could get ugly and people could lose face if it went that far. Kelly took her agenda out of her desk and started looking for CLAIR's phone number.

DISCUSSION QUESTIONS

1. What should Kelly and the other ALTs do now?
2. Why did conflict occur? How could it have been prevented?

Questionnaires

The Personal Bargaining Inventory

INTRODUCTION

One way for negotiators to learn more about themselves, and about others in a negotiating context, is to clarify their own personal beliefs and values about the negotiation process and their style as negotiators. The questionnaire in this section can help you clarify perceptions of yourself on several dimensions related to negotiation—winning and losing, cooperation and competition, power and deception—and your beliefs about how a person "ought" to negotiate. Your instructor is likely to ask you to share your responses with others after you complete the questionnaire.

ADVANCE PREPARATION

Complete the Personal Bargaining Inventory questionnaire in this exercise. Bring the inventory to class.

PROCEDURE

Option 1: 60–90 Minutes

a. Pick six to eight statements from Part I (rating yourself) and six to eight statements from Part II (rating people's behavior in general) that you feel most strongly about.

b. In groups of four to five (as organized by the instructor), discuss those statements in Part I that you feel most strongly about. Working around the group, each individual should reveal (1) the statements he or she selected, and (2) whether the statements are characteristic or uncharacteristic of him or her. Other group members may then ask questions of clarification. The group as a whole then should help the individual arrive at a two- or three-sentence summary description of that individual's *self-image as a negotiator.*

Note: The role of the group is *not* to challenge, confront, or attempt to change an individual's self-view. Group members are encouraged to be supportive of an individual's self-view and try to understand how that individual sees himself or herself.

Adapted from an exercise developed by Bert Brown and Norman Berkowitz.

c. Using the same groups, members should now proceed to Part II (on people's behavior in general) of the questionnaire. The same format and approach should be followed.

Individuals should identify the six to eight statements that they most strongly agree or disagree with. Each individual should state these to the group, and the group should then help each individual identify that individual's *philosophy of negotiation effectiveness*. Again, the purpose of the groups is not to talk an individual out of his or her beliefs, but to try to understand how people approach this process with very different beliefs and values. Individuals should work to understand how their own view is *similar* to or *different* from that of other individuals in the group and class.

d. One person from the group should be selected as spokesperson to prepare a report to the class. The reporter should *not* identify individuals, but should instead try to summarize the different "types" of individuals that were identified in the group.

Option 2: 60–90 Minutes

a. The instructor will give you six to eight 3 x 5 file cards. Select 6 statements from the first group of 23 that you feel most strongly about (statements that are either strongly characteristic or strongly uncharacteristic of you). Write each statement on a separate 3 x 5 card—statement number, full text of the statement, and whether it is characteristic or uncharacteristic of you.

b. Your instructor will give you further information on how to proceed.

Personal Bargaining Inventory Questionnaire

The questions in this inventory are designed to measure your responses to your perceptions of human behavior in situations of bargaining and negotiation. Statements in the first group ask you about *your own behavior* in bargaining; statements in the second group ask you to judge *people's behavior in general.*

Part I: Rating Your Own Behavior

For each statement, please indicate how much the statement is *characteristic of you* on the following scale:

1 Strongly uncharacteristic

2 Moderately uncharacteristic

3 Mildly uncharacteristic

4 Neutral, no opinion

5 Mildly characteristic

6 Moderately characteristic

7 Strongly characteristic

Rate each statement on the seven-point scale by writing in one number closest to your personal judgment of yourself:

Rating	Statement
_____	1. I am sincere and trustworthy at all times. I will not lie, for whatever ends.
_____	2. I would refuse to bug the room of my opponent.
_____	3. I don't particularly care what people think of me. Getting what I want is more important than making friends.
_____	4. I am uncomfortable in situations where the rules are ambiguous and there are few precedents.
_____	5. I prefer to deal with others on a one-to-one basis rather than as a group.
_____	6. I can lie effectively. I can maintain a poker face when I am not telling the truth.
_____	7. I pride myself on being highly principled. I am willing to stand by those principles no matter what the cost.
_____	8. I am a patient person. As long as an agreement is finally reached, I do not mind slow-moving arguments.
_____	9. I am a good judge of character. When I am being deceived, I can spot it quickly.
_____	10. My sense of humor is one of my biggest assets.
_____	11. I have above-average empathy for the views and feelings of others.
_____	12. I can look at emotional issues in a dispassionate way. I can argue strenuously for my point of view, but I put the dispute aside when the argument is over.
_____	13. I tend to hold grudges.
_____	14. Criticism doesn't usually bother me. Any time you take a stand, people are bound to disagree, and it's all right for them to let you know they don't like your stand.
_____	15. I like power. I want it for myself, to do with what I want. In situations where I must share power I strive to increase my power base, and lessen that of my co-power holder.
_____	16. I like to share power. It is better for two or more to have power than it is for power to be in just one person's hands. The balance of shared power is important to effective functioning of any organization because it forces participation in decision making.
_____	17. I enjoy trying to persuade others to my point of view.
_____	18. I am not effective at persuading others to my point of view when my heart isn't really in what I am trying to represent.
_____	19. I love a good old, knockdown, drag-out verbal fight. Conflict is healthy, and open conflict where everybody's opinion is aired is the best way to resolve differences of opinion.
_____	20. I hate conflict and will do anything to avoid it—including giving up power over a situation.
_____	21. In any competitive situation, I like to win. Not just win, but win by the biggest margin possible.
_____	22. In any competitive situation I like to win. I don't want to clobber my opponent, just come out a little ahead.
_____	23. The only way I could engage conscientiously in bargaining would be by dealing honestly and openly with my opponents.

Part II: Rating People's Behavior in General

For each statement, please indicate how much you agree with the statement on the following scale:

1 Strongly disagree
2 Moderately disagree
3 Mildly disagree
4 Neutral, no opinion
5 Mildly agree
6 Moderately agree
7 Strongly agree

Think about what you believe makes people effective negotiators. Rate each statement on the seven-point scale by writing in one number closest to your judgment of what makes an excellent negotiator:

Rating	Statement
_____	24. If you are too honest and trustworthy, most people will take advantage of you.
_____	25. Fear is a stronger persuader than trust.
_____	26. When one is easily predictable, one is easily manipulated.
_____	27. The appearance of openness in your opponent should be suspect.
_____	28. Make an early minor concession; the other side may reciprocate on something you want later on.
_____	29. Personality and the ability to judge people and persuade them to your point of view (or to an acceptable compromise) are more important than knowledge and information about the issues at hand.
_____	30. Silence is golden—it's the best reply to a totally unacceptable offer.
_____	31. Be the aggressor. You must take the initiative if you are going to accomplish your objectives.
_____	32. One should avoid frequent use of a third party.
_____	33. Honesty and openness are necessary to reach equitable agreement.
_____	34. It is important to understand one's values prior to bargaining.
_____	35. Be calm. Maintaining your cool at *all* times gives you an unquestionable advantage. Never lose your temper.
_____	36. Keep a poker face: never act pleased as terms are agreed upon.
_____	37. A good negotiator must be able to see the issues from the opponent's point of view.
_____	38. An unanswered threat will be read by your opponent as weakness.
_____	39. In bargaining, winning is the most important consideration.
_____	40. The best outcome in bargaining is one that is fair to all parties.
_____	41. Most results in bargaining can be achieved through cooperation.
_____	42. Principles are all well and good, but sometimes you have to compromise your principles to achieve your goals.
_____	43. You should never try to exploit your adversary's personal weakness.
_____	44. A member of a bargaining team is morally responsible for the strategies and tactics employed by that team.

_____ 45. Good ends justify the means. If you know you're right and your goal is worthy, you needn't be concerned too much about *how* your goal is achieved.

_____ 46. Honesty means openness, candor, telling all and not withholding pertinent information, not exaggerating emotion. One should always be honest during bargaining.

_____ 47. Imposing personal discomfort on an opponent is not too high a price to pay for success in negotiation.

_____ 48. Regardless of personal considerations, team members should accept any role assigned to them by the bargaining team.

_____ 49. There is no need to deal completely openly with your adversaries. In bargaining as in life, what they don't know won't hurt them.

_____ 50. There is nothing wrong with lying to an opponent in a bargaining situation as long as you don't get caught.

DISCUSSION QUESTIONS

Option 1

1. Which six to eight statements did you identify for Part I? What summary statement did you arrive at to characterize your self-image as a negotiator?

2. Which six to eight statements did you identify for Part II? What summary statement did you arrive at to characterize your philosophy of negotiation effectiveness?

3. How similar or different were you to other people in your group? In your class? Did this surprise you? Why?

4. What do you believe are the good and bad aspects of your self-image as a negotiator? Are there aspects that you would like to change? Which ones?

Option 2

1. Which six to eight statements did you begin with? Which six to eight statements did your group end with? How much do your statements still represent your own self-image?

2. How much influence do you think you had in the group meetings? If you had a lot of influence, how were you influential? If you had very little influence, how were others influential?

3. Are you comfortable with the group's statements? Do you wish you had behaved any differently in group discussions?

4. How do the groups' statements differ from one another? What does this say about personal views of negotiation?

The SINS Scale

INTRODUCTION

The purpose of the SINS (Self-reported Inappropriate Negotiation Strategies) scale is to inquire about your general disposition toward ethical issues in negotiation. It will help you draw the line between those tactics which most people see as ethical and those which most see as unethical. The instructor will explain how to score and interpret this questionnaire.

ADVANCE PREPARATION

Complete the SINS scale as specified by your instructor.

PROCEDURE

1. Complete the SINS scale.
2. Your instructor will hand out a scoring key for the SINS scale. Follow the key in order to score your questionnaire. A description of the groups of items in the questionnaire can be found following the questionnaire.
3. Be prepared to share your answers to the questions with others in a small-group or class discussion. Your instructor will also give you more information about your scores and their meaning.

Incidents in Negotiation Questionnaire

This questionnaire is part of a research study on how negotiators decide when certain strategies and tactics are ethical and appropriate in negotiations.

In completing this questionnaire, please try to be as candid as you can about what you think is appropriate and acceptable to do. You are being asked about tactics that are controversial; however, your responses on this questionnaire are completely anonymous, and no one will ever know your individual responses.

You will be asked to consider a list of tactics that negotiators sometimes use. You should consider these tactics in the context of a *situation in which you will be negotiating for something which is very important to you and your business*. For each tactic, you will be asked to indicate how appropriate the tactic would be to use in this situation. Then assign a rating to each tactic,

---

Questionnaire developed by Robert Robinson, Roy J. Lewicki, and Eileen Donahue. Used with permission of the developers.

evaluating how appropriate it would be to use this tactic in the context specified above, based on the following scale:

1	2	3	4	5	6	7
Not at all appropriate			Somewhat appropriate			Very appropriate

(If you have any need to explain your rating on a tactic, please do so in the margin or at the end/back of the questionnaire.)

Rating

1. Promise that good things will happen to your opponent if he/she gives you what you want, even if you know that you can't (or won't) deliver these things when the other's cooperation is obtained. _____

2. Intentionally misrepresent information to your opponent in order to strengthen your negotiating arguments or position. _____

3. Attempt to get your opponent fired from his/her position so that a new person will take his/her place. _____

4. Intentionally misrepresent the nature of negotiations to your constituency in order to protect delicate discussions that have occurred. _____

5. Gain information about an opponent's negotiating position by paying your friends, associates, and contacts to get this information for you. _____

6. Make an opening demand that is far greater than what you really hope to settle for. _____

7. Convey a false impression that you are in absolutely no hurry to come to a negotiated agreement, thereby trying to put time pressure on your opponent to concede quickly. _____

8. In return for concessions from your opponent now, offer to make future concessions which you know you will not follow through on. _____

9. Threaten to make your opponent look weak or foolish in front of a boss or others to whom he/she is accountable, even if you know that you won't actually carry out the threat. _____

10. Deny the validity of information which your opponent has that weakens your negotiating position, even though that information is true and valid. _____

11. Intentionally misrepresent the progress of negotiations to your constituency in order to make your own position appear stronger. _____

12. Talk directly to the people whom your opponent reports to, or is accountable to, and tell them things that will undermine their confidence in your opponent as a negotiator. _____

13. Gain information about an opponent's negotiating position by cultivating his/her friendship through expensive gifts, entertaining, or "personal favors." _____

14. Make an opening demand so high/low that it seriously undermines your opponent's confidence in his/her ability to negotiate a satisfactory settlement. _____

15. Guarantee that your constituency will uphold the settlement reached, although you know that they will likely violate the agreement later. _____

16. Gain information about an opponent's negotiating position by trying to recruit or hire one of your opponent's teammates (on the condition that the teammate bring confidential information with him/her). _____

Your instructor will give you a scoring key. This key will permit you to determine your "scores" on five different groups of tactics represented in this questionnaire.

Group 1, *Traditional Competitive Bargaining,* represents an aggregation of traditionally accepted tactics which are frequently advocated as necessary to successful distributive bargaining. Research shows that people who see these items as appropriate also tend to see them less as "types of deception" or dishonesty, and more as simply common tactics to be used in a distributive bargaining context. Given the general description of distributive bargaining presented earlier in this volume, the tactics are generally oriented toward maintaining the secrecy of one's own position, sending out false cues that will throw the opponent off the track, and thwarting the attempted secrecy of the opponent.

Group 2, *Manipulation of Opponent's Network,* represents a class of negotiation tactics in which the objective is to undermine the negotiator's support system within his/her constituency—talking to one's boss or one's network and undermining the negotiator's support, encouraging erosion of his support through defections, or threatening to embarrassing the opponent. Most negotiators understand the implicit (or often explicit) pressures on them by constituents to appear strong and competent, and the powerful impact that a negative evaluation can have on loss of face. They know that it is important to maintain the broader relationship with others "outside" the boundaries of a 1:1 negotiation.

Group 3, *False Promises,* includes tactics which use deception to force an opponent into dealing with the negotiator directly. These might be labeled as the common bag of negotiator dirty tricks, including making promises you don't intend to keep, or having your constituency do the same things. The common element in this group of tactics is that they use the power of future rewards to pressure the opponent to comply with the negotiator directly, but then renege on the actual follow-through in delivering these rewards.

Group 4, *Misrepresentation of Information,* includes tactics in which information is distorted in some manner to a "significant other" in negotiation—either to the opponent or to your constituency. While the tactics differ in the reasons why they are performed—justification of position, retribution against an opponent, preserving confidentiality or face saving—and while the respondents define sharp differences in the perceived appropriateness of the tactics, the common theme of misrepresentation unites them.

Finally, Group 5 is *Inappropriate Information Gathering.* This factor includes those items that address various forms of gathering information by paying for it, bribery, personal favors, and so on. The commonality in these tactics is not one of truth distortion, but of "cheating" on the informal rules of negotiation by paying for information which one would not otherwise have available. These tactics are included in a list of unethical negotiation tactics because many people clearly feel that negotiation should be a process of information which is freely gained and offered; "paying" for information or for leverage in negotiation is an inappropriate thing to do.

DISCUSSION QUESTIONS

1. What were your scores on each of the five categories? Do these scores surprise you? Why or why not?

2. How do your scores compare to those of other students in your class or study group? Does this comparison surprise you? Why or why not?

3. Your instructor may give you information about how other students at other universities have completed this questionnaire. How do your scores compare to those of the other groups?

4. How do *you* decide what tactics are appropriate or inappropriate in a negotiation? What factors related to the other person, the issues under negotiation, or the situation, might make you

   a. More likely to use some of these tactics?

   b. Less likely to use some of these tactics?

5. Do you think that negotiators need a clear "code of ethics" about what is OK or not OK to do? What might be some of the problems in developing, disseminating, or enforcing such a code?

6. Do you agree with the following quotation? (Think about it and discuss it with your classmates.)

   There is no such thing as an "honest bluff," as distinguished from the empty promise or the treacherous falsehood. If an "honest bluff" fails, the bluffer may be forgiven for trying a legitimate stratagem, but if he has lied, he may be cold-shouldered out of the game.[1]

7. Do you agree with the following quotation? (Think about it and discuss it with your classmates.)

   Falsehood ceases to be a falsehood when it is understood on all sides that the truth is not expected to be spoken. [Attributed to Sir Henry Taylor, British statesman][2]

---

1. Quotation from Albert Carr, "Is Business Bluffing Ethical?," *Harvard Business Review,* January–February 1968.
   2. Ibid.

The Influence Tactics Inventory

INTRODUCTION

The questionnaire in this exercise is designed to measure your predisposition to use different influence tactics at work. In responding to these questions, you will learn something about the influence tactics that you use, depending on whom you want to influence.

ADVANCE PREPARATION

At the discretion of the instructor.

PROCEDURE

Step 1: 5 Minutes

Identify three different people whom you have needed to influence at work. One should be a superior, one a subordinate, and the other a co-worker.

Step 2: 20 Minutes

Work completely through the questionnaire for *each* of the three people you have chosen, keeping only one person in mind at a time. Use the following scale to respond to each of the statements below. Be sure to respond to all of the statements for each of the three people.

5 I usually use this tactic to influence him or her.

4 I frequently use this tactic to influence him or her.

3 I occasionally use this tactic to influence him or her.

2 I seldom use this tactic to influence him or her.

1 I never use this tactic to influence him or her.

Step 3: 30 minutes

Your instructor will hand out a scoring key. Follow the key in order to score the questionnaire.

Adapted from "Intraorganizational Influence Tactics: Explorations in Getting One's Way," *Journal of Applied Psychology* 65, pp. 440–52, by David Kipnis, Stuart M. Schmidt, and Ian Wilkinson. Used with permission.

Superior	Subordinate	Co-Worker	Statement
_____	_____	_____	1. Kept checking up on him or her.
_____	_____	_____	2. Made him or her feel important ("only you have the brains, talent to do this").
_____	_____	_____	3. Wrote a detailed plan that justified my ideas.
_____	_____	_____	4. Gave no salary increase or prevented that person from getting a raise.
_____	_____	_____	5. Offered an exchange (e.g., if you do this for me, I will do something for you).
_____	_____	_____	6. Made a formal appeal to higher levels to back up my request.
_____	_____	_____	7. Threatened to notify an outside agency if he or she did not give in to my request.
_____	_____	_____	8. Obtained the support of co-workers to back up my request.
_____	_____	_____	9. Simply ordered him or her to do what I requested.
_____	_____	_____	10. Acted very humbly to him or her while making my request.
_____	_____	_____	11. Presented him or her with information in support of my point of view.
_____	_____	_____	12. Threatened his or her job security (e.g., hint of firing or getting him or her fired).
_____	_____	_____	13. Reminded him or her of past favors that I had done for him or her.
_____	_____	_____	14. Obtained the informal support of higher-ups.
_____	_____	_____	15. Threatened to stop working with him or her until he or she gave in.
_____	_____	_____	16. Had him or her come to a formal conference at which I made my request.
_____	_____	_____	17. Demanded that he or she do what I requested.
_____	_____	_____	18. Acted in a friendly manner prior to asking for what I wanted.
_____	_____	_____	19. Explained the reasons for my request.
_____	_____	_____	20. Promised (or gave) a salary request.
_____	_____	_____	21. Offered to make a personal sacrifice if he or she would do what I wanted (e.g., work late, work harder, do his/her share of the work, etc.).
_____	_____	_____	22. Filed a report about the other person with higher-ups (e.g., my superior).
_____	_____	_____	23. Engaged in a work slowdown until he or she did what I wanted.
_____	_____	_____	24. Obtained the support of my subordinates to back up my request.

DISCUSSION QUESTIONS

1. What was your score for each of the different influence tactics?

	Superior	Subordinate	Co-Worker
Assertiveness	_____	_____	_____
Ingratiation	_____	_____	_____
Rationality	_____	_____	_____
Sanctions	_____	_____	_____
Exchange	_____	_____	_____
Upward appeal	_____	_____	_____
Blocking	_____	_____	_____
Coalition	_____	_____	_____

2. Compare the influence tactics used with superiors, subordinates, and co-workers by your classmates. Which tactics are most frequently used with which role? Which are least frequently used? Why did this pattern occur?

3. Which is the most powerful influence tactic? Does this depend on situational factors? How?

4. When others are trying to influence you, which tactics do you think are most effective? Most ineffective? Annoying?

5. When you are trying to influence others, which tactics are you most comfortable using? Least comfortable?

The Trust Scale

INTRODUCTION

The purpose of the Trust Scale is to inquire about your general level of trust in another person before or after a negotiation. The instructor will explain how to score and interpret this questionnaire.

ADVANCE PREPARATION

Complete the Trust Scale as specified by your instructor.

PROCEDURE

1. Complete the Trust Scale.
2. Your instructor will hand out a scoring key for the Trust Scale. Follow the key in order to score your questionnaire. A description of the questionnaire and what it measures will be provided by the instructor.
3. Be prepared to share your answers to the questions with others in a small group or class discussion.

Trust Scale

Identify a *specific other person* for whom you have some level of trust. Then rate that other person on the following five-point scale:

1	2	3	4	5
Strongly disagree		Undecided		Strongly agree

	Rating
1. This person's behavior meets my expectations.	_____
2. This person wants to be known as someone who keeps promises and commitments.	_____
3. This person knows that the benefits of maintaining trust are higher than the costs of destroying it.	_____
4. This person does what he or she says he or she will do.	_____

Questionnaire developed by Roy J. Lewicki and Maura Stevenson.

Trust Scale (continued)	*Rating*
5. I hear from others about this person's good "reputation."	_____
6. I have interacted with this person a lot.	_____
7. I think I really know this person.	_____
8. I can accurately predict what this person will do.	_____
9. I think I know pretty well what this person's reactions will be.	_____
10. This person's interests and mine are the same.	_____
11. This person and I share the same basic values.	_____
12. This person and I have the same goals.	_____
13. This person and I are pursuing the same objectives.	_____
14. I know that this person will do whatever I would do if I were in the same situation.	_____
15. This person and I really stand for the same basic things.	_____

DISCUSSION

In recent years, a great deal of research has been conducted on the nature of trust and the role it plays in critical social relationships. Trust is essential to productive social relationships with others, and can play a critical role in negotiations, particularly integrative negotiations. High trust contributes to better negotiations, and more cooperative, productive negotiations are likely to enhance trust. Conversely, low trust may contribute to less productive negotiations, and less productive negotiations are likely to decrease trust.

There are many definitions of trust, reflecting different views about trust as either a core characteristic of one's personality or a set of situation-based perceptions and expectations shaped by what we know about the other party and the situation in which that relationship occurs. In discussing it here, we will define *trust* as an individual's belief in, and willingness to act on the basis of, the words, actions, and decisions of another.

Recent research on trust suggests that there are three different types of trust—calculus-based trust, knowledge-based trust, and identification-based trust:

> • *Calculus-based trust* is based on consistency of behavior—that people will do what they say they are going to do. Behavioral consistency is sustained by offering either the promise of rewards for people who do what they say they are going to do or the threat of punishment (e.g., loss of relationship) that will occur if consistency is not maintained (i.e., when people do *not* do what they say they will do). This type of trust is based on an ongoing, economic calculation of the value of the outcomes to be received by creating and sustaining the relationship relative to the costs of maintaining or severing it. Not only are these rewards and punishments given directly to the other, but we also can reward or punish the other by enhancing or destroying the other's "reputation" with friends, associates, and business partners if they honor or violate the trust.

- *Knowledge-based trust* is grounded in the other's predictability—knowing the other sufficiently well so that the other's behavior can be anticipated. Knowledge-based trust relies on information rather than rewards and punishments. It develops over time, largely as a function of the parties having a history of interaction that allows them to get to know the other well enough to understand how the other thinks, what is important to him or her, and how he or she is likely to behave in a variety of situations. There are several dimensions to knowledge-based trust. First, and most simply, information contributes to the predictability of the other, which contributes to trust. The better one knows the other, the more accurately one can predict what the other will do. Second, predictability enhances trust—even if the other is predictably unreliable—because we can predict the ways that the other might violate the trust. Finally, accurate prediction requires an understanding that develops over time in multidimensional relationships (similar to calculus-based trust). In knowledge-based trust, *regular communication* and *courtship* are key processes. Regular communication puts a party in constant contact with the other, exchanging information about wants, preferences, and approaches to problems. Without regular communication, we lose touch with each other—not only emotionally but in our ability to think like and predict the reactions of the other. Second, "courtship" is behavior that is specifically directed at relationship development, at learning more about a possible partner. Courtship permits actors to gain enough information to determine whether the parties can work together well.

- *Identification-based trust* is based on a complete empathy with or identification with the other party's desires and intentions. At this third level, trust exists because each party effectively understands, appreciates, agrees with, empathizes with, and takes on the other's values because of the emotional connection between them—and thus can act for the other. Identification-based trust thus permits one to act as an "agent" for the other and substitute for the other in interpersonal transactions. The other can be confident that his or her interests will be fully protected, and that no surveillance or monitoring of the actor is necessary. A true affirmation of the strength of identification-based trust between parties can be found when one party acts for the other in a manner even more zealous than the other might demonstrate; the parties not only know and identify with each other but come to understand what they must do to sustain the other's trust. One comes to learn what "really matters" to the other, and comes to place the same importance on those behaviors as the other does. When one watches very closely knit groups work together—such as jazz quartets, basketball teams, or very skilled work groups under pressure—we get to see identification-based trust in action.

In addition to proposing these three different types of trust, recent theorizing on trust suggests several additional aspects to this approach to trust:

- The three types of trust are linked sequentially; that is, in most relationships, calculus-based trust develops first, followed by knowledge-based trust and then identification-based trust.

- Not all relationships move to the identification-based trust level. Most relationships do not develop past calculus-based trust, while only the closest, most personal, and most intimate develop true identification-based trust.

- Trust probably develops slowly over time but can decline rapidly if the other side violates the trust.

- Repairing violated or broken trust is a very complex, difficult process.

DISCUSSION QUESTIONS

1. Think about the person you rated in this questionnaire. How close and personal (or distant and impersonal) is your relationship with that person?

2. Experiment with the questionnaire by rating several different people. For example, rate:

   - The person whom you trust the most.
   - A person whom you trust in a professional capacity (e.g., a doctor, counselor, financial adviser).
   - A person who has violated your trust.
   - A boss or colleague at work.

   How do your ratings differ for each? What does this say about the role of trust in the relationship with that person?

3. How do you build trust in order to make negotiation more effective? What kinds of things can you do to strengthen trust? What should you avoid if you do not want to damage existing trust?

4. Think about the person who has violated your trust. What happened in this situation? Why do you no longer trust that person? What would it take to be able to repair the relationship with that person?

Appendixes

Capital Mortgage Insurance
Corporation (B)

By late afternoon on May 21, 1979, Frank Randall and Jim Dolan had finished putting together Capital Mortgage Insurance Corporation's formal offer to purchase all the outstanding stock of Corporate Transfer Services, Inc. The offer they settled on was virtually identical to the draft that Jim Dolan had already prepared, with one significant addition: an offer to retain Elliott Burr as a consultant to help build a strong relationship between the relocation company and MetroNet.

Randall considered the offer to keep Burr actively involved as a key ingredient in the total package. As he told Jim Dolan: "Burr fathered this company, and now he's putting it up for adoption. I want to give him every assurance that we'll be an adequate foster parent. Besides, he can be a key link to MetroNet for us." The consulting arrangement would also be a way to provide Burr with some extra income beyond what he stood to make by selling his stock.

In addition to the purchase offer letter, Randall also prepared a letter formally stating CMI's interest in acquiring CTS. The letter (see Exhibit 1) opened by expressing Randall's gratitude to the four stockholders for their help and cooperation during the past several months. Randall planned to distribute this letter to the four men before discussing the formal purchase offer.

Once the purchase offer details were settled, Randall telephoned Elliott Burr again to arrange the details of their meeting. At Randall's suggestion it was agreed that he and Dolan would fly to Chicago on the morning of May 24 and meet with the CTS stockholders at the Burr and Lehman Real Estate office. Again, however, Randall was intentionally vague about his agenda for the meeting.

THE MAY 24 MEETING

When Randall and Dolan arrived in Chicago, they found only Elliott Burr, William Lehman, and Tom Winder in attendance. Burr explained that Michael Kupchak, the fourth stockholder, was tied up in a meeting in Gary, Indiana, and would not be able to get back in time.

Capital Mortgage Insurance Company (A)–(F), 9-480-057-062

Copyright © 1980 by the President and Fellows of Harvard College.

This case was prepared by James P. Ware as a basis for class discussion rather than to illustrate either effective or ineffective handling of an administrative situation. Reprinted by permission of the Harvard Business School.

EXHIBIT 1

Board of Directors and Stockholders
Corporate Transfer Services
Chicago, IL

May 24, 1979

Gentlemen:

The purpose of this letter is to express our sincere appreciation for the help and cooperation you and your staff have provided over the past several months to enable us to understand the employee relocation service business. You have been most liberal with your time and candid in the sharing of your knowledge of the industry.

As you know, we have conducted an extensive study of the employee relocation service industry and we realize there is still much for us to learn. During our analysis, we have gained a high regard for CTS and the manner in which you have conducted your business.

Capital Mortgage Insurance Corporation would like to acquire the ownership of Corporate Transfer Services. We will make every effort to do so on a mutually fair and equitable basis. We enter these negotiations with you fully aware of your personal feelings as individuals who have created and nurtured CTS for several years.

Upon acquiring CTS, I want to assure you that we are committed to building and expanding the operations on a nationwide basis that will continue the high business standards you have established.

Sincerely,

Franklin T. Randall
President

The five men sat down at a conference table in a private room in the back of the Burr and Lehman Real Estate office. Burr sat on one side of the table, flanked by Winder and Lehman. Randall and Dolan settled into the seats directly opposite. Randall opened the meeting with a brief but warm statement of thanks for all the help the CTS group had provided. He then distributed his formal letter of intent and expressed his continuing interest in developing a formal relationship with Corporate Transfer Services. Randall concluded:

> We appreciate the fact that you have created this company out of nothing, and that you care a great deal about its future. We understand those feelings, and we respect them. We are definitely interested in acquiring you, but we want to do so only on terms that will satisfy your concerns about the future of Corporate Transfer Services.

Elliott Burr then replied, "What is your offer?" Randall responded:

> We find it exceedingly difficult to put a price on your company. Most acquisitions are completed on the basis of a projected earnings stream; you don't have one. Most acquisitions involve a careful analysis of a company's management team; you have only one man.

You have only very small exposure to the MetroNet brokers, and your business is basically self-liquidating with no residual value. But we do want to buy you on the basis of your goodwill and reputation.

Burr:

What is your offer?

Randall:

We will pay you $400,000 above your audited net worth.

Burr:

We are very disappointed in that offer price.

Randall:

What did you have in mind?

Burr:

We wanted $5 million.

Capital Mortgage Insurance Corporation (C)

On hearing Elliott Burr's demand for $5 million for CTS, Frank Randall replied: "If you're serious, we might as well leave right now. But why don't you listen to our complete offer?"

Jim Dolan then read through CMI's formal offer letter, which spelled out all the details of the proposed agreement. Dolan took the CTS group slowly through the letter, explaining the meaning of each item in great detail.

Elliott Burr then suggested that they skip the price issue momentarily. He reviewed the offer step by step, asking questions to clarify the implications of each part of the proposal. Winder and Lehman remained silent during this exchange.

The tremendous difference in the asking and offering prices continued to be the major source of contention, however. After several minutes of open debate, Randall finally asked in exasperation, "How did you ever come up with that figure?" Tom Winder mentioned hearing that 60 percent of another employee relocation company had been sold recently for something in excess of $3 million.

Dolan:

How does that relate to us?

Winder:

Well, I guess it really isn't the same thing. I suppose we made a mistake using that as a base.

There was a long silence following Winder's comment. Finally, after several minutes, Elliott Burr said: "Let me tell you about Mike, who isn't here. I have his proxy, and he'll sell right now for $3.5 million."

Randall replied, "That's ridiculous."

The meeting then degenerated for several minutes, as Burr, Lehman, and Winder whispered among themselves. They finally announced their willingness to sell for $2 million.

Capital Mortgage Insurance Company (A)–(F), 9-480-057-062

Copyright © 1980 by the President and Fellows of Harvard College.

This case was prepared by James P. Ware as a basis for class discussion rather than to illustrate either effective or ineffective handling of an administrative situation. Reprinted by permission of the Harvard Business School.

Capital Mortgage Insurance
Corporation (D)

Frank Randall paused only briefly before saying, "That's still way too high."

Burr:

> But we control MetroNet.

Randall:

> No you don't; you have no control there—no ability to guarantee their performance.

Burr:

> You don't understand . . .

Randall:

> No, *you* don't understand. You can't deliver MetroNet. In fact, I'll have to live down your poor performance with MetroNet.

Dolan:

> Just how much time have you spent working with MetroNet?

Winder:

> Well, I spoke at half a dozen regional seminars in 1976. I made up a bunch of slides, passed out brochures, and answered a lot of questions. That was a lot of work.

Dolan:

> How much of that effort is still valid? Has it generated much business?

Winder:

> Well, I really don't know . . . I guess we probably haven't grown as fast as we should have to satisfy MetroNet . . .

Burr interrupted, cutting Winder off.

Burr:

> We're still awfully far apart. Can we work out a deal giving us some now and something more in the future?

Capital Mortgage Insurance Company (A)–(F), 9-480-057-062

Copyright © 1980 by the President and Fellows of Harvard College.

This case was prepared by James P. Ware as a basis for class discussion rather than to illustrate either effective or ineffective handling of an administrative situation. Reprinted by permission of the Harvard Business School.

Dolan:

If you want to take on some future risks, we'll pay your net worth now and a fixed dollar payout in the future, based on the ROE we can get. The fact is, the future performance of this company will depend a lot more on the capital we're going to put in than it will on what it's worth today.

Burr:

That's not acceptable. But I'm still certain we can work something out. You have a John F. Kennedy stadium in Philadelphia, don't you? I remember he used to say that people of goodwill can always get things done.

Randall:

You've got my geography misplaced. I'm originally from Missouri; you've got to show me. Besides, I preferred Harry Truman to J.F.K. I especially like one of his sayings: "If you can't stand the heat, get out of the kitchen." Look, why don't you all get together and discuss our offer in more detail. Maybe you can quantify your performance with MetroNet, and sign a written warranty or pledge to produce the business. Meanwhile, let's keep the lines of communication open. Come on, Jim, let's get back to the hotel. I want to get some dinner.

Capital Mortgage Insurance Corporation (E)

Randall and Dolan stopped only briefly at the hotel before going out for dinner; Randall was certain Elliott Burr would be trying to reach them before too long. Sure enough, when they returned to the hotel at 11:00 PM, there were several phone messages. They ignored the messages and went to bed, since they had to get up at 6:00 AM to catch their flight back to Philadelphia.

Promptly at 6:00 AM, Jim Dolan's telephone rang. As he groggily picked up the phone, a familiar voice said, "Good morning, Jim. This is your wake-up call. It's Elliott Burr. I tried to reach Frank and couldn't; but I would like to talk some more before you leave." Now fully awake, Dolan responded, "All right, I'll listen. But let's be clear that this is *not* a negotiating session."

Dolan met Burr in the hotel coffee shop at 6:30 AM after a quick shower and shave. Burr had CMI's offer letter with him. He had crossed out the offer to pay $400,000 over net worth and replaced it with $1 million. Jim was deliberately noncommittal in responding to Burr. All he said was that he and Randall were flying back to Philadelphia immediately, and he added, "Frank will let you know."

Capital Mortgage Insurance Company (A)–(F), 9-480-057-062

Copyright © 1980 by the President and Fellows of Harvard College.

This case was prepared by James P. Ware as a basis for class discussion rather than to illustrate either effective or ineffective handling of an administrative situation. Reprinted by permission of the Harvard Business School.

Capital Mortgage Insurance Corporation (F)

As the big jet banked over the city and began its final approach toward the Philadelphia airport, Frank Randall closed his briefcase and looked at Jim Dolan.

> Well, I don't know about you, Jim, but I think we're in good shape. We brought their price down into our range, and we established our feelings about CTS's intrinsic value—or lack of value.
>
> And I know my ceiling price; I won't go a dollar over it. If they won't accept it, we'll just forget them. But one way or another, we're going into the business.

FURTHER NEGOTIATIONS WITH CORPORATE TRANSFER SERVICES

Once again, Randall and Dolan let their relationship with Elliott Burr and his partners cool off a bit. There were several phone conversations over the next two weeks, but Randall often "forgot" to return calls, and he remained deliberately neutral in his discussions with Burr. The conversations that did occur tended to focus on technical matters such as alternate payout arrangements; the price issue was hardly mentioned.

Randall kept David Osgood of MetroNet up-to-date on the negotiations. During one of their conversations Randall told Osgood about Burr's claim that he "controlled" the MetroNet brokers and could "deliver" them. Osgood was incensed; he told Randall he was going to write a letter to Burr calling attention to CTS's failure to meet commitments the company had made to MetroNet.

During this time Randall also hired the consultant who had prepared the relocation industry report for MetroNet earlier in the spring. The consultant spent several days in Philadelphia helping Randall and Dolan think about how to structure and operate a relocation business, and suggesting the names of experienced managers they might want to recruit. The consultant also put Randall in touch with the parent organization of one of the well-established relocation companies. The consultant hinted that

Capital Mortgage Insurance Company (A)–(F), 9-480-057-062

Copyright © 1980 by the President and Fellows of Harvard College.

This case was prepared by James P. Ware as a basis for class discussion rather than to illustrate either effective or ineffective handling of an administrative situation. Reprinted by permission of the Harvard Business School.

the parent was not satisfied with its subsidiary and might be willing to sell it, even though it was one of the largest in the industry. Randall made an appointment for early June to "discuss matters of mutual interest" with the executive vice president responsible for the subsidiary.

Jim Dolan was beginning to question whether they really wanted to acquire CTS. The discussions with the consultant had given him new insights into the business, and now he not only had someone to compare Elliott Burr and Tom Winder with, but there was the possibility, however remote, of buying a much bigger and clearly more successful operation.

Finally, on June 5, Burr called again. He told Randall, "We've thought about your offer and talked it over. How about $750,000 over book value?" Randall replied, "We're not even sure we want to go through with it. I'll get back to you in a day or two."

Randall and Dolan spent most of June 6 rethinking their whole assessment of Corporate Transfer Services. As Dolan later recalled:

> At that point we had a chance to do some real soul-searching. It was fully in our hands; we knew we could get the company, and get it at a price we considered reasonable. The negotiations were in a sense over; the next move was our real commitment. We talked ourselves into and out of doing it several times, and we thought about our other options as well.

Finally, late in the day, Randall called Elliott Burr and offered $600,000 over net worth. Burr, without any hesitation, agreed.

Collective Bargaining at Magic Carpet Airlines: A Union Perspective (B)

JULY 21: SENIORITY AND FRINGE BENEFITS

On Monday, Mr. Irving was absent, so Mr. Orleans continued as chief MCA negotiator. He brought in a typed version of the agreed-upon sections. As the LFA negotiating committee reviewed them, they grew perplexed.

Hardy:

Mr. Orleans, I know we agreed not to change several clauses in the contract, but as I look through this, it appears to me that *nothing* is changed! In fact, the uniform clause is your initial, concessionary, contract proposal! Mr. Orleans, are you trying to pull a fast one on us? Because if you are . . .

Orleans:

Oh, I must have given the wrong pages to my secretary to type. Sorry. It won't happen again.

But it did happen again. Whenever his secretary typed any provisions, Mr. Orleans brought in a retyped version of MCA's initial concessionary contract provisions for one or more contract clauses. Repeatedly, Dixie sent it back to be retyped according to what they had actually agreed. Interestingly, this occurred only at meetings where Ross Irving and Tom Windham were absent.

Lee:

I propose that laid-off (or "furloughed") flight attendants continue to accrue seniority even while laid off. Also, flight attendants who had transferred out of flight attendant positions or into management positions should be stricken from the seniority list.

This case was prepared by Peggy Briggs and William Ross of the University of Wisconsin–LaCrosse, and is intended to be used as a basis for class discussion rather than to illustrate either effective or ineffective handling of the situation. The names of the firms, individuals, and locations; dates; conversation quotations; and financial information have all been disguised to preserve the firm's and union's desire for anonymity.

An earlier version of this case was presented and accepted by the refereed Midwest Society for Case Research and appeared in *Annual Advances in Case Research, 1991.* All rights reserved to the authors and the MSCR.

Copyright © 1991, 1997 by Peggy Briggs and William Ross.

Lamb:

I like your furlough proposal, but not your seniority proposal. Instead, I propose that people hired in these other positions be added to the seniority lists.

Lee:

Mrs. Lamb, I understand that you do not want your staff to lose their seniority rights. But those employees do not have the same concerns as our active LFA members. They should not get this benefit.

Lamb:

It was acceptable in the last contract, what's different now? You have to look out for the interests of your employees, and I have to look out for the interests of mine. I'm sure you understand.

After much wrangling, it was obvious that the two sides could not agree. So they recessed for lunch. During lunch, Mr. Sanders found the LFA group in the hotel restaurant.

Sanders:

I have an idea that might resolve this issue. Consider the following: Flight attendants transferring into other jobs will continue to accrue seniority, but if they want to return to flight attendant positions, they cannot "bump" existing attendants. Rather, they must wait until there is an opening and "bid" on that opening. In return for accepting that proposal, management will agree to the following: (1) flight attendants will be officially recognized as safety professionals, (2) two flight attendants will be allowed to attend each domicile's bi-monthly Safety Committee meeting, (3) two union officers can meet monthly with domicile managers to discuss flight attendants' working conditions, and (4) union officers can have one paid day off each month to conduct union business.

Lee:

Let us caucus.

Hardy:

What is he up to, coming to us at lunch like this? I am real suspicious of this all-or-nothing proposal. Besides, it sounds like he is trying to buy us off with added benefits for union officials.

Boaz:

These types of package deals are common; it's OK.

Lee:

Let's work up a counterproposal while we eat lunch.

After their lunchtime caucus, Dixie offered a counterproposal.

Lee:

We'll accept Mr. Sanders's offer, *provided* you give LFA officers three paid days off each month (*plus* free travel passes) for union business, and give all LFA attendants paid days off for jury duty or funerals.

Mrs. Lamb frowned. Mr. Sanders stroked his chin. It was now management's turn to caucus. Upon returning, Mr. Orleans offered the group's response.

Orleans:

Let's compromise on one day per month with free travel for union business. As for your other two suggestions, my first response is, Why pay people for not working? Besides, people will abuse the funeral leave. Every week, some step-nephew twice removed will pass away!

Lee:

Well then, what do you propose?

Orleans:

(*Pause while calculating costs.*) Jury duty at half-pay. And one extra personal leave day per year. If they want to use it to go to a funeral, they can. They can go fishing if they like. Just so they give us two days' advance notice.

Lee:

Make it two personal leave days and we'll accept it.

Orleans:

(*Another pause while calculating costs.*) Done.

With that, the parties agreed to adjourn until the next morning.

JULY 22: LADIES IN WAITING

LFA negotiators met at a nearby coffee shop and then proceeded as a group to the scheduled 8:00 AM meeting. The MCA managers did not arrive until 8:45 AM.

Lee:

Now for the tough one—wages. Wages should increase for starting flight attendants from $13.00 to $15.45 per hour, and from $20.20 to $25.55 per hour for attendants with five or more years of seniority. Further, we want the minimum pay increased from 65 hours to 70 hours per trip, because we are away several days on each trip. Finally, our attendants want guaranteed pay of 4.5 hours per day for showing up (in case weather canceled the flight).

Orleans:

We'll have to caucus on this proposal.

Seven hours later, the LFA team members still sat in the negotiation room, waiting. Gradually, they realized that the managers were not caucusing at all, but had probably returned to their normal work activities. At 5:00 PM, a secretary appeared at the door to announce that the MCA managers had decided that they would prefer to continue negotiations another day. Further, no manager could meet the following day—or any day until August 21.

That evening, Dixie called Tom Windham at home to complain about the delay. Mr. Windham promised to investigate. The next day, a very cordial Ross Irving called to ask if the union could meet earlier—Monday, August 4.

Lee:

I'm sorry, but that day, we'll be counting ballots from the LFA strike authorization vote. But I could squeeze y'all in on Tuesday. By the way, have you ever heard of CHAOS? You can read all about it on our union's Web page.

ROUND THREE

Before the Tuesday meeting, the union faced a decision. Dixie had become ill and could not attend. Marie and Jody had to work. Only Peggy and Ruth were available to negotiate. Although neither felt competent to serve as spokesperson, they agreed to meet anyway. By a toss of a coin, Peggy Hardy was chosen as spokesperson.

AUGUST 5: ARBITRATION RULINGS, HEALTH CARE, AND SICK LEAVE

The negotiators devoted the morning to modifying contract clauses in ways that incorporated previous arbitrator's rulings. They devoted the afternoon to arguing about the LFA proposal to increase health care coverage by 25 percent. Nothing was accomplished. The two sides agreed to move to other issues.

Hardy:

We are offering a fair sick leave proposal. Under this plan, workers receive pay for all time missed due to illness for the first month and then one-third pay for any days beyond one month.

Irving:

Peggy, this is unacceptable. I'm sorry. MCA already pays seven days off for illness, and we agreed to give you two personal leave days. The industry average is only to pay for 78 hours due to illness.

Hardy:

OK, increase the paid time off for illness from 56 hours (seven days) to 78 hours at full pay and then the remainder can be at half pay.

Orleans:

You girls are dreaming. Tell you what: I know that your flight attendants complain whenever they show up for work and their flights are canceled. That's why we guarantee 3.25 hours of pay—just for showing up. We'll increase your minimum daily guaranteed hours, if you agree to drop your sick leave proposal.

Hardy:

Now *you're* dreaming!

Taking a page from Dixie's book, Peggy sat silently staring at Mr. Orleans. After some fidgeting and a few calculations, Mr. Orleans paused and lit his 10th cigarette of the day.

Orleans:

We'll increase your daily guarantee to 3.5 hours and we'll increase your paid sick leave to 78 hours. Total. That's the best we can do.

Hardy:

Agreed.

Boaz:

Now, I think we should discuss wages—and no running away this time!

Orleans:

I was looking at your proposal and I saw you wanted duty rigs. No can do. Duty rigs are too costly!

Irving:

Your minimum guaranteed pay demand of 4.5 hours would bankrupt the company. That simply isn't feasible!

Orleans:

And your demands are outrageous. What do you think we are flying—gold-plated aircraft? The trouble with you union types is you only know one word—*gimme.*

Boaz:

Do you want to discuss our proposal? Or would you rather spend your time thinking up clever insults?

Orleans:

We are willing to negotiate, but negotiations can't be all one-way; we've got to see more give and less take on your part—especially in the area of wages.

Boaz:

Mr. Orleans, look at how MCA compares to other airlines! Our attendants earn less than those working for other national carriers of similar size.

Orleans:

There are reasons for that. We are smaller. We make less profit. We have to keep costs low, to keep our feeder contract. To put it simply, we can't afford to give you what you are asking for. We've been generous up to this point, but we've given about all we can give— that is true for wages and for health care. No more concessions! Sorry!

Boaz:

(*Standing.*) Then we have nothing further to discuss.

Irving:

Wait, Ruth. Would you like me to call the government and request a federal mediator?

Boaz:

Fine. (*Glancing at Mr. Orleans.*) Just pick someone who doesn't smoke.

With that, the meeting was adjourned.

Collective Bargaining at Magic Carpet Airlines: A Union Perspective (C)

AUGUST 26: MEDIATION

On Tuesday, August 26, the mediator arrived. Dixie, who had recovered from her illness, led the LFA team. The mediator, Cal Crenshaw, told of his 15 years of experience at handling airline negotiations. He also asked the negotiators if they had seen a recent issue of *Monthly Labor Reports* containing transportation worker wage and benefit averages. Everyone nodded.

Mr. Crenshaw then reviewed all areas of the contract that had been agreed upon and all sections still outstanding. Each side explained its position on the provisions in question. Mr. Irving tried to show the mediator that MCA could not afford the LFA requests. Dixie tried to show the mediator that the requests matched industry averages. This process took the entire day.

Tuesday, Mr. Crenshaw separated the two sides and met extensively with each side. He met with MCA first and then with the union.

Crenshaw:

First, I want to assure you that everything said here is confidential. Now, Dixie, can you accept anything else instead of your duty rig request?

Lee:

No.

Crenshaw:

Can we lump the wage items together into one dollar amount? MCA thinks in terms of 'total labor costs' and you'd be presenting the information in their lingo.

This case was prepared by Peggy Briggs and William Ross of the University of Wisconsin–LaCrosse, and is intended to be used as a basis for class discussion rather than to illustrate either effective or ineffective handling of the situation. The names of the firms, individuals, and locations; dates; conversation quotations; and financial information have all been disguised to preserve the firm's and union's desire for anonymity.

An earlier version of this case was presented and accepted by the refereed Midwest Society for Case Research and appeared in *Annual Advances in Case Research, 1991.* All rights reserved to the authors and the MSCR.

Lee:

No, each issue is important in its own right and should be considered separately.

Crenshaw:

Well, tell me, what do you really want in the area of wages? What is your bottom line?

Lee:

Sir, other flight attendants have duty rig provisions. We want them too. Also our wage proposal calls for a modest wage increase and the company's proposal offers nothing. Now which is more reasonable to you?

Crenshaw:

What offer could you give me to discuss with the other side? What concession could you make?

Lee:

The principle of the duty rig is more important than the specific pay level. So we are flexible on our demand for one hour's pay for every two hours of duty. We'll come down on health benefits too.

The remainder of the day was spent in such caucuses with the mediator, discussing wage and benefit issues. By the end of the day, the union had softened its duty rig demand to one hour's pay for every 2.5 hours of service and MCA management had agreed in principle to the concept, but not to any pay level. Finally, Mr. Crenshaw realized that progress was unlikely and adjourned negotiations until 9:00 the following morning.

AUGUST 27: WORKING CONDITIONS AND JOB SECURITY

To the union leaders, the morning of August 27 seemed wasted. The mediator caucused with each side. When with the union, he asked "What if" questions. He then presented hypothetical scenarios and observed Dixie's reaction.

Crenshaw:

If you gave up your demand for eight paid holidays at double time—holiday periods are big travel days for flight crews—what would you expect in return?

Lee:

Currently, if an attendant wants to trade routes with another attendant, he or she has to give a five-day notice to the company. What difference does it make to MCA who flies what routes? As long as all of them are covered, what do they care? We think a 24-hour advance notice is sufficient.

Mr. Crenshaw left. Two hours later, the mediator returned.

Crenshaw:

They accepted the compromise. They wouldn't have bought the 24-hour proposal if they had believed you had thought of it, so I told them it was my idea. I also kept pointing out that this would not cost them any money. Clever, eh?

That afternoon, discussion turned to job security. Mr. Crenshaw continued to caucus with the union.

Crenshaw:

As I understand it, you want two things: (1) the contract will remain binding in the event of any change in ownership, and (2) arbitration will be used to protect the seniority rights of all on the flight attendant seniority list.

Lee:

Right.

Crenshaw:

Let me offer a proposal: Have you ever heard of a "me-too" clause? That is where one group's contract determines the terms for another group.

Rogers:

I don't follow. What's your idea?

Crenshaw:

My sense is that MCA will never agree to your proposal because of who you are—flight attendants. However, clauses that are virtually identical to what you are requesting are found in both the pilots' and the mechanics' contracts. So I suggest you negotiate a clause that says that your group will be treated the same as those two unions.

Boaz:

I don't like the idea of leaving our fate to others.

Crenshaw:

Think about it. Planes can easily fly with scab flight attendants. Planes can't fly without the unionized pilots or mechanics. So you are allowing more powerful unions than your own to negotiate for you!

Lee:

What makes you think MCA will go for it?

Crenshaw:

Three factors. First, the costs are remote. I know that MCA is not planning any airline acquisitions or mergers within the next three years, so this doesn't cost management anything. Second, they don't have to renegotiate this clause with you in the future. Whatever they negotiate with the other unions covers you too. Third, if you let them pick the more favorable (to their side) of the two contracts—the mechanics or the pilots—they still feel like they are "managing." Either is better than what you can get on your own.

Lee:

I like it. We'll agree if they will.

But MCA did not agree. And the managers requested more joint meetings and fewer private caucuses. The joint meetings produced nothing but bickering. This continued throughout the week. By Friday afternoon, Mr. Crenshaw had had enough.

Crenshaw:

As you know, tomorrow is your last day to bargain before the present contract expires. It has become increasingly clear that I am no longer an asset to the negotiation process but a liability. Each side seems to be trying to make the other look bad in front of me. You are not far from an agreement and you can conclude these talks successfully, but you all have to want to settle. I've arranged to go back to Washington, so when you resume tomorrow, you must agree on your own.

TABLE 1   Changes in the Magic Carpet Air League of Flight Attendants Contract
as of August 30, 1997

Contract Provision	1994–97 Contract	Initial Union Proposal	Settlement to Date
Compensation			
Base wage	$13.00	$15.45	None
Wage after five years	$20.20	$25.55	None
Duty rig pay	None	1 hour pay per 2 hour duty (50%)	None
Daily guarantee	3.25 hours	4.5 hours	3.5 hours
Holiday pay	None	8 holidays at "double-time" rate	Two paid (regular rate) personal holidays
Job Security			
Successorship	None	Contract will still be binding	None
Protection of seniority rights in the event of a merger	None	Arbitrator combines MCA seniority list with that of other airline	None
Working Conditions			
Trip trading lead time	5 days	24 hours	24 hours prior
Shoe allowance	None	$100/year	$25/year
Winter coat	None	Total cost	$60/three years
Uniform maintenance	$16/month	$20/month	$18/month

As the meeting adjourned, the union members sat in stunned silence. Peggy looked at her notes, containing a chart of the issues (Table 1). She saw that the union was so close—and yet so far—from agreement. She wondered what would happen next.

Vanessa Abrams (B)

Beginning in the 1990–91 fiscal year, the commission system had been changed at S&G. Starting in September 1990, Vanessa Abrams and the other members of her sales group had been paid 3 percent commission on all new business brought in. There was no longer a commission on account management, and the 2 percent override was no longer part of Abrams's compensation package. She did receive 120 percent of base salary. The revenue goal for the New York office for 1990–91 had been $5.3 million, and even though the sales team was experiencing a general slowdown in their markets, Abrams said that she and her team were coming to the end of a phenomenal year. Abrams explained that in July–August 1991, business had dropped way off and, furthermore, the profit picture was bleak:

> In the best year we'd ever had, there were no profits to speak of. Jerry blew it. I remember how that felt. I was thinking, Why am I doing all this, for nothing? We were all frustrated, and morale was just terrible. Jerry kept talking about how much money "he'd" lost. In front of staff, in front of management. But it was the *business* that had lost, not *him*.

On Tuesday, November 12, 1991, things began to happen "fast and furiously," as Abrams put it. Jerry came into Vanessa's office at 6:00 on a Tuesday night saying that he had to talk to her. He said that there was a great deal to discuss in the next management committee meeting, scheduled for next week, Monday the 18th. He said that revenue forecasts, budgets used for marketing and sales expenses, and salaries would all be up for discussion. Bailey was vague, but Abrams realized that he was quite serious.

Then Bailey really caught Abrams off guard:

> He asked me what my plans were for the long term. I told him I really hadn't thought about it. I said that my kids were both going to be in college in a couple of years, my husband and I had talked about a few things, but that I really hadn't made any plans. I had this feeling that now that he had the nondisclosure from me, he was just going to come crashing down. I'd made good money in fiscal 1990–91, and this must have killed him, because I know how competitive he is. Maybe he made more than I did; I don't know. But still. The conversation was, well, strange.

This case was prepared by Deborah Kolb and Cinny Little for the Institute for Case Development and Research, Simmons Graduate School of Management, Boston, MA 02215.

After Jerry left her office, Vanessa was exhausted. She realized that she had a lot to think about and just a week before the management committee meeting. The first thing that came to mind was that Jerry was going to reduce her compensation as a cost-cutting move. She wondered whether she ought to assemble information on what her rights were before the management meeting. And if there were going to be extensive budget cuts, did that mean she was going to have to cut staff? Her staff were all people she had hired and whom she genuinely enjoyed working with, and the thought of letting people go distressed her. And Jerry had wanted to know about her "plans for the long term."

Clearly, there was going to be some negotiating with Jerry in Vanessa's immediate future—both in the management committee meeting and one-on-one. But at this point, the only thing she knew for certain was that her last negotiation with Jerry had been both unsatisfying and unsuccessful. Taking her lawyer Nick's advice to "get tough" had not seemed to work. She wondered what she should do, if anything, to prepare.

During the week, Abrams made a number of phone calls. First, she called a trusted friend of hers, Elizabeth:

> Elizabeth said that I should look at the big picture. She thought this might be an opportunity to think about other things and engage Jerry in looking at a wider perspective where I was concerned. Did Jerry want me to leave? Did *I* want to leave? Get out of health care altogether and do something else? I had thought in the past about writing a book, and Elizabeth said I should think about whether I wanted to do that now. Maybe I should take the summer off and write.

Abrams also had an informal talk with another attorney friend of hers, Juan. Abrams recalled:

> I told Juan that I just knew that Jerry was going to cut my compensation. I just *knew* it. I said I wanted to make sure I got my parachute, but that I didn't want to do anything that looked like resigning. I wanted to know what my rights were. We just had a brief, informal chat, and he gave me some language I could use. I was so close to just resigning on the spot at that point.

Vanessa Abrams recalled the management committee meeting on November 18, 1991:

> Jerry ran the meeting, and there was absolutely no opportunity for discussion. We were told we had to reduce our costs, immediately, by 20 percent. It looked like we were going to have to downsize. If my expense budget was going to be cut 20 percent . . . that includes salaries—mine and the people who work for me. I knew where Jerry was headed with that. Here comes the salary cut, I thought.
>
> We had expected bad news, but this was really shocking. He hadn't listened to what I'd said about our revenue forecasts and our expenses, and now this. Cutting staff and probably pay cuts for all those who remain. I felt sad. Personally very saddened by it all.

After the meetings, Abrams felt more and more confused. Questions continued to come to mind: Should she leave S&G? Should she take an extended leave of absence? Was it time for a career change? She could certainly use her track record and skills in another setting. Or should she stay and work part-time for S&G? She'd thought in the past about writing a book; would this be a good time to take some time off and do that? What about compensation? How would she work that out? Should she get tough, invoke her parachute now, and just leave the company?

On Wednesday, November 20, 1991, Vanessa Abrams went in to Jerry's office. Coming right to the point, she told him that she wanted to discuss her compensation. She wanted to know what he had in mind and she asked him to name a figure. Abrams recalled:

> I heard that number, and it just blew me away. He was naming a figure that was half of what I'd made in fiscal 1990–91. What he was saying was that they were going to change the commission structure. My base salary would remain intact, but my commissions would be gone. In its place would be a discretionary bonus. That meant that my total salary would be entirely up to Jerry's discretion. So, when he told me what he had in mind, I just walked out. I mean, not *walked out,* I just said, "Okay," and left. After I walked out, I went crazy. How could he do this to me and think I was going to take it? I needed to talk to somebody and try to figure out what rights I had and what I wanted to do next.

That day, Abrams retained an attorney, a specialist in employee relations highly recommended by her friend Juan. Gail, the attorney, suggested that Vanessa had some leverage because of the parachute that was attached to her nondisclosure agreement.

Abrams's understanding was that Jerry's action of cutting her pay in half was legally equivalent to "constructive discharge," or, in short, firing her. If indeed Jerry was firing her, she might well be entitled to a year's pay equivalent to what she had made in her best year, fiscal 1990–91. Gail thought Vanessa had a good case for setting the parachute in motion now. To Vanessa, that seemed an attractive idea at the moment.

Then Vanessa called her friend Elizabeth again. Elizabeth encouraged her to "focus on the psychological piece" of the negotiation. Elizabeth reminded her that she had talked about getting out of health care altogether, taking a leave of absence, writing a book, working part-time, and other options.

After these conversations, Vanessa said:

> Elizabeth convinced me not to make the same mistake I'd made last time. Last time, with the nondisclosure agreement, I'd used a negotiating style that was not my own, and it didn't work. This time, I'd be aware of the style I used to negotiate. On Thursday [November 21], I went in and talked to Jerry. I asked him what he wanted to have happen with me. I wanted to try to get at it. But that was too open-ended for him. I told him that I would be willing to work only part-time. He said that having me part-time was better than not having me at all, and he left it at that.
>
> I felt that he wasn't listening to me and that we weren't really getting anywhere.

Vanessa called Gail. The attorney, focusing on the changes in the compensation package, helped Vanessa write a letter to Jerry. The letter, which Vanessa gave to Jerry on Monday, November 25, is shown in Exhibit 1.

Toward the end of that Monday, Jerry came to Vanessa's office and said that he would be willing to talk with her but not until she "rescinded the letter," as he put it.

EXHIBIT 1   Abrams's Letter to Jerry Bailey, November 25, 1991

November 25, 1991
Jerry Bailey, President
S&G New York

Dear Jerry:

I have given a lot of thought recently to your change in my compensation package and how it impacts me not only relative to other professionals but also how it impacts my rights under the Employee Nondisclosure Agreement I signed in July 1990.

You have, in effect, slashed my compensation by 50 percent. The new compensation program you want me to agree to leaves my base salary intact but removes the commission on all New York–originated business. You have substituted a "discretionary bonus" that hasn't been fully defined. Although you have cut my income by 50 percent, you still expect me to lead the sales group to attain or exceed the 1991–92 sales goal of $5.1 million.

Last fiscal year, as you acknowledged in our recent management committee meeting, your board of directors and I warned you to reduce expenses. The warnings had no effect. Professional and administrative staff are going to be asked to take pay cuts. It is in this area that I have been particularly mistreated. Although the other executive vice presidents are being asked to take cuts of 20 percent or less, my cut is at least 50 percent. It is clear that I have been asked to take a disproportionate share of the reductions in compensation, because as executive vice president of sales, a significant portion of my compensation (and that of my staff) comes from commissions. You are asking me to do this with no decrease in my responsibilities.

I am particularly concerned about the impact that this unfair treatment will have on my rights under the Employee Nondisclosure Agreement. Under that agreement, if I am terminated without cause, I am entitled to receive pay for 12 months at the rate in effect on the day of termination. The new compensation structure also cut the value of my "parachute" by over 50 percent. I consider this a breach of the implied covenant of good faith and fair dealing which in part governs the Employee Nondisclosure Agreement and, very likely, constructive discharge.

Given my treatment under the new compensation structure, it appears that you want me to leave the company. I think it is imperative that we now sit down and talk frankly about my rights under the agreement and the implementation of those rights. Please let me know at your earliest convenience when you will be available to discuss these issues.

Sincerely,

Vanessa Abrams

INDEXES

Author Index

Title Index